HANDBOOK OF CONTEMPORARY PREACHING

MICHAEL DUDUIT
EDITOR

HANDBOOK OF CONTEMPORARY PREACHING

MICHAEL DUDUIT
EDITOR

BROADMAN PRESS
NASHVILLE, TENNESSEE

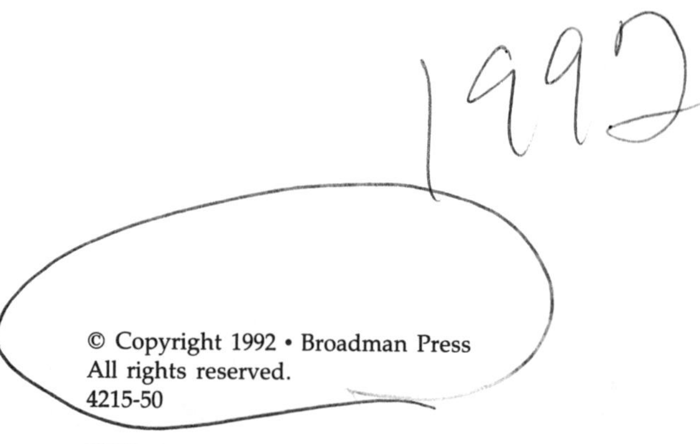

4215-50

ISBN: 0-8054-1550-5
Dewey Decimal Classification: 251
Subject Heading: PREACHING
Library of Congress Catalog Card Number: 92-9539
Printed in the United States of America

Library of Congress Cataloging-in-Publication Data

Handbook of contemporary preaching / Michael Duduit. editor/contributor.
p. cm.
Includes bibliographical references.
ISBN 0-8054-1550-5 :
1. Preaching. I. Duduit, Michael, 1954-
BV4222.H35 1993
251—dc20 92-9539
CIP

Contents

Introduction

Recent years have seen a resurgence of interest in preaching in all segments of the church. An avalanche of books, periodicals, seminars, and other programs testify to a hunger for information and assistance in strengthening the ministry of the pulpit. Likewise, scholarship in homiletics is producing a constant stream of stimulating and challenging ideas concerning the nature of preaching, new forms and techniques, and more.

This *Handbook* reflects the need to provide, in a single volume, an accessible overview of the contemporary preaching scene. Its purpose is to introduce a variety of homiletical topics and issues to readers—both preaching ministers and seminarians—and to suggest additional resources for further study. The *Handbook of Contemporary Preaching* will introduce readers to a host of vital issues relating to the preaching task—from biblical exposition to narrative preaching, from hermeneutics to the practical impact of preaching on such areas of ministry as pastoral care or church growth.

I am grateful to nearly fifty different contributors who helped make this volume possible. They represent the best among today's teachers and practitioners of the preaching craft. Without their willingness to share their own insights and experience, this *Handbook* would not exist.

The contributors to this volume represent a diversity of denominational families and approaches to the preaching task. Each is allowed to speak with his or her own voice and style. No attempt has been made to enforce a single style or approach on issues like the use of gender inclusiveness in language; writers are allowed to speak out of their own theology and tradition.

A careful reader will note that writers may take conflicting positions or significantly different approaches to similar issues. No attempt has been made to cover over such differences; they reflect the reality that great preaching involves the personality and gifts of the preacher as well as the message itself.

I am also thankful to my wife, whose assistance and encouragement were so essential to the completion of this project. She is a partner in ministry, for whom I am grateful.

My prayer is that this volume will be useful to you as you seek to carry out God's call in your own life, and that your preaching, like Paul's, will be "in demonstration of the Spirit and of power" (1 Cor. 2:4).

Michael Duduit
Editor

Part I
The Roots of Contemporary Preaching

Chrysostom (347-407)
"The Golden Mouth"

One of the first great preachers of the Christian church, the name Chrysostom is actually a nickname ("golden mouth") which was applied to John of Antioch long after his death.

Trained in rhetoric and law, as a young man Chrysostom felt drawn to a life of Christian devotion and study. He became a deacon in his native Antioch, and five years later was ordained to the priesthood over his own objections. Appointed chief preacher in the city, his clear and powerful proclamation drew great crowds and made a remarkable impact on the religious and political life of Antioch.

So popular was Chrysostom with the people that upon his appointment as archbishop of Constantinople, the populace objected vehemently to any effort to take him from Antioch. Chrysostom shared their lack of enthusiasm for the move; he was finally tricked into leaving the city whereupon he was escorted to Constantinople by troops of the Empress Eudoxia and installed as archbishop.

His preaching quickly prompted similar loyalty to Chrysostom from the citizens of the imperial capital, but his denunciations of clerical and civic sinfulness earned him enemies in high places. He was banished, but a popular riot led to his recall. The reprieve was temporary, however, and Chrysostom would eventually end his life in exile.

Like most early Christian preaching, the sermons of Chrysostom are mostly homilies—simply structured sermons which follow the text closely. Yet a wealth of illustration, practical application, and dynamic delivery in those sermons transformed John of Antioch into one of the most gifted preachers in the church's history.

R. Albert Mohler, Jr., Editor
The Christian Index, Atlanta, Georgia
and Associate Editor, Preaching Magazine

1 A Theology of Preaching

Preach the word! That simple imperative frames the act of preaching as an act of obedience (see 2 Tim. 4:2, NIV). That is where any theology of preaching must begin.

Preaching did not emerge from the church's experimentation with communication techniques. The church does not preach because preaching is thought to be a good idea or an effective technique. The sermon has not earned its place in Christian worship by proving its utility in comparison with other means of communication or aspects of worship. Rather, we preach because we have been commanded to preach.

Preaching is a commission—a charge. As Paul stated boldly, it is the task of the minister of the gospel to "preach the Word, . . . in season and out of season" (2 Tim. 4:2, NIV). A theology of preaching begins with the humble acknowledgment that preaching is not a human invention but a gracious creation of God and a central part of His revealed will for the church. Furthermore, preaching is distinctively Christian in its origin and practice. Other religions may include teaching, or even public speech and calls to prayer. However, the preaching act is *sui generis*, a function of the church established by Jesus Christ.

As John A. Broadus stated: "Preaching is characteristic of Christianity. No other religion has made the regular and frequent assembling of groups of people, to hear religious instruction and exhortation, an integral part of divine worship."[1] The importance of preaching is rooted in Scripture and revealed in the unfolding story of the church. The church has never been faithful when it has lacked fidelity in the pulpit. In the words of P. T. Forsyth: "With preaching Christianity stands or falls, because it is the declaration of the gospel."[2]

The church cannot *but* preach lest it deny its own identity and abdicate its ordained purpose. Preaching is communication, but not *mere* communication. It is human speech, but much more than speech. As Ian Pitt-Watson notes, preaching is not even "a kind of speech communication that happens to be about God."[3] Its ground, its goal, and its glory are all located in the sovereign will of God.

The act of preaching brings forth a combination of exposition, testimony, exhortation, and teaching. Still, preaching cannot be reduced to any of these, or even to the sum total of its individual parts combined.

The primary Greek form of the word "preach" (*kērusso*) reveals its intrinsic rootage in the *kerygma*—the gospel itself. Preaching is an inescapably theological act, for the preacher dares to speak of God and, in a very real sense, *for* God. A theology of preaching should take trinitarian form, reflecting the very nature of the self-revealing God. In so doing, it bears witness to the God who speaks, the Son who saves, and the Spirit who illuminates.

The God Who Speaks

True preaching begins with this confession: we preach because God has spoken. That fundamental conviction is the fulcrum of the Christian faith and of Christian preaching. The Creator God of the universe, the omniscient, omnipotent, omnipresent Lord chose of His own sovereign will to reveal Himself to us. Supreme and complete in His holiness, needing in nothing and hidden from our view, God condescended to speak to us—even to reveal Himself to us.

As Carl F. H. Henry suggests, revelation is "a divinely initiated activity, God's free communication by which He alone turns His personal privacy into a deliberate disclosure of His reality."[4] In an act of holy graciousness, God gave up His comprehensive privacy that we might know Him. God's revelation is the radical claim upon which we dare to speak of God—*He has spoken!*

Our God-talk must therefore begin and end with what God has spoken concerning Himself. Preaching is not the business of speculating about God's nature, will, or ways, but is bearing witness to what God has spoken concerning Himself. Preaching does not consist of speculation but of exposition.

The preacher dares to speak the Word of truth to a generation which rejects the very notion of objective, public truth. This is not rooted in the preacher's arrogant claim to have discovered worldly wisdom or to have penetrated the secrets of the universe. To the contrary, the preacher dares to proclaim truth on the basis of God's sovereign self-disclosure. God has spoken, and He has commanded us to speak of Him.

The Bible bears witness to itself as the written Word of God. This springs from the fact that God has spoken. In the Old Testament alone, the phrases "the Lord said," "the Lord spoke," and "the word of the Lord came" appear at least 3,808 times.[5] This confession brings the preacher face to face with Scripture as divine revelation. The authority of Scripture is none other than the authority of God Himself. As the Reformation formula testifies, "where Scripture speaks, God speaks." The authority of the preacher is intrinsically rooted in the authority of the Bible as the church's Book and the unblemished Word of God. Its total truthfulness is a witness to God's own holiness. We speak because God has spoken, and because He has given us His Word.

As Scripture itself records, God has called the church to speak of Him on the basis of His Word and deeds. All Christian preaching is biblical preaching. That formula is axiomatic. Those who preach from some other authority or text may speak with great effect and attractiveness, but they are preaching "another gospel," and their words will betray them. Christian preaching is not an easy task. Those who are called to preach bear a heavy duty. As Martin Luther confessed "If I could come down with a good conscience, I would rather be stretched out on a wheel and carry stones than preach one sermon." Speaking on the basis of what God has spoken is both arduous and glorious.

A theology of preaching begins with the confession that the God who speaks has ultimate claim upon us. He who spoke a word and brought a world into being created us from the dust. God has chosen enlivened dust—and all creation—to bear testimony to His glory.

In preaching, finite, frail, and fault-ridden human beings bear bold witness to the infinite, all-powerful, and perfect Lord. Such an endeavor would smack of unmitigated arrogance and over-reaching were it not for the fact that God Himself has set us to the task. In this light, preaching is not an act of arrogance, but of humility. True preaching is not an exhibition of the brilliance or intellect of the preacher, but an exposition of the wisdom and power of God.

This is possible only when the preacher stands in submission to the text of Scripture. The issue of authority is inescapable. Either the preacher *or* the text will be the operant authority. A theology of preaching serves to remind those who preach of the danger of confusing our own authority with that of the biblical text. We are called, not only to *preach*, but to preach *the Word*.

Acknowledging the God who speaks as Lord is to surrender the preaching event in an act of glad submission. Preaching thus becomes the occasion for the Word of the Lord to break forth anew. This occasion itself represents the divine initiative, for it is God Himself, and not the preacher, who controls His Word.

John Calvin understood this truth when he affirmed that "The Word goeth out of the mouth of God in such a manner that it likewise goeth out of the mouth of men; for God does not speak openly from heaven but employs men as His instruments."[6] Calvin understood preaching to be the process by which God uses human instruments to speak what He Himself has spoken. This He accomplishes through the preaching of Scripture under the illumination and *testimonium* of the Holy Spirit. God uses preachers, Calvin offered, "rather than to thunder at us and drive us away."[7] Further, "it is a singular privilege that He deigns to consecrate to Himself the mouths and toungues [sic] of men in order that His voice may resound in them."[8]

Thus, preaching springs from the truth that God has spoken in word and deed and that He has chosen human vessels to bear witness to Himself and His gospel. We speak because we cannot be silent. We speak because God has spoken.

The Son Who Saves

"In the past," wrote the author of Hebrews, "God spoke to our forefathers through the prophets at many times and in various ways, but in these last days He has spoken to us by His Son, whom He appointed heir of all things, and through whom He made the universe" (Heb. 1:1-2, NIV). The God who reveals Himself (*Deus Revelatus*) has spoken supremely and definitively through His Son.

Carl F. H. Henry once stated that only a theology "abreast of divine invasion" could lay claim upon the church. The same holds true for a theology of preaching. All Christian preaching is unabashedly Christological.

Christian preaching points to the incarnation of God in Christ as the stackpole of truth and the core of Christian confession. "God was in Christ, reconciling the world unto Himself" (2 Cor. 5:19). Thus, preaching is itself an act of grace, making clear God's initiative toward us in Christ. Preaching is one means by which the redeemed bear witness to the Son who saves. That message of divine salvation, the unmerited act of God in Christ, is the criterion by which all preaching is to be judged.

With this in mind, all preaching is understood to be rooted in the incarnation. As the apostle John declared, God spoke to us by means of His Son, *the Word*, and that Word was made flesh and dwelt among us (1:14). All human speech is rendered mute by the incarnate Word of God. Yet, at the same time, the incarnation allows us to speak of God in the terms He has set for Himself—in the identity of Jesus the Christ.

Preaching is itself incarnational. In the preaching event a human being stands before a congregation of fellow humans to speak the most audacious words ever encountered or uttered by the human species: God has made Himself known in His Son, through whom He has also made provision for our salvation.

As Karl Barth insisted, all preaching must have a *thrust*. The thrust cannot come from the energy, earnestness, or even the conviction of the preacher. "The sermon," asserted Barth, "takes its thrust when it begins: The Word became flesh . . . once and for all, and when account of this is taken in every thought."[9] The power of the sermon does not lie in the domain of the preacher, but in the providence of God. Preaching does not demonstrate the power of the human instrument, but of the biblical message of God's words and deeds.

Jesus serves as our model, as well as the content of our preaching. As Mark recorded in his Gospel, "Jesus came preaching" (1:14), and His model of preaching as the unflinching forth-telling of God's gracious salvation is the ultimate standard by which all human preaching is to be judged. Jesus Himself sent His disciples out to preach repentance (Mark 6:12). The church received its charge to "preach the good news to all creation" (Mark 16:15). Preaching is, as Christ made clear, an extension of His own will and work. The church preaches because it has been commanded to do so.

If preaching takes its ground and derives its power from God's revelation in the Son, then the cross looms as the paramount symbol and event of Christian proclamation. "We preach not ourselves," pressed Paul, "but Jesus Christ as Lord" (2 Cor. 4:5). That message was centered on the cross as the definitive criterion of preaching. Paul understood that the cross is simultaneously the most divisive and the most unifying event in human history. The preaching of the cross—the proclamation of the substitutionary atonement wrought by the sinless Son of God—"is foolishness to those who are perishing, but to those of us who are being saved, it is the power of God" (1 Cor. 1:18).

Any honest and faithful theology of preaching must acknowledge that charges of foolishness are not incidental to the homiletical task. They are central. Those seeking worldly wisdom or secret signs will be frustrated with what we preach, for the cross is the abolition of both. The Christian preacher dares not speak a message which will appeal to the sign-seekers and wisdom-lovers, "lest the cross of Christ be emptied of its power" (1 Cor. 1:17). As James Denney stated plainly, "No man can give at once the impression that he himself is clever and that Jesus Christ is mighty to save."

Beyond this, Paul indicated the danger of ideological temptations and the allure of "technique" as threats to the preaching of the gospel. Writing to the church at Corinth, Paul explained: "My message and my preaching were not with wise and persuasive words, but with a demonstration of the Spirit's power, so that your faith might not rest on men's wisdom, but on God's power" (1 Cor. 2:4-5, NIV).

To preach the gospel of the Son who saves is to forfeit all claim or aim to make communication technique or human persuasion the measure of homiletical effectiveness. Preaching is effective when it is faithful. The effect is in the hands of God.

The preacher dares to speak for God, on the basis of what God has spoken concerning Himself and His ways, and that means speaking the word of the cross. That underscores the humility of preaching. As John Piper suggests, the act of preaching is "both a past event of substitution and a present event of execution."[10] Only the redeemed, those who know the cross as the power and wisdom of God, understand the glory and the burden of preaching. To the world of unbelief, such words are senseless prattle.

To preach the message of the Son who saves is to spread the world's most hopeful message. All Christian preaching is resurrection preaching. A theology of preaching includes both a "theology of the cross" and a "theology of glory." The glory is not the possession of the church, much less the preacher, but of God Himself.

The cross brings the eclipse of all human pretensions and enlightenment, but the empty tomb reveals the radiant sunrise of God's personal glory. If Christ has not been raised, asserted Paul, "our preaching is useless" (1 Cor. 15:14, NIV). This glimpse of God's glory does not afford the church or the preacher a sense of triumphalism or self-sufficiency. To the contrary, it points to the sufficiency of God and to the glory only He enjoys—a glory He has shared with us in the person and work of Jesus Christ. The reflection of that revelation is the radiance and glory of preaching.

The Spirit Who Illuminates

The preacher stands before the congregation as the external minister of the Word, but the Holy Spirit works as the internal minister of that same Word. A theology of preaching must take the role of the Spirit into full view, for without an understanding of the work of the Spirit, the task of preaching is robbed of its balance and power.

The neglect of the work of the Spirit is one evidence of the decline of biblical trinitarianism in our midst. Charles H. Spurgeon warned, "You might as well expect to raise the dead by whispering in their ears, as hope to save souls by preaching to them, if it were not for the agency of the Holy Spirit."[11] The Spirit performs His work of inspiration, indwelling, regeneration, and sanctification as the inner minister of the Word; it is the Spirit's ministry of illumination that allows the Word of the Lord to break forth.

Both the preacher and the hearers are dependent upon the illumination granted by the Holy Spirit for any understanding of the text. As Calvin warned, "No one should now hesitate to confess that he is able to understand God's mysteries only in so far as he is illumined by God's grace. He who attributes any more understanding to himself is all the more blind because he does not recognize his own blindness."[12] This has been the confession of great preachers from the first century to the present, and it will ever remain. Tertullian, for example, called the Spirit his "Vicar" who ministered the Word to himself and his congregation.

The Reformation saw a new acknowledgement of the union of Word and Spirit. This *testimonium* was understood to be the crucial means by which the Spirit imparted understanding. This trinitarian doctrine produced preaching that was both bold and humble; bold in its content but uttered forth by humble humans who knew their utter dependence upon God.

The same God who called forth human vessels and set them to preach also promised the power of the Spirit. Martyn Lloyd-Jones was aware that preachers often forget this promise:

> Seek Him always. But go beyond seeking Him; expect Him. Do you expect anything to happen when you get up to preach in a pulpit? Or do you just say to yourself, "Well, I have prepared my address, I am going to give them this address; some of them will appreciate it and some will not"? Are you expecting it to be the turning point in someone's life? That is what preaching is meant to do. . . . Seek this power, expect this power, yearn for this power; and when the power comes, yield to Him.[13]

To preach "in the Spirit" is to preach with the acknowledgement that the human instrument has no control over the message—and no control over the Word as it is set loose within the congregation. The Spirit, as John declared, testifies, "because the Spirit is the truth" (1 John 5:6b, NIV).

Conclusion

J. I. Packer defined preaching as "the event of God bringing to an audience a Bible-based, Christ-related, life-impacting message of instruction and direction from Himself through the words of a spokesperson."[14] That rather comprehensive definition depicts the process of God speaking forth His Word, using human instruments to proclaim His message, and then calling men and women unto Himself. A theological analysis reveals that preaching is deadly business. As Spurgeon confirmed, "Life, death, hell, and worlds unknown may hang on the preaching and hearing of a sermon."[15]

The apostle Paul revealed the logic of preaching when he asked, "How, then, can they call upon the one they have not believed in? And how can they believe in the one of whom they have not heard? And how can they hear without someone preaching to them?" (Rom. 10:14, NIV).

The preacher is a commissioned agent whose task is to speak because God has spoken, because the preacher has been entrusted with the telling of the gospel of the Son who saves, and because God has promised the power of the Spirit as the seal and efficacy of the preacher's calling.

The ground of preaching is none other than the revelation which God has addressed to us in Scripture. The goal of preaching is no more and no less than faithfulness to this calling. The glory of preaching is that God has promised to use preachers and preaching to accomplish His purpose and bring glory unto Himself.

Therefore, a theology of preaching is essentially doxology. The ultimate purpose of the sermon is to glorify God and to reveal a glimpse of His glory to His creation. This is the sum and substance of the preaching task. That God would choose such a means to express His own glory is beyond our understanding; it is rooted in the mystery of the will and wisdom of God.

Yet, God has called out preachers and commanded them to preach. Preaching is not an act the church is called to defend but a ministry preachers are called to perform. Thus, whatever the season, the imperative stands: Preach the Word!

Notes

1. John A. Broadus, *On the Preparation and Delivery of Sermons,* rev. Vernon L. Stanfield (San Francisco: Harper and Row, 1979), iv.
2. P. T. Forsyth, *Positive Preaching and the Modern Mind* (Grand Rapids: Eerdmans, 1964), 5.
3. Ian Pitt-Watson, *A Primer for Preachers* (Grand Rapids: Baker Book House, 1986), 14.
4. Carl F. H. Henry, *God, Revelation and Authority,* Vol. 2 (Waco: Word Books, 1976), 17.
5. As cited in Martyn Lloyd-Jones, *Authority* (London: InterVarsity Press, 1958), 50.
6. John Calvin, *Commentary on Isaiah* [55:11], *Corpus Reformatorum* 37.291, cited in Ronald S. Wallace, "The Preached Word as the Word of God," in *Readings in Calvin's Theology,* ed. Donald McKim (Grand Rapids: Baker Book House, 1984), 231.
7. John Calvin, *Institutes of the Christian Religion,* IV.1.5, tr. Floyd Lewis Battles, ed. John T. McNeill, 2 vols. (Philadelphia: Westminster Press, 1960), 1018.
8. Ibid.
9. Karl Barth, *Homiletics,* tr. Geoffrey Bromiley and Donald W. Daniels (Louisville: Westminster/John Knox Press, 1991), 52.
10. John Piper, *The Supremacy of Christ in Preaching* (Grand Rapids: Baker Book House, 1990), 35.
11. Charles H. Spurgeon, *New Park Street Pulpit,* 5.211.
12. Calvin, *Institutes,* II.2.21, 281.
13. Martyn Lloyd-Jones, *Preaching and Preachers* (Grand Rapids: Zondervan, 1971), 325.
14. J. I. Packer, "Authority in Preaching," *The Gospel in the Modern World,* ed. Martyn Eden and David F. Wells (London: InterVarsity Press, 1991), 199.
15. Charles H. Spurgeon, *Metropolitan Tabernacle Pulpit* 39 (London: Alabaster and Passmore, 1862-1917): 170.

2 *Bill J. Leonard*
Professor of Religion
Samford University
Birmingham, Alabama

Preaching in Historical Perspective

"He went about all Galilee, teaching in their synagogues and preaching the gospel of the kingdom and healing every disease and every infirmity among the people" (Matt. 4:23). "Jesus came preaching," the Holy Scriptures declare. He sent out the apostles, charging them: "Preach as you go, saying, 'The kingdom of heaven is at hand,'" (Matt. 10:7, RSV). At Pentecost the Spirit was poured out on "all flesh," and observers reported: "We hear them telling in our own tongues the mighty works of God" (Acts 2:11, RSV). Peter recalled the words of the prophet Joel: "On my menservants and my maidservants in those days I will pour out my Spirit; and they shall prophesy" (Acts 2:18, RSV). After his encounter on the Damascus Road, the apostle Paul "went in and out among them at Jerusalem, preaching boldly in the name of the Lord" (Acts 9:28-29, RSV). Paul himself would assert that "it pleased God through the folly of what we preach to save those who believe" (1 Cor. 1:21, RSV).

From the beginning, the church of Jesus Christ was a preaching church. This chapter describes Christian preaching in historical perspective. It is an effort to delineate selected themes, issues, and persons related to the history of preaching. At best, these limited materials may point the reader to further study in greater detail.

Apostolic Preaching and Preachers

The earliest Christians struggled with the nature of their message and the role of their messengers. Almost immediately the first Christians were compelled to develop strategies for distinguishing true preachers from false ones. It was no easy matter. Initially, many of the churches were guided by various traveling "charismatics" who addressed particular spiritual and practical needs, exercising their specific spiritual gifts for the edification of the fledgling communities of faith. These included apostles, prophets, teachers, miracle workers, healers, helpers, administrators, and "speakers in various kinds of tongues" (1 Cor. 12:28, RSV).

As the Christian communities grew and matured, however, they turned to a more localized ministry composed of pastors (variously called elders, presbyters, or bishops) and deacons. Conflict soon developed between the settled ministers and the traveling charismatics. Paul described difficulties between himself and the so-called "super-apostles" in 2 Corinthians 12. The letter of Clement of Rome to the Church at Corinth, written around A.D. 96, illustrates a continuing controversy in that troubled church. It seems that the church had displaced the duly elected bishops (pastors) and deacons for the leadership of certain traveling prophets who had appeared on the scene. Clement wrote that the Corinthian church has "unjustly deposed" those "who were appointed by the Apostles, or subsequently by other eminent men, with the approval of the whole Church."[1] These preachers were known as those who "have ministered blamelessly to the flock of Christ in a humble, peaceable, and worthy way, and have had testimony borne to them by all for long periods."[2] Their reputations, as their doctrine, was tried and true.

The situation at Corinth remains a dilemma for the church. Who is a prophet and who is not, and how do you know the difference? One clue to the early church's response is found in an early second-century handbook called the *Didache* or *The Teaching of the Twelve Apostles*. The writer suggested: "But let every apostle that cometh unto you be received as the Lord. And he shall stay one day, and, if need be the next also, but, if he stay three, he is a false prophet."[3] So the first Christians developed a method for receiving all who claimed to be prophets and preachers and a plan for sending them on their way! Their experience teaches us that such questions concerning ministerial message, reputation, and authority are nothing new in the church.

The early Christian preachers had a formidable task. Their sermons dealt with morality and doctrine, with politics and pastoral care. On one hand they were apologists, defending the right of Christianity to exist in a sometimes hostile, sometimes indifferent world. Yet they were also polemicists, defining theological ideas and doctrinal positions for those inside the church. Tertullian, Cyprian, Justin Martyr, Clement of Alexandria, Origen, and Jerome were among those preacher/teachers who shaped the church's doctrines. They addressed and expanded on questions touched, but not elaborated on, in Holy Scripture. Who was

Jesus Christ? What was His relationship to the God He called Father? What was the nature of the human and the divine within Jesus? How were those two dynamic forces fused in Jesus of Nazareth? What was the Christian's relationship to the state? What was the meaning of baptism and the Lord's Supper? What was the nature of ecclesial and ministerial authority? Preaching was a means of dealing with controversies, addressing crises, and articulating beliefs. To read the early Christian preachers is to realize how timeless the struggles, needs, and debates are within the church of Jesus Christ in the second or the twenty-first centuries.

Augustine: *Confessions* of a Preacher

No writer, preacher, or theologian in the early church has had greater impact on the church's identity (at least in the West) than Augustine of Hippo. Augustine's conversion is described in his classic autobiography known as the *Confessions*. In that pilgrimage he reminded us of the impact of preaching on his own spiritual struggles. One powerful influence on Augustine came from the great preacher Ambrose, the bishop of Milan (339-397). Ambrose was a major factor in Augustine's final decision to move toward faith and baptism. Augustine's own words detail the significance of the bishop's preaching:

> To Milan I came, to Ambrose the Bishop, known to the whole world as among the best of man, Thy devout servant; whose eloquent discourse did then plentifully dispense unto Thy people the flour of Thy wheat, the gladness of Thy oil, and the sober inebriation of Thy wine. To him was I unknowing led by Thee, that by him I might knowingly be led to Thee. . . . And I listened diligently to him preaching to the people, not with that intent I ought, but, as it were, trying his eloquence, whether it answered the fame thereof, or flowed fuller or lower than was reported; . . . and I hung on his words attentively; but of the matter I was as a careless and scornful looker-on; and I was delighted with the sweetness of his discourse.[4]

Augustine's own sermons were usually preached without notes and recorded by secretaries in the audience. His sermons were "simple, direct, and to the point." He was often given to spontaneity and digression.[5] Like other preachers, he warned of the dangers of pride and self-centeredness, noting: "He is a vain preacher of the word of God without, who is not a hearer within."[6] Concerning words of the preacher and the Word of God, Augustine suggested: "We use words every day and they become very cheap. They just sound, and then they are done with—nothing but words. Yet even in man there can be a word that remains in his heart. What comes out of his mouth is sound. The word in his heart has a real existence; you can understand it from the sound you hear, but it is not the sound."[7]

Joseph Bernadin observes that the "chief characteristic" of Augustine's work as pastor and preacher appears to be "his penetrating insight into both divine and human nature, and his use of this insight in his dealings with the contemporary world and its problems. His advice and activity were conspicuous for sound common sense, breadth of view, psychological acumen, generosity, and fairness."[8]

John Chrysostom: Prophet in the Pulpit

St. John Chrysostom—John the Golden-mouthed—was perhaps the greatest preacher of the early Christian centuries. Born in A.D. 345, John was nurtured to the faith by his pious mother, Anthusa. His early religious education was shaped by Meletius, the bishop of Antioch, and Diodorus, the leader of a catechetical school in the city. Following his baptism in 369 (deferred baptism was common in the fourth century), John embarked on a hermit's life, endangering his health with certain ascetic practices. Ordained a priest in 386, his career as a preacher began in Antioch. John Chrysostom's fame as a preacher should not obscure the controversial nature of his moral and spiritual concerns. The fact is that his preaching frequently got him into trouble with the ecclesiastical and political establishment of his day.

In 398 he became bishop of Constantinople. There his fame as preacher increased along with his criticism of the immoral activities of the rich and their continued exploitation of the poor. In a homily on John 4:2-10, he attacked those "diseases of the soul"—"greed, sloth, melancholy, laziness, licentiousness"—which mark the beginning of folly. He asked: "Where there is satiety, it is not possible for desire to exist, and if desire is lacking how could there ever be pleasure? Therefore, not only should we find the poor more prudent and healthier than the rich, but even enjoying more happiness."[9]

Such criticisms soon created conflict within the court at Constantinople, particularly with the Empress Eudoxia who took his moral admonitions quite personally. Court intrigue led to a series of exiles and restorations. Ultimately, Chrysostom died in 407, again exiled, worn out from his travails.

Chrysostom's homilies are a treasure of spiritual insight. The sermons generally began with a "rather formal, and often quite stylized, introduction."[10] Next there was a commentary on the text of Scripture around which the homily was built. This was followed by a "moral exhortation," stressing particular virtues or vices to be promoted or forsaken. The sermon then concluded with a brief prayer and doxology.[11]

Chrysostom's works include an extensive collection of sermons on particular books of the Bible. He composed some 88 homilies on the Gospel of John, 90 on the Gospel of Matthew, and 32 on the Epistle to the Romans.[12]

Contemporary homileticians should take heart in Chrysostom's comments regarding the inattentiveness and distraction of his fourth-century listeners. In one sermon he noted: "To be sure, he who addresses an attentive audience has the consolation of speaking to receptive listeners. However, he who continues to preach, and, though not listened to, does not cease speaking, would be deserving of more credit, because, in accordance with what seems best to God, he is performing his duty completely, even though no one is paying attention."[13] Even "golden-mouthed" orators cannot keep everybody listening.

Concerning the preacher's task, Chrysostom declared:

> Now, my preaching is addressed to all and provides a remedy in common for those who need one, but it is the duty of each one of my listeners to take what is suited for his affliction. I do not know who are the sick, who are healthy. Therefore, I discuss subjects of every sort and suited to every ill: Now censuring greed, and again delicate living; at another time, attacking licentiousness; now praising and encouraging almsgiving, then again each of the other good works. . . . Indeed, in such a great crowd as this all the diseases of the soul must be represented, even if not all are in every man.[14]

Chrysostom's sermons have an inescapable timelessness which address the human condition in every age.

Bernard of Clairvaux: The Mystic Dogma

Christian monasticism brought renewal to the church through the cultivation of the life of prayer and contemplation. Bernard of Clairvaux (1090-1153) gave voice to monastic and mystical spirituality in the twelfth century. His presence and his preaching drew persons to the new French abbey of Citeaux (founded in 1098). When he joined the Cistercian Order in 1112, the community was struggling and its future seemed uncertain. C. H. Lawrence writes: "By the time of his death forty-one years later, it had dispatched colonies to all parts of Europe; and there existed 343 abbeys of Cistercian monks, of which 68 had been directly founded from Clairvaux."[15] During those years Bernard became the Cistercians' "foremost apologist and recruiting officer."[16]

Bernard was a complex personality, a mystic who called the church to follow the love of Christ. He was also a powerful controversialist with an almost obsessive concern to preserve and protect Catholic orthodoxy. The details of his early life are sketchy, shaped by the hagiographical admiration of his contemporaries and later devotees. He was a monastic, a mystic, an advisor to popes, and a well-known opponent of the brilliant and controversial philosopher Peter Abelard. Bernard also proclaimed the need for a crusade to preserve sacred sites in the holy land. He helped provoke great crusading fervor, but his effort ultimately collapsed due to internecine squabbling among the nobility.[17]

Through it all Bernard was a preacher. His sermons were "a call to total renunciation of the secular world, to follow Christ by embracing a life of poverty, austerity and prayer."[18] Indeed, Bernard preached a vision of salvation centered in the monastic life. It was "a spirituality based on experience."[19] In his introduction to Bernard's selected works, Benedictine scholar Jean Leclercq focuses attention to the biblical foundation of the mystic's homilies. Leclercq writes: "He assimilated the Bible so completely that it became part of himself and he had no need to refer to the text before quoting it to verify his statements."[20]

Among Bernard's best known sermons is a collection on the "Song of Songs," read in the allegorical hermeneutic of the times. They include some eighty-six homilies, none of which goes beyond the second verse of the first chapter of the book. In these sermons he stressed the intimacy of spiritual experience, "between the soul and Christ."[21] This method of biblical interpretation is evident in Bernard's reflection on the text: "Let him kiss me with the kisses of his mouth" (1:2). He declared: "It is with good reason, then, that I have nothing to do with dreams and visions, reject figures and mysteries, and even the beauty of angels seems tedious to me. For my Jesus outshines them so far in his beauty and loveliness (Ps 44:5). That is why I ask him, not any other, angel or man, to kiss me with the kiss of his mouth."[22]

As preacher, mystic, and monastic, Bernard was an articulate spokesperson for the spirituality of love, a theme that occurs throughout his homilies. Bernard never wrote down any of his sermons. They are known only through the transcripts recorded by his listeners. Some were dictated to a secretary. Many of his formal sermonic presentations were given in the style of the day, dictated to a scribe while pretending to be addressing an audience. They were widely circulated in a large collection of materials. His style was fairly simple. He began with an Old Testament response to a particular issue, discussed its dogmatic significance in the New Testament, and concluded with its moral and theological significance.[23] Leclercq writes that Bernard "drafted hundreds of liturgical sermons, none of which were actually preached in the form that has come down to us."[24] They are a blend of the dogmatic and the practical which became an important part of the mystical literature of the church, and are utilized to this day by those concerned with the quest for Christian spirituality.

Even saints are human beings, however. Bernard's ascetic tendencies affected his physiological condition. C. H. Lawrence notes that the saint could "not keep food down long after eating and he found it necessary to dig a receptacle in the ground beside his stall in choir. For a time his physical presence was so repellent to the brethren that he had to live in separate quarters."[25] William of St. Thierry, Bernard's early biographer, saw this as a sign of his spirituality. William concluded that in Bernard, "the spirit lusted against the flesh with such power that the weakly animal nature sank under the burden."[26] Bernard's asceticism shaped his work as preacher and monastic.

Bernard was certainly not the only medieval preacher and ascetic to captivate the faithful with his homilies and his holiness. The mendicant orders which thrived in the thirteenth century were composed of persons who sought to live the gospel literally from the pages of the New Testament. The mendicant orders of the middle ages were primarily preaching orders. Francis of Assisi, the best known of the mendicants, perceived a two-fold calling: to rebuild the church (he literally began with one small church outside Assisi), and to preach the joys of the kingdom of God. As he wrestled with his calling, Francis (1181/2-1226) heard the words of the Gospel of Matthew, read during the celebration of the mass: "Preach as you go, saying, 'The Kingdom of heaven is at hand.' " "Take no gold, silver, nor copper in your belts, no bag for your journey, nor two tunics, nor sandals, nor staff; for the labourer is worthy of his food." Thomas of Celano, Francis' earliest biographer, says that when he heard those words he cried: "This is what I wish, this is what I am seeking."[27]

The Franciscan Order which Francis founded was above all a community of preachers who were called to live according to the gospel, to preach the good news, and to depend on others for care and sustenance. They were to own nothing, roaming the country preaching repentance. Indeed, their life was the first phase of their preaching. C. H. Lawrence writes: "At the beginning, Francis and his disciples were an intimate fraternity of nomadic preachers, some clerics but most of them laymen, who moved from town to town in central Italy, preaching in the market-squares, attending services in the churches, and doing manual jobs or begging for their keep."[28] Francis encouraged all the Fratres Minores, the Little Brothers, to preach everywhere they went. One biographer writes:

> Braving all ridicule, he stood in the squares of Assisi and nearby towns and preached the gospel of poverty and Christ . . . revolted by the unscrupulous pursuit of wealth that marked the age, and shocked by the splendor and luxury of some clergymen, he denounced money itself as a devil and a curse and bade his followers despise it.[29]

Their word and their witness brought renewal to the medieval church.

The mendicants known as the Order of Preachers, however, were the Dominicans, the followers of Dominic de Guzman (1170-1221). The order was born of Dominic's desire to convert the Albigensians or Cathari, a heretical group prevalent in the Languedoc region of southern France. Approved by the Church in 1216, the Dominicans were given a world-wide preaching mission. They fostered a revival of preaching in the medieval church. Lawrence observes: "In their hands, sermon-making became a new art, which was inculcated in their schools through their writings."[30] They produced a significant collection of literature, including a work called *The Instruction of Preachers,* written by the Dominican Humbert de Romans. It admonished preachers: "Keep a middling tempo in delivery, so as not to speak too fast or too slowly; for rushing swamps the understanding of your hearers, and slowness generates boredom."[31] They also edited a number of biblical concordances to provide the preacher with effective texts. There were also collections of *exempla,* the medieval equivalent of sermon illustrations, taken from the lives of the saints and the moral lessons of daily life.[32] Dominicans also perfected a form of the sermon which had appeared in the 12th century, sermons *ad status,* addressed to particular subgroups within medieval society. These included knights, nobility, married couples, servants, and others. Education was seen as essential in preparing the preacher for his task. The Dominicans were among the most educated preachers of the Middle Ages.

Martin Luther: Wrestling with the Word

A. Skevington-Wood writes that Martin Luther "only became a reformer as he wrestled with the Word. Throughout his career he conceived his first duty to be that of preaching."[33] He made no distinction between classroom lectures and pulpit sermons. He was not only a professor at the University of Wittenberg, but he was also a preacher at the parish church there. His normal practice was to preach two to three times a week.[34]

Wood notes that in calling Luther a biblical preacher Luther's broader conception of the Word of God should not be undermined. Wood writes that Luther "did not equate the Word of God with the Bible, although he accepted the Bible as the Word of God. For Luther, the Word of God was not static, but active. It could never be imprisoned in a book—not even in God's Book. The Word of God is speaking. It is God confronting man in personal encounter."[35] This meant that in Luther's preaching he gave extensive attention to the role of paradox. He said: "When I preach a sermon I take an antithesis."[36] Likewise, his sermons gave great emphasis to the role of faith by which the truths of Scripture become reality in the life of the individual. He reminded his hearers that "faith comes from what is heard, and what is heard comes by the preaching of Christ" (Rom. 10:17).

For Luther, preaching was the central element of worship, but it could not be divorced from the entire worship event. Word and sacrament were inseparable. Luther wrote that the preacher "baptizes, catechizes, absolves you through the ministry of His own sacraments. These are the words of God, not of Plato or Aristotle. It is God Himself who speaks."[37] The Word permeated all the work of the preacher.

John Donne: Poet in the Pulpit

"Invention, and Disposition, and Art, and Eloquence, and Expression, and Elocution, and reading, and writing, and printing, are secondary things, accessary things, auxiliary, subsidiary things; men may account us, and make account of us, as of Orators in the pulpit, and of Authors, in the shop; but if they account of us as of Ministers and Stewards, they give us our due; that's our name to you."[38]

John Donne (1571/2-1631), "the preacher who remained always the poet," was one of the greatest preachers of the seventeenth century.[39] Language—speech—was central to Donne's sense of himself as a minister and preacher. "Breath is speech," he declared, "but Breath is life too."[40] Words were the expression of the Spirit of God in human beings.

Like many of his seventeenth-century contemporaries, Donne's sermons contain references to such early church writers as Jerome, Justin Martyr, Chrysostom, Ambrose, Cyprian, and Augustine, one of Donne's favorites. P. G. Stanwood and Heather Ross Asals survey Donne's "Theology of Language," noting his abiding, almost obsessive, concern for preaching. They explain that as he neared death, Donne stated his desire to die in the pulpit or, "if not that, yet that I might take my death in the Pulpit, that is, die the sooner by occasion of my former labours."[41]

Preachers, Donne said, were the "Trumpets, the Trumpetors" of the Word of God.[42] Preaching introduced the hearer to "the joyes [sic] of heaven."[43] As an Anglican preacher, Donne stressed the inseparable relationship between word and sacrament. They are, he said, "a powerful thunder, and lightning, that go together: Preaching is the thunder, that clears the air, disperses all clouds of ignorance; and then the Sacrament is the lightning, the glorious light, and presence of Christ Jesus himself. And in the having and loving of this, the Word and Sacraments, the outward means of salvation, ordained by God in his Church, consists this Irradiation, this Coruscation, this shining."[44] Both were necessary for the true proclamation of the gospel.

For John Donne, the preacher has a distinct "calling," a *Vocatio radicalis,* the calling that is the root and foundation of all."[45] The preacher is the messenger of the Word of God. Donne wrote: "It becommeth me to make my selfe as acceptable a messenger as I can, and to infuse the Word of God into you, as powerfully from the Word of God it selfe, quickened by his Spirit."[46] Preaching, therefore, was "God's Ordinance," whose end was to "beget faith." To do away with preaching would be to "disarme God, and to quench the spirit."[47]

John Donne was a master preacher and poet whose life was the pulpit. He is a bridge between the preachers of the early church and a new generation of Protestant pulpiteers. His work is an amazing blend of poetry and prose within the "radical vocation" of preaching. It is evident in his poetry/proclamation:

> Batter my heart, three-personed God, for you
> As yet but knock, breathe, shine, and seek to mend;
> That I may rise and stand, o'erthrow me, and bend
> Your force to break, blow, burn and make me new. . . .
> Take me to you, imprison me, for I
> Except you enthrall me, never shall be free,
> Nor ever chaste, except you ravish me.[48]

George Fox and the Quakers: Preaching in the Spirit

> That which I was moved to declare was this: that the holy Scriptures were given forth by the Spirit of God; and that all people must come to the Spirit of God in themselves in order to know God and Christ. . . . For as the Spirit of God was in them that gave forth the Scriptures, so the same Spirit must be in all them that come to understand the Scriptures.[49]

So George Fox (1642-1691) described the heart of the Quaker message, a word of the "inner light," which enlightens every human being and has only to be recognized. The early Quakers may have shared worship together in silence, but they were articulate preachers of the spiritual life, even in the face of imprisonment, persecution, and death. Fox preached to awaken the inner light in others. He preached in marketplaces, on hillsides, and even in Anglican worship services where the man in leather breeches would stand to challenge the priests on their own turf. In one such encounter Fox asked one priest: "Do you dare call this steeple house a church? Do you dare call this multitude of sinners a church? The true church is a pillar and ground of the truth, made up of living stones, living members, a spiritual household, which Christ is the head of; but he is not the head of this mixed multitude."[50]

The early Quakers, men and women alike, preached unashamedly, challenging the established religion of their day, calling for a new openness to the Spirit. All who discovered the power of the inner light were "ordained" to preach the gospel. Fox's wife, Margaret Fell Fox, spent years in jail for preaching the gospel of the light within. Likewise, Mary Dyer, a fearless Quaker preacher, was the first woman executed in America. Dyer was hanged by Boston Puritans in 1662 for preaching the gospel according to Quaker views.

Quaker preaching also challenged prevailing social attitudes of the day. Quakers challenged the death penalty, the just war theory, and class divisions of the time. God, they declared, was the Great Equalizer. All persons were to be treated the same. It was, and remains, a radical social ethic. The Society of Friends took their calling to it very seriously.

John Wesley: Proclaiming Grace for All

"Monday, 2nd April 1739. At four in the afternoon I submitted to be more vile, and proclaimed in the highways the glad tidings of salvation, speaking from a little eminence in a ground adjoining to the city (Bristol), to about three thousand people."[51] So John Wesley (1703-1791) described his decision to begin "field preaching," a revolutionary method for taking the gospel to 18th century Britain. Wesley's method was direct and simple: "I want thee for my Lord! I challenge thee for a child of God by faith. The Lord hath need of thee. Thou who feelest thou art fit only for hell, art just fit to advance his glory—the glory of his free grace. Believe in the Lord Jesus Christ and thou, even thou, art reconciled to God."[52] It was the message of free grace and free will that characterized the preaching of early Methodism.

Wesley's own sermons addressed numerous topics, but his abiding concern was with the doctrines of salvation by faith, assurance of salvation and sanctification, going on in grace.[53] He insisted: "It is our part to preach Christ by preaching all things whatsoever he hath revealed."[54] Wesley's message was clear: Christ has reconciled us to God. Sinners can be restored to fellowship with God and experience assurance of salvation. Salvation is not limited to an elect spiritual or economic elite. All who come to Christ by faith may receive God's grace.

Wesley urged his preachers to use language that was "plain, proper and clear."[55] He encouraged them not to preach lengthy sermons lest they lose the attention of their listeners. He noted: "People imagine the longer a sermon is, the more good it will do. This is a grand mistake. The help done on earth, God doth it . . . ; and He doth not need that we should use many words."[56] He advised them: "You are a Christian minister, speaking and writing to save souls. . . . Use all the sense, learning and fire you have; forgetting yourself, and remembering only these are the souls for whom Christ died."[57] Wesley himself must have used his own "sense, learning and fire" to declare the gospel. John Nelson, one of his early lay preachers, wrote of his first time to hear Wesley preach: "It made my heart beat like the pendulum of a clock and when he did speak, I thought his whole discourse was aimed at me. When he had done, I said, 'This man can tell the secrets of my heart.' "[58]

John Wesley was ever the "grand itinerant." For almost fifty years he traveled four to five thousand miles annually. It is estimated that during his lifetime he preached over forty thousand sermons. His work sparked a revival of preaching, worship, and social reform throughout Great Britain. The world has not ceased to be his parish.

The Shakers: When Women Preach

The Methodists were not the only religious group to begin in eighteenth-century Britain. New communities of "charismatic" Christians also took shape during this time. One of the most important of these new movements was the United Society of Believers in Christ's Second Appearing, or the Shakers. While their monastic, communitarian life has been studied extensively, little attention has been given to Shaker preaching, particularly in the early days of the order. The first members of the group were known as "Shaking Quakers" because of the ecstatic nature of their worship services. Begun in 1747, the members looked to women for leadership. Jane Wardley and Ann Lee were the most important. Jane Wardley was an articulate preacher who urged her followers to:

> Repent. For the kingdom of God is at hand. The new heaven and new earth prophesied of old is about to come. The marriage of the Lamb, the first resurrection, the new Jerusalem descended from above, these are even now at the door. And when Christ appears again, and the true church rises in full and transcendent glory, then all anti-Christian denominations—the priests, the church, the pope—will be swept away.[59]

Ann Lee joined them by 1758 and soon assumed leadership of the small community. The loss of four children in infancy created great trauma for "Mother Ann," as her followers later called her. She claimed numerous revelations regarding the fall of Adam and Eve and its relationship to sexual intercourse. She had become the "Mother of the new creation," who called her followers to confess their sins, give up all their worldly goods, and take up the cross of celibacy.[60] Her small community was soon known for its enthusiastic worship given to "singing and dancing, shaking and shouting, speaking with new tongues and prophesying, with all those various gifts of the Holy Ghost known in the primitive church."[61] The Shakers, as they were called, saw themselves as the avant garde of the kingdom of God, preparing the way for the new era when God's will was done on earth. In the kingdom, as in the Shaker fellowship, there was "neither marrying nor giving in marriage." Celibacy was a preparation for the kingdom.

By 1774, Ann Lee and some eight of her followers had immigrated to America, settling in New York. There they preached their doctrines and won a surprising following. Ann herself was a powerful preacher and charismatic personality, traveling around the colonies, particularly in New England, preaching her gospel views. When confronted about a female's right to preach, she responded that "all the children, both male and female, must be subject to their parents; and the woman, being second, must be subject to her husband, who is the first; but when the man is gone, the right of government belongs to the woman: So is the family of Christ."[62]

As their communities grew, women and men shared leadership of the Shaker communities. Women preached and received revelations as the Spirit fell upon them. Thriving on the religious enthusiasm of the first and second Great Awakenings, the Shakers declared their messianic, communitarian message with significant response. One early convert observed: "The wisdom of their instructions, the purity of their doctrine, their Christ-like deportment, and the simplicity of their manners, all appeared truly apostolical."[63] The Shakers represent a small but important utopian response to the gospel. Preaching in their communities knew no boundaries of gender, social class, or education. Their voice, though limited, must not be ignored.

The "Foolishness" of Preaching

There is so much more to tell: of Charles H. Spurgeon proclaiming the gospel from the pulpit of Metropolitan Tabernacle in words which caught the attention of a nation; of Nathan Soderblom proclaiming the unity of Christ's church as the modern ecumenical movement took shape; of Joseph Fort Newton and A. Maude Royden modeling shared ministry and homiletical insight from the pulpit of City Temple, London, in the midst of World War I. We could tell of Martin Niemoller and Dietrich Bonhoeffer declaring the gospel and putting their lives on the line in the face of Nazi oppression; and of Sojourner Truth and Martin Luther King, Jr. whose sermons against the oppression of African-Americans spanned a century of struggle for civil rights. The history of the church is, in one sense, the history of preaching. Truly it pleased God by the "foolishness of preaching" to save those who believed.

Notes

1. J. Stevenson, *A New Eusebius* (London: SPCK, 1970), 12.
2. Ibid.
3. Ibid., 128.
4. Augustine, *The Confessions of St. Augustine* (New York: Airmont Publishing Co., 1969), 78.
5. Roy W. Battenhouse, ed., *A Companion to the Study of St. Augustine* (Grand Rapids: Baker Book House, 1979), 72-73.
6. Ibid., 73.
7. A. P. Carleton, *John Shines through Augustine* (New York: Association Press, 1959), 18-19.
8. Joseph Bernadin, "St. Augustine as Pastor," in Battenhouse, *Study of St. Augustine*, 59-60.

9. St. John Chrysostom, *Homilies on the Gospel of John* (New York: Fathers of the Church, 1957), 221.
10. Ibid., xv.
11. Ibid.
12. Ibid., xi-xii.
13. Ibid., 295.
14. Ibid., 222-223.
15. C. H. Lawrence, *Medieval Monasticism* (New York: Longman, 1984), 153.
16. Ibid.
17. Ibid, 24.
18. Ibid., 154.
19. Bernard of Clairvaux, *Selected Works* (New York: Paulist Press, 1987), 8.
20. Ibid., 34.
21. Ibid., 9.
22. Ibid., 216.
23. Ibid., 29.
24. Ibid., 28.
25. Lawrence, *Medieval Monasticism*, 154.
26. Ibid.
27. Ibid., 199.
28. Ibid., 201.
29. Will Durant, *The Age of Faith* vol in *The Story of Civilization* (New York: Simon and Schuster, 1950), 8.
30. Lawrence, *Medieval Monasticism*, 208.
31. Ibid.
32. Ibid.
33. A. Skevington-Wood, *Captive to the Word* (Grand Rapids: Eerdmans Publishing Company, 1969), 85.
34. Ibid., 86.
35. Ibid., 88-89.
36. Ibid., 91, citing *WA* 36:181.
37. Ibid.
38. John Donne, *The Sermons of John Donne*, ed. Evelyln M. Simpson and George R. Potter (Berkley: University of California Press, 1953-62), 6:103-104, cited in P. G. Stanwood and Heather Ross Asals, eds., *John Donne and the Theology of Language* (Columbia: University of Missouri Press, 1986), 1.
39. Ibid.
40. Ibid., 2.
41. Ibid., 7.
42. Ibid., 46.
43. Ibid.
44. Ibid., 332, citing works, 4:104-105.
45. Ibid., 299, citing works, 4:109.
46. Ibid., 300, citing works, 8:272-273.
47. Ibid., 336, citing works, 4:196-197.
48. Glenn Leggett, ed., *12 Poets* (New York: Holt, Rinehart and Winston, 1958), 43.
49. George Fox, *An Autobiography* (Philadelphia: Farris and Leach, 1909), 176-177.
50. George Fox, *The Journal of George Fox* (New York: Capricorn Books, 1963), 92-93.
51. W. L. Doughty, *John Wesley the Preacher* (London: Epworth Press, 1955), 36.
52. John Wesley, "Justification by Faith," in Albert C. Outler, ed., *John Wesley* (New York: Oxford University Press, 1964), 209.
53. Doughty, *John Wesley the Preacher*, 85.
54. Ibid., 87.
55. Ibid., 141.
56. Ibid., 177, citing *Letters*, vii.70.
57. Ibid., citing *Letters*, IV.256-258.
58. John Pudney, *John Wesley and His World* (New York: Charles Scribner's Sons, 1978), 71.

59. Edward Deming Andrews, *The People Called Shakers* (New York: Oxford University Press, 1953), 6.
60. Ibid., 12.
61. Ibid.
62. Ibid., 19.
63. Ibid., 25.

Martin Luther (1483-1546)
"Preaching for Reform"

Martin Luther's preaching was one of the major tools he used to shake the foundations of Christendom and begin the Reformation.

An Augustinian monk, Luther became a professor of theology at the University of Wittenburg. Even as a young man, his preaching became popular because of its emphasis on the spiritual needs of people, in contrast to the dry theological treatises common to so many pulpits of his day.

Luther's study of Scripture led him to condemn the abuses of 16th century Catholicism—especially its emphasis on good works as a means to salvation which produced such excesses as the sale of indulgences—and led to the initiation of the Reformation. Luther's commitment to the study of Scripture was also reflected in his preaching which emphasized the biblical text and its meaning. Despite his own scholarship, however, Luther's preaching was noted for its clarity and simplicity. He was convinced that people must understand a sermon if it was to compel them to act on its message.

As his reforming work continued, Luther came to see preaching as the central element of worship. He was convinced the primary purpose of preaching was to proclaim Jesus Christ; as a result, the Gospels' texts occupied the largest part of his preaching schedule, although he often preached from the Epistles as well.

As with every other area of his life, Martin Luther approached the preaching task with boldness, vigor, and a powerful commitment to serve God and honor His Word.

3 *Michael Duduit, Editor*
Preaching Magazine and
Director of Development and Church Relations
Samford University, Birmingham, Alabama

The Preaching Tradition in America

American life has been shaped, to a great extent, by two forms of public address: political and religious. While political speaking has had a profound influence on the life of the nation—witness such examples as Lincoln's "Gettysburg Address" or Franklin D. Roosevelt's stirring address to Congress following the attack on Pearl Harbor—religious speech, particularly preaching, has had an equally important place in the life of the nation. Indeed, if one could measure the impact of preaching on the heart and soul of the American people over some three centuries, it is likely that religious speech has had the more significant influence in the shaping of the national mind.

Preaching in a New World

From the earliest colonial days—whether English, Spanish, or French—religion was an integral element of life in the new world. Missionary expansion as well as material exploitation combined to provide a compelling rationale for the development of colonies in the western hemisphere.

American Protestants would trace their own earliest American roots to the English colonization efforts, especially those in New England. Many of those who sailed the Atlantic for a new life in America did so primarily for religious reasons. The Puritan movement which emerged within the Church of England sought additional reform modeled on the work of the Swiss reformers, particularly John Calvin. Many early Puritan leaders had fled to Geneva during Mary's reign, and upon the succession of Elizabeth I they returned to their homeland ready to lead a similar reform of the Anglican church. Once home, they encountered strenuous resistance from both crown and clergy.

The first New England colony consisted of a portion of a Separatist congregation which had been formed in England. They lived for a time in the Netherlands (where they made an uneasy peace with the Church of England), then returned to England and, in 1620, departed from Plymouth aboard the Mayflower, destined for Virginia but actually arriving in the less forgiving territory of Cape Cod in Massachusetts. Since their pastor had died before joining them, the "Pilgrims" were led spiritually for several years by Elder William Brewster, who served as preacher.

In terms of its influence on the American religious scene, the more significant colonial settlement came a decade later with the establishment of the Massachusetts Bay Colony. In that year, a thousand colonists arrived to form the towns of Boston, Charlestown, and Newtown (later Cambridge) to join the existing town of Salem.[1] Not all the colonists were Puritan—indeed, only about 20 percent of the Colonists were even professing Christians—but all the ministers were Puritans, as were the leading laypersons.[2] Though the group did not formally break with the Church of England initially, they soon adopted a congregational form of church government which set the pattern for ecclesiastical life in New England.

The church became the center of village life. The ministers, many of whom had served churches in England before coming to America, were often the best educated citizens and quickly became leaders in the community in political, as well as religious, affairs. The sermon was an important element in this leadership role; through preaching, ministers influenced religious and moral attitudes.

Perhaps the first significant American preacher was John Cotton (1584-1682), who served as pastor of a British church for more than 20 years before his Puritan views caused him to flee to Massachusetts; he became pastor of the Boston church in 1633. Cotton had been strongly influenced by William Perkins, whose *Arte of Prophesying* (1592) was the primary text for young divines when Cotton studied at Cambridge. Influenced by Calvin, Perkins argued that "preaching must take as its field the Word and the Word alone. Nothing extraneous can be added to Scripture, and nothing, even of the most minimal nature, subtracted from it."[3] Despite Cotton's use of a "plain style" of preaching encouraged by Perkins (characterized by a simple formula of text-doctrine-reasons-uses), Cotton was nevertheless known as a preacher of great power, and the Boston church grew dramatically under his leadership.

This "plain style" characterized most of New England preaching, with the average sermon resembling a doctrinal lecture more than a contemporary sermon. Sermons tended to be logical, highly structured, and deductive in nature. They were written as manuscripts and usually read; length varied from thirty minutes to two hours or even more. Some preachers, such as Thomas Hooker (1586-1647), became known for their skill with "uses" or application provided at the end of the sermon in Perkins' model.

Although the first generation of Puritan colonists had come to a new world seeking to build a "holy commonwealth" that would provide a model for their native England, successive generations did not share the enthusiasm of their forebears. As new generations were born, and "as new immigrants brought new and old values to new and old settlements . . . they shattered the older Puritan hegemony not through a new-found atheism but through their simple indifference to the Puritan churches that had been the principal means of expressing Christian adherence in this quite remarkable society."[4] Immigration to New England now related to economic more than religious factors. Although church membership continued to grow, it fell behind overall population growth; many towns echoed the decline in Salem, where 83 percent of the town's taxpayers were not church members by 1683.[5] This situation prompted the frequent use of a sermon form described as a "Jeremiad"—"a lamentation concerning past failures coupled with a call to take up again the original task."[6]

On the heels of a revival among a series of Dutch Reformed and Presbyterian congregations in the Raritan Valley of New Jersey and Pennsylvania, the Great Awakening came to New England through the preaching of Jonathan Edwards (1703-1758), one of the most significant theologians in American history. The son of a Connecticut pastor, Edwards studied at Yale, preached and taught for a time, then joined his grandfather, Solomon Stoddard, at the Congregational church in Northampton, Massachusetts in 1727. Edwards became pastor in 1729, at his grandfather's death. He spent as many as 13 hours a day in study for his preaching and teaching; during the early years in the pastorate, he preached two sermons each week, which averaged about an hour in length (but could last much longer).[7]

During Edwards' ministry in Northampton, two remarkable spiritual awakenings—periods of religious fervor—swept through the church and town; the first was in 1734-35, the second and more significant in 1740-41. In the face of religious decline in New England, Edwards, who had experienced a profound conversion during his college years, appealed to both the hearts and the heads of his congregation; he offered an urgent and powerful appeal to the emotions, yet he did so in a setting rich with biblical content and doctrinal teaching. He was pointed in his attacks on moral failure and was unafraid to confront error where he saw it; his eventual dismissal from Northampton stemmed from his refusal to open the Lord's table to those who professed no Christian experience.

Although best known for his sermon *Sinners in the Hands of an Angry God*—probably the most famous sermon ever preached in America—Edwards' preaching was characterized by a pastoral concern for his people. Even his use of fear stemmed from "his conviction that sinful hearts of men and women could be turned only by extremely forceful and painfully direct preaching."[8]

One of the most gifted preachers of the colonial era was George Whitefield (1714-1770), an itinerant Anglican evangelist who spent some ten years in America on seven different preaching tours. Whitefield preached throughout the colonies, often preaching as many as forty hours in a week, using an extemporaneous style and dramatic delivery.[9]

A brief study of this kind cannot adequately deal with a variety of worthy topics. In addition to New England, much could be said of the Presbyterian and Reformed preaching in the middle colonies, of the Anglican worship that characterized churches in the South, and of the preaching of the Dissenting churches (like Baptists) that were beginning to make an impact on colonial society. Women were not yet present in the pulpit except among the Quakers; Mary Dyer was hanged because of her "Enthusiastick" preaching in Boston. African-Americans were also virtually excluded from preaching prior to the revolution, except on rare occasions when slave preaching was allowed among some Baptists.[10]

It is clear that preaching during the colonial era helped to shape the minds and hearts of those who would soon declare their independence as a new nation.

Preaching in a New Nation

The rise of congregationalism in New England, coupled with the progress of the Dissenting churches (like Baptists and Quakers), introduced the concept of religious liberty in the American colonies to an extent unknown elsewhere in the world. Enjoying such religious liberty—and faced with significant economic differences with England—the colonies were ready to demand political liberty as well.

When the first shots of the American Revolution were fired in 1775, the churches also faced a period of tumult. Most damaged was the Anglican church, which was severely split between loyalists and patriots. New England's Congregationalists faced a far different situation; such churches were almost universally in the patriot camp, and the ministers became outspoken advocates of the revolution. Presbyterians and Baptists were mostly supportive of the patriot cause, while Methodist ministers were instructed by John Wesley (a loyal subject to George III) to remain neutral; this neutrality led to beatings and even prison for some Methodists. Lutherans tended to side with the patriots, though they had a small minority of loyalists.[11]

The cause of liberty and revolution was a popular topic in pulpits leading up to and during the revolution. One Baptist minister in Boston, John Allen, delivered a sermon in 1772 that was widely reprinted and circulated. He urged:

> Has not the voice of your Father's blood cried yet loud enough in your ears, "Ye sons of America scorn to be slaves?" Have you not heard the voice of blood in your streets, louder than that which reached Heaven, that cried for vengeance. . . . Therefore, if there be any vein, any nerve, any soul, any life, or spirit of Liberty in the Sons of America, shew your love for it; guard your freedom, prevent your chains; stand up as one man for your Liberty; for none but those, who set a just value upon this blessing are worthy to enjoy it.[12]

In the years immediately following the revolution, the new nation was at a low ebb of religious fervor. Church attendance waned, religious interest among the young was rare, and even church leaders began to question if Christianity had a future in the United States. As bad as things were in the East, religious interest on the western frontier was even more rare. Yet, remarkably, the young nation would soon experience significant growth in both the number of churches and church membership. Baptists grew from about 100,000 in 1800 to a million adult members by 1860. Methodists grew even more, increasing from 70,000 in 1800 to nearly two million by 1860. Congregationalists and Presbyterians increased about seven-fold during the same period. Lutheran and Catholic growth was also large, primarily through immigration.[12]

Much of that growth can be attributed to the Second Great Awakening—a fresh outpouring of the Spirit that generated new vitality among the churches and drew hundreds of thousands into their ranks. In New England, the arrival of Methodist preachers who preached with a strong evangelistic emphasis drew many. Among Congregationalists, as well, signs of revival became apparent. Timothy Dwight (1752-1817), grandson of Jonathan Edwards, became president of Yale College in 1795, and challenged anti-Christian ideas in both the chapel and the classroom. He preached a series of sermons on "Theology Explained and Defended" which contributed to the outbreak of revival in 1802. One-third of Yale's student body was converted; similar awakenings took place at Dartmouth, Amherst, and Williams Colleges.[14]

Unlike the quiet awakening in the east, the western phase of the revival was characterized by the camp meeting, with its extravagant emotionalism among both preachers and congregation. James McGready (1758-1817), a Presbyterian minister noted for his powerful and emotional preaching, introduced the camp meeting in 1797 in Logan County, Kentucky, where he was a pastor. The idea spread across the frontier, culminating in the Cane Ridge revival of 1801 in Bourbon

County, Kentucky. More than 10,000 people gathered as a series of evangelists preached simultaneously, with remarkable results: people cried, got "the jerks," and fainted by the score.

A major difference between the First and Second Great Awakenings is that in the former, spiritual awakening was seen as solely a gift of God, to be prayed and waited for like the rain. By contrast, preachers in the Second Awakening came to believe that certain techniques, or "means," could be used to promote revival and result in decisions. The great figure of the Second Awakening was Charles G. Finney (1792-1875), a lawyer from New York who was converted at age 29 and became an effective evangelist. His preaching gave evidence of his legal training; his sermons were carefully prepared, highly structured, clear, and direct. Tall and commanding in the pulpit, Finney used simple language so that his hearers could not misunderstand his message, which called for conviction and repentance.

Lyman Beecher (1775-1863) was one of the pivotal figures of the American pulpit in the first half of the nineteenth century. Beecher thought of himself as standing in the lineage of the great Puritan divines; he has even been referred to as the last of the Puritans, for his ministry took place in an era when their influence, even in New England, shrank in the face of a changing society. He was in his sophomore year at Yale when Timothy Dwight assumed the presidency and the Yale revival began; that event shaped Beecher's life to a great extent, resulting in his conversion and convincing him of the efficacy of revivals. As a divinity student he joined classmates in preaching at revival meetings twice a week, and in his first pastorate a revival resulted in eighty conversions, primarily among the young people.[15] Other revivals followed. His preaching became known for its strong reformist impulse; his sermon against dueling was reprinted and circulated nationally. A series of sermons followed which were also widely circulated and established Beecher as an early temperance leader. His preaching was characterized by attacks on evils of all description, from profanity to Unitarians.

The early years of the new nation saw the first (though meager) movement of women into religious leadership in the traditional denominations. Women participated in revival meetings, which raised questions about their proper role. As early as the 1830s some official statements were issued by church groups condemning those who would allow "any of that sex who so far forget themselves as to itinerate in the character of public lecturers and teachers."[16] Some early nineteenth-century movements gave women a place of prominence in leadership (see the brief discussion of the Shakers in Part I, chapter 2 of this volume), but they were few in number. An increased role for women in church leadership awaited further social change, including the suffragist movement.

This was, however, a period when African Americans began to assume responsibility for their own religious life. In the South, white churches often featured black galleries, where slaves could sit during white-led worship services. With the creation of the African Methodist Episcopal (in 1816) and the A. M. E. Zion (1821) communions within Methodism, churches composed of and for African Americans were founded; simultaneously, black Baptist churches were beginning to sprout up in both the North and the South. The primary figure in such churches was the preacher, who not only provided spiritual teaching but also nurtured a hunger for freedom.[17]

Despite the significant growth experienced by the churches in the first half of the century, the nation's denominations would soon be shaken asunder by the growing regional division that was to split the nation and result in a battle between brothers.

Preaching in a Divided Nation

Among the reform movements which emerged from within the churches in the early nineteenth century, none was to have a more profound impact on the nation than Abolition. Gradually, more and more people in the North identified slavery as a great evil, while the South defended its "peculiar institution" and increasingly resented Northern interference. The battle lines were drawn, and they divided America's denominations. First the Presbyterians (1837), then the Methodists (1844) and Baptists (1845) divided into northern and southern bodies.

For the most part, Southern preachers defended slavery as justified by the Bible. In an 1837 sermon, Methodist Samuel Dunwoody argued that God provided precedent in Scripture for perpetual slavery. Since the New Testament requires Christians to obey the civil authorities, a slaveholder acting under such civil law could not be construed as a sinner—therefore, slavery was not an issue appropriate for consideration in the pulpit.[18]

In the North, meanwhile, anti-slavery attitudes increasingly found a place in the pulpit. Henry Ward Beecher (1813-1887), son of Lyman Beecher, began preaching against slavery while still a young Presbyterian pastor in Indianapolis. (The local Presbytery urged at least one such sermon a year.) Upon his move to Brooklyn's Plymouth Church in 1847, Beecher became an even more outspoken opponent of slavery and made the topic a frequent issue in his preaching. In addition to rhetoric, Beecher linked words and actions; he opened Plymouth Church to runaway slaves, creating what one historian would later call "the Grand Central Station" of the Underground Railroad.[19] While critical of the South for its treatment of slaves, Beecher also assailed the hypocrisy of the North for its refusal of education, employment, and the basic rights of citizenship to African Americans.[20]

Once the first cannon were fired on Fort Sumter on April 12, 1861, even preachers who had been silent on slavery tended to preach support of the national cause—with the specific cause determined by regional loyalties. Southern preachers tended to link God's will and the Confederate cause, while northern preachers were equally as strident in their advocacy of the Union. Sermons often included calls to support the war effort, sometimes encouraging young men to join the army. Revival services were sometimes held in the camps. Though the war would end in 1865, much of the regional bitterness between churches would remain well into the next century.

Preaching in a Growing Nation

With the war behind it, the United States entered into a remarkable period of growth and development characterized by extensive immigration and urbanization. As population moved rapidly to the cities, many urban churches grew to prominence under the leadership of "pulpit princes" who became popular throughout the nation as well as within their own congregations.

Henry Ward Beecher built Brooklyn's Plymouth Church into the nation's largest congregation. Hearing Beecher was a popular attraction for visitors to New York, many of whom read his sermons regularly in periodicals or pamphlets. Phillips Brooks (1835-1893), rector of Boston's Trinity Episcopal Church and later Bishop of Massachusetts, presented the Lyman Beecher Lectures on Preaching at Yale; it was during these lectures that Brooks provided his famous definition of preaching as "the bringing of truth through personality."

Another of the Yale lecturers (and the only Baptist to present them until 1979) was John A. Broadus (1827-1895), professor of New Testament and homiletics at the Southern Baptist Theological Seminary in Louisville, Kentucky. Much in demand as a preacher throughout the nation, he declined numerous prestigious pulpits and professorships to remain at the young seminary. His textbook, *On the Preparation and Delivery of Sermons* (1870), is the most widely used text on preaching ever published; more than a century later, it is still used in many colleges and seminaries.

The last half of the nineteenth century saw the emergence of a new emphasis on evangelistic preaching and revivalism, led by Dwight L. Moody (1837-1899). Moody preached at large meetings throughout the United States and Great Britain, delivering simple but engaging sermons that stressed God's love and the need for salvation through Christ. Moody's ministry was characterized by an interdenominational cooperation not always enjoyed by some of his successors.

The rapid growth of American industry following the Civil War, fueled by a new urban population of both native-born Americans and European immigrants, produced new concentrations of wealth along with new social problems. While many preachers applauded the great industrialists as divine instruments and condemned the growing labor movement (with its unions and strikes), an increasing number of preachers began to relate the gospel to the new social realities of the nation's cities. Washington Gladden (1836-1918), pastor of the First Congregational Church in Columbus, Ohio during the last 36 years of his life, has been called the "father of the Social Gospel." His sermons emphasized the application of Christian principles to economic and political life as well as for individuals.

By the early years of the twentieth century, American Protestantism was dividing along theological and ideological lines. The successors of Gladden—with their emphasis on social involvement of the churches, acceptance of the new theory of evolution, and a less authoritative view of the Bible—had moved away from what conservatives considered the basics (or "fundamentals") of the Christian faith. The resulting Fundamentalist-Modernist controversy of the 1920s resulted in great turmoil in the churches (primarily in the North), and the creation of several new denominations. The most prominent spokesman for the liberals was Harry Emerson Fosdick (1878-1969), the pastor of New York's Riverside Church. A gifted preacher, Fosdick stressed the significance of Christian experience and behavior rather than theology. His most famous sermon, "Shall the Fundamentalists Win?", was actually preached in 1922 while Fosdick was still pastor of the First Presbyterian Church in New York City (where he served until 1924). He became known to many Americans through his nationally-broadcast radio program. Fosdick is considered by many to be the greatest single influence on preaching in this century.

Standing in opposition to the modernists was Clarence Macartney (1879-1957), a Presbyterian minister who presented a conservative response to Fosdick, "Shall Unbelief Win?" As the leader of the anti-modernist forces in the Presbyterian Church, in 1924 he was elected moderator of the General Assembly. Macartney was a biblical preacher but not an expository preacher; he is perhaps best known for his biographical sermons.

During the decades following the Civil War, the church became the most important institution for African-Americans, and preachers became civic and political, as well as spiritual, leaders in their communities. Preaching emphasized not only Christian experience and personal morality but also social consciousness. The African Methodist churches moved south to embrace the newly emancipated slaves. Baptist congregations were also formed, leading to the creation of the National Baptist Convention in 1895.[21]

Some African-Americans, like many whites, were drawn to the new holiness and pentecostal churches that emerged around the turn of the century. Pentecostalism, which is characterized by speaking in tongues, healing, and other "gifts of the Spirit," otherwise shares much of the theological viewpoint of fundamentalism. One difference is the official status of women; since 1935, the Assemblies of God (formed in 1914) has permitted ordination of women (although less than 300 have held pastorates at any one time, out of some 13,000 congregations), and women are accepted as preachers among most pentecostal groups.[22]

Preaching in a Modern Nation

In the years immediately following World War II, America saw a revival of interest in religious activity. In the midst of an era of suburbanization, new mobility, and economic growth, Americans joined churches at a rate twice that of population growth. By 1960, about 70 percent of Americans were members of a religious body, and more than a billion dollars had been spent on church construction during the 15 years leading up to 1960.[23] A new generation of evangelical preachers emerged during that period. They often shared the conservative theology of their fundamentalist forebears, but they did so with a new willingness to abandon the cultural isolation of fundamentalism and adapt their style to communicate to the post-war generation.

Billy Graham (1918-), a young Baptist minister from North Carolina, became a national figure—almost a "national chaplain"—and the primary spokesman for Evangelicals through his mass crusades, known to millions of Americans through televised specials. Another preacher who became known through television was Norman Vincent Peale (1898-), a pastor of New York's Marble Collegiate Church for many years. Unlike Graham, whose sermons are characterized by traditional Christian teachings on sin and the need for salvation, Peale's message was one of self-help and positive thinking.

The decade of the 1960s was a time of social and political tumult that enveloped the churches in a variety of ways. As the "baby boomers" entered their college years and young adulthood, their arrival was accompanied by a host of social issues and divisions, including the anti-war movement, the women's movement, and the civil rights movement. Churches and theologians reacted in different ways. Some gladly adapted their values and teachings to the cultural and political revolutions under way, seeking to make Christianity "relevant" to a new age; some preachers held firmly to orthodoxy while trying to deal fairly with the need for legitimate social change; still others condemned all such movements and called for a return to the values and stability of the previous era.

The churches were at the forefront of the civil rights movement. African-American pastors led marches, faced water hoses and police dogs, and demanded equality of opportunity for all Americans. The key leader of the movement was Martin Luther King, Jr., (1929-1968), a Baptist pastor whose eloquence gave voice to those struggling to overcome centuries of oppression. His political rhetoric echoed the rhetoric of the Black pulpit, with its rhythmic structure and strong biblical imagery.

The demands by women for equal treatment in the political and economic realms were joined by increasing demands for a place for women in the pulpit. The early decades of the twentieth century had been marked by slow progress for women seeking to enter the pulpit in mainline churches. American Baptists began ordaining women as early as the 1890s. A woman in a Presbyterian church was first licensed to preach in 1912, but that action was revoked the next year; it was not until 1956 that full ordination was permitted for women. That same year, Methodists removed all sex-based restrictions on ordination. Although women are increasingly moving into ministerial roles in the mainline churches—and to a lesser extent among Evangelicals—the majority of women in ministry serve in associate roles or as senior pastors in smaller congregations; as a result, few women are as yet widely recognized among the better-known preachers in their denominations or the wider church.

Another trend in the contemporary church is the emergence of "mega-churches," very large congregations (often several thousand members) with multiple ministries. In such churches, the senior pastor often fills two primary roles: preacher and chief executive/team leader. The preaching in such congregations is one of the major unifying elements and key attractions for new members; thus, preaching is expected to be of a very high quality. Many such "mega-churches" have expanded their ministries by televising their worship services; among those pastors most widely known because of their televised services are Charles Stanley (First Baptist Church, Atlanta, Georgia), Lloyd Ogilvie (First Presbyterian Church, Hollywood, California), William Hinson (First United Methodist Church, Houston, Texas), and Ed Young (Second Baptist Church, Houston, Texas).

During the 1960s, many "experts" proclaimed the death of the pulpit; preaching, they claimed, was no longer relevant to the needs of the average American. Ironically, the last two decades have seen an explosion of interest in preaching within the American church; Evangelicals, mainline churches, and even Roman Catholic parishes are placing an ever higher priority on preaching. That trend seems likely to continue, as churches follow the model of those earliest Christian believers who "ceased not to teach and preach Jesus Christ" (Acts. 6:42).

Notes

1. Dewey D. Wallace, Jr., *The Puritans* (Wilmington, NC: Consortium Books, 1977), 53.
2. William Warren Sweet, *The Story of Religion in America* (New York: Harper & Brothers, 1950), 48.
3. Teresa Toulouse, *The Art of Prophesying: New England Sermons and the Shaping of Belief* (Athens: University of Georgia Press, 1987), 14-15.
4. Jon Butler, *Awash in a Sea of Faith: Christianizing the American People* (Cambridge: Harvard University Press, 1990), 55-56.
5. Ibid., 62.
6. Wallace, *The Puritans*, 81.
7. John Piper, *The Supremacy of God in Preaching* (Grand Rapids: Baker Book House, 1990), 69.
8. Patrick Pang, "The Pastoral Preaching of Jonathan Edwards," *Preaching*, Vol. VII, no. 4 (January-February 1992), 59.
9. DeWitte T. Holland, *The Preaching Tradition* (Nashville: Abingdon Press, 1980), 57.
10. Butler, *Awash in a Sea of Faith*, 162.
11. Thomas A. Askew and Peter W. Spellman, *The Churches and the American Experience* (Grand Rapids: Baker Book House, 1984), 55-59.
12. Quoted from Edwin S. Gausted, ed., *A Documentary History of Religion in America to the Civil War* (Grand Rapids: Wm. B. Eerdmans Publishers, 1982), 252.
13. Louis B. Weeks, *A New Christian Nation* (Wilmington, NC: Consortium Books, 1977), 11-12.
14. Sweet, *The Story of Religion*, 226.
15. Milton Rugoff, *The Beechers* (New York: Harper & Row, 1981), 17.
16. Barbara Brown Zikmund, "The Struggle for the Right to Preach," *Women and Religion in America*, I, Rosemary Radford Reuther and Rosemary Skinner Keller, eds. (San Francisco: Harper & Row, 1981), 194.
17. Weeks, *A New Christian Nation*, 124-125.
18. Hubert Vance Taylor, "Preaching on Slavery, 1831-1861," *Preaching in American History*, DeWitte T. Holland, ed. (Nashville: Abingdon Press, 1969), 175.
19. Noyes L. Thompson, *The History of Plymouth Church* (New York: G.W. Carleton & Co., 1873), 79.
20. Henry Ward Beecher, *Freedom and War* (Boston: Ticknor and Fields, 1863), 18-19.
21. Mary R. Sawyer, "Black Religion," *Dictionary of Christianity in America* (Downers Grove, IL: InterVarsity Press, 1990), 160.
22. E. L. Blumhofer, "Assemblies of God," *Dictionary of Christianity in America*, 86-87.
23. Askew & Spellman, *The Churches*, 196.

4

Craig Loscalzo
Associate Professor of Preaching
The Southern Baptist Theological Seminary
Louisville, Kentucky

The Literature of Preaching

Imagine going to the doctor and finding out that you need major surgery. Your doctor talks to you about the procedure; as you listen you begin to get nervous. Even your reading of the medical column in *Time* magazine makes you more informed than your physician appears to be. You ask the doctor about advanced procedures about which you have read. He nods in tacit consent. "Yes, I've heard something about that too. But I've not read about it. I'm so busy with my patients; I just don't have time to keep up with so many new things in the field. I'm just glad we had a course on your problem when I was in medical school."

You ask about medical school, and he tells you that he graduated about twenty years ago. You realize that many medical discoveries have taken place in twenty years, discoveries about which your doctor knows nothing. Your physician breaks the silence: "Well, are you ready to schedule your surgery?" What are you going to do?

You know exactly what you are going to do—you are going to find another doctor. I wonder how many ministers believe they can coast through the rest of their careers solely relying on their seminary experience. I venture to guess that there are more than we want to believe. Why do we demand excellence from other professionals—doctors, lawyers, accountants—and tolerate mediocrity in ministry? H. Grady Davis said that most preachers "are not willing to put forth a tenth of the effort required for excellence in comparable fields."[1] That indictment is often tragically true.

Demands on the modern minister are astronomical. The adage "a jack of all trades and a master at none" does not work for ministers. Churches expect us to be "a jack of all trades" and a master of *all*!

Pastoral counseling, church administration and leadership, preaching, evangelism, community action, and denominational service describe just a few of the hats churches expect their ministers to wear with excellence. Add to that walking on water and casting out demons and the demands of modern ministry are humanly impossible. In the face of such pressures, many ministers give up the pursuit of excellence for the rut of mediocrity. Ministry loses its lustre, serving the church becomes a job, and burnout is right around the corner. Yet it does not have to be that way.

Keeping a razor sharp edge for ministry is possible. Ministers who know the value of continual learning, who take time to listen to the wisdom of others, and who reap the benefits of the literature of their field seldom burn out. The purpose of this article is to analyze critical publications and events that inform contemporary preaching. The aim is to highlight some literature of preaching—books and periodicals—to help you in your pursuit of excellence for your pulpit ministry. An exhaustive analysis is not my intention for this essay. Some homileticians would include literature that I omit; others would omit literature that I include. I deal with representative types of literature about which preachers should be aware. Examples that I cite should be understood as just that—examples—and not the only valuable literature in the particular area.

Literature to Avoid

With the demands placed on ministers, the ever present temptation is to look for books and periodicals that promise a large return for a small investment. "Easy Outlines for Sermons on the Cross" somehow misses Jesus' admonition to take up our cross and follow Him. Perhaps the most enticing temptation comes in the form of pre-packaged sermons. At least once a month I receive an advertisement that promises to enliven my pulpit ministry by providing me with fifty-two biblical sermons complete with illustrations. The sermons even come in large print so they can be easily preached just as they are. Of course, you can modify them for your purposes, so they seem like yours. Other publications promise sermon outlines that make the busy preacher's sermon preparation easier and more efficient.

I find it hard to imagine the apostle Paul allowing someone else to do his thinking for him. That is exactly what these types of sermons help do—instant sermons in an instant age. No theological reflection is required, no hermeneutical struggle with the text is necessary, and there is no obligation to work on behalf of your hearers.

A similar threat is emerging with sermon aids on computer disk, making it easy to use pre-packaged sermons with minor modifications to make the sermon "seem" like you wrote it. Aside from the question of the ethics of such practices (see Raymond Bailey's chapter on "Ethics in Preaching,") generic sermons by someone else never accomplish what the dedicated preacher, struggling with a text for a particular congregation, can accomplish. I am not sure where modern preachers learned to develop sermons this way. No preaching textbook—from the most conservative to the most progressive—advocates sermon preparation by using a "sermon service." None of the preaching professors I know in the Academy of Homiletics, a group which represents preaching professors from various denominations across the country, teach this method in their classrooms.

Along the same line, be cautious of reading books of sermons merely hoping to preach them as your own. Reading sermons by others can be intellectually and spiritually rewarding as part of a discipline of study. As an opportunity to spark your thinking on a subject, to stimulate your searching, to challenge your theological understanding, to see what others are doing homiletically, to discover how another has interpreted a text are proper ways to use sermon books. Gardner Taylor's *Chariots Aflame* is a wonderful collection of sermons he preached as pastor of the Concord Baptist Church of Christ, Brooklyn, New York.[2] I found the sermons to be rich with imagery and imagination, challenging theologically, and masterfully crafted homiletically. *The Minister's Manual* and the *Best Sermons* series, both edited by James W. Cox, are fine sources for sermon study and worship planning.[3] *20 Centuries of Great Preaching* is an excellent source for sermons written by notable preachers from the first century to the modern era.[4] Such books are designed as aids, not substitutes, for sermon preparation. Reading these books—and others like them—deepens and widens your horizons. In other words, avoid literature designed to do the work for you.

I also caution preachers not to invest hard earned money in books of illustrations. The following advertisement crossed my desk recently:

> Your time is valuable. There are not enough hours in the day to do all that we have to do. Would an illustration book so well indexed that you could find just the illustration you want for your next sermon, be the very help you have been looking for? We now have that Illustration book.

Sounds enticing, does it not? Generally speaking, collections of illustrations contain dated and worn stories, lacking any contemporaneous connection with your hearers' life situations. No doubt, you will find and use some valuable illustrations and stories in such collections but the return on your investment in the book is small. Instead, create your own illustration books. You do not have to spend a lot of time looking for illustrations; they are all around: the daily newspaper, radio programs such as Paul Harvey and National Public Radio, television, bumper stickers, billboards, street signs, watching people in the mall, films, children's books, sayings on tombstones, television commercials, magazines, the things kids say, contemporary literature, lyrics of hymns, lyrics of songs (contemporary and classic), and the list goes on *ad infinitum*. Illustrations are all around; stories from life will enliven your preaching.

Classic Books and Lectures

You will notice in the "Bibliography" that preaching has developed a sizeable body of literature. To understand contemporary preaching, preachers must read widely, including a classic or two. An accessible example is Augustine's *On Christian Doctrine*.[5]

Augustine studied and later taught classical rhetoric. Many Christians of his day maintained a distaste for pagan rhetoric because of its flowery style and absence of content. However, Augustine saw a real value in reclaiming the classical aim of rhetoric and adapting it to Christian purposes. Between A.D. 396 and 426, he wrote the four books of *On Christian Doctrine*. The first three books provided preachers with the substance and form necessary for effective preaching. In essence, these books were interested in hermeneutics, the interpretation of Scripture.

Book four of *On Christian Doctrine* has been called "the first manual of Christian rhetoric."[6] Augustine emphasized rhetoric as a means of persuading Christians to lead a holy and righteous life. Augustine contended that knowledge of truth alone does not ensure effective communication. Purposeful and effective communication should not be a tool only at the disposal of the enemies of Christianity. Augustine wrote:

> Who dare say that the defenders of truth should be unarmed against falsehood? While proponents of error know the art of winning an audience to good will, attention, and open mind, shall the proponents of truth remain ignorant? While the [sophist] states facts concisely, clearly, plausibly, shall the preacher state them so that they are tedious to hear, hard to understand, hard to believe? While the one attacks truth and insinuates falsehood by fallacious argument, shall the other have too little skill either to defend the true or to refute the false?

Augustine claimed rhetoric as a foundation for preaching, a claim that has extended into the twentieth century.

In 1871, Yale College founded a lectureship in the department of pastoral theology that was to be called "The Lyman Beecher Lectureship on Preaching." The lectureship was "to be filled from time to time . . . by a minister of the Gospel, of any evangelical denomination, who has been markedly successful in the special work of the Christian ministry."[8] The lectureship has been filled by such notable preachers as Henry Ward Beecher (whose father was the namesake of the lectureship, Lyman Beecher), Washington Gladden, Charles E. Jefferson, Harry Emerson

Fosdick, George Buttrick, Paul Scherer, H. H. Farmer, Leslie D. Weatherhead, James Stewart, and D. T. Niles. Frederick Buechner, John Claypool, Fred Craddock, Henry Mitchell, and David H. C. Read are some who have delivered the lectures in recent years.

One of the first to deliver the Lyman Beecher Lectures was Phillips Brooks in 1877. Brooks was an Episcopal minister who served churches in Philadelphia and Boston, and later became Bishop of Massachusetts. His lectures were published under the title *Lectures on Preaching*, still a popular title in used-book stores.[9] Brooks saw two elements essential for preaching: the timeless truth of the gospel and the personality of the preacher. His definition of preaching provided the foundation for much modern homiletic theory:

> Truth through Personality is our description of real preaching. The truth must come really through the person, not merely over his lips, not merely into his understanding, and out through his pen. It must come through his character, his affections, his whole intellectual and moral being. It must come genuinely through him."[10]

In *Lectures on Preaching*, Brooks dealt with the life and work of the preacher, the development of the sermon, understanding one's congregation, and the role of ministry in the world. While the language of the lectures reflects a particular time, Brooks' wisdom still speaks to issues about preaching today. This work should be a part of every preacher's library.

Another classic text is *A Treatise on the Preparation and Delivery of Sermons* by John Albert Broadus.[11] Broadus, himself a popular preacher and Lyman Beecher lecturer (1889), taught homiletics at The Southern Baptist Theological Seminary in Louisville, Kentucky, and later became president of that institution. For years, the Broadus text was the authoritative work on homiletics used in colleges and seminaries in the United States. At a recent meeting of the Academy of Homiletics at Fuller Theological Seminary in Pasadena, David Hubbard, Fuller's president, remarked that his own seminary course in preaching used Broadus' text. This incident reminded me again of the wide usage experienced by this book.

The book shows the influence that Aristotle, Cicero, and other classical writers had on Broadus. The classical canons of rhetoric form the outline of the book. *Invention* is covered under the topic "Materials of Preaching." In this section Broadus dealt with such topics as selecting a text, doctrinal preaching, types of sermons, originality, plagiarism and borrowing, the cautions of sensational preaching, and the importance of argument in preaching. *Arrangement* of a sermon, *style, delivery* and *memory* (the four other canons), and a section on leading public worship form the remainder of the book. With over 540 pages of text, not including a bibliography detailing the critical works on homiletics of that day, *A Treatise on the Preparation and Delivery of Sermons* was the most comprehensive textbook available for some sixty years.

One could criticize Broadus' homiletical approach for relying too heavily on the preacher learning techniques and rules. Broadus reflected little understanding of preaching as a theological discipline in its own right, an understanding that is only now being acknowledged. Nevertheless, you will find this work helpful as resource for studying the roots of contemporary preaching.

Finally, one of the premier lectureships on preaching is the E. Y. Mullins Lectures on Preaching at The Southern Baptist Theological Seminary, Louisville, Kentucky. Named after Baptist theologian E. Y. Mullins, this lectureship, which began in 1941, continues to feature the pioneer thinkers and writers of preaching. William Lyon Phelps was the first to deliver the lectures. A list of subsequent lecturers sounds like a "Who's Who" of preaching: George Buttrick, Halford Luccock, H. H. Farmer, T. W. Manson, Robert McCracken, Paul Scherer, H. Grady Davis, Donald Macleod, Kelly Miller Smith, Edmund Steimle, D. E. King, John Claypool, Clyde Fant, Gardner C. Taylor, Ernest T. Campbell, Elizabeth Achtemeier, Fred Craddock, Calvin Miller, William Willimon, James Forbes, and Eugene Lowry.[12]

Contemporary Literature

We modern preachers are blessed with abundant resources to help us in our pulpit ministries. Textbooks, monographs, and journals abound, waiting to be devoured by hungry preachers.

Comprehensive Texts

Contemporary business theory talks about the need to change paradigms (the presuppositions of thought) to survive the rapidly changing business world. In 1958, H. Grady Davis, then the professor of functional theology at The Lutheran School of Theology at Chicago, offered a new paradigm for thinking about preaching. Preaching books talked about structuring and outlining sermons. Davis argued that good sermons are not the result of getting the points of the outline in order. Good sermons *grow*, an organic development of content and form.

Design for Preaching was the title of the book. A cursory reading of the table of contents shows that Davis was plowing fertile homiletical soil upon which many would sow and reap. He argued that substance and form could not be separated. He urged preachers to think inductively as well as deductively. He suggested that sermons might be a thesis supported. He also challenged preachers to think about sermons as stories. He chided preachers for writing for the eye and not for the ear; preachers must learn the difference between written and spoken language. The book is not easy reading, but, nearly thirty years after it was written, you will find much here that will enhance your composition of sermons.

While Davis focused on designing the sermon, Clyde Fant's *Preaching for Today* covered every aspect of preaching, from the role of the preacher to sermon development and delivery.[13] Fant is dean of the chapel and professor of Christian studies at Stetson University in DeLand, Florida. Fant's optimistic view about the role of the pulpit in the church is an encouraging word for all preachers. His call for incarnational preaching echoes Brooks' understanding that preaching is a divine/human endeavor. Fant's major contribution to sermon preparation and delivery is that preaching should maintain an oral character. He challenged preachers to develop an "oral manuscript" and to preach from a "sermon brief." The revised edition of this book (1987) is one of the first preaching texts to devote a section, though somewhat limited, to women and preaching.

Another complete text is *Preaching: A Comprehensive Approach to the Design and Delivery of Sermons* by James W. Cox. Known as a leading authority in homiletics, James Cox has taught preaching at The Southern Baptist Theological Seminary in Louisville, Kentucky for over thirty years. This work covers the waterfront of preaching theory: the theological rationale for preaching; preaching's contexts, with a focus on worship; the making of sermons, with an excellent section on the ethics of motivation; and sermon delivery. A major strength of this book is Cox's fluent conversation with homileticians from the past. Cox translates their earlier ideas into major contributions to contemporary theory.

One of the most popular preaching textbooks in seminary classrooms and preachers' studies is *Preaching* by Fred Craddock.[14] Craddock is Professor of Preaching and New Testament at Candler School of Theology, Emory University in Atlanta. Like his preaching, Craddock's writing style is conversational; rather than telling his readers what they need to know, he invites them to participate in the process of learning sermon preparation and delivery. Reading his book is like talking with a good friend about a subject you both love. Craddock's love and concern for preaching is breathed into every page. While the areas Craddock covers are not new to preaching, his approach to them enables you to discover things about preaching you knew but did not recognize. "Recognizing" is Craddock's way of teaching us something new about preaching. To the dismay of some academicians, this book contains no footnotes and is light on the use of theological and homiletical jargon. That alone should make you want to read it.

David Buttrick's *Homiletic: Moves and Structures* is the most aggressive undertaking at staking out new claims for homiletics.[15] Buttrick is professor of homiletics and worship at Vanderbilt University, Nashville,

Tennessee. The traditional wares of preaching textbooks—the character of the preacher, sermon delivery, the various contexts of preaching—are not Buttrick's major concern. Buttrick delves into the way sermons are created in consciousness and how they speak to the communal consciousness of gathered hearers. His discussions about language, image, and metaphor are provocative and enlightening. His unwillingness to separate homiletics and theology is a reminder to preachers of the wisdom attributed to Karl Barth—theology that does not preach is no theology at all. The impact of this book on the field of homiletics is yet to be measured.

I have a caution of which you should be aware. David Buttrick told a group of us at the Academy of Homiletics meeting in 1988 that this book was not written for preachers or seminarians at the master's level. He said his intention was to provoke teachers of preaching and the field of homiletics to rethink approaches, that is, paradigms. This book is a scholarly study to homiletics. If you are looking for a how-to-write-a-sermon book, look elsewhere; but I think parish ministers who are serious about their preaching will benefit immensely from wrestling with *Homiletic*.

The final contemporary textbook I want to offer is Tom Long's *The Witness of Preaching*.[16] Long teaches preaching at Princeton Theological Seminary, Princeton, New Jersey. Long's thesis is that preachers come from the pew to the pulpit. Preachers do not materialize *ex nihilo*—out of nothing. Preachers are products of the church; they have heard and responded to the call to preach as active recipients and participants of the church's nurturing. Preachers may be pastors. Their approach to preaching may be that of the herald or the story teller. However, Long opts for the image of a preacher as a witness. Long unfolds the implications of the witness model for preaching as he discusses such topics as biblical exegesis for preaching; the focus and function of the sermon, from desk to pulpit; and conversation along the pilgrim way. A major strength of the book is Long's lucid dialogue with the contemporary literature of preaching. One could read this work and become familiar with most of the major writers in the field of homiletics today. Tom Long's writing style is direct and clear. His use of humor and examples make *The Witness of Preaching* a delight to read.

Preaching Monographs

The plethora of preaching monographs deals with a variety of subjects: hermeneutics for preaching, sermon style, preaching and imagination, designing sermon forms, doctrinal preaching, theology and preaching. The list goes on, almost *ad infinitum*. Below are some works that I believe will whet your homiletic appetite.

I find Elizabeth Achtemeier's writing to be provocative and helpful.

Her books include *Creative Preaching, Preaching as Theology and Art, Preaching About Family Relationships,* and *Preaching from the Old Testament.*[17] She is an ardent scholar and church person who does not mince words about getting serious when it comes to preaching. Because she is a woman writing about preaching, some preachers will avoid her works. If that is your attitude, you will certainly come out the loser.

Raymond Bailey's two recent releases, *Jesus the Preacher* and *Paul the Preacher,* should be a part of your library.[18] Bailey considers Jesus and Paul as two different models from which contemporary preachers can learn a great deal. Bailey's writing style is lucid and interesting. Both books mix important preaching theory with practical guidance that can be incorporated to enhance your preaching ministry.

The Modern Preacher and the Ancient Text by Sidney Greidanus is an important contribution to preaching literature.[19] This conservative approach to biblical hermeneutics looks at a wide landscape of interpretive approaches and analyzes their strengths and weaknesses for preaching. While the book is pedantic in style, the content is well researched and provides valuable insights. Serious biblical and preaching scholars from across the theological spectrum will find this book useful.

Another book dealing with hermeneutics is Tom Long's *Preaching and the Literary Forms of the Bible.*[20] Long entreats preachers to consider both the form and content of biblical texts. His mandate is to consider the "form of the content" and not form and content separately. After an explanation of his approach, Long applies it to various forms of biblical literature: psalms, proverbs, narratives, parables, and epistles. The book is well written and is replete with wonderful and creative examples.

One of my favorite books to introduce to students is Eugene Lowry's *The Homiletical Plot.*[21] Lowry considers the sermon as a narrative art form. He discourages preachers from building sermons brick by brick because sermons are not things. Sermons are events-in-time. Lowry imports narrative theory as the paradigm for developing the sermon. He suggests a five step process: (1) upsetting the equilibrium, (2) analyzing the discrepancy, (3) disclosing the clue to resolution, (4) experiencing the gospel, and (5) anticipating the consequences. This book is not only helpful in viewing preaching in a new way, it is enjoyable to read.

Periodicals[22]

Again, the list is endless of journals preachers find helpful to read. While you cannot subscribe to even a portion of them, you should have some professional and academic journals crossing your desk regularly.

Homiletic, the journal jointly published by the Academy of Homiletics and the Religious Speech Communication Association, is a biannual review of books dealing with preaching and religious communication. Review topics include the following: preaching, sermons, history of preaching, biblical interpretation, theology, worship, arts and media, and human sciences and culture. In a single volume, you can learn about the latest in preaching literature.

Periodicals like *Interpretation* and *Review and Expositor* are quarterly journals that contain several scholarly articles and book reviews covering the broad spectrum of theological disciplines. This type of journal helps you to keep abreast of the pioneering thought in theology.

Professional journals like *Preaching* and *The Living Pulpit* are geared toward the practical side of pulpit ministry. Preachers are always looking for sermon ideas, preaching helps, and inspirational reading to enhance their ministries from the pulpit. These journals are written with the practicing preacher in mind.

Do not forget your own denominational publishing houses. Most denominations provide preaching aids aimed at the specific needs of their ministers.

We have not even scratched the surface of the literature available to help you in your task of proclaiming the gospel each week. The above books and periodicals are the types of literature designed to help you become the best preacher you can be. Paul admonished us to walk worthy of the calling to which we have been called (Eph. 4:1). The literature of preaching is here to help you in your walk.

Notes

1. H. Grady Davis, *Design for Preaching* (Philadelphia: Fortress Press, 1958), 10.
2. Gardner C. Taylor, *Chariots Aflame* (Nashville: Broadman Press, 1988).
3. *The Ministers Manual* and *Best Sermons* are published annually by Harper Collins Publishers, San Francisco, California.
4. Clyde E. Fant and William M. Pinson, eds. *20 Centuries of Great Preaching*, 13 vols. (Waco: Word Books, 1971).
5. Augustine, *On Christine Doctrine*, trans. D. W. Robertson, Jr., The Library of Liberal Arts (Indianapolis: Bobbs-Merrill Educational Publishing, 1958).
6. James J. Murphy, "Saint Augustine and the Christianization of Rhetoric," *Western Speech*, 22 (1958): 27.
7. Augustine, as cited in Charles Baldwin, *Medieval Rhetoric and Poetic* (New York: The Macmillan Company, 1928), 57.
8. From the records of the corporation of Yale College, April 12, 1871 as cited in Phillips Brooks, *Lectures on Preaching* (New York: E. P. Dutton & Co., 1877), v.
9. If you are interested in purchasing *Lectures on Preaching* or other out-of-print books dealing with preaching and theological subjects write: Theologue Books, 3618 Lexington Rd., Louisville, KY 40206; or Baker Book House, P. O. Box 6287, Grand Rapids, MI 49506.
10. Brooks, *Lectures*, 8.
11. John Broadus, *A Treatise on the Preparation and Delivery of Sermons*, rev. ed. (New York: Harper and Brothers Publishers, 1898).
12. See Don Aycock, *Preaching with Purpose and Power: Selected E. Y. Mullins Lectures on Preaching* (Macon: Mercer University Press, 1982). This book contains some of the Mullins lectures.
13. Clyde Fant, *Preaching for Today* (New York: Harper & Row Publishers, 1975).
14. Fred Craddock, *Preaching* (Nashville: Abingdon, 1985).
15. David Buttrick, *Homiletic: Moves and Structures* (Philadelphia: Fortress Press: 1987).

16. Thomas G. Long, *The Witness of Preaching* (Louisville: Westminster/John Knox Press, 1989).
17. Elizabeth Achtemeier, *Creative Preaching* and *Preaching as Theology and Art* (Nashville: Abingdon Press, 1980 and 1984 respectively); *Preaching About Family Relationships* (Philadelphia: Westminster Press, 1978); and *Preaching from the Old Testament* (Louisville: Westminster/John Knox Press, 1989).
18. Raymond Bailey, *Jesus the Preacher* and *Paul the Preacher* (Nashville: Broadman Press, 1990 and 1991 respectively).
19. Sidney Greidanus, *The Modern Preacher and the Ancient Text* (Grand Rapids: William B. Eerdmans Publishing Company, 1988).
20. Thomas Long, *Preaching and the Literary Forms of the Bible* (Philadelphia: Fortress Press, 1989).
21. Eugene L. Lowry, *The Homiletical Plot: The Sermon as Narrative Art Form* (Atlanta: John Knox Press, 1980).
22. For information about the periodicals listed, write the appropriate address: *Homiletic*, Lutheran Theological Seminary, 61 West Confederate Avenue, Gettysburg, PA 17325; *Interpretation*, 3401 Brook Road, Richmond, VA 23286-3402; *Review and Expositor*, 2825 Lexington Road, Louisville, KY 40280; *The Living Pulpit*, 5000 Independence Avenue, Bronx, NY 10471; *Preaching*, 1529 Cesery Blvd., Jacksonville, FL 32211.

Part II Contemporary Preaching Methods

John Calvin (1509-1564)
"Theologian and Preacher"

Although viewed today as one of the towering figures of his century and of the Reformation, John Calvin always saw himself primarily as a student and preacher of the Word of God.

A brilliant scholar, Calvin studied both law and theology; his legal training brought a special dimension to his theological writing and his preaching. At the age of 26, he completed his Institutes of the Christian Religion, *one of the most significant theological works ever written.*

As the leader of the Reformation in Geneva, Calvin's work spanned the spheres of church and state and resulted in much controversy, particularly related to his use of government to enforce moral behavior among the citizens of the city. Despite this involvement in political life, he devoted the majority of his time to studying, writing about, and preaching God's Word.

Unlike his writing—which was meticulously and carefully prepared through hours of study—his preaching was remarkably free and spontaneous. He carried no manuscript into the pulpit; indeed, because of his heavy schedule many sermons were preached without any specific preparation. Yet it would be incorrect to assume that they lacked preparation, for his prodigious biblical study (combined with a remarkable memory) allowed him to preach powerful, biblical sermons. His sermons had no introduction or conclusion; he simply opened the Word where he last studied it and began to teach.

Like Luther before him, Calvin's work as a reformer was inextricably linked with his service as a preacher of the Word.

5

Paul Borden
Executive Vice President
Denver Seminary
Denver, Colorado

Expository Preaching

Trying to explain expository preaching and how it is done is like trying to describe the U.S. Congress and how it works. Almost everyone believes that we need a congress that functions well, but few know how to describe its workings, and almost everyone agrees it governs poorly. So it is with expository preaching. While most preachers believe it is important, they have trouble describing what it is and how to do it. Much of what passes for expository preaching fails to qualify. John Knox once said: "It is possible to preach a quite unbiblical sermon on a biblical text; it is also possible to preach a biblical sermon on no text at all."[1]

My goal in this chapter is twofold: to provide a description of expository preaching, and to demonstrate how to produce an expository sermon from the selection of a text to the pulpit delivery. I bring to this task certain assumptions about interpretation and preaching, but since the purpose of this chapter is to assist you in preaching expository sermons, the assumptions, for the most part, will go unstated.

A Description of Expository Preaching

The standard texts on homiletics convey a variety of definitions for expository preaching. Rather than offering you another definition, I think it best to follow Walter Liefeld's list of the characteristics of an expository sermon.[2] It is crucial to set limitations on the characteristics, however, in order to be clear about what an expository sermon is.

First, an expository sermon contains a clear statement of the primary biblical idea that is legitimately derived from a passage or passages.

Every passage has a primary idea supported by secondary ideas. Well-trained students of the Scriptures can distinguish between them.

An expository sermon does not have to rest on a single passage, but careful exegesis is required of every passage used. If not, you will never know if you have reflected the passages accurately. A topical expository message is possible, but such a sermon is obviously easier to prepare when you have fewer passages.

Second, the structure of the sermon must be consistent with the structure of the text or texts. For example, a narrative does not have to be preached as a story, but most narratives do not fit into a three-point sermon outline. Therefore, if the passage is inductive, or the argument is circular, or there are only two points, the structure of the sermon should be consistent with the structure of the text.

Third, the sermon must be relevant to listeners. Sermons ought not to be exegetical lectures. Exegetical lectures on Sunday morning are a poor way to communicate even cognitive information. Sermons are relevant when the preacher integrates biblical truth with real life. Preachers need to learn to speak the way people listen. A sermon must be logical; however, it is just as important to develop it psychologically, since a congregation listens that way.

Fourth, sermons are like jigsaw puzzles. The idea, outline, applications, illustrations, and assertions must fit with each other as well as with the context and intent of the biblical text. The inability to connect an application to the text, for example, means the sermon is not strictly expository.

Assumptions About the Procedure

While my intent is not to examine basic exegetical and preaching assumptions, it is important for you to know certain reasons behind the procedure for expository sermons. Pastors are busy people who face endless responsibilities. You should know, therefore, the time and effort required to practice the procedure. Failure to carve out the time to follow proper procedures will result in preaching that is not expositional.

First, effective preachers are made not born. Preachers who work at the craft of preaching become—over time—good communicators. Poor preaching can often be traced to preachers who do not work at their craft; or, if they do, work only on aspects that come easily.

Second, a busy pastor, with myriads of responsibilities, can only preach one good sermon a week. You may be required to preach more often but you can only preach one *good* sermon and fulfill other pastoral tasks.

Third, the procedure for expository preaching will require 10-15 hours each week. Beginning pastors will probably spend at least 15-20 hours a week; as they become more proficient and learn exegetical short cuts, the time should decrease.

Fourth, the procedure for expository preaching assumes that the homiletical process will require as much time as the exegetical process. You might find help in imagining a mental wall in your study process. As you exegete, you must never wrestle with how you will preach a text. The homiletical questions are on the other side of the wall and cannot be asked during the process of exegesis. Once your exegetical idea and outline are complete, you are then free to pursue homiletical issues.

Spending equal time on both the homiletical and exegetical processes requires the use of exegetical shortcuts. There is no need to translate passages or parse verbs—unless this comes easy to you—if these things have already been done well by competent people. Use your linguistic skills for the problems and questions that are not explained by the scholars.

Fifth, to speak clearly and eloquently in the pulpit you must be willing to write a great deal in the study. Preachers work with ideas. Ideas are not communicated clearly and relevantly without writing. Many preachers do a lot of work in their heads and must rely on notes, since the sermon is not developed logically and psychologically. That is why the preacher cannot remember the content. Good writing is essential to good preaching.

Sixth, since most people think that expository preaching focuses on a single passage, the procedure is designed for preaching from a single passage. The same format, however, must be followed when dealing with more than one passage.

The Exegetical Procedure

Genre

Once you have selected a passage, the first requirement is to determine the genre of the literature from which the text comes. Failure to do this creates a genre error which will lead to faulty interpretation because the interpreter will ask the wrong questions of the text.[3] Many basic exegetical courses in seminaries only teach how to exegete didactic or epistolary literature. As a result, many preachers have no idea how to study, let alone preach, passages of poetry, narrative, proverb, apocalypse, and parable. The result is that many preachers preach frequently from the epistles since their literary form closely matches the sermon's literary form. It is much easier to fit a square into a rectangle than into a triangle. The lesson for preachers: the genre determines the literary tools you need to interpret a passage.

However, since many pastors do preach from the epistles and their literary form is closer to the sermonic form, this chapter assumes that you are preaching from the epistles.

Familiarity

It is helpful to become familiar with a passage before studying it in detail. Some preachers do this by reading the passage five to ten times in one or more translations and paraphrases. Some suggest it is helpful to read the passage aloud. Since much of Scripture was originally written for an oral culture, reading aloud may be of great benefit.

Another practice for gaining familiarity with a passage is to copy the text in long hand or on a computer. This enables you to leave lots of open spaces around the words. Some homileticians suggest copying the text in terms of apparent English thought patterns rather than verse by verse. This helps you to sort out the primary idea and the subordinate ones.

These practices help to move the text from the printed page with its divisions, margins, and print into the eye and mind of the preacher. It helps you visualize the text and its structure.

Interpretation

You are now ready to begin your exegetical work. Obviously, the study habits of an individual are as unique as a person's signature. Even so, I would like to make a few suggestions for busy preachers.

Remember, your goal is to understand what the author of the text intended when it was read to the original congregation. For example, in dealing with a paragraph, the purpose of studying its parts is to determine what the main ideas are in light of elements such as words, phrases, construction, context, argument, audience, and author.

Check the excellent Greek commentaries first for different kinds of data. Note the word studies, the division of the text, the grammatical points, and where the exegetical problems exist. Note the writer's interpretations and supporting data for the interpretations.

Finally, since the commentaries do not always provide the answer to your questions, decide where you will need to investigate the original text by using exegetical tools.

Your investigation of the text should enable you to determine what is primary and secondary. To determine that you can distinguish between primary and secondary ideas, write out the passage in terms of grammatical or thought development. Observe the primary statements since they are crucial to developing the exegetical idea.

Sample: Romans 8:31-39, NIV, Primary and Secondary Ideas

What, then, shall we say in response to this? If God is for us, who can be against us?

He who did not spare his own Son, but gave him up for us all—how will he not also, along with him, graciously give us all things?
Who will bring any charge against those whom God has chosen?
It is God who justifies.
Who is he that condemns?
Christ Jesus, who died—
More than that, who was raised to life—is at the right hand of God and is also interceding for us.
Who shall separate us from the love of Christ?
Shall trouble or hardship or persecution or famine or nakedness or danger or sword?
As it is written: "For your sake we face death all day long; we are considered as sheep to be slaughtered."
No, in all these things we are more than conquerors through him who loved us.
For I am convinced
That neither death nor life, neither angels nor demons, neither the present nor the future, nor any powers, neither height nor depth, nor any thing else in all creation,
will be able to separate us from the love of God that is in Christ Jesus our Lord.

Major thought divisions are reflected in the way I have written the text. These divisions are based upon interpretive decisions.

1. The division of the paragraph is 31-37 and 38-39. In verse 38 Paul used "for," spoke in the first person, and employed the perfect passive indicative to show that he had become convinced. He used the interrogative with the future indicative active in the first and third rhetorical questions in verse 33 and 35 to bracket all three questions. The three questions cannot be separated.

2. The basic question of verse 31 and Paul's answer in verse 38 are primary while the rest of the passage is secondary.

3. Note that verse 32 is placed above the other secondary verses. Paul used this historical event, written with emotional terminology, to answer the question of verse 31. He argued from the greater to the lesser. The death of Christ is the greater and the implications of verses 33-37 are the lesser. Therefore, verse 32 has precedence over verses 33-37. Paul was convinced (v. 38) by God giving His Son for him (v. 32). Verse 32, as well as verses 31 and 38, are significant. The exegetical idea is based upon these primary passages.

The sample illustrates how your interpretation produces structure and an exegetical idea. You may disagree with the interpretation. The point is not to convince you of the interpretation. Rather, the point is to demonstrate how the exegetical idea is formed.

The Exegetical Idea and Outline

The exegetical idea of the passage is determined by the context and the structure of the passage. The idea is not necessarily a theme or statement of a major theological teaching. The idea is what the text is discussing (the subject) and what the text is saying about that which is being discussed (the complement).

The idea is determined as much from the synthesis (overall interpretation) as the analysis (study of specific pieces of data) of the text. Since the sermon is ultimately a reflection of both the idea and the structure, the outline of the passage is as crucial as the idea. Therefore, the same sermonic format (the three points formula) cannot be imposed on every passage. Rather, the opposite is true; the sermonic format is derived from the passage. A good expositor knows the exegetical outline is as important as the exegetical idea.

The exegetical idea has both a subject and a complement. The subject answers the question: What is being discussed? The complement answers the question: What is being said about what is being discussed? State the subject in question form and answer the question with the complement. Then merge the subject and complement to form a declarative statement.

Sample: Romans 8:31-39, NIV, Exegetical Idea

What has God's demonstration of His love in giving His son, with all of its implications, convinced the apostle Paul of? (vv. 31-37).

That nothing can separate him or any believer from God's love through Jesus Christ (vv. 38-39).

God's demonstration of His love in giving His Son, with all of its implications, convinced the apostle Paul that nothing can separate him or any believer from God's love through Jesus Christ.

Note that the exegetical idea is quite long. That is because it reflects the overall intent of the passage. It is not simply a rehearsal of exegetical data.

The exegetical outline must be consistent with the exegetical idea. The entire outline must be written in complete sentences. The development of thought, the key interpretations, and the delineation of that which is primary (that which contributes to the exegetical idea) and secondary (that which supports the idea) must be in the outline.

The complement is found in verse 38. In order to demonstrate that the complement completes the subject, the subject is worded with part of the complement in it. Note, too, that Paul did not mention other believers in verses 38-39. Paul, however, was arguing that he was a representative of all believers.

The exegetical outline and the idea must be consistent with the structure of the passage. This means that the exegetical outline:

1. Must be written in complete sentences. Complete sentences demonstrate the development of thought.

2. Must reflect the major interpretations of the passage. If you cannot state the major interpretations, you do not understand them.
3. Must demonstrate how the parts of the passage form a meaningful whole. The whole passage must be understood as a whole. Without this understanding you cannot know the idea.

Note: A well-written exegetical outline is one tool the lonely pastor has to check the accuracy of his idea.

Sample: Romans 8:31-39, NIV, Exegetical Outline

Exegetical Idea: God's demonstration of His love, in giving His Son with all of its implications, convinced Paul that nothing can separate him or any believer from God's love through Jesus Christ.

I. The apostle proved that God is for His people by demonstrating what God did for them and detailing the resulting implications (vv. 31-37).
  A. The apostle offered proof that God is for His people (those He has called) (vv. 31-32).
    1. Paul affirmed this fact—that God is for us—which, if true, indicates one can be against us by attacking our salvation (v. 31).
    2. Paul's proof is that God deliberately gave up His Son for us, which was the most costly thing He could do, implying He'll do whatever else is necessary for our salvation (v. 32).
  B. There are a number of implications resulting from what God did in proving His love and these are now detailed by the apostle (vv. 33-37).
    1. God—by the act of justification—has made it impossible for any charge against us to stand (v. 33).
    2. The different aspects of Christ's work, leading to His continual intercession, make it impossible for anyone, including God, to make a judgment against us that would stand (v. 34).
    3. Christ's work in establishing us as God's heirs and sons makes it impossible for anyone or anything to separate us from His love (vv. 35-37).

II. God's proof of His love for Paul as seen in the death of Christ convinced the apostle that his salvation and ours is impregnable from any attack (vv. 38-39).
  A. Paul made the statement that he personally had become convinced of the impregnability of his salvation (v. 38a).
  B. The result of being convinced was the understanding that nothing in the universe could penetrate God's defense of Paul's salvation (vv. 38b-39a).
  C. Therefore Paul could never be separated from God's love (v. 39b).

Functional Questions and Purpose Statement

The work of interpretation is not yet finished. You must ask three functional questions of your idea. Pretend you are the biblical author asking questions of the biblical audience. The answers to the questions determine the biblical writer's purpose. The first question is, do they understand the idea and, if not, how do I explain it? Second, do they believe the idea and, if not, how do I convince them it is true? Third, so what, or what difference does the idea make in the way they live life?

When the author's purpose is clear it is possible to discover the psychological and logical development of the text. Knowing the purpose also helps you to recheck your interpretations.

This step in the procedure is important since the exegetical idea and outline must be consistent with the content and purpose of the text.

Sample: Romans 8:31-39, NIV, Functional Questions

Paul used rhetorical questions. He provided historical evidence couched in emotional wording (v. 32). He employed his own testimony to demonstrate that something convinced him (perfect passive). Paul quoted the Sons of Korah (Ps. 44) as authoritative proof. He argued from the greater to the lesser. These evidences point to the second functional question. Paul was trying to get this congregation to believe, and as a result, spent little time explaining or dealing with pragmatic applications.

This interpretation is further enhanced by the context of Romans 1-8. Paul was drawing his argument about the righteousness of God to a close. The immediate context argues that suffering precedes glorification. Paul wanted to convince these Roman Christians that such suffering does not separate them from God's love. His purpose is not to explain but convince.

This step is important since the exegetical idea and outline should reflect both the content and purpose of the text.

The Creative Cycle

As stated previously, an imaginary wall should be established to separate the exegetical part of the procedure from the homiletical part. When the exegetical idea is stated, the exegetical outline is written, and the purpose affirmed, the exegetical process is complete. You are now ready to tear down the wall and begin the homiletical part of the procedure.

However, it is important to complete the exegetical process one to two weeks before the homiletical process is initiated. During this time interval the preacher's mind interacts with the material consciously and unconsciously. There is time to collect stories and illustrations that are appropriate. Contact with people inside and outside the church provides opportunities for application, as you observe truth meshing with life.

The creative cycle takes no extra time. For example, if exegesis takes eight hours and homiletics takes eight hours, it makes no difference whether these two segments come back to back on a Friday or Saturday or a week apart.

The Homiletical and Preaching Ideas

The exegetical idea is long because the subject and complement are stated in a complete fashion. The biblical writer, audience, and times are reflected in the terminology. Due to these features the idea must be shortened and restated. The basic idea must remain. This process changes the exegetical idea to a homiletical one.

Just as rewriting ideas creates preciseness, the preaching idea, like the exegetical one, must be rewritten several times. It is difficult to shorten and restate the idea in contemporary terms the first time.

Sample: Romans 8:31-39, NIV, Exegetical and Homiletical Ideas

Exegetical Idea: God's demonstration of His love in giving His son, with all of its implications, convinced the apostle Paul that nothing can separate him or any believer from God's love through Jesus Christ.

Homiletical Idea: God's demonstration of His love convinces believers that separation from that love is impossible.

Note the wording of the homiletical idea is not first century in terminology but twentieth. Also, the qualifying phrases are deleted. Secondary ideas are often presented in the sermon but are not part of the homiletical idea.

After developing the homiletical idea, create the preaching idea. The preacher's primary tool is language. Therefore, create an idea that is both well stated and stated well. The idea must be consistent with the exegetical and homiletical ideas. In order for it to be remembered, the preaching idea is stated as succinctly as possible. A well-worded idea is remembered more easily. Create a catchy statement that sounds proverbial. Remember, the preaching statement is an idea. It may not be a complete sentence, but it has a subject and complement.

Writing and rewriting preaching statements is crucial. To be creative you must have time. You have the time when you employ the creative cycle.

Sample: Romans 8:31-39, Preaching Idea

Exegetical Idea: God's demonstration of His love, in giving His son with all of its implications, convinced the apostle Paul that nothing can separate him or any believer from God's love through Jesus Christ.

Homiletical Idea: God's demonstration of His love convinces believers that separation from that love is impossible.

Preaching Idea: An expensive love guarantees an eternal relationship.

Functional Questions—Again

Again ask the three functional questions. This time ask them as the preacher in relation to your congregation. The purpose of the sermon is determined by the answers to the questions. Remember, the author's purpose and the preacher's purpose may be different since audiences are different.

Even though you have the preaching idea, it is best to ask the questions of the exegetical idea. Assume that members of your congregation are handed a piece of paper with the exegetical idea written on it. Assume as well that they know the meanings of the words in the idea. You are now ready to ask the functional questions.

The first question is: Would they understand the idea? If your answer is no, then you will have to explain the concepts they do not understand. However, if the answer is yes, meaning no explanation is needed, then you will do little or no explaining in the sermon. Obviously, you ask this question first since people cannot believe or act without first understanding.

The second question is: Would they believe the idea? Belief means the congregation embraces this idea as truth both cognitively and affectively. Belief means the congregation actually lives life in light of this truth, they do not just assent to it. If the answer is no, people in my congregation do not believe this idea in part or in whole, then you will need to spend time convincing them it is true. Obviously, persuasion cannot occur without information. However, people are usually not persuaded to make life-changing decisions by information and data alone.

The third question is: What difference does it make? In other words, how will a person live differently in light of this truth? How will people feel, think, or act differently? Again, if it doesn't make a difference, take time to demonstrate the practical differences created by a person's belief in this idea.

Note that it is sometimes difficult to distinguish between the second and third question. Often people are convinced to believe an idea by specific examples of action. Also, people may believe but not know how to act. For example, a person who says airplanes can fly but will not board one has given mental assent, but has not exhibited genuine, full, or complete belief. On the other hand, an individual may want to fly but does not know how to buy a ticket or obtain a boarding pass.

The answers to the functional questions determine both the purpose of the sermon and the structure of the homiletical outline. The exegetical outline should reveal the biblical writer's intent and purpose. The preacher reflects intent and purpose in the homiletical outline. Major sections of a text cannot be divided since such actions violate meaning and intent. However, the preacher may rearrange major sections in order to communicate intent and purpose. This decision is based upon answers to the functional questions.

Write the purpose statement in terms that reflect what the congregation should know, believe, or do. Note whether you use words like know, convince, act, and so on. These terms determine the amount of time spent on informing, convincing, demonstrating, or doing all three. The purpose statement is as binding on the sermon as the idea. For example, a preacher who says the purpose is to convince and yet preaches an explanatory sermon demonstrates that the purpose statement did not impact the development of the sermon.

Homiletical Outline

Write the homiletical outline. As with the exegetical outline, write in complete sentences. Look for the development of thought, inconsistent interpretation, consistency between the idea and purpose, and parallelism between the sermon structure (even if it is rearranged) and the structure of the text. Make sure the passage is developed both logically and psychologically.

Be sure to insert the preaching idea into the outline at that place you will first state it. Write out the transitions in brief paragraphs between the points. Using brief phrases, list throughout the outline the illustrations and applications you intend to use.

Sample: Romans 8:31-39, NIV, Homiletical Outline

Purpose Statement: To convince believers that nothing can separate them from God or lessen their standing as a child of God.
Sermon Outline: Homiletical Outline (minus transitions, illustrations, and applications)

I. Great believers have been convinced that nothing can interfere with their relationship with God (vv. 38-39).
   A. Great believers have stated categorically that nothing can separate them from God (v. 38a).
   B. Great believers have pointed out that nothing—even extremes— can separate them from God (vv. 38b-39a).
      1. Things done in life cannot separate us.
      2. Circumstances cannot push one to a point of separation.
      3. Individuals cannot separate themselves.
   C. Great believers see God's love in Christ is irrevocable (v. 39b).

(Transition: This idea of no separation may be acceptable for great believers, but such believers do not face the struggles that we common, average Christians face.)

II. Most/many Christians struggle with issues that cause them at times to wonder about their relationship with Christ—either separation or standing—despite what the Bible says (vv. 33-37).
   A. Christians often struggle with:
      1. A life-style that seems to contribute to accusations of guilt that affect our relationship with God (v. 33a).
      2. The assumption that God will not put up with our continuing sinning (v. 34a).
      3. The belief that the circumstances of life demonstrate that God is displeased with us (v. 35).
   B. God's Word affirms that:
      1. No charge against us can stand (v. 33b).
      2. God will not condemn us (v. 34b).
      3. The sufferings of life are not an indication of God's moving away from us; in fact, we can succeed in the face of such adversities (vv. 36-37).

(Transition: It is nice to hear that no charge can stand, God will not condemn us, and that difficult circumstances are the lot of all believers. However, how do I know that these statements are really true for me? What proof do I have?)

III. God has demonstrated His love to us to prove that, since He has given us the most expensive gift He could, He will take care of that which causes us to fear separation (vv. 31-32).
   A. God affirms He is for us (v. 31).
   B. God's proof is that He gave His Son and will in turn do more (v. 32).
      1. He volitionally and emotionally gave up His Son for us.
      2. If He will give us His Son He'll make sure *nothing* can separate us.

(*Preaching Idea:* An expensive love guarantees an eternal relationship.)

1. Note the purpose statement for the sermon is the same as Paul's, to convince. Sections of the passage were rearranged, however, to persuade inductively rather than deductively. Since most people come to church with no understanding of this passage, it should be preached inductively, which means the preaching idea is stated last.

2. Even though sections of the text are rearranged for the sermon, they are not divided in a way that would violate the meaning of the text.

3. The outline is also in sentence form. You are able to follow the logical and psychological development of the sermon. Note the wording of the sentences focuses on the audience, not on the text.

Illustrations and Applications

Remember, a sermon is not an exegetical lecture, rather it is a persuasive speech about biblical ideas. How things are said is as important as what is said. It is not enough to develop a preaching idea, purpose statement, and homiletical outline. There is more. People listen psychologically more than logically. Logical sermons focus on the content, while psychological sermons focus on people.

Envision specific people in the congregation who each week you invite into your office for an imaginary visit. The group is a varied one. It may include a single mother, a businessman climbing the corporate ladder, an empty nester, a professional woman balancing career and family, a lonely teenager, an active senior citizen, and so on. Imagine where these individuals live, how they manage or mismanage life, as well as their needs and joys. Preach the sermon to these individuals, picturing where they would ask such questions as: "What in the world do you mean? Do you really expect me to believe that? How does that idea work in real life? Do you really expect me to change in light of that reason?" Their questions indicate the places where you must illustrate, convince, work on specific wording, and apply.

These imaginary meetings help to determine how to develop the sermon. They tell you where to start, where to end, and how to get from the beginning to the end. They help you to present truth emotionally and personally.

Introduction and Conclusion

Write the introduction and conclusion at this point. Now that you have the idea, purpose, structure, illustrations, and applications, you know where to begin and end. Until these parts of the sermon are determined, the introduction and conclusion remain a mystery.

Most pastors cannot and should not memorize their sermons. However, if you memorize any part, remember the first 25 words of the introduction. Since these words set the tone for the entire sermon they are crucial.

Introductions should do a number of things. The most important thing is to create a need to listen further. This is accomplished by creating tension in the minds of listeners. Raising felt needs or making unfelt needs felt, without providing solutions, creates tension. When the introduction is finished, people should be asking: "How is the sermon going to answer the question that has been raised and not resolved?" Since the preaching idea resolves tension, do not state it at the end of the introduction.

Develop the conclusion last. The conclusion drives home the idea and accomplishes the purpose. Since the conclusion is crucial and is what the congregation hears last, spend a good deal of time preparing it.

A good conclusion moves the congregation to interact with the idea and purpose of the sermon cognitively, affectively, and behaviorally. To use a salesperson's or evangelist's term, this is the *close*. Wording is crucial, legitimate emotion is necessary, and an invitation to change one's life is needed. Resolve the major need raised in the introduction and developed throughout the sermon. People should feel like they have been handed a beautifully-wrapped gift.

Preparing to Preach

The preacher does not focus just on ideas, purposes, outlines, applications, and illustrations. The preacher must also focus on words, the building blocks of verbal communication.

Write a paraphrase of the passage. A paraphrase helps you review your homiletical and exegetical work. A good paraphrase states the interpretation of the passage in modern words, reveals the structure, and reflects the major implications of the passage. A paraphrase takes time to write; however, it is the second major tool (after the exegetical outline) to assist a pastor in reviewing both the interpretation and communication of the passage.

Next, write a manuscript or an extended outline of the sermon. The introduction, conclusion, and transitions should definitely be written. Write out the illustrations and applications as well. The result is that you will say things well and efficiently.

The purpose of writing your sermon is not to memorize it. Rather, writing forces you to work on wording. You may not remember all the metaphors and figures of speech. Many will remain, however, and you will say things well. Focus on communicating abstract ideas in concrete terms or phrases. Writing takes the mist and fog out of what you say.

Finally, preach the sermon out loud at least two or three times. As you preach the first time listen to what you are saying. Does it make sense? Do you really believe what you are saying? Would you listen to you? Have a spouse or good friend listen to you when you finish these trial runs. Pay attention to the questions they ask. The questions and comments reflect areas that are unclear or illogical.

Even if you use notes in the pulpit, preach your sermon through without notes before entering the pulpit. Those words, phrases, or illustrations that cannot be remembered were developed illogically. Notes may help you get through that section in the pulpit but the person in the pew will not follow.

Work on gestures, facial expressions, emotion, pitch, rate, and volume the second time you preach the sermon. Remember, preachers communicate a great deal through body language and other external expressions.

You are now ready to preach an expository sermon that is both biblical and relevant.

Notes

1. John Knox, *The Integrity of Preaching* (Nashville: Abingdon Press, 1957), 19.
2. Walter L. Liefeld, *New Testament Exposition* (Grand Rapids: Zondervan Publishing House, 1984), 24.
3. Sidney Greidanus, *The Modern Preacher and the Ancient Text* (Grand Rapids: William B. Eerdmans Publishing Co., 1988), 17.

6 *Al Fasol*
Professor of Preaching
Southwestern Baptist Theological Seminary
Fort Worth, Texas

Textual Preaching

Textual preaching sounds like the kind of appellation every preacher would enjoy and the kind of sermon every congregation would appreciate. One would think that every preacher would want to be known as a textual preacher. To announce a biblical text and then preach on that text is or should be the goal of every preacher. When sermons are criticized, one of the stronger accusations is that the preacher announced and read a biblical text, but the sermon had little or nothing to do with that text. Textual preaching, then, should be one of the primary goals of a preacher.

Unfortunately, the terminology *textual preaching* has, in the writings of homileticians, run the gamut from full acceptance to full rejection. From a survey of preaching books written over the past 150 years, we learn that textual preaching was held in higher regard in the late nineteenth and early twentieth centuries than it is today. These progressively negative opinions of textual preaching have been the result of a vague definition foisted on textual preaching and of continuing refinements in our understanding of the principles of communication which have led to a refinement of a theology of proclamation. The chief problem, however, is the inadequate definition assigned to biblical preaching. As a result, the reputation of expository preaching, which is highly comparable to textual preaching, has been exalted while the reputation of textual preaching has declined.

Clarence S. Roddy offered the clearest of many suggested definitions of textual preaching:

> A textual sermon is one in which both the topic and divisions of development are derived from and follow the order of the text . . . the text controls and dominates both topic and development in this type.[1]

In a preceding section of his article Roddy wrote:

> The vital area of distinction (between topical, textual, and expository sermons) is the relation of the body of the sermon to the text, and particularly the relation of the divisions of the sermon to the divisions of the text.[2]

Several authors attempt to define a textual sermon in relation to the length of the biblical text. Those definitions are superficial at best. Those authors generally agree that a textual sermon has a text of one to three verses. A lengthier text classifies the sermon as expository. The discussions of text length for the textual sermon never answer the question of why three verses (or less) constitute a textual sermon, while four verses or more constitute an expository sermon. The textual sermon is an extension of the topical sermon because the textual sermon draws both its topic and its divisions from the text. As Roddy stated later in the same article: "Of course, there is liberty of expression, but the basic ideas of the text control the divisions."[3]

The venerable homiletician, John A. Broadus, praised textual preaching, but only faintly. Broadus also struggled with his own definition of textual preaching:

> 1. A single subject is drawn from the text, and stated . . . and then is discussed under such divisions as the text furnishes . . . but . . . it would still be called a text-sermon, if the divisions were actually derived from a contemplation of the text. In general, such plans are quite different from those which a logical analysis of the subject would suggest. Text-sermons of this sort are by some writers confounded with subject (topical)-sermons, because in both cases there is a definite subject. Others call them textual-topical.
>
> 2. In other text-sermons there is not one definite and comprehensive subject, but several topics presented by the text are successively treated. These, though they do not admit of being combined into one, ought to have such a mutual relation as to give the discourse unity. . . . As a rule we ought to have as close an internal relation among the topics of discourse as possible.[4]

To illustrate the "single subject" textual sermon, Broadus cited this sermon outline:

> Acts 9:4 (KJV): "Saul, Saul, why persecutest thou me?" (1) It is the general character of unconverted men to be of a persecuting spirit. (2) Christ has His eye upon persecutors. (3) The injury done to Christ's people, Christ considers as done to Himself. (4) The calls of Christ are particular.[5]

Broadus did not think, however, that this was a strong sermon. He suggested that the fourth point could be eliminated and advised that "one should not very often allow himself to construct sermons in so loose a fashion."[6]

As an example of a textual sermon with "several topics presented by the text," Broadus shared:

> Galatians 5:6: *What it is that in Christ Jesus avails*? (1) Neither circumcision nor uncircumcision. (2) But (a) faith, (b) which worketh, (c) by love.[7]

Broadus concluded:

> The people love to have their minds kept in close contact with the text, if it is done in an interesting and impressive way. . . . Yet it is always pleasing, when effected without artificiality, to see all the lines of development kept within the limits of the text.[8]

Austin Phelps, professor of Sacred Rhetoric at Andover Theological Seminary, found the terms topical, textual, and expository to be eminently practical. Phelps felt that "these distinctions are of great practical value in the labor of the pulpit."[9] Phelps, in fact, added the term "inferential" preaching to the list. To Phelps: "The textual sermon is one in which the text is the theme, and the parts of the text are the divisions of the discourse, and are used as a line of suggestion."[10]

Phelps described how Philippians 2:12-13 may be developed either as a topical, textual, expository, or inferential sermon. For his textual example, Phelps wrote:

> But we might make the text itself the theme of discourse, and might follow its line of thought by remarking:
>
> 1. The duty enjoined in the text, "Work out salvation;"
>
> 2. The individual responsibility for the soul's salvation implied in the text, "Work out your own salvation;"
>
> 3. The spirit with which salvation should be sought, "With fear and trembling;"
>
> 4. The dependence of effort to be saved upon the power of God, "It is God which worketh in you;"
>
> 5. Dependence upon God for salvation is the great encouragement to effort for salvation, "Work, *for* it is God which worketh in you." This train of thought developed would constitute a textual sermon.[11]

Andrew Blackwood devoted an entire chapter of one of his books to "The Value of Textual Sermons." Only one sentence, however, was given to a definition: "A textual sermon is one whose structure corresponds with the order of the parts in the text."[12] Blackwood offered some expansion of this definition in a section labeled "The Advantages of this Method." Blackwood listed four advantages, two of which were directly related to his definition of textual preaching:

1. The textual sermon *fixes attention on one part of the Scriptures.*
2. The textual sermon is comparatively *easy to prepare* because, once the preacher knows what the text means in its own setting, he should encounter few obstacles in helping the layman see the form of the text.
3. *The hearer can follow* the textual sermon with ease and satisfaction.
4. Textual preaching *brings the hearer close to the heart of the Bible.*

Blackwood warned: "The textual message does not lend itself to every passage. . . . Here and there the textual minded pastor . . . finds (the text) like the Master's seamless dress, all in one piece."[13] Blackwood felt Frederick W. Robertson to be the best example of a textual preacher.

For examples of textual preaching turn to Frederick Robertson. . . . When he dealt with Matt 5:48, "Be ye therefore perfect" he would bring out two aspects of the subject. . . . "The Christian Aim—Perfection," and "The Christian Nature—because it is right and Godlike to be perfect." When he started with John 8:32 "Ye shall know the truth and the truth shall make you free," he dealt first with "The Truth That Liberates," and then with "The Liberty That Truth Gives." . . . Other men, of course, employ the textual method in far different ways.[14]

As an example of one of the "different ways," Blackwood cited William P. Merrell: " 'The Practical Value of Religion'. . . . (1) 'They shall mount up . . . as eagles'—strength for keeping up ideals; (2) 'They shall run and not be weary'—strength for meeting crises; and (3) 'They shall walk and not faint'—strength for the daily routine.' "[15]

Ilion T. Jones, in 1956, began to raise doubts about the validity of the word "textual" as a label for a sermon. Jones concurred with the classical definition of textual preaching: "In a textual sermon the points of the discussion are found in the text itself."[16] After citing two examples of a textual sermon, Jones then expressed his grievances with the term "textual":

Someone has estimated that it would be difficult . . . to find in the whole Bible a hundred texts suitable for textual treatment.

Handling most texts in this manner readily becomes . . . artificial and tends to develop into what James S. Stewart called a form of "textual vivisection." . . . Much so-called textual preaching consists of taking passages apart rather than expounding them.[17]

Jones drew his illustrations largely from Blackwood's book on the preparation of sermons. Jones used Merrell's sermon "The Practical Value of Religion" as an illustration of a good textual sermon. Jones used Spurgeon's sermon on Mark 10:45 as an example of "textual vivisection."

(1) "The Son of Man"—humanity;
(2) "came"—antecedent existence;
(3) "Not to be ministered unto"—vicarious life;
(4) "But to minister, and to give his life a ransom"—vicarious death;
(5) "For many"—amplitude.[18]

Jones scathingly denounced Spurgeon's sermon when he said: "Vinet used to say that ministers are supposed to 'develop rather than to decompose the text.' Much so-called textual preaching consists of taking passages apart rather than expounding them."[19]

Donald Miller declared that *all* preaching is expository. He called for the elimination of the words "topical" and "textual" insofar as they are used as labels for sermons. To accomplish this, Miller submitted a broad definition of expository preaching:

An act wherein the living truth of some portion of Holy Scripture, understood in the light of solid exegetical and historical study and made a living reality to the preacher by the Holy Spirit, comes alive to the hearer as he is confronted by God in Christ through the Holy Spirit in judgment and redemption.[20]

Miller then concluded:

> If this broad definition of expository preaching be accepted, then it remains true that all real preaching is expository preaching; for if a pulpit discourse does not embody the elements included in our definition, it can hardly be classed as a sermon. . . . The ancient categories, therefore, of topical, textual, and expository are irrelevant from the standpoint of determining the biblical content of a sermon. Whatever validity they may have in the jargon of formal homiletical technique, they can do little but create mischief when they are used to delineate the relative biblical content of a sermon.[21]

Miller then shared an example of a sermon on Jonah 4, but denounced the example by writing: "It is highly doubtful that it could justly be called a textual sermon."[22]

H. Grady Davis, in his highly popular *Design for Preaching*, shared this dawning disdain for the term "textual." Davis, however, showed some ambivalence. First, Davis frowned upon the use of the word:

> The terms topical, textual, and expository, are used loosely and not at all uniformly in homiletical literature, and are of limited usefulness. Having a topic does not necessarily make a sermon topical. A good textual or expository sermon also has a topic expressed or unexpressed, a unitary idea, an inclusive subject with one or several predicates.[23]

Later, Davis decided to use the word in its classical sense, this time without any sense of disapproval. In an analysis of a sermon by Karl Barth, he used the label "textual" and at the same time offered a brief definition: "This is a textual sermon, that is, it draws not only its idea but also its structural elements from the text."[24] Thus, despite its "limited usefulness," Davis relied on the word "textual."

Brown, Clinard, and Northcutt—in the durable *Steps to the Sermon*—virtually avoided mentioning the words "topical," "textual," or "expository." Without specifically denouncing those words, Brown, Clinard, and Northcutt strongly implied that classifying sermons as topical, textual, or expository is an inadequate approach:

> For centuries sermons have been classified by form or by the source of the sermon points. In this classification . . . the textual sermon, an unusual blend of (topical and expository), secures its major points from the text and its main points from the title or from any other source.
>
> In some systems of classification the length of the Scripture passage has played a significant role. In this method . . . a careful treatment of a short passage of Scripture (two verses or less) is considered to be a textual sermon.[25]

The authors go on to suggest various other ways of classifying sermons and conclude that any system of classification should include a study of purpose and not just a study of form.

Brown, a few years later, took this approach a step farther. In the preface to *A Quest for Reformation in Preaching,* Brown declared that:

> For centuries, ministers have viewed sermons in terms of form—as expository, textual, and topical sermons—and have therefore severely limited the discipline of preaching. Authentic sermons must be understood in terms of authority, purpose, and form.[26]

In chapter nine, "Acceptable Sermon Form," Brown did not mention the words *textual, topical,* or *expository* at all.

William Thompson wasted no time in denouncing the terminology "expository" preaching, "textual" preaching, and "topical" preaching. The first page of the first chapter in Thompson's *Preaching Biblically: Exegesis and Interpretation* begins the attack with these words:

> My own tradition advocated "expository preaching" as the epitome of biblical preaching. In their classes and their books my seminary professors told us that expository preaching involved preaching on long texts, while textual preaching utilized short texts. My predecessor in the chair I now occupy in a different seminary taught a generation of students that when both main points and subpoints of the sermon were taken directly from the biblical material, it was an expository sermon; when only the main points came from the Bible, it was textual preaching; and when the points came from one's own brain, the preaching was topical. . . . What must we conclude? That the terms expository preaching and textual preaching are at least worthless—perhaps dangerous, if they keep us from understanding what *biblical* preaching is.[27]

Sidney Greidanus represents homiletical thinking on textual preaching in the 1990s.

> The term expository preaching cannot truly be contrasted with textual preaching or preaching on a single verse, since these terms describe preaching from different angles. Instead of contrasting these terms, therefore, one can easily combine them. . . .
>
> Textual preaching is preaching on a biblical text and expounds the message of that text. This definition implies that all textual preaching requires not only a text but also an exposition of that text. All textual preaching is therefore understood as expository preaching.[28]

The concept of textual preaching is still with us. However, Brown, Greidanus, Thompson, and others have pointed the way to a better understanding of preaching by assessing its biblical authority and its biblical purpose rather than by describing preaching by just its form alone.

Notes

1. Clarence S. Roddy, "The Classification of Sermons," *Homiletics* (Grand Rapids: Baker Book House, 1970), 34.
2. Ibid., 32.
3. Ibid., 34.
4. John A. Broadus, *A Treatise on the Preparation and Delivery of Sermons* (New York: George H. Doran Co., 1890) 311-312.

5. Ibid., 314.
6. Ibid.
7. Ibid., 316.
8. Ibid., 316-317.
9. Austin Phelps, *The Theory of Preaching: Lectures on Homiletics* (New York: Charles Scribner's Sons, 1914), 31.
10. Ibid., 31.
11. Ibid., 31-32.
12. Andrew J. Blackwood, *The Preparation of Sermons* (Nashville: Abingdon Press, 1948), 55.
13. Ibid., 59.
14. Ibid., 55.
15. Ibid., 56-57.
16. Ilion T. Jones, *Principles and Practice of Preaching* (Nashville: Abingdon Press, 1956), 82-83.
17. Ibid., 83.
18. Ibid.
19. Ibid.
20. Donald G. Miller, *The Way to Biblical Preaching* (Nashville: Abingdon Press, 1957), 26.
21. Ibid., 27.
22. Ibid., 32.
23. H. Grady Davis, *Design for Preaching* (Philadelphia: Fortress Press, 1958), 32.
24. Ibid., 63.
25. H. C. Brown, Jr., H. Gordon Clinard, and Jesse J. Northcutt, *Steps to the Sermon* (Nashville: Broadman Press, 1963), 134-135.
26. H. C. Brown, *A Quest for Reformation in Preaching* (Waco: Word Books, 1968), 6.
27. William D. Thompson, *Preaching Biblically: Exegesis and Interpretation* (Nashville: Abingdon Press, 1981), 9-10.
28. Sidney Greidanus, *The Modern Preacher and the Ancient Text: Interpreting and Preaching Biblical Literature* (Grand Rapids: Eerdmans, 1988), 123.

7

Francis C. Rossow
Professor of Homiletics
Concordia Seminary
St. Louis, Missouri

Topical Preaching

When I began my ministry in the late 1940s, the senior pastor of our congregation and I alternated in a planned and systematic way between a textual and a topical approach to our Sunday preaching. One year we would preach on texts assigned by the lectionary; the next year we would select topics and then preach on a biblical text (or texts) dealing with the topics under consideration. The latter practice—at least in my own church denomination—is a dying phenomenon. I think this is unfortunate.

It is my goal in this chapter to put in a good word for topical preaching: to defend the approach as a respectable and helpful homiletical alternative and to encourage the practice in the church-at-large without in any way disparaging the more traditional (and perhaps more defensible) textual approach to preaching. It is my contention that we "ought to do the one and not leave the other undone."

The Nature of Topical Preaching

To begin with, we need to be more precise about the distinction between topical and textual preaching than indicated in the opening paragraph—not for the sake of mere precision but for the sake of reader understanding. In their use of the terms "textual" and "topical," different homileticians sometimes mean different things. "The terms, topical, textual, and expository, are used loosely and not at all uniformly in homiletical literature, and are of limited usefulness."[1]

For example, one writer sees the difference between textual and topical preaching largely in terms of the *approach* to the sermon. "The textual sermon finds its theme and goal in a text. The topical sermon begins with a theme and goal in the mind of the preacher. . . . By 'topical' [this book] means the preaching on a subject which the preacher has begun to develop before he turns to a text to define it."[2] In the textual sermon, the text determines the choice of the topic; but in the topical sermon, the topic determines the choice of text. Note, however, that in both instances a biblical text is used for the sermon.

Another writer sees the difference largely in terms of the *development* of the sermon's structure. "Topical (subject) sermons are those in which the divisions are derived from the subject. The topic may be derived from the text, but the divisions come from the subject."[3] In this instance, the text, not the preacher's idea, is the starting point—in fact, the text may even suggest the topic—but what makes the sermon topical is that the sermon outline is developed in terms of headings natural to the topic rather than those dictated by the text.

Henry Grady Davis in his treatment of topical preaching suggested the possibility of *several biblical texts* rather than one.[4] J. Daniel Baumann in his recent publication hints at the possibility of *no specific biblical text* at all. Says Baumann: "Let us define a topical sermon as the elaboration of a topic, a textual sermon as the elaboration of a short text, and an expository sermon as the elaboration of a longer passage of Scripture."[5]

In this chapter I use the term "topical preaching" to include most of the senses described above. I call a sermon "topical" when the preacher is free to choose a text from the Bible rather than preach on a pericope assigned by the lectionary; when the preacher has an idea and then searches for a biblical text (or texts) treating that idea; even when the preacher writes on an assigned text but feels free to develop the sermon without rigid adherence to the structure of the text and without the compulsion to deal fully with every verse, phrase, or word in that text. Homileticians call this "free text preaching" and "synthetic outlining."

To this broad definition of topical preaching, I hasten to attach the following amendments. First, the topic selected must be a biblical topic, or, if not that, at least a topic treated—and resolved—from a biblical perspective. However chosen and however developed, the sermon topic must ultimately have a "Thus saith the Lord" quality to it; the authority of the Scriptures must prevail.

Second, even though the preacher may develop this theme in his own individual way and may not deal with certain aspects of the text, there must be considerable congruence between the content of the sermon and the content of the text. No topical sermon dare distort or disregard the meaning of the biblical text(s) with which it is associated.

Third, the topical sermon—like the textual sermon—must preach the gospel, the good news of God's saving and sanctifying help through the life, death, and resurrection of Jesus Christ, the Son of God. In fact, the gospel must not merely be present in the sermon—it must be paramount. Although the gospel may not necessarily claim the bulk of the sermon, it should be perceivable by the hearer as the solution to the problem posed or as the means to the end advocated. No matter what the topic, no matter what the text, the gospel must be seen as a principal ingredient in the sermon preached, as a major reason why the sermon was preached at all. Failure to include and highlight the gospel does not disqualify the sermon as a topical sermon—it simply disqualifies it as a sermon at all.

The Advantages of Topical Preaching

The advantages of topical preaching's counterpart, textual/pericopal preaching, are well-known. For the pastor, textual/pericopal preaching eliminates the often frantic and time-consuming weekly search for a text. It reduces the temptation of overt and inordinate subjectivism: reveling in cultural dilettantism, grinding an ax, preaching on pet topics, what James Cox calls "hobby preaching,"[6]

Although Davis warns that "a sermon is not necessarily unbiblical because it has no text, nor biblical because it uses one,"[7] and although Baumann concedes that "in spite of the criticism that has been leveled against topical sermons, it is not necessarily true that a textual or expository sermon is more biblical than a topical sermon,"[8] the fact remains that, in general, textual/pericopal preaching more clearly accents the authority and centrality of the Scriptures in human affairs than does topical preaching. For the congregation, textual/pericopal preaching provides a balanced fare of Scriptural texts and subjects over a long period of time.

Yet topical preaching also has its advantages that ought not to be overlooked or downplayed. For one thing, it is need-oriented rather than tradition-oriented. Although it is not impossible to adjust textual/pericopal preaching to specific congregational needs, it is obviously easier to meet such needs through a topical/free approach. The specific need to be dealt with will not be dragged in by the hair but will rather be the central concern of the text informing the sermon.

Further, freedom of choice can result in better written and better delivered sermons. It is a truth generally accepted among teachers of English composition that their students are more likely to produce quality work when they are permitted to write on topics of their own choosing rather than on assigned topics. One writes better on subjects that are within the range of one's own understanding, experience, and emotional involvement. Might not the same hold true of preaching?

There may be some truth to the contention that a competent homiletician should be able to produce a quality sermon on any assigned text, yet in practice it does not always work that way. Occasionally in textual/pericopal preaching the pastor confronts a text that does not "talk to him" at that particular moment in his life. It may pose some exegetical or hermeneutical difficulty; more likely it is a text whose truth the preacher has not experienced in everyday life—yet. As a result, he may approach the writing of a sermon on that text listlessly, an apathy that may surface in word choice and word arrangement and, above all, in sermon delivery.

Although such outcomes are by no means the inevitable results of preaching on assigned texts, they are less likely to occur when the pastor is free to choose and develop a biblical text that is within the range of his own understanding and whose truth he has encountered in either his living or reading experience. It is a homiletical platitude that "preaching is truth through personality." As long as the personality involved is indeed a sanctified personality, one under the rule of the Holy Spirit, there is little danger of the preacher grinding an ax, riding a hobby, or reveling in some cultural "high." Preaching is more than the explication of a text. It is more than the presentation of objective biblical truth. Preaching is rather the stirring proclamation of objective biblical truth warmed, charged, by the preacher's God-manufactured personal sanctification, enthusiasm, insight, experience, and emotional involvement.

There are two things to realize about subjectivity in preaching. The first is that it is inevitable. Seldom can even the most conscientious of us approach a biblical sermon text—including one assigned to us by a lectionary—in a vacuum, entirely devoid of personal input. Invariably, we bring something to the text as well as derive something from it. "There can be no sermon that was not first preceded by an idea or a theme."[9] This holds true for even the most ardent practitioner of strictly textual preaching. The only way I know that the preacher could even come close to avoiding subjectivity altogether would be to read the text in a very accurate translation and then promptly exit from the pulpit without having made any comment on the text at all. Such a practice might be construed as textual loyalty, but it would hardly be considered preaching! Because subjectivity is unavoidable in preaching, it does not follow that we should give it its head and let it run away with the sermon. We do, however, need to recognize that even under the most ideal conditions in our sermon preparation a degree of subjectivity is inevitable.

That leads us to the second thing we need to realize about subjectivity: it is not necessarily bad. Subjectivity is not intrinsically evil. What is crucial is the origin and character of what we bring to the text. Is our input the product of previous reading of the Scriptures? If not that, is our input at least in agreement with the Scriptures? It is possible to think we are bringing something of ourselves to a sermon text when, in fact, what we are bringing is God's gift to us through our previous use of His Word and through His gracious direction of our living and reading experiences centered in that Word.

In summary, the more we read the Scriptures and live under their sway, the more we understand a particular Scripture. The more we dwell richly in the Word (see Col. 3:16), the more meaning we see in a specific Word of God serving as a sermon text—whether that text has been assigned or voluntarily chosen. There is a give and take, a mutual interaction, between our study of a text and our previous Bible reading, In this area too our Lord's words apply: "Whosoever hath, to him shall be given; and whosoever hath not, from him shall be taken even that which he seemeth to have" (Luke 8:18).

Three final advantages to topical/free text preaching deserve brief mention. The first is that it enables the pastor to preach on many homiletically rich texts in the Bible not covered by pericopal systems (even when the pastor employs many different pericopal systems in the course of ministry). The second is that a topical approach allows a pastor who has the ability (and the necessary accompanying sense of responsibility— to use certain creative sermon formats—such as multiple texts, literary genres, extended analogies, monologue, dialogue, letter formats—and to match such formats with texts compatible to these formats. The third is that the pastor may consult individuals or groups in the congregation for their input to the choice of sermon topics and sermon texts, thereby increasing the likelihood of subsequent sermons being relevant to individual and congregational needs.

Obstacles to the Restoration of Topical Preaching

One of the factors discouraging the restoration of topical preaching in contemporary ministry is the character of the current system of homiletical helps. In many denominations, publishing house sermon aids and seminary journal homiletical helps are built around the contemporary lectionary. In order to utilize such aids pastors are tempted to preach only on the pericopes contained in the lectionary. In order to provide relevant aid to such pastors, publishing houses and seminary journals continue to focus their homiletical helps only on the pericopes in the lectionary that pastors are using. The process becomes circular, and self-perpetuating! Add to this the existence of admittedly convenient and useful published bulletin inserts containing all the elements for any Sunday and the process is entrenched.

Another factor currently inhibiting occasional topical preaching is, I fear, the gradual development of lectionary/pericopal preaching into a sacred cow. Pericopal systems are hallowed by time and tradition. They are blessed with an aura of objectivity and balance. They are richly liturgical. True as all this may be, I think we need to remind ourselves that whether we preach on a pericope from the lectionary or on a free text, a *human* choice has been made. In the one case the preacher makes his own choice; in the other case the preacher lets someone else make that choice for him. Accordingly, the preacher should not be intimidated by the existence of pericopal systems and assigned texts. They are human choices—time-honored and balanced to be sure—but human choices nonetheless.

Sources for Sermon Topics

Having established that topical preaching is a legitimate as well as a helpful homiletical alternative, it is now appropriate to ask: What are the sources for it? Where can the preacher get ideas for sermons?

The main source is the Bible itself. As we have already seen, textual preaching does not have a corner on that source. In the foregoing discussion, we have recognized the paradox that the topics we bring to our sermon preparation and for which we hunt appropriate texts are themselves often the products of our prior exposure to the Scriptures. They are frequently not "our" ideas at all but rather God's gifts to us through our previous use of His Word.

Hence it follows that successful topical preaching depends heavily upon the pastor's frequent and regular use of the Scriptures. The topical preacher, no less than the textual preacher, needs to be a student of God's Word. While confrontation with the Bible in weekly sermon preparation need not be an exclusively professional, academic activity, it is better if the pastor also encounters the Scriptures on a regular basis for personal edification apart from the impending demands of the Sunday sermon. How he does this is up to him—so long as he does it. However he does it, such devotional study is a key factor in enriching not only the pastor's daily life but also his supply of sermon topics. "Seeking the Kingdom of God first" in his approach to the Scriptures, the pastor discovers the "sermon ideas are added unto him."

The congregation the preacher serves is another obvious source for topical preaching. Often a pastor's sermon subject grows out of "a spark from the anvil of his ministry."[10] That is why it is so important that the pastor spend time not only in study but also among his parishioners. He needs to get into their homes and into their places of employment and recreation. Rubbing shoulders with his people, the pastor will hear their hopes and aspirations and become familiar with their needs and concerns. He will find plenty to talk about in Sunday-to-Sunday preaching, with the added confidence that what he talks about will be relevant to his listeners' everyday lives.

The pastor's own life experiences constitute still another source for topical preaching. With Spirit-opened eyes, the pastor recognizes the emergence of a pattern in God's various dealings with him. Among his joys and sorrows, his ups and downs, the pastor sees life whole. Among all the drab and colorful numerators of daily living, he sees certain common denominators that he attributes to God's grace. He then integrates what he finds, makes sense out of it, translates it into relevant sermon topics, and under these topics communicates the sense he has discovered to others through the sermons he preaches. From his own particular God-directed life experiences, the pastor formulates generalizations (informed by God's Word) which he then applies to his congregation.

A final source for topical preaching is the pastor's reading experience: theological books and journals, newspapers, magazines, reviews, and belletristic literature (novels, dramas, poems, and short stories). The value of the last-mentioned genre for topical preaching I can verify from my own experience. Writers like Austen, Camus, Cervantes, Donne, Dostoevsky, Fielding, Greene, Hemingway, Herbert, Marvell, Pope, Shakespeare, Steinbeck, Swift, Tolstoy, Trollope, Waugh, Wharton, plus many others, are seers of the soul—human beings who have wrestled intensely with the issues of life and death and have reported their findings in attractive, non-sermonic form. An occasional writer (for instance, C. S. Lewis, J. R. R. Tolkien) will even supply the reader with a new perspective on the gospel. Although belletristic writers cannot always be relied upon to narrate in any great detail the saving gospel, they can be relied upon to make clear our need for that gospel. If they do not suggest distinctively Christian themes, they supply a host of topics which we can view from the perspective of the Scriptures. If I seem to emphasize this source for sermon topics unduly, it is not because I regard it as more important than the other sources mentioned, but because it is the one we preachers are most likely to overlook or ignore.

A Final Appeal

It has not been the purpose of this chapter to denigrate or discourage textual preaching. It has rather been its purpose to restore topical preaching to its rightful place. In examining the two homiletical genres, we have not been looking at the difference between a homiletical virtue and a homiletical vice. Both are homiletical virtues—even though, customarily, textual preaching had been considered the greater virtue. Both genres have their place in the average preaching ministry.

Most of us will prefer one or the other. If you are inclined to be a textual preacher, then make sure that your sermon content and sermon language are related to audience need and experience. If you are inclined to be a topical preacher, then make sure that your sermon material is clearly informed by the witness of the Scriptures. As Richard Caemmerer warns, the textual sermon dare not become a lecture in exegesis and the topical sermon dare not become a review of the arts or of contemporary events.[11] I suggest that a pastor employ both the textual and the topical approaches, preferably in a programmed and systematic way in order to tap the unique advantages of both genres. Each will complement the other. Not only will the preacher "enjoy the best of both worlds" but the congregation will be the richer for it.

Ultimately, the two approaches are not all that different from each other. As I review my amended definitions of both genres above and as I reconsider the goals of preaching, it occurs to me that the two approaches blend together beautifully. Both proclaim law and gospel, sin and grace. Both acknowledge the authority of the Scriptures. Both reflect biblical doctrine. Both usually develop a biblical text, but in varying degrees of completeness. The textual sermon brings the biblical to bear on the secular; the topical sermon puts the secular into the context of the biblical. The outcome in either case is similar. As Caemmerer points out:

> Both textual and topical preaching have several things in common which are at the heart of the preacher's task. Both give the opportunity to preach the Gospel of Jesus Christ. Both draw the material by which God really helps them from the Bible. Both concern themselves with the relation of people to God. This means that in their final form they are not going to be too different from each other.[12]

Given a sermon that does these things—and does them in language that is attractive and understandable—it makes little difference whether we classify the sermon as textual, topical, or textual-topical.

Notes

1. Henry Grady Davis, *Design for Preaching* (Philadelphia: Fortress Press, 1958), 32.
2. Richard R. Caemmerer, *Preaching for the Church* (St. Louis: Concordia Publishing House, 1959), 133, 139.
3. John A. Broadus, *On the Preparation and Delivery of Sermons*; 4th ed., rev. Vernon L. Stanfield (San Francisco: Harper & Row, 1979), 55.
4. Davis, *Design for Preaching*, 48.
5. J. Daniel Baumann, *An Introduction to Contemporary Preaching* (Grand Rapids: Baker Book House, 1988), 101.
6. James W. Cox, *Preaching* (San Francisco: Harper & Row, 1985), 62.
7. Davis, *Design for Preaching*, 33.
8. Baumann, *Contemporary Preaching*, 101.
9. John Killinger, *Fundamentals of Preaching* (Philadelphia: Fortress Press, 1985), 44.
10. Caemmerer, *Preaching for the Church*, 134.
11. Ibid., 145.
12. Ibid., 76-77.

John Knox (1513-1572)
"The Thundering Scot"

Few preachers in history have so influenced the course of a nation's history as did John Knox of Scotland.

As a young man, Knox came under the influence of the Reformation, leaving the Catholic priesthood to join ranks with the Protestant cause. Imprisoned for a time, after his release Knox became a pastor—first in England, then in Germany. He also spent time in Geneva, where he associated with John Calvin.

Knox's return to Edinburgh in 1559 was marked by armed conflict as well as preaching. Led by Knox, the Scottish Protestants claimed control of the nation. Over the next several years Knox faced down Queen Mary who was determined to restore Catholicism to preeminence in Scotland; her eventual abdication secured the place of Protestantism in the political and religious realms.

Knox was known as a bold and fearless preacher who attracted great crowds to hear him in his Edinburgh pulpit. He ignored threats of imprisonment and execution in order to fulfill a divine calling to proclaim the gospel.

Sadly, only two sermon manuscripts from Knox's ministry exist today, so there is little material available to evaluate his preaching apart from its remarkable effect on the lives of people and the life of a nation. We do know he was a devout student of the Bible, and the two sermons we have consist primarily of exposition of his chosen text. Knox also was careful to show how the listeners could apply the message of the text in their own walk of faith.

John Knox was a dynamic preacher and leader whose words and actions changed the course of a nation.

8
Timothy George, Dean
Beeson Divinity School
Samford University
Birmingham, Alabama

Doctrinal Preaching

In a handbook such as this which features models of *contemporary* preaching, it is not at all obvious that there should be a chapter on doctrinal preaching. Expository preaching, creative preaching, evangelistic preaching, incarnational preaching, narrative preaching, yes; but *doctrinal* preaching? The very word *doctrine,* like its cousins *dogma* and *dogmatic,* has fallen on hard times. For many people it connotes authoritarianism, intellectualism, and legalism. When applied to preaching it comes out rigid and stultifying rather than dynamic and edifying.

Yet despite those misconceptions, the recovery of doctrinal preaching is essential to the renewal of the church. The crisis of identity which engulfs contemporary Christianity, especially in the West, has resulted in large measure from the loss of a persuasive message clearly proclaimed in the power of the Holy Spirit. What does the church have to say that no one else can say?[1] What does the preacher have to say that the psychologist, politician, stock broker, or social commentator has not already said with more passion and insight than most pastors can muster even on Easter Sunday? The credibility of the church's proclamation will not be restored by acquiring new communication skills or devising better sermonic forms, as helpful as these may be. The answer is a preacher in whom the Word of God burns as a fire in his bones, one who must speak because he cannot keep silent, one who preaches with fierce humility ("Who is equal to such a task?" 2 Cor. 2:16, NIV) yet also with unstinted audacity ("Such confidence . . . is ours through Christ," 2 Cor. 3:4, NIV) in the certain knowledge that God Himself is speaking in the faithful proclamation of His Word. Or, as Second Helvetic Confession (1566) put it even more succinctly:

"The preaching of the Word of God is the Word of God."[2] This is the burden of doctrinal preaching.

The strategy of this essay is first to examine the presupposition of doctrinal preaching, then to give practical suggestions as to how this approach might affect the craft of the sermon, and finally to present several examples of doctrinal preaching from the history of the church.

The Message Is the Medium

Without a doubt the most influential theologian between the Reformation and the twentieth century was Friedrich Schleiermacher, who died the same year that Charles H. Spurgeon was born (1834). While working out of the Reformed tradition, Schleiermacher defined religion not in terms of the doctrinal concerns of historic Christianity but rather a "feeling of absolute dependence." This principle enabled him to recast traditional Christian doctrines in terms of the relative God- or Christ-consciousness of the believer. Thus in his major theological work, *The Christian Faith*, he relegated the doctrine of the Trinity to a slight appendage at the end since it seemed to him to have little relevance to the religious experience or actual life-situation of the individual Christian.[3]

Schleiermacher was a preacher as well as a theologian. His homiletical theory provided a new paradigm for preaching in the modern world. According to this understanding, the preacher dares to step forward and address the congregation only in order "to project his innermost self as a subject of shared observation." His purpose is "to lead them to the sphere of religion, where they feel at home so that he can instill his [own] sacred feelings."[4] The emphasis is not on the content of the message, which may be quite irrelevant, but on the authenticity and self-expression of the messenger whose "inspired speech" gives concrete form to the religious sensitivities of the congregation. In this scheme the preacher is a divine *virtuoso*, a spiritual *guru*, whose role is to tap the innate yearnings and inner quests of his hearers. To this way of defining the preaching task, one can only ask with Karl Barth: "Where is the Word of God in this immanent sea of feelings? Where is the ongoing seeking if all that is done is simply the expression of an inner possessing?"[5]

Against the modern, subjectivistic understanding of preaching stands the earlier Reformation model of preaching as the central sacramental moment of worship. According to Luther: "The preaching and teaching of God's Word is the main part of all divine service."[6] The German word for worship, *Gottesdienst*, is a double entendre: it means not only our response to God in adoration, confession, thanksgiving, and praise, but also—and in the first instance—God's service to us, the Word of God addressed to us in law and gospel, promise and fulfillment, judgment and grace. For this reason we who have been called and appointed to preach have no business regaling the congregation with "our own prophetic booming," however eloquently expressed or aesthetically framed such booming may be. Our vocation is that of the postman: we have been entrusted with a message which has to be delivered. As John H. Leith has put it: "The message is in a real sense the medium, and the worst heresy in preaching is for the medium to become the message."[7]

If anything, Zwingli and Calvin stressed even more rigorously than Luther this uni-directional doctrine of preaching. In October, 1523, Zwingli addressed the ministers of Zurich on the true nature of ministry. He declared that the false shepherd or pastor was one who put forth his own ideas rather than teaching the "certainty and clarity" of Holy Scripture. The Reformation had been introduced in Zurich on January 1, 1519, when Zwingli entered the pulpit of the Great Minister and began a series of expository sermons through the Gospel of Matthew, discarding the "canned homilies" provided by the church authorities. In 1525 he began "The Prophecy," a regular seminar on preaching which met in the cathedral choir, in order to train Reformed ministers, presumably "true shepherds," in biblical exegesis and doctrinal theology.

Calvin carried this emphasis further still by insisting that when the Bible is purely preached, it is as if God Himself were speaking in person. Richard Stauffer has claimed that preaching for Calvin was not merely an essential task of the church and preacher but also an occasion for divine epiphany.[8] It is the work of the Holy Spirit and not the personality or skill of the preacher which produces such an occasion of transcendence. As we sing: "All is vain unless the Spirit of the Holy One comes down . . . Pray . . . while we try to preach." Thus true ministers of the divine Word—Calvin's preferred term for set-apart preachers—are to "invent nothing themselves, nor teach whatever they please, but faithfully transmit [only] what God has committed to them."[9]

The presupposition of doctrinal preaching is that the God who has once and for all come in Jesus Christ and once and for all spoken in Holy Scripture still comes and still speaks to His people through the faithful proclamation of His Word in the power of the Holy Spirit. "Doctrine" is not an abstract formulation of belief divorced from this saving reality and divine revelation. To the contrary, it is the irreducible content of this very reality, conveyed through God's authoritative, infallible Word and elucidated through what the church of Jesus Christ believes, teaches, and confesses on the basis of that Holy Word.

Preaching Doctrinally

What has been said thus far concerning the presupposition of doctrinal preaching could well apply in a general sense to the entire task of preaching in the life of the church. We must now examine more concretely how these principles are applied in the art of sermon construction.

It is unfortunate that "doctrine" and "Bible" are frequently pitted against each other as polar opposites between which the hapless preacher must choose. This dichotomy reflects a long-standing tension on theological faculties between biblical scholars on the one hand and systematic theologians on the other. Such turf wars may have their place in the obscure guilds of academic life, but they are disastrous in the pulpit. Every doctrinal sermon must be contextually rooted in sound exegesis; and every expository or biblical sermon should place a given passage in the widest theological framework possible. Both the unity and the historicity of the Bible demand no less.

Building on the insights of the Reformation, the English Puritans developed a pattern of preaching which was both biblically based and theologically responsible. Reacting against the "bare reading ministry" prescribed by statute and the rhetorical ornamentation practiced by many Anglican divines, the Puritans sought to cultivate a "plain style" of preaching, a style which focused on the message rather than the messengers who, as Calvin had warned, "must not make a parade of rhetoric, only to gain esteem for themselves . . . the spirit of God ought to sound forth by their voice, so as to work with mighty energy. . . for doctrine is cold unless it is given divine efficacy."[10]

One of the principal handbooks on preaching in the Puritan tradition was William Perkins's *The Arte of Prophesying* (1592). In this pithy treatise of eleven brief chapters Perkins summed up his homiletical methodology in four basic rules:

The order and sum of the sacred and only method of preaching

1. To read the text distinctly out of the canonical Scriptures.
2. To give the sense and understanding of it being read, by the Scripture itself.
3. To collect a few and profitable points of doctrine out of the natural sense.
4. To apply, if we have the gift, the doctrines rightly collected to the life and manners of men in a simple plain speech.

The sum of the sum:
Preach on Christ by Christ to the praise of Christ.
Soli Deo Gloria[11]

True preaching thus requires the measured reading of Holy Scripture and its proper interpretation, followed by doctrinal exposition and pertinent application. Concerning the third step, doctrinal exposition, Perkins distinguished those texts which are freighted with doctrinal meaning (for instance, Rom. 3:9-26) from other texts where the doctrine is implied rather than expressed in an obvious manner. In the case of the former, the preacher's task is like that of a weaver unloosing a braid; in the latter case the preacher must compare Scripture with Scripture in order to properly place a particular text within the *scopus* of the entire drama of redemption. Such "collections," as Perkins called this latter exercise, are to be soundly gathered and derived from the genuine and proper meaning of the Scriptures. They are not to be forced upon the text by the fancy of the preacher. Still, it is necessary and proper to "rightly divide the Word" in this sense because the Bible is not a hodgepodge of literary texts from the ancient world but rather the perfect record of God's dealings with humankind in creation and redemption, inspired and given definitive canonical shape by the Holy Spirit.

The sermon is not complete until the fourth step of application has been taken. The purpose of preaching is never merely to dispense information or to display the erudition of the preacher. Perkins was critical of sermons that were too "garnished with skill of arts, tongues and variety of reading."[12] The sermon is not a seminar! The preacher must apply the doctrine rightly collected from the text in such a way that its spiritual impact is felt by the hearers. In order to do this effectively, the preacher must be as good an exegete of the congregation as he is of the text. He will know how to reprove the wayward, comfort the disconsolate, rebuke the obstinate, encourage the disheartened, and extend the invitation of grace to the unsaved.

While the pattern of doctrinal preaching developed by the Puritans can still be used with great profit, it is not necessary to follow their precise order of presentation. All sermons should have a strong doctrinal content, but there are many special occasions and preaching opportunities which lend themselves to a particular doctrinal emphasis. The following suggestions may be helpful in planning a schedule of preaching throughout the year.

1. Use confessions and catechisms to give a framework for doctrinal sermons. Some preachers, including even renowned evangelical ones, have been reluctant to follow this method. They prefer the sermon to arise directly from the Bible and not from human formulations, not even very good ones.[13] However, it need not be either/or. After all, confessions and catechisms are derived from the Bible. They have no independent authority apart from the Bible, and they must always be tested by, and stand revisable in the light of, the Bible. They are deeply anchored in the history of particular faith communities and can be a useful device for passing on the faith intact to the next generation.

2. Preach on the grand events of salvation history throughout the church year. In Jesus Christ, God has redeemed not only individuals and the cosmos but also time itself. Christians celebrate this fact throughout the year by ordering their lives and worship around the events of Jesus' advent, birth, baptism, death, resurrection, ascension, and the pouring out of the Holy Spirit at Pentecost. Preaching with the aid of a lectionary will bring these themes into focus for sermon preparation.

3. Prepare for the celebration of baptism and the Lord's Supper by sound doctrinal preaching. One of the great themes of the Reformation was the coherence of Word and sacrament. The "visible words" of God in bread, wine, and water should always be accompanied by thorough instruction. Such sermons need not be restricted to the administration of the ordinances. A message on the unity of the church would be especially appropriate for the Lord's Supper, just as the theme of discipleship would comport with the meaning of baptism.

4. Use great hymns of the faith to accent the theological content of the sermon. In the absence of consistent doctrinal preaching, hymns have often been the primary carriers of Christian meaning for many believers. They are best used, however, in concert with sound theological exposition. Who could not preach on the grace of God after singing Charles Wesley's "And Can It Be?" or on forgiveness after "Praise, My Soul, the King of Heaven?"

5. Show the importance of doctrine in the lives of great biblical and church historical characters. Doctrine has both a propositional and an incarnational dimension. It is the truth of God's Word distilled and applied to fallen and redeemed human beings, but it is that truth lived out in the flesh and blood reality of the people of God. To show how Athanasius staked his life on the doctrine of the Trinity, or how Luther struggled against the fury of hell for the doctrine of justification by faith, is to impress on the congregation the gravity and relevance of the faith once for all delivered to the saints.

Three Examples

In conclusion, we want to look briefly at three examples of doctrinal sermons from the history of the church. Each comes from a different period of church history—Patristic, Reformation, Modern. Each represents a distinctive point of departure in preaching: the first is a sermon on the Apostles' Creed; the second, a sermon taken from the routine of an expository series; and the third, a thematic approach to a great doctrinal topic. All three, however, follow in varying measures the essential elements of the fourfold pattern outlined above.

The first sermon was preached by Saint Augustine to new Christians preparing for baptism. It is entitled, "On the Creed: A Sermon to the Catechumens." Augustine encouraged his hearers to receive, believe, and confess their faith in the words of the Rule of Faith, what he called the Apostles' Creed. This statement, he argued, is indeed a summary of the principal teaching of the Bible itself. "These words which ye have heard are in the Divine Scriptures scattered up and down: but thence gathered and reduced into one, that the memory of slow persons might not be distressed; that every person may be able to say, able to hold, what he believes."[14]

The biblical basis of each phrase of the creed is explicated. Special attention is given to the relation of the Son to the Father. Disputes over the Trinity were still troubling the church in Augustine's day, and he clearly affirmed the equality and co-eternality of the Father and the Son. "Hold ye therefore boldly, firmly, faithfully, that the Begotten of God the Father is what Himself is, Almighty."[15] He also discouraged those young believers from prying too inquisitively into the hidden things of God. Concerning Christ's ascension and session at the right hand of the Father, he admonished: "And let not your heart say to you, What is he doing? Do not want to seek what is not permitted to find: He is there; it suffices you."[16]

By treating the entire Apostles' Creed in one brief sermon, Augustine passed lightly over many deep truths of the faith. His purpose was to ground the catechumen under his charge in the essentials of the gospel. He sought to apply these truths by pointing out their relevance to daily Christian living: "He shewed us in the cross what we ought to endure, He shewed in the resurrection what we have to hope."[17] By using the framework of the Rule of Faith, Augustine was able to present a comprehensive statement of Christian theology within the confines of a single sermon.

Our second example, Calvin's "Sermon on the Passion of Our Lord Jesus Christ," is a more focused message based on a specific text, Matthew 26:36-39. Calvin presented a masterful interpretation of this passage which records the Gethsemane experience of Christ. Calvin claimed that the Scripture intends to confront us with three truths in this event: first, God's inestimable love toward us; second, our detestable sinfulness; and, third, that we should value the salvation won for us by Christ so dearly that we will forsake the world and find our true joy in the inheritance acquired for us at so great a price.

Calvin emphasized the voluntary character of Christ's suffering and the empathy produced by His ordeal. "For if he had not felt in his person the fears, the doubts, and the torments which we endure, he would not be so inclined to be pitiful toward us as he is."[18] Calvin also pointed out that Christ's fears were not merely confined to the physical agony, but stemmed from His experience of the eternal death and damnation which He endured as our substitute. "For even if there be only a single sinner, what would the wrath of God be?"[19] Calvin was careful to affirm both the full deity and true humanity of Christ in this most vulnerable moment of His incarnate life.

What is the purpose of rehearsing this event in the life of Jesus Christ? Calvin made a threefold application in this sermon. First, the contemplation of the sufferings of Christ should reorient us more fully to the things of God. In the second place, Calvin preached this sermon as a preparation for the celebration of the Lord's Supper which was to take place on the following Sunday in Geneva. Finally, the good news of Christ's suffering and atonement should inspire us to encourage one another and reach out to the lost. "Let us not grow weary in the middle of the journey, but let us profit so much day by day, and let us take trouble to approach those who are out of the road, let this be all our joy, our life, our glory and contentment, and let us so help one another until God has fully gathered us to himself."[20]

Our third example is a sermon on "The Perseverance of the Saints," delivered by Charles H. Spurgeon on June 24, 1877. Spurgeon did not believe that a preacher should ever plan a series of sermons in advance. Instead, he felt that the Spirit would guide the preacher to the appropriate text for each occasion. His text for this sermon was Job 17:9: "The righteous also shall hold on his way." Spurgeon declared: "I take our text as accurately setting forth the doctrine of the final perseverance of the saints."[21]

The sermon is divided into three parts: introduction, the proof of the doctrine, and its practical application. Since this particular doctrine had been hotly debated in the Calvinist-Arminian disputes, Spurgeon's presentation had a slight polemical tone, although he stayed close to the scriptural arguments and never indulged personal slurs or partisan remarks. He set forth seven arguments on behalf of the doctrine: the nature of regeneration, Christ's expressed teachings, the intercession of Jesus, the character and work of Christ, the covenant of grace, the faithfulness of God, and the work of the Holy Spirit.

Having marshaled his evidence in an impressive manner, Spurgeon turned to the impact of this doctrine for the life of faith. He found first that it is a great encouragement for those who are on the way to heaven. The divine assurance of a successful finish keeps the pilgrim on the road in the most trying of circumstances.

> One might hardly undertake a difficult journey if he did not believe that he would finish it, but the sweet assurance that we shall reach our home makes us pluck up courage. The weather is wet, rainy, blusterous, but we must keep on, for the end is sure. The road is very rough, and runs up hill and down dale; we pant for breath, and our limbs are aching; but as we shall get to our journey's end we push on. We are ready to creep into some cottage and lie down to die of weariness, saying, "I shall never accomplish my task;" but the confidence which we have received sets us on our feet, and off we go again.[22]

In addition, Spurgeon declared, this doctrine is an enticement to sinners who are seeking salvation. "I am happy to preach to you a sure and everlasting salvation. . . . Grasp at it, poor soul; thou mayest have it if thou dost but believe in Jesus Christ, or, in other words, trust thy soul with him."[23]

Of the three examples cited here, Calvin's sermon comes closest to fulfilling the requirements of the Puritan model. Augustine's sermon is strong on doctrinal content but weak in its exegetical basis. Spurgeon's sermon is thoroughly interlaced with Scriptural exposition but only related tangentially to his primary text. All three preachers took pains to apply doctrinal truth to the lives of their hearers. All three dealt with major concerns of the faith, not with obscure points of doctrine. Each preacher—Augustine, Calvin, and Spurgeon—spoke powerfully to his generation out of a core of conviction. Each desired to declare the whole counsel of God because each knew something decisive was at stake every time a minister of the divine Word stands to declare: "Thus saith the Lord."

The rich treasury of doctrinal sermons in the history of the church can help us to recover an endangered genre of preaching in our own generation. If our sermons are to be more than "cozy chats on small matters," we must apply ourselves to this challenge with all of the gravity and gladness of our souls.[24]

Notes

1. See John H. Leith, *The Reformed Imperative: What the Church Has To Say That No One Else Can Say* (Louisville: Westminster/John Knox Press, 1989). See also the chapter on preaching in Leith's *From Generation to Generation* (Louisville: Westminster/John Knox Press, 1990), and his "Calvin's Doctrine of the Proclamation of the Word and Its Significance for Today," *John Calvin and the Church: A Prism of Reform,* ed. Timothy George (Louisville: Westminster/John Knox Press, 1990), 206-229.

2. John H. Leith, *Creeds of the Churches* (Atlanta: John Knox Press, 1982), 131.

3. Friedrich Schleiermacher, *The Christian Faith* (New York: Harper and Row, 1963) 2:738-751.

4. Friedrich Schleiermacher, *On Religion: Speeches to Its Cultured Despisers* (New York: Harper and Row, 1986), 151. For a more positive appraisal of Schleiermacher, see B. A. Gerrish, *A Prince of the Church: Schleiermacher and the Beginnings of Modern Theology* (Philadelphia: Fortress Press, 1984).

5. Karl Barth, *Homiletics* (Louisville: Westminster/John Knox Press, 1991), 22-23.

6. *D. Martin Luthers Werke, Kritische Gesamtausgabe,* 58 vols. (Weimar: Böhlau, 1833), 19:78.

7. Leith, *From Generation to Generation,* 95.

8. Richard Stauffer, "Le discours à la première personne dans les sermônes de Calvin," *Regards contemporains sur Jean Calvin* (Paris, 1965). Quoted in Leith, "Calvin's Doctrine," 211.

9. Comm. Jer. 1:9-10. See William J. Bouwsma, *John Calvin: A Sixteenth Century Portrait* (New York: Oxford University Press, 1988), 226.

10. John Calvin, *Letters of John Calvin,* ed. Jules Bonnet (Philadelphia: Presbyterian Board of Publication, 1858) 2:190-191; Comm. John 17:1.

11. Ian Breward, ed., *The Works of William Perkins* (Appleford: Sutton Courtenay Press, 1970), 349.

12. Ibid., 327.

13. See, for example, D. Martyn Lloyd-Jones, *Preaching and Preachers* (Grand Rapids: Zondervan, 1971), 187.

14. Philip Schaff, ed., *The Nicene and Post-Nicene Fathers* (Grand Rapids: Eerdmans, 1980), 3:369.

15. Ibid., 370.

16. Ibid., 373.
17. Ibid., 372.
18. John Calvin, *Sermons on the Saving Work of Christ*, tr. Leroy Nixon (Grand Rapids: Baker Book House, 1950), 53.
19. Ibid., 60.
20. Ibid., 65.
21. Charles Haddon Spurgeon, *Sermons on Sovereignty* (Pasadena, Texas: Pilgrim Publication, 1990), 202.
22. Ibid., 212.
23. Ibid., 213.
24. Merrill R. Abbey, *Living Doctrine in a Vital Pulpit* (New York: Abingdon, 1964), 3. For a recent statement of this challenge, see John Piper, *The Supremacy of God in Preaching* (Grand Rapids: Baker Book House, 1990).

9

Calvin Miller
Professor of Communications and Ministry Studies
Southwestern Baptist Theological Seminary
Fort Worth, Texas

Narrative Preaching

Nearly thirty-five years ago, H. Grady Davis reminded us that while only one-tenth of the gospel is exposition, nine-tenths of it is narrative. Why then do our preceptual sermons so often roar on, entirely out of sync with the Bible's narrative mode?[1] Small wonder that Eugene Lowry and others are calling for narrative preaching as a primary sermon form.

At the outset, let me clarify that narrative preaching, as Lowry and others might call for it, is not a simple matter of using stories and illustrations to make the sermon interesting, instructive, or challenging. The narrative sermon, rather than containing stories, *is* a story which, from outset to conclusion, binds the entire sermon to a single plot as theme. Here and there sub-plots, separate illustrations or precepts may punctuate or ornament the narrative, but the theme narrative stays in force all the way through—from the sermon's "once-upon-a-time" until its "happy ever after." I will use the term *narrative sermon* in this story-as-sermon understanding.

First, let us begin by looking at five reasons why this form is a strong and advisable sermonic model. Following our affirmation of the form, we will look at some reasons to be cautious in its use. Finally—against what all pure narrative sermonizers would advise—we raise four cautions about the narrative sermon's pure induction and see what principles might be stated as to both the best use of the narrative sermon and the best use of narratives within a sermon.

Strengths of the Narrative Form

The first and most notable strength of the narrative sermon is that it speaks in a natural way to the story of both Scripture and contemporary culture. The Bible is largely narrative; therefore, it follows that, if we are going to preach the Book, we need to remember that the Book is a "story book." If the sermon is going to be the servant of the Book, it should serve in narrative ways. The Bible is not only a book of individual stories, but also the stories really serve in such a way as to comprise a single, comprehensive narrative that tells a single story of God being reconciled with humankind. If the Bible can be as diverse as it is and yet tell one story, the narrative sermon would seem to be wholly consistent.

Not only is the Bible a single story, but the great creeds of the church are single stories as well. To begin a creedal recitation with, "I believe in God the Father Almighty and in Jesus Christ His Son," tells the worshiper an elemental, single story is about to be confessed with which the whole church will concur. When the church recites a creed, it is collectively confessing the great narrative of its faith. If it then listens to a narrative sermon, it couples with the larger narrative confession of the church to bring a wholeness to all of worship.

Nearly as important as Bible and creed, our own culture—more than any other that has ever been—is a story-oriented culture. Literally thousands of new novels, movies, plays, and teleplays are released every year. All of these proclaim our age as the age of the story! In such a story-soaked age, the narrative sermon will naturally find a cultural acceptance which the precept-oriented or the exegesis sermon might never find. Typical congregations nourished on years of television dramas and popular video releases have been groomed to relate to the narrative sermon.

A second value of the narrative sermon is that it contains a generous barb to snag the three-minute interest spans that current church-goers bring to church with them. Fred Craddock once remarked that boredom is a form of evil.[2] Story snags interest and, like a child who will not be ignored, it grasps the parent's chin and pulls the face straight with the face of the narrator. Narrative sermons force our dull minds to pay attention far more than many older sermon models. Eugene Lowry speaks to the issue when he says his power of narrative is what makes a good novel so hard to lay down.[3] The magnificent component of narrative preaching that forces us to pay attention is *plot*.

Lowry defines *plot* as "the moving suspense of story from disequilibrium to resolution." All plots depend upon this movement and the easing of this tension. *Plot* is, as he so aptly says, the journey from itch to scratch.[4] Lowry (an excellent pianist), while lecturing on this unfulfilled itch, will often to go a piano in the middle of his lecture and play "almost" an entire scale from "do" to "ti." While the audience hangs for his completion of this "almostness," the point is made. None of us want unfinished scales in our lives. It is our hunger to have every itch scratched that makes the narrative sermon so all-consuming. We will attend to it with baited breath until the preacher finally arrives at some "happy ever after!" This unresolved tension pulls whole audiences along in our oft-maddening compulsion to find the sermon's resolution.

A third strength of the narrative sermon is that it is less preachy to the "me generation" of today and the "we generation" that's on the way. Many sociologists believe that the "me generation" of the '80s is folding into the "we generation" that will conclude the second millennium. The narcissists of the '80s did not like precept preaching as sermon form because its heavy imperatives came across as too "shouldy" or "musty" for the hang-loose, don't preach-to-me generation. Now as the decade of narcissism fades into the decade of consensus, the demand will be equally great that preaching not "talk down," like God aperch Sinai, to those who want to dialogue their way into the third millennium.

Stories are warmly inductive and make few imperative demands. They charm the listener to apply the point only as they wish. In this sense, narrative preaching is to homiletics what Carl Rogers was to psychology. In Rogerian counseling, under guidance counselees diagnosed their own issue and arrived at their own prescription and cure. The narrative sermon, like a skilled counselor, maneuvers a story through whole congregations of privatized needs and each applies the story to their own situation to arrive at the best individual application. Answers are arrived at without the austerity of "thou shalts" or "thou shalt nots." "Come now and reason together," cried the prophet (Isa. 1:18). The narrative preacher sees the sermon story as a dialogue of irresolute moving to the opening needs of the me-first-we-first age without sounding preachy.

A fourth strength of the narrative sermon has to do with the flow and fix of the sermon. By "flow" I mean the smoothness of the sermon's movement and by "fix" I refer to the memorability of the sermon. Stories move with an "oily" glide, that is not possible with the "jerky" and spastic plodding of the preceptual sermon outline. The oral exegesis sermon that characterizes so many evangelical pulpits moves by jolting the listener between its outlined subpoints. Each subpoint stops the mind to notch the point before banging its bumpy way on through the (oft-projected) outline.

Lowry says that just as our education system is geared to make "truth stand still," the same evil has also been a long-standing fault of sermons. If Jesus' parables are not "still-life" pictures but motion pictures, Lowry argues, why treat the studies as still life? As stories move through time, their very movement indicates that sermons also move through time, and a good word to describe the movement should be flow.[5] I never will forget the first time I heard a narrative preacher. The rattle-bang homiletics of all the one-two-threesy preachers of my youth dissolved sweetly like reels of old horror films in the charm of his narrative. From that time on, I was hooked on the idea. Recently while reading Elizabeth Achtemeier's "Yellow Bicycle," I was struck by the marvelous flow of her narrative sermon.

Can we, however, remember them later? Certainly far better than we might remember even the most cleverly alliterated outlines so common to evangelical, preceptual sermons. Markquart has reminded us that the ear needs an image to help us remember.[6] Stories have a way of staying in place when even the most cleverly contrived sermon outlines elude us. When anyone, in the dull gray fog of Wednesday, asks me what I preached on Sunday, I hate my sluggish mind for being so slow on the uptake. If I have preached a narrative sermon, my mind replies so fast I startle myself. The story so fixes the sermon, like a new artwork in a gallery, that it will not let us forget the tale that charmed us toward the truth.

I remember hearing a good friend of mine, Wendell Belew, preach a sermon, "The Last Rock Uncle Billy Ever Sat On." It was the first time I ever heard him preach. His story was told in a rare Kentucky way that fixed both his story and its truth into my mind. His sermon was the tale of "Uncle Billy," who once sat on a rock while resting from his plowing on a hot Kentucky day. The poor bloke had a heart attack and died, leaving a million furrows unturned. His dear friend Zeke, who found him dead, revered the last rock Uncle Billy ever sat on as some revere the traditions of the church. Zeke took the rock home and, while finding it cumbersome and in the way, kept it for years. In old age, Zeke, late one night, stumbled over the rock and was killed—so our death as institutions often result from the very things we revere. A writer of my acquaintance has written a book, *When the Horse is Dead, Dismount*. How clever is the story that fixes the best of truth so firmly in our minds.

The final strength of narrative preaching is its literary form and endurance. I save this value till last precisely because it is the least valuable. Sermons are good sermons if they live up to their intent, and their primary intent is not to be literary. Nonetheless, to remember Conwell's "Acres of Diamonds," or Peter Marshall's "Keeper of the Springs" speaks to the literary quality of narrative sermons. How long we treasure sermons which are well heard and *well written*.

Still, Niebuhr cautioned us against the need to write "pretty sermons" whose beauty overwhelms the mind and keeps it from achieving anything more than being pretty. Thus the sermon is treasured while its demands are lost to those who would rather idolize a sermon than obey one.[7] Nonetheless, may the narrative sermon propel us a long way in the direction of sermonic artistry. Such propulsion will likely not come from more preceptual homilies.

Weakness of the Narrative Form

So much for the outstanding strengths of the narrative sermons. What are its weaknesses?

The same argument that bolsters narrative preaching may be used to support a more traditional style: the Bible is *only* nine-tenths narrative. Any story, which is the basis of a good sermon, will be able to retain its "cliff-hanging" demands on the listener only once. Thus the well-known story cannot motivate attention like the brand-new story. It is, for instance, easier to watch half-a-video movie when we have seen the entire original earlier. The first time I saw *The Sound of Music*, it compelled me like it seldom has since.

Still, I do believe in repertory theater and, like many, do thrive on the oft-repeated story. When I pay $50 or $60 to see a Broadway musical, I do not want the producers to innovate merely because I know the story. As the biblical story is always welcome in my world, so the narrative sermon, twice heard, may feed me the familiar and leave me feeling good that while I know how the sermon story will end, my time is well-spent. In the case of repertory theater or a great movie, I am no longer propelled by waiting for the "ti" in the scale to be resolved in the "do." I know the "do" and am content to live through and enjoy the entire piece to its conclusion.

For the most part, the entire video movie industry is feeding those who want to repeat a story rather than hear it for the first time. What becomes the hook the second time around, when we feel no tension about how the plot is to be resolved? Why indeed do I like Shakespeare, Ibsen, or Beckett over and over? Because the stories bear such truth and identity in my life that every hearing quickens my interest and answers my need all over again. For such reasons the biblical narrative—like manna in Sinai—is picked up fresh every morning. The narrative preacher may assume too much that the story must hold some imperative hook to be new. In actuality, telling the familiar in a new way may need only the hook of doing it differently to eliminate the need for the hook of unrelieved tension.

The first self-proclaiming weakness of the narrative sermon may be thwarted induction. The narrative sermon may falsely assume that it can lead its hearers to supply their own life stories to arrive at their own conclusions. Some may not be motivated to see the connection between their own life story and that of the sermon. An even worse presumption is that when the story is concluded, the sermon story will have led the hearer to a clear understanding of how the hearer's own story should be amended, challenged, canceled, or redirected. Even if the hearer consents to amend his or her life story, is there any guarantee that the hearer will reach the best *biblical* conclusion? Rorschach's ink blots prove that no two of us see or tell stories to the same conclusion. While this may be a freeing quality of the narrative sermon, is it possible that the Word of God may not come to any real encounter in the auditor's life? If *the Word* is missed, has real preaching occurred?

A second weakness in a constant diet of narrative preaching is the loss of didache (or teaching) in the church. From the inception of preaching, it did tell stories (see the parables of Christ, Saint Stephen's sermon in Acts 7, or Saint Paul's sermon before Agrippa), but the sermon also was charged with the *didache* responsibility. The sermon must teach. Stories may do this, but they are less forthright in the matter. Deuteronomy, as the farewell address of Moses, or Simon's call to repentance at Pentecost ever remind us that sermons can sometimes best use precepts to teach.

More and more, we are unable to locate the visible doctrinal church of Christ. In the current salad bar, mix-and-match of church program and community activities, many theologians are growing concerned that the church is losing the ability to define and defend its faith. What does the church believe, and why does it believe? What are its tenets and why? Elizabeth Achtemeier warns us:

> In my own Reformed tradition, the minister is appropriately known as a "teaching elder," and under that rubric, he or she has two very important tasks. First of all, as the congregation's church theologian, the minister has the task of educating the congregation in the central beliefs of Christianity. This is not a task that is performed only in confirmation class or in the church school. For far too long we have turned the responsibility for Christian education over to the Sunday school, with mixed results. Long before there was a Sunday school, faithful clergy taught their congregations Christian theology in their Sunday sermons, and traditional Christian theology has been preserved in the church.[8]

It is precisely at this point that nearly all fundamentalists and most Evangelicals will not ascribe to too many narrative sermons lest the sermonic form soften the church's understanding of its role in the world and lose track of what its sacraments mean.

The third weakness of the narrative sermon is that it may connote that the sermon exists to fascinate rather than change. One of the great liabilities of the gospel invitation (or altar call) is it may tacitly support this notion that sermons do not exist to be heard, but to prompt a response. From Jonah to Jesus, the sermon has always existed to bear the demand of God. What is the sermon's demand? It demands that hearers "follow" (Matt. 4:19) or "go possess the land" (Deut. 1:8) or "go proclaim liberty" (Luke 4:18) or "repent and be baptized" (Acts 2:38). The inductive call of the narrative sermon may elicit strong inner decisions, but it might also allow the more biblical demands of sermons to go unheeded. In another context, James asked us to be more than mere hearers of the word (Jas. 1:22).

A fourth weakness of the narrative sermon is that in every congregation there exists a strong percentage of souls whose life orientation is less story-oriented. The narrative sermon's inductive enticement may miss these altogether. My own pulpit style is so story-oriented, I have had a difficult time remembering that many who hear me preach are so preceptually oriented that they are not equipped to hear me on a narrative level, nor are they able to perceive on such a level. For the most choleric of these, movies and novels do not exist. Fifty percent of Americans do not read books—even novels—period! For these, metaphors but entangle their brisk computerized minds in a thick, story-like molasses through which they cannot readily swim.

As there is a wide difference between the thick precepts of Paul (his sermons are a long distance from narrative preaching) and the smoothly flowing parables of Christ, these same differences exist in our own congregations. Narrative preaching may overlook or even overwhelm this significant segment of Christ's body.

The final weakness is that narrative sermons go only as far as the imaginative capacities of the hearers allow. Preachers are generally far more familiar with the world of metaphor than the average parishioner. This does not mean that the sermon narrative cannot be toned down, so that most can at least follow the story. It does mean that just as preachers are often accused of preaching over people's heads, they might just as easily "narrate" over people's heads. I recently read a narrative sermon in which my best powers of induction finally faltered and I was forced to ask: "Why did he tell that story?" Such a question was about the same as asking: "What was the preacher trying to say in his more preceptual sermon?" I have occasionally come back from a movie full of question marks. The plot of the movie did not move from tension to resolution; it just ended with tension. It should never be assumed that all narrative preaching leaves those who hear it resolved with total understanding.

Goals of the Narrative Form

I want to conclude this issue by determining what must still be expected of the narrative sermon. It must preserve three distinct goals, all having to do with a clear delineation of biblical authority (even in a day that generally pursues human consensus). The three goals are: "Thus saith the Lord," the answer to the question, "What must we do?" (Acts 2:37), and the heralding of the good news that "God was in Christ reconciling" (2 Cor. 5:19).

As to the importance of the first goal, "Thus saith the Lord," again Elizabeth Achtemeier rightly recalls that this quality is the sine qua non of the sermon.

> Books and teachers dealing with homiletics have therefore largely concentrated their attention in the past on the necessity of preaching from the Bible. They have rightly inveighed against sermons that do nothing more than dispense psychological and mental health principles, that impose the preacher's opinions on the Scripture, or that ignore the actions of God through the Scripture and exhort the people to rise to new moral levels on their own.[9]

This is not to say that stories cannot inductively cry, "Thus saith the Lord." Nathan's strong rebuke to David after the king's sin with Bathsheba made it clear that stories may powerfully speak with authority, but the narrative preacher must remember that all induction must be carefully employed so that it leads all to see the demand of God in the sermon. Jesus' powerful parable of the Good Samaritan, for instance, leads to the pricking of the heart: *"Which of these three was neighbor to him who fell among thieves?" (see Luke 10:36).* Certainly Stephen's historical narrative in Acts 7 also pricks the very heart of institutional Judaism. It was clear that the real message was "Thus saith the Lord."

I once read Martin Bell's *Barrington Bunny* as a major part of my sermon. One less-narrative type was angry at the story. Perhaps the old timer objected to *Barrington Bunny*, fearing the possibility of some future sermon when the high demand of God would not enter my sermon and the "Thus saith the Lord" would be missing, leaving the sermon full of only rabbits.

The second goal of the sermon is the question: "What must we do?"(see Acts 2:37), which follows Peter's Pentecostal sermon. This is an evidence that the Holy Spirit has moved in the homily and now the dumbfounded believers (or unbelievers), washed in His divine flame, wait for instruction. Sermons, narrative or otherwise, which do not end in this question from Acts 2 are incomplete sermons.

The conclusion of the sermon does what conclusions ought to do—namely, sum up the thought of the entire sermon and call for the desired response from the congregation.[10] Remember the response of the Ninevites? They had heard Jonah's word, and they waited for instruction as to what response they would make to God.

Perhaps the most important end of a narrative sermon is to remember a sermon can call itself a Christian sermon only in the sense that it reflects the central teaching of Christ. The preacher must understand why Christ came. Was it really to seek and to save that which was lost (Luke 19:10)? Is this the central charge of Christ, for the church to enter the world evangelizing, teaching, and baptizing? The narrative sermon may not just tell stories; if this be true, it must tell a *saving* story. Since Reformation times the thrust of the modern missions movement and the great awakenings found the church out to determine its preachment in terms of the *evangelium*: The great *raison d'être* of the Reformation church is always that God was in Christ reconciling (2 Cor. 5:19).

The emphasis in narrative preaching is weak at the point that it did not originate from the center of the Evangelical tradition but from the homiletic tradition of the old line denominations. Since many of these denominations have been in numerical decline since the mid 1960s, the question often raised among some Evangelicals might be: "Does the narrative sermon rise from the passionate center of evangelism and mission? Was it a last attempt to get people to listen to us as opposed to a strategic call to confront a needy crowd?" This does not mean the narrative sermon is not valid as a sermonic model for all Christians, but it does give us pause enough to cause us to be sure we demand that this model be a strong package for our missionary ecclesiology. Narrative sermons must stay in touch with an evangelistic compassion for the lost world for which God created the church.

What, then, is the place of a narrative sermon within the preaching ministry of the church?

There are many great Christian truths that comprise the full responsibility of the teaching of the church. I doubt that narrative preaching alone can adequately teach the entire gamut of truth for which the church is *Mater et Magistra* (to use John Paul XXIII's term). C.H. Dodd long ago charted this corpus of responsibility. He found within the New Testament itself a central kerygma or proclamation characteristic of the early church, which had approximately the following outline:

1. The age of fulfillment, or the coming of the kingdom of God, is at hand.
2. This coming has taken place through the ministry, death, and resurrection of Jesus.
3. By virtue of the resurrection, Jesus is exalted at the right hand of God as the messianic head of the new Israel.
4. The Holy Spirit in the church is the sign of Christ's present power and glory.
5. The messianic age will shortly reach its consummation in the second coming of Christ.
6. Forgiveness, the Holy Spirit, and salvation come with repentance.[11]

Sermons that deal with these subjects may have to look again at the word *discipline*. Narrative may make the sermon more fun to attend to than a more preceptual style. Yet pressing the truths of the church may mean the sermon will have to answer the issue of Christian content on a more taxing level not entirely possible with the narrative sermon alone.

Let us demand of every sermon that it be preached in such a way as to honor both the Bible as narrative and as propositional truth. Generally practicing only one form of any medium is in a sense extreme. To preach only narrative sermons would probably carry an admission that we were one-sided or even extremist. Fred Craddock is right when he reminds us: "Among the aids for generating listening experience, none is more effective than a metaphor. . . at the heart of the parables of Jesus is the metaphor."[12] This is certainly true, but there are other sound models for preaching in the Scriptures. Inductive narrative should serve where it may, but it should not necessarily be forced into sermonic service where another form might better fit. I believe that Buechner is largely right when he calls on us to emulate the sermonic style of Jesus. Still, he is remiss at some points when he advises us:

> The way to preach is the way he [Jesus] did. Not in the incendiary rhetoric of the prophet nor in the systematic abstractions of the theologian, but in the language of images and metaphor, which is finally the only language you can use.[13]

What is wrong with this advice? Well, first of all, Jesus did sometimes preach in the blistering rhetoric of the prophets (see his woes upon the Pharisees, Luke 11:39-44). Second, not all the systematic teachings of theology are abstract (see the concrete issues of Romans or Galatians). Third, I do not believe the language of metaphor is the only language available to us. Sometimes simple precepts may serve sermons from first to last, especially in the teaching ministry of the church.

Developing the Narrative Sermon

When the text and occasion seem to mandate the form, how is the narrative sermon to be prepared and delivered? Let us discuss the matter exactly as we would the preparation and delivery of any sermon—under these four categories: the approach, the writing, the delivery, and the calling of the sermon.

Approaching the narrative sermon deals with the sermon in its earliest stages of preparation: namely, arriving at a subject, text, and form for the sermon. For the lectionary preacher, these issues are largely there before the sermon preparation begins. For those whose long-range sermon planning has set the text early in the year (as my own does), at least the theme and text will already have been determined for the sermon. The first, most basic step in all sermon preparation has to do with an arrival at theme and text, and in that order. Only after we have determined what needs to be said (theme) can we begin to search out the text that says it best. Thus narrative sermons, like other kinds, proceed from theme to text to form by answering these questions: What do I need to say? Where does the Bible best say this? What kind or form of sermon is the best vehicle to allow the text to impact the hearer?

Briefly put, the theme is the *what* of sermon preparation which locates the text. The *how* of sermon preparation tells the preacher what form or style of sermon will say it best. Generally speaking, a narrative text will more easily suggest a narrative form for the sermon. Certainly this is not always the case. We might, for instance, be preaching a series on the Ten Commandments in which all ten of the precepts could be housed in ten dynamic narrative sermons. Once the form is arrived at, the writing may begin.

The writing of the narrative sermon begins as soon as it is determined this

PLOT

INTRODUCTION				CONCLUSION
Once upon a time (the O.U.A.T.)	EVENT	EVENT	RESOLUTION Happy ever after (the H.E.A.)	APPLICATION
Here we begin with a story situation that intrigues because the character or characters are located in a situation which will not free them. Their predicament will not free the audience either.	The events of the narrative sermon must complexify without miring	the audience to the point they lose interest in the conclusion.	Here at the end of the sermon the audience should breathe easier because the story is concluded.	The inductive power of the narrative sermon is usually best concluded with an inductive ending: a question, for instance, which calls for the listener to answer or respond.

Parable of the Good Samaritan
Luke 10:25-37

"A certain man went down from Jerusalem to Jericho" (v. 30).	He fell among thieves (v. 30).	Enter characters who pass by: priest and Levite (vv. 31-32).	The Samaritan took him to an inn and the man's life is spared (v. 35).	A question: "Which of these was neighbor?" (v. 36).

is the best form to use. The contriving of the narrative sermon will have *plot* for its primary ingredient. The plot is the unresolved tension that must remain unresolved until the final moments of the sermon. The simple way to say this is: "Keep the audience waiting for outcomes; don't even hint at the ending of the story until it is time for the story to end." The characters of the plot must be contrived and used in such a way as to contribute to the concealment of the resolution which the listeners are eager to discover.

Simplicity is the best rule for the twenty-minute sermon. The plot should be tense but not complex. The characters should be few but clearly presented. In this fast-moving age, with its three-minute maximum attention span, the narrative preacher should not try to "adjective" his or her way to success, but to "verb" it all the way. Simply put: keep the story moving. Verbs are movement words, full of high action and intensity; adjectives only describe. Adjectives may mire the plot, slogging the story to a stop.

Narrative sermons have a linear, not an Arabic numeral, outline.

As a model for this form of sermon, let us take Jesus' parable of the good Samaritan in Luke 10: 25-37 (see full page illustration).

The narrative sermon may be extended in length during the development from beginning to resolution by the introduction of supporting illustrative material, by adding secondary illustrations to clarify and intensify the original plot. This must be done without distracting the hearer from the "trunk narrative" which *is* the sermon.

The delivery of the narrative sermon should be gilded with the best, well-rehearsed techniques of oral interpretation and dramatic enhancement. This is perhaps the hardest part of narrative preaching. To whisper, shout, pause for effect, hurry the action, retard the action, and evoke emotions are the real stuff of compelling delivery. As I earlier counseled, the art of storytelling is not innate nor ever present in all preachers. Even those who can tell stories well need to rehearse the sermon several times to be sure it is well done.

In my book *Spirit, Word, and Story: A Philosophy of Preaching,* I have suggested paralleling as a way of bringing the best lines from great novels, plays, and poems into use in the story sermon (all properly acknowledged, of course). These parallel literary passages, however, will require memorization and rehearsal to make the narrative sermon smooth and professional.

If you decide, after a few trials, that narrative preaching is not your form (and the body language of your listeners will quickly inform you on the matter), I believe you would be wise to return to a form more natural to your own unique personhood.

The calling of the sermon should be obvious by the time the narrative is resolved. What is the text demanding of them? What does God require? How can they meet the issue? Is the issue clear? Why was the sermon preached in the first place?

No sermon should exist that is unsure of its calling. In my judgment, the calling of the sermon should surface as the narrative unfolds. It should be allowed to declare itself far ahead of the end of the story to give time for the calling of the sermon to make the demand of God (which issues from the text and not the preacher) clear. In churches which have invitations, the calling of the sermon must be abundantly clear when the invitation hymn begins. In churches which do not have invitations, the narrative sermon must still issue its call so clearly that all understand.

Is the inductive method strong enough to apply the sermon to all individual lives? Sometimes, yes, sometimes, no. When it is not, the narrative sermon's calling must be clearly stated and there must be a call for a response. The calling of the sermon always says: "This is God's word to you; it has been given, so you may be challenged to make such-and-such response." "Come now, let us reason together" (Isa. 1:18).

One final thing that should be said for the narrative sermon is that it often fits the largely narrative style of Scriptures. Yet the best sermons, I believe, fit the tone of the passages they expose. To make the simple baroque or the baroque simple does not let the tone of the passage shine through. Hamlet encouraged the players: "Suit the action to the word, /the word to the action."[14] Still, fitting the passage to the style will, for the most part, demand that we study and become masters at the inductive art of the narrative sermon. The day demands it, and the Bible exhibits it. Let us move therefore to make narrative a major sermon model for the calling of our world to faith.

Notes

1. H. Grady Davis, *Design for Preaching* (Philadelphia: Fortress Press, 1958), 157, cited in Edward F. Markquart, *Quest for Better Preaching* (Minneapolis: Augsburg Publishing House, 1985), 22.
2. Fred B. Craddock, *Overhearing the Gospel* (Nashville: Abingdon, 1978), 12, cited in Markquart, *Quest for Better Preaching*, 19.
3. Eugene L. Lowry, *Doing Time in the Pulpit* (Nashville: Abingdon Press, 1985), 54.
4. Ibid., 52, 65.
5. Ibid., 36.
6. Markquart, *Quest for Better Preaching*, 196.
7. Reinhold Niebuhr, cited in Elizabeth Achtemeier, *Preaching as Theology & Art* (Nashville: Abingdon Press, 1984), 53.
8. Achtemeier, *Preaching as Theology & Art*, 17.
9. Ibid., 9.
10. Ibid., 93.
11. C.H.Dodd, *The Apostolic Preaching and its Developments: Three Lectures with An Appendix on Eschatology and History* (1936; reprint, New York: Harper & Row, 1964), cited in Achtemeier, *Preaching as Theology & Art*, 10.

12. Craddock, *Overhearing the Gospel*, 134, cited in Markquart, *Quest for Better Preaching*, 135.

13. Frederick Buechner, *Telling the Truth* (San Francisco: Harper & Row, 1977), 62, cited in Markquart, *Quest for Better Preaching*, 135.

14. *Hamlet*, act III, sc. ii, lines 17-18.

10

Bryan Chapell
Vice President, Academic Dean
Covenant Theological Seminary
St. Louis, Missouri

Alternative Models

Old Friends in New Clothes

Best friends never seem to change. Proportions may vary and appearances may mature; but, deep down, best friends stay the same.

The same is true of preaching forms. Qualities that make them dear beacon through contemporary alterations for those who know them best. The sermons that communicate well demonstrate unity, organization, truth-establishment, creativity, and application. No matter how their proportions, order, and emphases vary, these old friends greet us warmly in the best messages. New structures do not force us to abandon sermon qualities that we love. Alternative models actually enable us to welcome these old friends in new clothes.

One way to see how contemporary sermons may vary from older forms without losing key characteristics is to consider the phases of their development.

Three-Phase Models

Though few preachers consciously plan for their sermons to fall into a standard three-phase structure, our academic training gears us to approach messages this way. In the sermon's first phase we introduce a problem and establish its seriousness. In the next phase of the message we propose a solution and prove that it is biblical. The last phase of the message provides the evidence that our solution works, or demonstrates the results of employing it.

The thought patterns of Western culture steer us into these phases of logical development in the message as a whole and even in its individual features. A single main point in a sermon may contain all three phases, or a major component of the sermon may be devoted to each phase as the message unfolds. A sermon that uses a main point for each phase forms a traditional "Problem/Solution Model." This model creates a convenient benchmark against which alternative forms using similar building blocks can be compared and understood.[1]

The introduction of the typical Problem/Solution sermon (see Fig. 1) describes the problem the message will address. The first main point—or first main phase—of the sermon then proves the extent, validity, and/or seriousness of the problem based upon scriptural evidence, logical argument, or facts from life. The second main point of the message offers biblical solution(s) for the problem the first phase addressed. Evidence that the solution will work, or biblical demonstration that benefits will result from employing the ideas in the second phase of the message, characterize the third main point.

Problem/Solution Model

Introduction	Problem Statement
Main Point #1	Problem Proof
Main Point #2	Problem Solution
Main Point #3	Results/Evidence
	Problem Emphasis
	Appeal
	Academic Mind

Fig. 1

The emphasis on problem solving in a Problem/Solution Model makes it very appealing to the academically trained mind. Young preachers almost always fall into this approach to sermonizing while they are in a seminary environment where they are testing ideas and trying to correct their own thoughts. Unfortunately, the strong emphasis on finding and establishing problems tends to put the preacher in an antagonistic stance toward the congregation. Each week the preacher has to prove that a problem exists. The sermon often sounds accusing from the beginning: "You have got a problem. There is trouble right here in River City. And if you don't believe that you have got a problem, I will prove it to you."

Now, of course, there are very appropriate reasons for preachers to accuse. Sometimes there is trouble right here in River City. If all the preacher knows to do is spend the opening third of a sermon wagging a finger at the world or the congregation, trouble is brewing nearer than the preacher imagines. Not only will the people despair or rebel at the weekly tirade, but despondency will be crouching at the door of the preacher. Pastoral burnout more often results from anger than fatigue. Such anger breeds in the hearts of preachers whose messages have a structure that causes people to become defensive rather than responsive.

A different tone resonates when pastors use the building blocks of a Problem/Solution message in different proportions to create alternative models. The "Need/Plan Model" also starts with a problem in the introduction, but the problem does not need proof (see Fig. 2). Instead the preacher uses the introduction to identify a need that is so patently obvious everyone will acknowledge its validity. No one will stand to argue with the preacher who begins: "It is hard to raise teenagers today." Everyone agrees the problem exists.

By creating a need all acknowledge in the introduction, the preacher's main task moves from proving a problem exists to offering a plan for its solution. Thus, in a Need/Plan message the main points, or the developmental features of the message, concentrating on presenting a biblically based plan of action. Each main point typically represents one plank in an overall plan. If the need created by the introductory comments is that raising teens is difficult today, then these plans for meeting that need could be offered as main points of the message: "We must provide teens with Christian peers;" "We must provide teens with Christian models;" "We must provide teens with Christian alternatives."

Need/Plan Model

Introduction	Creates Identifiable Need
Main Point #1	Plan Plank #1
Main Point #2	Plan Plank #2
Main Point #3	Plan Plank #3
	Solution Emphasis
	Appeal
	Congregational Mind

Fig. 2

Because the body of a Need/Plan message establishes plan planks, the overall emphasis is on the solution rather than on the problem. The shift in sermonic tone can be dramatic. "You've got a problem" becomes

"God offers help." There is no question which approach has more congregational appeal. Ordinary persons do not sit in the pew every week to have proven to them that they have problems raising teens, managing their resources, experiencing God's forgiveness, overcoming temptation, or handling a legion of similar difficulties. In almost every heart is this unvoiced plea: "Pastor, I know this is a problem. You don't have to prove it to me. Please help me find answers in God's Word." Mature pastors hear this plea and most frequently preach in this mode even if they do not consciously construct their sermons according to this model.

Less frequently used but strongly encouraging for congregations is a "Plan/ Motivation Model" (also known as a "Comparative Advantages Model"). The introduction not only presents a problem, but it offers a solution. The need is so apparent and the plan to handle it is so obvious that people do not require further proof of what is wrong or further explanation of what to do. Such a sermon assumes knowledge is not the problem; action is. People often struggle to do what they know the Bible requires. Sometimes what they need is not problem information or plan instructions, but motivation for obedience.

Presenting the comparative advantages of doing what we know we should do is a wonderful way of urging others to heed God's Word. In this way preachers encourage people with the benefits that will result from implementing their convictions. A Plan/Motivation sermon employs this dynamic by using each major component to develop a key benefit or advantage that will result from acting on the plan specified in the introduction.

Plan/Motivation Model

Introduction	Presents Need and Plan
Main Point #1	Motivation or Advantage #1
Main Point #2	Motivation or Advantage #2
Main Point #3	Motivation or Advantage #3

Results Emphasis
Appeal
Congregational Mind

Fig. 3

In a typical Plan/Motivation message the introduction can identify a problem such as the feeling of neglect by God that results from our infrequent prayer. Such an introduction will also imply or state the solution: pray! The difficulty is not that people disagree with the need nor are they ignorant of how to address it. Almost everyone sitting in the pews will agree that a sense of isolation from God would diminish if they spoke to Him more. What people need is sufficient motivation to pray as they wish they would. That motivation can be offered in the sermon's main points. The first main point might encourage prayer: "Those who pray will see the work of God." The second main point might say: "Those who pray will further the work of God." A final point could be: "Those who pray experience the blessing of God." Each point of such a Plan/Motivation message offers a biblical advantage for those who pray. The emphasis is on the results of obedience, and the appeal is in helping a congregation understand the true benefits of faith. A Plan/ Motivation message seeks to motivate with encouragement and often is the best approach to inspire a congregation to attempt great things for God.

No one of these three-phase models is right for all occasions and all sermonic purposes. Perhaps their relative strengths are best understood by evaluating how each would approach a topic like Father's Day. Every pastor knows that just as surely as the purpose of Mother's Day is to praise mothers, the purpose of Father's Day is to bash fathers. At least, that is the way many fathers feel during the sermon on their "special day."

If pastors do not want to sound accusing on Father's Day, we are wise to consider alternative models to the Problem/Solution message our academic training may have so ably prepared us to deliver. The need to establish the problems with fathers will force early portions of a Problem/Solution sermon to concentrate on their parental faults and failings. Proof may be offered in the form of statistics about the average amount of daily time the average father spends with his children. Biblical examples of the consequences of poor fathering may be produced. The priorities of fathers who will devote themselves to careers over family needs will be sharply questioned and biblically reproved. Overall the sermon will carry the message: "You're not the father you should be, and you ought to do better." Few will question whether the problem is valid, the principles true, or the reproof justified. Yet fewer still may leave better equipped and spiritually prepared for the high and difficult calling of Christian fathering.

To the traditional Father's Day reproof, a Need/Plan model offers a healthy alternative. The preacher could begin such a message with an introduction citing a need with which any busy father can identify: It is hard to balance a family and a career today. The introductory material does not try to prove the problem, it only seeks to create a need all want satisfied. An illustration, quotation, or set of statistics that captures the hurt fathers feel in not knowing how to prioritize career and family pressures is sufficient. Fathers then know the pastor understands what they are experiencing and will long to hear Scriptural answers. The answers come in the form of a plan drawn from Scripture. The first point in the sermon might be: "We must provide for our children's physical well-being by all we do." The second point: "We must protect our children's emotional well-being in all we do." The third point: "We must preserve our children's spiritual well-being above all we do." Overall this sermon carries the message: "It's tough to be a father today, but God gives us these principles to help sort out how to be the fathers our children need." The plan offers hope that there are solutions for the difficulties fathers face.

If the plan as well as the problem are obvious, then a Plan/Motivation approach may be the best for a Father's Day message. The introduction of such a message might identify the guilt many fathers feel in spending so little time with their children. The obvious solution to this common remorse is for fathers to allot more time for the kids, but everyone knows that answer before they sit in the pew. The plan of action is not obscure; the motivation to carry it out is.

The preacher can help encourage fathers to do what Scripture requires by focusing on the results or advantages of parental care. The message might unfold with these ways the Holy Spirit can use a father's regular influence: "Time with children molds minds"; "Time with children unites hearts"; "Time with children saves souls." The message seeks to fill fathers with the wonder that Christian parents have an advantage that no other parents share in raising children. The Spirit of God is at work in our lives. When we spend time with our children we are not simply heeding the advice of a current psychology; we bring the very presence of God into our children's lives. Such a perspective can inspire, empower, and motivate far more than the depressing brow beating of the traditional Father's Day message.

There are messages where it is far more appropriate to use a Problem/Solution emphasis. When the preacher is directly confronting a sin people have not acknowledged or will not confess, then time must be spent proving the problem and its seriousness. Each model has a legitimate place and purpose. When we fill our preaching tool cases with a variety of instruments we are simply better equipped for the variety of tasks to which Scripture calls us.

Two-Phase Models

We can better conceptualize some sermons, as well as components within them, by describing the two phases of their development. If the message first establishes general truth principles, and then applies them to particular situations, the sermon is called "deductive." The particulars are deduced from the principle (see Fig. 4). This sermon model also claims a rich history in the preaching traditions of Western culture.

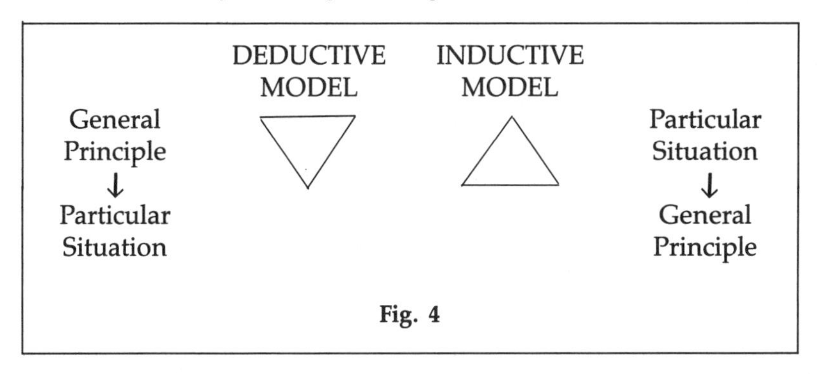

Fig. 4

Traditional Puritan sermons epitomize the deductive model. The first hour or two of a Puritan sermon focused on doctrinal development (see Fig. 5). The preacher exegeted a passage of Scripture or surveyed a number of passages to develop a biblical principle. Once the doctrine was established, the implications were spelled out in "numerous" applications—scores of applications in some sermons. Although modern preachers rarely copy the length of Puritan sermons, the form remains very common. If we preach on an epistle of Paul, deductive sermons naturally unfold if they follow his own pattern. Pauline Epistles open with a greeting, proceed quickly to doctrinal explanations, then generally offer the major applications in latter portions of the letter.

Though preachers may not know the technical designation, they often use a deductive model when first needing to lay a doctrinal foundation for applications they wish to make. There are some liabilities inherent in this model, however. Because the principles have to be developed before particulars are applied, it may take quite a while to get to what the congregation sees as relevant. This is not just a modern problem. The Puritan preachers who sent deacons down the aisles with feathers to tickle the noses of women who slept and staffs to clout the men who snored were aware—if not forgiving—of the difficulties people had in staying with deductive sermons. In this age of shortened attention spans, non-linear thinking, and doctrinal illiteracy the difficulty has certainly not decreased.

Some preachers have faced these difficulties and are exploring the potential of "inductive" models as alternatives to the traditional deductive pattern.[2] An inductive sermon does not so much abandon the components of a traditional sermon as invert them. Particulars precede principles (see Fig. 4). Rather than beginning with the development of doctrine, the preacher will often describe someone in a life-situation that needs scriptural answers. Relevance and application introduce the message and keep its focus even throughout the expositional features. Illustrations are frequent. Doctrinal abstractions are rare. The sermon as a whole, as well as its individual main points or chief features, begins with and returns to what is personal, interesting, and real. Principles and particulars remain in inductive messages but their order and proportions generally are the reverse of deductive messages.

The strengths of an inductive alternative are obvious. People simply want more to hear what strikes them as immediately relevant. The weaknesses of such an approach need honest appraisal. Preaching needs to concern itself with what people need to hear as well as with what they want to hear. Many of our churches are experiencing the agony of their people being so doctrinally unlearned that they do not know what principles to apply to their daily challenges. Preachers whose primary focus is life's particulars provide neither the biblical authority nor doctrinal perspective necessary to address our culture's complex challenges.

Doctrinal abstraction is not the answer either. Deductive messages that spend thirty minutes in detailed exegesis and two sentences of concluding application have no audience. Most people switched off the preacher within the first two minutes if they concluded that relevance was not soon coming. The same two minute warning will apply to every component of the message. If the exposition goes on and on without rather immediate relevance at least beckoning, mental channels have changed to another station. If a Puritan model is appropriate for the subject, it is still necessary that the doctrinal development portions be chock-full of illustrations, allusions, and statements of applicational intent that will keep everyone tuned in. It will do little for the kingdom to blame the people for not responding if the preacher does less to help them listen. The nature of the subject, the background of the congregation, the goals of the preacher, and the balance of a ministry all bear on the appropriateness of deductive or inductive approaches to any particular message.

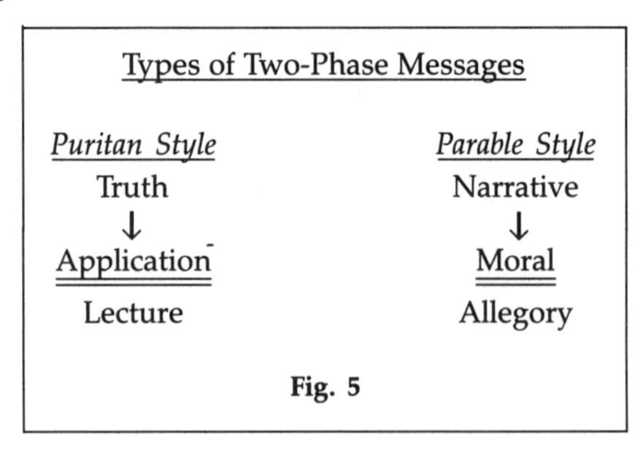

Fig. 5

A natural outgrowth of emphases on inductive models, as well as a number of other cultural forces undermining confidence in propositional forms of communication, is the current interest in narrative preaching models.[3] From a broad perspective a narrative message has a very similar structure to a Puritan sermon. The first part of the sermon establishes a truth and the latter portions apply the truth. The internal features are what make a narrative message so seemingly revolutionary. A narrative sermon establishes the truth it wants to advocate in a story rather than in propositional argument. The moral of the story is the application. What would function as illustrative spice in a traditional message is the meat of a narrative sermon or, at least, major components of it. The literary form of two-phase sermons changes from lecture to allegory in narrative preaching.

If one has been born and bred on expository sermons it may be a little difficult to accept narrative styles. Such sermons naturally draw the accusation often hurled at those who have drifted from preaching to entertaining: "All this preacher does is tell stories." Lest we malign such a model too quickly, we had best remember its most noteworthy advocate: Jesus! A narrative sermon is really a parable, or a series of them. Such preaching has Christ's imprimatur and rich historical precedent, particularly in testimony services, mass media ministries, rural and African-American traditions, and Eastern cultures.

Three-quarters of Scripture is historical narrative, image or parable. Preachers who are committed to preaching the truths of the Scripture should not fear communicating in its forms.[4] We should also remember, of course, that the Bible includes sufficient propositional content to explain what its stories mean. Even though Jesus "did not say anything to them without using a parable," when he was in private "he explained everything" (Mark 4:34). A congregation fed *only* stories will be malnourished.

Single-Phase Models

Single-phase messages are essays presented in oral form. Major sermon divisions disappear. One paragraph of thought leads to the next in straightforward logical development. This "upward plane of glass" model tends to need a great deal of energy or thoughtfulness in expression since the absence of main points leaves the listener without sermonic landmarks to orient thought or give an impression of progress. Some of the greatest sermons ever preached are single-phase messages. They are often the product of months or years of thought that has boiled internally, then bursts forth in a rush of thought that would only be constrained by traditional sermon structures.

Few preachers preach these essay sermons weekly since their passages and portions are difficult to deliver well without a great deal of memorizing. Essay sermons will tend to have all the components of traditional sermons (exposition, illustration, and application), but the elements are more integrated and the divisions less distinct. Often essay sermons are used in social issue preaching where most of the sermon's material is drawn from cultural analysis rather than biblical exposition. Topical sermons and special occasion sermons such as those presented at weddings, funerals, devotionals, dedications, commencements, etc., also may lend themselves to single-phase approaches since the messages tend to be short and often are not intended to explain specific biblical texts.

Mass Media Models

Preachers who have been trained in an expository tradition are often perplexed by television and radio preaching. Somehow people that struggle to stay awake on a Sunday morning still appreciate listening to someone else preach on a car radio. What are the mass media preachers doing?

Broadcast sermons sound very similar to traditional messages, but there is an energy or, at least, a technique that keeps listener interest and involvement focused. Of course, there is no real secret to what the mass media preachers are weighing consciously or unconsciously. Somewhere in their minds is the image of a listener with ten fingers, each of which is only inches from a channel select button or remote control. Listener interest must be maintained not over thirty minutes, but over fractions of every minute if the broadcast ministry is to survive. Media pressures have forged the model for a typical broadcast sermon.

Not every preacher faces these pressures, of course, but there are lessons to learn from those who do. We church preachers have people in our congregations who struggle to hear what we have to say. It is not fair or honest to blame them for their inattention if we have not examined every tool that will help us communicate—even if we do not use it all the time. The broadcast model is such a tool and we need not fear that it will force us to abandon all that we hold dear. Here, again, the sermon components are not as novel as is their organization (see Fig. 6).

Distinctives of a "Communication Model" are easily seen by comparing a single main point in its structure to a main point in a traditional "Information Model." An Information Model (which could also be called a "Detail Model" or "Exegetical Model") usually begins a main point with a statement of some biblical principle or instruction. Subpoints follow which prove or develop the main point statement with exposition of Scripture. Each subpoint contains a paragraph or two of information and, thus, the exposition of a main point is likely to take three to seven

Information Model vs. Communication Model

Information Model ("Detail" or "Exegetical" Model)	*Communication Model* ("Application Model")
Characteristic Main Point Structure:	
Statement of the Main Point 1. subpoint 2. subpoint 3. subpoint	Statement of the Main Point [Immediate proof, explanation, or definition; 1-2 sentences]
Illustration	Illustration
Application	Applications -Developed -Particularized -Qualified -Scripture tied -Enablement identified
Strengths:	
1. Dealing with didactic or epistolary passages 2. Exploring small portions of Scripture 3. Proving intricate or complex logic	1. Dealing with large themes or grouping complexity 2. Distilling large portions of Scripture 3. Applying truth with power and development
Weaknesses:	
1. Often dull or belabored 2. May lose people in detail 3. Little time for application	1. May inadequately expound 2. May inadvertently become topical legalism
Assumptions:	
1. Complexity = Seriousness 2. Higher Order Truths = Orthodoxy 3. Universal→particular	1. Sincerity = Seriousness 2. Applicability = Orthodoxy 3. Particular is universal

Fig. 6

minutes. After proving the truth of the main point the preacher typically then demonstrates that truth with an illustration. The illustration leads into application which, because of the time and energy expended in exposition, all too commonly simply reiterates a sentence or two of abstract principle developed earlier. Information is emphasized, application minimized, and relevance often sacrificed.

The "Communication Model" (which could also be called an "Application Model") attempts to maintain relevance and interest throughout. A main point within this mass media approach will begin with a statement of some biblical truth, or a question of what someone should do in a particular situation that is answerable with such a truth principle. The preacher then follows the truth statement with an immediate proof, explanation, verse recitation, or definition that corroborates the principle. This corroboration typically occurs in one or two sentences and concludes the "exposition" of this main point. Knowing that listeners will not have the mental stamina or tolerance for lengthy explanations, the preacher quickly progresses to illustration.

The illustration of a Communication Model sermon usually is life-situational with a strong taste of realism that suggests how the truth previously stated can be applied in everyday life. Application is really the heartbeat of this model, dominating both its emphases and proportions. The applications that follow the illustration take full advantage of this dynamic. The terms used and concepts developed thus far in the main point prepare for specific instructions. The preacher presents applications with enough detail that listeners know that God requires in particular situations and devotes enough time to the application so that important qualifications or limitations can be added. There are no vague generalities here. Whether you agree with the application or not, there is no arguing that they are specific and concrete. Frequently the preacher will quote additional Scripture verses to further clarify or authorize the applications and to remind listeners that they can only do what God requires as they seek His enablement. By the end of the application listeners know what to do, where to do it, and how to do it. *Why* is not this model's strength. Whatever other components of a traditional sermon structure may be slighted, application and the riveting relevance it creates are never lacking.

Debating the appropriateness of Information Models versus Communication Models displays lack of real discernment. Each has its strengths and weaknesses. The exegetical focus of the Information Model makes it a far better tool for explaining the intricacies of the epistles or other strongly didactic passages. This same advantage will enable the preacher to explode the rich implications of small portions of Scripture and to really prove theological principles with the occasionally complex logic that good doctrinal development requires. The broad brush of the Communication Model enables the preacher to deal with general themes and group ideas without unnecessary complexity. This may actually help the preacher to deal with larger portions of Scripture than the exegetical model typically allows and, thus, give the preacher and the listeners new insights into the ways the Bible develops truth. Lengthy biblical narratives are often made plainer when the preacher distills truth rather than covering an event (which may run for chapters) line by line. Still, the real strength of the Communication Model is its communicability, which is so enhanced by the resources it devotes to application. Listeners simply do not walk away without knowing what the preacher says God expects today. In an age where profession of faith seems to have so little impact on the conduct of life, this is no small contribution.

Each model had obvious weaknesses. The detail orientation of the Information Model can make it boring. Without great sensitivity to the biases of one's own academic training the preacher may belabor the instruction and lose people in unnecessary detail. Time for application can get swallowed in exposition, and the preacher may feel self-satisfied even if the people still hunger to know what God's Word means for them today. The Communication Model has real vulnerabilities also. The most obvious is that it will simply not adequately expound the text and, therefore, degenerates into opinion and legalism addressed to topical issues of personal origin.

Rather than trying to determine which model is right, it is more important to assess what specific purpose a sermon, or even a single main point, needs to achieve. Preachers should use the model that best serves the immediate sermonic task. Appropriate models may vary between sermons, or even between divisions of a single sermon, depending upon the message's purpose, proportion, rhythm, focus, and subject.

More important than sensing the strengths and weaknesses of any sermon model is understanding its underlying assumptions. The assessment you make of these not only determines how you will evaluate the model, but also how you will develop your own approach to each preaching task. The Information and Communication Models have enough competing assumptions to put some important issues in stark contrast. Again, it is not necessary to label any of these assumptions as entirely right or wrong. It is critical for every preacher to determine when and why these assumptions apply if we are to be equipped for the full range of tasks in our calling.

Though perhaps they never directly state it, consistent practitioners of the Information Model assume that complexity equals seriousness. Deep down they believe that the way they demonstrate they are serious about the Bible is by detailing its beautiful intricacies. These preachers believe the people who really appreciate the Bible expect them to preach at this level of complexity because it proves that the people are serious, too. Some ministers think they should speak with complexity even if the people do not want it because such preaching—like vegetables—is good for them.

Contrasting with this attitude is the conviction evident in the assumptions of Communication Model preachers. They tire of the "head games" the exegetes play. Communication oriented preachers believe simple sincerity equals seriousness. Deep down they believe you cannot really speak from the heart if you are on a "mind trip" into esoterica. Plain truth plainly spoken is their passion.

Preachers of the Information Model assume that developing higher order truths demonstrates orthodoxy. By using biblical proofs to back up statements of universal truth, these preachers believe they have laid the foundations for orthodox commitments in every sphere of life. Information preachers expect properly articulated universal principles to trickle down to correct decision-making in every particular situation. The Communication Model adherents scoff at such stratospheric abstractions. They think the high-blown doctrinal precepts show you are not willing to roll up your sleeves and deal with the real issues of life. For these preachers applicability equals orthodoxy. They believe that when we concentrate our messages on the particulars of life we make the most universal statements, since "No temptation has seized you except what is common to man" (1 Cor. 10:13, NIV).[5]

Of course, the assumptions above are stereotypical and stated more baldly than any informed preacher would say. The absurdity of each position taken to an extreme underscores the need of every preacher to be sensitive to the task at hand when choosing a sermon model. The alternative models are not wrong simply because they are new. The older models are not outdated simply because they are tradition-worn. We are best equipped for a lifetime of feeding God's family when our pantries are full. Understanding each model's assumptions as well as its structure will provide the Lord's servants with the options we need for the occasions He provides.

Notes

1. Alan Monroe's "motivated sequence" for persuasive speaking supplies the seminal thought for the Problem/Solution Model and its derivatives. For an extensive discussion of the motivated sequence, see Douglas Ehninger, Alan H. Monroe, and Bruce E. Gronbeck, *Principles and Types of Speech Communication*, 10th ed. (Glenview, IL: Scott, Forestman and Co., 1987).
2. For the key work on this subject for evangelicals, see Ralph Lewis with Gregg Lewis, *Inductive Preaching* (Westchester, IL: Crossway, 1983).
3. See Eugene Lowrey, *The Homiletical Plot* (Atlanta: John Knox Press, 1980); and Wayne

Bradley Robinson, ed., *Journeys Toward Narrative Preaching* (New York: Pilgrim Press, 1990).

4. See the author's *Life-Situation Illustrations* (Grand Rapids: Zondervan, 1992).

5. Norman Neaves, *Preaching the Story*, ed. Edmund A. Steimle, Morris J. Niedenthal, and Charles Rice (Philadelphia: Fortress Press, 1980), 108.

Part III Preparing the Sermon

Jean Baptiste Massillon (1663-1742)
"The French Prophet"

Though privileged to preach before the elegant French court of Louis XIV, Jean Baptiste Massillon was not afraid to apply the Word of God to the problems of materialism, injustice, and political corruption that plagued the French nobility.

As a young priest, Massillon felt inadequate to the task of preaching and tried instead to devote his ministry to teaching. As he began preaching more often, however, news of his gift spread widely. In 1699, he preached for the first time before the French court, and preached there frequently over the next few years. Even in the corridors of power, Massillon preached boldly on the pressing social evils of his day—evils that ultimately led to the French Revolution a generation later. Little wonder that near the end of his life, Louis XIV no longer sought out the gifted preacher whose messages indicted the activities of king and court.

Not only was Massillon a preacher of social reform, he was also an evangelist. His sermons earnestly called people to repentance and faith. He did not demonstrate the elegant oratory of many other French court preachers, but his clear and forceful proclamation gave his preaching a power and impact the others lacked.

Surely few moments in the history of Christian preaching were more electrifying than when Massillon stood in the great Notre Dame Cathedral to preach the funeral sermon of Louis XIV. Amidst the wealth and power of France in all its glory, he began his sermon with the words, "God only is great."

Though not widely known among English–speaking preachers, Jean Baptiste Massillon is a worthy model of one unwilling to compromise the gospel he has been called to proclaim.

11

Frank Pollard
First Baptist Church
Jackson, Mississippi

Preparing the Preacher

"Good sermon, preacher!"

"It was the Lord."

"It wasn't *that* good."

We never will preach that good. The complimented preacher should have ditched the humble "It was the Lord" statement for a grateful "Thank you." Yet we do want to preach good sermons, and that means more than a well-prepared text. It involves the well-prepared preacher.

On Saturday mornings I write the sermon I have been working on all week. In the middle of this exercise, about 9:30, I go to the empty worship center. It is a beautiful place. I thank God for it and the wonderful people who built it. I touch and rub the pulpit and thank God for the privilege to stand there and preach.

Then I go and sit in the pews. I will sit where a widow usually sits and think about her and what she may expect when she comes to worship. I sat for a long time one Saturday morning in the place a fifteen-year-old occupies on Sunday morning at the eleven o'clock service. It changed me. It changed the way I thought about young people. It caused me to pray differently and more ardently for young people in our society. It made me want to preach sermons to which the young man would listen and be benefited.

This simple Saturday morning exercise has challenged me to do the best job of communicating the Word of God I possibly can. Preachers must be more than sermonic disc jockeys playing others' creations or maybe their own (flip side on Sunday evening). Well, what must a preacher be? How does one prepare oneself to communicate God's Word effectively? Some of the solution is found in answer to these questions:

"Have you bought what you're selling?"
"Can you do without it?"
"Is the main thing the main thing?"
"Are you real?"
"Who is in charge of your career?"

Have You Bought What You're Selling?

Watch your life and doctrine closely (1 Tim. 4:16, NIV).

The first question which must be asked is: "Have you been to Jesus for the cleansing power?" An unsaved preacher is an armless person teaching the art of pitching a baseball. It is a bankrupt person teaching economics and investments. It is an alcoholic lecturing on abstinence. It is a guide showing people things he has never seen, taking them to places he has never been.

In my youth, the richest man in our county of less than a thousand people bought an old car to drive while soliciting votes for the county commissioner. He pretended to need the job while all knew he was living a lie. He received one vote. His wife would not even vote for him.

The most pitiful picture in all the showcase of miserable examples must be the unconverted preacher. How sad is the idea of churches empty of people. A thousand times more tragic is the thought of a pulpit filled with a Christ-less preacher.

We who do know Him must beware the gradual falling away from our walk with God. Many of my friends in ministry who are much more gifted that I have fallen by the way. The enemy has compromised them. Each has said in remorse, sitting like Job in the ashes and pain of a lost opportunity: "I neglected my quiet time. I stopped having a close walk with my Lord."

Our Lord does indeed hit straight licks with crooked sticks—huge licks with small sticks. We are not likely to do the most for Him unless we are at our best spiritually. When we are doing our daily spiritual workout, when we are building our devotional muscles, we are most likely to be used. How tragically easy it is to be so busy making talks about God that you have no time to talk with Him.

No Christian is more tempted than the preacher. The slings and arrows of the evil one are aimed directly at your heart. Equip yourself with the whole armor of God. Make sure you have bought what you are selling. Do you know Christ as personal Savior and Lord? Are you walking daily with Him? Use this checklist, or one of your own making, regularly:

Do I know Jesus Christ as Lord and Savior of my life? I can no more tell what I do not know than I can come back from where I have not been.

Is my walk with Christ up-to-date? Are my sins confessed and forgiven? "The hand that makes another clean cannot itself be dirty."

Do I preach to communicate His truth or my cleverness? It is a good thing for preachers to be clever or they will not likely be heard. It is a better thing to honestly evaluate my motivation for preaching.

Do I pretend to be more spiritual than I am? I cannot act like Mother Teresa if I have no ministry to the needy.

Can You Do Without It?

> Yet when I preach the gospel, I cannot boast, for I am compelled to preach. Woe to me if I do not preach the gospel (1 Cor. 9:16, NIV).

Consider calling, the special way God draws people into His ministry. As president of a seminary, I found many committed Christians studying for the vocation of a minister who should not have been there. They somehow believed that the highest level of dedication to God is a lifetime of vocational Christian ministry. After much counseling, these dear people were sent joyously back to the office, the shop, or the factory having gratefully learned that rededication and call to ministry are not the same thing. It is my conviction that a godly layperson is worth at least five preachers in the impact of witness to a lost world.

An impressive and handsome young attorney told me: "I am thinking about entering the ministry." I said: "Forget it if you can. If you can do anything else, do that." Disappointed in my discouraging counsel, he visited the president of a seminary. The president said to him: "Forget it. If you can get the monkey off your back any other way, get it off."

Then the young man came again to me. He said: "I can't help it. I must do it. My greatest desire is to preach the gospel." He left his lucrative law position and worked his way through seminary. I see him often. He is joyously consumed with a passion to communicate the Word of God.

God's call is desire, not ability. It is love for Him and a desire to do the thing He had compelled us to do. We do not emerge full-blown and gifted if we are called. We may not preach like Billy Graham the first time or maybe even the last time we preach. We will never arrive. We will struggle to learn to preach all our lives. We will never preach the sermon we feel is worthy of our Lord or His people. Yet we will burn with a desire to learn to preach all the days of our lives.

In preparing for this assignment, I found something I wrote as a young man. It is now many years later. For what it is worth, this is still true: "I am preacher for the same reason that Moby Dick was a whale. I can't help it. It is what I was born to and created for. My only ambition is to be a communicator of God's truths found in His Word. My one goal is to state the great, old truths of the Bible in simple, fresh ways. My only tools are words, short, simple words born in the love of God. It is as impossible for me to see preaching as dull, tedious work as it is for a bird to dread to fly. I've tried to arouse my interest in many hobbies, but each dulls quickly as the desire to share His good news in new ways constantly claims the passion of my heart. This is God's will for me. It is good!"

Neglect, personal sin, love of the world, all those things which short-circuit the power from God to you and me can put out the fire and chill our calling. Read Paul's letter to Timothy as he laid out the pitfalls to sidetrack our calling. It is a thing to treasure and build. Paul urged his young friend Timothy to guard his calling (1 Tim. 6:20; 2 Tim. 1:14). Hear the testimonies of others called to preach:

> "I wanted to preach." C. H. Spurgeon
> "An irresistible urge . . ." R. G. Lee
> "Preach! Preach! He seemed to cry in my heart." Lee Scarborough

Don't do it if you can. But if you have to do it, give it your all.

Is The Main Thing the Main Thing?

> It would not be right for us to neglect the ministry of the word of God (Acts 6:2, NIV).

There are obvious reasons that the work of preaching should be our priority. Who else will do it? If we do it poorly, every program in the church will suffer. The message, the gospel, is our priority. "How then will they hear without a preacher?" (see Rom. 10:14).

When Henry Ward Beecher began his ministry, the results were underwhelming. There was no response, no growth, no sign of awakening. The indifferent remained indifferent. The lost remained unreached. One day a thought grabbed him and shook him awake. "There was a reason why when the apostles preached they succeeded, and I will find out what it is if it is to be found out." What a sound strategy and how immediate was the reward!

May our Lord drive all of us back to the New Testament to seek the secret of the success of that early band of bold ministers of our Lord. They had a message which consumed them like a flame and through them set the world on fire. Their message was no theory, not something they had simply learned. It was no propaganda of beautiful ideas of the brotherhood of mankind. It was not an argument but an announcement. It was not a debate but a declaration. It was infecting, contagious proclamation of the mighty acts of God. Its keynote was: "That which we have seen and heard declare we unto you that you also may have fellowship with us. Truly our fellowship is with the Father and with his Son, Jesus Christ" (see 1 John 1:3).

Preaching's priority centers in the Person it proclaims. Of course, our message will confront His people with ethical, social, and moral challenges. However, preaching that only tells people what to do is dull and ineffective. All of our preaching ministry is built on the solid foundation of the wonderful thing God has done for us in Christ.

"I came to town," writes John Wesley in his journal, "and offered them Christ." Make that the priority of your preaching, and preaching will not only become the priority but the power of your ministry.

Are You Real?

> The teachers of the law and the Pharisees sit in Moses' seat. So you must obey them and do everything they tell you. But do not do what they do, for they do not practice what they preach (Matt. 23:2-3, NIV).

With the news of every ministerial scandal comes a lessening of every preacher's credibility. We must not play the role of a Christian leader; we must be Christian leaders. This demands honesty. We must begin by being honest with ourselves. If we are not honest with ourselves, we cannot be perceived by our people to be honest.

In 1 Thessalonians 2, Paul was reviewing his conduct and presentation of the gospel while in Thessalonica. For all called of God to Christian ministry, for all who want to make a maximum impact for the Gospel, these words are more than a pattern. They contain insight into what God must have had in mind when He said: "Now I'll make me a preacher."

Verse 4 combines both the agony and the ecstasy of our calling—words which simultaneously humble us to the dust and inspire us to the utmost: "We have been approved by God to be entrusted with the gospel so we speak" (NASB). In this portion of Holy Scripture, we are given a glimpse at the heart of a messenger:

> You know we never used flattery, nor did we put on a mask to cover up greed—God is our witness. We were not looking for praise from men, not from you or anyone else. As apostles of Christ, we could have been a burden to you, but we were gentle among you, like a mother caring for her little children. We loved you so much that we were delighted to share with you not only the gospel of God but our lives as well, because you had become so dear to us (vv. 5-8, NIV).

By example constantly and on several occasions specifically, our Lord clearly stated that His idea of leadership is not that of this world's. "He that is greatest among you shall be servant of all" (see Mt. 20:26; Mk. 9:35; and Mk. 10:43-45). Paul is Exhibit A, a sterling example of this kind of servant leader. "I did not use flattery to manipulate you," he reminded. "I was not motivated by greed, power, position, glory, or money." Leave your ambition, your career, and your wealth in His hands. Whatever He gives you will be more than you deserve.

Paul went on: "I did not assert my authority as an apostle." Perhaps one of the best indications of serious spiritual illness among us is our preoccupation with authority. The world will never be won by the egomaniac who guards his authority but by the loving servant who gives self away, saying to those to whom they minister: "I impart to you not only the gospel of God, but also my very own life because you have become so dear to me."

Strive for that. Pray for that. And above all, be real. Say to your people: "I can't be all I preach. God's Word is the ideal and I have not arrived." Yet also say honestly: "I want to get there, and I want to urge you toward that goal." Then, your preaching will be authentic and it will be powerful.

Who's In Charge of Your Career?

The life I live in the body, I live by faith in the Son of God, who loved me and gave himself for me (Gal. 2:20b, NIV).

J. D. Grey wrote a helpful little book titled *Epitaphs for Eager Preachers*. From his experience, he was warning young ministers of the pitfalls which may lead to the death of ministry. One chapter is titled: "He Died Climbing."

How do you handle your ambition? May I simply suggest you take your ambition to the top and leave it there? Tell the Heavenly Father your dreams, desires, and goals. Tell Him and no one else. If He cannot make it happen, who can? If He does not make it happen, should it happen?

One great secret of outstanding ministry is confidence—not self-confidence but God-confidence. Humility is not weakness. This God-confidence is vital to peace and effectiveness in our work. Without it we will be pulled apart like a grasshopper in a biology class.

Our people have many hidden contracts with us. Each one expects us to be like their often inflated memory of a much-loved pastor of years gone by. Some have unrealistic ideas of what a pastor should be. They think the role is filled by someone who is a combination of Jesus, Johnny Carson, and Lee Iacocca. You are expected to preach like Billy Graham, lead like a corporate CEO, visit like a hospital chaplain, counsel like Joyce Brothers, and manage financially like E. F. Hutton.

Some imagined a pastoral search committee drawing up this profile:

"We are looking for a young man with the wisdom of one ripe in years who visits all the members and is always available in his office, who will expound the Word of God without fear, and who will tell us with authority exactly what we want to hear." I wish that were more humor than truth.

How do you handle those kinds of expectations? By trusting your career, your security, your calling to God. There is confidence in being able to say: "I am doing what I'm doing because God called me to do it. I am doing it where I'm doing it because He put me here."

I have stated the ideals. It is important to me that you know that I do not pretend to measure up to what I have stated, but these are the goals. To be authentic and prepared to preach, one must struggle with the questions:

Have I bought what I'm selling?
Can I do without it?
Is the main thing the main thing?
Am I real?
Who is in charge of my career?

12

David Dockery
Dean of Theology
The Southern Baptist Theological Seminary
Louisville, Kentucky

Preaching and Hermeneutics

Biblical preaching is the task of bringing about an encounter between people of our times and the written Word of God, composed in another language, another time, another culture. Hermeneutics is a term from the Greek, *hermeneuien*, meaning to express, to explain, to translate, to interpret. Traditionally hermeneutics sought to establish the principles, methods, and rules needed in the interpretation of written texts, particularly sacred texts.

Contemporary hermeneutics differs from traditional hermeneutics in that it is no longer equated with a theory of exegetical method, but is a description of what constitutes the phenomenon of understanding as such. Our understanding of hermeneutics, or the task of interpretation, focuses on discovering the historical meaning of the biblical text. The task of preaching relates the ancient text to the people to whom the preached word is now spoken again as a living word. Our goal in this article is to discover how to interpret the biblical text in its historical setting in order to expound the meaning and significance of the biblical text for the contemporary world.

The History of Hermeneutics: An Overview

From the beginning of the church a dual heritage developed: (1) one that maintains that Scripture's meaning is found only in its primary historical sense, and (2) another that considers Scripture's ultimate meaning to rest in its plenary, or full sense. From these distinctions several models and combinations of models developed for interpreting Scripture in the early church.

The Early Church

The apostolic fathers in the second century found the true understanding of the Bible in the teachings of the apostles. The rise of false teachings (particularly gnosticism) and challenges to accepted orthodoxy created confusion in interpretation. To demonstrate the unity of Scripture and its message, theological frameworks were implemented by such scholars as Irenaeus (about A.D. 140-202) and Tertullian (about A.D. 155-225). These frameworks served as guides for faith in the church. Continuing the Christological emphasis of the first century, the rule of faith outlined the theological beliefs that found their focus in the incarnate Lord. Sometimes, however, the interpretation of Scripture through this theological grid forced the biblical text into a preconceived set of theological convictions. This approach resulted in a safeguard for the church's message but reduced the possibility of creativity among the individual interpreters. It also tended to divorce the biblical text from its literary or historical context.

Creative biblical interpretation reached new levels with the rise of the school of Alexandria in the third century. The innovation of allegorical interpretation developed in this context. Allegorical interpretation assumes that the Bible intends to say something more than what its literal wording suggests. It seeks to draw out the deeper, mystical sense beyond the words themselves. The two great representatives of the Alexandrian school were Clement (about A.D. 150-215) and Origen (A.D. 185-254).

Those in this tradition understood biblical interpretation as a state of ecstatic possession. Therefore, it was appropriate that the biblical words imparted in this way should be interpreted mystically if their inner significance was to be made known. They affirmed the importance of the literal sense of Scripture. The literal sense, however, was not the primary meaning of Scripture. Origen particularly thought it absurd that a God-inspired Bible could not be interpreted spiritually. From this supposition followed Origen's threefold hermeneutical approach. He maintained that the Bible had three different yet complementary meanings: (1) a literal or a physical sense, (2) an allegorical or a spiritual sense, and (3) a tropological or a moral sense. Yet in some instances the Alexandrians ignored the literal sense and found numerous spiritual meanings in a single passage, thus creating an entire scale of allegorical interpretation. Alexandrian interpretation was primarily practical. The work of these allegorical interpreters cannot be understood until this is realized.

The successors of Origen were challenged by the school of Antioch, which emphasized a literal and historical interpretation. The great Antiochene interpreters included John Chrysostom (about A.D. 347-407) and Theodore of Mopseustia (about A.D. 350-428). They conceived of biblical inspiration as a divinely given quickening of the writers' awareness and understanding in which their individuality was not impaired and their intellectual activity remained under conscious control. The Antiochenes focused on the biblical writers' aims, motivations, usages, and methods. They believed the literal-historical sense of Scripture was primary and moral applications were made from it. The mature exegesis of Theodore and Chrysostom, while literal, was not a crude or wooden literalism that failed to recognize figures of speech in the biblical text. In continuity with the previous practices of Jesus and the early church, the Antiochenes read Scripture Christologically through the application of typological interpretation.

As the church moved into the fifth century, an eclectic and multifaceted approach to interpretation developed, which sometimes emphasized the literal and historical, and sometimes the allegorical, but always the theological. Augustine (A.D. 354-430) and Jerome (about A.D. 341-420) established the directions for this period. The biblical text was interpreted in its larger context and understood as the biblical canon. The biblical canon established parameters for validating both typological and allegorical interpretations so that the historical meaning remained primary, even though the deeper spiritual meaning was not ignored. Neither the allegorical practices of Alexandria nor the historical emphases of Antioch dominated. A balance emerged, influenced by pastoral and theological concerns. The Bible was viewed from the standpoint of faith, producing interpretations that emphasized the edification of the church, the love of neighbor, and primarily a knowledge of and love for God.

The Medieval and Reformation Period

From the time of Augustine, the church, following the lead of John Cassian (died about A.D. 433), subscribed to a theory of the fourfold sense of Scripture: (1) The literal sense of Scripture could, and usually did, nurture the virtues of faith, hope, and love. When it did not, the interpreter could appeal to three additional virtues, each sense corresponding to one of the virtues. (2) The allegorical sense referred to the church and its faith, what it was to believe. (3) The tropological or moral sense referred to individuals and what they should do, corresponding to love. (4) The anagogical sense pointed to the church's expectation, corresponding to hope. For example, the city of Jerusalem, in all its appearances in Scripture, was understood literally as a Jewish city, allegorically as the church of Jesus Christ, tropologically as the souls of men and women, and anagogically as the heavenly city. The fourfold sense characterized interpretation in the Middle Ages.

Martin Luther (1483-1546), the great reformer, began by using the allegorical method but later claimed to have abandoned it. It was Erasmus (1466-1536), more than Luther, who rediscovered the priority of the literal sense. John Calvin (1509-1564), the most consistent interpreter of the Reformation, developed the emphasis on the grammatical-historical method as the foundation for developing the spiritual message from the Bible. Luther's stress on a fuller sense found in the Christological meaning of Scripture linked the reformers with Jesus, the apostles, and the early church.

It is commonly believed that the followers of the reformers shrank from the freedom in interpretation employed by Luther and Calvin. While this is an overstatement and an oversimplification, it is true they conducted their exposition along new theological boundaries, establishing a new Protestant scholasticism. This new form of scholasticism resulted in an authoritative and dogmatic interpretation. Almost simultaneously, enlightenment thought began to develop. This movement rejected both authoritative and dogmatic approaches, resulting in two reactions: (1) a new found pietism associated with Philipp Jakob Spener (1635-1705) and August Herman Franke (1663-1727), and (2) a historical-critical method that stressed the importance of the historical over the theological interpretation of the Bible. The modern era has generally continued in one of three directions: the Reformation, the pietistic, or the historical-critical approach.

The Modern Period

The "father of modern hermeneutics," F. D. E. Schleiermacher (1768-1834), argued that interpretation consisted of two categories: grammatical and psychological. Prior to Schleiermacher, hermeneutics was understood as special hermeneutics *(hermeneutica sacra)* and general hermeneutics *(hermeneutica profana)*. Special hermeneutics was concerned with how the Bible ought to be interpreted and general hermeneutics was for interpreting other kinds of literature. Schleiermacher, however, insisted that the understanding of linguistic symbols, whether biblical, legal, or literary texts, should be derived from a consideration of how understanding in general takes place.

Schleiermacher saw that what was to be understood must, in a sense, be already known. Acknowledging that this appeared circular, he nevertheless maintained this was true to the facts of everyday experience. People must relate new words to what is already known. If not, the understanding of words would remain meaningless. On the other side, argued Schleiermacher, people must assimilate something alien or universal that signifies a resistance for the original vitality. To that extent it is an accomplishment of hermeneutics, Schleiermacher added, that since understanding new subject matter depended on positive relations to the interpreter's own known horizons, lack of understanding was never completely removed. Therefore, interpretation or understanding constituted a progressive process, not simply an act that can be definitely completed. He contended that a preunderstanding must take place before interpretation can happen. For Schleiermacher, interpretation was grounded in the biblical author's intention.

The early Schleiermacher articulated in his discussion on grammatical interpretation some of the most incisive statements found in all hermeneutical literature on the principles for grasping what a biblical author willed to communicate. His grammatical hermeneutics were largely dependent on the work of Ernesti's *Institute Interpret's Nov. Testament* (1761). The grammatical meaning, however, was not enough for Schleiermacher. He argued that the theme of an author's text was a product of the author's nature. The ultimate aim, therefore, involved getting through to an author's unique individuality with a psychological interpretation. Understanding required a knowledge of grammatical concerns and a divinatory intuition through empathy with and imagination of the author's experience.

The interpreter's goal, then, focuses on sharing a life-relationship with the author. Understanding involves more than re-thinking what an author thought. It includes re-experiencing what was in the life of the author who generated the thought. Schleiermacher suggested that if this re-experiencing could take place, the interpreter could understand the author's work as well as, or even better than, the author.

Toward a Hermeneutical Model

The prominent approach to biblical studies in both Protestant and Roman Catholic schools of interpretation until the middle of this century was an author-oriented approach in line with the Schleiermacher tradition. This view has been called the "literal-grammatical," "historical-contextual," or "historical-critical" method of interpretation. All the different aspects of this approach define interpretation in terms of discovering the meaning intended by the human author and understood by the original readers. Followers of this hermeneutical approach consider the meaning of the biblical situation. The task of interpretation includes furnishing the original—reconstructing the transaction of the author to the original audience by way of the text.

Contemporary theorists, such as E. D. Hirsch, Jr., have distanced themselves from the Schleiermacher tradition by maintaining that it was not the task of the interpreter to determine the mental processes by which an author produced a work. Instead, they affirm that the author's verbal meanings can be grasped because the interpretation of texts is concerned with sharable meanings. They contend that authors choose language conventions that will bring to mind in others the things they are attempting to communicate. Therefore, the readers can know what the writers wanted to share with their audience by words. The meaning of words is limited by a context that has been determined by the author. We cannot, then, understand what writers mean except by what they have actually written.

Following Hirsch, we can distinguish between *meaning* and *significance*. *Meaning* is what the writer meant when addressing the original readers. There is one primary normative meaning—that which the author intended. The more important or meaningful a text is, however, the greater the possibility of deeper, fuller meanings. The *significance* of the text includes all the various ways a text can be read and applied beyond the author's intention.

We can distinguish exegesis from preaching in a similar manner. Exegesis focuses on the primary normative meaning of the biblical text. Preaching entails expounding the fuller meaning or significance of the text in accord with the way the early church read Scripture. Since the second century, this has been through the vehicles of typological and allegorical interpretation, plus the developments of *sensus plenior* (the fuller meaning of the text) and the analogy of faith.

The goal, then, of interpretation is not to psychologize an author, but to determine the purpose of an author as revealed in the structure of the text. Another way of summarizing this approach is to say the goal of interpretation concerns itself with what the author achieved. We should remember when reading the biblical text that the human author is not present to be questioned about ambiguous meaning in the text.

A text's meaning is intelligible across historical and culture distance. Because of the nature of writing, the biblical text opens a possible world to the interpreter (the text-world); the interpreter may enter into that world and appropriate the possibilities it offers. When that occurs, the meaning of the text is actualized in the interpreter's understanding. What is understood or appropriated is the text itself, the result of the author.

From Text to Sermon

The question for the preacher is how to apply this hermeneutical approach in preparing sermons. Here we can identify seven steps (see chart) and appropriate questions involved in this process. The first four steps are preliminary. The final three steps make up the heart of the process.

Step 1. Introduction

The sermonic process begins with prayer. God's direction and enablement must be sought at each step. Then we bring our questions to the

Introduction	Observation	Translation	Basic Exegesis	Interpretation	Theology	Proclamation
Step 1	Step 2	Step 3	Step 4	Step 5	Step 6	Step 7
Ask:	Ask:	Ask:	Ask:	Ask:	Ask:	Ask:
What presuppositions do I have when I approach this text?	What are the limits of the text?	What is the text?	What kind (genre) of text is this?	What does the text mean in its context?	What does the text mean to the contemporary reader?	How can the hist. meaning and contemp significance be communicated?
What is the historical situation?	Basic translation	Establish the text	Advanced observation	Why was it said this way? canonical meaning?	What cultural factors need to be contextualized?	How will the text be heard and understood today?
What is the cultural context?	Observe structure		Lexical Exegesis	see commentaries	What is the theological significance?	
	paragraph		What does the text say?	survey history of interpretation		
	sentence		macro-structure			
	words		plot			

text at hand. Three questions help us deal with introduction issues. First and foremost we must ask: "What presuppositions do we bring to the biblical text?" Basic assumptions pertain to the nature of the biblical text and hermeneutical models undergirding the interpretive process.

The basic assumption concerns the full inspiration of the Scriptures, including the belief that they constitute a truly, truthful, divine-human book. The next two questions focus on matters related to the historical situation and cultural context of the final form (or canonical shape) of the text. We must seek to determine: "What is the historical situation behind the author?" and "What is the cultural context out of which the author wrote?"

Step 2. Observation

As we observe the text under consideration we ask: "What are the limits of the text?" We must look for keys or structural signals (such as conjunctions, particles, and so on) in the structure of the text. While the basic unit for consideration is the paragraph, we must pay attention to sentences and word meanings as well. Unfortunately, much that is identified as interpretation is little more than word studies. Viewing the text's structure in paragraph units will enable us to see the text's major idea.

Step 3. Translation

Here we ask, "What is the text?" Through textual criticism and comparison of various translations we establish the text from which we are working. It is likely that most preachers work from one basic (favorite) translation (NIV, NRSV, NASB, KJV, and so on) and do minimal comparisons from this foundation.

Step 4. Basic Exegesis

Before moving to our primary steps, we need to ask: "What kind (genre) of text are we interpreting?" Is it poetry, narrative, prophetic, parabolic, gospel, epistolary, or apocalyptic? Then we can begin to do basic work with Bible dictionaries, concordances, and grammars. Diagramming a sentence flow at this point can be extremely helpful for seeing the major emphases of the text. For certain genres, discovering the plot or macro-structure of the text will be necessary at this point.

Step 5. Interpretation

This is the most important step in seeking the textual meaning from an author-oriented perspective. We bring the question: "What did the text mean in its historical setting to the initial readers?" Here the question moves from "what" to "why." We move beyond asking, "What does the text say?" to "Why was it said in this way?" Now we must examine commentaries, trace the history of interpretation of our passage, and move toward seeing the meaning in its literary and canonical context.

We should view Scripture as a commentary on Scripture, thus affirming the analogy of faith (the picture of comparing Scripture's clear teaching with sections that are less clear) and the *sensus plenior* (the fuller meaning) of Scripture. We must expect illumination from the Holy Spirit to assist in interpretation.

Step 6. Theology

Three important questions will help us seek the theological significance of the passage. First: "What does the text mean to the contemporary reader?" Second: "What cultural factors need to be contextualized or retranslated?" Third: "What is the theological significance of the passage?" In answering these questions we should expect the Bible to speak to the reader's contemporary concerns. Ultimately we must interpret the Bible in light of the centrality of Jesus Christ.

Step 7. Proclamation

Finally, we must raise two questions: "How can the historical meaning and contemporary significance be communicated to our contemporary world?" and "How will the text be heard and understood today?" This final step obviously includes applications, illustration, and motivation as well (matters discussed elsewhere in the *Handbook*).

Conclusion

We have offered a hermeneutical model that grounds the meaning of the biblical text in the author's purpose or result. Sometimes hermeneutics is prized in theology or philosophy, but neglected in preaching. We have seen that preaching and hermeneutics join hands as the means of expressing Christian truth in the modern world. They stand between the two worlds of "the then" and "the now." Contemporary trends— combined with gaps in time, culture, and language between the biblical world and ours—demand that preachers interpret our world as well as the biblical text. Preaching involves both the construction and communication of sermons since preaching is concerned not only with communication but also primarily with the message of Scripture.

Note

1. See step-by-step instructions in Gordon Fee, *New Testament Exegesis* (Philadelphia: Fortress Press, 1983), 60-77.

13

Joseph Byrd, Pastor
Stewart Road Church of God
Monroeville, Michigan

Methods of Preparation

In high school and college speech courses, most of us learned four methods of presenting a speech: impromptu, reading a manuscript, reciting a memorized manuscript, or extemporaneous speaking from a brief outline. While homileticians cringed at the very thought of an impromptu sermon, the other methods of presentation were part of many early twentieth-century preaching textbooks.[1] Homiletics has changed in the last part of this century, and with the change in conceptualizing the sermon, a need for new methods of preparation has emerged. However, no single method of preparation stands as the "ultimate" method.

Preachers have different personalities and abilities which make certain methods of preparation more helpful than others. In one sense, they are "tools" for the preacher. Tools intended for one activity are different from those to be used in another. One does not usually use kitchen utensils to repair automobiles. In the same way, a method of sermon preparation should be guided by the desired product of the process. In other words, one may find great difficulty in preaching an inductive sermon while reading a manuscript. Yet the same preacher can also find difficulty preaching a deductive sermon using brief and sketchy notes. Methods of preparation must coincide with abilities and preferences as well as the kind of sermon one desires to preach. Each method has its strengths and its weaknesses, but all have their place and purpose.

Manuscripts

During the years when sermons were frequently published, preachers often used full manuscripts in preparing to preach. Preaching textbooks described the process of sermon preparation as culminating in writing out the sermon as one would preach it. The rise of non-literary media demanded more "freedom" in delivery. Today, while preparing full manuscripts has certain weaknesses in terms of a "free" delivery, particularly if one "reads" the manuscript, the benefits of a manuscript must not be overlooked by contemporary preachers.

While publication was a motive for writing many manuscripts in times past, preaching textbooks of that era instructed the preacher to guard against the sermon manuscript losing its aural style. One could distinguish between a manuscript written to be "read" by "readers" and a manuscript written to be "heard" by a "congregation." Therefore, even if the manuscript were to be read, it was to be written in an aural style, crafted for the listeners' ears.

Contemporary Manuscripts

Today, preparing a full manuscript can relieve some of the anxiety of preachers who are unsure of their recall ability. The manuscript can provide clear direction for the sermon so that the preacher does not wander around the countryside of the text or the topic at hand. Time limitations can be more easily negotiated with a full manuscript, particularly if a worship service is broadcast live on radio or television. Also, the manuscript provides the preacher with a written record of what was preached at a particular time. This written record can be the basis of a later article or chapter of a larger work. If the preacher has a detailed written record of what has been preached in previous messages, the manuscripts can be reviewed for direction in plotting the theme of the sermon at hand. A manuscript will also be helpful if one chooses to preach a "topical" style of preaching. Preachers will find it particularly tempting in topical sermons to stray into foreign discussion without a manuscript to guide their presentation.

An important use for a manuscript in contemporary preaching is dramatic monologues. In the process of creating a dramatic monologue sermon, the preacher lives out of the context of a Scripture text in order to make the Scripture come alive. The preacher must "visualize" the scene and get the "feel" of the character.[2] In order to accomplish this task one must carefully think through the "script" of the sermon. The preacher must consider what, when, and how each part of the narration is to be properly expressed. Obviously, the preacher will not read from the manuscript during the dramatic monologue, but preparing a manuscript will be essential to the organization of the monologue.

Disadvantages of Manuscripts

Certain weaknesses and disadvantages of manuscript preaching surface when used regularly in our preaching, particularly if one reads the manuscript. A primary problem with manuscripts is that most of us are not gifted oral readers who can read a manuscript with inflection and proper enunciation so that listeners are glued to our every word. Heads of state use manuscripts knowing that every word will be evaluated by the world; no small slip of the tongue is excused in that public forum. The situation during a presidential speech demands the listeners' attention; congregations seldom feel the constraint to listen that closely to preachers.

Contemporary homiletics emphasizes the oral and aural nature of preaching and notes that too few can preach from manuscripts in an aural style. Preachers do not prepare a sermon to be read; they prepare sermons to be heard. Chaining ourselves to a manuscript that is meant for the eye and not the ear can result in agony for the preacher and the listeners.

Another disadvantage to manuscript preaching is the time required to write out every sentence in the sermon. Contemporary homileticians note that spending valuable time used for "writing" the manuscript can be more appropriately used for orally rehearsing the sermon.[3] The schedule of a busy pastor hardly allows adequate time for sermon exegesis, let alone typing a full manuscript, particularly if the pastor must preach more than one each Sunday.

Suggestions in Using Manuscripts

Given some of the disadvantages of using a manuscript, one can be sure that creative use of a manuscript is essential in order to gain all of its benefits. In preaching a dramatic monologue, the script must be so organized that one can commit the script to memory without too much anxiety. If one uses a manuscript to preach other types of sermons, continuous printed paragraphs intended for the eye should be eliminated. Major sections should be appropriately marked. The preacher should embolden or highlight key sentences, phrases, or words. If lists of words or pairs of parallel images are used, the section should be blocked together. These suggestions will allow the preacher to move through the manuscript with little problem.

Rote memorization of a manuscript is asking more than most preachers can accomplish. However, the preacher should be very familiar with the manuscript, even rehearsing it aloud several times if possible. In light of the time that is required to type a manuscript and the pressing schedule of modern preachers, the use of computers with word processing capabilities is essential.

Some preachers consider using a manuscript essential to the success of their preaching. Successful use of a manuscript may be enhanced by the above suggestions as well as increase the aurality of manuscript sermons.

Oral Manuscripts

We have noted that several contemporary homileticians stress the importance of an oral/aural style in preaching. In his textbook, *Preaching for Today,* Clyde Fant states that too often the use of written manuscripts for sermons results in stiffness and impersonality in preaching. Fant suggests a variation on the preparation of a written manuscript which he calls an "oral manuscript." An oral manuscript is prepared through a process of preaching thoughts out loud as the sermon is developed. Fant describes the following process of preparing an oral manuscript.[4]

One begins the oral manuscript much like any other sermon through careful examination and reflection upon the text. A tentative plan for the sermon is developed in rough notes from this study. While developing this plan the preacher considers such issues as determining the theme or direction of the sermon, and a tentative arrangement of basic directional sentences or steps in developing the theme of the sermon.

After the initial study and rough notes are given some basic arrangement, each directional sentence is written on a separate sheet of paper. The preacher then preaches each idea aloud using free association, stopping only to note key phrases that emerge. Each directional sentence introduces a "thought block" which takes one or more minutes to develop. The preacher should experiment by saying the development of the thought block aloud, using various arrangements within each development. The notations taken should indicate the strongest arrangement of the "thought blocks" and their development. These notes constitute a rough oral draft.

The rough draft is refined while reviewing the notations and preaching the entire message aloud. The preacher should preach without reference to the material. Any changes should be made that assist ease in speaking. This process allows the preacher to listen in the privacy of the study to determine if the sermon fits together, avoiding the consequences of discovering problems while preaching to a congregation in worship.

After a final draft of the manuscript has been created, the preacher creates a "sermon brief." The sermon brief is one to two pages in length. It is composed of an introduction of about three to five sentences; six to ten sentences (thought blocks) which discuss the biblical text and the contemporary situation; and a three to five sentence conclusion. The three sections are connected with "basic directional sentences." Spacing, underlining, and indenting should be used to make the sermon brief visual. Fant considers the sermon brief "more than an outline and less than a manuscript . . . but superior to both."[5] The preacher may find that it is not necessary to use the sermon brief in the pulpit.

The strength of the oral manuscript is in its emphasis upon the oral nature of the sermon. The sermon brief, however, looks very similar to traditional deductive outlines which are in a vertical format. Contemporary homiletics has directed preachers to use inductive models which are reversals of the traditional outline format.

Outlines and Notes

Most homileticians suggest that the preacher put some type of notes or outline on paper for use in delivery. While others suggest preaching without notes or an outline, we shall concern ourselves here only with the general use of notes. Two types of outlines or notes emerge in contemporary homiletical thought: deductive and inductive. Deductive sermons are designed with a general thesis statement or proposition which is supported by specific major points. Inductive sermons move from specific points to narrative material leading the congregation to a general conclusion which they discover through their own intellectual faculties. The notes or outlines of these two kinds of sermons will differ and need to be discussed separately.

Deductive Sermon Outlines

The proper outline structure is essential to preaching a traditional deductive sermon. Although he advocates inductive-narrative sermons, James Cox provides a detailed discussion about deductive sermon outlines. Cox explains that the deductive sermon is only as strong as the outline because the outline "organizes" the preacher's ideas. Ideas are organized in groups and arranged for logical sequence and communicative effectiveness.[6]

The most common outline is the full sentence outline in which the preacher writes the proposition and the major supporting points in complete sentences and appropriate outline form. Often the introduction and conclusion of the full sentence outline is fully written out in brief paragraphs. The outline should be on a single page if possible. Underlining and emboldening important key words and phrases will assist the preacher in delivering a sermon from a full sentence outline.

Preachers who use full sentence deductive outlines for their sermons will find it helpful to write down the title, topic, and specific purpose of the sermon at the top of the outline. From researching the topic or passage of Scripture, the preacher should be able to succinctly state the basic premise of the sermon in a single and complete sentence; this is the *proposition*. The final proposition should be written on the outline either after the specific purpose or after the introduction, depending on when the preacher plans to state it orally.

The major points of the sermon should be developed after the topic has been chosen and the proposition and specific purpose have been determined. These major points (usually three to six in number) are statements which logically support the proposition. These should be honed into succinct, clear, and complete sentences which address the topic, directly support the proposition, and work to achieve the specific purpose of the sermon. Any subpoints needed to develop the major points should be briefly noted underneath the related major point.

After the body of the outline is in mind, most people find it easier to write the title, introduction, and conclusion. The introduction should gain the interest and good will of the preacher's audience. The conclusion should summarize the proposition and call the listeners for a response related to the specific purpose of the sermon. The title of the sermon should catch the attention of the listeners, but not promise more than the sermon will provide. The title may be a brief indicator of the proposition. Generally speaking, the typical deductive sermon outline will follow a basic pattern and resemble the following:

Title:
Topic:
Specific Purpose:

Introduction:
Proposition:

Body:
- I.
  - A.
  - B.
- II.
  - A.
  - B.
- III.
  - A.
  - B.

Conclusion

Inductive Sermon Notes

Contemporary homileticians discuss inductive and narrative preaching at great length. Yet little, if any, attention is given to what is put down on paper in terms of notes or outlines.

Inductive sermons are created with different designs and movement from traditional deductive sermons; therefore, the inductive sermon requires a different process of notes or outlining. The inductive sermon resists the formal and rigorous organization of the full sentence outline. The function of inductive sermon notes is not to organize ideas, but to serve as a guide or road map for an oral journey to discover the meaning of a biblical text. The journey moves toward an intentional end in its discovery process. The intentional end has been described as the "aha" moment; that is, when the listeners discover the meaning of the biblical text for themselves.[7]

One can conceive an inductive outline as moving in the opposite direction of the deductive outline. That is, one begins with the subpoints of the last major point working backward toward the proposition, such as:

C.
B.
A.
II.
C.
B.
A.
I.

Proposition

Fred Craddock is one of the most influential among the early proponents of inductive preaching. Much like Clyde Fant, Craddock believes that orality should regulate sermon preparation. He suggests the preacher should put the sermon on paper in five steps.[8] The preacher first writes the preliminary issues of the sermon, similar to the full sentence outline we have already noted. The text, the theme sentence, and the subject should be written on the front and center of the page. Second, information and ideas from notes taken during reading and study should be written in phrases down the page. Third, each phrase should be clear and amended if it needs illustration, elaboration, or analogy. Fourth, portions of the sermon which are more tedious should be written in full sentences or brief paragraphs. Finally, Craddock suggests the preacher should edit and rearrange the notes in light of the text, theme, and subject.

Another contemporary homiletician, David Buttrick, suggests that sermons should be designed or "plotted" in *moves*. Moves are blocks of sentences which present a single idea in no more than three internal developments. A sermon consists of about five or six moves which are each three to four minutes in length.[9] The moves are not connected with transitional sentences, but they are connected logically according to the order in which they are plotted.

Once the basic idea of each move included in the sermon is established, Buttrick suggests that the preacher create an expanded "sermon sketch." Each move in the form of a simple sentence is expanded in the sermon sketch through theological understanding and relation to lived experience.[10] The preacher is able to work through the sermon sketch, rearranging and expanding each move as needed. The final structure becomes more than a sketch but less than a manuscript. Buttrick's examples of sermon notes include listing the sermon text, a brief paragraph introduction, short enumerated paragraphs (each one is a move), and a brief paragraph for a conclusion.[11]

In their final form, neither Craddock's nor Buttrick's sermon notes seem very different from the formal full sentence outline. The movement and presentation of the sermon is quite different but the notes or outline created does not look as different as one might first imagine. However, one other possibility for inductive preaching should be mentioned that would demonstrate the difference; that is, diagramming the sermon.

Diagramming a Sermon

The idea of diagramming a sermon is to place all the needed data on a single sheet of paper in a manner which will visually demonstrate the design of the sermon. The preacher need not become an artist to diagram a sermon. To write a sermon diagram, one may use simple blocks, lines, and arrows. It will be helpful to turn the paper on its side to diagram the "directional sentences," "moves," "stages in a plot," "scenes of a narrative," and so on.

The benefit of this method is that we know we have the entire sermon before us while we are preaching. We know how a certain statement relates to following statements in the sermon. If the sermon moves toward a climax, blocks can be constructed which look like a set of stairs with the important phrases written inside the blocks. We can see at any time during delivery where we are headed in the sermon and our notes give us a visual impression of where we should be, given our immediate place.

One may believe this process to be too time consuming. On the contrary, the diagramming of a sermon can assist the preacher in determining the movement within the text as well as in the sermon. In fact, the diagram may be more helpful in aiding preacher's memory than linear notes or outlines. Each movement of the sermon or directional sentence should be placed in a block or shape with pivotal words which will aid the preacher's recall. The visual elements of a diagram, such as an arrow or an equal sign, allow the preacher to see the relation of the sermon movements at just a glance.

In observing preachers who have attempted to use diagrams in the pulpit for sermon notes, one usually notices an improvement in freedom of delivery. Less time spent staring at a manuscript or outline means more time communicating with the congregation eye to eye. With a diagram, it is easier to keep a mental picture of the entire sermon. It is helpful to include text and title on the page with the diagram; even more importantly, one should place the objective of the sermon clearly at the bottom or top of the page. That is, what does the preacher hope to accomplish in the lives of the congregation as a result of this sermon? Direction and clarity of the sermon should be maintained without the problems of a lengthy and cumbersome manuscript.

All the methods of preparation mentioned here have those who are for as well as against them. Each preacher will work with a method that coincides with habits, abilities, and personality. The conscientious preacher should try various methods with different kinds of sermons. With regular use, most methods will find their place in the preacher's sermon options.

Notes

1. See John A. Broadus, *On the Preparation and Delivery of Sermons*, rev. Jesse Burton Weatherspoon (New York: Harper and Row, 1926), 315.
2. See Raymond Bailey and James Blevins, *Dramatic Monologues: Making the Bible Live* (Nashville: Broadman Press, 1990), 11-15.
3. See Clyde Fant, *Preaching for Today*, rev. ed. (San Francisco: Harper and Row, 1987) 166-169; Eugene Lowry, *Doing Time in the Pulpit* (Nashville: Abingdon, 1985), 101-102; idem., *How to Preach a Parable* (Nashville: Abingdon, 1989), 41.
4. The following description of Fant's method follows his suggestions in *Preaching for Today*, 165-169.
5. Ibid., 171.
6. James Cox, *Preaching* (San Francisco: Harper and Row, 1985), 137.
7. For a more detailed discussion and comparison of the deductive and inductive sermons, see Thomas C. Long, *The Witness of Preaching* (Louisville: Westminster/ John Knox Press, 1989), 76-86; 92-111.
8. Craddock's discussion is found in his *Preaching* (Nashville: Abingdon Press, 1985), 192-193.
9. See David Buttrick, *Homiletic: Moves and Structures* (Philadelphia: Fortress Press, 1987), 5-28.
10. Ibid., 313.
11. Ibid., 357-360.

Diagrammed Sermon
Sermon Title: Wind, Waves, and Faith
Mark 4:35-41

vv. 35-36	v. 37	v. 38a	v. 38b	vv. 39-40	v. 41
Ordered to cross over in a boat ——— They were doing what the Lord told them to do	Furious storm comes up without warning ——— Life's storms emerge without warning: they catch us off guard	Jesus is asleep in the bottom of the boat! ——— God often seems distant when we are in the midst of difficulty	The Disciples Respond Luke 8:24: "Master we're going to perish." 1) they thought they knew all of the elements involved in their crisis and they decided their fate. 2) We often think we know the entire situation and the "real problem." We know our fate! ——— Matthew 8:25: "Lord save us, we perishing!" 1) Not only do they think they know their fate, they think they know what God needs to do! 2) Often, we think we know the problem and how God should resolve it. ——— Mark 4:38: "Lord, don't you care?" Why would God let me undergo this?	Jesus Rebukes 1) The wind and waves: brings calm 2) The Disciples Why do you fear? Have you no faith? ——— These seem unfair: -fear was natural -lack of faith expected HOWEVER, their lack of faith is unreasonable because Jesus is still in the boat!	Identity The cause of their fear is they do not know who Jesus is! ——— We often forget who God is and who we are in Christ! We are His children!

Jonathan Edwards (1703-1758)

"Revivalist and Philosopher"

Jonathan Edwards is recognized not only as the preeminent preacher of America's colonial period, but also as one of the finest philosophers the nation has ever produced.

The son and grandson of Congregational ministers, Edwards had a religious experience during his studies at Yale and became a pastor soon after. In 1727, he joined his grandfather, Solomon Stoddard, as co–pastor of the Congregational church in Northampton, Massachusetts. Stoddard died two years later, leaving Edwards as pastor.

A careful and diligent student, Edwards focused his energies on the preaching task. During his Northampton pastorate, a time of spiritual renewal—the first Great Awakening—swept through much of New England, and Edwards became a primary advocate for the revivalist spirit.

Though not entirely characteristic of his preaching ministry, Edward's sermon "Sinners in the Hands of an Angry God" is the most famous single sermon ever preached in America. Edwards' preaching consistently reflected a thoroughgoing Calvinism and a demand for moral righteousness.

Dismissed from his pastorate because of his insistence that the Lord's table be limited to Christians, Edwards for a time became a missionary to the Indians, then President of Princeton College. His presidency lasted only a month before Edwards died of smallpox at age 54.

A powerful thinker and writer, Edwards was and continues to be the consummate American model of the preacher–theologian.

14

Hugh Litchfield
Professor of Preaching
North American Baptist Seminary
Sioux Falls, South Dakota

Outlining the Sermon

To Outline or Not to Outline

What do you think about when someone mentions outlining the sermon? For years, it usually meant "three points and a poem." Many sermons were developed along the idea of "tell them what you're going to say, say it (usually in three points), and tell them what you've said." For many preachers and congregations, that worked well. It was very logical. You found a thesis, proved it, and called for the people to act upon that truth.

In recent years, there has been a revolt against that type of sermon form. Tired of the sameness of the traditional "three point form," new forms and ways to outline a sermon have been suggested. For example, David Buttrick, in his massive work *Homiletic*, stated:

> For years, preachers have talked of making *points* in sermons. The word "point" is peculiar; it implies a rational, at-a-distance pointing out things, some kind of objectification. Of course, for many decades preachers did seem to suppose that there were fixed truths "out there" to be talked about or pointed.[1]

Buttrick substitutes the word "moves" for "points." "Sermons, no matter how intricately arranged, involve sequential talking, a series of language modules put together by some sort of logic."[2] So a sermon will be outlined around a series of "moves."

Others have talked about the sermon being a "plot" to be developed[3] or a narrative to be told as a story.[4] The debate is helpful as a reminder that there are a variety of ways through which we can present the truth of God. In trying to outline a sermon, there is not one way to do it. We must seek to play the whole scale of development possibilities. "Three points and a poem" may, at times, be the best outline for a sermon. At other times, the conflict/resolution approach of a plot may be the best way to present it. I agree with Clyde Fant when he wrote:

> If a form suits the meaning and message of the sermon, if it follows meaningful methods appropriate to good theology of proclamation, and if it is the form that allows the historic revelation to speak most distinctly to its contemporary congregation—it is good structure, whatever its arrangement.[5]

As we discussed the process of outlining a sermon, we must also keep in mind that as important as outlining is, other factors are involved in determining the effectiveness of sermon factors such as language use, illustrative material, and delivery. Variety is the spice of sermon development. We must be open to that.

There are many hearers for the new forms of sermon approaches. We must be thankful to God for that. However, James Earl Massey speaks the truth when he said:

> . . . Many voices are being raised advising that the old forms and approaches need to be adapted in the interest of greater variety and wider public appeal. There is much to be said for increased appeal and the need to move beyond the limitations of stilted stereotypes . . . but when I hear discussions about some sermon form being outmoded I recall something musician Richard Wagner reportedly remarked upon hearing Johannes Brahms play his scintillating *Variations* and *Fugue on a Theme* by Handel. Although Wagner was not especially fond of Brahms, he was so moved by the composer's genius that he declared, "That shows what may still be done with the old forms provided someone appears who knows how to treat them.[6]

In the light of that, how do we go about outlining a sermon?

Starting Points

"The most important single device for achieving boldness of attack in preaching is a well-constructed outline."[7] If that judgment by James Cox is correct, what is the basis for our "boldness of attack?"

There are two concepts I am assuming that we, as preachers, will have in hand before starting an outline. The first of these is a controlling idea for the sermon. "No preacher has the right to look for points until he has the point."[8] From all the study, exegesis, and reflection upon the biblical passage, what idea has emerged as the one needing to be preached? When all is said and done on a Sunday, what one idea do you want the congregation to have heard? This has also been called the thesis, or proposition, or focus idea of the sermon. If we do not know what we want to say, it will be hard to develop a good way to say it.

The other part of the sermonic puzzle is the purpose or intention of the sermon. What do we hope to accomplish through this sermon? What do you want the sermon to do, with the people or through the people? It should go without saying that a sermon must go somewhere. However, the purpose of a sermon is often clouded in mystery. If we aim at nothing, we will probably hit it.

The shape of the sermon is often determined by its purpose. How will we get from the controlling idea to the purpose? What is the best way we can make that trip? What is the best road map? Such is the purpose of an outline: to provide the best possible way to get the controlling idea to come to life in the lives of the people.

For example, here is one sermon idea from the parable of the rebellious son in Luke 15. (Throughout this chapter, I will use this text to illustrate most of the outline.)

Main Idea: God loves everyone unconditionally.
Purpose: That they would accept God's unconditional love.

What would be the best way to develop such a sermon? The possibilities are many:

1. Deductively
   The Way of God's Love
   I. Is patient - waits lovingly
   II. Is forgiving - accepts lovingly
   III. Is generous - restores him to sonship

2. Telling the Story
   I. Boy's Story
      a. Rebelled
      b. Repented
      c. Was accepted in love

   II. Our Story
      a. Have rebelled
      b. Have felt bad about it
      c. Can find God's accepting love
      (Or we can reverse the order - Our Story/Boy's Story)

3. Comparison/Contrast - between the Father's reaction and the elder son's reaction
   I. Elder Brother's Reaction
      a. Bitterness - that he got away with it
      b. Punishment - he should get what he deserved
      c. Rejection - he would not go in

II. Father's Reaction
 a. Joy - over the son's return
 b. Grace - gave what was not deserved
 c. Love - accepted younger son as a son again

These are just a few of the possibilities. Each one seeks to help present the unconditional love of God in such a way that the people will come to trust in it themselves.

The sermon needs to have a "skeleton, a cardiovascular system, flesh, and muscle."[9] How can we develop outlines that will help breathe life into a sermon?

Qualities of a Good Outline

As we develop this skeleton idea of the sermon, what qualities of an outline do we need to keep in mind?

1. Unity

Every point (or move, or section, or step) of the outline is controlled by the main idea (thesis). The points will develop the idea of the thesis. Any point that does not contribute to the thesis is material for another sermon. Example:

Main Idea: God's love is unconditional
 I. God's love is patient
 II. God's love is accepting
 III. Sin has terrible consequences
 IV. God's love is forgiving

In that outline, point III is out of place. It certainly is a true statement and can be supported by the text, but the sermon is about the love of God, not the consequences of sin.

A well-constructed outline will have unity. It will help us to stay on the road and avoid side trips that could get us lost in unfamiliar places. The question to keep in mind as we continue the sermon is this: Does each point contribute to the development of the sermon?

2. Balance

An outline will help us keep the sermon in balance by giving each point the development it deserves. One of the problems with sermons is that often one point gets more attention than it needs. As a result, the other points suffer in comparison. The preacher will spend ten minutes on point one and not have adequate time to deal with points two or three.

The idea is to keep the points in proper balance. Therefore, if you preach a twenty-minute sermon and have three points, ideally you need to give each point about five minutes. An outline gives the overall road map of the journey and highlights the different roads to be taken. Each road should be given the proper "driving time."

The question to be asked in outlining a sermon is this: Are we giving each point the time needed to develop it properly?

3. Movement

A sermon should move swiftly to accomplish its purpose. An outline is the road map of how that trip is to be taken. The sermon should move toward a climax, where the celebration and challenge of the sermon idea is experienced. Each point should lead to the next one, so the points should be in the proper sequence. A leads to B, which leads to C, and so on. The outline moves to the conclusion in the proper way.

Fred Craddock has talked about "building anticipation" into the sermon. He stated: "If one's whole point has been stated in the introduction or fully made five minutes into the sermon, why should anyone continue to listen?"[10]

The hope is that we will take the congregation on a search, looking for the answer of the gospel to their particular needs. A sermon hopes to keep the excitement alive. An outline can help the movement of the sermon. The question to ask in writing an outline is this: Are the points moving the sermon to a climax?

Deductive/Inductive Approach

In developing an outline, we must first determine how we will develop the "flow" of the sermon, deductively or inductively. In my judgment, an outline can serve either approach. What are these approaches?

1. Deductive

In a deductive approach, these principles hold true:

a. The sermon starts with the biblical principle and then moves to the needs of the people.

b. The thesis is stated in the introduction and the points then "prove" the truth to it. The sermon moves from a general idea to specific applications.

c. The approach is very logical, majoring on a clear, linear development of the idea.

For years, this has been the basic structure for most sermons. An example of this type from Luke 15:

Main idea: God's love is unconditional

I. God's love is patient—waits long for our return
II. God's love is accepting—takes us as we come
III. God's love is forgiving—it wipes the slate clean

The sermon points are logically adding up to the thesis that God's love is unconditional. Each point is a proof that this is true.

The deductive approach appeals to those who think in very clear, logical ways. It appeals to the mind, providing information on the faith and affirming the proofs of it. Such an outline is often used for the expository sermon—the giving of exposition or a running commentary on the biblical text.[11]

2. Inductive

The basic principles of the inductive approach are these:

a. Start with the experience of the people and then move them to the text. In an inductive sermon, you do not start with the text. "You move through situations or problems of life, and perhaps illustrations of them, toward the text."[12] The sermon seeks to touch the experience of the people. Having sensed the sermon is talking about a truth that matters to them, we can more easily move them to the text to show how it speaks to the life situation.

b. The thesis is stated in the conclusion. The inductive approach is like a mystery that will be solved in the final act. Fred Craddock feels that the "preacher should retrace the steps that caused him to arrive at the conclusion—see if the hearers come to the same conclusion."[13]

I liken the difference between the deductive and inductive approaches to a murder mystery on television. The deductive approach lets us know who the murder is right away, and the rest of the show gives the clues that proves to others what we already know. In an inductive approach, we do not know who the killer is. We are involved in the search to discover who he is, just as the characters in the program are. How good we feel if we are able to figure it out!

c. The inductive approach appeals to the experiences of life, moving from them to the logical truth. It moves from specific applications to a general truth.

Ralph Lewis, in his book *Inductive Preaching*, writes the inductive outline this way:

Illustration A
Illustration B
Illustration C
Therefore: Central Idea and Conclusion[14]

The illustrations come from human experience and then lead into the biblical truth they illustrate. A sermon outline of the parable of the rebellious son might appear:

A. We have run from God
B. We have suffered because of our choice
C. We need mercy
Therefore: We must trust God for it (as the boy in the text did)

Another inductive outline has been given by Fred Craddock.[15] His scheme is as follows:

    1.
    2.
  A.
    1.
    2.
  B.
I.

In this outline, you have two truths that lead to the thesis idea. We might sketch such an outline this way:

    1. We are unhappy with life
    2. We have forgotten God
  A. Rebellion against God leads to unhappiness (pig sty)
    1. We realize we need help
    2. We realize only God can help us
  B. Repentance sets us in the right direction
I. God will accept us back as faithful children

These are possible ways an inductive sermon may be presented. This approach has the possibility of sustaining greater interest because it starts with the experiences of the people where they are, helping them to see how this sermon will matter to them. I also feel that this approach is valuable in preaching to those who are unbelievers, who do not accept the authority of Scripture. To tell them "the Bible says" this or that, may make little impact. Yet if we start with their real life experiences and then show how the Bible understands and deals with them, they may listen to the Word more easily.

In deciding how to outline, which approach will you take? Deductive or inductive? The decision will influence the way you create your outline.

Unlimited Possibilities

Tom Long of Princeton Seminary has written: "In the simplest of terms, a sermon form is an organizational plan for deciding what kinds of things will be said and done in the sermon and in what sequence."[16] There are unlimited possibilities to this "organizational plan." It seems to me that the outline will either rise from the text itself or from some logical outline that we impose upon the biblical material. Ideally, the outline will come from the text. Sometimes this will be in the form of an analytical biblical outline where the form of the biblical text becomes the form of the sermon. Expository sermons are often after this pattern.

In addition to that, there are several other options.

1. Order of Time

The points are presented chronologically in the order in which they happened.

I. Repentance - "He came to himself"
II. Confession - "Father, I have sinned"
III. Forgiveness - "My son is found"

2. Order of Place/Space

Sermon points organized around specific locations. One can imagine a photograph of the events.

Peter's Struggle Toward the Faith

I. Caesarea Phillipi — "I won't deny you"
II. The courtyard — "I do not know him"
III. The seashore — "Peter, feed my sheep"

3. Thesis/Antithesis/Synthesis

This form is modeled after G.W. F. Hegel's philosophy of history.

Getting in God's Graces (Eph. 2:8-10)

I. Thesis: We may try the way of good works
II. Antithesis: We may assume that God is pleased already
III. Synthesis: God is pleased by those who trust Him completely and live out a right relationship with him through good works.[17]

4. Synopsis Outline

Milton Crum organized sermons around these headings.

I. *Situation.* Like the young man in the parable, we have rebelled against God.

II. *Complication.* Our rebellion, like the young man's, gets us into trouble.

III. *Resolution.* Like the young man, we can go home and discover a loving God waiting for us.

The synopsis outline arranged the content of the sermon text. Crum felt that such an outline could be the basis for any sermon.[18]

5. Story Outline

Edmond Steimle, who taught preaching at Union Seminary in New York, popularized this approach to sermon development.[19] He felt the sermon ought to be the weaving together of three different stories:

A. *God's Story*. This is the story of how God has worked and is continuing to work as recorded in Scripture. This story is the biblical truth.

B. *The Preacher's Story*. How has God's story interacted with the life of the preacher? Hopefully, the sermon can tell how the biblical truth has worked in the life of the preacher.

C. *Their Story*. How will the truth of God's story make a difference in the lives of the hearers? How will it change them, comfort them, challenge them? The biblical truth needs to "take up residence" in their lives.

Such is the basic understanding that lies behind the story outline. In the simplest form, a sermon on Luke 15 could look like this:

I. God's Story: The young boy took his money, left home, made a mess of his life, landed in a pig sty, made a decision to go home, and found the Father's love.

II. Preacher's Story: "I know the way the boy felt. I rebelled against my father. I spent a period in my live rejecting values he taught me—not going to church, drinking, and making other self-centered choices. I finally came to my senses, said I was sorry and found a father ready to love and forgive me."

III. Their story: Have you ever rebelled against God? Do you feel bad about it? There is a God waiting for you to come home right now, waiting with arms of love and forgiveness.

Whatever the outline, the weaving together of the three stories is essential. God's story is presented through the preacher's story with the hope that it will become part of their story.

6. Narrative Outline

Another recent emphasis in homiletics is the narrative approach to sermon construction. Eugene Lowry has been noted for his work in this genre. In his book, *The Homiletical Plot*, he wrote:

> A sermon is a plot (premeditated by the preacher) which has as its key ingredient a sensed discrepancy, a homiletical bind. Something is "up in the air"—an issue not resolved. Like any good storyteller, the preacher's task is to "bring the folks home"—that is, resolve matters in the light of the gospel and in the presence of the people.[20]

The idea is that a sermon is developed like a plot. Lowry outlines such a sermon this way:

A. Upsetting the equilibrium—"oops"
B. Analyzing the discrepancy—"ugh"
C. Disclosing the clue to resolution—"aha"
D. Experiencing the gospel—"whee"
E. Anticipating the consequences—"yeah"[21]

This kind of outline creates the tension and then finds the release for it. In light of the parable of the rebellious son, a narrative outline might take the following shape:

I. Son gets his freedom—"oops"
II. Son loses all he had, lands in trouble—"ugh"
III. Son "comes to himself" and decides to go home—"aha"
IV. Son finds a forgiving father —"whee"
V. Son is restored as a son—"yeah"

The narrative outline that Lowry presents does provide an exciting way to preach narrative material. James Cox, in dealing with the narrative sermon, has pointed out three possible ways to present the sermon:

1. Alternate between narrative detail and application.
2. Follow simple historical narration by the drawing out of lessons from the story.
3. Tell the story in such a way that the application is implied.[22]

The narrative form provides a variety of ways to present the biblical story.

7. Problem/Solution

This is one of the easiest ways to organize a sermon. You find a problem and then give the biblical solution for it. Lowry believes that every biblical passage has an "itch" (problem) and a "scratch" (solution).[23] If you find the itch and the scratch, you have your sermon outline.

I. Problem—rebellion against God
II. Solution—forgiveness from a loving God

Many inductive sermons use this approach. Similar to this type are Conflict/Resolution, Question/Answer, and Comparison/Contrast type outlines.

8. Chase Outline[24]

In this outline, you "chase" down possible answers to a problem until you get to the right one.

How Does Forgiveness Come?
I. Can we earn it? No.
II. Can we deserve it? No.
III. Can we trust God for it? Yes.

This outline will help involve the hearers in a search for an answer to the problem.

9. Cause to Effect

This outline names the cause and then shows the effect.

Cause: Sin comes
Effect: I. It destroys
II. It poisons
III. It leads away from God

10. Effect to Cause

You begin with the effect and then the points develop the causes.

Effect: Life is a mess.
Causes: I. Due to selfishness
II. Due to indifference to God
III. Due to rebellion against God

11. Case Study Approach[25]

You take a biblical character, tell his or her story, and draw some conclusions about life.

I. Story of the character
II. Lessons drawn from that story that matter to us

There are several kinds of outlines that can be based on the biographies of Bible persons.[26]

12. Explanation/Application

This sermon simply tells the biblical story and then applies it.

I. Explanation — tell the story or explain the text
II. Application — how the text applies to the needs of the hearers

13. Analogy Outline

The outline is built around a similarity or relationship between the subject and things.

Christ Is Our Shepherd (How is that so?)
I. Christ cares for the sheep

II. Christ knows the sheep
III. Christ is willing to die for the sheep

These are just some of the outline possibilities. Some other kinds are Order of Acceptability (move from most acceptable to least acceptable); Order of Familiarity (move from most familiar to least familiar); Order of Utility (arranges points in a sequence needed by the hearer to understand what is to follow); Order of Complexity (from less complex to more complex).[27] As we deal with the text, more creative ways will come to mind for outlines. There is no one book that contains all the ways sermons can be outlined. These are just some suggestive possibilities.

Some Tips to Ponder

While doing research for this chapter, I discovered many "dos and don'ts" of outlining. As a final section, I will simply list these suggestions:

1. The points must not equal the thesis. The points are subservient to the thesis.
2. Do not let points stray from the thesis. Keep it unified.
3. "Only subdivide if forced to by the text."[28]
4. Do not be verbose. Keep point statements brief and simple.
5. "Each point should be a statement, not a question . . . the points in the outline should answer questions, not raise them."[29]
6. Watch the overlapping of points. Each point should be a separate unit.
7. Watch strained alliteration. It can be overdone. "The blessed, beautiful, bountiful, beloved Bible" is a bit too much.
8. Strive for balance and proportion between the points.
9. As a general rule, put points in complete sentences or phrasal form. Organize them in a parallel form.
10. Quotations of Scripture and illustrations are not really considered points.
11. Strive for contemporary language. If possible, put points in present tense.
12. Remember, the main divisions in a sermon serve to amplify, explain, or prove the thesis.[30]

Such are the "tips." Hopefully, they might be helpful in developing your outlines.

Conclusion

Outlining a sermon is not an easy task; once done, however, it can provide a useful road map for the preacher and the congregation as to where the sermon will go. The outline is the heart of sermon development. Variety is the key to outlining. Do not get stuck in only one way. Enjoy the creative possibilities of outlining that wait before you. Good outlines lead to effective preaching.

> Sermon forms are not innocent or neutral. The shape of a sermon is not merely a convenient or logical way to arrange content; it is an invitation to—perhaps even a demand upon—the hearers to listen to the content according to a particular pattern. As such, form significantly influences what happens to the hearer in and through the sermon.[31]

With that final word, may we never underestimate the importance of a good sermon outline.

Notes

1. David Buttrick, *Homiletic* (Philadelphia: Fortress Press, 1987), 23.
2. Ibid., 24.
3. Eugene Lowry, *The Homiletical Plot* (Atlanta: John Knox Press, 1980).
4. Edmund Steimle, Morris Niedenthal, and Charles Rice, *Preaching the Story* (Philadelphia: Fortress Press, 1980).
5. Clyde Fant, *Preaching For Today* (San Francisco: Harper and Row, 1987), 24.
6. James Earl Massey, *Designing the Sermon* (Nashville: Abingdon, 1980), 24.
7. James Cox, *Preaching* (San Francisco: Harper and Row, 1985), 137.
8. Fred Craddock, *As One Without Authority* (Nashville: Abingdon, 1979), 105.
9. Ian Pit-Watson, *A Primer for Preachers* (Grand Rapids: Baker Book House, 1986), 60.
10. Fred Craddock, *Preaching* (Nashville: Abingdon, 1985), 167.
11. John Killinger, *Fundamentals of Preaching* (Philadelphia: Fortress Press, 1985), 53.
12. Harold Freeman, *Variety in Biblical Preaching* (Waco: Word Books, 1987), 172.
13. Craddock, *As One Without Authority*, 57.
14. Ralph Lewis, *Inductive Preaching* (Westchester, Ill.: Crossway Books, 1983), 82.
15. Craddock, *Authority*, 152.
16. Thomas Long, *The Witness of Preaching* (Louisville: Westminster/ John Knox Press, 1989), 93.
17. James Cox, *A Guide to Biblical Preaching* (Nashville: Abingdon, 1976), 77.
18. Milton Crum, Jr., *Manual on Preaching* (Valley Forge: Judson Press, 1977), 32-33.
19. Steimle, Niedenthal, and Rice, 41ff.
20. Lowry, *The Homiletical Plot*, 15.
21. Ibid., 24.
22. Cox, *Preaching*, 70.
23. Lowry, *The Homiletical Plot*, 20.
24. H. C. Brown, Jr., Gordon Clinard, and Jesse Northcutt, *Steps to the Sermon* (Nashville: Broadman Press, 1963), 113.
25. Lewis, *Inductive Preaching*, 87.
26. See Roy DeBrand, *Guide to Biographical Preaching* (Nashville: Broadman Press, 1988).
27. See Brown, Clinard, Northcutt, 108-118.
28. Fant, *Preaching for Today*, 183.
29. Haddon Robinson, *Biblical Preaching* (Grand Rapids: Baker Book House, 1980), 131.
30. Lloyd Perry, *Biblical Preaching for Today's World* (Chicago: Moody Press, 1973), 53.
31. Long, *The Witness of Preaching*, 97.

15 *Lloyd John Ogilvie, Pastor*
First Presbyterian Church
Hollywood, California

Introducing the Sermon

Ernest Hemingway said that his most anguishing hours as a writer were spent deciding how to begin a novel. After he had developed the plot, story line, the main and supporting characters, he would sit with a blank page before him wondering how to start in a way that would grip his readers.

Finally, he would sit in front of the fireplace with an orange in his hand. He would carefully peel the orange and let the peelings drop into the fire. As the blue flames sputtered and flickered, Hemingway tried to focus on the one thing he wanted to communicate. When that was clear, the opening paragraphs formed in his mind; and he was ready to return to his desk and fill the blank page, and hundreds of pages after that.

As preachers, we can certainly emphathize with Hemingway's stress over getting started. I can remember many Tuesday afternoons (when I write my sermons) sitting at my desk with everything in an outline completed except the introduction. The sermon had been planned the summer before while I was on study leave. Ideas and illustrations had been gathered in the subsequent months. Monday and Tuesday morning had been spent on indepth research and Bible study. Now it was time to write the sermon. How would I begin?

The purpose of this essay is to share what I have discovered over thirty-six years of Tuesday afternoons spent waiting, praying, and sometimes pacing until the most effective introduction to the sermon came. And when it did, I knew it was the gift of the Holy Spirit, the result of a lot of hard work in the preparation of the main points of the body of the sermon, a profound love for my listeners, and a longing to communicate with them.

The first three minutes of the sermon determine the effectiveness of the whole message. Whether we preach twenty minutes or a half-hour, during these three minutes of the sermon it is crucial to "set the hook." What we write in the first two pages of a ten to fifteen page manuscript will either win or lose our audience.

The introduction of a particular sermon must be consistent with our purpose in preaching. The sermon is our part of an ongoing dialogue with our people. It arises out of listening to them and to God in our study of the Word and prayer. We listen to our people in conversation and counseling with sensitivity to what is going on in them, their relationships, and their struggle with the soul-sized issues of justice and righteousness in our society. We need to know their deepest needs and most urgent questions, their greatest hopes and hurts. I have found it helpful to do a yearly survey of what is on my people's minds and hearts.

Listening to our people helps us live on the "growing edge" with them. This does not mean that people's expressed needs limit the preaching of the full gospel or the full counsel of God in Scripture. When we feel led to preach on an aspect of the gospel that has not been articulated in these expressed needs, that too gives us a spring board for our dialogue. If we have taken time to really know our people, we will know when an *unasked* question about discipleship, evangelism, or social justice exposes an even greater need. Planning a whole year's preaching ahead of time in our summer study leave enables us to be sure that, having listened to God in our prayers and Bible study, we have included messages for both their expressed needs and those we have discerned beneath the surface. In our introduction to the sermon, we can establish in words and attitude our empathy, caring, and how the message is going to make a difference in people's lives.

The next thing I have learned about effective introductions to sermons is that they should be written out *after* the outline of the sermon has been completed. During my research, I have three sets of paper handy: one for the introduction, one for the body of thought, and another for the conclusion. On the introduction pages, under Roman numeral "I," I put "A—Opening paragraphs to be completed later." Then under "B," I write out a statement of the purpose of the message. "C" is for illustrations, stories, or anecdotes that may be useful in writing the introduction when the outline of the body of thought and the conclusion have been fully assembled.

The purpose statement, "B" of the outline of the introduction, is strategic and of primary importance. Leslie D. Weatherhead, for years distinguished preacher of the historic City Temple in London, said:

> It is my practice, when I am trying to make a sermon, to write out at the head of a sheet of paper the aim of the sermon—what I hope the sermon will achieve.

It is a good thing for the preacher to keep that in mind lest he preach a sermon of interest, and perhaps, usefulness to himself, but to very few others. Let him set down in black and white what he expects his discourse will do.[1]

Without that kind of clarity and purpose, the sermon will aim at nothing and hit it. The lack of a clear purpose statement will also make writing the introduction very difficult. The goal of an introduction is to state the purpose of the message in the most effective and varied form.

We preach in a day of "media bites" and secular television communicators who have polished the art of capturing and keeping people's attention. Lengthy, rambling introductions to our sermons that might satisfy our own need for rapport with our people will not work today.

A parishioner described his pastor's introductions to sermons in a colorful way: "Ever see a bull at a bullfight when it's getting ready to run headlong toward the matador's red flag? It moves about nervously, sniffs and snorts, rakes the ground with it's front hooves, then finally focuses on the target and goes for it with gusto. Well, our pastor is like that in the first minutes of his sermon. Once he gets going, it's pure gold, but oh, the agony of the beginning—for him and for the congregation!"

This pastor's proclivity distracts from the content of the body of the message. Chances are that he has not topped-off his extensive research with a carefully prepared introduction.

This will require both writing and memorizing the introduction. Writing is the expression of refined and polished thought. Memorizing our introductions frees us to look our people in the eye and establish communication. It need not be word for word, but repeated readings of it plus saying it out loud will fix it in our verbal memory patterns.

So, the content of the introduction should clarify the purpose of the message, establish empathy, hold out the promise of what the "take away" from hearing the message will be; and it should be one of a variety of different types.

Predictability is the preacher's bane and the congregation's boredom. A preacher who always starts with an anecdote, three points, and a poem deserves the "ho-hum" attitude he eventually receives from his congregation. To avoid this, it is good to actually keep a log of the types of introductions used and be sure they have been rotated. Here are the types I have found most effective:

1. A personal story from my own life pilgrimage, followed by application of the biblical text and statement of purpose.

2. A real-life story that gets to the essence of what you feel called to preach, followed by the purpose of the message and the biblical text.

3. An anecdote or parable from contemporary life or history that exposes the central issue of the biblical text. Then state the purpose and press on with the thesis and points of the body of thought.

4. A direct statement of the biblical text and what it promises for our contemporary life.

5. A sympathetic reference to a need expressed by many in the congregation and how the biblical text offers a promise to meet that need.

6. The dramatic retelling of the story line of a biblical account with "you are there" intensity and sensitivity. State the purpose and, with empathy, hold out the hope that what happened then can happen now.

7. The straightforward statement of a contemporary problem, moving to the biblical text and the idea that the truth therein is the solution to that problem.

8. Asking questions that get to the core of a human need. These "Do you ever. . ." questions should be followed by an "Of course, we all do" kind of empathy, and then the statement of how God can meet the need and how this message will help explain what He is ready to do.

9. A clearly stated paragraph of the essential truth which the entire message will elucidate. Then break down into the points to be covered and press on.

10. Recounting of a current news item that is on people's minds, dilating the contemporary focus for the biblical text to be preached. This opens the way to show how the Bible speaks today, answers our "why" questions, and meets our deepest needs.

As you can see, all of these types of introduction prepare the way for biblical exposition. A verse or portion of Scripture must always be the basis of the sermon. Even topical preaching must be rooted to the authoritative Word of God. Though we draw from the rich biblical passages to illustrate the basic verse or paragraph of Scripture on which the sermon is based, we should thoroughly explain the primary position with which we are dealing. This provides lasting biblical education as well as inspiration for our people.

When we do a series of sermons or move through a book of the Bible, verse by verse, focusing on a verse or paragraph each week, it is best to do the transitional explanation prior to the reading of the Scripture rather than at the beginning of the sermon. The continuity lines like "Last week we considered" or "Today we move on in our exposition of ______" will become cumbersome and ineffective in the introduction. A sermon is to be a focused laser beam that begins its penetration into the listener's mind and heart from the very beginning.

In any and all the types of introduction to a sermon I have listed, there must be a note of urgency, authority, and vulnerability. A congregation needs to know that the sermon is crucial for their lives, now and for eternity. Since we are not simply proclaiming our views but God's good news, we should communicate a "thus says the Lord" sense of intrepid conviction.

At the same time, we must indicate that the truth we are about to proclaim has had an impact on our own lives. Thus we do not stand over or above our people, telling them something *they* need to know which we have long since digested and are living to perfection. Rather we stand with them as mutual recipients of what the Lord has to say through His Word.

Now, let us go over the types of introductions I listed and consider some examples of each of them. The actual wording of some of these types will appear in bold type:

One of my favorite stories is about the Episcopal priest who went out into the chancel of a cathedral and spoke the traditional words, "The Lord be with you," to which the people were to respond "and with your spirit." Since the nave and the chancel were divided by a distance, the priest was totally dependent on the public address system. The congregation had not heard his opening words because two little wires in the microphone were disconnected. Catching the eye of a fellow priest in the chancel, he banged the microphone in his hand. As he did, the two little wires were reconnected and what he said to his fellow priest was broadcast loudly throughout the sanctuary. "There's something wrong with this microphone!" he shouted. And the people, with rote, patterned response said, "And with your spirit."

This story then can be followed by something like these transitional lines: **All of us at times have something wrong with our spirits, our dispositions, and moods. You and I have a mutual problem: sometimes our dispositions contradict what we say we believe. But what do you do when you feel down or have a rotten disposition? I know from experience that trying to talk myself into a new attitude with glib thought conditioners doesn't work. Know what I mean? I know you do. We are cut from the same cloth, you and I, when it comes to wardrobing the future.**

Often we panic, blame others or circumstances, react with fear, or pretend we've got it all together. It's then that we need grace, the grace of the Lord Jesus and His Spirit to transform us. Paul's final benediction in his letter to the Galatians is more than a traditional postscript. Backed up by a living Lord, it is a promise that we don't have to stay the way we feel. "May the grace of our Lord Jesus Christ be with your spirit." We are offered a grace-captivated disposition! Now let's discover what that really is, how we can receive it fresh every day and how we can become communicators of grace.

Another example of a personal story introduction that points away from ourselves and puts preacher and people in a position to receive the transforming power of Christ is what happened to me at a luncheon in Darien, Connecticut: **A woman stood up to introduce me as the speaker of the luncheon. What she said put panic in my soul. "We have**

someone with us today who will change our lives. He will give us hope, new self-esteem, and power to live a dynamic life!" she said confidently. I wanted to crawl under the table as she continued: "Meeting this person will be like the rivers of your life will stop and flow in a new direction. You'll experience freedom, joy, and gusto in your life." The woman paused, smiled and said: "This person's name is Jesus Christ and here is Lloyd Ogilvie to tell us about Him." It was one of the best introductions as a speaker I've ever received. It explains why I'm alive, why I feel called to preach, and what is my essential message: Christ; Christ crucified; Christ risen and reigning; Christ indwelling as Lord.

Telling that story really works as the introduction to a sermon on the new creation and what it means to be a new creature in Christ. This story also prepares the way for an exposition on a text like Romans 15:29: "I know that when I come to you, I will come in the full measure of the blessing of Christ" (NIV).

In an introduction to a sermon on hope, I used my own experience of discovering hope when I crushed my leg in a traumatic hiking accident in Scotland. The following opening paragraph set the scene and enabled me to share my own witness of Jeremiah 29:11: "I know the plans I have for you . . . to give you hope and a future (NIV).

I might have died . . . but God had other plans.

In what turned out to be one of the most traumatic episodes of my life, God gave me new excitement for the future through a dramatic experience of authentic hope.

The use of true stories of other people can be very effective as an introduction. The story should exemplify the essence of the main point and purpose of the sermon. If the account is of a contemporary person, be sure to get permission, and if historical, be sure to get the facts straight.

A couple allowed me to use the account of a turbulent counseling session with me before they were reconciled and began a new life together. The account opened a sermon on Christian marriage:

The couple sat on the couch in my study. They sat as far apart as the arms on the two ends of the couch would permit. The husband went on endlessly in a tirade about all that his wife refused to be for him in their marriage. The woman, feeling unjustly accused, sat in stony silence until she could endure it no longer. She leaped to her feet, walked to the other end of the couch, and burst out in anger: "What will it ever take to satisfy you?"

That's the essential question, isn't it? What would it take to satisfy you in your marriage? Sooner or later we are forced to discover that only Christ can satisfy our deepest needs. And when He does, we are set free to serve our mates rather than keep a running account of the deficits of what he or she has not done.

One Easter I opened my sermon by telling about a man who had received the risen, reigning Christ as Savior and indwelling Lord. The shocker was that he had been a church member for years and had been to forty-five Easter services in his fifty-five years of life. His story led into the basic theme: "For Resurrection living there's Resurrection power."

A woman I will call Julie gave me permission to share what happened one Sunday morning. It provided a personal account of forgiveness for the opening of a message on God's indefatigable love. The introduction went something like this:

As I greeted the congregation streaming out of the sanctuary, a woman named Julie shook my hand and urgently asked if she could talk to me after I finished. I knew something was wrong when I was finally able to talk with Julie that Sunday morning. She threw her arms around me, sobbing compulsively. Then I looked into her lovely face that drugs and hard living had plowed with furrows beyond her years. Her eyes were filled with pain.

"Lloyd, I stumbled! Is there hope for me?" Julie sobbed. She had slipped back into her addiction in a two-day binge. Since then she had been staying away from church because she couldn't imagine that the Lord would forgive her, or that she would be accepted by her new Christian friends.

Well, you be the judge. Is there hope for Julie? Or for you or me, whatever we've done or been? Is there ever a time when God stops loving us or offering us forgiveness?

Accounts of historical characters also provide a launching-pad lift to an introduction. The sources seem endless. Excavating the treasure of these accounts comes from reading extensively in biographies and autobiographies as well as general history.

An account of Bishop Jean Massilon's funeral oration for Louis XIV gave me exactly what I needed to open a message on pride and the grace of God:

Notre Dame Cathedral was filled to overflowing in a spectacular moment in a secular age. The glorious, proud reign of Louis XIV had ended. His casket was placed at the center of the chancel with only one large candle beside it. That's the way the King had arranged it in his will for his funeral. Massillon mounted the pulpit. The audience fell silent. Massillon announced his text from the Vulgate, Ecclesiastes 1:16: "I spoke in my heart, saying, 'Behold, I have become great, and have advanced in wisdom beyond all who were before me in Jerusalem.'"

After a long pause to allow the text to have it's full effect, Massillon said: "God only is great, my brethren; and above all in those last moments when He presides at the death of the kings of the earth, the more their glory and their power have shown forth, the more vanishes:

then do they render homage to His greatness; God then appears all that He is, and man is no more at all that which he believed himself to be."

Massillon finished his sermon and left the pulpit, walked to the casket and solitary candle. He snuffed out the candle and repeated: "God only is great!"

After a story like that, it takes only a few transitional sentences to get into the body of thought for a message on the greatness of God and our false pride!

One of the best introductions I have ever heard for a sermon on 2 Corinthians 4:7, "We have this treasure in earthen vessels," was: **An English preacher was holding meetings in northern Ireland. The preacher returned to his lodging and as he stepped into the room, a hand grasped the locks at the back of his head and swung him around the room in anger. The assailant was not a member of the IRA, but the preacher's termagant, shrewish wife. The year was not in the later twentieth century, but around 1771. The woman's name was Mary, but she went by the name Molly. And her husband's name was John Wesley![2]**

Our idea that our heroes and heroines had it all together is wrong. They, like all of us, hold the treasure in earthen vessels.

Last summer, on study leave in Scotland, after reading thousands of responses to my survey of the needs of my congregation and radio and television ministries, I decided that a series of messages, and eventually a book, was needed on the promises of the Covenant. The rainbow, the sign of the Covenant, became the symbol of my studies. You can imagine my delight when I came across a little know fact in a biography on George Matheson, the blind scholar and preacher of a previous generation. It gave me the title and thrust of the series. When Matheson first wrote the hymn, "O Love That Will Not Let Me Go," the third verse read:

> O Joy that seekest me through pain
> I cannot close my heart to Thee,
> I climb the rainbow through the rain,
> And feel the promise is not vain
> That morn shall tearless be.

The Hymnal Committee of the Church of Scotland insisted that line, "I climb the rainbow in the rain," be changed to, "I trace the rainbow through the rain." Matheson was not happy about the change. For him, "climbing the rainbow" meant claiming the promises of the Covenant.

I had an opening for the completed outline of the first message on Noah! The phrase "climbing the rainbow" became the theme of the whole series on the Covenant and subsequently the title of a book.

Another poet provided an introduction to a sermon on God's providence: **In despair, William Cowper decided to drown himself in the**

Thames. He left his home and hired a horse-drawn cab to take him to the river. After hours of searching in heavy London fog, the cab driver ended up at the door of Cowper's home. Cowper stumbled into his house, fell on his knees, and gave his life to God. Then he wrote the famous poem and hymn, "God moves in mysterious ways His wonders to perform."

Life around us today is also filled with living parables. They are in newspapers, magazines, novels, and contemporary biographies and autobiographies, as well as other books on psychology and management. For example, Tom Peters' best-seller on the management revolution provides a wonderful starting place for a sermon on pressure and stress. The book is entitled *Thriving on Chaos*. As Christians, we thrive *in* chaos; what a difference! From that concept, it is only a short step to introducing John 16:33 and Jesus' promise of courage.

Another method of introduction to a sermon is the statement of the text and what it promises for contemporary life. Arthur John Gossip, one of the great preachers of Scotland in the 1920's, often expressed a Scot's directness by simply stating the text from the Scripture and then launching into his consistently magnificent exposition. His sermon, "That Queer Complex, Human Nature" is a good example. He gave his text from Luke 3:38, "The son of Adam, the son of God," and opened by saying: **"There you have it, thrown down bluntly and vividly for all to see, the littleness and the greatness of man, that baffling self-contradiction, carried to such unbelievable lengths . . . that stares at and confuses all of us. A son of Adam, a mere transient nothing; earthly and of the earth; and yet a son of God, with real unquenchable spark of the divine in him! How both? Yet, is it not so we are formed, and from the jar and noisy clashing of those two opposites in us there arise all our unrest and all our glory?"**

You can be sure that opening paragraph did not come ad-lib and off-the-cuff. No, it was the result of polished writing and rewriting.

Congregations enjoy varied openings to sermons. After several weeks of sermons opening with stories or anecdotes, it is a welcome change for the preacher to begin by saying: "Let's get straight to the point." Then give a statement of the basic presupposition, the thesis of the message, and the biblical truth to be expounded. However, there should be a vivid illustration early on to give the people an opportunity to feel as well as conceptualize the thrust of the message. Martyn Lloyd-Jones was the master of this method.

James I. Packer, in an evaluation of Lloyd-Jones' preaching, wrote this about his introductions:

> He first announces his text, usually with some variant of the formula: "I should like to call your attention to . . ." The formula means just what it says. Lloyd-Jones is an expository and textual preacher and the whole concern of his

sermon will be to make us attend to the message which his text contains. Next, he begins to talk around some problem of life or thought today, or some issue arising from the congregation's circumstances, on which the text will in due course be heard to speak; or perhaps he will point to the way in which some feature of the text or context exposes and questions us today. . . . The style of these opening minutes is conversational, informal and unstudied, yet at the same time serious and business like: You are made to feel at once that Lloyd-Jones knows exactly where he is going and that his perception of life's issues is such that he will be well worth accompanying.[3]

The dramatic description of a biblical account, putting our listeners in the scene, is also an effective method. Some time ago, I did a message entitled "Drop That Stone!" in which I described the John 8:1-11 account of a woman caught in adultery from the accuser's point of view. After a full description of the passage from inside the skins of all involved, I had four points about judgmentalism and forgiveness of others and ourselves. During the entire sermon I held a large stone which I forcefully dropped at the end of the message, while calling everyone to drop the stones of condemnation and unforgiveness they had been carrying.

When doing a topical sermon on a contemporary problem it is important to state the problem clearly, show what it is doing to us, and progress to the biblical mandate. For example, in a message on pornography, I opened with a statement: **It is alarming to discover that 90 percent of the pornographic literature, magazines, films, and videos are produced within a radius of eight miles from where you are sitting in this beautiful, historic sanctuary! Today, I want to confront what pornography does to pollute the American mind, its motivating influence on rape, dehumanization of women and men, and child abuse.** This was followed by illustrations and statistics.

Another effective way of opening the sermon is with personal questions. My professor, James S. Stewart, was a master craftsman of many different methods of introducing the sermon. I am indebted to him for the lasting, indelible impression of great preaching. In a sermon on the omnipotence of God, Dr. Stewart displayed the use of questions as the introduction: **"What is the biggest fact in life to you at this moment? What is the real center of your universe? 'The biggest fact in life?' replies one man. 'Well, I reckon it is my home. That for me is the center of everything.' A very noble thing to be able to say! 'The main fact in life to me,' says a second, 'is, without any shadow of doubt, my work. If you take that away from me, you just take everything.' 'The central thing for me,' declares a third, 'is health and happiness. As long as I have that, I'm quite content. I can't bear to be unhappy.' But what is your answer?"** In one brief paragraph, Dr. Stewart involved the listener and drew him or her into mental dialogue.

It was said of Methodist Bishop James Kennedy that he began the sermon where you might expect him to end. He affirmed his audience in his introduction by assuming growth and willingness to get down to the application of convictions held, but which needed to be lived. He spent a great deal of time writing his introductions.

So did Robert J. McCracken, distinguished pastor of the Riverside Church in New York City for many years. In his book, *The Making of a Sermon,* he explained how important the introduction is to an effective sermon. He would do the first draft of the sermon outline on Tuesday. He sorted and sifted his source materials accumulated over a period of time. Then he would begin to sketch an outline. By Wednesday morning he was at work on the introduction of the sermon. He writes:

> Experience has taught me that this may take some considerable time. . . . I have written and rewritten the introduction over and over again. And I have discovered that once satisfied with the introduction, the remainder of the sermon can be done more rapidly. The introduction takes time because here considerations of style are especially paramount. A well-constructed sentence is like a sharpened tool. If the sermon opens with sentences that are concise and precise, it will arouse interest and it may linger in the memory. . . . What are the requirements for a good introduction? It should never be lengthy. Any tendency to become expansive or discursive, as if all the time in the world were at our command, must be resisted. We ought to come to grips at once and forthrightly with our subject. It should be as interesting as we can make it.[4]

The introduction is especially crucial when the sermon is in response to a particular crisis or tragedy in the congregation, community, nation, or world. The situation or concern is already on people's minds. Once again, allow me to illustrate. A couple of years ago, one of the outstanding young men in our congregation was killed in a tragic auto accident. The parents were devastated. Daily they had claimed the promise that God would protect their children. What could people say to this family? The following Sunday, we could not proceed as if nothing had happened. So the sermon was rewritten to give pastoral care to the whole congregation. The grief of one family had stirred the unhealed grief in many others. And so I began: **It's on all our minds. So let's talk about it. One of our families has endured a heart-shattering loss. Deep questions have been stirred in all of us. How could God have allowed this to happen? Why is there suffering?**

No less concern must be expressed in community and national crises. The preacher's introduction to his or her sermon is an opportunity to comfort and bring a decisive, caring message from the Word of God.

A concluding word about introductions to sermons must acknowledge that some of the best preachers of history differ greatly in how they started their sermons. Robert Murray McCheyne's introductions were generally weak, almost nonexistent. He usually began with an exposition of words and phrases of his text and only occasionally did he make a statement of his theme. A contemporary of John Henry Newman commented on his preaching: "Three things impress us. First, the directness of the address. He gets to work promptly, drives straight at his mark, and closes with direct appeal." Studying the sermons of Washington Gladden reveals that his introductions were always brief.

As an admirer of the sermons of G. Campbell Morgan, I was surprised to read a first-hand account of his introductions. Alexander Gammis, in *Preachers I Have Heard,* wrote: "Morgan appeared stiff and awkward at the beginning of the sermon. But once he had plunged into his subject, there was a wonderful transformation. The whole man appeared to palpitate with an uncontrollable energy."[5]

Karl Barth stuck to biblical introductions, believing that the preceding portions of the service served as introductions so that he did not need to do much introducing. Dietrich Bonhoffer did not believe that he should depend heavily on the introduction or complicated scheme of construction. He believed that the text gave form to the sermon and the sooner into the text, the better. His sermons were composed of the three elements of teaching, edification, and evangelism.

Helmut Thielicke, on the other hand, gave a great deal of attention to his introductions. He used them to establish immediate contact with his audience and state the theme of his message. He established rapport with the contemporary mind and laid the groundwork for the theme of the message. Penetrating questions, which he answered in the body of the sermon often served as the main thrust of the introduction.

Some who gave little attention to their introductions could have been even more effective if they had given more attention to them, and the success of others was measurably increased because of time spent polishing their preparation for the strategic opening minutes of their sermons.

Now to summarize, allow me to put what I have tried to communicate into several positive admonitions for the introduction of the sermon:

- Vary the types of introductions.
- Write them out with great care.
- Prepare the introduction after your research is completed and the thrust of the sermon is clear in your mind.
- Be sure the introduction meets the five tests: arrests attention, establishes your empathy, states the biblical text, clarifies the purpose of the sermon, and promises what the "take away" will be for the listener.
- Memorize the introduction so you can give it, looking the congregation in the eye.

May it always be said of us what was said of Phillips Brooks after his preparation of the sermon manuscript was completed. "The sermon was now in Brooks himself, like a banked furnace waiting to break forth with heat."

Notes

1. Leslie D. Weatherhead, *That Immortal Sea* (New York: Abingdon Press), 191.
2. John Pudney, *John Wesley and His World* (New York: Charles Scribner's Sons, 1978), 101.
3. Clyde E. Fant and William M. Pinson, Jr., *20 Centuries of Great Preaching,* vol. 11 (Waco, TX: Word, 1971), 269-270.
4. Robert J. McCracken, *The Making of the Sermon,* 91-93.
5. Alexander Gammis, *Preachers I Have Heard,* quoted in Fant and Pinson, *20 Centuries of Great Preaching,* vol. 8, 1971), 12.

16

Stuart Briscoe, Pastor
Elmbrook Church
Waukesha, Wisconsin

Developing the Sermon

When W. E. Sangster, the gifted Methodist preacher, learned that he had contracted a fatal disease he wrote:

> I long to go into every manse and vicarage in the land and confront men in the ministry with this question, "Do you really believe in preaching as the primary means by which God brings man to salvation, and, therefore, as your primary task, to the accomplishment of which you will devote your best hours and your greatest energies?"[1]

This is a significant question to those of us who seek to minister the Word of God effectively in the midst of busy lives surrounded by people with clamoring needs and endless problems. If, because of secular attitudes and theories, our confidence in the effectiveness of preaching has been eroded, or through sheer tiredness and busyness our enthusiasm has become jaded, then our interest in sermon preparation will automatically have been downgraded. On the other hand, as we constantly refresh ourselves in the Word and relate it to the needs of our world, there should be challenge and encouragement enough through the Spirit to lead us to devote our "best hours and greatest energies" to preaching, starting, of course, with preparation. How should the hours be spent and the energies be expended?

Obviously the sermon starts somewhere with an idea. Dr. D. Martyn Lloyd-Jones relates how the idea for his famous series of sermons on "Spiritual Depression" came to him while dressing one morning. He said: "All I had to do was to rush as quickly as possible to put down on paper the various texts, and the order in which they had come to me."[2] He did explain, however, that while he had not thought of preaching such a series he had been collecting all the requisite material without recognizing the central idea behind it.

Once the idea has been conceived, the embryo of the sermon will start to develop. The idea will often come from the preacher's study of the Scriptures. A case in point is a series I have preached entitled: "Where to Find Help." This was impressed upon my spirit as I read: "Let us then approach the throne of grace with confidence, so that we may receive mercy and find grace to help us in our time of need" (Heb. 4:16, NIV).

On other occasions the idea will be planted by careful observation of the specific circumstances of the people being addressed, or by concerns generated by events in the culture in which the people live or, perhaps, by traumatic and dramatic happenings which need to be addressed. In all the cases where the idea is not derived directly from Scripture, it will be necessary for the preacher to go immediately to Scripture in order to have something of eternal significance to say. As John Stott rightly asserts: "It is my contention that all true Christian preaching is expository preaching." He added: "The expositor pries open what appears to be closed, makes plain what is obscure, unravels what is knotted and unfolds what is tightly packed."[3]

This means the preacher heads for the study with the idea to discover what God has to say on the subject. As Keith Price, the Canadian expositor once told me: "I must know what God is saying before deciding what I will say." In the case of my "where to find help" idea, which was based on Hebrews 4:16, I started to read and re-read the epistle numerous times. As I did so I became aware not only of the vast amount of material contained therein, but also of the many different preaching approaches that could be taken. W. E. Sangster in his classic book, *The Craft of the Sermon,* said that sermons can be classified by "their subject matter—the actual content of the sermon" including "Biblical Interpretation," "Ethical and Devotional," "Doctrinal," and "Evangelistic."[4]

Using his classification system it was clear that the series could be preached as biblical interpretation (Hebrews needs a lot of that for modern congregations), ethical and devotional (Hebrews is full of "let us therefore" passages which cry out for practical application), doctrinal (the "high priest in the order of Melchizedek" holds many mysteries and teachings close to his priestly garments which need careful explanation), and evangelistic (the urgent, "How shall we escape if we ignore such a great salvation?" holds its own powerful appeal).

As I meditated on the passages it became clear to me that it would be necessary to incorporate all of the above at one time or another in the series. I did not wish the series to extend beyond eight weeks. It would not be possible, therefore, to cover the complete epistle adequately. Given the key idea, "Where to Find Help," it was not difficult to identify specific areas in the epistle which addressed the kind of issues with which the people to whom I minister are dealing. I began, therefore, to plan out the specific passages we would explore together on the understanding that I would briefly outline the intervening passages to maintain continuity in much the same way that a jeweler concentrates on the pearls without ignoring the string that holds them together. As a result, I worked out the following outline:

1. Where to Find Help—Cleaning Up Your Life (Heb. 1:1-4).
2. Where to Find Help—Coping with Your Fears (Heb. 2:14-18).
3. Where to Find Help—Facing Up to Your Frustrations (Heb. 4:1-13).
4. Where to Find Help—Dealing with Your Temptations (Heb. 4:14-16).
5. Where to Find Help—Seeing Beyond Your Problems (Heb. 5:7-14).
6. Where to Find Help—Handling Your Insecurities (Heb. 6:13-20).
7. Where to Find Help—Clearing Your Conscience (Heb. 9:1-14).
8. Where to Find Help—Maintaining Your Faith (Heb. 10:19-39).

Having identified the passages of Scripture we would address together and having also picked a dominant theme for each passage (stated in the title), it was time to begin the work of exegesis. I have on my shelves about ten commentaries on Hebrews; these in addition to such resources as *The Dictionary of New Testament Theology* and *Theological Dictionary of the New Testament* gave me more than enough answers to the basic exegetical questions—"What does it say?" and "What does it mean?"—which lead eventually to the essentially practical question: "How does it apply?" Or as a youth pastor friend says: "What?" "So What?" and "Now What?"

The "What does it say?" question is answered by attention to the author's line of reasoning, use of vocabulary, and points of emphasis. There are many aids to understanding the text which will greatly benefit us if we take the trouble to utilize them! The "What does it mean?" question may not be answered as simply as some people would like to imagine. For those whose approach is basically "The Bible says it, I believe it, that settles it!" there may be some rude and requisite awakenings when they begin to study—as they must—such matters as the author, the recipients, the purpose, and the date of the epistle. This is particularly true in Hebrews which has more than its share of passages which do not easily yield simple answers.

I write the products of my exegetical work in a notebook reserved for that purpose, making special notes of definitions of key words and other uses of these words first in the immediate context, then in the epistle as a whole, and, if necessary, in other biblical books. So, for example, in the first message of the series I made special note of such words as "prophets" and "purification," taking time to trace both important concepts back to the Old Testament. This was particularly important because the epistle written to Hebrews assumes much about the recipients' knowledge of Old Testament religion which many modern Westerners do not possess. So we must learn about it if we are to begin to understand the relevance of this Scripture to the recipients first, and then to ourselves.

In passages like Hebrews 1:1-4 there is so much truth packed into a small space that a preacher may be tempted to linger long in its fertile fields. Generally speaking, it is not advisable to contemplate each phrase at length. Granted, since it is truth, it will be beneficial to study it; but there is a danger inherent in this approach. We may become so enamored of detail that we miss the panoramic view which the author intended us to see. This is not to suggest that we should ignore parts of what has been written, but we should give the author credit for having a purpose in writing by endeavoring to identify that purpose and making correct application of it to our lives. The apparent intent of the author in the introduction to Hebrews was to show to some professing believers with a background in Judaism that their apparent intention to revert to their former religious experience and practice was a dangerously ill-advised path to take because of the marked superiority of the Lord Jesus to the various tenents and dogmas of the religion to which they were being drawn.

It was quite clear to me that if the sermon was to carry any weight whatsoever it would need to communicate convincingly the meaning and the significance of *sin*. In my experience this is not an easy task because of modern man's perceptions or misperceptions of the subject. Craig Skinner has pointed out:

> The preacher will be speaking with many who are ignorant of the specific knowledge he possesses. He may address those whose views of religious truth may differ from his, or who may be opposed to him. Any speaker who assumes that his audience thinks and feel exactly as he does will always be wrong.[5]

This is particularly true when the subject is sin. As I looked over the materials that I had gleaned from exegesis of the passage, my attention was drawn to the fact that God had spoken; my immediate question to myself—or more accurately to the Scripture—was: "God has spoken, but what did He say?" The text itself did not give specific answers to the question, but it did say He had spoken "through the prophets" and "by His Son." Noting that the communication "through the prophets" had come "at many times and in various ways", I was drawn to consider in a little more detail the nature of the prophets' communication, with particular reference to the subject of human sin.

Care had to be taken at this stage to avoid becoming too intrigued with what God had spoken through the prophets. It would have been too easy to wander down prophetic pathways never to return to the Hebrews' highway. On the other hand, it was necessary to identify what

God said through the prophets concerning His offer of forgiveness with particular reference to the promised Messiah/Suffering Servant and the principle of atonement. Having carefully noted these developing lines of thought, my attention then turned to the second way in which God had spoken: "by His Son."

I addressed the data concerning the Son through Whom God had spoken with a view to finding further answers to the question: "God has spoken, but what did He say?" Two phrases, packed with meaning, "The Son is the radiance of God's glory" and "the exact representation of His being," pointed unerringly in the direction of an answer. It occurred to me that God had spoken about His purposes through the prophets and about His person through the Son. The words "radiance" and "representation," both of which merited further study, conveyed the idea that God had revealed something of His essential nature and person through the Man, Christ Jesus. The twin themes of His radiant holiness and His incredible grace and mercy needed to be explained and proclaimed.

By this time, as a result of exegetical study, prayerful meditation, and careful thought about direction and structure, I was ready to write down an outline. I must admit at this juncture in my preparation I felt like Ezekiel when he saw a great many bones on the floor of the valley, "bones that were very dry" (Ezel. 37:2). Strewn across my desk by this time were very many books and notes and scribbled ideas and I was wondering to myself: "Can these bones live?" My "bones" needed to "(come) together bone to bone" with or without "a noise, a rattling sound" (Ezek. 37:7). I began to write down the beginning of a skeleton outline as follows:

"Where to Find Help—Cleaning Up Your Life" (Heb. 1:1-4).

I. God has spoken, but what did He say? (vv. 1-3a).
  A. About His Purposes—through the prophets.
    1. His desire for fellowship—ruined.
    2. His offer of forgiveness—provided.
      a. The promise of Messiah.
      b. The principle of atonement (see Heb. 9:22).
  B. About His Person—through the Son
    1. The radiance of His glory.
    2. The representation of His being.

Having completed the skeletal structure of the first section it was now time to return to the exegetical notes still strewn across my desk like bones in the valley. I needed a second main heading that would relate in some way to the first one—"God has spoken, but what did He say?" —but which would also serve to develop the theme of the next section. My attention began to focus on the significant statement: "He sat down at the right hand of the Majesty in heaven." This is a dominant theme in Hebrews, being mentioned on five separate occasions and, as the overall theme of "Where to Find Help" points to "the throne of grace," (Heb. 4:16) it obviously needed to be highlighted.

As I thought about it there seemed to be a certain rhythmic connection between "God spoke out" and "Christ sat down." I do not always look for such connections, but they often seem to jump off the page! Christ's glorious Ascension was very much on the author's mind. It is sad that there is a marked lack of appreciation of its significance today. Even where Christmas and Easter are recognized, and, if it doesn't interfere with Mothers' Day and Pentecost, there is often little interest in the fact that Christ "sat down at the right hand of the Majesty in heaven." So the question that came to mind was: "Christ has ascended, but what did He accomplish?" A sense of structure and rhythm was beginning to form in my mind:

I. God has spoken, but what did He way? (vv. 1-3a)

II. Christ has ascended, but what did He accomplish? (v. 3b)

To answer that question it was necessary to explore the significance of "sat down," "right hand," and "the Majesty in heaven."

I came to the conclusion that "sat down" spoke of the work of redemption completed in the same way that God rested after completing His initial creative work. "At the right hand" addressed the fact of Christ being greatly honored on His return to heaven after His humiliating time on earth, and "the Majesty in heaven" referred to the authoritative position He now fills. But, and this was very important in the development of our theme, He did all this "after He had provided purification for sins." There were, therefore, two main accomplishments: "He provided purifiction for sin" and "He sat down at the right hand."

Looking over the sermon developed thus far I noted that I had not addressed a considerable amount of material that described Christ, and I was convinced that if the significance of "purification" (or cleaning up the life) was to be pressed home, it was to a large extent dependent on an understanding of sin which I was not convinced was as yet established. As I thought about this it seemed that if the status of Christ was underlined as described, and a contrast between Him and us could be made, our sinfulness would be shown in sharp relief. So "He appointed Him heir of all things"—the fact that everything, including us, rightfully belongs to Him—was set in stark contrast to our rejection of Christ-rule in favor of self-rule. The fact that He is the One "through whom He made the universe" was contrasted with the pitiful and dangerous self-delusion of the self-made person. The reminder that He is busy "sustaining all things by His powerful Word" clearly contradicts our concepts of self-sufficiency. These stark denials of Christ which are so common in contemporary society are unmistakable evidences of the sin which lies at the root of our problems. Nobody needs much convincing that people naturally prefer the self-ruled and self-sufficient life-style of the self-made person to a life characterized by the "obedience of faith"!

There remained the statement of Christ's superiority to the angels which was obviously extremely relevant to the author, presumably because the Hebrews had developed a special interest in angels similar to or identical to that of the members of the Dead Sea sect. Persons today have little or no interest in angels, except occasionally in the "fallen" variety. Therefore it would not be wise or profitable to spend much time on this section, but this did not warrant ignoring the statement altogether. It occurred to me that angels were known to serve God with great and glad enthusiasm until one of their number, dissatisfied with his status, determined out of pride to establish a higher position for himself. His action led not only to a monumental fall but his attitude found a fertile resting place in the heart of mankind—another evidence of sin. Most people know that "pride comes before a fall"; what they need to know is that it was angelic pride that led to the original Fall and humanity's insistence on repeating the exercise perpetuates the problem. Musing on this, the thought crossed my mind that when mankind (made lower than the angels) tries out of pride to rise higher, mankind (made higher than the animals) proceeds out of passion to sink lower.

Attention now had to be given to the key phrase "purification for sins." This had been "provided" by Christ because it was necessary and because no one else was capable of doing it. I also noticed the special emphasis in Hebrews on the unique activities of the Old Testament High Priest and his marked limitations. The meticulous attention to detail both in the ceremonial cleansing of High Priest and people, the awesomeness of God insulted by the presence of sin, and the utter helplessness of mankind to provide their own cleansing, served to highlight the fact that human beings are incapable of cleaning up their lives; yet they are accountable. In contrast, Christ (by virtue of His perfect sacrifice) demonstrated that His ability to cleanse is as great as the responsibility He assumed for us.

It was now time to see if the bones would shake together to form the next part of the skeleton. Here is the result:

II. Christ has ascended, but what did He accomplish (v. 3b)?
   A. He provided purification for sins.
      1. The reality of sin.
         a. He is heir of all things—we prefer self-rule.
         b. The Universe is made through Him—we prefer being self-made.
         c. He sustains all things—we prefer self-sufficiency.
      2. The repercussions of sins.
         a. Made lower than the angels—pride lifts us higher.

b. Made higher than the animals—passions drag us lower.

3. The responsibility for sin.
   a. We are accountable and incapable.
   b. Christ demonstrated ability as He accepted responsibility.

B. He sat down at the right hand of God.
   1. He was humiliated on earth but honored in heaven.
   2. He concluded purification work but continues intercessory work (Rom. 8:34).

Having concluded the two main sections of the sermon's outline the question to be addressed was: "Has the material explained been adequately applied?" J. I. Packer has pointed out this extremely important question:

> To pass on biblical context, unapplied, is only to teach, not to preach.... Preaching is teaching-plus, that is, application of truth to life. One's adequacy as a preacher, interpreting God's Word to God's people, is finally determined not by the erudition of one's exegesis but by the depth and power of one's application.[6]

In some instances the application may best be left until the end of the sermon, in which case it may be presented in the form of the famous third point of a three-point sermon so beloved by many preachers. In many instances the application can be made more effectively as the sermon progresses. For instance, in the section II. A. 1. a-c above, the most natural and effective way of making the application was at the time of presentation. There is, however, no necessity to try to drive a wedge between the two approaches; and it may be that a little of both in each type of sermon is needed. The force of the application is found in the way the preacher courteously and carefully, but firmly and lovingly, on the basis of what God has said, addresses the mind, emotions, and will of the hearer with a view to serious thought and response.

In applying truth to the mind there should be a pointed request or challenge to the hearer to determine whether what they think on the issue at hand is in line with what God thinks. As for an appeal to emotions (beware of an emotional appeal which can easily become manipulative and unethical), the appeal should be one to those motivating dynamics in our lives which lead us to action either in continuing and persevering in what is right or in making changes in areas that are clearly wrong. This leads to the challenge to the will—the citadel of mankind—which can be approached through the gate of mind or emotion (preferably both). Every preacher has met people (including the preacher) who have intellectually grasped the truth and been emotionally moved by the truth but have resisted the changes demanded by the truth.

As Ian Pitt-Watson has pointed out: "The special kind of truth of which the Bible speaks is a holistic truth in which intellectual assent, emotional involvement and volitional commitment are fused together when we wholeheartedly embrace the Christian faith."[7] To bear this in mind in our application is to avoid the sterility of purely intellectual teaching, the shallow response called for by excessively emotional preaching, and the self-righteous activism that results from exclusively volitional preaching.

Even though I planned to make application throughout the sermon, I was convinced I needed a third section to reinforce what had been said. Looking back over the two previous main headings I needed another which would bring some symmetry to the sermon, a sense of order, at least in my own mind, even if not recognized by anyone else. Spurgeon's remark to his students had been firmly lodged in my thinking: "Order, which is heaven's first law, must not be neglected by heaven's ambassadors."[8]

The focus was now on application and response and, therefore, on the hearers and what the sermon was intended to mean to them. So I decided on:

III. We have heard, but what did it mean?

I must admit that I tend to produce sermons with three points, but I do not belong to the school that insists on "an introduction, three points, and a conclusion." This is possibly because many years ago I was told a story about a young seminarian who was required to produce a homiletical outline of that vintage for his professor. He apologetically said: "My subject is, 'The man who was sick of the palsy.' I'm afraid I couldn't think of an introduction, I arrived at no conclusion, and I could only come up with two points." His professor, singularly unimpressed, asked what the two points were. The young man replied: "The first is, 'The man had the palsy,' and the second is, 'He was sick of it!'" The professor sighed deeply!

My conclusion from that story was: "If there aren't three points, don't go looking for them. If you struggle to find two, settle for one, and if you can't find one, do something else!" Some people seem to have a gift for outlining and headings like the famous preacher Alexander McLaren of whom it was said: "He fed the sheep with a three-pronged fork."[9] In some instances the headings seem to fall quite naturally into an alliterative mode. This can be helpful both for its sense of order, symmetry, and beauty; but, if forced, it can draw attention to *itself* rather than serving to bear along the message. Skeletons are extremely valuable for body structure but are particularly gross when viewed alone. Martyn Lloyd-Jones, with characteristic forthrightness, said what he thought about alliterative outlines: "For myself, I am acutely allergic to the practice and generally find it to be a hindrance to the truth and an annoyance."[10]

To return to the third point, I was anxious to reinforce three simple but basic points, two of which should have been heard and the third which needed to be introduced. These points were designed to show not only the necessity of response, but also how practically to make it.

So the final section read:

III. We have heard, but what did it mean?
   A. The significance of sin must be acknowledged.
   B. The offer of salvation must be accepted.
   C. The danger of drifting must be addressed (Heb. 2:1).

The basic structure of the sermon was now complete. An introduction designed to get people's attention and to lead into the sermon was now necessary. I was interested in showing the people how God had found a way to communicate with us. This is particularly motivating when we realize how difficult it is for humans to communicate with each other.

I told the story of the little girl who, on seeing her Daddy disappear into his study as usual after supper, asked why he did it. "Because he has work to do which he couldn't finish at the office." To which the bewildered child responded, "Well, why don't they put him in a slower grade?" This type of story relaxes people, builds a bridge, and draws them into thinking about the difficulties of communicating with, and to, a child. Then I talked about the best selling book, *You Really Don't Understand,* which deals with male/female communication. A couple of humorous and readily identifiable examples from the book further established the problems we humans have communicating with each other and quite naturally led to a consideration of God's remarkable way of overcoming the difficulty of communication with human beings.

By way of conclusion I often give the congregation "Points to Ponder." Is my life in need of a clean up? Do I recognize the reality of my sin? Am I prepared to respond to Christ? These "Points to Ponder" lead into prayer designed to help people in their individual responses.

The final part of sermon preparation is usually the insertion of illustrations and occasional quotations. The latter are helpful if they say better than you can what needs to be said or if the person saying it strikes a chord with the hearer which you may not strike. A few days ago I was told of a young woman who, half-listening to my talk, suddenly came alive as I quoted Jean-Paul Sartre's words spoken shortly before his death, in which he tacitly renounced the nihilism for which he was notorious. She explained after the talk that she had long been a disciple of Sartre but had never heard that he finally believed in a Creator Who had created him. This led to a five-hour discussion and the appreciative acceptance of a Bible with a promise to read John's gospel.

As for illustrations, they are designed to throw light on the subject and act, as Spurgeon said, as windows. Phillips Brooks, however, goes a step further and insists:

I think that we confine too much the office of illustration if we give it only the duty of making truth clear to the understanding, and do not also allow it the privilege of making truth glorious to the imagination. . . . Love the truth, and then, for your people's good and for your own delight, make it as beautiful as you can.[11]

People of all ages love stories. They appreciate occasional glimpses into the personal life of the preacher. Humor delights them and the application of mundane everyday happenings to higher principles intrigues them. So I keep my eyes and ears open all day, everyday, not so much looking for sermon material as knowing that life around me is so rich that, as I draw from it, I will also have a rich resource from which illustrations should flow.

I have tried to walk you through the preparation of one particular sermon. In conclusion, let me mention two important considerations. The first is that I have illustrated the development of one kind of sermon; you could call it a doctrinal sermon. This book covers not only a number of needs for which help is available but also utilizes different styles of sermons which, of course, require slightly different preparation approaches.

Second, the sermon when prepared is like Ezekiel's bones which had so developed that "tendons and flesh appeared on them and skin covered them, but there was no breath in them." So Ezekiel prayed, "and breath entered them: they came to life and stood up on their feet—a vast army" (Ezek. 37:8-10). May it be so in all our preaching.

Notes

1. Related by Eric J. Alexander at the Spiritual Life Convention, Toronto, January, 1989.
2. D. Martyn Lloyd-Jones, *Preaching and Preachers* (London: Hodder and Stoughton, 1971), 190.
3. John R.W. Stott, *Between Two Worlds* (London: Hodder and Stoughton, 1982), 125,126.
4. W.E. Sangster, *The Craft of the Sermon* (London: Epworth Press, 1954), 22.
5. Craig Skinner, *The Teaching Ministry of the Pulpit* (Grand Rapids: Baker Book House, 1973), 95.
6. Richard Allen Bodey, ed. *Inside the Sermon* (Grand Rapids: Baker Book House, 1990), 188.
7. Ian Pitt-Watson, *A Primer for Preachers* (Grand Rapids: Baker Book House, 1986), 99.
8. Charles Haddon Spurgeon, *Lectures To My Students* (London: Marshall Pickering, 1989), 77.
9. Wallace E. Fisher, *Who Dares to Preach?* (Minneapolis: Augsburg Publishing House, 1979), 134.
10. Lloyd-Jones, *Preaching and Preachers*, 209.
11. Phillips Brooks, *The Joy of Preaching* (Grand Rapids: Kregel Publications, 1989), 132.

17

Stephen Brown, President
KeyLife Ministries, Key Biscayne, Florida
and Professor of Preaching
Reformed Seminary, Orlando, Florida

Illustrating the Sermon

It is said that Sydney Smith, the British clergyman and author who helped found the *Edinburgh Review,* was once praying out loud. A friend overheard him say: "Now Lord, I'll tell you an anecdote."

It is possible, I suppose, that the Lord did not want to hear the anecdote or that He was even offended—but I doubt it. You see, when He gave us His Book, He did not give us a list of doctrines, a confessional statement, a systematic theology, and an index. That is what we gave Him, and it is not a half bad gift to give to God when we get close to the truth. When He gave us His Book, He mostly gave us a Book of illustrations. Not only that, He created people who like and respond to stories.

Richard Pratt, my friend and colleague at Reformed Seminary, in his excellent book on Old Testament interpretation, *He Gave Us Stories,* talks about his consuming academic pursuit of Old Testament interpretation. He writes: "But more than this, it has been a driving spiritual quest since I came to know the mercy of God in Christ and realized that He gave us stories."[1]

He did, you know, give us stories.

It then behooves any communicator of a message from God to tell stories, too. No matter how accurate our truth or how deep our message, if there are no illustrations, we have missed the very clear methodology of God: to make truth relevant with stories that illustrate that truth.

Before we become practical about illustrating, let me give you a principle: *If you can't illustrate it, don't preach it.*

By that principle, I do not mean that every point must have an illustration, or that without illustration, God cannot use the preaching of His Word. However, by that I do mean that if you cannot think of an illustration—a person, a story, a situation to which to apply the truth—then the truth is at best irrelevant or at worst simply not true. Truth that does not apply to real life is not worth preaching.

One of the most terrible things happening in the modern church is the proclivity we have of acquiring knowledge without seeing the necessity of applying that knowledge. When I was in seminary (that was just after the Noahic flood), there was a rather bizarre theory that once the lay people in the church understood modern theological thought and biblical scholarship there would be some kind of renewal of the church. That sounded silly to me at the time, but I was, after all, only a young theological student with very little understanding of how God brings renewal.

At any rate, small study groups were formed in churches all over the country. Those study groups, with the sophisticated help of the informed pastor, studied large portions of the writings of modern theologians and biblical scholars. They were required to reduce those portions to ever decreasing paragraphs until the essence of modern theological thought was understood and expressed in a sentence or two.

Do you know what happened? Most of the study groups were still born, and those which survived spawned lay people who knew a lot about a lot of things but did not know what to do with what they knew. The questions were quite to the point: "So now that I know about the Graf/Wellhausen documentary hypothesis, what am I going to do about my guilt? Now that I understand Niebuhr and Barth, how can I handle my lust? Now that I am familiar with higher criticism, where can I take my loneliness?"

Whenever truth is taught, the preacher needs to ask: "So what?" If there is no answer, the preacher ought to go on to something else. If there is an answer, the preacher has the beginning of an illustration that will provide those who hear with a reality that the simple articulation of the truth never will.

Where Do I Find Illustrations?

Most illustrations come from life and from being sensitive to it. Bishop William Quayle once gave a sermon for preachers in which he named observation as one of the major tasks of a preacher. He said:

> When this preacher comes to a Sunday in his journey through the week, people ask him, "Preacherman, where were you and what saw you while the workdays were sweating at their toil?" And then on this preacher we may say reverently, "He opened his mouth and taught them saying: 'And there will be another, though lesser, Sermon on the Mount.' And the auditors sit and sob and

shout under their breast, and say with their helped hearts, 'Preacher, saw you and heard you that? You were well employed. Go out and listen and look another week; but be very sure to come back and tell us what you heard and saw.' "[2]

Every encounter with real people—every hurt heard, every occupation observed, every life lived—provides illustrative material for sermons. Someone had said that the art of writing is the art of observation. That is as true for the preacher as it is for the writer. Anyone can write a sentence, punctuate correctly, and use a dictionary to spell properly; but only those who observe life have anything to say. Ask God to make you sensitive to what is going on around you. Ask Him to make you an observer of what people say, think, and do. Then use what He has taught you.

While you are observing, do not forget to observe what goes on *in you*. Preachers cannot comment on the human race as an outsider. (Airports do not have separate bathrooms for men, women, and clergy.) After some twenty-eight years as a pastor, I have discovered that the things that frighten, tempt, and inspire me, frighten, tempt, and inspire nearly everyone else. As a result, I have found that one of the greatest sources of illustrations is myself and what is going on in my own life.

One time I was speaking in Chicago and was staying at the airport hotel. The next morning I woke up earlier than I had expected and decided to catch an earlier flight. As I was leaving the room, I picked up the travel alarm clock I carry with me and put it in my attache case. I forgot to turn the alarm off. The fact became apparent when the alarm went off at some thirty thousand feet in the air as we were on the way back to Miami.

Do you know all those calm, courageous people who say they are never afraid of flying? They do not exist. When the alarm went off, the man next to me who was reading the *Wall Street Journal* almost had a coronary, and the woman across the aisle screamed. The couple in front of me began to pray, and the woman behind me looked like she had seen a ghost. I learned something that morning. I learned that most folks are like me, and if I talk about what is going on inside of me, I will most likely be talking about what is going on inside of most other folks.

Another place to get illustrations is, of course, by reading. The preacher who does not read is going to be in some serious trouble. You ask: "What should I read?" Everything. Read the advertising on cereal boxes, read billboards, read magazines, and read every book you can.

One of the reasons many preachers "miss the mark" with the people in the pews is that we only read theology. If religious books and magazines are not a part of your reading schedule, then you will be bereft of the truth you need to apply. If your reading is exclusively theological, you will not know where to apply the truth you know and understand. There are, of course, certain experiences no preacher can experience without losing his or her job. However, you can read about those experiences and, by your reading, apply the truth you know to the reality of human experience.

Do not forget television and radio. I weary of preachers who are constantly on the war path with the media. As a former commercial broadcaster, let me tell you a secret: no industry is more sensitive to what people want than television and radio. Commercial broadcasting exists by finding out what people want and then giving it to them. I do not like that any more than you do, but it is a fact. Because it is a fact, the preacher who is not aware of what the electronic media are doing is going to miss the "real" place where people live. One of the best sources of illustrative material is in television and radio.

Another source of illustrative material is books of illustrations. I know, I know. Your homiletics professors told you that it was an abomination to use illustration books. The reason they told you that is they only had to preach one sermon a month, and they had already preached that sermon in ten different churches. If they had to turn out three or more sermons a week, they would buy every book of sermon illustrations they could find!

Most sermon illustration books are not very good, but if you get three or four good illustrations from a book, it is worth the price of the book. Of course, you should not put the illustration books in a prominent place on your library shelves. Prominence on library shelves should be reserved for Kittle and Keil/Deilitzch. Make sure that you keep—in a plain, brown paper wrapper if necessary—some good books of sermon illustrations.

The best resource I know for sermon illustrations is the people to whom you preach. Make it clear to your congregation that you would "sell your soul" for a good illustration, and those dear folks will become your research assistants. Not only that, they will enjoy hearing a story or quote they have given to you and that enjoyment will increase their desire to give you more. Preaching should never be a private affair. Real preaching involves the congregation, and one of the best ways to involve the congregation is to ask them to help you with finding sermon illustrations.

How Do I Store Illustrations?

The second practical question is this: How does one save and file sermon illustrations? As you know, there are very good computer software programs for organizing sermon illustrations, and may good books on preaching will give you a system for categorizing and filing illustrations. Let me suggest that you check out those systems and skip what follows because I am going to give you my system—and it may be the worst system of organizing sermon illustrations in the history of the church.

I carry a notebook almost every place I go and there is a section in the notebook for illustrations. When I read, hear, or observe something that would be a good illustration, I write it down in the notebook. When I use the illustration, I draw a line through the illustration I have used. "You mean, that's it?" Yes, that's it. I certainly do not suggest that it would work for everybody, but it does work for me and I am too old to change.

One of the interesting things about my system is that, in almost every case, the illustrations I have written down in the notebook are all used within a two or three week period. It is a constant source of fascination for me to see the illustrations I have written down become "just the right one" for a particular sermon I was working on at the time.

How Do I Use Illustrations?

Now let us turn to the final question: Once the preacher has the illustration and the truth of God's Word, how does he or she put the two together? I have ten principles I follow in using illustrations.

1. Good Illustrations Should Not Be Wasted.

If the illustration is better or more important than the point, do not use it. One of the dangers of illustrating a sermon is the danger of making the illustration more important than the truth that is being taught. Spurgeon's oft quoted comment that illustrations are windows to truth is a good one. However, no one wants to live in a house that has only windows.

Most preachers, after they learn the importance of illustrations and after they see the reaction of their people to the use of illustrations (especially if the preacher has not been using illustrations), have a tendency to become overly impressed with the power of the illustrations.

I can remember that happening to me. I was preaching a sermon without notes and I got to a particular point in the sermon that I could remember the story but not the point. I decided, at that moment, that I had been called to be a preacher and teacher of God's Word, and not a storyteller.

There is a dangerous proclivity in the heart of most preachers who know the power of a good illustration and make it fit the point—even it if does not. Like sin, one cannot completely get rid of this proclivity until glory. However, the frequency of its practice reflects a lack of concern with revealed, propositional truth. The road to hell is paved with stories without a truth.

2. Good Illustrations Suffer from Bad Illustrators.

Illustrating a sermon is an art. The art of illustrating is beyond the scope of this chapter, but let me say that the art of illustrating does not come easily or quickly. It is here that preachers need to listen for the reactions of the people in the pews.

I listen and watch for reactions to illustrations. I adjust my illustrative style to solicit a positive response from the people. Often, if I have a good story or illustration, I will try it out in normal conversation with my wife or some close friends to see their reaction. I take very seriously what people say about the illustrations I use.

The point of an illustration is to make a truth clear. If people do not like the truth, there is very little you can do. If they do not like (or perhaps "respond" would be a better word) an illustration, I need to change the illustration.

3. The Most Important Place for an Illustration Is in the Opening and Closing Moments of a Sermon.

When I was in commercial broadcasting, I learned the importance of a "stinger." A stinger is a phrase or a statement which causes the listener, at the beginning, to listen to a commercial and, at the end, to remember and be interested in what has been advertised.

That is as true for a sermon as it is for a commercial. The opening and closing illustrations are the first and final strikes of the hammer to the nail that one needs to drive. It is very important, it seems to me, that what one says in the first and last thirty seconds of a sermon be thought through very carefully.

The preacher who opens a sermon with, "Today we are going to study the Bible," will spend the first ten minutes of his sermon trying to get the congregation to even care about studying the Bible. The preacher who closes a sermon with, "Now let me review what we have learned . . ." will find that during that review the dear saints are already reaching for their coats. It is far better to have a "stinger" illustration, quote, or memorable story at the end. It has often been said that the beginning and the end of a sermon are the most important parts. The body of your sermon, where the meat is given to the congregation, is the most important part; however, from a communications standpoint, an illustration at both ends of a sermon can make a difference. In the beginning it can prompt a congregation to listen, and in the end it can cause them to remember what they have heard.

4. Good Illustrations Are Generally Short Illustrations.

If the illustration or story is long, special precautions must be used. When you have a long illustration you have used the most precious commodity you have in a sermon: time. A preacher must make sure that it is worth the investment, that it is a good story, that you do not make a mess of it when you use it, and that, when you have finished, the point you have made has been made clearly in the minds of the people.

If you "blow" a short illustration, it is not a great loss. You can make the point in another way or try another illustration. If you have committed a number of minutes to an illustration and you see, once you are committed that it is not working—you are stuck.

Let me give you some rules for using long stories or illustrations: First, make sure you have practiced it enough to be comfortable with it. Second, if you have to use notes in order to use a long illustration, you should not use it because you are not familiar enough with it. Third, memorizing a long illustration is not a bad idea.

5. Always Give Credit . . . But Not Always Specific Credit.

So many good illustrations are spoiled by an oversensitivity to naming the source. Preachers ought to have a tender conscience; however, a tender conscience often will destroy a good illustration. By the time proper credit is given to a good illustration, a preacher can lose the congregation. For instance, if I say: "Let me tell you a story I read in Sam Smith's book, *The Care and Keeping of Dogs,* that Dr. Smith got from Sara Sloan's book, *How to Bury a Dead Cat*. Dr. Smith tells, quoting from Sara Sloan, of a woman who loved. . . ." Do you see what I mean? Most folks do not care where you got it.

The only thing from an ethical standpoint that you have to do is to make clear that it is not your story. Saying, "Let me tell you a story I read the other day. . ." or "Someone has said . . ." or "There is a great story Sam Smith tells . . ." is sufficient. It is probably wise to note in your sermon manuscript or notes the complete source of the illustration, but do not feel constrained to do that when you are preaching.

6. Never Be Afraid to Share Illustrations.

It is a ministry to your fellow preachers. I love the fellowship of preachers. There is nothing I would rather do than to sit around with a group of preachers and share "war stories." However, illustrations are better than war stories. The best illustrations I get are from other preachers; and, I might say, some of the best illustrations they have are from me.

Illustrative material is never yours exclusively. The business of a preacher is to be a part of a glorious band who have been called to proclaim the truth. We are a team. If one basketball player refuses to pass to a team mate, that basketball player is going to be part of a losing team.

I can remember calling up a preacher acquaintance of mine and asking him for some details on a story I had heard him give in a sermon. Do you know what he did? He refused to help me with it. He said: "I worked hard for that illustration, and you should work hard for yours."

He certainly had the right to do that, but in life and in sermon illustrations, to whom much is given much will be required. Learn to share the gospel *and* good illustrations. God will bless you for both.

7. People Remember Illustrations Longer Than They Remember a Point.

Explain, illustrate, and then explain again. It is very important that what is illustrated is made very clear. Above, I said that an illustration more important than a point should not be used. This point is similar, but with a twist.

Over the last few years some people have come to think of me as a storyteller. I do not mind that reputation as long as the stories are remembered for the points they illustrate. I have a practice of saying to someone who has just complimented me on a story: "I'm glad you liked it. What did it say to you?" The answers I get can be embarrassing, both to me and the person to whom I direct the question, but the answers are revealing too. Those answers reflect whether or not those to whom I preach are "getting the point." If they are not, it is not their fault.

8. Historical Illustrations Require Historical Accuracy.

Poetic license can be used with most "common domain" stories, but not with history. There are thousands of generic sermon illustrations. You hear them all the time, and they can be effective. Not only that, those stories can be adjusted to fit material you are presenting.

For instance, you have probably heard the story of the preacher who asked his congregation how many were going to heaven. Not only that, he asked those who wanted to go to heaven to stand. One little boy remained seated and the preacher singled him out. "Son," he asked, "do you mean to say you don't want to go to heaven when you die?"

"Sure," replied the boy, "when I die. I thought you were getting a bunch together to go today."

That illustration can be adjusted. The little boy can become a little girl, the preacher can become a Sunday School teacher, and the emphasized point can be fear of death, hope of heaven, or the childlike requirement for the kingdom.

However, if your illustration concerns Martin Luther or Henry VIII, you have to check the facts and make sure you are accurate. One time I used a portion of a poem and named my source as Tennyson, when it had come from Browning. An English teacher in my congregation was so bothered that she got nothing more out of the sermon except the fact that I attributed the poem to the wrong poet. She, of course, should not have centered in on that fact, but human nature is easier to work with than against.

9. Care Must Be Given to the Use of Illustrations from the Bible.

My friend, Jay Adams, in his book *Preaching With Purpose,* says that preachers should not use biblical illustrations. He said:

> Now, one last comment. Many preachers use Scripture, especially the Old Testament, illustratively. Don't do it. Always use the Bible authoritatively; never illustratively. Scripture was not given merely to illustrate points; it was written to make points. If you don't pay attention to this warning, the first thing you know, you will find yourself making points you want to make and using (misusing) the Bible to illustrate and back up your ideas. Psychologizers do this all the time.[3]

This is a subtle temptation because those who use Bible illustrations think that, by doing so, they will become more biblical than those who, with Christ, talk about birds and flowers. Nowhere do New Testament preachers use the Old Testament illustratively; whenever the Bible is quoted, it is quoted as God's authoritative Word on the point at issue.[4]

While I would not be as absolute as Jay on this point, I think the point is well taken.

10. Illustrations Should Be Geared to the Congregation to Which They Are Given.

I do a daily radio program that is heard on a number of radio stations across the country. I record that program in a studio. After I had left the pastorate and began to teach at Reformed Seminary, I found that much of the Bible teaching I was doing on the broadcast was losing its reality. I started reading a portion of the letters that came in from the listeners. Because of the great volume of mail generated by the broadcast, I generally let the staff deal with the correspondence. However, somewhere I lost touch with the people God wanted me to teach.

Now, reading the letters allows me to adjust the truth I know to the people God asked me to teach. I am not against preaching behind a pulpit, but pulpits, if one is not careful, can become a barrier between you and people. If one's tradition requires standing behind a pulpit, one must work very hard at somehow breaking down that barrier.

Preaching is not just an act of worship between you and God—though it is that. It has to do with God's people. The point at which a preacher touches the people is at the point of a good illustration. If you cannot find a good illustration for a truth you are teaching, it probably means that you need to spend less time in the study and more time with your people. The incarnation is a good illustration of that point.

Illustrating may not be the most important aspect of preaching, but it is terribly important. After all, God did a fair amount of preaching and illustrating. But when He wanted to really make His point, He sent His Son who, among other things, is the consummate illustration. I sometimes forget the preaching of Moses, Isaiah, and Jeremiah; I have trouble on occasion remembering the wisdom of the Proverbs or the inspiration of the Psalms; but I can't get Jesus out of my mind. That's the nature of a good illustration.

By the way, did you hear the story about. . . .

Notes

1. Richard L. Pratt, *He Gave Us Stories* (Franklin, Tennessee: Wolgemuth and Hyatt Publishers, 1990), xvi.
2. Bishop William Quayle, quoted from Gerald Kennedy, *With Singleness of Heart* (out of print).
3. Jay E. Adams, *Preaching with Purpose* (Grand Rapids: Zondervan Publishing, 1981), 103.
4. Ibid.

18

James Earl Massey, Dean
Anderson School of Theology
Anderson, Indiana

Application in the Sermon

In homiletics, "application" involves the work of linking the import of the truth stated in the text and sermon with a hearer's situation and need. It is that section or sentence in the sermon that urges the acceptance of what has been stated, so the hearer will act upon its counsel. Simply put, "application" in the sermon points out the relation of what has been said to the hearer's life; it calls attention to how what has been spoken is to be used, and why it is important to do so. In his now-classic text *On the Preparation and Delivery of Sermons,* John Albert Broadus explained:

> Application, in the strict sense, is that part, or those parts, of the discourse in which we show how the subject applies to the persons addressed, what practical instructions it offers them, what practical demands it makes upon them.[1]

The application portion of the sermon can be an extended section within the conclusion. When this is so, it is usually an appeal that follows a restatement of the sermon focus, and it is a call for action based upon what has been thematically presented. It thus signals closure to the sermon and direction to the hearer.

Application can also be done by strategic sentences throughout a sermon. The best sermon organization will allow for this. Along with the usual principal parts of what homileticians refer to as "sermon organization" (for example, order, unity, proportion, movement, illustration, example, and interestingness), application-linkage places must also be considered. When sermon organization allows for these linkage places, application of the message can be immediate as the movement flows, and then intensified as the sermon closes.

General Guidelines For Application in a Sermon

1. First, any true application will be *related:* (a) to what has been said, and (b) to those who heard it said. It must link some truth or wise counsel with a person's life.

The relation between what has been said and the hearer's need should be immediately obvious. There should be no need for the meaning to be assumed; the direction must be immediately clear, so that all necessary action can be readily taken by the hearer who receives it with appreciation. Many examples of such immediacy and relation could be cited, but one might suffice to illustrate how this can be wisely done.

In his sermon, "A Sad Memorial" (1 Chron. 10:13-14), Gardner C. Taylor dealt with the grim problem of failed human potential, using the tragic downward career of selfish King Saul to illustrate it. In the sermon introduction, Taylor set the stage by quoting a maxim he heard his college president voice to him and his undergraduate classmates many years earlier. "What you are today will largely determine what you will be tomorrow." Taylor went on to qualify that college president's meaning:

> Now, this is not to say that tomorrow cannot be different from today. He said, rather, that tomorrow is largely, not solely, shaped by today. To be sure, tomorrow can be different.

Then, with a sense of immediacy, Taylor made an application of the president's point, saying pastorally: "We can change. Old habits can be beaten and banished from us. The grip of a bad disposition can be broken, and ugly ways can be transformed."[2] Still within the introductory section of his sermon, Taylor once more applied the wisdom of the saying he had quoted:

> We have got to stop letting ourselves off with our bad manners and impolite attitudes . . . you and I ought to be ashamed of being nasty, brutish, unfeeling, and savage in the way we talk to each other. We can do better.[3]

Actually, the wording in his initial application became the focal thrust within his sermon, and throughout the sermon the periodic link was evident between what one should be and what one must do in order to so become. In Taylor's sermon, the application-points are many; the places where he linked his message and the lives of its hearers are strategically interspersed, although he also closed the sermon with a fuller appeal for wise choices and action:

> Saul needed not to come to such an end. He had God and he had Samuel. He threw his chances away. Day by day he sank into ruin. We have less reason for such an end and such a memorial. We have Jesus Christ to make everything so much clearer.[4]

A sermon can be organized to allow application of its message all along the course of hearing, even though a full formal appeal is planned as part of the conclusion.

2. Whether intermediate or final, application in a sermon should always *summon to a decisive action*. One does not miss this in the preaching of Jesus. The conclusion of the parable of the good Samaritan is a case in point. Jesus, answering the listener who had raised the question about what being "neighbor" is supposed to mean, portrayed a neighbor as someone whose heart allows boundless deeds of mercy to flow from it in the direction of someone with needs. He then added the focal word of application after the parable: "Go and do likewise" (Luke 10:37, NIV).

Rightly understood, the application in the sermon deals with the true object of the sermon. As William Pierson Merrill explained it in the Lyman Beecher Lectures in 1922: "We need to bear in mind that in preaching the object is even more important than the subject. Every sermon aims at definite action. It is meant to make a difference in the lives of the hearers, or it is no true sermon.[5] The application helps the hearer of the sermon to keep that needed difference in focus.

3. The application, whether a sentence or larger section, should *grip and motivate the hearer*. The application is that point beyond argument or statement or illustration where appeal is made; it is that aspect of the sermon which addresses what to do and how to do it. It is that aspect of the sermon within and by which the hearer gains an immediate sense of what is both real and necessary, what is truly vital and important. It is that aspect of the sermon which helps to link the hearer's intellect with feeling, touching the heart by immediate appeal so as to stir a feeling about what is being said. Nothing base, unworthy, threatening, or manipulative is meant here; rather it is an honest and humane result of a truth-awakened, truth-stirred self that the preacher is hoping to achieve in his hearers. As John Henry Jowett expressed it: "Our ultimate object is to move the will, to set it in another course, to increase its pace, and to make it sing in 'the ways of God's commandments.'"[6]

4. Then, too, the application may either be *indirect* or *direct*. The debate continues concerning which approach is best, and homileticians are equally divided over the question. Actually, the same sermon might well include both approaches. There is in 2 Samuel 12 an instructive example of this. Nathan the prophet had to get behind King David's selfish intelligence and grip his conscience after his adulterous affair with Bathsheba—and his murder of her husband Uriah.

The prophet's approach began with a parable, the message of which allowed a disturbance to enter the king's mind under disguise; the prophet's intent was to stir the king's sense of moral outrage. He succeeded, and King David pronounced a judgment about the fate of the insensitive man described in the parable. Then came Nathan's courageous response—a direct application of why he had told the parable: "You are the man!" The message was initially shared by a story—an indirect method, while the application of the story was direct. The confrontation achieved its proper end.

A study of the predominant preaching method of Jesus (the parable form) shows that the Master was usually direct in applying His message. While we must recognize that some of the parables in the Gospels have been given a secondary setting (due to re-use for a changed audience), form critical studies have made evident the very fact that so many of the parable-messages still have a direct application in the secondary setting; this might well suggest that this method of Jesus has been transmitted with greater fidelity than one might otherwise think. Even when the framework of some Gospel narrative is secondary—and this is the case with so many of the Gospel parables as C. H. Dodd, Joachim Jeremias, and John Dominic Crossan have all studiously shown[7]—the intentional restatement of his message might well be accompanied by a restatement of the *method* used in applying it. If so, then His predominantly used method was direct application in preaching. The concern of Jesus was creative and constructive, even when the effect was at times confrontational. The direct approach was His way to ensure that the hearers of the parables would not only see the action within the dramatic parables but also sense God's demand upon their lives as a result of that seeing. Such is the purpose of application in preaching.

Persuasion as the End in Application

Application in the sermon, both throughout and as a concluding act, must be focused upon persuading the hearer—stirring the hearer of the sermon to act upon the truth that was shared. Persuasion is a key concern in the preaching task because pulpit utterance must have both its art and its aim. Preaching is deliberative, using both information and inspiration to achieve its end: acceptance of the Word and action because of its importance. All rightful handling of a text in preaching is motivational in the end.

Persuasion is based upon a shared understanding of the given Word. That understanding can be by statement, explanation, example, illustration, testimony, or guided pondering. A climax of impression is planned and attempted through the sharing. A call must finally be made to identify with the meaning and import of it all, so that the claim of the truth can be answered to the hearer's benefit. Very strategic in all of this is the kind of appeal the preacher has made in the handling of the text and its message.

Persuasion is usually linked with appreciation for the message one has heard. The appreciation will reflect an attitude of openness to the promise in that message, to the value sensed in it by the hearer. Appealing promise is a characteristic element in the gospel, since "good news" bids one to appreciate what can benefit the person.

Persuasion will involve the reason—which is why understanding must be fruitfully engaged in preaching. Persuasion will involve the emotions—since preaching at its best is a whole-person action that makes a whole-person claim upon another. What is first heard as the preacher's word is finally sensed as God's claim. It is by strategic application, at intermediate stages and in a formal closing appeal, that the claim of God is stated and the self is called upon to act with decisiveness on that claim.

There are many rhetorical means by which a final application can be made in a sermon. One means is to simplify it by direct statement about the significance of acting on the message one has heard. Another means is to amplify it, reinforcing the point of the message by dramatic examples of outcomes. Still another means is to dignify the message by a planned cadence of strategically ordered words and climax-building phrases, so that the zeal and enthusiasm of the preacher can speak even more warmly to the feeling-level of the hearer, "moving" them to identify fully with it all. This can be most important in stirring the hearer to a positive, personal, and passionate commitment to some truth one not only believes but also *feels*. Persuasion, then, not only involves comprehension but also contagion! One need only read Paul's sweeping rhetorical statement in Romans 8:35-39 about his experience of Christ to sense the extent to which this is so.

For Further Reference:

Merrill R. Abbey, *The Word Interprets Us: Biblical Preaching in the Present Tense* (Nashville: Abingdon Press, 1967); Aristotle, *Rhetoric and Poetics of Aristotle*, trans. W. Rhys Roberts and Ingram Bywater (New York: Modern Library Edition, 1954); Aurelius Augustine, *On Christian Doctrine*, trans. D. W. Robertson (New York: Library of Liberal Arts, 1958); John A. Broadus, *On the Preparation and Delivery of Sermons*, rev. ed. (Nashville: Broadman Press, 1944); Kenneth Burke, *A Rhetoric of Motives* (New York: Prentice-Hall, 1952); David Buttrick, *Homiletics: Moves and Structures* (Philadelphia: Fortress Press, 1987); James W. Cox, *Preaching* (San Francisco: Harper & Row, Publishers, 1985); Wayne C. Mannebach and Joseph M. Mazza, *Speaking From the Pulpit: A Guide to Effective Preaching* (Valley Forge: Judson Press, 1969); Henry H. Mitchell, *Celebration and Experience in Preaching* (Nashville: Abingdon Press, 1990).

Notes

1. John A. Broadus, *On the Preparation and Delivery of Sermons*, rev. ed. (Nashville: Broadman Press, 1944), 211.

2. Gardner C. Taylor, "Shaping Sermons by the Shape of Text and Preacher," *Preaching Biblically: Creating Sermons in the Shape of Scripture*, ed. Don M. Wardlow, (Philadelphia: Westminster Press, 1983), 137-152.

3. Ibid.

4. Ibid.

5. William Pierson Merrill, *The Freedom of the Preacher* (New York: Macmillan Co., 1922), 35.

6. John Henry Jowett, *The Preacher: His Life and Work* (New York: Harper and Brothers Publishers, 1912), 172.

7. C. H. Dodd, *The Parables of the Kingdom*, rev. ed. (London: Nisbet, 1961); Joachim Jeremias, *The Parables of Jesus*, rev. ed. trans. S. H. Hooke (New York; Scribner, 1963); John Dominic Crossan, *In Parables: The Challenge of the Historical Jesus* (New York: Harper and Row, 1973).

John Wesley (1703-1791)

"Preaching That Changed a Nation"

So remarkable was the preaching of John Wesley, it may have been the single greatest factor in averting revolution as Great Britain entered the Industrial Revolution in the Eighteenth Century.

Son of an Anglican priest and a devout Christian mother, the young Wesley went to America as a missionary to the Indians; within two years, he returned to England convinced of his own spiritual emptiness. Converted on May 4, 1738, at a Moravian service on London's Aldersgate Street, Wesley soon joined his friend George Whitefield in open–air preaching services.

Though his sermons included earnest pleas for moral living, the heart of Wesley's preaching was an invitation to personal religious experience. At a time when the cities were becoming ever more crowded, with unemployment common, and with industrial society declining, Wesley's preaching touched the hearts of tens of thousands of common people and offered them hope. Huge crowds—as many as 10,000 or 20,000 at a time—would turn out to hear this messenger of God's love and grace.

Few, if any, preachers have more faithfully given themselves to the proclamation of the gospel. He travelled Great Britain on horseback, covering some 20,000 miles a year, and preaching an average of 800 sermons annually. In addition to his own preaching, Wesley called out and equipped hundreds of Methodist preachers who would carry on and expand his own life's ministry.

The preaching of John Wesley was used to bring a powerful revival to Great Britain, and continues to influence and encourage those who preach today.

19 *Brian L. Harbour, Pastor*
First Baptist Church
Richardson, Texas

Concluding the Sermon

On the way home from church, the father asked his ten-year-old son what he thought of their new pastor. "I like this one better than the one we had before," the little boy said. "Why do you like him?" came the father's query. "Well," the boy explained, "this preacher said, 'In conclusion,' and he concluded. The other preacher said, 'Lastly,' and then he lasted and lasted and lasted!"

Many preachers have that problem. They make a strong beginning, develop a masterful outline, punctuate their message with vivid illustrations, and then destroy the impact of their message because they do not know how to bring the sermon to a conclusion. The twin dangers of finishing a sermon before it is done or finishing a sermon after it is done have destroyed many a pulpit venture.

Perhaps the reason for ineffective endings is a failure to understand how important the conclusion is. Andrew Blackwood once wrote: "Apart from the text, the most vital part of the sermon is the conclusion."[1] Being the last part of the sermon the listener will hear, the conclusion needs to summarize, restate, illustrate, or apply the sermon in such a way that the listener can take home the essence of the message. Effective preaching demands an effective ending.

After building the foundation of the sermon and having delivered the message of the sermon, how can we maximize the effect of our sermon in the conclusion? Let us approach the subject from both the negative and positive perspectives.

Pitfalls to Avoid

Before looking at some positive suggestions for concluding the sermon, let us approach the subject from the negative standpoint. We need to avoid some common pitfalls as we bring the sermon to its conclusion.

The Runaway Train

Some sermons are like a runaway train. They have tremendous power and move rapidly forward, but they never seem to end.

One worshiper, who slipped out of the early service, was asked by one of the people waiting for the second worship service: "Is the preacher through?" "The preacher is through," said the worshiper, "but he is not finished yet."

The most disastrous error in preaching is simply failing to plan how to conclude the message. When preachers make this error, the congregation might say to themselves: "If I ever get off this runaway train, I'm never going to get back on it again!"

The Triple-Double

The *triple-double* is a term used in basketball to describe an outstanding effort by a player in three different categories. For example, the player may have reached double figures in scoring, rebounding, and assists. That is referred to as a triple-double. In basketball, the term is a term of achievement.

In concluding a sermon, a triple-double is a perjorative term. A preacher scores a triple-double when he concludes the same sermon two or three times. Often, a preacher cannot decide which ending to use, so he opts out of his dilemma by including both of the endings.

Knowing what to leave out of a sermon is one of the most difficult parts of the homiletic process. Without proper preparation, a preacher can end up with a triple-double.

The Repeat

Sometimes, instead of summarizing the salient points of the sermon in the conclusion (see following), the preacher will preach the same sermon again. Perhaps the preacher is not satisfied with what he said earlier, so he tries to improve on it during the conclusion. Or, maybe, the preacher leaves out an important quote or a good illustration. The conclusion provides an opportunity to use the neglected material.

One of the greatest compliments a preacher can receive is for his people to say: "You said what you had to say and then you sat down!" Unfortunately, the people often say instead: "The preacher missed several good opportunities to quit!" Such ministers are guilty of "the repeat."

The Postscript

This is similar to the double-triple, except that in the postscript the preacher throws in all of the extra ideas and thoughts which he could not find a place for earlier in the message. Like a postscript in a letter, the postscript conclusion has little connection with the rest of the sermon and shows little organization. It is simply a hodgepodge of last minute thoughts.

One successful lawyer suggested he used only 20 percent of his research material in his presentation. Preachers should follow a similar practice. Many ministers mistakedly believe the congregation wants to hear everything they know. The result is the postscript conclusion.

The Form Letter

In one of my churches, worship planning was done according to a form. Worship followed the same order each week, and included the same ingredients. Worship planning consisted of filling in the blanks with the hymn number or the name of the anthem.

Some preachers use this method to conclude their sermons. They conclude every sermon in the same way every week. They simply fill in the blank according to the subject and text for the day.

Even if a person loves steak, he needs a change in his menu occasionally. Likewise, those who come to be fed God's Word desire and deserve some variety in the way the message is served to them.

Patterns to Follow

Effective preaching demands more than just avoiding the pitfalls discussed above. Positive patterns must be discovered and followed. Over the centuries, several different patterns have been used to bring sermons to a conclusion. Most are still valid methods for today.

Summarization

One of the most common ways of bringing a sermon to a close is to summarize the major points of the sermon or the central theme of the sermon. Repetition is one of the most revered methods of teaching. Repetition reinforces key ideas. Summarization adopts this proven teaching method.

I concluded in this way a sermon on John 13:34-35 entitled: "An Anatomy of Love." I began with an oft used anonymous poem which expresses the difficulty of love:

To dwell there above,
With those that we love,
That will be glory.
But to live here below
With those that we know,
That's another story.

In the sermon, I described four distinct demonstrations of love: encouragement, assistance, forgiveness, and appreciation.

In the conclusion I said: "Jesus gave us a new commandment to love one another. And if we will put into practice just the elements of love I have discussed today—encouragement, assistance, forgiveness, and appreciation—then we can change that ditty with which I began the service to say:

To dwell there above
With those that we love
That's the future story.
But to live here below
With those that we know
That's the real glory.

And we will not have to tell anyone we are Christians. They will know it by our love."

The value of summarization is that it reaffirms the major points of the message for the congregation. The danger is that many preachers repeat too much of the sermon in the conclusion rather than just summarizing the sermon's salient points.

Illustration

Another effective way to conclude a sermon is with an illustration or story. The concluding story will flesh out and paint a portrait of the central theme of the sermon or its main points. Illustrations are both windows and mirrors. An effective illustration will enable us to see the truth discussed in the sermon. An effective illustration will also enable us to see our own life as it compares with the truth discussed in the sermon. In either case, the illustration or story will imprint the message on the listener's mind.

I used this method to conclude a sermon on salvation. Based on Romans 6:23, the sermon was entitled: "The Plan of Salvation." I presented Romans 6:23 as God's plan for the salvation of mankind. In the sermon, I delineated the basis of God's plan, which is grace, and the instrument of God's plan, which is Christ. Then I presented the explanation of God's plan. I went to the New Testament for explanations of God's plan, pulling out several images used in the New Testament: the financial image in Mark 10:45; the military image in Colossians 1:13-14; the sacrificial image in Hebrews 9:11-12; and the legal image in Romans 8:1.

I concluded with the story, told in several versions, of the man who was on a bus heading for Florida. He had been in prison and was on his way back home. He did not know if his wife would accept him back so he gave her instructions to tie a white cloth on the old oak tree right outside of town. If he saw the white cloth, he would stop. If not, he would keep on going. As he approached the edge of town he spotted the tree. And tied to the tree were a dozen pieces of white cloth! Then I offered this concluding remark: "That is what God did on the cross. On the cross He left a message for sinners: I still love you, so come on back home!"

The value of illustration is that it visualizes the truth of the message in a way which will make an impact on the listener. The danger is that many preachers use an illustration which does not fit the sermon or one which is so long it swallows up the sermon.

Application

In a day when 42 percent of our inactive church members dropped out of the church because of irrelevant sermons, we need to learn to apply the sermon to the lives of our people. This can be done, and should be done, throughout the message. However, the conclusion provides a final opportunity to answer one of the three questions those in our congregation are asking: What can we do? Why should we do it? And, how can we do it?

I used this approach to conclude a sermon from Psalm 73 about human suffering. In the body of the message, I discussed some of the explanations for suffering in human life. I reminded the listeners of the similar struggle the Psalmist had with suffering. The question which arose naturally from the message is the question: "What then can we do about it?" Based on verse 28, I suggested three things in concluding the sermon. The Psalmist got as close to God as he could. That is, he deepened his relationship with God. He said: "But as for me, the nearness of God is my good." Then, he committed himself and his very life to God. As he put it: "I have made the Lord God my refuge." Finally, he proclaimed what a good God we serve. In his own words: "That I may tell of all thy works." This conclusion, which provided the congregation with some concrete steps to apply the message to their lives as they faced suffering, was an application of the message.

The value of application is that it brings the message from the biblical world into the contemporary world and provides answers to the what?, why?, and how? questions. The danger is that many preachers do not draw the application out of the truths of the text but out of their own personal convictions.

Exhortation

A method of concluding the sermon which is as old as Pentecost is to close the message with an exhortation. Luke told us: "Now when they heard this, they were pierced to the heart, and said to Peter and the rest of the apostles, 'Brethren, what shall we do?' And Peter said to them, 'Repent, and let each of you be baptized in the name of Jesus Christ for the forgiveness of your sins; and you shall receive the gift of the Holy Spirit' " (Acts 2:37-38, NASB). An exhortation is a challenge to respond, a call to do something specific in response to the message.

I used this method to conclude a sermon entitled: "What Every Person Needs to Know About God."[2] Acts 17:16-33 was my text. In Paul's sermon to the Athenians, he described God as an existing God, an eminent God, an embracing God, and an exacting God. The fourth point of the sermon was the conclusion. Using verses 30-31, I pointed out that this existing, eminent, embracing God makes a demand on our lives. What does He demand? He demands a choice. He presents His gift of love to us, and we must either receive it or reject it. He demands that choice. What makes this choice so urgent is that someday we will all stand before God and give an account of our lives.

When I preached the message I concluded like this: "Are you ready for that hour? You can be by aligning yourself with God's Son, Jesus Christ, and becoming a joint heir with Him to all of the glories God has prepared for those who love Him. Will you do it? Will you do it today?"

The value of exhortation is that it reflects the purpose of a sermon to motivate people to action. As Blackwood put it: "One difference between the sermon and the essay is that the essay entertains or instructs, whereas the sermon leads to moral and spiritual action."[3] The danger is that many preachers use manipulation and intimidation to try to force decisions instead of exhorting the congregation to simply respond to the truths presented in the message.

Versification

A popular method of concluding in the past, which is not in vogue as much today, is closing the sermon with a verse from poetry and hymnody. Much of the preaching I remember hearing as a youth was characterized by this method of conclusion.

I used this method to conclude a sermon on Jesus and even took the title for my sermon from the hymn I would use to conclude the message. The title of the sermon was "Hallelujah! What a Savior!" The text was Hebrews 2:1-4. In the introduction, I affirmed that the basic message of Christianity is the message of Jesus Christ. Then I presented several conclusions about Jesus. I suggested first that Jesus is history's inescapable fact. Then I described Jesus as the church's sole foundation. Finally, I presented Him as the sinner's only Savior. I concluded the sermon with these words: "When we realize again that salvation is made possible by Jesus Christ, by the love He had, by the life He lived, and by the sacrifice He made, then we know what the hymn writer meant:

> Man of sorrows, what a name
> For the Son of God who came
> Ruined sinners, to reclaim
> Hallelujah! What a Savior!

The value of this approach is that the words from some of the gifted poets and composers of the past express the central truths of Christianity in unique and distinct ways. The danger of versification is that many preachers do an inadequate job of speaking the poem or hymn. Such ineptness in presentation neutralizes the impact of the words.

Textualization

Preachers commonly begin with the text. The text is either read prior to the message or is introduced early in the message. Sometimes, however, a preacher can end with the text and allow the text to be the conclusion. I call this method "textualization."

I used this method of concluding in a sermon entitled: "The Ministry of Encouragement." My text was Hebrews 10:24-25. However, I did not begin with the text. I began with a story from Og Mandino's book, *The Greatest Miracle in the World*.[4] He told the story of Simon Potter who lived during the depression. Simon spoke of the ragpickers who picked up rags and other waste materials from the street to earn a livelihood. He explained that he was not that kind of ragpicker but a ragpicker who searched out waste materials of the human kind. I suggested that the greatest need in our world today is ragpickers of the human kind, men and women who major in the ministry of encouragement.

In the first point of the sermon, I pointed to Jesus as the model of this ministry of encouragement. Then I described the motivation for this ministry of encouragement, the low self-esteem which plagues most Americans today. Point three of the message was the method of this ministry of encouragement. How can we go about it? I presented two primary avenues: our communication (what we say) and our compassion (what we do). Ephesians 4:29 provided a basis to discuss how our words can encourage others. James 2:15-16 provided a basis to explain how our actions can encourage others. I concluded the sermon by saying: "By what we say and by what we do, we can once more become involved in the ministry described in our text: 'Let us consider how to stimulate one another to love and good deeds, not forsaking our own assembling together . . . but encouraging one another' " (NASB).

The value of textualization is that it magnifies the text by building up to it and allowing it to be the last words said. The danger in this approach is that many ministers present their opinions on various issues and then use the text to legitimize what they have said.

Which method is the best? Which method is the most effective? No single answer can be given to those questions. Each of the methods can be the best in certain situations. And each of the methods can be effective when properly used. The key is to vary your approach. Even if you feel most comfortable with one way of closing your sermon, use some of the other methods occasionally to break the routine and stimulate your people.

Principles to Remember

Choosing which method to use and which way to conclude your sermon is a challenging undertaking for most ministers. Keep the following principles in mind when deciding how to bring your message to a close.

The Conclusion Needs to be Appropriate

The conclusion needs to be appropriate for the occasion, for the crowd, and for the sermon. For example, if you choose the application method to conclude your sermon, make sure the application applies to the individuals in the congregation. If a central theme is sounded over and over throughout the sermon, the summarization method might not be as effective as using an illustration to conclude the sermon. If you choose the illustration method to conclude the sermon, make sure the illustration fits the understanding, interests, and experience of the listeners.

Here is the first guideline—when you have prepared your conclusion, ask the question: "Is this conclusion appropriate for the occasion, the crowd, and the sermon?"

The Conclusion Needs to be Clear

The conclusion needs to be understandable. If you use the exhortation method of concluding the sermon, the congregation needs to clearly understand what you are challenging them to do. If you conclude your sermon with an application, the conclusion needs to provide a coherent answer to the what?, why?, or how? questions. If you close the sermon with a verse, make sure the meaning of the words in the verse are comprehensible to the listener. Nothing destroys the impact of a conclusion faster than to have to explain what it means.

Here is the second guideline—when you have prepared your conclusion, ask the question: "Can everyone clearly understand what I am saying?"

The Conclusion Needs to be Personal

The conclusion needs to convince the listener that it was meant just for him or her. When a listener feels like you have been reading his mail, when she asks the question, "How did the preacher know I was struggling with this issue?", when the worshiper rejoices that he was at church to hear that message, then the conclusion has been personal.

Here is the third guideline—when you have prepared your conclusion, ask the question: "Will this touch the listeners where they really live?"

What a shame to destroy a well-prepared, Spirit-inspired, biblically-based message simply because we do not know how or when to stop!

Notes

1. Andrew Blackwood, *The Fine Art of Preaching* (Grand Rapids: Baker Book House, 1976), 125.
2. Brian L. Harbour, *From Cover to Cover* (Nashville: Broadman Press, 1982), 178-181.
3. Blackwood, *The Fine Art*, 134.
4. Og Mandino, *The Greatest Miracle in the World* (New York: Bantam Books, 1975).

20

James W. Cox
Professor of Preaching
The Southern Baptist Theological Seminary
Louisville, Kentucky

Evaluating the Sermon

The quality of preaching is basically a matter of the inner life. Those who deeply feel God's call possess the first qualification for effectiveness. This may appear to be too sweeping a statement, for we all know preachers who profess God's call, yet who do not fulfill our expectations, not to mention God's expectations and their own. Nevertheless, within that call lies the potential motivation for all the study, self-examination, prayer, and work needed for effective preaching. If we can assume those qualities, then we can go on to consider other—and very important—measurements of homiletical prowess.

This series of questions should prove helpful in evaluating your preaching.

1. Do Your Sermons Give a Fair Representation of All the Scriptures?

Some preachers limit their preaching to their own private canon—those texts they consider important to themselves. This means they preach mostly from the Old Testament, or exclusively from the New Testament, or from prophetic and ethical teachings of the Bible. Also, there are preachers who avoid—consciously or unconsciously—texts that might judge them; conversely, others might preach on texts that reflect preoccupation with a personal weakness the preacher might be struggling with or trying to hide.

Pastors would do well to check their preaching against the texts of a lectionary, such as the *New Common Lectionary,* to see if they are habitually neglecting important texts. Some pastors would do even better to preach systematically on the lessons in the lectionary, being assured that representative texts are getting a hearing, that they themselves stand under the judgment of the Scriptures, and that the hearers are getting a more comprehensive knowledge of the Bible.

Many have found it useful to preach straight through books of the Bible, alternating between an Old Testament book and a New Testament book. Such a series could begin with an introductory sermon on a main theme of the Bible book as a whole, then continue week by week, paragraph by paragraph, or chapter by chapter to the end.

There is no reason to believe that long-range systematic planning will limit the Holy Spirit. The series can be interrupted to take care of some obviously pressing sermonic need.

2. Does the Preaching Provide Systematic Treatment of Important Biblical Themes?

Expository preaching, important as it is, may not be able to do all that a sermon sometimes must do. Often the hearers need to see a doctrine treated systematically, that is, discussed from all important angles. No individual biblical text does just that. Thus it is necessary to bring together in a logical fashion all of the Bible teaching about that doctrine and perhaps even relate it to, let us say, what philosophy, sociology, or science might contribute to our discussion.

This question can be answered in the affirmative if the preacher preaches a single sermon on the particular teaching, giving a comprehensive treatment; or, if the preacher presents a series of messages that give a fair account of the various aspects of the teaching.

3. Is the Preaching Relevant to Present Needs of the Hearers?

It is easy to make sermons that sound very biblical and that therefore, seem to be authentic preaching when they actually are not authentic preaching. Sermons can be full of material from the Bible and fail as sermons. Why? They are mere historical recitations and lectures. Everything said in them may be important in its own place and even in a certain context in an authentic sermon; but, to qualify as real preaching, the sermon has to connect with life today.

This is not to say that a sermon must always be immediately or obviously relevant. Some sermons are cumulatively and hiddenly relevant. Still, preachers ought to ask: Why am I preaching this sermon? What am I saying that will make a real difference in the lives of the people who hear me, if they take my message seriously?

Some preachers have discovered that bringing together a group—

perhaps a committee—from the congregation to discuss the text with the pastor on a regular basis will uncover relevance and heighten interest. Other preachers have formed homiletical study groups with their fellow pastors and have not only found the congenial fellowship stimulating, but also have been the recipients of fresh insights, pointed applications, and apt illustrations.

4. Does the Preaching Reflect the Preacher's Own Involvement with the Message?

In theory, it is possible to preach so that anyone—even an atheist—could preach the sermon just as well as the preacher. In other words, the preacher might be little more than a town crier who hardly listens to what he is saying and could care less. No doubt there will be times when the preacher, who ordinarily wrings sermons from the soul entwined with the Bible, will feel cold and detached. Such preachers should not feel guilty that there are dry spells, that dark nights of the soul come and impair one's customary sense of inspiration and fervor.

Yet Phillips Brooks was at least partly right when he defined preaching as "truth through personality." Truth came through the personality of our Lord Jesus Christ, and, though it is an awesome thought, truth may come through our own personalities as preachers of the same Christ.

Admittedly, the way we live, the carelessness with which we throw together our sermons, and our indifference to genuine human need can obscure the truth, distort it, and hold it up to ridicule. An important aspect of the preacher's task is to be not only proclaimer, prophet, or teacher, but also *witness,* so that the hearers recognize *that* the preacher believes as well as *what* the preacher believes.

5. Does the Sermon Have a Clearly Stated Central Idea?

A sermon needs unity, and a clearly stated central idea can give it—provided it is brief and the preacher pays attention to it in developing the sermon from start to finish. The central idea is simply what the sermon says—no more, no less. We sometimes call it the theme, the thesis, the proposition, or the gist of the message.

Use the simplest words that will convey the thought accurately. Get rid of as many qualifying words, such as adjectives and adverbs, as you can conveniently omit; there will be the entire sermon to expand this generic, generating idea. Reduce the statement of the central idea, if possible, to one sentence.

This central idea should be in your thoughts as you sketch out your sermon and/or write it in full. Whether you begin with the idea and proceed to unpack it in a deductive sequence, or whether you move toward the idea step-by-step as the last idea in an inductive process does not really matter. What is important is that it is a controlling factor—it will not permit the sermon to go astray in meaningless, though perhaps tempting, digressions.

It will not be necessary to state the central idea formally, whether it comes first or last as a creative force in the sermon. However, it may be desirable to state it at one point or the other. If your sermon is a teaching message, you might help your hearers by stating directly what you propose to explain, develop, elaborate, or apply. If your sermon is an argumentative message, you might boldly state what you propose to prove. In any case, as to the central idea—do not leave your study without one!

6. Does the Sermon Have a Sharply Defined Aim?

A central idea without a definite aim is like a ship without a rudder, a car without a steering wheel, an arrow without a target. Now it is true that one sermon will sometimes serve several aims, whether on purpose or not. The sermon ought to do its work more surely if one specific aim dominates, while other aims perhaps fulfill subordinate goals.

What should a sermon do anyway? It can inform, or it can explain something; it can prove something; it can edify the hearers (that is, build up and revitalize them); it can move them to action. Choose one of these aims. Let it dominate your approach to your subject and your audience, and it will determine the form the sermon takes, the type of illustrations you use, your word choice and style, and the way you deliver your message. This will save you and your hearers from wandering in a homiletical wilderness and never entering the land that your sermon title promises.

7. Do the Sermons Let Both the Content of the Message and the Nature and Needs of the Hearers Suggest Variety of Structure?

Some preachers jam most, if not all, of their sermons into the same homiletical mold—thus the old cliché about "three points and a poem."

Given the variety of texts as to both form and content, and given the variety of human personality and need, there is no excuse for sameness in structural approach. Indeed, as to the form of the biblical text, the sermon in some cases might find additional strength in following the configuration of the text. For example, if the text is a question, perhaps the sermon should take an interrogative approach throughout.

In any event, here are some basic structural forms, among other approaches, that offer solid biblical content and potential variety.

The best expository preaching finds a center of gravity in a text—a central idea—and lets that become the organizing principle for the entire sermon. The central idea may focus on one verse, one phrase, or even one word. What makes it an exposition is that it exposes and emphasizes the content of the passage on which it is based.

The best thematic preaching is broadly biblical but does not necessarily focus on one text. It may, as we have seen, systematize the teachings of various parts of the Bible. It may, as well, deal logically with some philosophical issue not explicitly biblical, yet a matter of Christian concern. Also, it may come to expression in a psychological structure with all the dynamics of a sales transaction, after the fashion of Alan Monroe's "Motivated Sequence" or Eugene Lowry's "Homiletical Plot."

This leads directly to the question: What about narrative sermons—sermon as story? The method is as old as the Bible and as modern as sermons heard increasingly from contemporary pulpits. It is a fad; it is not a fad—both are true. However, it must be said that the preacher who routinely ignores the power and possibilities of story—both as vehicle for the entire sermon and as illustrative material—is less than biblical and more than shortsighted.

A mere narrative—that is, a string of events—will not suffice. Tension, the power of drama, must be present to transform the narrative into a story—a story with characterization and attendant interest in the people with whom the hearers can identify and thus relive their own experience.

8. Does the Sermon Follow a Definite Logical or Psychological Progression?

It was said of the sermons of the old Scottish preacher Thomas Chalmers that they moved on hinges rather than on wheels. In other words, they went nowhere! His sermons were powerful in their own way, but in spite of, not because of their arrangement.

Some examples of logical arrangement would be: past, present, future; then, always, now; inner, outer; symptoms, disease, remedy; problem, solution; not this, but this; thesis, antithesis, synthesis. Examples of a psychological arrangement would be Alan Monroe's "Motivated Sequence": Attention Step, Need Step, Satisfaction Step, Visualization Step, and Action Step; and Eugene Lowry's "Homiletical Plot": Upsetting the Equilibrium, Analyzing the Discrepancy, Disclosing the Clue to Resolution, Experiencing the Gospel, and Anticipating the Consequences.

Sometimes both the logical and the psychological will combine in one sequence.

9. Does the Sermon Use a Variety of Developmental and Supportive Material?

This question has to do with what is popularly known as *illustration.* Many sermons fail, not because they are not based on sound exegesis, not because they are not arranged carefully or because they are not expressed precisely. They fail because preachers often take the people for granted. They use few or no examples to illustrate what they are talking about or to emphasize its reality, few or no comparisons to throw light on the subject.

If the preacher is using a narrative text, it may not be necessary to go outside the text itself for concrete, graphic material. A preacher with imagination can find most of the best examples and illustrations in the texts themselves—texts like The Parable of the Prodigal Son, Jacob Wrestling with the Angel, or The Call of Isaiah.

Various writers and preachers have found the following types of material indispensable in all kinds of public speaking, including preaching.

Restatement simply reiterates a thought in other words, perhaps in several sentences until that thought has a chance to be understood or properly felt. As the preacher piles sentence upon sentence, the original assertion goes deeper and deeper into the thought processes or the emotions. The ideas expressed are the same, but the words are different.

Examples give concrete instances of what the preacher is saying. They may be as brief as a word or as long as a story. Ingratitude may be exemplified by the mere mention of a thankless child or by telling the story of The Ten Lepers in the Gospel of Luke.

Comparisons help people to understand or appreciate certain truths. They are not examples or instances but they often make an idea more credible or impressive. A comparison may be as simple as a simile that says our sins are as scarlet, or it can be as elaborate as an analogy, perhaps a speech that makes numerous points of comparison, telling us: "Life is like a football game." The parables of Jesus fall into this category, with their (usually) one-point comparisons.

One minister takes the congregation on a scenic journey with interesting characters and events, and the congregation lives through the experiences, with laughter and tears, inspiration and suspense, faith and doubt. The sermons seem to be about a real God and real people! In contrast, another minister takes the congregation on a relentless trek across a parched desert of theological abstractions, and God seems to get lost in a sandstorm of propositions. Which preacher, do you think, will receive the best hearing?

10. Can the Hearers Identify in Ethically and Religiously Significant Ways with the People in the Stories and with the Allusions?

Some stories stimulate interest and support but do not cause the listeners to see themselves in the stories. The listeners may be caught up in the dynamics of the drama without experiencing any important new learning, believing, feeling, or decision making.

To begin with, a story, whether factual or fictional, must possess verisimilitude; that is, likeness to truth. Fiction, even in a sermon, is a legitimate literary device, provided that it is not represented as factual. Some, if not all, of Jesus' parables were probably fictional; if so, the hearers understood they were not factual, though true in another, more profound sense. If a story is not believable, then the preacher has no credibility and the message goes begging.

A preacher can tell the story of the prodigal son in such a way that a bitter, grudging father could have his hard heart softened and turn toward a wayward son or daughter with compassion and forgiveness; or a wayward son or daughter could dare hope that forgiveness from those they have hurt is possible; or a jealous, self-righteous person like the elder brother in Jesus' parable could see that he may be a greater sinner because of his resentful, unforgiving attitude toward his repenting brother. A father, then, could say: "If God can forgive us who sinned against Him, I ought to be able to forgive my own child." A penitent son or daughter could say: "I've made a mess of things, but there is hope for me." A pharisaical person could say: "This hits me right between the eyes. I need to get off my high-horse and think about how other people hurt and hope."

Storytelling is an art, but an art that can be learned. Learning to live into or feel into a biblical incident or a contemporary life-situation is a matter of sympathy, resentment; love, hate; hope, despair; courage, defeat—emotions that one feels when entering into the house or getting under the skin of another person.

11. Does the Sermon Use a Variety of Sentence Types?

Our problem here may be a tendency to say everything in declarative sentences—one statement after another, with no relief whatever from an occasional question. Isn't the use of questions truer to real life? Doesn't it make the sermon more like a conversation? It would be ironic, wouldn't it, if preachers known as delightful conversationalists, who know how to carry on interesting dialogue, give the impression when they preach that they are always laying down the law, even suggesting that their every statement carries the weight of "Thus saith the Lord"?

In everyday speech, we use a wide variety of sentence types: long sentences, short sentences, fragmentary sentences, exclamations, complex sentences, compound sentences, simple sentences. Preachers who know what they want to say discover unusual help as they look into the faces of their hearers and read their expressions. They learn how to say things differently as they enter into conversation with these increasingly involved and interested listeners.

12. Is the Language Clear and Understandable?

The problem: sermonic language is often technical, academic, literary, or just fuzzy. When I was a student in seminary, I went to hear a scholarly preacher in one of the leading churches near that seminary. A personality profile in a local newspaper reported that this preacher usually spent twenty hours each week on his Sunday morning sermon. I loved the carefully constructed intellectual sermons, but I noticed that few people listened: men and women gazed out an open window, thumbed through hymnbooks, yawned and dozed, and seemed to welcome any and all distractions. As I reflected on what I had witnessed on several occasions, I concluded that nothing was wrong with the content and structure of the sermons; the problem was with the word choice, the language. Heavy academic theological terms sank the homiletical ship for nonseminarians.

Rudolf Flesch, Robert Gunning, and others have proven that simple, mostly Anglo-Saxon words can express with clarity, color, power, and beauty almost anything we wish to say. Still, there are many words that come from the Latin element in our language that are just as clear as the Anglo-Saxon, words like *color* and *beauty*. Oversimplification is much to be preferred to denseness, provided that we do not falsify the matter under discussion.

13. Is the Language Concrete and Sensuous?

Professor H. H. Farmer noted that a lack of concreteness is one of the worst faults of sermons. These sermons make no appeal to the senses. The listeners hear words strung together in abstract arguments or explanations, but the sermons do not engage and involve the listeners in vital ways.

To talk about the Bible in this way seems strange when we consider that the Bible, our primary textbook, is very concrete: "I John saw the holy city, new Jerusalem, coming down from God out of heaven, prepared as a bride adorned for her husband" (Rev. 21:2). "God heard their groaning, and God remembered" (Ex. 2:24). "He smelled the smell of his raiment" (Gen. 27:27). "Suffer me that I may feel the pillars" (Judg.

16:26). "I did but taste a little honey with the end of the rod" (1 Sam. 14:43) "I am tormented in these flames" (Lk. 16:24). "He casteth forth his ice like morsels: who can stand before his cold?" "If thou hast run with the footmen and they have wearied thee?" (Jer. 12:5).

Such is the language of the people—most of them. The good news of Jesus Christ is told in such terms in the New Testament, just as the mighty acts of the Father in the Old Testament are made known. It does make sense that if we are in the same business today we should take seriously the way in which our biblical predecessors conveyed their message.

14. Does the Language Achieve the Desired Emotional Effect?

The gospel is good news, and as such, it should be proclaimed in words that confirm its positive, healing, cheering message. There are exceptions, of course. In this world we see unhappiness, fear, suffering, and death—not very bright subjects but matters that we have to deal with from the pulpit. Sin and injustice are real, and the preacher who ignores them is not a friend to the people.

The issue here is a matter of control, of saying what we intend to say the way we intend for it to be received. Consider the preacher who makes every sermon sound like a funeral dirge. These words and phrases appear constantly: death, judgment, mourning, weeping, desert, famine, pain, despair, defeat, loneliness. Why does the preacher do this? In this case, he may never have experienced deeply the liberating power of the gospel and the joy of the Spirit. His life may be lived mostly under law, rather than under grace. He may actually be seeking company for his private, somewhat unregenerate misery. Thus the emotional effect may be more or less what he desires. Should he desire it? Is it Christian?

John Wesley said we should preach faith until we have it. Consider the radiant words that tend to stimulate faith, hope, and courage, words like *love of God, joy, surprise, laughter, smile, feast, cheers, kindness, friendship, music, and dancing*. The language of Scripture is so often the language of celebration, from the rejoicing in the Psalms to the hallelujahs in the Book of Revelation.

It is true, the Bible does speak of the cross, of sufferings, but through and in it all, of joy and glory.

15. Are the Sermons Delivered in a Manner that Best Communicates the Message?

The preacher's delivery, apart from the words, can convey its own message. An evangelist I heard years ago knew that and apologized repeatedly in his sermons for his harsh voice, which he knew sounded angry. This enabled the hearers to make mental adjustments and allowances. Some preachers, however, seem unaware of the impression they create. To smile broadly while talking about divine judgment could suggest that the preacher is sadistically enjoying the prospect of sinners suffering for their sins or that the preacher is making a joke of the entire matter.

It may be asking too much to expect the average preacher to be able to express a kaleidoscopic variety of emotion with hair-trigger responses to subject matter and audience, but is it too much to expect that the preacher's body language confirm the gospel as good news, and judgment as bad though reliable news?

16. Is There Creativity and Reciprocity in the Act of Delivery?

This question would seem to suggest the need to preach without a manuscript, perhaps even without any visible notes. Creativity implies struggling with words and ideas in the very moment of delivery. Reciprocity implies eye contact with listeners and paying attention to their body language.

Preaching can be a chore, or it can become an event. The preacher can help the listeners to feel they are a part of the sermon; and, while that is happening, the preacher will sense the joy of creativity. Transcripts of Augustine's sermons, I am told, indicate that Augustine would sometimes let the presence of a particular person in his congregation lead him into what we would consider a digression, but which no doubt was the preacher's effort to deal faithfully with a real situation. Charles Spurgeon's account of his own conversion describes how a lay preacher, reading the misery written on the face of a teenage boy, said a word so personal and direct that young Spurgeon responded in a commitment that changed his life. Spurgeon compared some sermons to sheet lightning, which fills the sky with its brightness but which hits nothing. Other sermons, he suggested, are pointed and, like daggers, strike their object with telling effect.

This is not to suggest that the ideas and language have to await the moment of delivery to be born. Far from it! Preachers who are thoroughly saturated with the ideas, who follow a viable sequence for these ideas, and who have at their command multiple ways of expressing their thoughts—these are preachers who will have the freedom and sensitivity necessary to engage in "dialogue" with those who hear them.

17. Does the Speaking Voice Receive Proper Attention and On-going Care?

Attention to the voice does not imply the development of what has been termed a "ministerial tone." Even in the nineteenth century, two highly visible and successful preachers received plaudits for the naturalness of their delivery. It was said that evangelist Dwight L. Moody talked to people from the pulpit in something of the same manner in which earlier as a shoe salesman he had talked with people about shoes. London pastor Charles Spurgeon spoke in a conversational style to his five thousand congregants, though it was obviously conversation "enlarged." No doubt their being "real" contributed to the popularity of these two preachers.

On the other hand, there are, in some cultures, certain audience expectations that make acceptable a style of delivery that is more like singing than speaking. Who is to say that this is unacceptable, since it is obviously accepted and celebrated? At the same time, who is to say that a different style would not be more acceptable and ultimately more effective given exposure and a ripening appreciation?

In any event, the preacher should speak clearly, which means that there must be no swallowing of words at the back of the throat, no slurring in pronunciation. Such faults can be detected by the offenders themselves, by listening to recordings of the voice in the actual event of preaching. Then a program of reading aloud, privately, with special effort to carve out the consonants should gradually carry over into public speech, especially if the preacher practices in everyday conversation.

18. Is the Sermon an Event in Which the Holy Spirit Is Truly at Work?

All the homiletical mechanics and techniques are of no lasting avail if God is not somehow at work in what the preacher does. For our comfort, if not for our complacency and laziness, it is heartening to know that throughout the ages God has overruled and used human inadequacies to get His work done. To challenge us, but not to discourage us, it is sobering to consider that more people could have been helped and brought to God if we who preach had paid more attention to what and how we preach.

19. Does the Preaching Exalt Jesus Christ?

All of our preaching ought to be an effort to catch up to the exaltation that God has already given to His Christ, so that people may know what God has done and what this eternal God is like and is doing.

21

Ronald Allen
Professor of Preaching
Christian Theological Seminary
Indianapolis, Indiana

Preaching and the Christian Year

The preacher seeks for the gospel to be born and reborn in the listening community. The Christian Year—and its frequent companion, the lectionary—can be important midwives to preaching for they provide themes and biblical texts which help the gospel to give birth in the hearts, minds, and wills of the congregation.

I will first review the background, purpose, and relationship of the Christian Year and the lectionary. I will then point to the Christian Year and the lectionary as helps and hindrances to the preacher.

The Christian Year

The Christian Year (sometimes known as the Church Year or the Liturgical Year) is an annual calendar which brings to consciousness many leading aspects of the Christian faith. As the twentieth century draws to a close, an increasing number of congregations in many denominations and movements follow it.

From the dawn of human consciousness, people have yearned to know the significance of the passing of time. What can we count upon? Mircea Eliade points out that human beings feel anxious and fearful when time passes without interpretation. Eliade refers to this dread as the "terror of history."[1] Terror increases when human survival is precarious and when random events of suffering and evil befall the community. One of the major functions of religion is to assure the community that time (and hence the continuation of human and cosmic life) is not chaotic and threatening but is orderly, meaningful, and trustworthy.[2]

The calendar and rites of worship help the community live in time with a sense of purpose and freedom.[3]

The religion of the ancient Hebrews and their descendants invested time with meaning. The observance of the Sabbath was a foundation of Jewish life. The Sabbath was a weekly reminder that the world is created and tended by a loving God. Major festivals dramatized God's providence through the cycles of nature (for instance, Feast of Weeks, Feast of Booths) as well as God's redemptive presence in history (for instance, Passover, Day of Atonement, Purim).

The earliest Christians initially followed Jewish patterns of worship. Soon Christians began to develop their own rites. They took with them Jewish notions of God's providence and presence (as experienced through Jesus Christ). They also adapted themes from the larger religious environment of the first centuries of the Common Era.[5]

Sunday, "little Easter," was the first component of the Christian Year to emerge (see 1 Cor. 16:2, Acts 20:7, Rev. 1:10) because it was the day of Jesus' resurrection. The observance of Sunday as a day of worship and teaching is the foundation of the Christian Year.[6] In the midst of the principalities and powers, Sunday reminds us of God's promises, presence, and purposes as revealed through Christ.

Easter was the first Christian festival and was observed annually as early as the second century. It quickly became an occasion for baptism. By the fourth century, the church had gathered other days and periods around Easter—Good Friday, Palm Sunday, Maundy Thursday, Holy Saturday (the day before Easter), and periods of fasting.[7] Lent emerged as a forty-day period of preparation for Easter with a double focus: as a time of preparation for baptism and as a period of fasting and penitence.

The church regarded the fifty days after Easter as an extended celebration of the resurrection climaxed by the day of Pentecost. Pentecost flows integrally from Easter to show that the power revealed in the raising of Jesus is continually in the church. Thus, today we think of the worship which stretches from Ash Wednesday (the first day of Lent) through Pentecost as an Easter cycle, a single complex of movement and meaning.

The earliest Christians discerned revelation in Jesus' life and teaching and in the incarnation. This interest reached liturgical expression with the commemoration of Christmas. The church attached Advent to Christmas and transformed the meaning of Advent. Advent was originally focused on Jesus' return in glory but when joined to Christmas, it added a sense of preparation for Christmas. Eschatological emphasis persists as the first Sunday of Advent anticipates Jesus' return. Hence, Advent is a transition season which is both the climax and the beginning for the Christian Year.

The western church placed Epiphany (from Greek, "manifestation") twelve days after Christmas. Epiphany points to Christ as a manifestation of God's grace. Advent through Epiphany is a Christmas cycle.

This accounts for all but two periods of the Christian Year: the weeks after the days of Epiphany and Pentecost. These weeks interpret the significance of God's presence, purpose, and power and the great events of redemption for daily life (ordinary time).

The Christian Year as a Guide to Preaching

The Christian Year is governed by Christology. The Year teaches those who do not know the Christian story. It reminds those who forget aspects of it. Those who follow the story year after year often discover riches which they have previously missed.

Each season lifts up parts of the story: anticipation of Jesus' coming (Advent), incarnation (Christmas), manifestation (Epiphany), preparation for baptism and Jesus' death (Lent), resurrection (Easter), life in the Spirit (Pentecost), growth in discipleship and witness (Ordinary Time), and return in glory (Advent).

The sermon refracts the gospel through the lens of the season. During Christmas, for instance, the message draws the congregation to consider the significance of Jesus' incarnation. The preacher does not just preach a biblical text but asks: "How does this text illumine the season?" and "How does the season illumine the text?"

The Lectionary

A lection (from Latin, "to read") is a single reading from the Bible. A lectionary is a collection of readings from the Bible which are systematically joined together as a basis for preaching, teaching, or devotional meditation. The observance of the Christian Year is often accompanied by the use of a lectionary.

Lectionaries are usually organized according to one of two patterns. (1) *Lectio continua* (continuous reading). The readings proceed sequentially through a book of the Bible. Peter Bower calls this a beeline approach.[8] (2) *Lectio selecta* (selected reading). The readings are drawn from various books of the Bible in order to support the main themes of the lectionary. Peter Bower refers to this as a leapfrog approach.[9]

Most historians of the lectionary think that Judaism used a lectionary by the beginning of the Common Era.[10] This lectionary probably combined both *continua* and *selecta,* calling for the continuous reading of the Pentateuch over three years with a discrete pericope from the prophets (*haftarah*) selected to accompany the individual readings of the Pentateuch.

By the fourth century (and perhaps much earlier) the church developed lectionaries. These usually combined *selecta* and *continua.* Some readings developed as traditional in connection with specific days. However, the components of the various lectionaries varied from the fourth century to the Reformation.

Three approaches to lectionary use emerged from the Reformation. (1) The Roman Catholic, Lutheran, and Anglican churches solidified use of selected lectionaries. (2) The radical Reformers almost exclusively adopted continuous reading. (3) Calvin combined the two, preferring continuous reading but selecting lessons for particular celebrations.

A common theme permeates the development of lectionaries: the lectionary is the servant of the gospel and the purpose of the church. A lectionary is not an end in itself but is a way of helping the church stay in touch with dimensions of the Christian tradition which are essential for the identity, life, and witness of the Christian community.

Two factors spark the current surge of interest in the Christian Year and the lectionary: (1) the growth of the ecumenical movement and the search for Christian unity (even among churches who do not participate in the ecumenical councils); and (2) the lectionary reform initiated by the Roman Catholic Church following Vatican II which was first published in 1969. The Roman Catholic lectionary of 1969 was modified by the Consultation on Common Texts, an interdenominational body, and was issued in 1983 as the Common Lectionary[11] and revised in 1991 as the Revised Common Lectionary.

The Common Lectionary is organized in a three-year sequence with each year centering around a different synoptic Gospel (Year A: Matthew, Year B: Mark, Year C: Luke). The Gospel of John is interspersed. Three readings are appointed for each Sunday: one from the Hebrew Bible—except at Easter when this reading is replaced by one from the book of Acts—one from a Gospel, and one from an Epistle (or other document from the canonical literature from the hand of the earliest churches). A Psalm, intended principally for liturgical use, is also assigned. Any text(s) can serve as the basis for a sermon.

The Christmas and Easter cycles are structured as *lectio selecta* while Ordinary Time is structured as semi-continuous reading. Thus, in the Christmas and Easter cycles, the Gospel reading strikes the main notes for the day with the other readings in support. In Ordinary Time this principle gives way to semi-continuous reading of the Gospel, of Epistles, and of sections of the Hebrew Bible. In Ordinary Time, the lessons seldom interrelate.

The Christian Year and the Lectionary as Helps to Preaching

The most important value of the Christian Year and the lectionary is this: they help the church to sense God's continuous presence and to see who we are (loved unconditionally by a gracious God) and what we are to do (witness to God's love and justice).[12] The great themes of the year thus lead us to live freely and purposefully in the present and to greet the future with openness and trust.

The Christian Year and the lectionary center on God's promises and initiatives and thus help guard the church against moralism and works righteousness. At the same time, the Year and its readings reinforce the qualities of personal and social life which flow from Christian identity (ethics).

Christians live in the midst of many calendars, for instance, the calendar year, the fiscal year, the academic year, the agricultural calendar, and the Christian Year. The Christian Year does not coordinate precisely with other calendars and thus helps the church realize that we live by a system of values which transcend the world.

The Christian Year and the lectionary tell the story of Jesus. We thus continually rediscover that the event of Jesus Christ is the doorway through which the Christian community comes to God. Although some criticize the Christian Year and the lectionary as excessively Christocentric, we need to keep in mind that every good Christology is ultimately theocentric.

Most lectionaries bring the Hebrew Bible into the consciousness of the congregation. This helps us remember and be instructed by our Jewish heritage. It works, also, to correct Christian tendencies to ignore or to misrepresent Judaism.

The lectionary leads the congregation to a large and representative body of sacred Scripture and hence to far-reaching concerns of the Christian church. Pastors who switch from randomly choosing a text week by week to following a lectionary usually report two things: (1) the lectionary vastly broadens their range of preaching texts, and (2) the lectionary encourages them to wrestle in a positive way with difficult texts which they would otherwise avoid. As Dan Mosely puts it, the lectionary works against the preacher's idolatry of turning repeatedly to a limited group of texts and themes.[13]

By conversing with specific texts, the lectionary preacher tends to cast the gospel light on the community in a fresh, specific way and is less likely to let the sermon disappear in a fog of vague generalities. This also helps the congregation sense the diversity of Scripture. Furthermore, when the lections are well chosen on a given Sunday in the Christmas or Easter cycles, the readings help the congregation understand the interelatedness of Scripture.

The Revised Common Lectionary provides for both selected readings which illumine the calendar as well as for semi-continuous readings in Ordinary Time. It thus manifests the best of both approaches.

The Christian Year and the lectionary are apropos for our time. Much of current U.S. culture is individualistic, narcissistic, and even self-worshipful. The current liturgical renewal seeks to replace these destructive tendencies with a vision of life which is communal and is centered in a transcendent God. J. Irwin Trotter concisely says that "behind this lectionary lies an ecclesiology that is communal, organic, sacramental."[14]

The knowledge that we are accepted by God releases us from self-infatuation to a realistic (we are sinners after all) but hopeful appraisal of ourselves and our world. It frees us to lose ourselves in the new social world which is emerging in response to God's leading. The willingness of preacher and congregation to follow the Christian Year and to use a lectionary is a way of embodying this vision. To use a lectionary is to join congregations around the world in bending together on a given Sunday to hear the Word God would speak to us all.

Our era is also a time of historical and theological amnesia. Many parts of the church have become so fixated with psychology, sociology, economics, political analysis, and institutional maintenance that we forget the *raison d'etre* of the church: to reflect on life from the perspective of the gospel. The Christian Year reminds us of the importance of our past and its significance for the present and the future. It also reminds us of our reason for being.

The Christian Year and the lectionary also encourage the church to restore its weekly worship to the full pattern of the Word in the context of sacrament. Of course, the Roman Catholic lectionary was conceived for worship which climaxes in the Lord's Supper. While few Protestant congregations receive the Lord's Supper weekly, the values of the lectionary find their fullest expression as a part of a service of the Lord's Supper.

The Christian Year and the lectionary are also of practical value to the preacher. The season and the text provide places to start sermon preparation. The seasons and the lections allow for long-range planning which can include all involved in worship planning. The changes from season to season (and from week to week) bring variety and interest to worship. The widespread use of the Year and the lectionary encourages pastors to join together in weekly, ecumenical lectionary study groups. By publishing the lections in advance, the congregation is lured to prepare for worship by reading the lessons.

Lectionary preaching saves energy at the point of research: the minister can study the background of the Synoptic Gospels for the year (or for any of the books which appear in continuous reading) and draw upon that research for several weeks and months. This can also result in continuity for the listener. Instead of jumping week by week from continent to continent and from one speech to another, the listener's appreciation of a single Bible world can enlarge Sunday by Sunday. In addition, we now have an abundance of aids to lectionary preaching.

The Christian Year and the Lectionary as Hinderances to Preaching

While every good Christology is ultimately theocentric, the Christocentrism of the Christian Year and the lectionary can become almost exclusive. Though God is known to the church first through Jesus Christ, God is also known in other ways, for example, through the Hebrew Bible and even through the face of nature. Even though the latter appear in the lections, they are subordinate to the Gospel lesson. Therefore, the Year and the lectionary can have the effect of diminishing our other sources of the knowledge of God.

In the Christian Year, the canon is subordinate to the calendar, especially in the two major cycles. Scripture does not speak its own interepretive word but speaks through the filters of the seasonal themes. Proponents of the current liturgical revival point out that this is precisely what is intended. However, it can dull a vivid passage of Scripture.

Many of the deepest misgivings about the Common Lectionary (and about most lectionaries) come in regards to the Hebrew Bible. The Gospel lesson always sets the theme for the week. The reading from the sacred Scriptures of Judaism never does so. Of course, the pastor can preach from the Hebrew lection, but the lectionary assumes the priority of the Gospel. In fact, in the two great cycles, the lection from the Hebrew Bible is chosen because it provides background for the Gospel. Often, the relationship between the two is interpreted as that of prophecy and fulfillment, as if the sole function of our Jewish heritage was to prepare for the coming of Jesus. The church infrequently hears the sacred Scriptures of Judaism in their entirety.

In the Sundays after Easter, the lection from the Hebrew Bible disappears altogether. Furthermore, while the first thirty-nine books of the Bible are nearly eight times the length of the final twenty-seven books, the former represents only about one fourth of the readings in the Revised Common Lectionary. These things not only devalue the literature, history, and religion of ancient Israel but reinforce the church's neglect of the Hebrew Bible and contribute subtly to anti-Judaism.[15]

The Christian Year downsizes some essential themes of the Christian faith. For instance, the Year never focuses on the meaning of creation.[16] This minimizes the church's exposure to resources which could be valuable as the possibility of "ecocide" grows daily. Imaginative preachers supplement the fare of the Christian Year.

Critics point out that any lectionary enshrines the biases of the body which prepares and authorizes it. The Common Lectionary is often criticized as downplaying the Bible's persistent call for social justice and the concerns of women and other oppressed groups.[17] The lectionary softens some of the Bible's radical claims. The Revised Common Lectionary is designed to ameliorate these criticisms. Nonetheless, any lectionary is a hedgerow which stands between the Bible and the preacher.

The beginning and ending points of the lections are sometimes arbitrary. This is also true when a single lection is created by means of gerrymandering (a few verses from one part of a chapter and a few verses from another part) or when a portion of Scripture is subdivided into individual readings for separate Sundays. Thus, the preacher is advised to determine that the passage is a meaningful unit.

The lectionary does provoke preachers to wrestle with difficult texts which we might otherwise flee. Yet it does not include some of the texts which raise the most difficult moral and intellectual issues. Thereby, it can allow the pastor to bypass significant teaching opportunities.

The lectionary may immediately increase the diversity of voices of Scripture which speak in the worshiping community. The fact of repeating the same readings every three years, however, minimizes diversity. Indeed, the congregation which gets its Bible primarily in worship may lose consciousness of the rest of the Bible.

Congregations can be confused about the progression of readings from week to week. In the Christmas and Easter cycles, why do we jump from one setting in a synoptic Gospel to John and back to an altogether different setting in the synoptic Gospel? It is not always clear why a given reading appears on a given day. The congregation's experience of the Christian Year is enriched when the coordination of the Year and the lection is explained.

On many Sundays, three lessons are read but only one is interpreted in the sermon. This is often wise, since the freight of a single text is usually sufficient for any given day. Yet some preachers feel repeatedly compelled to deal with multiple lections and hence posit artificial connections among them. Occasionally I hear a sermon which travels from one text to another without relating the texts; the result is a series of unrelated sermonettes within one sermon. At the same time, some lections are so problematic to today's hearer that it is pastorally irresponsible to read them without commentary.

Preachers sometimes lament that lectionary readings on a particular Sunday do not "meet the needs" of the congregation at that moment. However, longtime lectionary users marvel not at how seldomly the lectionary speaks to the moment but at how seldomly it does not do so, even in times of crisis. Nevertheless, the lectionary can become a golden calf. The lectionary is the servant of the gospel and not the master of church or preacher. One of the preacher's principle interpretive responsibilities is the selection of the text. In most ecclesial communities the preacher is free to go outside the lectionary in response to the questions and needs of the community.

The Christian Year and the lectionary do not solve the preacher's every problem. Yet when regarded judiciously and critically, they, like midwives, can help deliver the gospel and place it in the hands of an eager, anticipating congregation.

Notes

1. Mircea Eliade, *The Myth of the Eternal Return,* trans. Willard R. Trask (Princeton: Princeton University Press, 1954), 139-162, especially 149-154. My colleague, Keith Watkins, called my attention to this notion.
2. Ibid., 159-162. Compare Clifford Geertz, *The Interpretation of Cultures* (New York: Basic Books, Inc., 1973), 87ff.
3. Eliade, *The Myth of the Eternal Return,* 159-162. Victor Turner explains how worship functions in his *The Ritual Process* (Ithaca: Cornell University Press, 1969).
4. For example, see Roland de Vaux, *Ancient Israel: Its Life and Institutions,* trans. J. McHugh (New York: McGraw-Hill Publishers, 1961), 484-508.
5. For example, see Adolf Adam, *The Liturgical Year,* trans. Matthew J. O'Connell (New York: Pueblo Publishing Co., 1981).
6. See Willy Rordorf, *Sunday,* trans. A.A.K. Graham (Philadelphia: Westminster Press, 1968).
7. See J.G. Davies, *Holy Week: A Short History* (London: Lutterworth Press, 1963).
8. *Handbook for the Common Lectionary,* ed. Peter C. Bower (Philadelphia: Geneva Press, 1987), 17.
9. Ibid.
10. For a concise review of lectionaries to 1977, see John P. Reumann, "A History of Lectionaries," *Interpretation* 31 (1977): 116-130.
11. See Horace T. Allen, Jr., "Introduction" in *Common Lectionary: The Lectionary Proposed by the Consultation on Common Texts* (New York: Church Hymnal Corporation, 1983), 7-27.
12. My evaluation is similar to that of many others. Note especially Shelley Cochran, *Liturgical Hermeneutics* (Ph.D. dissertation, Drew University, 1990).
13. Dan P. Mosley, "Lectionary: Guard Against Heresy," *Biblical Preaching Journal* 2/1 (1989): 46.
14. J. Irwin Trotter, "Are We Preaching a 'Subversive' Lectionary?" *School of Theology at Claremont Bulletin* 28/2 (1985): 1.
15. See James A. Sanders, "Canon and Calendar: An Alternative Lectionary Proposal," *Social Themes of the Christian Year,* ed. Dieter T. Hessell (Philadelphia: Geneva Press, 1983), 257-263. Here he proposes that a part of the lectionary cycle center upon readings from the Hebrew Bible.
16. This was noticed long ago by A. A. McArthur, *The Christian Year and Lectionary Reform* (London: SCM Press, 1958).
17. Ruth C. Duck, *Touch Holiness* (New York: Pilgrim Press, 1990), 129-135. Here she offers alternative readings which center upon women.

Part IV Preaching and the Biblical Text

George Whitefield (1714-1770)

"A Voice for God"

Benjamin Franklin, who was not known for his religious motivation, once heard George Whitefield preach on behalf of building an orphanage. Franklin determined at the outset to give nothing to the cause, but after hearing Whitefield's compelling sermon ended up emptying his pockets into the collection plate!

Whitefield was born the son of a wine merchant who died when the boy was only two. His early life was characterized by misconduct until a profound religious conversion changed his life forever.

At Oxford, Whitefield became friends with John and Charles Wesley. Following graduation, he felt compelled to preach, but his enthusiastic oratorical style was not welcomed in many Anglican pulpits. So Whitefield began the open–air preaching which would become such a central part of his ministry, both in England and in the American colonies.

Whitefield had a powerful voice, and it was an instrument he developed to full advantage. It was not uncommon for him to address more than 20,000 persons in open–air services; one Scottish meeting was estimated to include more than 100,000 persons with some 10,000 converts.

His preaching was dynamic, emotional, replete with illustrations, and delivered without a manuscript, though carefully prepared. He earnestly called his listeners to repentance.

A contemporary of Jonathan Edwards, Whitefield's preaching contributed to the First Great Awakening which had such a profound influence on the American colonies in the mid–eighteenth century.

22

Elizabeth Achtemeier
Adjunct Professor of Bible & Homiletics
Union Theological Seminary
Richmond, Virginia

Preaching and the Old Testament

If the Christian preacher wishes to preach the whole gospel, he or she must preach from the Old Testament as well as from the New. When the books making up our canon were collected together in the fourth century, and when the shape of that canon was then reworked by the Protestant Reformers in the sixteenth century, our forbears in the faith decided that it was absolutely necessary to put the revelation found in the Old Testament alongside that found in the New. Thus, the Old Testament now makes up two-thirds of our Bible and is understood as an integral part of our one authority for faith and practice.

Old Testament in Church Canon

The decision to include the Old Testament in the canon of the church was not an arbitrary one, however. Rather, it was based on the witness of the New Testament itself, for the New Testament's authors are quite convinced that it is impossible to know who Jesus Christ is apart from the Old Testament.

The first thing that Matthew told us about our Lord is that He is a descendant of Abraham and of David (1:1), and that His significance must therefore be understood in connection with God's promises to those two Israelites (compare 2 Cor. 1:20). John 1:45 and Luke 24:44-45 both indicate that the figure of Jesus is to be understood in the context of the Law and Prophets and Psalms of the Old Testament. Repeatedly, Jesus' life is seen as the fulfillment of Old Testament Scripture (for instance, Mark 14:21; 1 Cor. 15:3-4).

Although the theologies of the New Testament are several and varied, all of them point to Jesus of Nazareth as the completion and fulfillment of the sacred history of the Old Testament. For those New Testament writers who dealt with the Royal Traditions of the Old Testament, Jesus was the Messiah, the long-awaited Son of David, the Shepherd-Prince promised by Ezekiel, the High Priest after the order of Melchizedek, and the royal davidic Son of God who had been exalted to the right hand of the Father as the Lord over all enemies and powers. He was the one to Whom the traditions of David and the Royal Psalms pointed, the ruler whose coming inaugurated the beginning of the kingdom of God.

For those New Testament authors who told the story of Jesus' earthly life and death, Jesus was a new Moses, the prophet like Moses who was to come, and the Suffering Servant who gave His life as a ransom for many. He was the one who freed Israel from her final slavery, who instituted the new Sinai covenant of the prophets in His blood, and who made the perfect sacrifice for sin once and for all. He was the stone which the builders rejected, which had become the head of the corner, the rock of stumbling for the Jews and foolishness for the Gentiles. He was the ideal righteous Man of the Psalms, suffering and praising His Father from the cross. The exodus, Passover, Sinai, hexteuchal, and prophetic traditions all found their goal in Him, and the plan which God began with His first release of His people from Egypt was brought to completion in the story of the crucifixion and resurrection of Jesus Christ.

For those New Testament witnesses who concentrated on the fullness of His incarnation, Jesus was, in various traditions, the new obedient Son, Israel, the incarnate temple or the cornerstone of the new congregation of faith on Zion, the incarnate covenant and light and lamb, the Servant, Wisdom made flesh, the true vine, the true manna, the bread and water of life. In short, Jesus Christ was understood as the Word of the Old Testament incarnate, the light given by the Word which shone in the darkness. He was even the incarnate promised land, the place of rest offered to all who faithfully held fast to Him.

This means then, that according to the New Testament, Jesus Christ is not some mysterious figure suddenly dropped from the blue. Rather He is the culmination, completion, and final reinterpretation of God's two thousand year history with Israel. Apart from Christ's connection with that history, He could have been viewed in the first- to third-century Mediterannean world as another mythical savior in a mystery religion or gnostic sect. Still today, His connection with the history of Israel prevents our Lord from being understood as a projection of theological speculation, as a myth or symbol of a new human self-understanding, or as a humanistic model of a righteous man for others.

Jesus Christ is the completion and final interpretation of God's Word to Israel. He is God's act whereby God brings His sacred history to that climax which illumines all our past, present, and future. If preachers wish to preach Jesus Christ, as the New Testament presents Him, then they must preach from the Old Testament as well. Only from the whole Bible can the preacher make clear just who Jesus Christ is, what He has done, and what He will do.

This is not to say that there is nothing new in the New Testament. There is much that is new. With the appearance of Jesus, there was present Someone greater than Solomon and Jonah (see Luke 11:31-32), Someone greater than Abraham (see John 8:53-59) and Moses (see Mark 9:2-8 and parallel passages, Matt. 5:21-48; John 1:17). Jesus Christ is the beginning of that new age for which the old Israel could only hope (see Matt. 13:16-17; Luke 10:23-24), and the participants in that new age become greater than even the greatest of the prophets (see Matt. 11:11). Yet it is precisely the theologies and words of the Old Testament that are used to tell who this new Word is, and without the old the new cannot truly be proclaimed.

Similarly, preachers must preach from the Old Testament if they wish to make clear to their people just who their congregations are as the Christian church. In the New Testament, the church is called the body of Christ and the household of God. Paul also called the church "the Israel of God" (Gal. 6:16) and the "true circumcision" (Phil. 3:3, RSV). He said that we are the wild branches who have been grafted into the root of Israel (see Rom. 11:17-20). In Ephesians, the cross of Christ has now brought us into and made us one with the "commonwealth of Israel" (2:11-22). Therefore, in 1 Peter 2:9-10, the church is addressed with the same words that were spoken to Israel at Mount Sinai. We are now "a chosen race, a royal priesthood, a holy nation, God's own people" (RSV; compare Ex. 19:5-6).

Church as the New Israel

The Christian church has now become, through Jesus Christ, a part of God's covenant people Israel. That fact immediately raises the questions: Who is Israel? How did she come into being? What was the nature of her life, and what was she supposed to be and do? None of those questions can be answered apart from the Old Testament. The preacher must therefore preach from the Old Testament if the church is to understand fully its nature and mission in the world.

When the Old Testament is used to illumine the character and role of the church, it becomes apparent that the church's life in many respects parallels the life of Israel. The prophets of the Old Testament promised that the life of the new people of God would recapitulate that of the people of the old covenant (for instance, Isa. 40—55). That is exactly what we find when we compare our life as the Christian church with the life of Israel in the Old Testament.

Parallels Between Israel and Believers Today

Consider the parallels that may be drawn between Israel's life with God and ours: Both Israel and the church are freed from slavery by the redemptive act of God, before either of us has done anything to deserve such mercy—Israel is freed from her slavery in Egypt; we as the church are freed from our slavery to sin and death. By that undeserved redemption, both of us are adopted as the sons and daughters of God (see Ex. 4:22-23; Hos. 11:1; Gal. 4:4-7; John 1:12), and thereby have the foretaste of the glorious liberty of the children of God.

After their redemption, both Israel and the church are brought to the table of the covenant, the Lord's Supper. There God promises to be our God and to keep us as His people, and we promise to serve and worship Him alone as our only Lord.

In the covenant relation, both Israel and the church are given commandments by which their life is to be guided and sustained. At the same time, both are called to be God's holy nation, set aside for His purpose alone. Both are designated a kingdom of priests that mediates the knowledge of God to the rest of the world.

Both Israel and the church are set on a pilgrimage toward a promised place of rest, and both are accompanied every step along the way on that pilgrimage by the presence of God himself. "Lo, I am with you always, to the close of the age" (Matt. 28:20, RSV; see also Deut. 31:6; 1 Ki. 8:57). Both Israel and the church journey toward the kingdom of God, in which every knee will bow and every tongue will confess His Lordship (see Isa. 45:23; Phil. 2:10-11), and in which the knowledge of God will cover the earth, as the waters cover the sea.

Israel's Story Is the Church's Story

In other words, the story of Israel is the church's story. The Christian church has now become Israel, through the work of Jesus Christ. We see ourselves written on the pages of the Old Testament. We find there the parallels, the analogies, the types, the foretastes of our life with our Lord. If the preacher will preach the stories, the commandments, the poetry, the songs, and prophecies of the Old Testament, we will be aided in discovering who we are as the covenant people of God and what it is we are supposed to be and do in His service. For the modern preacher to neglect such proclamation is not only to leave a congregation without a full understanding of its identity and mission, but is also to refuse to guide them along their way with the signposts and instructions that God has mercifully given them through two thousand years of relationship with their Israelite forbears. "These things . . . were written down for our instruction," said Paul (1 Cor. 10:11, RSV). Our faith in Jesus Christ has brought us into the covenant people. Not to make known the nature and course of that unique, historical community is finally to ignore the full implications of the good news of Jesus Christ.

Further Reasons to Preach from the Old Testament

There are, however, further reasons why modern preachers will want to preach from the Old Testament, for there is much in the Old Testament that is simply presupposed in the New.

Creation

For example, it is in the Old Testament that the full shape of the church's understanding of the created world and of God's relation to it is set forth. We moderns, with our scientific world views, tend to view the world of nature as a closed system. That system, we think, proceeds entirely by natural law, and we rarely ascribe to God any happening in the natural world. That means that ours is a totally secular worldview, from which God is absent.

Yet the Old Testament affirms that God not only created the world but also sustains it and all of its processes by His faithfulness. For example, the round of the seasons is the result of God's faithfulness to His promise: "While the earth remains, seedtime and harvest, cold and heat, summer and winter, day and night, shall not cease" (Gen. 8:22, RSV). Everything is dependent on God's continual working. Apart from that working, the world would return to chaos (compare Gen. 1; Job 38:9-11). Jesus, therefore, can teach that it is God who feeds the birds of the air and clothes the lilies of the field in a glory exceeding Solomon's, or that not one sparrow falls to the ground without the Father's will (see Matt. 10:26-29). God is the Creator, Sustainer, and Lord of all nature. "The earth is the Lord's and the fulness thereof" (Ps. 24:1). The Old Testament spells out the meaning of that, and the New Testament then presupposes that meaning.

Human Nature

By the same token, it is the Old Testament that fully explicates the church's understanding of human nature. Once again, we moderns tend to have totally secular views of ourselves, believing that we are independent, free, self-governing, and self-fulfilling individuals, with immortality inherent in our souls. Certainly many modern philosophies and ideologies attempt to understand humankind solely in psychological, sociological, economic, or political terms. The Old Testament tells us that we can only be fully understood in our relation to God. He has made us in His image, responsible to Him for all human life and for our stewardship over all creatures and creation; and there is no way we can escape that responsibility or our relation to the Creator who has made us. If we try to do without God, we fall into sin under His wrath. The Old Testament also tells us that we are dependent on God for our very breath of life and that apart from God we die. So Jesus Christ, in the New Testament, heals our relationship with God and thereby offers us eternal life. Our Lord presupposes the view of human nature that is given already in the Old Testament.

Nature of God

Only from the Old Testament's revelation, presupposed by the New, can we also have a full understanding of the nature of God. Much of religion in our day is largely characterized by an emphasis on the immanence of God. There are even theologies and ideologies in the land that wish to identify God with the creation or that see the divine inherent in all things and persons, in modern forms of pantheism, panentheism, and natural religion. Certainly the God of the Bible works in the world through the media of His Word and Spirit. It is principally from the Old Testament that we also learn that God is "holy," which means that He is totally other than anything that He has created, and that, therefore, He is not to be identified with or worshiped in anything "that is in heaven above, or that is in the earth beneath, or that is in the water under the earth" (Ex. 20:4-5, RSV). In the Old Testament, God is revealed not only as immanent, but also as transcendent Lord, in all His majesty and glory. Unless congregations hear that transcendence proclaimed, they really cannot understand, for example, what was revealed to Peter, James, and John on the Mount of Transfiguration (see Mark 9:2-8 and parallel passages, Matt. 17:1-13; Lk. 9:28-36), or just what the the full nature of the God is who confronts us in the person of Jesus of Nazareth.

Purposes of God

To go further, apart from the Old Testament, we cannot truly grasp the nature of the purposes of God, for those purposes are set forth at the very beginning of the Old Testament. The Old Covenant tells us that in the beginning God created the world "very good," full of life and running over with abundance. Yet in the story of us all in Genesis 3—11, it also recounts how our attempts to be our own gods and goddesses have corrupted God's good world and all His gifts, and brought upon the whole creation God's judgment and the curse of evil and disharmony, violence and death. Therefore, in the call of Abraham, God set out to turn that curse into a blessing by making a new people, in a new covenant relation, through whom He could bring His blessing on all the families of the earth and restore to the earth the goodness that it was intended in the beginning to have. The entire story of the Bible, then, concerns the manner in which God is fulfilling that promise. Unless we know from the Old Testament what the promise was and why it was given, we cannot understand what God is doing in our world.

Moreover, it is from the Old Testament that we first learn that God's purpose in the world is a universal and cosmic purpose, spanning all time, all nature, and all history, from the first moment of creation until the kingdom comes. The New Testament presupposes that universal, cosmic view and can therefore testify that as the creation had its beginning from the Word of God, so it will be brought to its completion by that Word. In Christ, the Word was made flesh, and in the fullness of time, all things in heaven and on earth will be united (see Eph. 1:10). Only by preaching a history which spans the period from Genesis to Revelation can the preacher set forth the purposes of God and what God is accomplishing in our universe, and indeed, in each one of our individual lives.

Pair Old Testament Texts with New Testament Texts

However, while we want to emphasize the importance of preaching from the Old Testament, it is also necessary to remember that the Old Testament is not alone in our canon. The custom of many preachers, when using a text from the Old Testament, is to give a general reference to the gospel at the end of the sermon, in order to give the sermon a Christian setting. The gospel is not given to us in general! It comes to us through very specific words and deeds recorded for us in the New Testament. Therefore, when preaching from the Old Testament, the preacher should pair the Old Testament text with one from the New.

Old Testament Incomplete

In one sense, the Old Testament is an incomplete book. Its whole story strains forward toward the future, when God's Word does not return to Him void but accomplishes that which He purposes. We have to ask what happened to those words that we find in the Old Testament. Did God in fact keep His words to Israel, or were those words allowed to fall by the wayside, without effect and fulfillment?

That question applies not only to God's promises in the Old Testament, however, but to all of the Old Testament's writings. We have to ask if, through a descendant of Abraham, God has brought blessing on all the families of the earth (see Gen. 12:3). We also have to ask if the judgment announced by the prophets has come to pass, or if the assurance given by a psalmist has become reality, or if the words of a Wisdom writing have proved true. The only way we can finally decide is by searching the total story, by tracing God's actions through both Old

Testament and New. Then the whole revelation of God's dealings with us is made known, and we find our lives encompassed by a holy history that we learn is still continuing in our time.

This obviously does not mean that we read the New Testament or Christ back into the Old Testament. The revelation given us through the Old Testament has its own integrity and its own historical context, and the preacher leaves every Old Testament text in its actual setting.

Nor does the attention to the whole canon mean that, in a sermon, every Old Testament text is finally overshadowed and made less important than the text from the New Testament with which it is paired. I made it clear, I hope, that the Old Testament in and of itself bears a revelation absolutely necessary for our understandings of Christ and the church, of the world, and of the nature of God. The preacher, however, should study the Old Testament with an eye to that ongoing history of which the Old Testament forms the first part and tries to show how God's Word has been active throughout that history to accomplish the divine purposes.

Pairing Shows Contemporary Relation

The pairing of the Old and New Testament texts also is the means by which any Old Testament text is related to our contemporary lives. We have very little difficulty believing that a New Testament text is spoken directly to us, because we stand in historical continuity with the New Testament church, the Body of Christ, and have been incorporated by baptism into it. The case is different with Israel. We do not feel ourselves directly connected with her covenant community.

As we have seen, however, we have been grafted into the root of Israel and become members of the commonwealth of Israel through the work of Jesus Christ. Through Him, we now identify with Israel, and the revelation given to Israel is now given also to us. Through Christ, the Old Testament's story with God becomes our story—but only through Christ. By pairing an Old Testament text with one from the New, we acknowledge such facts. We enter into Israel by means of the gospel, and hear God's ancient words spoken to her as words spoken now also to us; and we experience God's judging and saving acts done to her as acts done now also to us.

Methods of Pairing Texts

There are several methods by which texts from both Testaments may be paired.

The most obvious is by use of the scheme of promise and fulfillment. The Old Testament text contains a promise. It may be a promise of judgment or of salvation but it concerns some action which God is going to carry out. The New Testament text then relates how the promise has been fulfilled. For example, Amos 5:18-20 tells us that the day of the Lord, the day of judgment, will be a day of "darkness and not light." Should that, then, be linked with the story of the crucifixion in which we read that "when the sixth hour was come, there was darkness over the whole land until the ninth hour" (Mark 15:33; compare parallel passages, Matt. 27:45; Lk. 23:44)?

Old and New Testament texts can also be paired on the basis of analogy. This is probably the most frequent way we use narrative texts from the Old Testament; they form analogies, types, or foreshadowings of events and texts in the New Testament. For example, Israel's entire story up through the time of the wilderness wanderings is analogous to the church's story. The redemption of Israel in the exodus is parallel to our redemption by the cross of Christ, to name just one analogy. There are hundreds of such analogies that can be drawn between Israel's life with God and ours. To give another, Jeremiah pointed out in his famous Temple sermon (7:1-15), that Judah in his day was trying to use Temple worship as a magical guarantee and hiding place ("den of robbers," v. 11) from God's judgment on sin. Surely that mirrors the attitude that we sometimes bring to church; certainly it parallels the misuse of God's Temple and the abuse of this worship which Jesus denounced (compare Mark 11:17). Drawing such parallels between Israel's life and the church's provides rich resources for preaching.

Old and New Testament texts can also be joined on the basis of common motifs. Again, there are hundreds of these that link the two Testaments. Some of them are well-known: covenant, circumcision, exile, pilgrimage, sacrifice, water of life, way, election, and so on. It can also be very fruitful to use a concordance and see what both Testaments do with the figure of the vine, or cup, or yoke. A study of light and darkness in both Testaments yields rich results, as does one that deals with figures for the sea, and both of those studies take the preacher back to Genesis 1 and the traditions concerning the primeval chaos. Jesus' use of the figure of the good shepherd, in John 10, goes back to Ezekiel 34, just as every title for our Lord in the New Testament has its basis in the Old. By tracing out the Testaments' mutual use of terms, motifs, and figures, much can be illumined.

Then, too, texts from Old and New Testaments can be paired simply to let one text illumine the other. Paul spoke of our slavery to sin (see for example, Rom 6:6). The story of Israel in captivity in Egypt can make that phrase graphic. Jeremiah 13:23 expresses such slavery in four short lines.

Sometimes texts from the two Testaments contrast with one another. For example, Hebrews 12:18-24 contrasts with the Old Testament's story of Israel at Sinai, but the preacher must be careful not to leave out the emphasis of either text. The God we know in Jesus Christ is the same God who spoke to Israel at the Mount of Covenant, and one text must not be used to negate the revelation given through the other. Far too often, preachers and people alike have tended to use the Old Testament as outdated or made irrelevant by the New Testament. Both are joined together by God's ongoing activity in the life of His people, and no part of that activity can ever be irrelevant for the church.

Old Testament Effect on the Language of Preaching

Let me finally mention the effect that the use of the Old Testament can have on the language of preaching. If a minister preaches from Old Testament texts at least half of the time—and that should be every minister's intention—he or she is not very likely to get lost in ethereal, vague generalities. If the story of Israel is anything, it is earthy, it is vivid, and it is full of concrete details. There is no other religion in the world that takes the life of this earth so seriously as does the biblical faith.

The preacher who studies the Old Testament will find, therefore, that it deals with the basics of human life—birth and death, love and hate, tenderness and violence, suffering and evil, unbelief and trust, enemies and friends, fathers and mothers and children and all of their multitudinous relationships. The Old Testament tells the graphic stories of real people, living in particular locations, at specific times. All of those stories are encompassed by the presence of an almighty, loving, judging, weeping, saving, calling, merciful God, who has adopted Israel as His own peculiar treasure out of all the peoples that are on the face of the earth. If preachers cling to all of those particularities, and talk of them in sermons, and use their vivid language and pictorial, human details, they may discover that the sermons preached are beginning to deal with real life, as it actually is.

Far too often we think to find God in beauty and peace and quiet. The Old Testament knows Him in the midst of the dust and swirl, the agonies and violence, the noise and clamor—and yes, sometimes quiet times—of everyday human life. There God has met us, and revealed Himself to us, and called us into His service as His chosen folk. The Old Testament can give our people a renewed sense of that marvelous revelation and a new certainty that God is indeed with them, in every circumstance, even to the end of the age.

23

Ken Mathews
Professor of Divinity
Beeson Divinity School
Samford University, Birmingham, Alabama

Preaching in the Pentateuch

Christian preaching requires the expositor to preach from the Pentateuch, since the heart of the New Testament's proclamation is grounded in the Hebrew *Torah*. Contemporary preaching often neglects the Jewish parentage of the church's birth. The apostolic tradition, however, did not ignore the ideological and cultural "Bethlehem" of its message; it is inseparably wedded to God's promissory blessing to the Fathers and the nativity of Israel at Sinai.

Consider, for example, Paul's theology: the apostle's understanding of justification by faith (compare Rom. 4:1-3,16-25 with Gen. 15:5-6; 17:5); the first Adam and the new humanity of Christ (compare Rom. 5:12-21 with Gen. 3; 1 Cor. 15:35-49 with Gen. 1—2; 2 Cor. 5:17 with Gen. 1); the relationship of law and faith (Gal. 3 with Gen. 12:3,7; 15:6; Lev. 18:5; Deut. 21:23; 27:26); the supremacy of Christ (Col. 1:15-23 with Gen. 1); the election of the saints (Rom. 9—11 with Gen. 21:12; 25:23; Ex. 33:19); and the nature of Christian ministry (2 Cor. 3—4 with Ex. 34:33-35)—all are indebted to Moses' books. From the people and events of the "Five Books," Paul detected paradigms for Christian practice: Adam and Eve contribute to understanding proper order in public worship (1 Cor. 11:1-16; 1 Tim. 2), Hagar and Sarah clarify law and grace (Gal. 4), and the exodus and wilderness wanderings are like illustrated sermons exhorting Christian devotion (compare 1 Cor. 10 with Ex. 16:2-36; Num. 9:15-23; 20:2-11).

Hebrews, by itself, interprets Jesus as the new Adam (chap. 2), the new Moses (chap. 3), the new Melchizedek (5:6-10; chap. 7), and as the new tabernacle and sacrifice (chaps. 9—10). Indicative of the gospel's dependence on Israel's beginnings are the opening words of the New

Testament: "A record of the genealogy of Jesus Christ the son of David, the son of Abraham" (Matt. 1:1, NIV).

The difficulty for the Christian preacher, therefore, is not justifying the relevancy of the Pentateuch for preaching but how to set it in our Christian framework without violating the integrity of the ancient context. This is not altogether the case, however, since we are puzzled as how the ceremonial and civil aspects of the Mosaic law might be relevant pulpit material. Also, we are befuddled as to what to do with Genesis 1—11 which reads so alien to our post-Enlightenment era.

We will first discuss what preachers must know of the Pentateuch's character so that they might approach the task properly. Second, we will give special attention to the problems of Genesis 1—11 and the relevancy of the Mosaic law. To help us see how this works for a specific passage, throughout this chapter we will consider as our sample the fourth commandment: "Remember the sabbath day by keeping it holy" (Ex. 20:8-11, NIV). This serves us well when we consider the special problems of the primeval history and the Mosaic law since the Sabbath motif occurs in both sections (Gen. 2:1-3; Ex. 20:8-11; Deut. 5:12-15).

Text and Context

Any real estate broker will agree that the three most important factors in the buying and selling of property are "location, location, location!" Like the rule of real estate, the maxim for preaching in the Pentateuch is "context, context, context!" The preacher must avoid the temptation to plunge into the passage without due consideration for its circles of context. These circles of context are its: (1) literary configuration, (2) historical/cultural conditioning, and (3) canonical-theological contours. Of course, these three circles are not mutually exclusive but for our purposes of discussion we have isolated each.

Literary Configuration

Like a jigsaw puzzle, the Pentateuch bears the features of a unified whole while also possessing discontinuities. At a distance a jigsaw puzzle appears to the eye as one piece, but a closer view reveals its irregular parts buttressed together to form a literary mosaic. The Pentateuch is a whole but betrays a compiling of literary blocks into a harmoniously arranged union. The "Five Books" of Moses, as Jewish tradition has called them, are in fact one story—stretching from creation (Gen. 1:1) to the death of Moses (Deut. 34)—which is constructed of, more or less, five distinguishable parts or "books."

The five part arrangement can be analyzed as chiastic (inverted):

A Genesis
  B Exodus

C Leviticus
B′ Numbers
A′ Deuteronomy

Genesis and Deuteronomy come closest to being independent works but by themselves they lack a satisfactory denouement. Genesis is the prologue to the collection and Deuteronomy recapitulates the works of Exodus through Numbers, but no effort is made by it to echo Genesis. The center books of Exodus, Leviticus, and Numbers are the most interdependent; together they tell of the migration of Israel from Egypt to the plains of Moab. Exodus and Numbers form a distinctive matching pair. Numbers presupposes a knowledge of Exodus; for instance, the striking of the rock by Moses (Num. 20:11) can only be rightly understood if it is known that he was commanded to do so in Exodus 17:5-7.[1]

However, the present canonical shape of five books does not reflect the *inherent* literary pattern of the Pentateuch.[2] It consists of these two unequal divisions: (1) Genesis and (2) Exodus through Deuteronomy. These two divisions in turn consist of two subdivisions:

(1) Genesis	(A) Gen. 1—11	Universal History
	(B) Gen. 12—50	Patriarchal History
(2) Ex.—Deut.	(A) Ex. 1—Num. 10:10	From Egypt to Sinai
	(B) Num. 10:11—Deut. 34	From Sinai to Moab

The element that holds Genesis together internally is the genre of genealogy, as evidenced by the repetition (11 times) of the phrase "these are the generations of." The cohesive factor that holds the second division together is the life of national Israel under Moses' leadership. These two major divisions are bound by this theme: *God's promissory blessings*.

The second division above, which dominates the content of the Pentateuch, is made up of two major blocks each preceded by a preparatory account, telling of Israel's journeys:

(1) From Egypt to Sinai	(A) Ex. 1—18	Journey to Sinai
	(B) Ex. 19—Num. 10:10	Events at Sinai
(2) From Sinai to Moab	(A) Num. 10:11—36:13	Journey to Moab
	(B) Deut. 1—34	Events at Moab

These two major blocks (Ex. 19—Num. 10:10; Deut. 1—34) focus on the Sinai revelation since Deuteronomy is an interpretive rehearsal of the Sinai event first given in Exodus. It is apparent therefore that the focus of the Pentateuch's narrative interest is *God's meeting with Israel at Sinai*. For our consideration of the Sabbath commandment, it is important that the commandment occurs in each of the major blocks (Ex. 20:8-11; 23:12; 31:12-17; Lev. 23:3; Deut. 5:12-15)

Literary Diversity.—A closer look at the Pentateuch shows a diversity of subject matter within the umbrella unity of the Five Books. The topics range from the cosmic to a particular Hebrew family to an emerging tribal confederacy. The scene shifts within the context of the Levant, including the three great centers of ancient civilization—Mesopotamia, Canaan, and Egypt. Scenes include urban, agrarian, and desert backdrops; palaces, sanctuaries, and tents; along with dreams, visions, and divine epiphanies.

Another literary feature of the Pentateuch is its makeup of diverse genre: narrative discourse, genealogy, census records, some poetry, and sermons (or prophetic oracle). Such diversity can be illustrated by the many different kinds of narrative discourse occurring in Genesis which coexist without serious disruption. The narrative of the universal history (1—11) makes greater use of symbol, such as the "trees" of the garden (2:9-11). This contrasts to the traditional epic style of the Abraham account (12—25) and the story form of Joseph (chaps. 37—50).[3] The Pentateuch is not a literary monolith. Each literary genre encountered by the expositor requires its own hermeneutical, homiletical rules of interpretation and proclamation.

In the case of the Sabbath commandment, its genre is apodictic law, and the Ten Commandments as a whole are modeled after an ancient political treaty form. This ancient treaty form was used in covenant agreements between the "Great King" and a vassal; bilateral commitments were made and both parties were under obligation to fulfill the stipulations. The biblical Ten Commandments have adopted the secular treaty form to communicate the stipulations of the covenant between God, the Great King, and the tribes of Israel, His vassals.

A micro-study of the Pentateuch further shows lines of discontinuity. There are differences in language, vocabulary, and style between and within the books. The various literary units do not always flow naturally from one to the other (for instance, Gen. 4:26 with 5:1). Also, for example, the legal collections in Exodus and Deuteronomy do not follow the same order and there are significant differences between them. There are duplicate accounts with variations, such as the second giving of the Decalogue upon tablets (Ex. 34; Deut. 10) and the laws for clean and unclean animals (Lev. 11; Deut. 14). Differences exist between the two recitations of the Sabbath in Exodus and Deuteronomy. In the case of Exodus, the reason for Sabbath observance is the example of God's creative week (Gen. 2:1-3). The second giving of the Decalogue is set in the plains of Moab where Moses expounds on the law by relating it to the redemption of Israel at the exodus (Deut. 5:12-15).

Literary Unity.—Nevertheless, the unity of the Pentateuch, also known as "the *book* (sg.) of Moses" (Ezra 6:18; Neh. 13:1; 2 Chron. 25:4), is assured by a narrative framework which links the patriarchs and the history of Israel from Sinai to its encampment on the plains of Moab. As noted earlier, the core is the Sinai event where the covenant-law is delineated: the preparation for the giving of the covenant-law (Ex. 1—18); the worship of God provided by Sinai's covenant-law (Ex. 19—Lev.—Num. 10:10); and the experiences of God's people living under the covenant-law (Num. 10:11—Deut.). The Hebrew canon reflects this by designating the Five Books as *Torah* ("Law"). However, the title "Law" may be misleading to the modern audience if it is thought that the Pentateuch is primarily a collection of codified laws; on the contrary, the laws are subordinate to the narrative framework (for instance, "the Book of the Covenant," Ex. 21—23). The Hebrew word *tôrâ* means "instruction" in a broad sense; this teaching concerns the way of the Lord in its entirety. The Five Books therefore defined for future generations the normative expression of Israel's religious way of life. Although the contents of Genesis antedate the Sinai revelation, they introduce the Sinai event by recounting the origins of Israel's ancestors (Gen. 12—50). Genesis 1—11 is an appropriate preamble to the whole work by setting Israel's experience in the framework of cosmic history. The God of covenant was the God of the universe.

This means that the Sabbath command is part of the central focus of the entire Pentateuch; nevertheless, it is still subject to the narration of Israel's story and must be understood as a step in Israel's progression to the land of Canaan. Additionally, the Sabbath was the "sign" for the covenant-law as a whole (Ex. 31:13); this alone magnifies the importance of the passage for defining the relationship between God and His people.

The unity of the Pentateuch is also indicated by the role of Moses. The same cannot be said of Abraham or any other figure for the Book of Genesis. The birth (Ex. 2) and death of Moses (Deut. 34) bracket the composition of Exodus through Deuteronomy, forming a literary *inclusio*. While Genesis covers chronologically many millennia, these four books are solely devoted to the 120 years of Moses' life. The setting of Genesis is spread across the three great geographic centers of Mesopotamia, Egypt, and Syria-Canaan, while Exodus through Deuteronomy is limited to Egypt and the desert of Sinai and the Negev.

Finally, the Pentateuch is unified by its common theme. By "theme" we mean the proposition that explains the content, structure, and development of the work. The theme of the Pentateuch is *the partial fulfillment (or "filling up") of God's promissory blessing to the patriarchs.*[4] Since it is critical to our topic that the expositor understand how this thematic thread holds the work together and how a given passage contributes to that theme, we will detail how the theme unites the Five Books.

1. *Genesis*—The patriarchal blessing is first stated in the calling of Abraham (Gen. 12:1-3; compare 15:4-5,9-21; 17:4-7,19-20). This Abrahamic covenant consists of three promises: a patriarchal homeland, a posterity, and the promise of a relationship with God. By virtue of Abraham's relationship to God, he can be a source of blessing (or cursing) for all the families of the world. This universal aspect of the promise echoes the original intention of God's blessing on all humankind at creation (1:28; compare "blessing" in 1:22; 2:3). The realization of that blessing, however, is postponed by the disobedience of mankind and the ensuing accounts of society's encroaching wickedness. The preamble (Gen. 1—11) includes God's "curse" against the serpent (3:15), the soil from which the first man was made (3:17), Cain's murder of Abel (4:11), the earth for the wickedness of society (8:21), and Noah's "curse" against Canaan (9:25). As though countering the five-fold cursing, God's promise to Abraham contains a five-fold repetition of "blessing" (12:1-3).[5] The divine "blessing" of Abraham (18:18; 22:17) is repeated for Isaac (26:3-4) and Jacob (28:13-14; 32:29), which results in the trilogy "the God of Abraham, Isaac, and Jacob" (for instance, Ex. 3:16). Yet, the "blessing" is not fully realized by Abraham or his offspring. Genesis ends with a mere "seventy souls" living under the protective custody of Egypt's royal house, and Joseph dies in Egypt (50:26). Nevertheless, Joseph's last words hold out hope for the return of Jacob's descendants "to the land which he [God] swore to Abraham, to Isaac, and to Jacob" (50:24, RSV).

2. *Exodus*—The prologue of Exodus (1:1-7) ties the book to Genesis by rehearsing what happened to Jacob's children as told at the close of Genesis. The deliverance from Egyptian bondage is explained as God making good on His prior commitment to the patriarchs (6:3-8); the Ten Commandments give formal expression to God's possession of Israel as His people. Therefore, the Sabbath relates to the third promissory blessing of relationship between God and Abraham. Although the relationship with Israel is sealed and ratified (20:2; 24:7), the people remain at Sinai and have come no closer to receiving the promises as the book ends. Yet, the conclusion contains a hopeful, proleptic comment on Israel's future: "For the cloud of the Lord was on the tabernacle by day, and fire was on it by night, in the sight of all the house of Israel during all their travels" (40:38).

3. *Leviticus*—The third book begins and ends with Israel in the same spot at the "door of the Tabernacle" (1:1; 27:34). There is no advance-

ment toward Canaan but this book is not motionless; it depicts the animated life of Israel's cultic institutions.[6] The worship system and detailed holy requirements sustained the God-people relationship already inaugurated at Sinai (11:44-45; 19:2; 20:26). This holy relationship presupposes the Exodus covenant: "I will remember the covenant with their ancestors whom I brought out of of Egypt . . . I am the Lord" (26:45, NIV).

4. *Numbers*—Israel continued encamped beneath the shadow of Sinai, but now at last preparations are under way for departure (1:1—10:10). Yet, their efforts are again thwarted by unbelief (chaps. 13—14); ironically, the spies fear the very land that Abraham had been promised. The following accounts tell of Israel's vagabond wanderings, but the promise of land remains its hope and goal (chaps. 15—32, especially chap. 20). The last chapters close with a review of Israel's travels from Sinai to the plains of Moab (ch. 33) and their final arrangements for possessing the land (chaps. 34—36). The book ends with Israel "in the plains of Moab by Jordan"; the promises remain just out of reach.

5. *Deuteronomy*—Moses delivered a series of sermons from the same site where the book of Numbers had closed—"on this side of Jordan, in the land of Moab" (1:1,5). The opening address (chaps. 1—4) recalls the events of Numbers, and the book concludes (34:9) with the succession of Joshua already announced in Numbers 27:18-23. The second address (chaps. 5—26) presents a theologically-reflective *re*statement of the Sinaitic covenant-law as first revealed in Exodus. The theme of patriarchal blessing continues, emphasizing the land element of the promises: "The Lord will bless you in the land which the Lord your God gives you as an inheritance to possess" (15:4, RSV). It is described as a land "flowing with milk and honey" which was promised to Israel's "fathers" (6:3; 11:9; 26:9,15; 27:3). The final chapters (27—34) contain warnings about Israel's anticipated life in the land; failure to abide by God's covenant-law will result in Israel's expulsion (chap. 28). The last recorded words of God to His servant Moses reiterate the long-awaited promise: "This is the land which I swore to Abraham, Isaac, and Jacob, saying, 'I will give it to your descendants'" (34:4, NASB). The book ends, however, with Israel not one step closer to the land than at the beginning; the elusive land still awaits them. The final depiction of Moses, looking upon the land from the distant Mount Nebo, captures the condition of Israel still waiting. The Pentateuch concludes "open-ended," looking ahead to the fulfilling of the promises.

Historical/Cultural Conditioning

We have already alluded to the complex historical setting of the Pentateuch, ranging from earliest recorded memories of human beings set in Mesopotamia and Canaan to the era of Moses in Egypt and the desert. It is not our purpose here to elaborate on the details but to point out the necessity of interpreting the Pentateuch in the light of our increasing knowledge of the ancient world, its language, customs, and geography. The Bible was not written in a cultural vacuum; it is imperative that the expositor consider its cultural setting in order to recognize the distinctive message of the Bible.[7]

Our particular interest is the practice of Sabbath observance in the ancient Near East.[8] There is no clear parallel. The Babylonian "evil days" were specially recognized each month; they were based on the lunar cycle, related to the quarterly appearances of the moon. Some restrictions were practiced because of the superstition associated with those days. *Shapattu* was the day of the full moon on the 15th of each month which consisted of ceremonies appeasing the gods. Israel's Sabbath shows a much different attitude. Not only was it unrelated to the moon's cycle, the Sabbath was a day of joyous celebration in which everyone, whether master, slave, or work animal, ceased for a day of rest. Exodus 20 ties it to the creation of God, giving it a universal significance, while Deuteronomy 5 relates it to the deliverance of Israel from Egypt. The Sabbath also became an integral part of the agricultural life of the people; a Sabbatical year was the year of release from indebtedness to creditors (Deut. 15:1). The point is that the land and its people belonged to God, and He alone dictated the use of the land and the release of obligations.

This is sufficient to show that the Sabbath was unique to Israel and thereby distinguished the people as the special possession of God. It conveyed the grace of God who as a beneficent landowner tended the needs of His tenants, Israel. It functioned as a memorial to the creation and redemption of Israel. It spoke of God as Cosmic Ruler and personal Savior.

Canonical-Theological Contours

The literary character of the Pentateuch has led us to see that it ends without a satisfying conclusion. The people of God remain encamped on the wrong side of the Jordan. What is the significance of the Pentateuch's abrupt end? What does the Pentateuch hope to say by this incomplete plot?

Looking Back to the Future.—We have discovered that the theme itself—the yet-to-be-realized promissory blessings—causes the Pentateuch to look beyond itself toward the future. This prophetic/eschatological perspective to Moses' books is attested with the *Torah* as a "witness" to future generations (Deut. 31:26). Essentially, the sermon of Moses in Deuteronomy 32—33 closes the Pentateuch with a prospective look at Israel's future life in the land. It anticipates the Former Prophets (Joshua—2 Kings) which interpret the rise and fall of Israel's monarchy in light of Moses' words. The final paragraph of the Pentateuch celebrates its focal figure as the quintessential prophet: "Since then no prophet has risen in Israel like Moses, whom the Lord knew face to face" (Deut. 34:10).[9]

This eschatological perspective also impacted the compositional scheme of the final form of the Pentateuch.[10] Literary "seams" occur at three major junctures which fasten together an extended narrative and a poetic speech. This approach is attested several times in Genesis 1—4; the pattern is narrative + poetic speech + brief epilogue (2:23-24; 3:14-24; 4:23-26). This same technique occurs for the Pentateuch as a whole at the macrostructural level. The three junctures are the blessing of Jacob (Gen. 49), the oracles of Balaam (Num. 23—24), and the Song of Moses (Deut. 32—33) which concludes the whole work. A closer look at the connective literary "tissue" at each juncture reveals the use of the same language and motifs. In each case, the major character (Jacob, Balaam, or Moses) summoned his audience and declared his intentions to speak of future events in "days to come." This expression, "days to come" (*be'ahar/H/Wt hayyāmîm*) introduces the poetic speech to follow (Gen. 49:1; Num. 24:14; Deut. 31:29). The occurrence of this phrase at only one other place in the Pentateuch (and that, too, at an interconnective seam, Deut. 4:30) indicates that the composition orients the reader to the future, not the past.

This eschatological perspective sees the past as a prototype for the future. Thus, Paul could speak of the past as examples, "and they are written for our admonition, upon whom the ends of the world are come" (1 Cor. 10:11). This means that the hermeneutic of the final composer was to establish the Pentateuch as the normative expression of Israel's faith and thus speak to future generations with the same authority as the contemporary Mosaic community. Hence, the prophet Moses is typological of the eschatological Second Moses to whom the Pentateuch looks (Deut. 18:15,18).

Also, evidence of this eschatological purpose is the use of narrative as a typology for the future. Smaller narrative episodes in Genesis prefigure events in the life of Israel. The route of Abraham into Canaan by way of Shechem, Ai/Bethel, and the Negev (Gen. 12:1-9) is repeated by Jacob upon his return from Haran (Gen. 33:18-20; 35:14-15,27); both patriarchs build altars of worship at Shechem and Bethel. The pattern of traversing these three regions is echoed in the conquest narratives of Joshua: Ai/Bethel (compare Josh. 7:2; 8:9 with Gen. 12:8), Shechem where an altar is built (Josh. 8:30), south of Ai/Bethel toward the Negev (Josh. 10) and then north of Shechem (Josh. 11). Again, the narrative of Abraham's sojourn in Egypt parallels the later account of Israel's experience in Egypt from Joseph to the Exodus (Gen. 41—Ex. 12). This indicates that the lives of the patriarchs were a foreshadow of the life of Abraham's descendants, Israel.[11] In the same way, the life of Israel in the Pentateuch became a picture of Israel's future history, particularly its exile (Egypt and Babylon) and return (under Moses and Ezra).

Realizing the Past.—What does this mean for preaching? The community life of Israel informs our understanding of "community" among the people of God today. The Mosaic community is a prototype for the Church today. B. K. Waltke has said: "The message of Christ is not something tacked on to the OT; he is at the heart, for the Spirit of Christ was in the prophets predicting 'the sufferings of Christ and the glories that should follow' " (1 Pet. 1:11).[12] The Old Testament is a resource of types and symbols for the spiritual kingdom which was initiated by the Messianic Lord and realized in His own person. Israel's worship (sacrifices), holy days (new moons, Sabbath), and institutions (priest and tabernacle) point to the spiritual kingdom we enjoy (Heb. 7:18-20; 8:1—10:18).

How does the Mosaic community serve as a foreshadowing of the church? There is an analogy or correspondence between the Old and the New. First, since the Pentateuch is prophetic (proclamation) and eschatological (unrealized), preaching the Pentateuch means proclaiming the forthcoming creation of the people of God as it is being realized in the body of Jesus Christ. Salvation history culminates in Christ and His church who defeats His enemies and brings to pass God's blessing on the elect (Gen. 3:15; 12:1-3; Rom. 16:20; Gal. 3:16). The New Testament identifies the church as "filling up" the three-fold promissory blessings to Abraham: (1) the establishment of a righteous nation (seed) (Gen. 12:2; Rom. 4:11,16-21; Gal. 3:8-9,16,29; Deut. 10:16;30:6 with Rom. 2:28-29); (2) the blessing of relationship in its universal aspect (Gen. 12:3; Gal. 3:6-9); and (3) the possession of a land as the eschatological home of Abraham and his "spiritual" descendants (Gen. 12:1; Heb. 11:8-10 with 12:22 and 13:14; also Heb. 3:7—4:11).

Second, the preacher declares the coming of the Second Moses who is realizing what Moses could not (Deut. 18:15,18). Whereas Moses saw God "face to face" (Ex. 33:11), it is Jesus Christ who fully "exegetes" the Father (John 1:16-18). Thus, Jesus is declared by the apostles as the "prophet" whom the Pentateuch anticipates (John 1:21,25,45; 5:46; 6:14; 7:40; Acts 3:22-26; 7:37).[13] Jesus is the true successor to Moses who consummates the household of God by uniting Jew and Gentile in the body of Christ.

Third, the old covenant carved on stone was abrogated by the sin of Israel, but God provided the New Covenant inscribed in the heart (Jer. 31:31-34), as anticipated already by Moses (Deut. 10:16; 30:6), through the crucified Christ. Jesus instituted the covenant at the Lord's Supper (Mark 14:12-25, and parallel passages, Mt. 26:17-30; Luke 22:7-23) so that the Church could enjoy the superior ministry of the New Covenant (Heb. 8:8-12). Jesus is superior to the old mediator, Moses, and administers the New Covenant from heaven itself (Heb. 8:1-6).

Fourth, Israel's worship has been superseded therefore by Christ and His heavenly tabernacle. Christ Himself is our Passover (Ex. 12:11; 1 Cor. 5:7); in Him are found all the holy festivals and days (Col. 2:16-17). Moses' tabernacle was only the earthly pattern of the heavenly reality (Heb. 8:5; Ex. 25:9,40; 26:30; 1 Chron. 28:11-12,19). Jesus has entered the very presence of God in the heavenly "holy of holies" where, as high priest, He achieves the Day of Atonement perfectly, once for all (Ex. 25—40; Lev. 16:13-15,24; with Heb. 7:26-28; 8:1—10:18; especially Heb. 8:1-2; 9:11).

Fifth, the struggling life of faith by Moses' community as they journeyed under the guidance and provision of God encourages and forewarns the church (1 Cor. 10:1-13). The people of Israel were united in their common salvation and in their submission to Moses' leadership. God led them through the sea to salvation (Ex. 14:22,29) and guided them through the wilderness by cloud and fire (Ex. 13:21-22; Num. 9:15-23; 14:14; Deut. 1:33). The "rock was Christ" (1 Cor. 10:4) from which poured the waters of life and provision that secured their survival (Ex. 17:1-7; Num. 20:2-11; John 6:30-35).

Therefore, we preach that Jesus Christ is Abraham's seed who is the mediator of God's promises for all peoples on the earth (Gen. 12:3; Gal. 3:16; Acts 3:25-26). God, through the baptism of the Holy Spirit (1 Cor. 12:13), is gathering all those who are the recipients of the promises (Gal. 3:29) into a spiritual kingdom (Rom. 4:17-21).

Problems and Preaching

There are three special problems facing the expositor of the Pentateuch: (1) the significance of Genesis 1—11 for the modern world, (2) the relevance of the Mosaic law, and (3) the relationship of law and the Church.[14] In discussing each problem, we will suggest ways the preacher can derive pulpit material.

Preaching Creation and Early Mankind (Genesis 1—11)

The modern audience will be troubled by these opening chapters of Genesis since they are so foreign to our contemporary way of reporting on human events. The times and events are not like anything we know; they occur in the distant past in almost surreal circumstances. We are much more at home with the patriarchal stories; they seem closer to our experience and therefore easier to accept and understand. For this reason, Genesis 1—11 are often chalked up to "myth" or "theology" and relegated to an antiquated view of human existence—a once-quaint but now obsolete view of origins. On the other hand, for those who hold to their historical veracity, these chapters have become a battle line in the defense of biblical orthodoxy.

Preachers are caught in a dilemma: do they tackle the scientific and historical problems headlong? Or do they cut these early accounts free from the realities of cosmos and history and stick to talking of "theological stories"? The ballet danced around this problem by esoteric theologians who drive a wedge between historical reality and faith (to save the latter) is not welcomed by the common-sense layperson in the pew. Nor is the congregation helped by the preacher who pretends to be a scientist, subjecting the authority of Scripture to modern reconstructions of the earth's beginnings.

A better approach is to explain these early chapters in light of ancient cosmogonies. It is in the ancient context that the intention of the text can be best appropriated for the modern reader who is trying to make sense of it all. When it is understood against the background of ancient thought, it becomes apparent that Genesis 1—11 is not "myth," but in fact anti-myth, and yet not solely a historical (not to mention scientific) account in our modern sense.

An Ancient Pattern of Telling.—Genesis appears to be following an ancient pattern for the way origins were told among the peoples of the Near East.[15] The closest parallels are the Akkadian *Atra-hasis* (1600 B.C.) and the Sumerian *Eridu Genesis* (1600 B.C.) which give an account of creation to the great Flood.[16] Other parallels to Genesis may be drawn from such myths as the Akkadian *Enuma Elish* and *Epic of Gilgamesh*. There is no evidence that outright borrowing occurred between the Hebrews and others; rather, there was a general knowledge of early traditions shared by all antiquity. The text of Genesis 1—11 addresses the topics common to the telling about beginnings.

The primary reason modern persons dismiss the opening chapters of Genesis as useless historically is because of the difference between how the Bible speaks of origins and how people speak of them today. This does not mean that Genesis 1—11 is not historical reality; it chooses to speak of those real (time, space) events in a way that was expected by its ancient audience but not in the way we tell history. These historical memories of early events also stand for universal truths. So the first man is both a real, individual "Adam" (compare the genealogy of Gen. 5; also Luke 3:38) and "Everyman" (*'ādām*, meaning "humankind"; compare Rom. 5:12-21); the serpent in the garden is more than a reptile, since it is the "Adversary" (Rom. 16:20; Rev. 12:9,20:2); and the two trees in the middle of the garden are unlike the other trees in that they are also symbols for knowledge and life (Rev. 22:2,19).

Also, the account follows a topical arrangement at places and not a strictly chronological one; thus, the Table of Nations (chap. 10) can precede the Tower of Babel (11:1-1) although the latter occurred first and explains the listing of the nations. Furthermore, the creation week does not necessarily follow a strict chronological arrangement of events.

Finally, the expositor must recall that the Genesis account does not attempt to be exhaustive; therefore, information that a modern account would include might be irrelevant to the purposes of the ancient composition.

Creation and Flood.—Significant differences between Genesis and pagan thought clarify the theological significance of Genesis 1—11.[17] Ancient cosmogonies were crude polytheistic and magical accounts of origins. Actually, the Mesopotamian stories tended to focus on the origins of the gods themselves, offering a theogony rather than a cosmogony. The God of the Hebrews, on the contrary, has no biography! Also, ancient people blurred the boundaries between the divine and the physical. For them, the universe itself was alive; a mystical union existed between physical phenomena and the gods. Genesis declares that God is Creator, distinct from His creation, though intimately concerned for His creation. The ancients also believed that creation was the result of a titanic struggle between primeval forces which was settled in the subjugation of chaos by the gods of cosmos followed by the emergence of heaven and earth. Yet, the biblical depiction has a God who *speaks* creation into existence by the authority of His word; no rival threatens Him, and no force disobeys. The biblical account is polemical, deliberately opposing the false notions of the pagans.[18]

Unlike the Bible, the pagan versions show the creation of human life as an afterthought; human beings were formed to serve the gods who had become too tired to obtain their own food for survival. Pagan accounts also had no record of woman's beginning. The Bible, however, celebrates the creation of man and woman; they are specially honored by their Maker and invited to rule over the earth. God graciously provides food for animal and human life.

Another significant difference lies in the variant interpretations of the Flood's purpose. *Atra-hasis* and the *Eridu Genesis* attribute the Flood to the last desperate attempt of the gods to rid themselves of the overpopulated, bothersome humans. The survival of their "Noah" was unintended and only accepted by the gods after a compromise. The Bible, on the other hand, presents the population of the earth as good in the eyes of God; procreation is a blessing and will bring to pass God's reign on earth through Adam's lineage. More importantly, the Flood is God's judgment against the encroaching world-wide practice of human sin. The Bible, unlike its ancient counterparts, shows that human civilization became increasingly sinful. This pessimism concerning the history and future of human society, apart from the moral intervention of God, was not shared by the ancients.

Tower of Babel.—No parallel to the Table of Nations in the ancient world has survived. It uniquely speaks to the universality of God's reign and explains the origins of the nations as related to one progenitor,

Noah.[19] It shows that human life is united as one family and yet divided by language, territory, tribal heritage, and political state. The dispersion of the nations at Babel (Gen. 11:1-9) explains that the origins of the nations are the result of God's judgment. Nevertheless, the dispersion which leads to the "filling of the earth" still accomplishes God's plan for blessing the human family (compare Gen. 1:28 with 9:7). The background to this account is Babylon and the Akkadian *Enuma Elish* which attributes the building of the city and its tower to Marduk, the patron deity of Babylon. Whereas the ancients perceived it as a source of pride for the builders, Genesis presents a satire on the futile attempts of these empire builders to achieve power and immortality. The key wordplay of the account is a pun on the name "Babel" by the Hebrew *Bālal*, translated "confused" or "to babble" (11:9).

Modern Science.— Before concluding this section, a word is needed concerning the relationship of Genesis 1 and modern science. The Christian community has responded with a legion of varying approaches. Many preachers are unaware that there is more for the preacher to consider than the two extremes of literalism (recent creationism) at one end of the spectrum and theistic evolution on the other. Alternative opinions, such as progressive creationism, are gathering a growing audience among scientists who hold steadfastly to Christian beliefs. The important factors to recall are: (1) the ancient text should not be manipulated by the exegete to answer questions never considered by the ancient writer, and (2) the genealogical framework of Genesis ("these are the generations," occurring 11 times in the book) clearly indicates that the accounts of creation and early human beings are reflecting historical reality.

Seventh Day.—In our sample passage, the fourth commandment relates Sabbath observance to the seventh day of the Creation Week. Just as God rested after His creation activities, His people are exhorted to follow the divine pattern of labor followed by rest. The traits of the seventh day (Gen. 2:1-3) distinguish it as the most important: (1) it is the only day "blessed" and "sanctified" by God; (2) God is silent since there is no creative word ("Then God said"); and (3) there is no cessation formula ("There was evening and there was morning"). The implication of the passage is that the seventh day is eternal, because it is related to God's special celebration of the created order. This indicates that God is ruler over time as well as space. God's people are invited to enter into that celebration in two ways: first, to celebrate God's creation and deliverance through Israel's weekly Sabbath, Sabbath-year, and jubilee; and second, to enter God's eternal rest through faith (not work!), a rest that still remains to those who believe (Heb. 4:1-11). In this way, the Sabbath functions as a foreshadow (Col. 2:16-17) of the eternal rest God inaugurated and enjoyed at creation. Today the gospel offers this rest.

Preaching the Mosaic Law

Law in the Biblical World.—The Pentateuch is largely made up of three bodies of laws (Ex. 21—23; Lev.; Deut). Our understanding of ancient law has been advanced by the recovery of law codes from Israel's neighbors from as early as 2500 B.C. In particular, the laws of ancient Mesopotamia correspond in striking ways to the biblical laws as well as having important differences.[20] Scholars have discovered that the exercise of ancient law was quite different than the modern conception of law. Only when biblical law is set against its ancient context will the contemporary audience come to appreciate its value.

The major misconception by modern readers is that the "law" of the ancient world was promulgated as a binding, statutory law as in our modern sense of law. It is commonplace in modern law to specify penalties when that law is breached; in other words, modern laws are promulgated with the view of specific enforcement, and the authority of the lawmakers is the basis for prosecuting an offender. Ancient Near Eastern law, however, is not a codified law which is referenced by the court. In fact, among the thousands of cases recovered from ancient records there is no evidence that courts appealed to a written law as the authorizing basis for a judgment.

Ancient law was rather a collection of laws which reflected existing case precedents. They described the existing legal tradition rather than promulgating a new one. Therefore, ancient laws were specific cases which illustrated the "policies" of society (societal attitudes). This is evidenced by the limitations of the ancient law codes. No ancient law code, including the Old Testament, is exhaustive; they are incomplete and selective, focusing on exceptional situations. This means that the laws of the Old Testament must be understood as a reflection of the *values* held by the Hebrew community.[21] For example, the tenth commandment (prohibiting covetousness) expresses a value concerning the attitude of the inner person. These values are expressed by the Ten Commandments which guided judgments rendered in specific cases. Old Testament law then does not emerge from the principles of law as much as it does the practice of law.[22]

Related to this is the covenant aspect of the Mosaic laws. Scholars generally agree that the Sinai revelation imitates the literary form of a vassal treaty or covenant. In the Mosaic covenant, the Ten Commandments are the stipulations to which the two parties, God and Israel, subscribed. Israel had two forms of law: case law and apodictic law. Case law, common to the whole ancient world, gives a specific case and ties a particular solution or sanction to it ("If a bull gores a man or a woman to death, the bull must be stoned to death" [Ex. 21:28, NIV].). Apodictic law, on the other hand, is a direct command, prohibition, or instruction (often in the second person). The Ten Commandments are apodictic in form; also, there is no specific sanction given. It is only in the examples of case law that the penalty of death is discovered. The best explanation for Israel's emphasis on apodictic laws lies in how Israel interpreted the source of its law as divine. The law codes of the pagans were given by kings, but God gave the law of Moses. In particular, the Ten Commandments were written by the "finger of God" (Ex. 31:18).

Another significant feature of Hebrew law is its inclusion of civil and sacral laws. Ancient law codes tended to exclude religious law whereas Hebrew law saw no difference. This reflected the Hebrews' view of their daily life as wholly under the governance of God. Israel's community knew no such thing as the "secular," because their covenant relationship to God came to bear on every aspect of their existence. Since the law was holy by virtue of its divine source, any breach of the law was considered a sin. This also explains why Hebrew law makes so much of the "clean" and "unclean." The law regulated every aspect of Hebrew life and distinguished Israel as *holy*, a people distinctly related to God.

Biblical Values.—The laws expressing these underlying principles are the values the preacher should expound. What were the values Israel's society held? In addition to the stipulations of the Ten Commandments, the Hebrew laws reflect values that contrasted with those of the unbelieving world. Biblical law prized human life above property. Mesopotamian laws gave inordinate attention to theft or damage of property; also, they often accepted monetary compensation for the loss of animal and human life. Biblical law is based on the principle of Genesis 9:4-6, requiring the blood of animal and person when homicide or negligence can be shown (for example, Ex. 21:28-36). Monetary compensation among the Hebrews was also avoided since it favored the rich. The preacher must declare that human life is most sacred to God.

The law also protected the oppressed such as the poor, slaves, aliens, and widows. The Hebrews gave special attention to slaves since they considered themselves the descendants of Egyptian slaves. For example, Mesopotamian law applied the law differently between social classes, but the Bible prescribes the same penalties for crimes regardless of class.[23] The Covenant Code (Ex. 21—23), for example, begins with laws bearing on slaves; also, Hebrew society provided a safe haven for runaway slaves from foreign countries (Deut. 23:15-16). The covenant-law repeatedly ensures comfort, protection, and restoration for the lower social classes (Ex. 22:21-22; Lev. 19:10; 24:22; Deut. 10:18; 24:12-14). This is the reason why the prophets so often pointed to the oppression of the poor by the ruling class as clear evidence of covenant unfaithfulness (Isa. 1:17; 3:14; Jer. 22:15-17; Amos 2:7; 4:1; 5:11). This is the heart of true religion (Jas. 1:27). The life of Jesus reflected this (Luke 14:13). Social justice and God's provision for the socially disenfranchised should be preached.

Finally, there is room for preaching the mercy of God. Modern audiences are confused by the biblical practice of talionic sanctions, expressed by the formula "an eye for an eye, a tooth for a tooth" (Ex. 21:23-25; Lev. 24:18-20; Deut. 19:21). Some attempt to vilify Old Testament religion by appealing to this phrase as typical of Hebrew law. Talionic law only means that the penalty matched the severity of the offense—equal retribution. This was practiced as well by the pagans, but they carried the principle to the extreme. For example, in Babylonian law, if a debtor is forced to give up his son as a bondservant to a creditor and that son dies due to the creditor's mistreatment, the son of the creditor will be put to death. Hebrew law, however, prohibits this vicarious form of retribution unless there is guilt. For example, in the case of an ox goring a man to death, Hebrew law insists that the owner of the ox, if found to have been negligent, be put to death as well as the ox (Ex. 21:28-32). In Hebrew law, the talionic formula is not calling literally for bodily mutilation, although this was practiced among the Mesopotamians. The talionic expression occurs in Deuteronomy 19:21 which clearly has nothing to do with bodily injury; it is merely a retaliatory formula calling for a stiff penalty. Talionic law does not advocate brutality but in fact restrains blood vengeance by restricting the response of the victim's family; the "eye for an eye" formula is a call for justice and a prevention of excessive reprisal.[24] Many other examples can be cited, but the clearest is the law of refuge. It provides six "cities of refuge" where the manslayer may flee for a fair hearing; if the offender is innocent of premeditated murder, he may remain in the city protected from the victim's blood avenger and can return to his home upon the death of the high priest (Num. 35:6-34; Deut. 19:1-14).

Preaching Law and Gospel

Ceremonial Laws.—Another puzzling aspect of the Pentateuch to the Christian audience is circumcision and the cultic laws of sacrifice. Circumcision was a puberty rite in Egypt but was not a custom among the Canaanites, Israel's closest neighbors. The Abrahamic Covenant (Gen. 17:10) required it of all male descendants, as well as those who were aliens living in the patriarch's household; also, it was commanded in the Mosaic tradition (Ex. 12:48; Lev. 12:3). The significance of the rite was to distinguish Israel by a mark in the flesh as the people of God. The apostle Paul drew an analogy between the circumcision of the flesh and the circumcision of the heart, indicating that the distinguishing mark of the Christian was special devotion to God as a part of God's household. This spiritual circumcision was required of the true believer in the Mosaic community also (Deut. 10:16; 30:6).

Like circumcision, the sacrificial system as a whole was designed to distinguish Israel as the people of God. Yet Israel's religious calendar and cult were not created in a cultural vacuum. The formal rites of the Old Testament had similarity to Canaanite customs, but the differences are more striking. For example, Canaanite religion interpreted the sacrifice of animals as feeding the gods and as a means of winning their favor. Since their religion was a fertility cult, the Canaanite festival calendar focused on the seasons of harvest which celebrated the procreation of the gods. The Israelites, on the other hand, offered sacrifices to God as expressions of worship and thanksgiving. Unlike the Canaanites, who did not emphasize appeasement for sinful behavior, biblical sacrifices also functioned as a reconciling atonement for their disobedience to God's holy expectations.

The clearest example is *Yom Kippur* ("Day of Atonement") which has no parallel in Canaan. Leviticus 16 spells out the elaborate ceremonial requirements for this most sacred day of the year in the life of the nation. It was the only day when the high priest entered the most holy place of the tabernacle; there, the high priest sprinkled the blood of the victim (goat) upon the "mercy seat" of the sacred chest ("ark of the covenant") which made propitiation for the sins of the nation. When the high priest placed his hands upon a second goat and confessed the sins of Israel, the animal symbolically becomes Israel's "scapegoat" which bore away Israel's sins out of the camp.

Through this rite of blood victim and scapegoat, God provided a ceremonial means whereby Israel could continue its relationship with God. The impact of this rite on the New Testament's interpretation of Jesus' death cannot be overstated; the character of the vicarious nature of the atonement was construed as a foreshadowing of the cross event. Jesus is depicted as the Suffering Servant (Isa. 52:13—53:12) who suffers vicariously as an innocent victim on behalf of the guilty (1 Pet. 2:21-24; 3:18). He is the "mercy seat" (="propitiation," Rom. 3:25, KJV) by whose own blood the sin of Jew and Gentile alike are covered. Hebrews makes it clear that no animal's blood could satisfactorily remove the sin of Israel; this feature of the past was only a temporary measure until the effectual offering of Christ's sacrifice had come to pass (Heb. 10:3-7).

This issue is part of the larger question of the relationship between the Old Testament's law and the New Testament's emphasis on salvation by grace. The sacrificial laws were never designed to "save" Israel from its sins (Heb. 10:1-3). The observance of the law was an *expression* of a person's devotion to God as Israel's covenant Lord. The *basis* for salvation in both testaments is the same: "[God] chose us in him [Christ] before the creation of the world" (Eph. 1:4, NIV). God elected Christ before the creation of the world to redeem sinners by His "precious blood" (1 Pet. 1:18-21). The means of salvation is *faith* and the *object* is the living Lord. Faith always took precedence over the law; before Moses' institution of the law, salvation was by faith, since Abraham believed

God and it was credited to him as righteousness (see Gen. 15:6; Rom. 4:3). For the Christian, the object of our faith is clearer, and the breadth and depth of God's love has now been fully manifested in the Cross event (1 John 4:9-10), but there is no difference between Old and New Testaments in the salvation God achieved.

Law and the Church.—Since all God's people enter this common salvation, the question arises as to how the law relates, if at all, to the church. The Gospels present Christ as the fulfillment of the "Law and the Prophets" and also the key to their interpretation (Matt. 5:17; Luke 24:27,44; John 5:46). The authority of the law was not disputed by Christ (John 10:35), although he gave a new interpretation (as with the temple) in light of the eschatological "Day of the Lord" initiated by His coming. In particular, He differed with the traditional application of the law by the Pharisees whose views often perverted the original Mosaic tradition.

It was left, however, to Paul to spell out the Christian's response to the law. Paul showed how the Christian integrates the Mosaic tradition in the present age of the Spirit.[25] While Paul never treated the subject exhaustively in any one place, Romans and Galatians give special attention to it. However, we must remember that Paul was commenting on the law in an adversarial discussion in which "Judaizers"—Christian Jews who imposed the Law on Gentile converts—had distorted the gospel and had misrepresented Paul's views. Judaizers were insisting on circumcision, dietary regulations, and Sabbath observance as prerequisites for Gentile inclusion in the church. These customs were historically the distinctive features of the Jews which had promoted Israel's ethnic pride and had driven the wedge between them and the Gentiles. Paul opposed using the law in this fashion.

Romans 6—8 sets the law of Moses in contrast to the "law" of grace. By virtue of Christ's death, the life-giving reign of the Spirit has begun; the dominion of the old order has passed. Galatians 3—4 argues that the law is no longer obligatory for the Christian. From these passages, it would lead one to conclude that Paul's assertion "Christ is the *telos* of the law" (Rom. 10:4) should be rendered "end" in the sense of cessation. This is further suggested by 1 Corinthians 7:19 where circumcision—the preeminent sign of the Old Covenant—is judged irrelevant for the Christian profession. Elsewhere, Paul drew on the imagery of Jeremiah's New Covenant (compare 31:31-34 with Ezek. 16:60; 34:25; 37:26) and declared the superiority of the New Covenant inaugurated by the death of Christ (2 Cor. 3:7-14). Those who preach the gospel are ministers of the New Covenant (2 Cor. 4; Heb. 8).

Despite this assertion that the Old Covenant is obsolete, the apostle appealed to the law as an authoritative voice and even continued to practice it on at least some occasions (Acts 16:3; 24:17-18). The church was entreated to practice holiness, echoing the motif of sanctification common to Leviticus (compare 1 Thess. 4:1-12 with Lev. 11:45). Also, the heart of the law was still effectual for Paul when he exhorted his Galatian readers to take up the "law of love" (compare Gal. 5:14 with Lev. 19:18). Paul, wrongly perceived by his opponents as antinomian (Acts 24:14; 25:8), declared that the law came from God, was holy, and was competent for its purposes (compare Rom. 7:12,14 with 7:22).

Was Paul ambivalent toward the law? The Christian audience today often senses conflict about the role of the law in Christian living. On the one hand, they hear in the Pentateuch the voice of God and are moved by the powerful spirit it conveys. On the other hand, the church knows that the sacrificial system (Heb. 10:3), dietary laws (1 Cor. 9:19-23), and numerous other unsung laws are inappropriate for the disciple today. This intuition that the law is obsolete yet that something of the law continues is a good one.

Paul was not ambivalent toward the law. He could maintain that the Mosaic law was still effectual for its intended purposes of instruction about holiness and its conviction of sin, but at the same time obsolete as a standard of conduct for the believer today. First, the law was a whole, not susceptible to the dissection of moral versus ceremonial. These distinctions made by preachers would be foreign to the Israelite and would be objectionable to Paul as a Jew (Gal. 5:3). Second, the law was never intended to *create* a righteous people, but rather to *identify* a holy possession belonging to God (Gal. 2:21). The law's intent was to expose the sin inherent in the Israelite (Rom. 7:5,7,13); it was never designed to justify since it could not be wholly obeyed. Anyone who chooses to submit to a part is responsible for all, and no one can achieve it all (Gal. 2:21; 3:10-11; 6:13). Third, the law was given as a temporary instructional device, a *pedagogue* or trainer (Gal. 3:23-25), and, therefore, was never expected to be perpetually binding. Evidence of this is the promise given to Abraham which antedated the Mosaic legislation (Rom. 4:1-25, especially vv. 2-3). The patriarch was saved by faith in God's promise (Gen. 15:6) before the introduction of circumcision (Gen. 17:10) and before the works of faith (see Gen. 22, the sacrifice of Isaac).

The avenue of faith has always been open to all—both Jew and Gentile (Gal. 3:6-9). The law was never opposed to promise, however, since it was the expression of faith in that promise (Gal. 3:21-22). Yet, the works of faith (that is, law) never could be substituted for faith since they did not produce the righteousness brought about by faith. Salvation from Egypt came first and was later followed by the creation of a covenant-keeping people, a holy nation for God (Ex. 19:3-6). The law was operational but never salvific, and it is Christ who has realized fully the promise of faith for us by the giving of the Spirit (Gal. 3:12-14). Now, it is "Christ's law" (Gal. 6:2) which is operational and to which the disciple is bound (1 Cor. 9:20-21). Thus, we "live by the Spirit" (Gal. 5:16-26) to whom we yield and by whom we are empowered to be the holy people of God, His peculiar possession (Rom. 8).

Therefore, Christ is also the "*telos* of the law" (Rom. 10:4), in the sense of "goal" as well as its "end," for it points to the law of Christ as its fulfillment (Matt. 5:17) and its successor (Gal. 3:24) who has brought us into "sonship" with God (Gal. 4:4-7). Those values expressed by the covenant-law are holy and remain to be emulated by the church, but the law as a formal code is obsolete. Thus, Paul could say: "These things happened to them as examples and were written down as warnings for us, on whom the *fulfillment* of the ages has come" (1 Cor. 10:11, NIV). The eschaton of the Spirit has come, and now the law of God is implemented by the regenerating and sanctifying power of the indwelling Spirit.

Application of the Covenant-Law.—How shall we preach and apply the covenant-law? Let it accomplish through our preaching what it was intended to do. First, *condemn!* The law functions like the "light" of Christ which exposes the evil of sinful persons which lurks in the darkness (John 3:19-21). An exposition of the law will show how encompassing God's holy demands are and how miserably short of them men and women live. The effect will drive people to confess their inadequacy to live obediently before God and their utter dependence on Christ who alone has satisfied the demands of God. It is Christ who has borne the curses of the law in our behalf.

Second, *challenge!* The law is a *pedagogue* to teach and illustrate the character of God, the devoted life of a covenanted-people, and God's provision for maintaining the God-human relationship. For example, the prohibition against eating blood (Lev. 17:10-14) has no exact parallel for Christians since we live under the principle of 1 Corinthians 10:31, that is, we are free to eat or drink whatever as long as we do it for the glory of God. Nevertheless, the Levitical prohibition is significant for us because it reflects the value placed by the Hebrew community on the sanctity of life, "because the life of every creature is its blood" (Lev. 17:14, NIV). Another example is Exodus 23:19 (also Deut. 14:21) which exhorts: "Do not cook a young goat in its mother's milk." This is a directive surely lost to the Christian audience! It, too, speaks of the sanctity of life and the unnaturalness of the mother participating in any way in the destruction of her own young. Furthermore, in this case, scholars surmise that this was a Canaanite custom prohibited by the Hebrews to avoid assimilation; therefore, a second lesson is sanctification as illustrated by this law in its original setting.

Third, *color!* Since the law was a trainer pointing to Christ, it functions like a primer for a child. The sacrificial system with its elaborate cult setting is a "coloring book" for the Christian to use in learning about Christ as sacrifice and mediator. A child's coloring book has either a scene or portrait which is drawn in outline; the child colors in between the lines to give the scene or portrait the colors of life. In the same way, the tabernacle cult is the portrait of Christ drawn in outline, and the New Testament's revelation fills in the colors to identify the "Lamb of God."

Sabbath.—What does this mean for our sample passage on the Sabbath? The abrogation of the Mosaic covenant as a code of conduct indicates that Sabbath observance—the very sign of the Old Covenant—is no longer binding on the Christian. The calendar prescriptions are only shadows of the true substance, namely, Christ (Col. 2:16-17) and, therefore, no longer a basis for conduct. Of the Ten Commandments, this is the only one which was not reissued in the New Testament. As with circumcision and dietary laws, the New Testament has no injunction for Sabbath observance. These have been reinterpreted eschatologically: we are circumcised in heart (Rom. 2:29); we are declared clean, and what we eat will not defile us (Mark 7:17-19; John 15:3); and we have entered into God's eternal Sabbath-rest (Heb. 4:9-11). Therefore, every day is sacred to the Christian (1 Tim. 4:3-5; Rom. 14:5,17).

The Christian community, first made up of Jews, continued the custom of Sabbath worship but early adopted the first day as a special day of remembering the Lord's resurrection (Acts 2:1; 1 Cor. 16:1-2). Soon, the first day was the focal day of Christian worship. Observance of communal worship is enjoined by the church, not on the basis of Mosaic law but because we live in the new age (compare Heb. 10:25). This is reminiscent of Jesus' attitude, who opposed the Pharisaic accretions to the Sabbath; rather, the Sabbath was designed to release mankind and never given to enslave (Mark 2:23—3:6, and parallel passages, Matt. 12:1-14, Luke 6:1-11; see also John 5:1-18). Therefore, the Christian community convenes to recognize the lordship of Christ; it is their proclamation that the Messianic Age has come and that they have identified with the new creation in Christ.

Notes

1. For this example and others, see Y. T. Radday, "Chiasmus in Hebrew Biblical Narrative," *Chiasmus in Antiquity*, ed. J. W. Welch (Hildesheim: Gerstenberg, 1981), 84-86.

2. For this discussion of the main parts of the Pentateuch, see R. P. Knierim, "The Composition of the Pentateuch," *SBL 1985 Seminar Papers*, ed. David Lull (Atlanta: Scholars Press, 1985), 393-415.

3. See the treatment of R. Longacre, *Joseph: A Story of Divine Providence* (Winona Lake, IN: Eisenbrauns, 1989).

4. For a detailed discussion, see D. J. Clines, *The Theme of the Pentateuch, Journal for Study of Old Testament Supplement* 10 (Sheffield: University of Sheffield, 1982).

5. Gordon J. Wenham, *Genesis 1-15*, vol. 1 in *Word Biblical Commentary* (Waco: Word, 1987), 51.

6. B. S. Childs, *Introduction to the Old Testament as Scripture* (Philadelphia: Fortress Press, 1979), 129.

7. See G. Herbert Livingston, *The Pentateuch in Its Cultural Environment* (Grand Rapids: Baker, 1974); John H. Walton, *Ancient Israelite Literature in Its Cultural Setting* (Grand Rapids: Zondervan, 1988).

8. *Harper's Bible Dictionary*, ed. Paul Achtemeier, s.v. "Sabbath" (San Francisco: Harper and Row, 1985).

9. Thomas W. Mann, *The Book of the Torah* (Atlanta: John Knox, 1988), 157.

10. This discussion is derived from the detailed analysis of J. Sailhamer, "Genesis," *Genesis, Exodus, Leviticus, Numbers*, vol. 1 in *Expositor's Bible Commentary* (Grand Rapids: Zondervan, 1990), 6-8.

11. U. Cassuto, *A Commentary on the Book of Genesis: Part II From Noah to Abraham*, trans. I Abrahams (Jerusalem: Magnes, 1964), 303-306; Sailhamer, "Genesis," 112-113, 116-117.

12. B. K. Waltke, "Kingdom Promises as Spiritual," *Continuity and Discontinuity: Perspectives on the Relationship Between the Old and New Testaments*, ed. J. Feinberg (Westchester, IL: Crossway Books, 1988), 278; see his article for a lively discussion on the correspondence of the Old and New.

13. The "covenant community" (Essenes) known from the Dead Sea Scrolls anticipated three eschatological figures, one of which was a prophet like that of Moses (also a messiah of David and Aaron).

14. See Wenham, "The Perplexing Pentateuch," *Vox Evangelica* 17 (1987): 7-21, for a discussion of the first two of these problems.

15. For a commentary addressing these issues, see Wenham, "Introduction," *Genesis 1-15*, xxi-liii.

16. I. M. Kikawada and A. Quinn (*Before Abraham Was: The Unity of Genesis 1-11* [Nashville: Abingdon, 1985]) have gone so far as to suggest that Genesis is written as a reaction to the prevalent views of the time as illustrated by *Atra-hasis*; though there are remarkable similarities between the structure of the two accounts, the evidence does not warrant a direct knowledge of the Akkadian version by the author of Genesis 1—11.

17. For a comparative discussion of ancient cosmogonies, see Walton, *Ancient Israelite Literature in Its Cultural Setting*.

18. G. Hasel, "The Polemic Nature of the Genesis Cosmology," *Evangelical Quarterly* 46 (1974): 81-102.

19. See the discussion by A. Ross, *Creation and Blessing* (Grand Rapids: Baker, 1988), 233-248.

20. For a convenient listing of comparisons, see S. Greengus, "Law in the OT," supplementary vol. in *Interpreter's Dictionary of the Bible* (Nashville: Abingdon, 1976), 533-534.

21. G. Mendenhall, "The Conflict Between Value Systems and Social Control," *Unity and Diversity*, eds., H. Goedicke and J. J. M. Roberts (Baltimore: Johns Hopkins, 1975), 169-180.

22. H. J. Boecker, *Law and the Administration of Justice in the Old Testament and Ancient East*, trans. J. Moiser (Minneapolis: Augsburg, 1980) 17, 55-56.

23. T. Frymer-Kensky, "Tit for Tat," *Biblical Archaeologist* 43:4 (1980): 233.

24. Ibid; Boecker, *Law and Administration*, 163-165, 174.

25. My discussion has been influenced by D. Moo, "The Law of Moses or the Law of Christ," *Continuity and Discontinuity*, ed. J. Feinberg, 203-218, and by my colleague, F. Thielman, "Law (in Paul/Paul and the Law)," *The Dictionary of Paul and His Letters*, ed. R. P. Martin *et al*. (Downers Grove, IL: InterVarsity, forthcoming).

24

Paul House
Associate Professor of Old Testament
Taylor University
Upland, Indiana

Preaching in the Historical Books

Preaching is both serious and joyous at the same time. It is serious because the preaching event affects the eternal destiny of men and women inside and outside the church. As John Piper says:

> This is simply stupendous to think about—that when I preach the everlasting destiny of sinners hangs in the balance. If a person is not made earnest and grave by this fact, people will unconsciously learn that the realities of heaven and hell are not serious.[1]

Given the high stakes of preaching, and the fact that not all hearers are ready and willing to accept correction, at times the preacher must urge an audience to act. Such urging often means denouncing sin and disobedience.

On the other hand, preaching is joyous because it is God's chosen vehicle for salvation for unbelievers and instruction for Christ's church. In his classic work on preaching, John A. Broadus wrote: "In every age of Christianity, since John the Baptist drew crowds into the desert, there has been no great religious movement, no restoration of Scripture truth, and reanimation of genuine piety, without new power in preaching both as cause and effect."[2] This confident joy in preaching often manifests itself through encouraging a congregation to continue good work or to keep the faith during hard times.

These twin emotions of gravity and joy are particularly relevant for all who preach from the Old Testament historical books. These texts were written to warn hearers not to repeat the mistakes of the past, but also to encourage them that Israel's past was not *all* bad, and that they can have a great future if they will serve the Lord. The books stress that during its history from Moses to the post-exilic period (about 1250-450 B.C.), Israel experienced its own set of agonies and joys. The people conquered the promised land (Joshua), became virtual slaves within it due to their sins (Judges), re-established their autonomy (1—2 Samuel), and finally lost the land because of their disobedience to God (1—2 Kings). After a seventy-year sojourn in exile, they returned to their homeland, this time to rebuild and recapture their former glory (Ezra and Nehemiah). Tragic and comic events combine to explain what happened to God's people and why the incidents occurred.

Obviously, human beings create positive and negative events. History is shaped by command and extraordinary individuals and countries. Therefore, the historical books focus on vital characters. Like all good communicators, the authors present their characters in interesting, honest, and creative ways. They use characters to set spiritual standards for their readers and to warn audiences about what happens to wicked persons.

Even with such weighty historical concerns, the books never forget that theology is their main priority. Their readers must develop a personal relationship with the God of Israel. Events and characters are therefore presented in a way calculated to build individual and national faith. The stories are not just entertaining or quaint tales from the past, then, nor are they a simple set of character sketches intended to inspire good deeds. Rather, they proclaim the nature and acts of the living God, a task all effective preachers recognize as their main goal in preaching.

Viewed this way, the historical books provide excellent material for preachers who want to challenge and encourage their congregations to develop their relationship with God by gaining a stronger grasp of biblical theology. Indeed, these books attempted to accomplish the same goals with ancient readers and hearers.

Perhaps a cautionary note should be added, though, lest modern ministers think communicating like the authors of the historical books is easy. The biblical writers knew the Scriptures well and possessed powerful and vivid storytelling abilities. In their books, Israel's history comes alive. All who proclaim their messages after them must have a similar commitment to careful exegesis and creative application. Those who accept the challenge will soon sense the texts' suitability for addressing modern history and modern history makers.

Few preachers (or other Bible readers for that matter) are truly familiar with the historical books. There are several reasons for this situation, but perhaps the most-repeated excuse is that the books are dull. After all, the books are about *history*, a word that means *boring and tedious* to some. Many people claim history is boring because it speaks of past, not current, issues. Others simply refuse to "wade through a bunch of kings" just to gather theological truths they think are more accessible in the New Testament. Such complaints usually arise from individuals who have never really read the books in a systematic way, or who have had bad experiences with unimaginative preachers and teachers.

Preachers who desire to communicate effectively can overcome this bias against the historical books by enthusiastically communicating the texts as they were proclaimed by their original authors. How does a modern preacher attain this ability? First, preachers must read the books themselves until their plot, characters, settings and themes are thoroughly understood. Only then can individual texts be interpreted properly within their context. Readers must recognize that the history is one continuous story. Each individual book provides its own portion of the history.

Second, preachers must learn a method of analyzing and interpreting individual passages that serve as the main text of a sermon. With the overall context in mind this task is easier. Still, much work must be done before the message is preached. Each particular detail the preacher discovers leads ever closer to an effective, viable sermon.

Third, preachers need a method for taking the data gleaned from the larger and smaller contexts and applying them to today's congregation. Many preachers want to apply texts without doing the difficult work already mentioned. Those who resist shortcuts, however, find that application is less difficult than they had imagined. With a few solid principles in mind, the preacher can ask a series of questions that will make every step of the interpretative process seem extremely practical.

Fourth, preachers need traits that no class or book can give them. They need imagination, courage, and discipline. Imagination helps individuals "see" events that happened years ago. Courage allows the minister to speak with the conviction of a prophet. Discipline keeps the preacher doing the necessary labor required of those who stand before a congregation week after week and are determined to have something interesting and timely to say. Though these essential qualities cannot be attained simply by reading this article, they can be gained by anyone who reads and applies the historical books to his or her own life.

Reading the Historical Books as a Whole

To call certain texts "the historical books of the Old Testament" is to say more than we think. This designation implies that the books are history, literature, and theology at the same time.[3] After all, they offer accurate accounts of Israel's past, so they are historical in nature. Further, they are literary because they are creative, selected accounts, not just bland catalogs of facts. Finally, they are considered Scripture by the church, which indicates their theological value. Each of these characteristics must be considered, then, for the books' overall context to be understood.

Many congregations are intimidated or "put off" by words like "history" and "theology." They are usually more comfortable with language from literature. Therefore, this section deals with grasping Israel's history and theology, but it does so by using terms such as "setting" for "historical background," "plot" for "historical event," and "theme" for "theological emphasis." Literary terminology also fits the nature of the books themselves.

Extent of the Literature

The English Bible designates Joshua, Judges, Ruth, 1—2 Samuel, 1—2 Kings, 1—2 Chronicles, Ezra, Nehemiah, and Esther as "historical books." This ordering offers the reader two rather complete histories of Israel. The first stretches from Joshua to 2 Kings, and the second encompasses 1 Chronicles through Esther. The two accounts tell many of the same events, yet have different purposes, which allows readers more than one perspective on what happened. [4] In general, the first history emphasizes the reasons for the nation's downfall, while the second stresses Israel's strong points and God's determination to redeem the chosen people.

In the first history, Joshua continues the story begun in the Pentateuch. The second generation of post-exodus Israelites conquered the promised land under the able leadership of Joshua. Once this faithful generation died, however, their descendants became idolaters, which caused the Lord to punish the nation (Judges—Ruth). Samuel, Saul, David, and Solomon helped restore Israel's prominence (1—2 Samuel), but the people finally forfeited their homeland by sinning against God (1—2 Kings). Obviously, this history does not say what happened to Israel after the exile. The nation is left in foreign lands, with seemingly little hope for the future. Thus, this history warns its readers of the seriousness of sin.

The second history has a more positive tone, though it in no way ignores Israel's sin. It begins with 1—2 Chronicles, a very upbeat recounting of Israel's past that seeks to encourage its audience by stressing the nation's solid heritage. These books say as many positive things as possible about Israel. Clearly, Kings and Chronicles present Israel's history differently. Both viewpoints are accurate; they simply choose divergent approaches to their task.

First and 2 Chronicles cover Adam's life through the fall of Jerusalem. They emphasize David's greatness, and often say good things about Israel's other kings as well. Ezra and Nehemiah continue the saga of Israel by noting how the people survived exile and returned to their ancestral home. Esther concludes the story by showing that Israel can and will endure even the harshest treatment in exile. Clearly, the second telling of the story claims that Israel's future is bright, in part because their past has been impressive.

Plot

A survey of a book's contents does not explain its plot. Plot analysis deals with cause and effect. It explores how one event leads logically to the next. In a widely quoted definition of plot, E. M. Forster states:

> A plot is also a narrative of events, the emphasis falling on causality. "The king died and the queen died" is a story. "The king died, and the queen dies of grief" is a plot. The time sequence is preserved, but the sense of causality overshadows it.[5]

In Biblical terms, "The Babylonians conquered Jerusalem" is a simple story, but "God sent Babylon to destroy Jerusalem because of Israel's sin" is a plot. Preachers must know what happened and why it happened.

Joshua—Kings portrays a tragic plot. That is, the story takes Israel to the heights of national glory, then sends the nation crashing to its lowest depths. Israel's highest point comes during David and Solomon's reigns. The nation had secured its homeland and had become quite prosperous in it. *Because* of idolatry, though, the nation splits into two parts, and eventually disappears altogether (2 Kings 17).

Given this focus on the causes of Israel's decline and fall, readers need to observe how each new leader or event hastens or delays this impending destruction. For instance, the author blames Jeroboam and Manasseh more than other kings for the nation's fall, and the defeats of Samaria and Jerusalem signal Israel's death as a nation. On the other hand, Josiah and Hezekiah were righteous rulers who stalled the people's well-deserved punishment.

Chronicles—Esther mentions the destruction of the nation, but guides readers to consider the more pleasant subject of God's continuing purpose for Israel. This history leaves the reader with visions of good leaders, like Ezra and Nehemiah, and with the impression that Esther and her Jewish brothers and sisters will defeat all their enemies. The same causes for Israel's downfall allow the nation to emerge from the ashes: Jewish leaders and foreign countries. This time the nation has proper leadership and the *favor* of foreign powers. Why? Because the Lord decides to restore them to their land.

Thus, preachers are offered two plots that allow two methods of addressing their audiences. Congregations who need warning and a sense of consequences of sin may respond best to messages from the first history. Groups who are discouraged and weary may need the comfort and hope that the second history affords.

Setting

Readers should know when the major events in the historical books occurred and where they took place. It is wonderful if all the dates of Israel's leaders and events can be memorized, but most people cannot retain that data. It is probable, however, that all serious readers can learn a few basic dates. Knowing seven main dates will give readers a usable historical framework.

First, Israel conquered the promised land by about 1200 B.C.,[6] which began their journey as a legitimate nation in their own geographical setting. Second, Saul became Israel's first king (about 1050 B.C.), thus instituting the monarchy. He, David (1010-970), and Solomon (970-930) served as the only three kings of a united Israel. Third, when Solomon died, the country divided into two parts, a larger (10 tribes) northern kingdom and a smaller (2 tribes) southern kingdom. Samaria became the capital of the north, and Jerusalem became the capital of the south.

Fourth, the northern kingdom was destroyed by Assyria in 722 B.C., and the southern kingdom was defeated by Babylon in 587 B.C. These two horrible events signal Israel's loss of homeland, monarchy, autonomy, and worship center. Every significant institution ceased to exist. Fifth, the exile lasted from 587 until 538 B.C. During this time Israel faced many dangers from its enemies and from the natural temptation to worship their captors' gods and life-styles. Sixth, Israel returned to the promised land in 538 B.C., and eventually rebuilt the temple (about 520-516 B.C.). Seventh, Ezra and Nehemiah worked after the return, sometime near 450 B.C. Once back home, Israel renewed its ties with God and began to restore their distinctive national heritage.

Most of the events in the historical books take place in Israel, particularly in the capital cities of Jerusalem and Samaria. Esther occurs in Persia, where many Jews were exiled after 587 B.C. Significant enemies include Assyria and Babylon, the conquerors of Israel; Syria, a constant regional foe; and less-powerful nations like Moab, Ammon, and Edom. In general, Israel only prospered when no major world power (for example Assyria, Babylon, or Egypt) dominated the Middle East.

Characters

Numerous characters enliven the historical books. Since it is impossible to mention them all, only the most vital to the total story will be introduced. Joshua is the first great individual in these books. When Moses died, Joshua was chosen to guide the nation. Though initially unsure of his own abilities (Josh. 1:1-9), he became a "strong and courageous" general, as well as an effective spiritual head of Israel. The people prospered as long as he lived.

After Joshua died, Israel ceased to worship the Lord exclusively. They plunged into idolatry, a topic the Book of Judges discusses extensively.

This moral slide lasts for decades, during which a series of colorful, but unstable, leaders called "judges" guided Israel. Samuel, the last of the judges, helped check this moral slide. Few biblical characters have his versatility. He acted as prophet, judge, and military leader during his long career. Despite his accomplishments, however, the people asked God for a king, so they could be like other nations—secure and protected. Though this request amounted to a rejection of God's rule (1 Sam. 8:7), the Lord granted their wish.

Saul was Israel's first king. Initially, he was a humble, self-effacing man. After some early successes, though, he became proud and irreverent. God decided to replace him with David (1 Sam. 16:1-14).

David was the most significant individual in the historical books. He defeated all Israel's enemies (1 Sam. 17—31). He refused to rejoice when his political foes were murdered (2 Sam. 1—4). Once established as king, David defeated all Israel's regional enemies, made Jerusalem his capital, and centralized worship there (2 Sam. 5—6). Most importantly, God recognized his spiritual strength, and made a permanent covenant with him (2 Sam. 7:1-17). The Lord pledged to establish David's kingdom forever, and maintained a special relationship with him despite some obvious moral flaws (2 Sam. 11). This promise was the basis for the prophets' conviction that the Messiah would come from David's family.

Many of David's descendants followed him on the throne, but only three of them that ruled in Jerusalem earn much praise in Scripture. Solomon, David's wisest son, ruled nobly for many years, but fell into idolatry in his old age (1 Kings 1—11). Hezekiah (about 715-687 B.C.) and Josiah (about 640-609) were godly kings who slowed Israel's moral decline. The rest of David's "sons" tended to act like Ahab, Jezebel, and the other corrupt northern leaders. God's decision to send the Assyrians and Babylonians to destroy the chosen people seems just, given the text's description of Israel's rebellion against God.

Prophets tried to warn the people to repent. The most famous of these important preachers were Elijah and Elisha, who dominated the story from 1 Kings 17 to 2 Kings 13. Whether as speakers, miracle workers, king makers, or advocates for the poor and oppressed, these two men spoke for God, calling Israel back to God. They were lonely moral voices in an age when Israel seemed to have lost its collective conscience.

Ezra and Nehemiah helped Israel's returning exiles to rebuild their devastated homeland. When the people began to come back from Babylon in 538 B.C., they discovered that the temple was a ruin, the land was barren, and squatters possessed Jerusalem (Ezra 1—5). Things had changed little by the time Ezra and Nehemiah arrived in Jerusalem (about 450), though the temple had been rebuilt (about 520-516). Ezra revitalized Israel's faith, while Nehemiah rebuilt Jerusalem's defenses and residences (Ezra 7—Neh. 13). Both types of leadership were needed for the nation's full restoration.

Preachers need to analyze characters carefully, avoiding the temptation to view them as one-dimensional. Joshua, David, Ezra, and Nehemiah were great people, but they had faults and fears too. Thus, their lives can instruct contemporary people who recognize their own potential and limitations.

Themes

Several ideas appear repeatedly in the historical books, giving the stories continuity and theological significance. Martin Noth concludes that many of these vital themes emerge from the fact that the histories were written by authors influenced by the standards set forth in Deuteronomy.[7] Because of this influence, kings were assessed by spiritual, not strictly secular, criteria. Likewise, the people were judged according to their faithfulness to God, not merely by their success in war or their material wealth.

Five basic themes explain the historical books' main concerns. First, Israel must honor its covenant with the Lord. When God delivered Israel, the people promised to obey the Mosaic covenant. God promised blessings for obedience, but consequences for rebellion (Deut. 27—28). Therefore, Israel's destruction was presented as the natural result of long-term sin. Second, the Lord is the only God (Deut. 6:4-9). Idols are merely the creation of human hands, and thus have no power. All who worship such images are foolish, break the covenant, and deserve punishment.

Third, God had chosen Jerusalem as the place to offer sacrifices and worship (compare Deut. 12:5-7). Therefore, worship anywhere else was forbidden, which explains the historical books' love for Jerusalem and hatred of high places. Fourth, Israel's rulers were to be just and kind (Deut. 17:14-20), rather than greedy and oppressive (compare 1 Kings 21). Fifth, prophets must speak only the words God gives them, and they must teach the people to serve the Lord exclusively (Deut. 18:14-22). Lying prophets would exist but would be judged by the Lord (compare 1 Kings 22:1-28).

Preaching these themes will help congregations to understand that the Old Testament is not some harsh, even cruel litany of an angry God's condemnation of a people. Israel agreed to abide by certain standards, yet broke their word. God waited centuries and sent warning prophets before giving Israel to Assyria and Babylon. If anything, the books reveal a patient God who worked on behalf of Israel. Modern people also need to keep faith with the God who always keeps faith with them.

Interpreting Shorter Texts in the Historical Books

Now that a sense of the historical books' larger context has been gained, it is necessary (and easier) to learn to analyze short parts of the books for the preaching event. This process is known as exegesis, which Douglas Stuart defines as "a thorough, analytical study of a biblical passage."[8] By "useful" he means useful for proclaiming God's Word to a congregation. As Walter Kaiser said:

> Preparation for preaching is always a movement which must begin with the text of Scripture and have as its goal the proclamation of that Word in such a way that it can be heard with all its poignancy and relevancy to the modern situation without losing one iota of its original normativeness.[9]

Only preachers who understand their sermon text within its context have any chance of meeting such lofty goals.

The first decision a preacher must make is the length of the sermon text.[10] Unfortunately, most modern audiences have short attention spans, so the minister can only read relatively brief passages. A congregation's "tolerance" for Scripture can be increased over time, but even then the text length must be fairly short. Therefore, it is usually necessary to be sure that a sermon comes from one specific scene or episode in the historical books. The text should be a complete unit: one that has a discernible beginning and end.

Next, examine the passage's setting. Where does the text fit in the major events of the historical books mentioned above? Does it occur during wartime or peacetime? Does it happen before or after the kingdom divides, the destruction of the nation, or the return from exile? Answering these questions helps the interpreter collect vital information about the story's characters, plot, setting, themes, and purposes. History can come alive when its components are truly understood.

Then note the text's literary context. Because both of the histories are consecutive accounts, knowing a text's historical setting leads to knowing its literary context, and *vice versa*. Note what part of a story a passage portrays. For example, is it the beginning, middle, or end of a story? What happens directly before and after an account? Observe thematic and linguistic links between the text and those that surround it.

Further, discern the passage's structure. Outline the text by dividing it into its appropriate parts. These sections occur when new subjects, scenes, speakers, or themes emerge. Patterns such as "repetition and progression" may also help readers identify structure,[11] as will linguistic keys like conjunctions and adverbs. Once the major sections are identified, they can be used as the main points in the sermon. The sermon outline should, then, be biblical, logical, and of an appropriate length.

With these aspects in mind, analyze any words, phrases, and grammatical points that are unclear, or will add interest to the sermon. Only what makes the text more understandable to the congregation should be included in the actual message. Audiences tire of preachers who attempt to parade their knowledge from the pulpit. Still, they appreciate speakers who use their expertise to make a passage "come alive."

Finally, it is important to examine how the text is quoted, alluded to, or otherwise mentioned in the rest of Scripture. For example, the prophets influence both one another and the New Testament writers. Elijah is used as a symbol of God's power and judgment in various Old and New Testament books. If the passage is not quoted directly, observe how the Scriptures approach the same subject. Collect data on the similarities and differences in how topics are treated in the Bible as a whole. Knowing how the Bible interprets itself should help preachers understand how to apply specific texts to current situations.

When this process has been completed, the preacher has accumulated a great deal of information on the chosen passage. A basic grasp of the story itself, its place in the Bible and history, its main themes and characters, and its outline has been gained. The process is not over. The textual outline must become a sermon outline. Themes must become the topic of the sermon. Characters must illustrate the sermon. In other words, the passage must be applied to modern needs.

Applying the Historical Books

Application of texts frustrates many preachers. They simply have a hard time making the transition from the ancient to the modern world. For those who understand some basic principles, however, applying the historical books to today's congregation is no harder than applying other biblical books. In fact, these basic principles are even simpler for interpreters who have done the analysis recommended in the previous section.

Effective application requires relevant interaction between the Bible, an audience, and a preacher dedicated to communicating life-changing truth. Therefore, it is necessary to link the needs of a congregation, the skills of a minister, and the guidance of God's Word. Perhaps there are many ways to unite these items, but one very logical way is to ask the text a series of questions based on what the passage and the audience have in common, or ought to have in common. This process is faithful to both the original intent of the historical books and mindful of the current situation.

Since the passage's original intention is the key to application, it is necessary to review the material gleaned from reading and interpreting the selected text. First, *remember the text's original setting and situation.* Were the people obeying God or sinning? Did they need correction or encouragement? What was their financial position? Modern congregations face similar situations and have many of the same problems.

Second *review the plot*. What does the text say about how the people were living? What causes and effects placed them in their present situation? What external factors (enemies, natural disasters, etc.) affected their lives? What were the results of decisions they made? Identifying causes and effects in the biblical world leads to understanding how and why events happen and the impact similar events have on today's congregation.

Third, *note the original themes*. What does the text teach about God, the human race, or other significant Bible doctrines? This knowledge helps the preacher realize how the audience needs to relate to God and others now. It also instructs individuals about salvation, commitment, and service.

Fourth, *take a second look at the story's characters*. Note their faults, strong points, relationship with God, and attitudes. Remember that it is the people's sin or obedience that dictates the action in the historical books. Use this category to analyze the Lord's character again as well, since helping people know God better is the goal of preaching. Character studies can be used as illustrations or the basis for sermon topics. Presenting biblical characters also helps modern audiences identify with individuals who, like themselves, have families to raise, careers to build, governments to serve, and relationships with the Lord to maintain.

Fifth, *examine the passage's original tone*. Texts that are biting and ironic should be presented that way. Stories that are optimistic (for instance, the conquest) should be preached in a way calculated to encourage congregations. The accounts in 1—2 Kings ought to warn audiences about how easily individuals and nations can slide into long-term sin and disaster. In other words, the original intention of Scripture helps the preacher with presentation *and* interpretation.

These five steps attempt to unite the text and the congregation. It is now time to link the sermon to this process. Most ministers tend to shape their sermons in the traditional three-point format. Others, though, use techniques such as dramatic monologue or storytelling. The historical books offer all types of opportunities to share truth creatively.

For example, it is possible for those who used the three-point approach to examine a text, and then find three aspects of the nature of God, three facets of leadership, three attitudes that harm our relationship to the Lord, and so on. All points will come from the text and will fit the preacher's normal manner of proclamation. Likewise, speakers who use storytelling or dramatic techniques have a wealth of material, especially since the story format of the literature itself matches the preferred method of presentation.

Conclusion

Thus, the preacher who knows a congregation well, reads and analyzes the chosen text carefully and accurately, and matches speaking strengths to the material can preach effectively from the historical books. As was stated in the introduction of this article, however, good preaching is normally the result of courage, discipline, and imagination. It does not happen by accident, nor does it ever become easy to accomplish. It is satisfying to the preacher, is often appreciated by congregations, and, most importantly, is very pleasing to God. When done from the historical books, it also makes the most neglected 25 percent of Scripture regain its original flair and relevancy.

Notes

1. John Piper, *The Supremacy of God in Preaching* (Grand Rapids: Baker, 1990), 55.
2. John A. Broadus, *A Treatise on the Preparation and Delivery of Sermons*, 22nd ed. (New York: A. C. Armstrong and Son, 1897), 19.
3. See Richard D. Nelson, *First and Second Kings, Interpretation* (Louisville: John Knox, 1987), 1-14, for a readable analysis of how these aspects mesh.
4. This list follows the Latin Bible, and differs from the Hebrew order. The Hebrew text includes the same books, but places them in a different sequence, and also calls them "former prophets" (Joshua, Judges, Samuel and Kings) or "writings" (Ruth, Esther, Ezra, Nehemiah, Chronicles). For an analysis of the importance of the Hebrew order, read Brevard Childs, *Introduction to the Old Testament as Scripture* (Philadelphia: Fortress, 1980). For a less technical approach to the same subject, read Paul R. House, *Survey of the Old Testament* (Nashville: Broadman Press, 1955), 86.
5. E. M. Forster, *Aspects of the Novel* (New York: Harcourt Brace Jovanovich, 1955), 86.
6. This date reflects the position that the exodus occurred c. 1290-1250 B.C., rather than c. 1450 B.C. Note R. K. Harrison, *Introduction to the Old Testament* (Grand Rapids: Eerdmans, 1969), 315-325, for an excellent survey of the issue.
7. Martin Noth, *The Deuteronomistic History* (1957; reprint ed., Sheffield: Sheffield Academic Press, 1981).
8. Douglas Stuart, *Old Testament Exegesis: A Primer for Students and Pastors*, 2nd ed. (Philadelphia: Westminster, 1984), 21. This book is an indispensable tool for preaching from the Old Testament.
9. Walter Kaiser, *Towards an Exegetical Theology: Biblical Exegesis for Preaching and Teaching* (Grand Rapids: Baker, 1981), 48.
10. Broadus, *A Treatise on the Preparation and Delivery of Sermons*, 38-50, suggests excellent principles for thoughtful text selection.
11. Stuart, *Old Testament Exegesis*, 36.

Charles Finney (1792-1875)

"Revivalist and Reformer"

Charles G. Finney established a pattern of evangelistic preaching that has survived nearly intact into our own era.

Raised in a non–Christian home, Finney trained as a lawyer and set up his practice in Adams, New York. As a young man he underwent a profound conversion experience that altered his life completely—and the life of his community. As he proclaimed what God had done in his life, revival swept through the entire city.

Finney became a Presbyterian home missionary and preached revivals in the villages and cities of New York. By 1832 he had become a pastor in New York City where his evangelistic preaching continued to draw large crowds. Three years later, he joined the faculty of Oberlin College as professor of theology, a school he would later serve as president.

As a revivalist, Finney was known as an advocate of the "new methods," such as the anxious bench and the public invitation. His sermons reflected his legal background in their clarity, conversational style, and persuasive appeal. He preached to a congregation as if he was an attorney standing before a jury.

Finney not only preached for personal conversions; he also preached on the social issues of his day, particularly slavery. A committed abolitionist, he denounced the sin of slavery in his sermons and warned of the danger to the nation if such evil was not eliminated.

The father of American mass evangelism, Charles Finney demonstrated that evangelism and social concern can go hand in hand.

25

C. Hassell Bullock
Professor of Biblical Studies
Wheaton College
Wheaton, Illinois

Preaching in the Poetic Literature

Some of the most powerful literature in the Old Testament for preaching in the postmodern age is that found in the so-called "poetic books." These books include Job, Psalms, Proverbs, Ecclesiastes, and the Song of Songs, to use the English canonical order. They are given the general designation "poetic books" because they are, for the most part, written in poetic verse. Yet the designation is not precise, for much of Ecclesiastes is written in an elevated prose.

Three of these books, Job, Proverbs, and Ecclesiastes, constitute the *wisdom literature* of the Old Testament, along with a few psalms.[1] Some scholars would even include the Song of Songs with them, but this book is probably best assigned to a category of its own, that of love poetry.

The poetic books belong to that category of the Jewish canon known as the *Writings* (or *Ketuvim*), and three of them (Job, Proverbs, and Psalms) were singled out for special attention by the Masoretes, the medieval Jewish scholars, who gave them a special set of poetic marks for reading purposes. However, the presence of these five books in the *Writings* makes a statement about their relationship to the *Torah* (Pentateuch) and the *Prophets*—they are neither Law nor Prophecy. In fact, their view of the world is quite different from that of *Torah* and *Prophecy*, even though they share many similarities.

The Book of Psalms, however, must be considered in a separate classification because it is hymnic material which drew heavily upon the tradition of both *Torah* and *Prophecy*. There are a number of sources which describe this literature more fully, and the reader can refer to them.[2]

Preaching Textually and Theologically

Most expository preaching is based upon a particular text of Scripture, and the preacher explains, expounds, and illustrates that text in various ways. Yet expository preaching can take two basic forms. It can expound the meaning of a limited passage of Scripture (what I am calling *textual*), or it can take a more synthetic approach and expound the theological meaning of books, themes, or several related passages. That is, it becomes more of an effort in the direction of *biblical theology*. Obviously, however, preaching upon a single text is *theological*, and expounding the wider theological dimensions of a book, books, or group of texts is *textual*. I am using the designations to distinguish between one method, *textual*, which tends to be basically *exegetical* and the other, *theological*, which tends to be more *synthetic*. In the following discussion I will try to draw out the differences more clearly.

Preaching on the Textual Kingpins

In ancient architecture a structure—for example, the roof of a building—was sometimes designed so that its coherence and strength to hold together were concentrated in a single centerpiece called a *kingpin*. Biblical texts are sometimes like that. A particular set of verses, or even a single verse, will sometimes hold an entire pericope together. If we want to be faithful to the biblical text, then we will look for such a textual center or focal point. Robert Gordis, for example, suggests that the Book of Ecclesiastes is composed of nineteen pericopes, each ending in one of four themes: (1) the weakness or transience of human accomplishments, (2) the uncertainty of human destiny, (3) the impossibility of attaining true knowledge in this world, and (4) the need to enjoy life.[3] If we follow Gordis, then we will look for the conclusion to each pericope, and that will in some way become the *kingpin* or the "glue" that holds the thought system together. Generally speaking, Qoheleth, "the Preacher" (1:1), will build toward the particular conclusion, or *kingpin*, of a given pericope.

The preacher should keep this in mind and allow this textual center to color the passage as it was intended to do. It is an effort to take the context seriously, an interpretive principle which every good exegete will observe. This method poses fewest problems for preachers as they work through a particular book. It can be done by choosing one or two good commentaries on a single book, grasping the main ideas and issues of that book, and then working through the text methodically to develop sermons on the *kingpin* texts or text centers. When preachers work through a book for the first time, this is probably the best way to approach the task. It allows time to absorb the book bit by bit.

Many of the Psalms can be readily preached like this.[4] For example, Psalm 73, one of the wisdom psalms, deals with the prosperity of the wicked as a theological problem. As the psalmist worked through the problem, frustrated that satisfactory answers just did not come, he went to the sanctuary and there discovered an answer:

> But when I thought how to understand this,
>   it seemed to me a wearisome task,
> until I went into the sanctuary of God;
>   then I perceived their end (73:16-17, RSV).

That is, he found an answer within the context of worship. It was both an answer to his problem, in that he perceived that God *does* bring them to judgment (vv. 18-20), and it was an answer in the sense that in worship, in the presence of God, he found strength and wisdom to deal with his question. This is reinforced in verse 28:

> But for me it is good to be near God;
>   I have made the Lord God my refuge,
>   that I may tell of all thy works (RSV).

The *textual kingpin* in this psalm is the importance of worship and the psalmist's participation in it for dealing with life's pressing issues.

An example from Job may further illustrate this method. Job and his "friends," as a matter of speaking, sometimes fight with the same sword. They all talk about the wonders of creation and God's powerful control of it. Yet as Job was responding wearily to the third speech of Bildad, Job struck again with this two-edged sword that both he and the friends had used from time to time—they to cut down Job's criticism of God's strange way of working in Job's life, and he to trim down the friends' inflated egotism that claimed a firm grasp of wisdom and a knowledge of God's ways. In fact, as preachers work with this beautiful speech of Job in chapter 26, they will find that sarcasm exudes from almost every line. The first line sets the tone:

> How you have helped him who has no power!
> How you have saved the arm that has no strength! (26:1, RSV).

Then Job picked up Bildad's sword and struck back with it. Bildad had argued that the Creator "makes peace in his high heaven" (25:2, RSV), and that even the planets are not clean in His sight, so how much less a man like Job! (25:5-6) Sarcastically Job talked about the awesome effect of the friends' words on the creation (26:5-6), and then moved into the beautiful description of God's creative activity (26:7-13), a point on which they would all agree. Then Job declared that a mere *knowledge* of the Creator and His creation is insufficient. Only an *encounter* with Him gives one that special edge:

> Lo, these are but the outskirts of his ways;
> and how small a whisper do we hear of him!
> But the thunder of his power who can understand? (26:14, RSV).

Only the reader, by dramatic irony, and God Himself know that Job is soon to receive that special edge that he has just described, for Yahweh will soon speak to him out of the whirlwind (38:1). The powerful message of the text is that the full knowledge of God can only come in *personal encounter*, a point that Job had been making throughout the dialogue as he insisted that God make His allegations known in some kind of personal appearance.

Psalm 16, to offer a third example, is among the immortal psalms which, like Psalm 23, live and activate the human heart in every age. After a brief petition (v. 1), the psalmist established the basis for his trust in Yahweh: "I have no good apart from thee" (RSV).[5] In this postmodern world, as western culture emerges from the Judeo-Christian ethic that has characterized our way of life, the preacher might consider the topic of "moral goodness" and raise the question whether it can exist apart from the Judeo-Christian ethic. Glen Tinder's article, in which he draws upon the power of *agapē love* as the key to the Christian ethic, may prove to be very helpful for thinking through this difficult but critical issue. He raises the question whether or not western cultures are merely "living on moral savings accumulated over many centuries but no longer being replenished."[6] I would suggest, however, that the preacher give this sermon time to mature before it is preached. Then, when it is ready, it will be a compelling message for the contemporary church.

Preaching on the Theological Arches

The arch is recognized to be one of the strongest architectural structures, and while the truth of the metaphor does not transfer automatically to the study of Scripture, it is generally recognized that the strongest doctrines of the Bible are those that have a prominent and continuing emphasis and development in Scripture. Admittedly, this is a more difficult approach to preaching because it presupposes *both* the exegete's *technical knowledge* of Scripture and the biblical theologian's *synthetic knowledge*. That is, it presupposes the preacher's ability to put the picture together and give the congregation a view of the larger portrait. It is the difference between standing close to the portrait and seeing only one spot and standing back from it and seeing the whole.

This kind of knowledge comes from a prolonged study of the poetic books and from absorbing their ideas over a long period of time. To preach *on the theological arches*, following ideas through the biblical text, means preachers must be involved in Bible study apart from mere sermon preparation. Sometimes they deliver a sermon which is still in its infancy or childhood and needs time to develop its adolescent stage and finally reach full maturity. That is one of the reasons I find it beneficial to rethink and rewrite sermons I have already done.

As a matter of personal discipline, and as a matter of listening to the voice of the Holy Spirit over a sustained period of time, each new preaching of a sermon should be prefaced with this rethinking/rewriting effort. In fact, preachers should be constantly alert to ideas that may enhance a particular sermon. I have found that a good system is to jot these ideas down when I come across them in my reading or in my everyday experience and file them in the folder with the sermon, so they will be available when I begin to rethink and rewrite this sermon. The *synthetic* type of sermon takes longer to mature, but when it does, a heightened sensitivity to life and biblical theology goes along with it. It is well worth the effort and time expended. The following are some examples of how this kind of preaching can be done with single sermons and a series.

Single Sermons: "A Negative Image for a Negative Age"

One interesting way the preacher can use the Books of Job and Ecclesiastes together is to focus on the negative image of life and faith evidenced in both of these books. That is, Job looked at his dilemma and felt hung between his personal catastrophe and a God who hid Himself. Convinced of his innocence, Job desperately needed to lay his case before God and present his personal defense, but God kept hiding from him. If He was there at all, Job felt that He was operating in an adversarial role (for instance, Job 16:11-14). As Job sorted through the irregular pieces of his life's jigsaw puzzle, he at first believed that faith made no provision to fill the chasm between what he perceived as reality and what he knew about God:

> There is no umpire between us,
> who might lay his hand upon us both (Job 9:33, RSV).

Yet as he clashed repeatedly with a senseless universe, Job began to see that, in spite of appearances, there had to be some better rationale permeating the order of faith—the Creator simply could not have neglected to provide some kind of arbitrator, some kind of mediator, who could stand between a nonsensical world and an insensitive God:

> Even now, behold, my witness is in heaven,
> and he who vouches for me is on high (Job 16:19, RSV).

It is a desperate faith that has to find its way out of meaninglessness, and as it catapults him from one end of the maze to the other, he momentarily gets a glimpse of a world where such a mediator *does* exist, where meaning is restored, and where justice takes hold of life:

> For I know that my Redeemer lives,
> and at last he will stand upon the earth;
> and after my skin has been thus destroyed,
> then from my flesh I shall see God,
> whom I shall see on my side,
> and my eyes shall behold, and not another (Job 19:25-27, RSV).

But this glimpse, capable of transforming the universe and making life tolerable, is fleeting and soon gone. Immediately he reached the other end of the trajectory and fell again into the maze of his suffering: "My heart faints within me!" (Job 19:27, RSV).

This negative image of faith in Job is complemented by another negative perception which Job verbalized several times. That is, he insisted that God's transcendence—Job might call it aloofness—models another deficiency in His relationship with human beings. He simply does not understand what it is like to be human:

> For he is not a man, as I am, that I might answer him,
> that we should come to trial together (Job 9:32, RSV).

The climax of this negative perception comes in 10:4-6, where Job said, if he could be convinced that God really understood what it was like to be human, it would make his suffering at least tolerable:

> Hast thou eyes of flesh?
> Dost thou see as man sees?
> Are thy days as the days of man,
> or thy years as man's years,
> that thou dost seek out my iniquity
> and search for my sin (Job 10:4-6, RSV).

To continue following the arch from the book of Job to Ecclesiastes, this author, like Job, urged that the world is a closed system:

> Is there a thing of which it is said,
> "See, this is new"?
> It has been already,
> in the ages before us (Eccl. 1:10, RSV).

Just as Job believed that God would not interrupt the system (except to show Himself to be Job's adversary), Qoheleth believed that God no longer breaks into the system:

> I know that whatever God does endures for ever; nothing can be added to it, nor anything taken from it (Eccl. 3:14a, RSV).

Unlike Job, he refrained from arguing the issue. Job roared like a lion about the deficiencies he perceived in the universe and the way God related to men and women, while Qoheleth whimpered like a defeated dog when he recognized that the world is a closed system and that God no longer breaks into it:

> Whatever has come to be has already been named, and it is known what man is, and that he is not able to dispute with one stronger than he. The more words, the more vanity, and what is man the better? (Eccl. 6:10-11, RSV).

His position is one of accepting the fact and learning to live with it as best he can: "God has made it so, in order that men should fear before him" (Eccl. 3:14, RSV).

Both of these books delineate the gaping hole in the universe that is made when God does not speak, when God hides himself, when He makes no provision for the man or woman who is caught between the rock of human suffering and the hard place of God's silence. That is the human dilemma in every age, and both Job and Ecclesiastes spoke forthrightly about it.

In contrast, the prophets of the Old Testament give a *positive image* of the Messiah; that is, they described the messianic person. However, in the poetic books, especially Job and Ecclesiastes, there is a *negative image,* which simply means that these books delineate the *need* or the *necessity* for such a person in human history. To make sense out of the injustices of life and the inequities of human existence, the human dilemma demands that there be some provision in the divine economy to cover these injustices and inequities. At this point the preacher must look beyond the poetic books to the New Testament where God has revealed himself in Jesus Christ and provided an *incarnate* answer to the human dilemma. Robert Short has provided a helpful discussion of the "Christ-shaped vacuum" in his book *A Time to Be Born, A Time to Die.*[7] His very practical analogy is that of the photographic negative which already has a picture on it (in the case at hand, Ecclesiastes), yet it needs the second penetration of light to transfer the image from the film negative to the paper. This second penetration of light (to draw out the analogy) is, of course, God's revelation in Jesus Christ. To illustrate the difference between the Old Testament image of the Messiah and its New Testament revelation in Jesus Christ, I have sometimes used the analogy of the Polaroid photo, which, as one watches, develops from a quite faint image, to a sharp and distinct picture.

The point is that both Job and Ecclesiastes delineated a spiritual vacuum in their knowledge and experience of God which is, in the progress of revelation, filled by the image of the Messiah found in the prophets, and tangibly fulfilled by the New Testament incarnation of God in Christ. Particularly in the case of Job, he circumscribed the vacuum in the human heart, the human desperation at so many unanswered questions, and the need for a personal encounter with God. When God spoke to him out of the whirlwind, it was God's answer to Job's need, but it was nevertheless a temporary solution. The permanent solution would come in a much more tangible form, in fact, in the form of God in human flesh who would do precisely what Job had suggested would be such a good idea—that God would look at the human dilemma through human eyes and feel how suffocating the awareness was that death was the only way out.

While all of the facets of this complex of ideas might not be considered in a single sermon, some connection with the thought of Ecclesiastes might augment the power of the sermon and better prepare us for the mystery and overwhelming power of the incarnation. In this connection preachers should take into account the fact that Ecclesiastes also delineated a vacuum in human experience, but one where we feel truly alone and God does not come; where God does not speak at all, not even out of a whirlwind. Then, to put the theological capstone on the sermon, the preacher can appeal to the incarnation of God in Christ—an eternal reality to be sure, but one which, according to Scripture, could never be understood outside the historical manifestation in Jesus Christ.

To follow the theological emphasis of the substitutionary atonement, Christ not only died for us, but entered into the spiritual vacuum of the soul to fill the emptiness. Christ as Savior descended into the utter nothingness of this vacuum and cried out on the Cross: "My God, my God, why hast thou forsaken me?" (Matt. 27:46, RSV). Did God understand the void in the human heart, the nothingness that fills the human soul? Indeed He did, and in His substitutionary death He entered its depths so that He might fill the vacuum. The utter abandonment that Job felt, and the spacious vacuum of the human heart that alarmed Ecclesiastes would never have the same power over the human soul after Christ had filled the vacuum. I am reminded of the gracious and powerful words of the writer to the Hebrews,

> But we see Jesus, who for a little while was made lower than the angels, crowned with glory and honor because of the suffering of death, so that by the grace of God he might taste death for every one (Heb. 2:9, RSV).

A Series: "Recovering the Essentials of Faith and Life"

I am inclined to preach sermon series because they give a sense of continuity and also commit me to thinking through the wider theological spectrum of a book or a concept. Personally I do not like a long series because it is difficult to sustain the congregation's interest for lengthy periods of time, and it also restricts the preacher to the thought frame of one book or the spectrum of one concept. I believe congregations need to be exposed to a variety of biblical books and genres and theological ideas even in the space of a single preaching year. In my view, when a series stretches out longer than a quarter, the preacher should ask just how he or she will be able to sustain interest, and whether or not such a concentrated effort on one series will deprive the congregation of needed exposure to a wider range of biblical books and theological ideas.

A suggested series that could cover the gamut of the poetic books follows:

1. The Recovery of God's Presence (Job)
2. The Recovery of Piety (Psalms)
3. The Recovery of Righteousness (Proverbs)
4. The Recovery of Joy (Ecclesiastes)
5. The Recovery of Love (Song of Songs)

Here again the preacher is *preaching on the arches*, and this presupposes a solid grasp of the theology of these books. Each of these sermons would feature a crucial concept in each of the poetic books. I will briefly indicate lines along which these topics might be developed.

1. *The Recovery of God's Presence (Job).* When one reads through Job, one senses that he feels utterly forsaken by God. The prologue sets the stage by relating the story of Job's loss of family and property (chap. 1), and then the author superimposes upon that loss Job's loss of health and physical well-being (chap. 2). The following dialogue (chaps. 4—31) records Job's physical suffering and emotional trauma, his struggle with the world, including family and friends, and most painfully, *his loss of a sense of God's presence*. The preacher can find much material in the dialogue that will help draw out the pain and much to connect Job's experiences with our own. The sense of abandonment that he felt serves to underscore the need for recovery of God's presence and highlights all the more the satisfaction he experienced in learning that God really could and would speak to him again:

> I had heard of thee by the hearing of the ear,
> but now my eyes sees thee (Job 42:5, RSV).

The experience of abandonment brought Job to a new level of relationship with God. It was the difference between hearing and *seeing*. Out of the crucible of suffering God brought forth an awareness of His presence more keen than anything Job had experienced up to that time. If the preacher wants to widen the field of the sermon to include the biblical theme of "God is with us" (*Immanuel*), a theological study of this theme can be most rewarding.[8]

2. *The Recovery of Piety (Psalms).* Piety is a spiritual stance which recognizes and practices a two-dimensional relationship to God and to one's neighbor. It is not, as its detractors would satirize, some kind of super-spirituality that soars above the day-to-day routine of life. It is the kind of relationship whose paradigm we see modeled in the Ten Commandments, which first regulate our relationship to God, and then our relationship to our neighbor. Jesus knew this so well, and He paired the greatest commandment, to love God with all one's heart, with the second greatest, to love one's neighbor as oneself (Matt. 22:34-40). This involves a spiritual posture that neglects neither of these dimensions.

The wisdom literature and the Psalms speak about the *fear of the Lord*, which, in its broadest sense, is religion itself. Yet it is also the ancient way of talking about a *personal relationship with God*. The Psalms and wisdom literature teach us that the *fear of the Lord* is not merely the vertical relationship (divine/human), but the horizontal, too (human/human). It includes both dimensions of life. A world view in which the horizontal is primary is a distorted view of reality. In that framework of thought, one can neither understand mankind nor God. The Psalms, contrary to the work of the form critics, contain so much that is personal and speaks directly to the question of personal piety. They guide us in ways of dealing with life's problems in a context of faith in God, the Creator and Redeemer. Through them we can recover our *spirituality*, whether we call it *piety*, *personal relationship*, or some other name.

3. The Recovery of Righteousness (Proverbs). In a world where personal righteousness is an outmoded concept, and in the church where it has declined to a non-emphasis, the Book of Proverbs can call us back to the crucial importance of a style of life that restores the unity between *believing* and *doing*. The preacher might begin the preparation of this sermon by the inductive method, and read through Proverbs without the aid of commentaries, noting the occurrence and usage of the words *righteous* and *righteousness*. The next stage could be an examination of these terms in several basic commentaries. It is better to study the terms first within their context of Proverbs before venturing too widely and examining them in the rest of the poetic books and the Old Testament at large. Before the study has advanced very far, the preacher will note that the concept of *righteousness* is one of both *faith* and *practice*, one of both *believing and doing*. It is a "real life" concept, and it involves how one *walks* (personal behavior) and how one *talks* (personal conversation). This truth can become an antidote for a popular theology which insists that Christianity is mostly *believing*, or that it is largely a matter of intellect. On the other hand it can put the social gospel, a *doing* faith, in the light of a *believing* faith. If the preacher feels more comfortable to pair an Old Testament text to a New Testament one, the Epistle of James—with its insistence on the union of faith and works—is a good source for this emphasis (Jas. 2:18-26).

Moreover, the concept of righteousness puts one in relationship to a moral code, and thus to God. Although the law (*Torah*), the moral code which underlies the Book of Proverbs, is not flaunted before the readers, it undergirds the moral system of the Book nevertheless. It is not a code developed merely in relation to social and cultural demands, but one whose origin is in divine revelation. Therefore, within the theological scope of Proverbs, moral relativism is unthinkable as an ethical option. A nondescript moral code which stands in between the gospel that makes demands of us and the culture that urges toleration of all life-styles, falls outside the circle of righteousness drawn in the Book of Proverbs.

4. *The Recovery of Joy (Ecclesiastes).* Despite the morose spirit that hovers over the Book of Ecclesiastes, there is a feature, among others, that lifts the theology of the book to a level worthy of both an ancient and a modern hearing. While Qoheleth struck his theme of vanity on numerous occasions, he nevertheless insisted that it was possible to extract joy from life. It is not what we call "fun," but it is a deep sense of pleasure and satisfaction at being a participant in the activities of living. Ironically enough, and often contrary to our "weekend" mentality, it is found in the *routine* of life, in eating and drinking and working (Eccl. 2:24-25; 3:12,22; 5:18-19; 6:2; 8:15; 9:7). This way of speaking does not mean that one should "live it up." Rather it is a metaphor for the routine of life, for doing the "daily dozen," for fulfilling one's duty.

Endemic to the thought of Qoheleth is the notion that God has constructed the universe and ordered life in such a way that despite the adversities and injustices of the world, one can extract a bit of joy from life's routine. The preacher can augment this message by that powerful passage on joy in G. K. Chesterton's book, *Orthodoxy*[9], and George A. Buttrick's beautiful statement on the quality of joy that dominated Jesus' ministry, even on His way to the cross.[10] Although most of us want to do those things in life that will give us the greatest amount of joy, so many of us find ourselves involved in activities and situations that in reality bring little joy. On the contrary, they produce generous quantities of boredom. I urge my students to make this an operating principle of life: "Learn to enjoy the things you do, rather than do the things you enjoy." There is certainly nothing wrong with the latter part of the dictum, but few of us are so fortunate as to receive the necessary components for turning this formula, doing the things we enjoy, into reality. The joy of life can be so easily lost in the *routine* of living and the fulfillment of responsibility, but not for a man like Qoheleth, and not for those who emulate his example. It is God's gift to humankind. It is the way He has ordered the world and life:

> There is nothing better for a man than that he should eat and drink, and find enjoyment in his toil. This also, I saw, is *from the hand of God* (Eccl. 2:24, RSV, author's italics).

5. *The Recovery of Love (Song of Songs).* Few pulpiteers find the Song of Songs a source of inspiration for preaching unless they appeal to the allegorical interpretation of the Song.[11] I personally am not opposed to the allegorical method but prefer to look at the Song more literally, as a book about the love between a man and woman. This theme, so firmly grounded in biblical theology, is also worthy of a book of Scripture. My own interpretation of the Song of Songs follows the *shepherd hypothesis,*

which holds that there are three main characters in the book: Solomon, the maiden, and her shepherd lover. Solomon tried to win over the love of the Shulammite maiden, already deeply in love with a simply shepherd boy, and none of Solomon's powerful overtures can dissuade her affection from the object of her love. When the Song reaches its climax in 8:6 with the declaration that "love is strong as death," the exemplary love of the maiden is held up as the ideal, rather than a love that appeals to physical and material enticements to woo its object.[12] In our world where *erōs love* dominates the media and seeks to shape our view of love, we Christians have an answer to the problem. We have *agapē love,* which gives and expects nothing in return. It is the only love worthy of the name.

Once the power of the poetic books for preaching is discovered, preachers will find they are a platform on which to stand within the circle of biblical faith and raise the pressing issues and question of our postmodern world. It is indeed a lavish provision in the canon of holy Scripture that the Holy Spirit should have provided this platform, especially the skepticism of Job and Ecclesiastes, *within* the arena of faith. Yet the sustained and sustaining faith of the Psalms is unmatched in the Old Testament and moves us in the direction of theological affirmation. We can be grateful for these spiritual provisions and exhibit our gratitude by exposing ourselves and our congregations to the ideas of this potent literature.

Notes

1. For a treatment of wisdom literature for preaching, see Ronald E. Clements, "Preaching from the Wisdom Literature," *Biblical Preaching: An Expositor's Treasury,* ed. James W. Cox (Philadelphia: Westminster, 1983), 84-101.

2. C. Hassell Bullock, *An Introduction to the OT Poetic Books,* rev. ed. (Chicago: Moody Press, 1988), 20-31; James L. Crenshaw gives a description of the wisdom movement in his *Old Testament Wisdom: An Introduction* (Atlanta: John Knox, 1981), 11-54.

3. Robert Gordis, *Koheleth—The Man and His World* (New York: Bloch, 1955), 252.

4. There are several helpful articles on preaching from the Psalms: Elizabeth Achtemeier, "Preaching from the Psalms," *Review and Expositor* 81 (1984):437-449; William E. Hull, "Preaching on the Psalms," *Review and Expositor* 81 (1984):451-456; Donald Macleod, "Preaching from the Psalms," *Biblical Preaching: An Expositor's Treasury,* ed. James W. Cox (Philadelphia: Westminster, 1983), 102-118; Alton H. McEachern, "Preaching from the Psalms," *Review and Expositor* 81 (1984):457-460.

5. Although the Hebrew word *bal* may function as a negative or affirmative particle, in either case the idea is that the psalmist's security and welfare, his "goodness," cannot exist apart from God. See Peter C. Craigie, *Psalms 1-50,* Word Biblical Commentary (Waco, Texas: Word Books, 1983), 155. On page 154 Craigie lists a bibliography where the options are discussed.

6. Glen Tinder, "Can We Be Good without God," *The Atlantic Monthly* (Dec., 1989):69-85. He deals with the above issue on page 82.

7. Robert Short, *A Time to Be Born, A Time to Die* (New York: Harper & Row, 1973), 97-112.

8. The preacher might begin with the theme of creation as laid out in Genesis 2, where God is present with His human creatures, and would not even leave them alone in their

disobedience, as Genesis 3 attests. The theme continues as God reaffirms His ongoing presence with the human race in Genesis 1—11 and confirms His presence in a personal way with Abraham. While He does not affirm His presence with this patriarch in so many words, He does to Isaac (Gen. 26:3), Jacob (Gen. 31:3), and Joseph (in narrative form, Gen. 39:2,23). Some insist that this is the meaning of the affirmation to Moses in Exodus 3:14. This same message of divine presence is reissued to Joshua (Josh. 1:9) and given prophetic form in the Immanuel prophecy of Isaiah 7:14. Ezekiel further reiterates the theme in the final words of his book as he renames Jerusalem "The Lord is there" (Ezek. 48:35). As one follows the theological arch, one finds the keystone in the fulfillment of the Immanuel prophecy in the birth of Christ (Matt. 1:18-23). Christoph Barth has chosen this theme as the keystone of his Old Testament theology, and a study of this book might further enhance the preacher's understanding of the significance of this biblical message. See Christoph Barth, *God With Us: A Theological Introduction to the Old Testament*, ed. Geoffrey W. Bromiley (Grand Rapids: Eerdmans, 1991), 517.

9. G. K. Chesterton, *Orthodoxy* (Garden City: Doubleday, 1959), 159-160.

10. George A. Buttrick, *The Parables of Jesus* (New York: Harper and Brothers, 1928), 224-225.

11. William P. Tuck offers some homiletical insights on the Song of Songs from a literal hermeneutical point of view, "Preaching from Daniel, Ruth, Esther, and the Song of Songs," *Biblical Preaching: An Expositor's Treasury*, 165-167.

12. See C. Hassell Bullock, *An Introduction to the OT Poetic Books*, 234; Robert Gordis, *The Song of Songs* (New York: The Jewish Theological Seminary of America, 1954), 26; Christian D. Ginsburg, *The Song of Songs and Coheleth* (New York: KTAV reprint, 1970), 188.

26 *Thomas G. Long*
Professor of Preaching
Princeton Theological Seminary
Princeton, New Jersey

Preaching in the Prophets

Old Testament prophets are widely misunderstood figures, both inside and outside the church. The typical impressions of who the prophets were and what they did could, in many respects, hardly be farther from the truth. Ask most people about the word *prophecy* and they inevitably talk about predicting the future. Anyone who can successfully forecast the rise and fall of the Dow Jones average or the winner of the Superbowl is, in our culture, justifiably called a "prophet." So, the conventional wisdom goes, the prophets in the Old Testament were simply earlier versions of such nimble prognosticators. Their main role was to point the finger toward the distant horizon of history and to predict what the future holds.

Who Were the Prophets?

The Old Testament prophets were stirred into action by the keen awareness that the God of Israel was about to perform a "new thing," and, as such, the prophets often did point toward these future events. However, these announcements of God's future must be seen in the context of a more comprehensive and complex understanding of prophetic activity. The Old Testament prophets were not simply futurologists or crystal ball gazers, and they were not interested in the future as a matter of general concern.

Rather, they were focused upon the character and activity of God. Their task was to preach more than predict the future and to give voice to the working and will of God among the people—past, present, and future. Indeed, the prophets looked backward to Israel's past as often as they leaned forward toward its future. The message of the prophets activated the memory of the religious tradition, of what God had done before, as much as it anticipated what God was yet to do.

Even among those who are aware of this more complex nature of Old Testament prophecy, another sort of mistaken view of the prophets persists. Generally, educated folk within the church are fully aware that the prophets were not merely clairvoyants and soothsayers. "The prophets were 'forthtellers,' not 'foretellers,'" goes the old saw. Students of the Bible know that the prophets spoke their messages to the people of Israel in all sorts of conditions and situations, sometimes disclosing God's action in the future but other times speaking in the past or the present tense. The churchly misapprehension of the prophets, then, has less to do with mistaking the prophets as soothsayers and more to do with a larger misunderstanding of what prophets were like as personalities and what their social roles were.

Within the church, the prophets are often seen as lonely eccentrics, powerful visionary personalities, and zealous social agitators. Like the counter-cultural revolutionaries of the late 1960s, the prophets are thought of as those who roam the countryside issuing rolling thunder pronouncements against the status quo, kicking down the walls of institutions; the prophets are viewed as righteously indignant reformers, persistently scolding the people for their failure to address this or that social ill.

Again, there is a measure of truth in this caricature of the prophets. Their pronouncements were often connected to issues of social justice, and their prophetic messages did include calls for radical, even unstabilizing, social change. Recent research, however, has underscored the fact that the prophets, far from being lonely misfits, were "an integral part of their society."[1] Prophecy appears to have been, for many of the prophets, an activity in which they occasionally engaged, not a full-time occupation or a comprehensive identity. Many of them held other positions in society: serving in the Temple, in the royal court, as priests, or in such secular occupations as shepherding and agriculture.

Also, most of the prophets whose words appear in the Old Testament were speaking in the context of considerable community sanction and support. Some of the prophets had liberal access to the king and represented broad constituencies within Israelite society. They were silenced or disciplined only when their messages were perceived as especially rancorous or threatening.[2]

Moreover, the message of the prophets rests upon a deeply traditional base: the theological claim of the covenant between God and Israel. Thus, the prophets were never merely freewheeling social critics. They were theologians whose vision of justice and righteousness and their call to renewed obedience were rooted in the richest soil of traditional

Israelite religion. Von Rad has aptly pictured the prophets as forging their message from the interplay of three factors: the ancient covenant tradition of Israel's election, God's new word for Israel today, and the concrete realities of some particular social situation.[3]

Indeed, the best way to grasp the role of Old Testament prophecy is to begin with the third of von Rad's factors: the particular situation. Prophets were channels through which God's message was spoken to people in a specific set of circumstances. Indeed, the more urgent the situation, the more likely the appearance of the prophet. Prophecy, therefore, was never abstract. Prophets did not spin timeless truths. The prophetic message was a divine word delivered on target.

Beyond the observation that all of the prophets spoke a fresh word concerning Israel's covenant relationship to God and spoke this word into a concrete situation, little can be said of the prophets in general. From this common root there grew a fascinating display of variety in prophetic message and style. The prophets pressed their language imaginatively to the task, employing every possible rhetorical strategy, even radical forms of expression and caricature.[4]

In sum, then, the prophets were, as Eric Rust has observed, like present-day preachers—concerned with speaking God's message to a particular time, place, and people[5]—and the prophets' messages are as diverse in theme, purpose, language, and local markings as are contemporary sermons. The preacher who preaches on the prophets should not assume that the prophetic sermon is an extraordinary case, a sermon requiring more than the normal measure of moral outrage, an extra dollop of ethical instruction, or an overflowing scoop of terms like "justice" and "oppression." To the contrary, the prophetic task is the enduring, week in and week out, task of preaching. Sometimes comforting, sometimes confronting, the prophet's role is to speak that which the culture could never generate on its own, the dramatic and life-giving Word of God to real people struggling with genuine issues.

Continuing the Prophetic Ministry Through Preaching

To preach on the prophetic literature is to continue the ministry of the prophets. What is that ministry? Walter Brueggemann maintains that the people of God are called to a peculiar way of being in the world and that this "alternative vocation" is always in danger of being domesticated. The ministry of the prophets, then, is aimed at preserving that alternative vocation, and "the task of prophetic ministry is to nurture, nourish, and evoke a consciousness and perception alternative to the consciousness and perception of the dominant culture around us."[6] The basic vision of the prophet is that the people of God are called to an identity and mission shaped by the will of God, one that is at risk of being compromised in and by the larger culture. God will not leave the community of faith to its own devices and, thus, is continually confronting, judging, and passionately renewing this people. The task of the prophet is to bring this divine activity to human speech.

Thus, prophetic ministry, maintains Brueggemann, entails two functions, one typically thought of as "liberal"—criticizing—and the other typically viewed as more "conservative"—energizing. Criticizing, the liberal tendency, involves pointing out where the present order is unfaithful to the covenant and call of God and, therefore, worthy of rejection. Energizing, the conservative tendency, calls to remembrance the relationship between God and the people and discloses God's promise of another way of living and serving, fervently anticipating what God will do to bring in this newness.[7] Prophetic ministry, states Brueggemann, "does not consist of spectacular acts of social crusading or of abrasive measures of indignation. Rather, prophetic ministry consists of offering an alternative perception of reality and in letting people see their own history in the light of God's freedom and his will for justice."[8]

What this means for preachers is that preaching from the prophetic literature involves the preacher in two broad tasks: (1) viewing life through the lens of God's covenant and imaginatively proclaiming the vision of human society, both in personal and social dimensions, living in responsiveness and obedience to God; and (2) truthfully and courageously naming the discrepancies between this vision and the way people are presently living.

Reclaiming Imaginative Prophetic Speech for Preaching

When the prophets spoke, they did not speak with a single rhetorical voice. The prophets proclaimed the lively and active Word of God into a myriad of social situations, and this interaction between Word and context evoked from the prophets a rainbow of rhetorical colors. Poetry and prose, subtle humor and outrageous puns, startling images and scalding satire—these and many other styles of discourse were in the prophetic repertoire.

When a preacher prepares to preach on a prophetic text, the first step is to recover the rhetorical character of the text at hand. Westermann, among others, has identified what he calls "the basic forms of prophetic speech"—the characteristic oral and literary patterns into which the prophets' messages can be sorted.[9] The preacher should see these forms as elementary types of prophetic speech, recognizing that the prophets improvised freely from these types and that individual prophetic texts display tremendous variety and creative departure from the standard forms.

Building upon the work of earlier scholars, Westermann named three major kinds of materials in the prophetic literature: (1) accounts, (2) prophetic speeches, and (3) prayers. Accounts consist of the narrative sections of the books that provide details of the prophet's life, circumstances of his activity, and so on. The prophetic speeches, comprising most of the material in the prophetic books, are the messages received from God and delivered by the prophet. The prayers are, in contrast to the speeches, words from humanity to God, and, like the psalms, they consist of both lament and praise.[10]

Accounts

The material that Westermann calls "accounts" is essentially the narrative glue that holds together the prophetic books. The accounts relate how the prophet was called, the circumstances of particular prophetic speeches, and the reactions of the prophet's hearers to his message. Some prophetic books, like Nahum, contain no such material, while others, like Jonah, contain almost nothing else.

The preacher who chooses to preach on one of the accounts will want to explore the text as a narrative. Who are the characters? What is the tension, the conflict, that motivates the narrative? How is resolution, full or partial, achieved?

We can explore, as an example of the account form, Amos 7:10-14. In this text Amaziah, the priest of the shrine at Bethel, opposed the prophetic ministry of Amos in two ways: Amaziah sent a negative report regarding Amos to King Jeroboam. Amaziah also confronted Amos directly, ordering him to prophesy in his home territory, Judah, and not at Bethel, the sanctuary of the king.

Amaziah's actions set up two tensions that fueled the narrative flow. First, he raised the issue of authority. Who is in charge here? Amaziah's words and deeds clearly disclose that he thought King Jeroboam was in charge. There is nothing surprising about this; it is simply the conventional wisdom (the "prevailing consciousness," to use Brueggemann's term) about power. The king is the authority, and the authority of all others is derived from royal power. So Amaziah did what functionaries of the royal court usually do: he covered his flanks by tattling to the king (7:10-11), and he wrapped himself in the flag and attempted to pull rank (7:12-13).

The second issue raised by Amaziah is one of vocation. Amaziah was a working man, a priest who served at Bethel. He assumed that Amos was a working man, too—a full-time prophet. The problem, then, was that Bethel was not big enough for both of them. "I've got a job; you've got a job," claimed Amaziah. "Why don't you do yours elsewhere, in Judah? Earn your bread on a different payroll. Bethel is the king's chapel, and there are no openings for prophets" (see 10:12-13).

Amos' reply to Amaziah, though brief, quickly redefined both the issue of authority and that of vocation. In terms of authority, Amaziah appealed to the king; Amos appealed to Yahweh. Amaziah had put on his most resonant voice and attempted from a human base to do that which only God has the authority to do: to issue a prophetic call to Amos. He had the words right ("O seer... go prophesy back home in Judah!") but, like the Wizard of Oz, when all is said and done, it is just the little man, Amaziah, in the box. Amos knew the difference between sanctimonious speech that imitates the Word of God (but really only expresses the word of the culture) and the real thing: "The Lord said to me, 'Go prophesy to my people Israel'" (10:15, NRSV), replied Amos, replacing the counterfeit word with the genuinely divine one.

In regard to the second issue, Amos made it clear that he was a prophet by vocation and not by occupation. "I am no prophet," he claimed. "I am a herdsman and a dresser of sycamore trees" (10:14, NRSV). In other words, Amos would not put the word "prophet" in the occupation blank on his tax form. He was not "earning his bread" (to use Amaziah's phrase) from his prophetic activity; he was fulfilling the commission of God.

Preachers have here a fascinating text to explore regarding its bearing on the contemporary situation. Where, preachers may ask, can we see evidence that the larger culture assumes that the prophetic ministry of the church is beholden to the two basic forces in society: power and money? Where does the culture exert its muscle to say: "Listen, we don't mind your prophetic activity, just not here. Do it over there, on your own turf. There's no money in it here, but over there you can earn your bread quite handily"?

Judgment

Many of the speeches of the prophets involve what Brueggemann termed "prophetic criticizing," disclosing the discrepancies between the will of God and the present circumstances. This activity finds expression in the prophetic speeches of judgment, directed toward both individuals and nations.

One example of this form of speech can be found in the attack on idolatry in Isaiah 44:9-20. The text is highly imaginative, provocative, and even witty. The prophet began with a taunt, a dare: "All who make idols... will be put to shame" (44:9, NRSV). Then he proceeded to follow through on this challenge by calling a meeting of the international association of idol makers: "Let them all assemble, let them stand up; they shall be terrified, they shall all be put to shame" (44:11, NRSV).

Having gathered his audience, the prophet enacted a little skit, a parody of the idol maker's craft. He depicted the ironsmiths, woodcarvers, and other artisans at their work, forging the metal, chopping down trees, planing wood, taking a break for lunch. There is a lot of physical exercise here; the verbs in the text—fashioning, forging, fainting, stretching, marking, cutting, planting, kindling, baking—are almost exhausting just to read. By a deft use of language, the prophet exposed one of the fatal flaws of idolatry: it exhausts human energy. Idolatry is hard work, with no replenishment. The prophet was poking fun here, quipping that one of the problems with being an idolater, with serving a God who cannot nourish or even move, is that it involves a lot of heavy lifting.

The prophetic satire does not stop here. He pictured the idol maker tossing the wood scraps onto the factory stove: "Ah, I am warm, I can feel the fire," coos the idolater, failing to note the rich irony in roasting lamb over the wood shavings left over from "god." Half of the wood block he burns in the fire, the other half he cries out to for deliverance. "Is this god, or is this firewood?" the prophet mocked. "It's so hard to tell" (see 44:15-17).

Preachers can find powerful connections between this passage and our own situation. The sermon can even take on the playful tone of the text itself, poking fun at the sheer energy we expend to maintain our idolatries. For example, we experience the exhaustion of trying to maintain a certain life-style because we are persuaded that it will give us freedom. The fact that we are trapped and exhausted by that very style of life which we have fashioned in the hope of comfort and liberation is an irony that would not be lost on the prophet Isaiah.

Another example of the prophetic judgment speech can be found in Micah 2:1-5. Here the prophet pronounced doom on those who, in defiance of the sacred law, greedily seize the land of others. The language is graphic; the prophet pictured these characters as dreaming up their schemes at night and then carrying them out in the daylight (2:1). Their plot, evidently, was to acquire land unscrupulously, probably by using loansharking to leverage out the rightful owners.

Whatever the details, the basic scheme is familiar. It recurs in every time and society. These people had learned how to work the system to their own advantage, using the legal structures of society not as they are intended, to provide justice, but rather to milk the weak of what little they do have.

In the face of this situation, the prophet had some news from God: bad news if you are one of the land-grabbers, good news if you hunger for fairness. God will punish these greedy shysters, and the punishment—quite deliciously—will fit the crime. They grabbed land; it will be grabbed from them. They laughed all the way to the bank; they will be taunted and mocked (2:4). They worked the system to their advantage; they will have no one to represent them when the land is redistributed. The party is over!

The preacher can hear and proclaim in this oracle of judgment a word of grace. Junk bonds, leveraged buyouts, greedy foreclosures, under the table deals, and political payoffs have left us jaded. "Well, that's the way the world is," we say. "Always has been, always will be." Not so, claims the prophet! The world still belongs to God, and the judgment of God is at work to expose and destroy the greed that sucks the marrow out of human life. When the final results are in, the heartless chuckles of the selfish will be replaced by their weeping lament.

Salvation

The prophets not only spoke judgment but also announced God's promise of deliverance, what Brueggemann calls "prophetic energizing." The prophet (and the preacher of prophetic texts) portrays with passion and creativity that which God has promised to do and will surely achieve. "It is the task of prophetic imagination," Brueggemann claims, "to bring people to engage the promise of newness that is at work in our history with God."[11]

These promises of newness and redemption are found in texts known as "oracles of salvation," and a good example of this form is Isaiah 46. The text begins with the familiar prophetic theme of idolatry, but this time the prophet was less concerned with the sting of judgment than he was concerned with painting the backdrop against which the announcement of salvation may be heard. With bittersweet humor the prophet imagined the Babylonians fleeing the city before Cyrus' invading forces. Among the possessions being loaded onto the backs of animals are statues of their gods, Bel and Nebo. The people have bowed down and humbled themselves before these gods, but now the tables are deliciously, sadly, ironically turned: "Bel bows down, Nebo stoops, their idols are on beasts and cattle" (46:1, NRSV).

This wry picture of Bel and Nebo being dragged away unceremoniously says it all. That which was thought to be the source of refreshment and nourishment turns out, when the chips are down, to be one more burden to be carried, one more piece of baggage to add to the pile.

It is over against these images of toil and the loss of energy that the prophetic oracle takes on its graphic power. The voice of the living God breaks into the weariness:

> Listen to me, O house of Jacob,
> all the remnant of the house of Israel,
> who have been borne by me from your birth,
> carried from the womb;
> even to your old age I am he,
> even when you turn gray I will carry you.
> I have made, and I will bear;
> I will carry and will save" (46:3-4, NRSV).

The images in these verses invigorate the imagination by their direct countering of the heaviness of the previous verses. The Babylonian idols must be borne by cattle; God had borne the people of Israel. The idols seemed sufficient in a day of ease, but the day of crisis exposed their emptiness; God had been present and faithful throughout the seasons, carrying Israel since birth. The idols were burdens that must be dragged through the streets, exhausting both humans and beasts, draining social resources; God does the carrying, refreshing the people with creative energy. The idols must be dragged away for protection; God has made, will bear, will carry, and will save His people.

Preachers who engage this text honestly will find insight, if not shame, in this picture of the weariness of idolatrous religion. They will not have to search far to identify those places where people find the church promising refreshment but offering only a burden to be shouldered, a drain of their energies. The aim of the passage is not shame, however, but refreshment. Into the midst of this toilsomeness God acts, renewing the faithful imagination of the people. Any idea of a God who must be borne by us, a God on our backs, is swept away by the bold announcement of this God whose "purpose shall stand" (46:10, NRSV) and who is even now shaping life toward redemption (46:13).

Another image-rich example of a prophetic salvation oracle is found in Hosea 14, the final chapter of that book. The prophet began by rehearsing the people in a prayer of confession (14:1-3) and then moved to God's response to that confession—a vow of redemption.

Preachers would do well not to sprint through this text, but to view it as a wandering path through a lush garden and to pause to rest and reflect along the way. What is it that God promises a truly repentant people? First there is healing, not a generalized therapy, but a salving of their "disloyalty" (14:4, NRSV) and a bathing of their wounds in the liberality of God's love. These medical images are quickly followed by metaphors of growth. God will provide the "dew," the precious moisture, necessary for growth, and the people will prosper not only in ways that can be seen—the "blossom"—but in the deeper, hidden ways as well—the "root" (14:5, NRSV). The benefits of this growth will be felt in an expanding arena. The "shoots shall spread out" and the "fragrance" of their renewed life will fill the air (14:6, NRSV). In Palestine the enemy of growing plants was drought from the merciless heat of the sun. God promised to provide not only the rare moisture required for growth, but also the protection of shade, so that the people will "flourish as a garden" (14:7, NRSV). Now, the images shift again; it is God who is compared to a plant. "I am like an evergreen cypress," strong and caring in and out of season (14:8, NRSV).

A sermon on this text could explore each of these images, letting them take root in the imaginations of the hearers, pointing to ways in the faithful community and in the larger culture where God's healing, nourishing, protecting hand can be felt.

Prayers

While the priests were in the sanctuary, it was often said, the prophets were in the streets. Like most simple assessments of the prophets, this one, too, falls before the evidence. Much of the prophetic literature is punctuated by worship, by doxology and lament. Prophets spoke not only to the society, they spoke also to God, crying out in pain, wonder, and praise.

The early Isaiah is called to his prophetic ministry in a moment of ecstatic worship, marked by hymns of awe, wrenching confession, and vows of commitment (Isa. 6). His prophetic message was heard in the street, but it led the people to the altar: "And you will say in that day: Give thanks to the Lord, call on his name" (Isa. 12:4, NRSV). Jeremiah, placed in stocks for his disturbing words, lifted up his voice in a sometimes angry prayer of lament that moved back and forth between regret and commitment (Jer. 20:7-18).

What can preachers make of these prayers woven into the fabric of the prophetic messages? Each one of them contains, of course, its own theological vision and its own expression of the depths of human life opened up before the divine presence. Each of these deserves sermonic treatment on its own ground. Apart from their specific content, however, these liturgical interjections reveal the intimate connection between prophecy and praise, between worship and justice. Indeed, sometimes the prophets move seamlessly from a call to righteousness to a call to worship (see Amos 5:6-9). Where there is no doxology, there can be no hope of a renewed human society. Where there is no quest for justice, doxologies become empty, sanctimonious, and burdensome.

A Chorus of Prophetic Voices

The study of the diverse forms of prophetic literature makes it clear that Old Testament prophecy is a multifaceted jewel. The prophets spoke not in a single fashion but in many voices. They wept and sang, spun yarns, and cracked jokes. They thundered, and they whispered. They poked with a sharp stick, and they soothed with a tender hand. They conjured up courtrooms in the imagination and called forth witnesses to testify. They provoked with parables and puzzled with riddles. They used their own lives—their marriages, their children, their occupations—as allegories. They irrigated the fields of faithful memory, but also called the people to forget the former things. They felt their messages burning like fire in their bones, and they felt their own fear like acid on their tongues. They carried on disputations with the people in the name of God, then turned the other way to state the people's case against God, the charges of those who wonder if God's arm has lost its power and mercy. There is a melody in the prophetic books, but it is fashioned from many voices. There is a harmony of sorts in this material, but it is not an easy one. The prophets sang together, but in parts.

Preaching in the prophets, therefore, frustrates the preacher with a too easy scheme of analysis and a fixed set of assumptions. What is required is a flexibility of mind, and openness of spirit, and a willingness to attend to the text. Preachers must be willing to trace the contours of the text's thought, to savor its images, to feel its rhetorical power. The goal is not to repeat what Isaiah or Jeremiah or Amos has said, but to allow the force of the text to be regenerated in the sermon. When the preacher is open to both the judgment and the promise of the prophetic word, there is the hope that the sermon may become an instrument of renewed vision, a channel through which the Word may be heard and the people, in the words of Isaiah, "shall renew their strength . . . shall run and not be weary. . . shall walk and not faint" (40:31, NRSV).

Notes

1. Robert R. Wilson, "Prophet," *Harper's Bible Dictionary* (San Francisco: Harper & Row, 1985), 829.
2. Ibid.
3. Gerhard von Rad, *The Message of the Prophets* (London: SCM Press, 1968), 101.
4. von Rad, *The Message*, 100.
5. Eric C. Rust, "Preaching from the Minor Prophets," *Biblical Preaching: An Expositor's Treasury*, ed. James W. Cox (Philadelphia: Westminster Press, 1983), 133.
6. Walter Brueggemann, *The Prophet Imagination* (Philadelphia: Fortress Press, 1978), 13.
7. Ibid.
8. Ibid., 110.
9. See Claus Westermann, *Prophetic Oracles of Salvation in the Old Testament* and *Basic Forms of Prophetic Speech* (Louisville: Westminster/John Knox Press, 1991).
10. Westermann, *Basic Forms of Prophetic Speech*, 90-91.
11. Brueggemann, *The Prophetic Imagination*, 62-63.

27

Robert Sloan
Professor of Religion
Baylor University
Waco, Texas

Preaching and the New Testament

It would be hard to overestimate the importance of preaching for the rise and spread of the Christian faith. Certainly Jesus' preaching of the kingdom of God as well as the earliest apostolic preaching are in no small way significant for both the genesis and spread of Christianity. Typically an act of speaking, preaching is a highly demanding art form in which both past and present are consciously brought to bear upon one another in an event of communication intended to take place between speaker and listeners. In the case of Christian preaching, both ancient and modern, the past is most commonly represented by a text, or series of texts, and the present is represented by the experience of the preacher and the audience.

Preaching the New Testament, therefore, is the act of communication between preacher and audience which involves the translation of the history, thought, and experience represented by that collection of documents called the New Testament into the present-day life and experience of the church and the world. Almost every Christian would agree upon the importance of preaching the New Testament, but, having said that, there has been and remains ample room for discussion and creativity as to how to carry out that task.

In trying to analyze what does, or should, take place in the preaching of the New Testament, we are immediately taken into a storm of swirling historical issues. There are textual problems, historical debates, and theological matters of considerable import, each involving questions related to the situations of both the original writer and the audience, to say nothing of the dynamics of the relationship between the two.

These historical issues alone—leaving aside matters pertaining to speech, rhetoric, and the modern audience—are daunting enough for the would-be preacher. To attend to any one of the texts in the twenty-seven "book" collection known as the New Testament is immediately to be confronted with the history of that text: for instance, the history of the translation being used, as well as the manuscripts and scholarly endeavors (generally referred to as "textual criticism"[1]) which lie behind it; the ancient conventions of speech, now "fossilized" in the text itself, which the writer brought to the task of communication; and the respective environments of the author and the originally addressed readers. Such historical issues are further compounded by the intellectual history—the theological issues—reflected in the text and in the interpretive history of the use of that text.

These historical issues cause us to insist upon, contrary to some who participate in the modern discussion of texts, the fact of meaning within the text.[2] That is, every text (whether sacred or not) exerts some legitimate and legitimating control over the parameters of meaning which may be plausibly derived from it. No text has a meaning *for me* until I read it or am otherwise confronted by it. The obviously subjective dimensions of any task of reading and interpretation should not cause us to dismiss as completely unknowable the parameters of meaning which any text carries with it—parameters we must assume to exist unless we are prepared to accept as utterly random the various uses to which any text may be put.

If that is so, why bother with any text at all? Put another way, historical questions such as those referred to above immediately force us to assume, given the historical genesis and background of any text, that there are some readings which are historically plausible—more consistent with the physical and intellectual history of the text—than others. What has traditionally been called "the intention of the author" is no longer in vogue as a way of speaking for those who participate in the modern discussion of texts and their meaning.[3] However, while no one should claim to understand fully the "mentalistics" of even one's own self, much less another contemporary—and still less an ancient author—it is nonetheless reasonable to use something which we may call "intentionality." This refers not so much to the psychological state of the author as to those meanings which may or may not be presumed as historically plausible based upon the clues in the text and everything else we know about the historical situation of both author and audience.

If texts do in this way influence our readings of them, and if texts have authors (which surely requires little imagination to assume), then texts do reflect, in however limited and historically derivative a way, "authorial intention" in terms of those readings which are historically more plausible than others. Thus, this author assumes: (1) that texts do have meaning; (2) that the meaning of a text may reasonably be assumed to be consistent with what the author or authors "intended" to say; and (3) that we may with the proper application of historical tools, intuitions, and deductive reasoning—all of which must be seasoned heavily at times with generous quantities of imagination—reconstruct with greater or lesser degrees of probability and/or historical plausibility the thought patterns of the ancient author, as represented in a given text.

In what follows, we shall deal with issues related to the meaning, or theology, of the New Testament, the text of the New Testament, and, very briefly, the audience of the preacher.

New Testament Theology

To attempt the art of preaching the New Testament is to be confronted immediately with the New Testament as a *collection*. That is, we are dealing with a body of literature which is comprised of individually composed units. These separate units are literary pieces composed within a much more narrowly confined period of time than their biblical counterparts, the books which comprise the Old Testament, but they are nonetheless pieces written at different times and places by different authors who attempt to speak to different situations.

Among other things, the fact that the New Testament is a collection which was used alongside and ultimately bound together with another collection forces us, first of all, to appreciate its relationship to what Christians came to call the *Old* Testament. Therefore, as a collection, the New Testament stands both in continuity with and in juxtaposition to the Old Testament. Thus, in many ways it is fair to say that the New Testament represents a rereading of the Old Testament.[4]

Early Christian leaders primarily conveyed their message through preaching. However, for varied reasons, the evangelistic and didactic materials propagated and perpetuated in the earliest decades of the church were also employed in the formation of written materials. The composition of at least four Gospels, the laying out of a historical narrative regarding the spread of the Christian faith to the ends of the earth, and various other documents largely conceived as pieces of correspondence from one place to another became, in literary form, the particular embodiment of at least the leading themes and traditions in the first century of Christian preaching.[5]

Since much of early Christian preaching was in fact carried out in both continuity and dialogue with the Jewish Scriptures and the traditions of synagogue Judaism throughout the Mediterranean world, it is not surprising to see Old Testament citations, allusions, and echoes used throughout the New Testament. It is therefore not inappropriate to think of the New Testament as a literary collection which embodies many of the earliest Christian traditions—traditions originally formulated in profound connection with the history of Jesus as interpreted through the conceptual matrix of the Jewish Scriptures and then propagated through the act of preaching.

Second, because it is a collection of different pieces, the New Testament must be approached with a view to both its variety and its unit.[6] On the one hand, the reader must consider the unique nature of the various texts. The individual nuances, the theological and literary variety, and the historical and verbal distinctives of each book must all be appreciated if the true character of the New Testament and its component parts are to be understood. On the other hand, the fact that the New Testament is a collection of materials must lead to the question of its unity. Why should these twenty-seven different pieces have been collected with one binding and under a single label such as the "New Testament?" Put another way, what is the historical and/or theological consensus which would cause the earliest generations of Christians to appreciate the unity of witness which these twenty-seven books, in all their variety, represent?

Before considering what that theological unity might be, it is important to understand the mutually reinforcing nature of the relationship between the theology of a given "book" of the New Testament (or even smaller units within that book) and the theological unity of the New Testament as a collection. Preaching the New Testament must work within the dialectic of the individual text versus the canonical whole. To understand the message of the New Testament is a synthetic task which arises from the examination of the various books of the New Testament. On the other hand, an understanding of any given book or passage within a book is greatly dependent upon the larger theological parameters within which the smaller pieces exist. Put another way, the interpretation of any given passage is immeasurably helped by a proper understanding of the overall message of the New Testament. Thus, as modern Christians we are involved in an interpretive circle which causes us constantly to revise our understanding of the whole in light of the parts and to interpret the parts in light of everything else we know.

When I preach a given passage from the New Testament, I am constantly aware of its place within the framework of the larger theological unity of the New Testament. Of course, I am assuming that there is a unity to the New Testament; but, given the historical fact of the collection of these books by the earliest generations of Christians—an activity which has been perpetuated for nearly two thousand years—I think such an assumption is intellectually credible.[7]

The discovery of the theological unity of the New Testament is a task which stays under discussion among New Testament scholars. Let it be sufficient to say here, however, than an analysis of (1) the earliest sermons in the book of Acts, (2) the earliest hymns, creeds, and confessional fragments embedded within the New Testament, and (3) the common themes which may be synthetically deduced from the New Testament writings all lead to certain conclusions which may be reliably drawn as to the core of early Christian theology and preaching. The earliest Christians believed, among other things: (1) that God had powerfully acted for their salvation through the life, and especially the death and resurrection, of one Jesus of Nazareth; (2) that this same Jesus was now enthroned at the right hand of God, having been exalted following His resurrection to the status of supreme heavenly Lord, now sharing the titles and prerogatives of Yahweh Himself; (3) that this same Jesus had poured forth His Spirit upon all His followers; (4) that all who would come to Him in a humility of trust and obedience, declaring Him Lord and following Him in an initiatory ceremony of baptism, would not only be His people, but also find the salvation long anticipated by the Jewish prophets; (5) that such salvation would constitute the followers of Jesus as the authentic and regathered Israel of God; (6) that this same Jesus would come again, manifesting Himself in heavenly glory to all the earth, thereby bringing to a final conclusion this present evil age and also ushering in the long-awaited age to come; and (7) that all of these dramatic saving events were accomplished in fulfillment of the ancient (Jewish) Scriptures.[8]

It is vain for any preacher to assume that he or she comes to any task in life, much less the reading of the text of the New Testament, with no preunderstanding or theological bent. The question is whether our theological predispositions have plausible historical and Christian warrants. Modern preaching and belief illustrate well the fact that theological "preunderstandings" often characterize our approaches to preaching and the New Testament. Whether we assume the five points of Calvinism before we approach a text, whether we have a charismatic understanding of the gifts and the baptism of the Spirit, whether we are predisposed to the perfections of holiness, whether we are primarily committed to the missionary task of evangelizing, or whether we focus upon the social mandates associated with historic Christianity, we all have preunderstandings which influence our reading of New Testament texts.

The widespread use and ongoing popularity of, for example, the Scofield Reference Bible, with its attendant theological "dispensationalism," bears witness to the very natural desire to have interpretive handles whereby we may come to grips with the Scriptures. What Christian has not sought for systematic handles with which to organize his or her faith? Preaching the New Testament, however, if it is to be done in a way which takes seriously and responsibly the necessities of historical plausibility, must attempt to use as hermeneutical guidelines the theological categories, themes, and emphases of the New Testament writers themselves. The seven central, common convictions enumerated above are a good place to start.

Third, an analysis of the New Testament as a collection raises the question of "interpretive directionality." The matter of which Testament interprets the other is of perennial concern. Do we interpret, for example, New Testament eschatology based upon Old Testament anticipations which are uninformed by New Testament light? Or, do we read the Old Testament in light of the New? Given the fact that the New Testament writers consistently interpreted their Scriptures in light of the events which had recently transpired with respect to Jesus, especially His death and resurrection, it is hardly surprising to note that various Old Testament motifs have come in for some rather dramatic reinterpretations. This is not to say that New Testament writers ultimately misread or distorted the Old Testament; but, it is to say that the New Testament writers often interpreted the Old Testament in ways which were spiritually, literarily, and theologically innovative.[9]

Given the general pattern of the New Testament use of the Old, it seems to this author that, while the Old Testament provides the theological, verbal, historical, and literary background to the New Testament, it is nonetheless the case that, for the purpose of securing a *Christian* reading, one must finally interpret the Old Testament in light of the New Testament's already "re-presented" interpretations of it.[10] Thus, I can no longer read of Ezekiel's future temple without being profoundly influenced by Paul's understanding of the people of God as a living, spiritual temple (1 Cor. 3:16-17; 2 Cor. 6:16; Eph. 2:19-22; compare 1 Pet. 2:2-5; Rev. 11:1-2; 13:6) constituted by those who are "in Christ." My "directionality" for interpreting Scripture thus moves from New to Old.

The Text

The New Testament text itself is rather obviously composed of words as the essential element of written communication. Each word has a history of participation in previous texts and language experiences, and there is a legitimate sphere of inquiry which deals with the history of terms and their various significations and meanings in other texts and situations. Words stand in relationship to other words in the same text, and therefore the study and analysis of what has traditionally been called grammar and syntax are vitally important. There is thus room for a historical discipline which understands the history of various terms in their own right, and there is also room for the study of the contextual relationships of words within a given text.[11] Both kinds of study are essential for sermon construction.

Some older styles of preaching from biblical texts were often a kind of "word study." Preachers would focus upon the individual history, or picture, of a given word or word group.[12] In more recent days focus has shifted away from the "word study" method toward a more contextualized treatment of words and passages. There is room for both approaches. Words not only have meaning in grammatical and syntactical relationship to other words of the same text, but each word also has a prior significance which led the New Testament author to choose and employ it in the composition of the text and which informed the original and subsequent readers, consciously or subconsciously, as to the meaning of the given term within a text. Thus, both writers and readers have prior histories of and with a given term and bring that prior understanding to the tasks of writing and reading. The history of a word *and* its relationship within a text, as used and understood by both author and readers, give words, phrases, and passages their significance. These basic facts of language are relevant for the construction as well as the delivery and reception of a sermon.

It is incumbent upon the preacher to use all the means of reading which are available. Every historical and literary tool which the mind can both devise and employ for the extraction of meaning from a text is appropriate.[13] The use of such methods, however, though absolutely essential, must not be permitted to obscure the fact that preachers are attempting to work with the text, and all the knowable history of that text, *as we have it*. We must deal with a text in a sympathetic way, where sympathy not only involves an attentive listening to the text and all its available nuances, but also a desire to read the text holistically. The application of historical critical methods, though necessary for understanding the text, must not be employed in such limited ways that we fragment the given text and ultimately ignore, or even obscure, larger issues of sense and meaning.

The more recent applications of rhetorical[14] and literary methods to biblical texts have reminded us to be alert to larger question of correspondence within a text and to listen for the flow, the thought, and the dynamic of a text. The chapter and verse designations of the New Testament are not part of the inspired text. They are remarkably "reader unfriendly" in terms of the often unconsciously misleading fragmentation of the argument and thought flow of a text which they induce. In this respect, it is critical for the sensitive reader of a text to pay attention to the relational terms (and not the chapter and verse divisions) which give sentences and paragraphs their flow and dynamic. Words such as "therefore," "nevertheless," "if," "not only. . . but also," establish relationships between phrases within a sentence and even larger patterns of thought and argument. Preachers have best understood a text, it seems to me, when they are able to "anticipate" a text. The underlying emphases, themes, and motivations of a text are best understood when there is such a sympathy with the author and the text that the reader is able to follow the flow of the text, to understand the various shifts in argument, and even on occasion to anticipate where the argument will go next. Assuming that the author has coherency and certain central convictions which govern the whole of the text, a reader may know that he or she has understood a text when the rhetorical movement of its argument is comprehensible and justifiable.

In understanding the whole of a text, it is especially vital to understand the genre of the text.[15] Genre analysis is the attempt to establish the type of literature with which one is dealing. To understand other pieces of literature which are of the same type and of the same time period enables the reader to know what to expect from a text. There are times when we ask too much of a text, or when we ask the wrong things of a text. There are times when a text is silent on the kinds of questions we would like to ask, and there are times when a text answers questions that we have not thought to ask. An appreciation for the historical situation and the kind of literature involved better enables the preacher to identify with the concerns of the text and thus to hear more precisely the distinctive voice and the rhetorical message of the given text. These insights in turn help the preacher translate the text into sermon form for a modern audience.

Finally, there must be a constant interplay between given texts—as they are broken down in terms of words, history, grammar, rhetoric, and genre—and, in the case of the New Testament, the unity of early Christian theology which seemingly holds all of these texts together. If the New Testament does have a theological unity, then another test for sound and plausible reading is the extent to which the individual books and/or given passages within those books, as interpreted, are not only rhetorically consistent within themselves, but also participate in the larger pattern represented by New Testament theology. A proper understanding of the larger theological emphases which stand "behind" a text, together with a knowledge of the historical circumstances which have motivated the author to shape that underlying theology literarily for the given historical occasion, help the preacher to understand the flow and argument of a text.

The Audience

It is at this point that the task of the preacher reaches its most critical stage. If there is failure at this point, all is lost. It is vital for the preacher to understand the theological whole which historically justifies the New Testament as a collection and canon of Holy Scripture. It is also vital for the preacher to understand the given text, the smaller book or literary unit which occupies the attention on a given occasion. This latter task involves the careful and meticulous study of words, phrases, historical settings, genre, and all the various patterns of textual relationship. However, if the preacher's knowledge of the history and theology of the New Testament as a whole and a given text in particular is not sufficiently communicated to the audience, then the act of preaching has not occurred.

The final task of preaching involves a human and spiritual dynamic between the preacher and audience for which there is no substitute. Theological and textual issues are essentially matters of relationship between the preacher and the text and/or the history of the text. The relationship between preacher and audience, however, involves a translation of the meaning or meanings gleaned from a given text to a living audience. This relationship between preacher and audience, however accurate and plausible the preacher may be with respect to the text, must involve a significant overlap of concern or no communication will take place. There must be a sense of community between the preacher and the audience (either by personal experience, pastoral concern, a common situation, or the honest use of rhetorical skills which for the occasion express and/or establish an overlap of concern). An empathy of experience between the preacher and audience must exist if the New Testament is to be successfully preached. As Thomas Long has so well stated:

> Preachers come to the pulpit from *somewhere*, and unless we can name that place, we risk misunderstanding who we are and what we are supposed to be doing in the pulpit. When we who preach open the sanctuary door on Sunday morning and find a congregation waiting there for us, it is easy to forget that we come *from* these people, not *to* them from the outside. We are not visitors from clergy-land, strangers from an unknown land, ambassadors from seminary-land, or even, as much as we may cherish the thought, prophets from a wilderness land. We are members of the body of Christ, commissioned to preach by the very people to whom we are about to speak.[16]

The New Testament itself represents a collection of documents designed—by genre, personal appeal, and a pastoral/rhetorical use of the historical situation—to establish an empathy of experience between writers and readers sufficient to create a psychological and moral justification for the given messages of exhortation, correction, and/or encouragement in each document.

The work of the Spirit may and must certainly be understood as a part of the preacher's task of preparation, a task which is both historical in method and artistically imaginative in character. The work of the Spirit is nowhere more vitally needed than in the establishing of a sympathetic relationship of concern between speaker and audience.

The preacher may never presume upon the moving of the Spirit. The preacher may never dictate the moving of the Spirit. Nor may the preacher ever claim to have definitively sensed the moving of the Spirit, for "the wind of the Spirit blows where it wills" (John 3:8). The New Testament clearly asserts the presence of the Spirit in worship (Rom. 8:12-27) and the presence of the Spirit in the preaching and teaching of the gospel and its implications (1 Cor. 2:4-16). Moreover, it is primarily in the body of Christ and in the experience of worship that the Spirit, as reflected in the New Testament, is in attendance and at work (1 Cor. 12—14). Thus, the authentic work of the Spirit is reflected in sound theology—and especially a sound Christology (1 Cor. 12:1-3; 1 John 4:1-6)—in unity among the people of God (1 Cor. 3:16-17), and in the edification of the saints (1 Cor. 14). These are the true marks of authentic New Testament preaching. Such preaching will have similarly positive results for both the preacher and the audience as they, by the power of the Spirit and in a mutually responsive relationship of communication, come into dialogue with the history, theology, and ultimately the significance of the New Testament for the totality of life under the lordship of Jesus Christ.

Conclusion

When I was first starting to preach, I was told that there are basically two types of sermons, the "topical" (that was normally said to be "bad") and the "expository" (much to be preferred). I have now come to believe that these are simply different ways of organizing texts and sermons for presentation to a given audience. So-called "expository" sermons and "topical" sermons may be equally biblical or unbiblical, depending upon the use of the texts involved and the application made of them for the audience.

I have come to prefer what I like to call "theological preaching"—a kind of preaching which has done its homework in terms of the history, grammar, and theology of the text; has also attained pastoral and relational legitimacy with the given audience; and then attempts to proclaim in the power of the Spirit a message which is not so much a theological extrapolation of the words and phrases of Scripture, as it is both a description and application of the underlying theology. Assuming that the given New Testament authors had coherent convictions, we must appreciate the fact that their literary productions gave written expression to such convictions. Therefore, the meaning of any given literary expression is best understood as significantly involving the recovery of the situation and theology which originally gave rise to the text. Thus, I seek to preach more the meaning "behind" the text, a meaning which, I believe, if truly touched upon (though never fully comprehended), gives a deeper and more holistic appreciation for the text as we have it. When such an experience occurs for both the preacher and the audience, then the kind of historical and theological understandings which make for a living involvement with the text for both preacher and audience can take place. Such engagement with the text can create a context in which the Spirit engenders the kind of living application which may lead to a more genuine obedience to Christ the living Lord.[17]

Notes

1. Compare Bruce M. Metzger, *The Early Versions of the New Testament: Their Origin, Transmission and Limitations* (Oxford: Clarendon, 1977); see also Metzger, *The Text of the New Testament: Its Transmission, Corruption and Restoration* (Oxford: Oxford University Press, 1968).

2. Representative examples are Stanley Fish, *Is There a Text in This Class?: The Authority of Interpretive Communities* (Cambridge: Harvard University Press, 1980); Susan Suleiman and Inge Crosman, eds., *The Reader in the Text: Essays in Audience and Interpretation* (Princeton: Princeton University Press, 1980); Stephen O. Moore, *Literary Criticism and the Gospels: The Theoretical Challenge* (New Haven: Yale University Press, 1989); and Edgar V. McKnight, *The Postmodern Use of the Bible: The Emergence of Reader-Oriented Criticism* (Nashville: Abingdon, 1989).

3. For a contrasting view, however, see E. D. Hirsch, *The Aims of Interpretation* (Chicago: University of Chicago Press, 1976); Northrup Frye, *The Great Code: The Bible and Literature* (New York: Harcourt Brace Jovanovich, 1982); and Leland Ryken, *Windows to the World: Literature in Christian Perspective* (Dallas: Word Publishing, 1990).

4. See Richard B. Hays, *Echoes of Scripture in the Letters of Paul* (New Haven: Yale University Press, 1989). Hays discusses not only Paul's use of Scripture but also larger issues of intertextuality, hermeneutics, and the normative value of scripture.

5. Compare R. E. Brown, *The Churches the Apostles Left Behind* (New York: Paulist Press, 1984); James L. Kugel and Rowan A. Greer, *Early Biblical Interpretation*, in Library of Early Christianity, ed. Wayne E. Meeks (Philadelphia: Westminster, 1986).

6. Compare James D. G. Dunn, *Unity and Diversity in the New Testament* (Philadelphia: Westminster, 1977). Although I think there is more unity than Dunn allows, his book is a good place to start with respect to this issue.

7. Robert Sloan, "Unity in Diversity: A Clue to the Emergence of the New Testament as Sacred Literature," *New Testament Criticism*, eds. David A. Black and David S. Dockery (Grand Rapids: Zondervan, 1991), 437 ff.

8. Ibid., 438-439.

9. See Robert Sloan, "The New Testament Use of the Old Testament," *Reclaiming the Prophetic Mantle: Preaching the Old Testament Faithfully*, ed. George Klein (Nashville: Broadman Press, 1992).

10. Compare G. F. Hasel, *Old Testament Theology: Basic Issues in Current Debate* (Grand Rapids: Eerdmans, 1972).

11. Compare James Barr, *The Semantics of Biblical Language* (Oxford: Oxford University Press, 1961).

12. A. T. Robertson's *Word Pictures in the New Testament*, 6 vols. (Nashville: Broadman Press, 1930) is still an excellent resource for the preacher.

13. For example, H. Conzelmann and A. Lindemann, *Interpreting the New Testament: An Introduction to the Principles and Methods of N.T. Exegesis*, trans. Siegfried S. Schutzmann (Peabody, Massachusetts, 1988); and David Aune, *The New Testament in Its Literary Environment*, in Library of Early Christianity (Philadelphia: Westminster Press, 1906).

14. For example, Jeanne Fahnestock and Marie Secor, *A Rhetoric of Argument* (New York: McGraw-Hill, 1982) is a general introduction to rhetoric in a form that is highly useful for any speaker; see also Burton L. Mack, *Rhetoric and the New Testament* (Minneapolis: Fortress Press, 1990).

15. An excellent introduction to this issue of genre and preaching is Thomas G. Long, *Preaching and the Literary Forms of the Bible* (Philadelphia: Fortress Press, 1989); see also David M. Brown, *Dramatic Narrative in Preaching* (Valley Forge: Judson Press, 1981).

16. Thomas G. Long, *The Witness of Preaching* (Louisville: Westminster/John Knox Press, 1989), 11.
17. It would be improper to end this essay without expressing my appreciation for and growing indebtedness to Fred B. Craddock's *Preaching* (Nashville: Abingdon, 1985).

28

Sidney Greidanus
Professor of Homiletics
Calvin Theological Seminary
Grand Rapids, Michigan

Preaching in the Gospels

The Gospels are ideal sources for contemporary preaching, for they are rooted in the preaching of Jesus and His disciples and are themselves a form of preaching. Specifically, the Gospels preach the kingdom of God that has come in Jesus Christ. Mark opened his Gospel as follows: "Jesus came into Galilee, preaching the gospel of God, and saying, 'The time is fulfilled, and the kingdom of God is at hand; repent, and believe in the gospel' " (1:14-15).[1] Later Jesus sent out the twelve, charging them: "Preach as you go, saying, 'The kingdom of heaven is at hand' " (Matt. 10:7). After His resurrection, Jesus charged His disciples: "Go therefore and make disciples of all nations, baptizing them . . . teaching them to observe all that I have commanded you" (Matt. 28:19-20).

Still later the evangelists Mark, Matthew, Luke, and John wrote their Gospels as a permanent record of the good news of the kingdom of God that came in Jesus Christ. Since this good news was addressed to specific churches, the Gospels themselves are a form of preaching. Contemporary preaching of the Gospels, therefore, is a natural extension of the Gospels themselves. Preachers need only redirect to the contemporary church the good news the evangelists preached to the early church.

Although preaching the Gospels is less complicated than preaching Old Testament narratives, in preaching the Gospels preachers will need to be aware of various options they can employ and various hazards they will wish to avoid. We shall follow the major steps in sermon preparation and, with each, present the options as well as the hazards.

Selecting a Preaching-Text from the Gospels

The preaching-text must be selected with care, lest one make the text say what the evangelist did not intend to say. A fragment of a passage can be made to say almost anything. John Stott recalls an instance where preachers managed to use fragments of the same verse to preach messages that were diametrically opposite. The verse was Matthew 18:17 where Jesus said: "If he neglect to hear the church, let him be unto thee as an heathen man and a publican." Preachers of the Oxford Movement frequently used the fragment "hear the church" to drum up support for their high view of the church's authority. This misuse provoked Archbishop Whately to preach the opposite message on the fragment: "If he neglect to hear the church, let him."[2]

To guard against falsifying the Gospels in the very act of selecting a preaching-text, it is imperative to select a literary unit as preaching-text.

A Literary Unit

Literary units can be discerned most easily by paying attention to the contents: a change of contents means a new literary unit. Repetition is also a good indicator: as long as a key word is repeated, one is dealing with a single unit. For example, the ninefold repetition of "blessed" marks the beatitudes of Matthew 5:3-12 as a literary unit. Sometimes rhetorical criticism can help identify units by discerning rhetorical structures such as inclusion and chiasm which at the end of the unit circle back to the beginning. For example, in Matthew 19 the words "lay his hands on them" of verse 13 are repeated in verse 15, thus forming an inclusion which marks verses 13 to 15 as a literary unit.

Frequently, inclusion and chiasm will mark large units of literature—perhaps too large to be covered responsibly in one sermon. For example, the whole Gospel of Matthew is enveloped by the inclusion of "God with us" (Matt. 1:23 and 28:20). The entire Sermon on the Mount (Matt. 5—7) is thought to reflect a chiastic structure.[3] One could, of course, preach a sermon on the entire Sermon on the Mount and possibly even on the whole Gospel of Matthew. With such large preaching-texts, one would be forced to omit many details. As a rule it is preferable to select from these large literary units a smaller unit which can be adequately explored in one sermon.

A Pericope

In general, one should think pericope when selecting a preaching-text from the Gospels. Form criticism has shown that the basic preaching units underlying the written Gospels are the "pericopes"—roughly corresponding to paragraphs in our English Bibles. Dwight Moody

Smith states: "When the pericopes of the Gospels are taken as texts for preaching, one is in close touch with their original intent and purpose."[4] Since these pericopes now form part of larger literary units (Gospel sections, the Gospel, the Bible), they cannot be preached in isolation but must be interpreted in their present literary contexts.

Sometimes there are occasions when a larger or a smaller unit would be more appropriate. For example, to select as text only one paragraph from a scenic narrative which relates a story in several paragraphs is to court misuse of the story. With scenic narrative which relates one scene per paragraph, one will usually need to select several paragraphs as a preaching-text. By contrast, for the sake of congregational retention, one may wish to focus on a single verse: say, the heart of a chiasm, or the conclusion of a pericope, or a single beatitude. The danger of misusing the Gospels by preaching on fragments can be avoided if one makes it a point to interpret and preach these small units in their larger contexts.

A Series of Sermons

The Gospels lend themselves well to preaching a series of sermons. Narratives as well as composite discourses (for instance, Matt. 5—7; 10; 13; 18; and 24—25) are excellent sources for consecutive treatment. By preaching a series of sermons on a larger Gospel unit, one can take advantage of the similarity of the pericopes by sketching the background material only once and concentrating in subsequent sermons on reinforcing and expanding the main point.

Combining Verses from Different Gospels

Sometimes preachers like to mix and match their preaching-texts by combining verses from different Gospels. Especially in preparing the Good Friday message, the temptation is great to combine verses from various Gospels in order to preach on "The Seven Words from the Cross." However, it is not advisable to create one's own preaching-text by combining verses from different Gospels. Such a hybrid preaching-text mixes decidedly different literary and historical contexts and makes it extremely difficult if not impossible to do justice to the intention of each Gospel writer. To pass on the message of the Gospel as intended by the inspired evangelist, a preaching-text ought to be selected from a single Gospel.

Theocentric-Christocentric Interpretation

For the sake of doing justice to the selected preaching-text, one must next seek to understand it according to the intent of its author. This concern calls for understanding the text in the context of the overall message of the evangelist. In all four Gospels that overall message has to do with God, more precisely with the kingdom of God. In fact, Mark speaks of "the gospel of God" and identifies the content of this good news as "the kingdom of God" (1:14-15).

Further, all four Gospels tie this central message of the kingdom of God to the person and work of Jesus Christ. With the coming of Jesus, the kingdom of God has not only "come near," but according to Jesus Himself, "the kingdom of God has come upon you" (Matt. 12:28), and will come in perfection (for instance, Matt. 25:34; 26:29; Luke 22:16-30). This all-encompassing good news of the Gospels—that in Jesus Christ the kingdom of God is coming near, has come, and will come—calls for a theocentric-Christocentric interpretation of each individual preaching-text from the Gospels.

Christocentric Gospels

Mark opened his Gospel: "The beginning of the gospel of Jesus Christ, the son of God" (1:1). Matthew alluded to the genealogy pattern of Genesis while focussing on Jesus: "The book of the genealogy of Jesus Christ, the son of David, the son of Abraham" (1:1). In his second volume Luke wrote: "In the first book, O Theophilus, I have dealt with all that Jesus began to do and teach, until the day when He was taken up" (Acts 1:1-2). John informed us that he wrote his Gospel "that you may believe that Jesus is the Christ, the Son of God, and that believing you may have life in His name" (20:31). The heart of all four Gospels is Jesus Christ.

Narrative criticism confirms that Jesus is central in the Gospels. Jesus is described as "the central figure," "the subject around which every narrative turns,"[5] "the major character," "the protagonist," "the supreme exponent of God's evaluative point of view."[6] Sermons that would be true to the Gospels ought to transmit this Christocentric focus of the Gospels.

Anthropocentric Sermons

Unfortunately, in preaching the Gospels, preachers frequently focus on the "secondary characters" and move them center stage in the sermon. Popular series include sermons on each of the twelve disciples and on the women in the Gospels. Preachers who are inclined to engage in biographical or character preaching should at least ask themselves if they are still true to the Gospels or have in fact allowed other characters to upstage Jesus.

Often this switch from Jesus to other characters is made for the best of reasons: relevance. One Sunday the sermon may be about Mary and her submission to the Lord and the congregation is encouraged to imitate her godly attitude. The next Sunday the sermon may be about Judas and his betrayal of Christ and the congregation is warned never to betray

Christ like Judas did. However, this kind of example preaching is basically moralistic and subverts the Gospel when it turns the Christocentric Gospel message into an anthropocentric sermon.[7] Ironically, in the process such sermons lose the real relevance of the Gospel, for the relevance of the Gospel is found not in the good and bad behavior and attitudes of the various characters but in the good news about Jesus Christ.

Questions to Ask

Accordingly, in preaching the Gospels one of the first questions to ask is: What does this passage tell us about the good news of Jesus Christ, His love for us, His mission, His suffering, death, and resurrection, His coming kingdom, His will for us and society?

Preachers who are inclined by tradition or habit to turn Bible characters into moral examples should further ask: Was it the intention of the evangelist to sketch these characters as moral examples for the early Christians? If this was not the intention of the inspired author, contemporary preachers of the Gospels have no business seeking relevance in that direction.

The next question related to Bible characters is: If Mary, Judas, or Peter may not upstage Jesus, what is their place in the sermon? Genuine biblical preaching, it seems fair to suggest, should seek to give the same place and function to these persons in the sermon as they have in the Gospels. In other words, one needs to ask how the Gospel writer has used these characters in presenting his Gospel.

The Function of Gospel Characters

Narrative criticism has made clear that the characters in the Gospels function not independently but as parts of an overall "plot." This fact also argues against the practice of isolating characters for the sake of presenting them as moral examples for the congregation, for the plot structure entails that these characters ought to be understood and preached in the context of the whole story. That whole story, of course, is the story about Jesus Christ. Thus every character in the Gospels stands in relation to Jesus, and every Gospel sermon, when considering these characters, can be genuinely Christocentric.

Narrative criticism has further shown that some characters function simply as catalysts for other characters to exhibit their traits or to move along the action in a scene. Other characters, however, function as foils to contrast and highlight certain traits of Israel or of the disciples. For example, Matthew contrasted the wise men's faith in Jesus with Israel's unbelief (2:1-12); later, he contrasted the Roman centurion's faith with Israel's unbelief (8:5-13). When we realize that Matthew's Jewish audience would tend to recognize itself in Israel, his polemical as well as his homiletical point comes into view. Again, Matthew contrasted the faith of the leper with the disciples' "little faith" (8:2,26) and the faith of the father of an epileptic with the disciples' "little faith" (17:14-21). When we realize that the early church Matthew addressed would identify particularly with Jesus' disciples, the point of his message comes into view.[8]

For Christocentric, relevant sermons, one need only follow the lead of the Gospel writer. For example, just as Matthew (for instance, 9:10-13; 12:1-14; 15:1-20) used the Pharisees as a foil to accentuate the freedom Jesus brings from legalism, contemporary preachers can do likewise. Similarly, contemporary preachers can make the same use of Zacchaeus that Luke (19:1-10) did when he used the wealthy, chief tax collector to proclaim that Jesus is able to save even rich swindlers. By closely following the lead of the Gospel writers, contemporary preachers can pay appropriate attention to the various human characters while retaining center stage for Jesus and His teachings.

Historical Interpretation

In our discussion of Christocentric interpretation we have already touched on historical as well as literary interpretation. This intermingling points out the fact that one cannot, strictly speaking, use these three kinds of interpretation one after the other but must use them concurrently. For discussion purposes, however, we can treat each in turn.

Historical interpretation in particular raises the questions: Who wrote this passage, to whom, when, where, and why? To answer these questions preachers will be aided by introductions to the New Testament and the introductions in specific Gospel commentaries, dictionaries, and atlases.

Aside from the issue of historical reliability,[9] the major homiletical question in historical interpretation of the Gospels is: Which homiletical horizon is to be used as a basis for contemporary preaching? The horizon of Jesus preaching to the Jews? Or the horizon of the disciples (and early church) preaching? Or the horizon of the evangelists Mark, Matthew, Luke, and John?

The Horizon of Jesus

Many preachers almost automatically opt for the horizon of Jesus, preaching sermons on Jesus calling His disciples, Jesus preaching to the crowds, Jesus healing the sick, Jesus challenging the Pharisees, and so on, and applying Jesus' message from that original setting to the church today.

The question may be raised, however, as to whether this approach does full justice to the written text. This method does use the written text, but only as a transparent window pane through which to view the historical Jesus and His words and actions. The Gospels, however, as a comparison of the four will show, are not transparent window panes but distinctly colored presentations of the historical Jesus. To look right through the written text to Jesus' historical horizon is to miss the kerygmatic point made by the Gospel writer in a later horizon. Preaching exclusively at this level fails to do full justice to the inspired Gospels.

The Horizon of the Disciples

A few preachers opt for the horizon of the disciples and the early church. Under the influence of form criticism, this horizon was seen as the formative stage of the Gospels. The early church preserved and transmitted the Gospel tradition in the unique kerygmatic units we now call "pericopes." William E. Hull sees the main homiletical value of form criticism in its delineation of the life setting of each pericope. If we can match the form of a pericope with a particular life setting, we have discovered the aim or goal of the pericope.

> Thus, for example, we may infer that liturgical forms (for instance prayers) were used in a worship context, that didactic forms (for instance, aphorisms) were used in a catechetical context, that controversy stories (for instance, debates) were used in a polemical context, and that testimonial forms (for instance, Old Testament quotations) were used in an apologetic context. The enormous relevance of this approach for preachers should be immediately apparent. Obviously preachers will try to meet a pressing need in their own situations by preaching on a passage that was designed to address that very same need in the early church.[10]

However, also at the horizon of the disciples the question may be raised if preaching at this level does justice to the inspired Gospel of which the pericope now forms a part. Surely one may not interpret and preach a pericope in isolation of its biblical context. A further problem in preaching at this level is that the form critical results are rather speculative and can hardly be considered a solid basis for preaching the Word of God.

The Horizon of the Evangelist

A third group of preachers seeks to preach the Gospels from the homiletical horizon of the Gospel writers. They try to detect the message Matthew proclaimed to the Jewish Christian church, or the message Luke formulated for the church of Theophilus, and transfer that message to the church today.

For support, this approach can appeal to the fact that the church received as God's inspired Word the written Gospels and not our reconstructions of the historical Jesus or of preaching settings in the early church. As well, it can appeal to Jesus' promise to His disciples: "When the Spirit of truth comes, he will guide you into all the truth" (John

16:13). Only *after* Jesus' resurrection and the outpouring of the Holy Spirit did the apostles begin to understand what had taken place in Jesus (see Luke 24:25-27; John 14:25-26; 16:12-15).

However, preaching at this level of the evangelists may also have its drawbacks. For, as some reaction-critics have demonstrated in their approach, it may slight the historical referents in the Gospels.[11] In other words, it may overlook the very reason for which the Gospels were written, namely to convey the meaning of the life, death, and resurrection of the historical Jesus.

A Combination of Horizons

A more thorough approach than any of the above would be to work with all three ancient horizons, especially those of Jesus and the evangelists. Since one learns about the historical Jesus only through the evangelist, one needs to begin at the level of the evangelist.

To understand a Gospel, one should have a good idea of the kind of church the evangelist addressed. What were its needs? Fred Craddock observes: "Since the Gospels were written not just 'to whom it may concern' but to particular Christian communities, then one would expect the needs of those communities to be addressed. The churches needed to be equipped for the usual task of evangelizing, teaching new converts, and worshiping."[12] In addition there might be special needs that had to be addressed—false teachings of Judaizers and of those who denied that Jesus was resurrected and that Jesus was the Messiah, the tendency to negate the present life because of the near expectation of the parousia, early Gnostic tendencies, threats of persecution, poverty, death, and others.

Having determined as closely as possible the needs of the church addressed, the next question is how the selected preaching-text seeks to respond to those needs. Here literary interpretation (see below) dovetails with historical interpretation. In general we can observe that the evangelists addressed those needs of the churches by relating the story of Jesus Christ. This state of affairs enables us to dig deeper in the Gospels and explore the horizon of the historical Jesus. What kind of people did Jesus address? What were their needs, their expectations, their attitudes, their life-styles? At this level, too, one can ask: How did Jesus meet those needs? How did He teach, reprove, correct, train in righteousness? One can probe for the point Jesus made as He taught His disciples or the crowds with sayings, parables, or miracles. Next one can investigate how Matthew in a later setting used that original message or even to bring the same or a revised message for a different time and place. Finally, one can reflect on the significance of this point for the church today.

Although in interpretation one necessarily starts with the horizon of the evangelist, in the sermon itself one can frequently start with the point made by Jesus in His setting, then explain how the evangelist applied this to the church in his day, and finally show the implications of this point for the church today.

For example, suppose one's text is Matthew 28:16-20. In the sermon, one can begin the exposition at the level of Jesus commissioning His eleven disciples "to make disciples of all nations" and promising them for this awesome task His abiding presence. Next one can show how Matthew in his later horizon introduced this mandate with a reference to "the mountain" (v. 16), thus reminding his Jewish readers one more time that Jesus is indeed the new Moses, the new Mediator between God and His people, the Lawgiver of the new covenant (compare Ex. 19:20; Matt. 5:1; 17:1). Matthew further noted that the disciples "worshiped Him" (v. 17) as Jews would worship only God. This sets the stage for Jesus' astounding statement: "All authority in heaven and on earth has been given to me" (v. 18). After this assurance, the King of kings commands His disciples to go and "make disciples of all nations" (v. 19). As Matthew projected this message to the early church, his hearers would identify with the disciples and know themselves to be mandated by the Lord Himself to "make disciples of all nations." Along with this mandate the early church also received Jesus' empowering promise: "I am with you always, to the close of the age (v. 20). Once the message has been understood in both of these horizons, its implications for the church today will be evident: The Lord of the church also commands and empowers His church today to make disciples of all nations because He is Lord of all.

Literary Interpretation

In literary interpretation one concentrates on analyzing words, grammar, syntax, figures of speech, rhetorical structures, and plot in order to determine the intended meaning of a passage. At this stage preachers are aided by concordances, dictionaries, grammars, rhetorical studies, and commentaries. In addition, since we have not one but four Gospels, we have frequent opportunity for comparing parallel passages in other Gospels. A synopsis like Aland's will prove helpful in locating the parallel passages and in discerning the differences between them.

The Unique Context of Each Gospel

Each preaching-text must be interpreted not as an isolated unit but as a unit in the context of a particular Gospel. By studying the composition of each Gospel and by comparing it with the other three Gospels, one becomes aware of the differences among the Gospels: they offer not four identical photographs of Jesus but four unique portraits. These distinct views of what Jesus did and taught are not a liability for contemporary preaching but an advantage. The unique portrait of Jesus each evangelist paints reveals the homiletical use to which he put the received traditions. Each distinctive slant may reveal the relevant point for a particular early Christian church.

Comparing Parallel Passages

The uniqueness of each preaching-text can be discerned even more exactly when, because of double or triple traditions, one has opportunity to compare parallel Gospel messages. Since preachers are interested not so much in who changed what as in discerning the specific emphases in each Gospel and in each passage, the most dependable method for preaching purposes is carefully to compare the preaching-text with parallel passages in other Gospels and to note the differences.[13] Such a comparison will reveal the kind of material each Gospel writer selected for transmission and how they rearranged and/or modified it. This information, in turn, will lead to understanding the homiletical interests and purposes of each writer and provide insight into the point of the preaching-text.[14]

For example, suppose one has selected as a preaching-text the pericope of Luke 18:15-17, the story of parents bringing their children to Jesus. One can compare Luke's version with that of Mark (10:13-16) and of Matthew (19:13-15) and thus get a sense of Luke's homiletical interests. First, in contrast to Mark and Matthew, Luke preceded this story with the parable of the Pharisee and the Tax Collector. Luke thus set the preaching-text in the context of the contrast between self-righteousness and humility. In fact, he ended that pericope with Jesus' words: "He who humbles himself will be exalted" (v. 14). That is a clue for understanding the preaching-text that follows immediately. Second, in contrast to Mark and Matthew, Luke changed the Greek word for children in verse 15 to a word denoting infants or babies. With this change Luke sharpened Jesus' point for his particular audience: "Whoever does not receive the kingdom of God like a child [the way a helpless baby receives its nourishment] shall not enter it" (v. 17). A sermon on Luke 18:15-17 would, therefore, seek to emphasize our utter inability to contribute anything towards receiving the kingdom of God and encourage us to place our complete trust in our heavenly Father who through Jesus freely provides this indispensable gift.

Formulating the Theme of the Text and of the Sermon

Having carefully studied the passage in its literary and historical contexts, one is ready to formulate the theme of the preaching-text.

The Theme of the Preaching-Text

The theme is a summary statement of the unifying thought of the preaching-text. It should be written out as a brief sentence (subject and predicate) which states succinctly what the text is saying.

Some homiletic textbooks suggest that for variety one can formulate the theme one time from the perspective of one character in the narrative and the next time from the perspective of another character. However, this procedure would bypass the evangelist who, as the author of the passage, ought to be allowed to determine its meaning for us. If one would be true to the Gospels, one has no choice but to formulate the theme from the perspective of the evangelist.

The Theme of a Narrative Text

Questions have been raised recently about the propriety of formulating a theme for a narrative text. For example, David Buttrick writes: "The preacher treats the passage as if it were a still-life picture in which some*thing* may be found, object-like, to preach on. What has been ignored? The composition of the 'picture,' the narrative structure, the movement of the story, the whole question of what in fact the *passage* may want to preach."[15]

Although Buttrick's warning against a rationalistic, scholastic approach is well taken, one must also maintain that every meaningful narrative has a theme. A narrative without a theme is like a ship without a rudder—it wanders around but goes nowhere in particular. Dan Via has helpfully compared plot and theme and calls them the "two sides of the same formal principle with plot being theme in movement and theme being plot at a standstill."[16] The theme of a narrative is its plot at a standstill. That description makes clear that the theme of a narrative is not the narrative itself but only an abstraction, a summary statement which the preacher requires temporarily to prepare a sermon in line with the text.

As an example, let us look again at Luke 18:15-17, the story of parents bringing their children to Jesus. As Luke related this story, it is obvious that he made his "point" in verse 17 with Jesus' words: "Truly I say to you, whoever does not receive the kingdom of God like a child shall not enter it." We have to look for the theme of this narrative, therefore, in this final verse. Formulating the theme positively, we could state it as follows: "Only those shall enter the kingdom of God who receive it like a child." Or in a more direct fashion: "We must receive the kingdom of God like a child." Mindful of Luke changing "children" to "babies" in verse 15, we should let this idea also echo in the theme: "We must receive the kingdom of God with the dependence and trust of a baby."

The Theme of the Sermon

Before formulating the theme of the sermon, one ought to compare the textual theme with other passages ("compare Scripture with Scripture") to see if any adjustments need to be made to the theme in the light of the whole Scripture. With Gospel texts the textual theme can usually function directly as the sermon theme. So Luke's message to the early church can be the heart of the message today: "We must receive the kingdom of God with the dependence and trust of a baby."

Formulating the sermon theme precisely is important for several reasons. First, it keeps the sermon true to the message intended by the evangelist. Carefully formulating the above theme rules out other possible themes such as: "Parents bring their children to Jesus," or, "Jesus loves little children," or, "The kingdom of God belongs to children." Although these may be worthy themes, they are not the point of this particular text. Second, the sermon theme keeps the sermon unified throughout if one follows its track from the beginning of the sermon to its conclusion. Preachers ought to be on guard especially against being side-tracked by the so-called practical remarks some commentaries offer with every verse. Typical remarks on our passage might be: verse 15a, as parents we are obliged to bring our children to Jesus; verse 15b, church elders and other adults ought not hinder parents from bringing children to Jesus; verse 16, Jesus invites our children to come to Him. These asides are beside the point made by Luke; moreover, they destroy the unity and punch of the sermon.[17]

Formulating the Goal of the Evangelist and of the Preacher

If the theme of the sermon is like the ship's rudder, the goal is the sermon's objective, the ship's destination.

The Goal of the Evangelist

The goal of the evangelist ties in with the "why" question of historical interpretation. Why did the evangelist transmit this passage in this form to this particular church? The answer to that question is his goal, or objective. The goal of Luke in the foregoing example is clearly to teach the church that salvation is not by our works but by God's grace alone—hardly a surprising teaching for a companion of Paul. In connection with that goal, Luke may also be trying to correct people who thought that they could at least contribute something towards gaining the kingdom of God. "Babies," Luke emphasized, are totally helpless, totally dependent, wholly trusting—that is how we receive the kingdom of God. By formulating the goal of the evangelist we give expression to the relevance of this passage for the early church. Past relevance is the only solid bridge to present relevance.

The Goal of the Preacher

The preacher's goal with the sermon cannot always be exactly the same as that of the evangelist, but it ought to be at least in *harmony* with it. For example, the preacher's goal with a sermon on Luke 18:15-17 can be similar to the goal of Luke for the early church. Depending on the local church, the goal could be to teach that salvation is by grace alone, or it could be to correct people who think they themselves can earn at least part of their salvation, or it could be to encourage people to enjoy the peace of a baby by wholly entrusting themselves to God's grace for their salvation. All these goals are appropriate because they are in harmony with Luke's goal. Inappropriate goals for a sermon on this passage would be to persuade parents to bring their children to Jesus, or to encourage the adults in the congregation to be kind to children, or to teach children that Jesus loves them. Although these are worthwhile goals in themselves, they are inappropriate for this text because they are not in line with Luke's goal.

Formulating one's goal for a sermon is important not only because it reveals whether or not one is making proper use of a passage but also because it expresses the relevance of the sermon. The goal articulates what one seeks to accomplish with the sermon: to teach, to encourage, to comfort, to warn, to correct. Moreover, the goal functions as a compass, setting the direction of the sermon and focusing it for the desired congregational response. The sermon goal will influence the form one selects for the sermon, its structure, and how one writes the sermon, especially its conclusion.

Selecting the Sermon Form and Structure

The Form of the Sermon

Since Gospel texts come in many different forms—from sayings to narratives and from prayers to hymns—one must pay careful attention to the form of the text not only in interpretation but also in selecting a sermon form. The sermon form need not necessarily be the same as the form of the text but should at least respect its characteristics. While didactic texts from sayings are usually best served by the logical, didactic form, narrative texts are usually best served by a narrative form. The development of each form can be either deductive or inductive or a combination of both.

The Structure of the Sermon

Every sermon requires a sermon structure—a frame or outline which supports it and provides it with coherence, movement, and clarity. A text from Jesus' sayings which is developed in a didactic form should normally have a logical outline with points and subpoints supporting the theme. By contrast, a narrative text which is developed in a narrative form should normally have a structure that follows the "moves" of the story line or plot. In either case, it is advantageous to follow the text step by step, wherever feasible, since this procedure enables the hearers to trace in their Bibles the development of the sermon, to test the sermon for biblical validity (compare 1 Thess. 5:20-21), and to recall it later.

The Context of the Gospels

As indicated above, the relevance of preaching the Gospels is not to be sought in moral examples but in the story of Jesus Christ. Jesus is the reason why the evangelists wrote their Gospels. Yet, as we also noted, in the Gospels the story of Jesus is part of a larger story: the story of the coming kingdom of God. This larger story is seen most clearly when we view the Gospels in their biblical context.

John, for one, pointed out that not even the story of Jesus is an isolated incident but part of a larger whole. He began his Gospel: "In the beginning was the Word . . . and the Word was God. . . . All things were made through him. . . . In him was life, and the life was the light of men" (John 1:1-4). John, like the other evangelists, saw the story of Jesus in a much broader context than just Jesus' own historical horizon. The story of Jesus ties right in with the history the Bible relates from the beginning of Genesis, the history of God's coming kingdom. This history began with God's good creation (Gen. 1), continued its up and down course despite the fall into sin (Gen. 3:1-7), and will come to completion with the new creation (Rev. 21—22). The Gospels proclaim that the coming of Jesus is God's mightiest act in this history of God's coming kingdom. The Word that was with God in the beginning "became flesh and dwelt among us" (John 1:14).

Jesus Himself preached "the gospel of the kingdom" (Matt. 4:23), defeated Satan (the pretender to the throne), and established a major beachhead for God's kingdom on earth (Matt. 12:28). Jesus, in turn, commanded His disciples and church to spread the gospel of the kingdom and "make disciples of all nations" (Matt. 28:19; see 10:7). The evangelists responded to this mandate by writing their Gospels of King Jesus and the kingdom of God.

Today preachers may respond to Jesus' mandate by using these Gospels to pass on the good news of Jesus Christ, to challenge and comfort their hearers with the marvelous vision of the kingdom of God which Jesus re-established on earth, and to give them hope as they discern the presence of that kingdom today and eagerly anticipate its perfect establishment when Jesus comes again.

Notes

1. Unless noted otherwise, all biblical quotations are from the RSV.
2. John R. W. Stott, *Between Two Worlds: The Art of Preaching in the Twentieth Century* (Grand Rapids: Eerdmans, 1982), 131.
3. See John W. Welch, *Chiasmus in Antiquity* (Hildesheim: Gerstenberg, 1981), 235-236.
4. Dwight Moody Smith, *Interpreting the Gospels for Preaching* (Philadelphia: Fortress Press, 1979), 20.
5. Paul J. Achtemeier, *Mark* (Philadelphia: Fortress Press, 1986), 53.
6. Jack Dean Kingsbury, *Matthew as Story* (Philadelphia: Fortress Press, 1986), 10-13, 36.
7. See further Sidney Greidanus, *Sola Scriptura: Problems and Principles in Preaching Historical Texts* (Toronto: Wedge, 1970), 56-120; and Greidanus, *The Modern Preacher and the Ancient Text: Interpreting and Preaching Biblical Literature* (Grand Rapids: Eerdmans, 1988), 161-166.
8. These examples are found in Kingsbury, *Matthew as Story*, 25-27.
9. For arguments for the historical reliability of the Gospels, see Greidanus, *The Modern Preacher*, 24-47, 80-101, and 269-277.
10. William E. Hull, "Preaching on the Synoptic Gospels," *Biblical Preaching: An Expositor's Treasury*, ed. James W. Cox (Philadelphia: Westminster, 1983), 174. Compare Smith, *Interpreting the Gospels for Preaching*, 21: "One may in preaching decide to work with the form and meaning of a pericope in the pre-Gospel tradition, that is, at the form-critical level. That would be a legitimate procedure. More often than not, however, the preacher will and should inquire into the meaning of a story or saying in the Gospel of which it is a part."
11. Greidanus, *The Modern Preacher*, 56-57.
12. Fred B. Craddock, *The Gospels* (Nashville: Abingdon, 1981), 26.
13. Gorden D. Fee walks students through a synopsis in his *New Testament Exegesis: A Handbook for Students and Pastors* (Philadelphia: Westminster, 1983), 103-116.
14. See further Greidanus, *The Modern Preacher*, 271-273.
15. David G. Buttrick, "Interpretation and Preaching," *Interpretation*, 35/1 (1981): 47.
16. Dan Via, *The Parables: Their Literary and Existential Dimension* (Philadelphia: Fortress Press, 1967), 96-97.
17. See further, Greidanus, *The Modern Preacher*, 163-167.

Frederick W. Robertson (1816-1853)

"Faithful in the Face of Opposition"

F.W. Robertson is widely considered one of the greatest English preachers of his century—yet he was virtually unknown until after his death.

A gifted scholar and committed student of the Bible, he entered the Anglican ministry after graduation from Oxford. He worked long days, determined to maintain his hours of biblical study while also throwing himself into ministry among the poverty–stricken people of his parish. This schedule contributed to the breakdown of his health that would end his life at the age of 37.

As rector of Brighton's Trinity Chapel, Robertson attracted large crowds from among the working class, but his preaching drew hostility and opposition from the aristocrats who visited or retired in the seaside resort. Continuing criticism and poor health prompted a severe and growing depression which plagued Robertson's final days.

Only one of Robertson's sermons was published during his lifetime, but with the posthumous publication of other sermons he became an important influence in the lives of preachers throughout Britain and America. His sermons are carefully crafted and organized; they demonstrate the power of Robertson's remarkable mind and the many hours of study given to each sermon. Though thoroughly prepared, Robertson carried only brief notes into the pulpit; he wrote out his manuscripts only after the sermons had been preached.

As one who considered his own life a failure, F.W. Robertson can provide encouragement to those who sometimes wonder if their service will ultimately count for the work of God's Kingdom.

29

Peter Rhea Jones, Pastor
First Baptist Church
Decatur, Georgia

Preaching in the Parables

You will be glad if you "preach in the parables" and so will your congregation. They know and love the stories already and have accorded them a place. You can strum the chords of the familiar powerfully yet bring a fresh and lively word from beyond. Fred Craddock among others has reminded us of the power of the familiar. These familiar parables were originally crafted as vehicles of communication designed by that oral Poet from Galilee.

Though numerous daunting critical theories gather around the celebrated corpus of stories and popular misconceptions still cling to them, the parables themselves beckon to both preacher and listener alike. While definite directions are advocated here unapologetically, preaching on the parables by their particular nature encourages individuality, flexibility, and creativity. There is no need to be uptight because there is not one correct and acceptable means of preaching the parables. Rather allow these guides to empower and equip and inspire. In that spirit start with the stories themselves.

Scanning the Stories First on Your Own

How do you preach on the parables? Not rigidly from one construct or model, and not slavishly following "critical orthodoxy." Variety exists among the parables themselves, making rigorously following a single methodology indefensible. Rather, begin with one book open, focus fiercely on the text, trust yourself, and interact with a firestorm of associative responses. Polyvalence or multiple layers of meanings do exist within the texture of the text, though idiosyncratic exegesis based upon personal whims can lead to erratic outcomes. Subordinated allegorical dimensions are sometimes present, especially as relates to the ministry of Jesus, but the reader does well to seek the center as well as the periphery. Let us recall some of the leading characteristics of parables in order to be able to perform direct exegesis personally.

With one book open pore over the text intently, letting it engage your mind and imagination. This first encounter benefits intangibly and immensely, subjectively as well as objectively, metaphorically as well as abstractly, intuitively as well as rationally, hermeneutically and homiletically as well as exegetically. Look at the parable holistically. Is it general situation (like the parable of the mustard seed), or specific situation (like the compassionate Samaritan)? Can you find the internal juxtaposition, the comparison or contrast within the parable (such as the compassionate father [Luke 15:20] and the angry brother [15:28])?

Underline all the direct discourse. Notice how the speeches function within the narrative as a whole. What do they achieve? Imagine how each came across when Jesus animatedly presented the original. Pay particular attention to final speeches (Luke 15:22-24 and 15:31-32) since meaning often lurks within.

Is the text an awakening parable? Does it disturbingly challenge things as they are? After all, the parable of the rich fool alarms and can awaken. The account of the prodigal son preached in contemporary fashion can assist nothing less than a coming to oneself. In cultural context, what "paradigm shift" does the parable precipitate? That is, how does it challenge things as they seem in the eschatological light of the will of God? David Granskou points out that Jesus did not directly answer the original question about the identity of neighbor (Luke 10:29). Rather, "the method of the parable is to restate questions, so that new perspectives for life appear."[1] What element of surprise do you detect?

How does the parable correlate with the central thesis of Jesus, the kingdom of God? Sometimes parabolic introductions address the topic explicitly, but often deeper insight uncovers revelations about the will of God inherent in the story or context. For example, the parable of the compassionate Samaritan does not include specific reference to the kingdom at all and neither does the parable of the rich man and Lazarus, yet the former amounts to a midrash on the love command and the latter dramatizes the judgment of God upon those who ignore the responsibility to love neighbor as self.[2] The will of God is centrally expressed in the love command.

Is there any genuine "Christological penetration" within the particular parable? For example, consider the celebrated instance in the parable of the strong man bound (Mark 3:23-27). In context the exorcism of demons becomes an opportunity for opponents to link Jesus with evil. The counter claim is remarkable. Jesus asserted that the stronger one had bound the strong one in a ministry of liberation. This kind of discovery, where applicable, can keep the sermon theological.

What function did your particular parable play in the historical ministry of Jesus? Was it a polemical weapon in controversy with critics exposing hostile positions and extolling the kingdom or explaining the ministry? Is the parable actually a theodicy suggesting a possible contemporary use? Do you note any bona fide allegorical aspects inherent in the original story interpreting the messianic ministry of Jesus? Examples such as the parable of the sower and the parable of the wicked husbandmen are two prime possibilities. Do you observe any special emphases of the evangelist that spark exegetical and hermeneutical implications (Luke 18:1)?

Take a moment to characterize the parable as a saying, parable proper, or narrative. If a narrative, divide it into unfolding scenes. Even in a brief parable like the lost sheep (Luke 15), picture in your imagination the first scene set in the wilderness and the second at home in the village. Like John Donohue, be sensitive to meaning, plot, characters, and point of view.[3]

Metaphorically speaking, does the particular parable belong to a larger complex united by a common metaphor (like seed or servant)? John Crossan, through his early book, heightened awareness to the prominent metaphors used repeatedly by Jesus.[4] In my studies I came across the householder metaphor favored by Jesus. In these parables the householder is also called *lord*, one who has the power to give the word. In each of these particular parables, the will of the master is challenged. This set of stories works well as a grouping related to the will of God.[5] Also look within a single parable for a recurring metaphor (as in the parable of the persistent widow in Luke 18).

One other major aspect of scanning is to pay attention to audience, a critical consideration that may very well influence your ultimate sermon. Parables themselves are explicitly addressed to disciples, crowds, and critics, but note the subtle presence of audience *within* some of the stories. Obviously the elder brother (Luke 15:25-32) points toward those who castigate Jesus for offering table fellowship to sinners (15:2), but they are addressed while their guard is down and while they are permitted to see the dinners with sinners in a new light, see sinners as individuals, see their own attitudes exposed, and experience the parable as unfinished and their personal freedom to change as available. Likewise the sinners would see themselves and God in the segment about the prodigal son.

Consider other audiences within. In the parable of the six brothers (Luke 16:19-31), the five living brothers suddenly realize they are addressed in the hope that they will be jarred awake, see their brother and his life-style in a new light, see hungry and sick people compassionately, and repent. Seeing their lives in juxtaposition to the hungry at the gate is a powerful angle of vision or re-vision. Life is not merely a matter of individual existence or even human development but of interrelatedness. The audience, then and now, can see the outcome of their current trajectory. They are permitted to see the presumptions upon which their lives are predicated and the illusions they hold regarding money.

In the parable of the sower an eager crowd motivated by dramatic healings listened breathlessly on the shore of the lake. As they heard the type of communication utilized deftly by Jesus they probably recognized it as a Palestinian parable. Ostensibly they would wonder and reflect and shuffle away puzzled and perplexed. Perhaps an alert auditor on the spot began to have her eyes opened, or later in the day "the penny dropped" and a disclosure developed. Whenever hearers start to see themselves in the story told, they are startled. Such questions may surface: Am I like a thirty-day wanderer or a convert on the first ballot? Am I a pawn of Satan? Is my commitment shallow or non-existent? Am I more interested in the world than in the Galilean?

In the parable of the wicked husbandmen, a current storm center for scholars, surely the wicked workers are "the chief priests, the scribes, and the elders" of Mark 12:12. The Sanhedrin itself stood exposed in its murderous intent, and the audience even then could reconsider, receive rather than reject. Aaron Milavec is certainly on target when he observes the impact of "unsettling the onlooker by tearing away those religious assurances which shield one from the terrible judgment of the living God."[6]

As you consider the audience for preaching you may well ask, like the lost boy in Peter Pan: "Am I in this story?"

After scanning the text on your own, write down your personal interpretation of the original historical meaning and your first impression of the contemporary meaning. Only now are you ready to turn to the rich resources that can steal your creativity if consulted too soon.

Consulting Exceptional Bibliographical Resources

Great anthologies of sermons on parables, expositions that make you want to preach, substantial exegetical resources, and actual guides on how to preach on the parables abound. There is no shortage of vital books and articles.

Consider first whole books of sermons selected only from parables. You are in for a treat when you read Leslie Weatherhead's book *In Quest of a Kingdom*, which contains remarkable illustrations and applications, though the exegesis is underwhelming. Helmut Thielicke's *The Waiting Father* is a virtual classic, retelling the narratives in contemporary, powerfully existential style, containing quotable remarks and sensitive insights. "The Word of God," says Thielicke, "is not a feast for the ears but a hammer. A man who comes from it unbruised need not think it has taken root in him."[7] Lloyd Ogilvie offers good, evangelical exposition as well as attractive sermon development in *The Autobiography of God,* which includes strong life changing stories out of his ministry rather than canned illustrations.

Robert Capon, currently quite the rage, brings his Greek expertise and theological interest to bear in his trilogy, *The Parables of Grace, The Parables of the Kingdom,* and *The Parables of Judgment.* These creative and highly stimulating sermons are conversational, informal, and communicative. The series amounts to a tour de force concerning the triumph of grace. Be aware he is given to overstatement and has a penchant for pushing universalism even in the most unlikely places.

Charles H. Spurgeon's sermons on the parables are available in *The Parables of our Lord* in *Miracles and Parables of our Lord,* volume three. Gerald Kennedy offers lively sermons with a decidedly contemporary touch and with winsome stories in *The Parables.* Charles Allen tells his inimitable stories in *When the Heart is Hungry.* A. M. Hunter in *The Parables for Today* not only provides expected exegetical insight but stories and quotable observations. It only suffers from brevity.

David Redding in *The Parables He Told* presents his messages with electrifying English that will make an audience sit up and take notice and will inspire the preacher. Convinced that prayer is not any good unless it is persistent, Redding maintains that "God won't read the third class mail." And: "God is sales resistant to the random request." And: "Those who take prayer so lightly they can't remember what it was they meant to pray for and never pray for the same things two weeks in a row, who assume one mention is enough, at least to be mad about it if He doesn't answer within the hour, make prayer a pity."[8]

Expository studies are equally abundant and excellent, the sort that will compel you into the pulpit. One of the finest is the classic by George Buttrick entitled *The Parables of Jesus.* Buttrick is hauntingly poetic as he reflects on the infinite power of the little, or as he subjectively selects three key words out of the parable of the lost sheep ("lost," "seeking," and "until") to unloose the parable. It will preach. William Barclay is sometimes marvelous with his background insight and his illustrations in *And Jesus Said.* It includes exquisite stories and quotes. The rich fool, allows Barclay, remembered the wrong things, himself and the world; and he forgot the essential things, such as his neighbors, time, God, and the fact that people are what they are and not what they have.[9] This is a traditional outline of great power.

Hugh Martin's book, *The Parables of the Gospel,* is a sleeper repaying reading, and A. M. Hunter's *The Parables Then and Now* is high quality exposition. Halford Luccock brought numerous individual insights and gave excellent illustrations and applications in *Studies in the Parables of*

Jesus. J. S. Glen, *The Parables of Conflict in Luke,* writes from the standpoint of a well informed New Testament professor with a good touch for application. The book could become the launching pad for a sermon series.

In addition to appealing expositional studies, serious exegetical explorations are available in large supply. R. H. Stein in *An Introduction to the Parables of Jesus* offers a good starting place. C. H. Dodd's *The Parables of the Kingdom* is a classic earlier study of major influence containing significant insight, frequently offering a single sentence that captures essence (although his emphasis on realized eschatology is overdrawn). C. W. F. Smith, *The Jesus of the Parables,* is underrated and overlooked, comprehensive and incisive. David Wenham's recent book, *The Parables of Jesus,* is attractive to conservative evangelicals, is non-technical but practical, is based upon good scholarship, and is readable. Simon Kistemaker is a conservative and highly informed scholar who has produced a valuable study, *The Parables of Jesus,* though it is not as thorough as his in-depth work on Hebrews. Eta Linnemann, *Jesus of the Parables,* teaches that one should look for the "interlocking" as a means of noting the concessions to common experience.

Joachim Jeremias gave much of his life to an incredible understanding of the message of Jesus through the parables. This great academic achievement is expressed primarily in *The Parables of Jesus.* Jeremias was obsessed with a desire to know the original meaning in the day of Jesus. His work deserves consultation on every parable. Jeremias insisted on the polemical nature of most parables, required the interpreter to take seriously the Teller, and saw clearly the crisis nature of many parables and the implicit call to decision. In his own way Kenneth Bailey, a veteran missionary to the Mideast, has advanced upon Jeremias and brought new insights from early Arabic commentaries and the culture he knows so well. He has written *Poet & Peasant* and *Through Peasant Eyes.*

Dan Via published one of the first major literary studies, entitled *In Parables,* which is quite creative with its novel use of the dramatic categories, both comic and tragic. His book could start the preacher on a sermon series, especially in a college church. J. D. Crossan, who has published profusely on parables, taught us to be far more sensitive to the master metaphors (seed, servant) appearing in numerous parables. The alert preacher could develop a different kind of Advent series based upon Crossan's advent of the Kingdom section. Bernard Scott has weighed in with two major studies, *Jesus, Symbol-Maker for the Kingdom,* and *Hear Then the Parable.* He emphasizes oral performance, has turned over every rock, and stands in the current literary approach. His bottom line interpretations are unusual and debatable.

A. M. Hunter brings the insights of the best of scholarship in an easily accessible form in his book *Interpreting the Parables*. John Donohue, in *The Gospel in Parable*, is on the cutting edge and is deceptively creative. In my own study, *The Teaching of the Parables*, an effort is made to be hermeneutical in application as well as substantive in exegesis. Direct discourse is emphasized along with other literary considerations.

Books and articles exist which address directly the topic of preaching on the parables. Martin Scharlemann published a good model with his *Proclaiming the Parables*, though it is limited to a small number of parables. It contains traditional outlines and even better exegetical insight. David Granskou, *Preaching on the Parables*, has an excellent manual with a consistent methodology, comprehensive coverage of many parables, and terse applications. Dwight Stevenson, veteran professor of preaching, offers a seasoned outlook in the relevant chapter of *In the Biblical Preacher's Workshop* that leaves the preacher with a variety of options for preaching strategy rather than a single approach. Thomas Long, rising star in homiletics, warns that while the parables look "preacher friendly" on the surface they are like a field with hidden treasure. He is quite willing to read the parable from the "intuitive chair" (as Craddock would say) and in their canonical form. Recognizing differences among parables, he speaks of code, vessel, and object of art.

David Buttrick, in a major and controversial volume on preaching, *Homiletic*, sees parables as having "stock plots into which surreal detail is inserted to disrupt our conventional world."[10] Very much opposed to the reduction of a parable to a main point, he points out the traveling action of the plot in the consciousness. Rather than analyze a parable at a distance, he believes we should preach it in the mode of immediacy. Rather than teaching the congregation through the parable, walk with the congregation to a discovery of the rule of God. Parables have lean plots and each must be experienced. Leave out extensive reports of first-century customs, design the sermon episodically in a contemporary manner, and let each move imitate our conscious hearing of the story. Here is a definite program that will engage some creative preachers.

Were your budget to limit you to a handful of books, consider all three volumes by Hunter, the one by Barclay, and the major work by Jeremias and Buttrick or Redding.

Shaping the Strategy for Presentation

The next step calls upon the preacher to move from analysis to creative design for the purpose of communication, an exciting and intimidating phase exceedingly open to individual touch more than rigid rules. You may identify creatively with a character and a point of view, or paraphrase the parable in provocatively contemporary language. You can devise a traditional but attractive expository outline. Since a parable usually conveys a primary point, you can single out the basic disclosure the parable intends and devise a design. Taking Luke 12:20 as his text, Martin Luther King, Jr. preached on "The Man Who Was a Fool." He asserted that the man was a fool: 1) because he permitted the ends for which he lived to become confused with the means by which he lived, 2) because he failed to realize his dependence on others, and 3) because he failed to realize his dependence on God.[11]

However, consider designing sermons in accord with the different kinds of parables and even in response to the distinctiveness of an individual parable. For example, scholars recognize numerous parabolic sayings in the Synoptic Gospels, a grouping that would benefit from more academic research. Many of these sayings appear in Matthew and particularly in the Sermon on the Mount. Examples include the blind leading the blind (Luke 6:39), the mote and beam (Matt. 7:3-5), and the tree and the fruit (Matt. 7:16-29). Treat the selected saying as a choric device and reiterate it throughout the sermon, adding a further touch of interpretation each time. Insert an appealing story, enhancing the saying each time, and make a terse but striking application. Such a presentation may give another look to your preaching and gain a wider hearing. The figurative saying itself may well stick in the minds of the hearers. And after all, true biblical preaching lets the text happen again.

The medium sized parable—generally called a parable proper or similitude or simple parable—is more than a picture. It is a picture expanded into a story. The paired parables of the lost sheep and the lost coin (Luke 15:3-10) are two among many. One strategy to consider is to move from the universal truth (accentuated by Juelicher) to the historical meaning during the ministry of Jesus (as emphasized by Jeremias) to an existential application (as stressed by Geraint Jones and Dan Via). This particular approach allows the preacher to begin where the people are, establish a natural "point of contact," move then to the specific meaning as intended by Jesus, and to close personally, including both how the text has healed and awakened the preacher and how it touches the water table of our common existence. The parable of the mustard seed, with its serene sensitivity to the infinitude of the little, offers a natural possibility for this model since it obviously has a universal meaning, yet Jesus intended something further. Indeed, before you are finished you may commend Christianity and infect someone with hope as does *The Grand Canyon Suite* when it signals with distant drops of rain the coming cloudburst.

The parable of the lost sheep (Luke 15) fairly invites proclamation about recovering the lost. Those who accept the concern of the shepherd personally, leave the ninety-nine and go out looking for the lost *until* they are found, and those who discover the extraordinary satisfaction in finding the lost are the best interpreters of this familiar similitude.

Those who emulate the action of Jesus, who follow the instruction of the parable, and who resonate with the attitude of God toward the lost are those who genuinely understand. Pastoral and evangelistic experience, the "pastor's heart," lend much empathic comprehension that can be conveyed in the act of preaching far beyond any subtle academic technique.

The historical cause of this remarkable gush of parabolic creativity derived from cutting criticism of the company Jesus kept (Luke 15:2). Jesus responded, not with blind anger but with a paradigm shift. His critics looked traditionally and conventionally at reinterpretation of what they had already seen with their own eyes. Jesus presented a glimpse of God without the frowning Puritan face, a picture of God in heaven who "knows just when to fling his crown for joy, how to make the angels laugh." (Redding). The sermon shape could grow out of the experience in the wilderness and the celebration at the shepherd's house.

A sermon on this parable might be entitled "The Catcher in the Rye," recalling the book by that title and the experience of the teenager Holden Caulfield desperately trying to find himself. In conversation with his sister Phoebe, he began to have a more focused if idealized idea of what he wanted to do with his life. He pictured little kids playing in a big field of rye with no one around to look after them. If one started to go over the cliff he would come out from somewhere and catch them. It was the only thing he would really like to be.

A more traditional expository sermon can be preached on Luke 13:1-9 as "The Parable of the Second Chance." You can move from (1) The Question of Sin and Suffering (vv. 1-5), to (2) The Law of Usefulness (vv. 6-8), to (3) The Grace of Another Chance (v. 9). Thus the first movement can be sensitively pastoral, the second portion prophetic, and the third evangelistic.[12]

Perhaps the greatest current interest in this era of narrative preaching lies with the longer stories. It is surely preferable not to look upon the art form of parable as merely a disposable envelope of little use once the main point is determined. We have begun to re-learn "the primacy of story and parable, as expressing truths that cannot be expressed in any other way."[13] The so-called narrative parables are enticing as opportunities to preach in a manner that may delay the truth rather than divide the truth into abstractions. So preach the parables in order that the primacy of the story may be kept rather than commit the "intentional fallacy" that imagines you can restate the meaning of a literary piece in analytical language and then disregard the form.

Separating the narrative parables into scenes provides a basis for dramatic development and allows the story to stay. In an exceptionally creative turn, Wade P. Huie addressed the parable of the rich man and

Lazarus. He recommended that his readers imagine a first act entitled, "The Rich Man seemed to be rich, and the Poor Man seemed to be poor." The second act contains the reversal in its caption, "The Rich Man became poor, and the Poor Man became rich." Then with some poetic license he contributed a third scene he called, "The Rich Man needed the Poor Man, and the Poor Man needed the Rich Man."[14] The parable conveys a strong missionary implication inasmuch as Albert Schweitzer felt called to foreign missions under the influence of this text, and with Huie recognize the social application, similar to the parable of the six brothers inviting the living to awaken, repent, and make a decision about the Teller.

The parable breaks naturally into two begging scenes, one earthly and the other otherworldly. In the first, Lazarus was begging and the rich man feasting while in the second the rich man begged Abraham and the poor man feasted at the heavenly banquet. A warning sermon might even end on a negative note, (heresy!) since it is downright unlikely the five brothers or sisters were going to let go of their aggressive greed or do anything about their eternal destiny. They may have put their lives on cruise control. They were going to keep on doing what they had been doing. They were not going to church where they could be exposed to the rules of reality. They did not read their Bible anymore, though they did peruse *Self* and *New Woman* and scoop up *GQ* to be cool. She dated a guy who did not give a flip about anything lasting. He was not even in the market for salvation but was sold on success. The poor never eat at fern bars. These affluent brothers and sisters were choosing brunch instead of the Bible on Sunday, sleeping in rather than sitting in the sanctuary, emphasizing Saturday night rather than Sunday morning. They did not acknowledge the claim of God in their lives. They may very well wind up keeping company with their brother unless . . . they repent!

Turn attention now to the most famous of all the narratives, Luke 15:11-32, knowing full well that new insights and fresh sermonic approaches are all too rare. The famous outline about the prodigal son—which takes the hearer from his badness to his sadness to his gladness—will preach, but it has grown hackneyed. While on a mission visit in Kenya a missionary shared a memorable approach unfamiliar to me. First, the prodigal saw something that is hard to see: he saw himself. Second, the prodigal said something that is hard to say: I have sinned. Third, he did something that is hard to do: he went home. One can also follow the narrative under the theme of a portrait of authentic repentance as follows: a great awakening (v. 17), a returning to the father (v. 18), a confessing of sin (vv. 18-19, 21), and an entering into the joy of the kingdom (vv. 22-24). A more narrative development of the "Story of the Second Son" pictures him leaving home (vv. 12-13a), living in the far country (v. 13b), surviving in a famine (vv. 14-16), coming to himself (vv. 17-19), returning to the father's house (v. 20a), and being received and accepted (vv. 20b-25). During a minister's conference when we shared program responsibilities, Robert Dale divulged a student sermon he prepared while a seminary student and called "The Even Whens of God." God loves us even when we rebel against Him, even when we use God as a last resort, and even when we bring a wasted life.

Looking at the parable as a whole, you can detect a dramatic contrast between the compassionate father (v. 20) and the angry brother (v. 28). These are contrasting ways of receiving sinners, a strong starting point for a sermon. The elder brother episode invites focus on the "Sins of the Spirit," such as envy and jealousy, lovelessness, contempt for others, and self congratulation. Yet another angle of vision yields two pictures of God, a God with extravagant love for the lost and a God who allows a frightening freedom of choice. What kind of community arises in response to such extravagant love? A community that knows how to celebrate, a community of restored self esteem, and a community that accepts. Leonard Markham, while a student, was privileged to sit before the fire at the home of his homiletics professor and discuss preaching on this parable; George Buttrick diffidently suggested a simple development:

Part One: the younger son
Part Two: the older son
Part Three: the Son who came to save them both

The second most famous parable, that of the compassionate Samaritan, can be preached quite naturally as a narrative. Long before Charles Rice became a published scholar on narrative preaching, he shared his own student sermon on the Samaritan. He began with those who hurt, moved to those who are hurt, and climaxed with those who heal the hurts of others. Such poetic sensitivity brings new life to the grand old story and reminds us to care about the victims of crime. This slender story, amounting to a handful of lines, has left behind it a path of power and promises to inspire and energize kindness to an amazing degree in the future. How can you participate in this "path of power"? You can identify with those who hurt because you are hurting yourself. You can reject hurting. You can distance yourself from self-centered religion. (The robbers were not the only ones to leave the scene of the crime.) You can participate in the path of power by developing a compassionate spirit, as you hear the cry, bring the hurt into your own heart, and take action.

Eugene Lowry, in his book *How to Preach a Parable,* introduces some subtle and varied strategies for preaching the biblical narrative. The book title is a bit of a misnomer—in that three of his four sermonic examples are not sermons on parables—but all four of the techniques exemplified are portable. Strongly affirming the narrative sermon, Lowry sees the sermon as an event in time that moves from opening disequilibrium, through escalation of conflict, to surprising reversal, on to closing denouément. His first option, running the story, consists of following the biblical story. He also commends the strategy of delaying the story for pastoral reasons or because the story is so very familiar. Suspending the story involves beginning with the biblical narrative until it runs into trouble, after which flashbacks or flashforwards come into play. In alternating the story, the biblical narrative is divided into vignettes with other kinds of material interspersed.[15] Here are some new forms to lead others through the drama of the parable. Surely Donohue has it right as he maintains: "The story must be re-presented before it can be truly present."[16]

Leaving individual parables, it still remains to envision the possibility of sermon series.

Projecting Sermon Series

A plethora of possibilities suggest themselves for sermon series, even the parables of the Old Testament, the parables of the Fourth Gospel,[17] and the enacted parables of Jesus. The parables of Matthew 13 make a suitable collection, as do the "refusal parables."[18] Theologically oriented preachers could prepare a series on Jesus as a parable of God. On the theology of hope, sermons could be planned on the parable of the sower, the mustard seed, the seed growing on its own, and the leaven.

One pastorally attractive option, mentioned above, is the corpus of stories utilizing the master metaphor of the householder. I stumbled upon them while reading the parables in Greek and observing the prominence of *oikodespotē* and *kurios* in the same narrative. If you look at this quartet of parables simultaneously, you will discover kingdom of God concerns but all dealing with the will of God. In every case the authority of the householder is challenged. There is sabotage, criticism, seizure, murder, resistance, and rejecand strained against his reins. Berry consoled the bad-tempered animal, managing to calm him somewhat by the time she anarticular parables are theodicies—answers to genuine questions about how God relates to the world. In each of these parables freedom is allowed for resisters, but inevitably the will of the householder goes forward. So we see wisdom in the parable of the tares, creative aggressiveness in championing grace despite criticism within the parable of the laborers in the vineyard, courage in the wicked tenants, and determination in the parable of the great banquet. Church members and ministers facing opposition to their ministry wonder about the apparent eclipse of God's will in the world and even wonder if they are on the winning side. Four sermons could emerge of a creative and pastoral sort on "The Will of God."

A prophetic series could be projected with the following as sources:

1. Call to National Repentance (Luke 13:1-9)
2. Call to Caring (Matt. 25:31-46)
3. Challenge to Religious Leadership (Mark 12:1-12)
4. Exposure of Inauthentic Living (Luke 12:13-21)

Such texts feature the demand side of faith.

And an evangelistic series or revival sermons are easily developed, with the following among the choices:

1. Recovering the Lost (Luke 15:1-10)
2. Receiving the Lost (Luke 15:11-32)
3. Turning Your Life Around (Luke 15:11-24)
4. Call to Decision (Luke 16:1-8)
5. Crisis of Choice (Luke 16:19-31)

All these passages are Lukan, the Gospel that reports Jesus' intention to seek and save the lost (19:10). Luke 16:1-8, perhaps the most difficult of the texts, reflects the desperate plight of the dishonest manager who received an inescapable summons from his master. Like him, today's hearers will be challenged by the unavoidable "either/or" summons of the Lord, the dangerous opportunity of both warning and promise in His gospel.

Situational or existential messages can be creatively designed and related to life from the perspective of different parables. As a provocative beginning try the following:

1. Life in the Light of Grace (as parable of Pharisee and publican)
2. Life in the Light of Nature (as parable of mustard seed and sower)
3. Life in the Light of a Moment of Truth (as parable of the compassionate Samaritan)
4. Life in the Light of National Crisis (as parable of barren fig tree)
5. Life in the Light of Death (as parable of rich fool, rich man and Lazarus)
6. Life in the Light of the Final Judgment (as parable of sheep and goats)

Authentic illumination can ensue.[19]

A brief series of three could be fashioned on the vital theme of discipleship with the following as a beginning:

1. The Imperative of Forgiveness (Matt. 18:21-35)
2. The Imperative of Love (Luke 10:25-37)
3. The Imperative of Perseverance (Luke 18:1-8)

Other sermons edifying believers could include the thoughtful commitment implicit in the parable of the tower builder (Luke 14:28-30), joy in hidden treasure (Matt 13:44), boldness in the unjust steward (Luke 16:1-13), and responsive hearing in the two houses (Matt. 7:24-27).

Re-experiencing the Parable during the Sermon Delivery

The questions included in some of the introductory formula for the parables, the questions left open at the end, elements of surprise and alarming awakening, beginnings based upon common consent—all these aspects point to interaction on the part of the original audience. The parable by its nature is not monologic but dialogic. The preacher leads into an oral event, even reading the response of the audience along the way. When it is appropriate, the preacher seeks to elicit an early nod, an easy concurrence with the picture part of the parable. This is a classic characteristic of persuasive speech, and when established early on can engage the listeners and lead them into disclosures and discoveries.

Also, be sure to envision the story as you read publicly and represent it. If you actually envision it, the congregation will as well. Read the parable in *The Cottonpatch Translation* or involve a youth or drama group in a simple dramatization prior to the sermon. Again, station a reader in the balcony reading all the narration and scatter persons presenting the speeches of the individual characters elsewhere. Memorize the speeches of the characters both for more enlivened reading of the passage, possibly delivering each in a distinctive manner for enhancement of the sermon.

Involve the element of surprise in your sermon as it is presented to your contemporary congregation and even indulge in shock to effect the awakening as intended in the original parable. Leave the hearers with a decided responsibility to answer.

Finally, and what may be itself a surprising comment, preach the parables *of* the heart *from* the heart. Modern techniques can be letter-perfect, but unless certain parables are preached from the heart to the heart the emotive connection originally inherent will not reoccur. A certain pathos carries power in any sermon. An Australian journalist visiting in the services of Alexander Maclaren wrote:

> A wondrously pathetic little bit in the sermon about Abraham and Isaac going up Moriah will not soon be forgotten. Here the voice changed, softened, and seemed to linger over the words: "Where is the lamb?" While the answer, "My son, God will provide himself a lamb," was like the wail of a breaking heart."[20]

Such feeling communicates memorably, and in certain parables of the heart is a necessity. Obviously, those parables that actually use the word *compassion* belong to this category. The parable of the compassionate

Samaritan lionizes a warm-hearted stranger with a concern for the wounded. Such empathy for a wounded person abandoned on a desolate road can be transferred to the wounds of a recently divorced person or the surgical wounds of by-pass surgery, either as overt examples or remembered in preparation and delivery. The father responds to the prodigal effusively and emotionally with compassion. This father cares deeply and perhaps understands himself the allure of the far country—that the bright lights are bright, some prostitutes are pretty, spending money freely is exhilarating—and that returning is humbling. In the parable of the unforgiving servant, the king does react emotively in the first scene to the pleading of the highly indebted servant.

Beyond these three parables are many others that display the secrets of the heart through internal soliloquies. The parable of the Pharisee and the publican is so much about the heart. Through each man's prayer, the reader is allowed to see the heart of each. In the Pharisee's prayer we see the spiritual hazards of stuffy, long-term goodness and an absolute loss of compassion or understanding of sinners. The people around him who are moral failures only earn his disdain. The Teller of the tale understands how overwhelmed the tax collector is with his sense of shame and guilt. "Poor in spirit," he throws himself upon the mercy of God. Since God's own heart is moved by such a prayer, the preaching of this parable must be from the heart to the heart.

In this sense, the parable of the rich fool is about the heart, albeit an evil heart. In the parable of the rich man and Lazarus we feel the plight of desperate Lazarus and identify with street people freezing to death in warehouses. The congregation hearing this parable needs to sense emotionality as well as intentionality, and this is best communicated in delivery and choice of words. The parable of the lost sheep is, frankly, an emotional story. The shepherd surely loved all the sheep, yet left the ninety-nine and went looking with a great concern for the one lost. When he found the sheep, he was as joyful as a halfback who dances in the end zone after catching the touchdown pass. Coming home the shepherd spontaneously calls his friends to a party. Jesus himself could be quite emotional as He looked upon the sheep not having a shepherd (Matt. 9:35-38). Good exegesis and the latest technique are not enough for the preaching of the parable of the lost sheep; a heart is also needed.

Preach in the parables. You are never any nearer to the mind of Christ. You will be glad you did and so will your church. Interact with the texts on your own, research strong resources, strategize presentations creatively, project series, and let the nature of the parable influence your manuscript and delivery.

Notes

1. David Granskou, *Preaching on the Parables* (Philadelphia: Fortress Press, 1972), 82.
2. See Peter Rhea Jones, *The Teaching of the Parables* (Nashville: Broadman Press, 1982), 219-239, 142-165.
3. John Donohue, *The Gospel in Parable* (Philadelphia: Fortress Press, 1988), 20-25.
4. See John Crossan, *In Parables* (New York: Harper & Row, 1973).
5. Jones, *Teaching*, 53-54.
6. Aaron Milavec, "A Fresh Analysis of the Parable of the Wicked Husbandmen in the Light of Jewish-Christian Dialogue," *Parable and Story in Judaism and Christianity*, eds. Thoma and Wyschogrod (New York: Paulist Press, 1989), 111.
7. Helmut Thielieke, *The Waiting Father*, trans. John Doberstein (New York: Harper, 1959), 56.
8. David Redding, *The Parables He Told* (New York: Harper, 1962), 39.
9. William Barclay, *And Jesus Said* (Philadelphia: Westminster Press, 1970), 121-126.
10. David Buttrick, *Homiletic* (Philadelphia: Fortress Press, 1987), 348.
11. Martin Luther King, Jr., *Strength to Love* (New York: Pocketbooks, 1968), 62-70.
12. For good resources on this parable see William Neil, *The Difficult Sayings of Jesus* (Grand Rapids: Eerdmans, 1975), 73-78; and Paul Duke, "Spared," in *Southern Baptist Preaching Today*, ed. Earl Allen and Joel Gregory (Nashville: Broadman Press, 1987), 80-85.
13. Thoma and Wyschogrod, eds., "Introduction," in *Parable and Story in Judaism and Christianity*, 1.
14. Wade P. Huie, "Poverty of Abundance," *Interpretation*, 22 (1968): 403-420.
15. Eugene Lowry, *How to Preach a Parable* (Nashville: Abingdon Press, 1989).
16. Donohue, *The Gospel in Parable* 25. For a superb update on narrative preaching, see John McClure, "Narrative and Preaching: Sorting it all Out," *Journal for Preachers*, 15 (1991): 24-29.
17. A. M. Hunter, *According to John* (London: SCM, 1968), 78-89.
18. Jones, *Teaching*, 58-59.
19. See Jones, "Parabolic Preaching: Perspectives on Life," *Preaching in Today's World*, ed. James Barry (Nashville: Broadman Press, 1984), 73ff.
20. Quoted in Clyde Fant and William Pinson, eds., *20 Centuries of Great Preaching* (Waco: Word Books, 1971), 5:11.

30

Scott Hafemann
Professor of New Testament
Gordon-Conwell Theological Seminary
South Hamilton, Massachusetts

Preaching in the Epistles

The goal of preaching in the Epistles is the same as the goal of preaching in any other portion of Scripture, namely, to affect the congregation with the theological truth of the text, both emotionally and intellectually, in order that God might be glorified. In a word, "the goal of preaching is the glory of God in the glad submission of his people."[1] In preaching the Epistles, as in preaching *per se*, the character of God revealed in the biblical text is the sermon's foundation and prevailing subject. The sermon must therefore look in two directions. In viewing the biblical text, the sermon must be faithful to the original intention of the biblical author.[2] At the same time, in viewing the congregation, the preacher must convey this intention in a way that makes sense of the Scriptures, in a way that the Scriptures make sense to them, and in a way that moves their inclination to the point of resolve and action by stirring up their affections.[3] The preacher stands between the Bible and the church as the mediator of the message of the Scriptures, whose calling it is to bring the text to the church, and the church to the text, in order that God's people might hope in God more and sin less (compare 1 John 2:2; Rom. 15:13; Eph. 3:14-19; 1 Pet. 3-9; Heb. 10:19-25).

Preaching the Epistles in View of Their Theological Character

The first point to be made about preaching the Epistles, therefore, is that they too, like all the books of the Bible, are thoroughly *theological* in character. Their subject matter is the holy and righteous God, who was manifest in Jesus Christ and is now at work in and through the church as the "temple of the Holy Spirit," in continuing fulfillment of God's commitment to His creation and to His covenant history with Israel (compare 1 Cor. 3:16-17; 6:19; 12:12-27; Eph. 2:21-22; 4:12, 15-16; Gal. 6:15-16; Rom. 8:18-25; 11:1-32; Heb. 3:1—4:10; 8:1—10:18; 1 Pet. 2:9-10). Hence, one preaches the Epistles, like the Bible as a whole, ultimately to declare God's glory, to make clear His relationship to the world He has created and sustains, and to expound the nature of the covenant which God has made with those whom He has redeemed.

This knowledge is not to be preached for its own sake. One *preaches* the Epistles in order to make the glorious character of the God of Israel and the Church clear, in all its facets, *so that* God's people may continue to repent from their sin as they increasingly entrust their lives to God. Conversely, we desire to learn of God *so that* our response as His "workmanship, created (anew) in Christ Jesus for (the purpose of) good works, which God prepared before hand, that we should walk in them" (Eph. 2:10, AT), might be pleasing to Him and *thereby* also satisfy the deepest longings of our hearts. To quote Piper again, preaching the Epistles is thus done in the confidence that:

> the wonder of the gospel and the most freeing discovery this sinner has ever made is that God's deepest commitment to be glorified and my deepest longing to be satisfied are not in conflict, but in fact find simultaneous consummation in his display of and my delight in the glory of God.[4]

Convinced of this, preaching the Epistles becomes an essentially theocentric endeavor, in which the ultimate subject of every sermon is God. Sidney Greidanus has rightly emphasized, therefore, that the fundamental questions to be asked in interpreting the Epistles and answered in preaching them, as in interpreting and preaching any part of Scripture, are: "Why was this text preserved in the canon? What does God reveal in this text about himself and his will? And what does this message mean in the context of the whole Bible?"[5] Preaching from the Epistles, like preaching from the Bible in general, is not preaching until it has answered these questions.

Preaching the Epistles in View of Their Occasional Nature

In view of the shared theological character of the Epistles, the first aspect which makes preaching in the Epistles distinct within the canon is not their function or role in preaching, but the *occasional nature* of epistolary literature. To a degree more pronounced than in the other literature of the New Testament, the Epistles are *historically specific* in disposition. While all of the New Testament documents were written to particular historical circumstances and communities, the Epistles speak to these circumstances and communities *directly*, in the form of a second person address, rather than indirectly through a predominantly third person narrative form. Indeed, as their general genre designation indicates, the "Epistles" are all various types of "letters," which, broadly conceived, are the written expression or corollary of oral, person to person communication.[6] More than the Gospels and Acts, or the Book of Revelation, the Epistles are singularly aimed at a particular church, churches (in the case of Galatians, Ephesians, James, and the "Catholic Epistles"), or individuals (i.e., the Pastorals, Philemon, and 2—3 John), and in each case they address specific situations or problems.[7]

The occasional nature of the Epistles means that they are not to be preached in the same way that one would read and preach universal maxims, which are based on what unifies people in their common human experience and written to a broad, largely unknown audience. Nor are they to be read as narratives of past events retold for the sake of demonstrating the faithfulness of God. They should also not be read and preached as prophetic revelations of God's will for His people, as a people, or as compendiums of systematically outlined theology. In short, the Epistles are not proverbs, historical-theological narratives, Torah, poetic wisdom literature, or prophecy; nor are they treatises on general religious principles such as the *Summa theologiae* of Thomas of Aquinas or Calvin's *Institutes.* Although the Epistles contain elements of all of these literary forms, and although the Epistles are thoroughly theological in character, the truths expressed in the Epistles are all expressed *in relation to* and *for the sake of* the concrete situations and problems being addressed.[8] In the Epistles the reality of God's glorious presence and the contours of His will and work are all made evident in the *specific* situations of life to which the letters of the New Testament are addressed.

As a result of their occasional nature, preaching the Epistles thus demands that one understand and expound the letter against its own historical backdrop in order to make sense of the letter itself and to make sense of it for the congregation. As all beginning students of the New Testament learn, the letter-structure, rhetorical devices, terminology, imagery, affirmations, disavowals, argumentation, and theology of the Epistles must all be understood against the backdrop of the language, literature, literary conventions, world-view, and historical circumstances common to the author and audience of the letters. In preaching the Epistles, one must ascertain the meaning of the *particular* point being made in terms of the literary conventions it employs in speaking and against the backdrop of the historical circumstance to which it speaks. The theology presented in the Epistles is a theology which is not only expressed in terms of a specific historical context, but which also comes to expression precisely *because* of that context and is expressed in *application* to that context.

This does not mean that the underlying and explicit theological truths of the Epistles, together with their inseparable corresponding implications, were not meant by their authors to be taken as true in the broadest sense of that word. As the self-understanding of their authors and the authority of the letters themselves demonstrate, the Epistles were specific, but not private; occasional, but not haphazard; familiar, but no less binding for the community.[9] Practically this means that in ascertaining the particular point of a passage, the preacher must be careful to interpret it *against the backdrop to which it was written,* in order to ascertain not only its meaning, but its *significance* as well.[10] For in the Epistles, it is the application of the author's theology to a concrete situation which provides the clue to the larger theological import of the text.[11]

In approaching the Epistles, a clear and unavoidable hermeneutical circle therefore exists between the message of the text and its historical context which has direct implications for preaching. The more one understands the letter's historical context, the more the meaning and significance of the letter become clear, and vice versa. This also means, however, that one's understanding of the historical context will greatly influence *how* one understands the text, and vice versa. Faced with this hermeneutical circle, especially in the Epistles where the historical context impinges so directly on the text, one should always *begin* by trying to understand the concrete text as well as possible *before* reconstructing its historical background. Beginning with a historical reconstruction, which one then brings *to* the text as the *key* to its meaning, leads to a hopeless circularity in which the very texts to be interpreted on the basis of one's historical reconstruction have also inevitably provided the data for the reconstruction itself. Knowledge of the historical backdrop of any given text should therefore be brought to the text only *after* one has ascertained the flow of the author's argument and its theological assertions and implications to the best of one's ability on the basis of its literary and canonical context. Preaching the Epistles in view of their occasional nature thus requires that one ask, first, *what* is being said in a given passage, understood in its *literary* context. Having ascertained as well as possible the content and flow of the argument, the interpreter/preacher must then go on to ask *why* it was said, and why it was said *in this particular way,* given its *historical* context.

As soon as the importance of the occasional nature of the Epistles and of the corresponding hermeneutical circle involved in understanding them is recognized, an even graver danger in preaching the Epistles must be avoided. The occasional nature of the New Testament letters does *not* mean that one ought to preach their historical background *per se.* Given their theological character, a sermon from the Epistles should include only those aspects of the historical background of a passage which are *absolutely essential* for explaining the intention and theological significance of the text at hand. In spite of the historical specificity of the Epistles, one must avoid allowing the sermon to degenerate into a history lesson on the first century.[12] Preaching is the proclamation of the theological truth of the text and its constituent implications, not a lesson in the circumstances and politics of the New Testament era, its language, or social problems and customs. One's preaching must thus be focused first and foremost on the *theological* message of the text and its implications, even though the context and expression of this message are thoroughly historical. In the words of Greidanus, by a theological message we refer:

> not to theory or the discipline of theology, but to *God*, specifically the revelation *of* God and the revelation *about* God. Theological interpretation seeks to hear *God's* voice in the Scriptures; it seeks to probe beyond mere historical reconstruction and verbal meanings to a discernment of the message of God in the Scriptures; it concentrates on the prophetic, kerygmatic dimension and the theocentric focus.[13]

The preacher of the Epistles must therefore penetrate to the theological dimension of the passage by ascertaining the view of God and His will which informs the concrete message and manner of the text as its expressed or unexpressed foundation. In addition to paying special attention to a passage's explicitly theological issues and affirmations, this will also entail asking *why* an author responded in the way he did to a particular problem or circumstance, recognizing that for the biblical authors, every issue, at heart, is a theological issue.[14]

Preaching the Epistles in View of Their Discursive Structure

The second aspect which makes preaching in the Epistles distinct is the *discursive structure* of epistolary literature. Unlike the other biblical genres, in which there are periodic discursive sections, the epistles are characterized by their thoroughgoing propositional argumentation. This means that the flow of the argument of the Epistles is established by a series of interrelated assertions in which the various statements are related to one another *logically.* The movement of thought in the Epistles is intricately tied to the order and manner of presentation of these propositions, so that the message of the text moves in a logical stair-step fashion up and down in accordance with the indicated logic of the discourse. Hence, as Daniel P. Fuller has emphasized:

> Just as the syntactical relationships between words in a proposition must be grasped in order to understand it, so one must see how propositions relate as they succeed one another in order to grasp the text as a whole. John Calvin, one of history's greatest exegetes, spoke of the necessity to trace out *le fil du texte* (the thread of the text). One stands no chance at all of grasping what an author intended until he has thought his way after him, proposition by proposition, and has seen how successive propositions join together.[15]

Thus, the basic building block of interpretation, and consequently also of preaching, is the individual assertion or proposition, not the isolated word or phrase, as if words could "carry" meaning in and of themselves.[16]

Within discursive literature, due to its style of argumentation, even individual propositions express very little meaning apart from the paragraph to which they belong. The discursive nature of the Epistles therefore demands that we take as the smallest unit of meaning to be interpreted, not the word or the proposition, nor even a compound sentence, but the *paragraph.*[17] In the same way, sermons from the Epistles should correspond to one's analysis of the paragraphs which compose the text, regardless of their length. Depending on one's purpose in the sermon (and time constraints), longer paragraphs, such as Ephesians 1:3-14 or Philippians 2:1-11, might require a series of sermons, all intricately related, in order to cover the terrain thoroughly. In doing so, each sermon should be related to the paragraph as a whole, keeping in mind that the purpose of a paragraph is to present an argument in support of a particular point of view or exhortation.[18]

It thus becomes apparent that in preaching a paragraph from an Epistle, the first step is to read the passage carefully enough to be able to determine and separate its individual assertions. The best way to do this is simply to list them in the order of their sequence in the text. This is one of the great values of knowing Greek, since from the Greek text one can delineate in a precise manner the specific assertions of the text, the order in which they are presented, and the way in which they are logically related. If one has no facility with Greek, a very literal translation such as the New American Standard Bible is strongly recommended for sermon preparation. Its literal nature leaves the original syntactical and propositional structure more evident than in those translations which aim at a more dynamic equivalent and colloquial style, such as the New International Version. In addition, when analyzing the constituent parts of a text's argument, keep in mind that a proposition consists of any clause which has its own subject and verb and thereby makes its own statement. As a rule of thumb, every verbal form, apart from nominal uses of the infinitive and substantival and adjectival participles, normally conveys a proposition and should be treated as a separate assertion (even when subjects and/or verbal forms must be supplied). Moreover, in some contexts, even prepositional phrases and absolute nominal clauses can be elevated to propositional status if their function in the sentence is to further the argument in some way.[19]

As an example, the paragraph found in 2 Peter 1:3-4, when translated literally and analyzed for its constituent assertions, has at least five propositions:

3a His divine power has bestowed to us all things
pertaining to life and godliness

3b through the knowledge of the one who called us to His own glory and virtue
4a through His own glory and virtue the precious and sublime promises have been given to us
4b in order that through them you might become sharers of the divine nature
4c having escaped the corruption in the world in passion

It is at this point in one's sermon preparation that the occasional nature and linguistic-cultural-historical-theological context of the text can be brought to bear on the passage. In doing so, one seeks to clarify the meaning of ambiguous or significant words, images, and allusions, as well as the meaning of the passage in relationship to what can be known concerning the situation of the author and addressees. For example, in 2 Peter 1:3-4 significant study will need to be done within 2 Peter and within its historical context in order to determine what is meant by "sharers of the divine nature" in verse 4b and by the "passion" in which the "corruption in the world" in verse 4c is found, or by which it is produced (the determination of the function of the phrase "in passion" is also a matter of exegetical and theological significance). The explicit content of the promises referred to in verse 4a will need to be mapped out within 2 Peter, and in view of the early Christian heresy being faced by the church to which 2 Peter was written, so that, in turn, one's own congregation will know just what can and cannot be expected from God according to this text! In addition, an examination of the Old Testament texts and/or early Christian traditions quoted or alluded to in the text will significantly influence the way in which one understands the argument of the passage as well. For example, the divine "power," "glory," and "virtue" referred to in 2 Peter 1:3 are later used up and explained in 2 Peter 1:16-21 in relationship to the transfiguration of Jesus and its implications for the content and surety of God's "prophetic word." Any understanding of these aspects in 2 Peter 1:3-4 must therefore take this larger historical and theological context into consideration.

After having separated out the propositions of the text and studied them within their original literary, historical, and theological context, the next important step in preaching in the Epistles is to return to the passage as a whole in order to determine the logical relationship that exists between *each* proposition and those which precede and follow it. The first clues to pursue are the conjunctions which the author himself provides. These connecting words and phrases must be understood precisely and taken seriously as essential indications of the author's intention, keeping in mind that even conjunctions can represent a variety of different meanings. "Context is king" here, as in all interpretive steps. Second, one must look to the general flow of the argument in order to determine the role of those statements which have no explicit conjunction introducing them, or in which the conjunction itself is ambiguous. Finally, one must ascertain the function of those verbal clauses, such as participial and infinitive clauses, in which the logical relationship is implied, not expressed and of those propositions which the interpreter has established based on nonverbal phrases.

The key at this point is to use common sense, since linguists have isolated only 18 different logical relationships which can exist between propositions, no matter what the language is.[20] The technical names for these relationships are not ultimately important. What *is* important is that one can explain *how* one idea in the argument leads to another. Only when one is able to trace the actual way in which the argument develops within a paragraph has the text been understood well enough to preach it. To preach in the Epistles does not mean to remove one of its propositions (not to mention concepts!) out of its literary and/or historical context in order to interpret it against a context foreign to it (whether a biblical context or the preacher's context). Nor does it mean to focus in on the "big ideas" in the passage, as if these ideas stand alone apart from what is said concerning them, why it is said, and for what purpose it is said. Instead, preaching in the Epistles means to construct a sermon which is faithful to the author's original intention as expressed in the various assertions in the text *in their original context*, which is first and foremost the *literary* context of the argument in which they "live and move and have their being." It is the *author's* points and arguments which we preach, not our own abstraction of them.

Preaching the Epistles in View of Their Main Points

When focusing in on the individual propositions of the paragraph, the preacher must be careful, however, not to lose the central thrust of the text. The final and most important step in preaching the Epistles, therefore, is *to ascertain the main point of the paragraph being preached*. The main point of the text is that *one* assertion, which may be restated in various ways throughout the passage, which is supported by *all* of the other propositions in the paragraph, and which itself supports *no* other proposition in the passage. One is ready to preach from the Epistles when one can state explicitly what the main point of the text is, and how it is supported throughout the text. It is the main point of the paragraph which becomes the main point of the sermon, even if it is not the main *emphasis* of the sermon.

For example, an analysis of the flow of thought in 2 Peter 1:3-4 produces the following representation of the argument, with the logical relationships between the individual propositions italicized for the sake of clarity:

3a His divine power has bestowed to us all things pertaining to life and godliness
3b *by means of* the knowledge of the one who called us to His own glory and virtue
4a *and by means of* His glory and virtue the precious and sublime promises have been bestowed to us
4b *in order that* through them you might become sharers of the divine nature
4c *as a result of* having escaped the corruption in the world in passion.

The main point of this passage is verse 4b, the *purpose* that one might become a sharer in God's own nature. The means to this end is twofold. First, God has granted to us through His own *power* everything we need in order to partake in His nature (v. 3a). Second, God has granted to us His own "precious and sublime *promises*" in order that we might partake in His nature (v. 4a). Together then, God's power and promises make possible and bring about our being able to share in His own nature. As verse 3b makes clear, both God's power and His promises are made available to us through the knowledge of God which He grants to us in our calling. According to verse 4c, our sharing in God's divine nature comes about directly as a result of our having escaped the corruption in the world by means of God's power and promises. Rearranged in accordance with its logical development, the argument of 2 Peter 1:3-4 can therefore be displayed in the following way:

1. God gives us knowledge of His own glory and virtue when He calls us (v. 3b).
2. *Through this knowledge* His power grants to us everything we need to live a godly life (v. 3a),
3. *and through this knowledge* God's promises have also been granted to us.
4. *The purpose of the display of God's power and granting of His promises in our lives is that* we might escape the corruption of this world caused (!) by passion
5. *in order that as a final outcome* we might share in the divine nature.

In preaching this text, or any epistolary passage, the sermon must remain faithful to both the main point and argument of the text. Indeed, the structure of the sermon itself is often best attained by following the structure of the passage in view, so that the points of the text become the points of the sermon.

At this juncture, one must determine whether the needs of the congregation indicate that the *emphasis* (not content!) of the sermon should also be on the main point of the text, or on one of the subsidiary supports for it. Even if one decides to focus on one of the subordinate assertions in the text, the congregation should always come to understand how this point fits into the overall argument of the text and how it relates to the author's main point. In the example before us, the sermon should make clear that the purpose of one's call as a Christian, as well as the purpose of the power and promises of God which the believer experiences, is to bring about our participation in God's own nature. Moreover, in the context, this divine nature must be clearly defined against the backdrop of verse 4c and the continuation of the argument in 2 Peter 1:5-11, so that its ethical content becomes clear. Given the needs of the congregation, however, the focus of the sermon may be on the nature and content of the promises of God and how they function to bring about the righteous pattern of life described in verses 5-7. Indeed, due to its density and crucial theological/practical significance, 2 Peter 1:3-4 could easily produce a series of three sermons, each one carefully integrated into the argument of the passage as a whole.[21] In any case, the preacher will endeavor to make clear how both the basis and goal of the Christian life as expressed in 2 Peter 1:3-4 finds its meaning and significance in *God* in the knowledge of *His* glory and virtue, in the display of *His* power and promises, and in the experience of *His* holy character. This requires that the sermon itself explain and illustrate the text in ways accessible and desirable to the congregation, since their willingness to join in the life of godliness aimed at in this passage, as in all others, will only be as strong and consistent as the clarity of their understanding of the compelling nature of the majesty, holiness, and beauty of God Himself.

Preaching the Epistles in View of Their Imperative Exhortations

The Epistles are thoroughly theological in character, occasional in nature, and discursive in structure. Preaching in the Epistles must therefore be based on an analysis of the argument of the text in the context of its literary and historical setting, and with a clear and constant view of the character and will of God revealed in it. This means that preaching in the Epistles must be focused on the explicit assertions and main points of the text, and *not on the general theme or subject matter of a passage.*[22] It is an indictment on the sinking quality of biblical interpretation and preaching today that many preachers are no longer able to determine the specific main point of a paragraph, nor how it is supported. Instead, they must be content with ascertaining only the general subject matter of a passage. This is especially evident in the Epistles, where the argument is rhetorically dense and conceptually intertwined. As a result, in preaching in the Epistles, preachers often focus either on too little, ripping a phrase or sentence in which the main theme appears out of its context, or on too much, roving quickly from one high point to another as they stick out of the horizon of the passage. In either case, the preacher is ignoring the argument of the text itself, which is the *only* thing that gives the points of the text their meaning, foundation, coherence, significance, and gravity.[23]

As the nature and structure of the Epistles demonstrate, in preaching a passage about "love," one does not preach a sermon on the abstract nature of love, nor on one of the statements about love from the text, but on the main point of what the author actually says about love, how he supports it, how these assertions are related to God, and what their inextricable implications are for our lives. Even more important, however, one must be careful not to preach sermons *about* God in the abstract. Rather, the theological focus of the sermon should be on the *specific* assertions made in the Epistles as they relate to the unfolding biblical revelation of the nature of God and His character made clear in history. The specific, occasional nature of the Epistles and their discursive structure are powerful reminders of this fact. When read carefully, the Epistles force the preacher to see God at work in and through the lives of people in concrete circumstances. Conversely, the challenge in preaching the Epistles is to penetrate through the specific situation to the character of God and the contours of His will, so that the implications of God's character and His will become evident for the life of congregations separated by culture, geography, and time from those in Corinth or Rome, the Diaspora or Jerusalem.

Yet, because of the theological character of the Epistles, it should not be surprising how much of the Epistolary literature is cross-culturally relevant with very little adaptation, once the language, culture, historical milieu, and social setting of the Epistles are taken into account. Moreover, this same theological character of the Epistles means that the question of relevance and application in preaching the Epistles is best answered by not trying to transform specific applications of theological truth in the first century into general principles of behavior for today. Furthermore, since all of the Bible is culturally expressed, both historically and theologically (it is impossible to speak apart from one's culture), it is naive and impossible to try to separate out "trans-cultural" statements from those which are culturally expressed. Rather, the preacher's task is to determine what is being said about God and His will as they are manifest in the specific historical and cultural situation of the text, in order to then ask how this same divine character and will are to be expressed in the contemporary context. For it is God and His will which never change, and it is God and His Will which are the indicative subjects of the sermon.

As students of the Epistles know well, the main points of the larger units of the letters are *imperatives*, not indicative formulations about God, His will, or some other aspect of reality. The reason for this is: the theology of the Epistles is aimed at the way of life or ministry of the church or individual. From the perspective of the biblical authors, to make a statement *about* God includes making a statement *to* His people, over whom He reigns sovereignly and with whom He has entered into a covenant relationship.

The danger in preaching the Epistles, therefore, is that the imperatives of the text will be separated from the indicative theological statements upon which they are inseparably based, or from the fulfillment of the promises to which they inevitably lead. When this occurs, the gospel of God's grace is perverted either into a demand for a life lived out before God on the basis of human achievement on the one hand, or into the kind of "easy believism" which fails to recognize that the growing life of obedience which inextricably flows from trusting in God's promises in the power of the Spirit *is* the evidence of genuine conversion on the other hand. Thus, in preaching in the Epistles, the imperatives of the text must always be grounded in their indicative "substantiation,"[24] while the divine promises of the text must also be linked to the conditions of which they are an integral and constitutive part.[25] If one's goal in preaching the Epistles is to stir the affections in order to move the will and inclination, then *every* sermon should contain both the theological foundation *and* its intrinsic implications for one's thinking, feeling, and way of life as taught in the text.[26] Once again, the theological character, occasional nature, and discursive structure of the Epistles all combine to make such a sermonic wedding of indicative and imperative not only necessary, but unavoidable. For in the end, as 2 Peter 1:3-11 makes clear, the goal of preaching the Epistles is to reveal the knowledge of the glory and virtue of God (indicative foundation, vv. 3-4), in order that we might respond to God's presence in our lives by sharing more and more in God's own nature through taking on the character qualities of God Himself (imperative implications, vv. 5-7), so that God might be glorified and we might share in His kingdom and righteousness forever (contingent promise, vv. 8-11). Preaching in the Epistles, like preaching in the rest of the canon, is thus the divinely ordained path to heaven. Even more important, it is also the means by which God's glory is increasingly made know through the transformed lives of His people, both now and for all eternity (Eph. 3:10).

Notes

1. John Piper, *The Supremacy of God in Preaching* (Grand Rapids: Baker Book House, 1990), 39. I know of no other recent work which gets to the heart of the goal of preaching better than this one.

2. That the basis of the sermon is the biblical author's original intention is, of course, a matter of great recent debate. With the advent first of the "new hermeneutic" and then of "post-modern" biblical interpretation, many have become skeptical concerning the possibility of rediscovering and expressing an author's original intention. To enter this debate here is beyond our purposes, but the underlying assumption of this chapter is that such a

goal is possible and that the first job of the interpreter and preacher is to rediscover this authorial intention as accurately and completely as possible. For two of the best treatments of this question and for an argument in favor of the view taken here, see still E. D. Hirsch, Jr., *Validity in Interpretation* (New Haven: Yale University Press, 1967) (whose view may strike many as extreme, but as such it serves as a needed antidote to contemporary moods); and Mortimer J. Adler and Charles Van Doren, *How to Read A Book*, rev. ed. (New York: Simon and Schuster, 1972).

3. See again Piper, *The Supremacy of God in Preaching*, 82-86, for a good discussion of the role of the affections and mind in relationship to action, based on the thought of Jonathan Edwards. As Piper points out, Edwards made the changed behavior of his hearers his aim precisely by preaching to transform their affections as the spring of all action. Moreover, Edwards was clear that those affections which do not arise from a solid understanding of the truth are not to be pursued, since preaching, to be profitable, must give the hearer "good reason," and "just ground" for responding. It is in this context that Edwards declares that ministers are not "to be blamed for raising the affections of their hearers too high, if that which they are affected with be only that which is worthy of affection, and their affections are not raised beyond a proportion to their importance. . . . I should think myself in the way of my duty to raise the affections of my hearers as high as possibly I can, provided that they are affected with nothing but truth." (*Some Thoughts Concerning the Revival*, vol. 4 in The Works of Jonathan Edwards (New Haven: Yale University Press, 1972) 387, quoted by Piper, 82 ff.

4. Piper, *The Supremacy of God in Preaching*, 26. The scriptural basis and experiential confirmation of Piper's view of the goal of preaching as the glory of God are developed in his two important works, *Desiring God: Meditations of a Christian Hedonist* (Portland: Multnomah Press, 1986) and *The Pleasures of God: Meditations on God's Delight in Being God* (Portland: Multnomah Press, 1991) which are must reading for preachers. For Piper, preaching must be passionately committed to manifesting the glory of God as the ultimate answer to human needs and the motivating force for all holy human endeavor.

5. Sidney Greidanus,*The Modern Preacher and the Ancient Text: Interpreting and Preaching Biblical Literature* (Grand Rapids: Wm. B. Eerdmans, 1988) 102. This is the best full length, technical discussion available on the hermeneutical issues involved in preaching and their concrete application to the task of preaching the various biblical genres. In this context, see especially his chapter, "Preaching the Epistles," 311-341.

6. See Greidanus, *The Modern Preacher and the Ancient Text*, 314: he points out that "In the Greek tradition, a letter was a stand-in for its author. . . . Hence one can characterize the New Testament Epistles as long-distance sermons." For an extensive discussion of the Epistles as part of the genre of ancient letters, see David E. Aune, *The New Testament in Its Literary Environment* (Philadelphia: Westminster Press, 1987), 158-225. Aune, (p. 162), classifies Greco-Roman letters in terms of three basic categories: private or documentary letters, official letters, and literary letters. However, since the letter is the most flexible of ancient literary genres (p. 159), he resists drawing strict boundaries between them. Moreover, Aune points out, (p. 167), that during the first century A.D. the letter was used by moral philosophers as a "vehicle of instruction." The letters in the New Testament all more or less follow the basic pattern of an opening formula (= prescript, with identification of sender, addressee, and salutation; and thanksgiving), the central body of the letter (with all of its various combined and overlapping purposes), and a closing formula (with final benediction), with each section enlarged, modified, or eliminated as desired by the author or required by the historical situation (pp. 183-225).

7. Aune, *The New Testament in Its Literary Environment*, 199, concludes that "with few exceptions, early Christian letters were either written with a basically deliberative purpose. . . . The two basic forms of deliberative rhetoric, persuasion and dissuasion, included not only advice but also most of the features associated with moral and religious exhortation: encouragement, admonition, comfort, warning, and rebuke." But Aune is careful to emphasize, 203, that most early Christian letters "resist rigid classification" and are "mixed" in character. Each letter must therefore be analyzed on its own terms, taking into account the complex nature of the letter and situation to which it was addressed, though there are letters with one distinct nature and purpose, such as the letters of recommendation of Philemon and 3 John. In treating the New Testament letters, Aune thus opts for only the two very broad categories of "(1) *circumstantial*, or dialogical, letters,

which are closely linked to specific historical situations, and (2) *general*, or monological, letters, which are unconnected to specific historical settings" (204; compare 204-214, 217-222).

8. See Gordon D. Fee and Douglas Stuart, *How to Read the Bible for All Its Worth: A Guide to Understanding the Bible* (Grand Rapids: Zondervan, 1982), 44-46 for an easily accessible discussion of the occasional nature of the epistles. Though they make too much of the distinction between letters and "epistles," their emphasis on the fact that in the epistles all theology is "task theology,"—"theology being written for or brought to bear on the task at hand... It is always theology at the service of a particular need" (p. 46), and its implications for interpreting the epistles (pp. 46-56), are helpful.

9. Thus, as Thomas R. Schreiner, *Interpreting the Pauline Epistles* (Grand Rapids: Baker Book House, 1990), 24ff., emphasizes, Adolf Deissmann's paradigmatic distinction between Paul's "letters" as quickly written, non-literary writings, which were aimed only at the immediate and specific context; and the more artistically and self-consciously produced "epistles," which were intentionally written for a broader audience and for posterity, has been rightly and seriously called into question by the nature of the Pauline epistles themselves. As Schreiner points out, Paul's letters are not to be paralleled to the papyri of his day; nor does their occasional nature take away from the care of their composition, the apostolic authority with which they were written (compare 1 Cor. 14:37-38; Gal. 1:8; 1 Thess. 2:13; 5:27; 2 Thess. 3:14); or Paul's own expectation that they would be circulated, even beyond the primary community to which they were sent (compare Col. 4:16). This is all the more true of Hebrews and the "Catholic Epistles."

10. I am using the terms "meaning" and "significance" in the technical sense established by Hirsch, *Validity in Interpretation*, 8: "*Meaning* is that which is represented by a text; it is what the author meant by his use of a particular sign sequence; it is what the signs represent. *Significance*, on the other hand, names a relationship between that meaning and a person, or a conception, or a situation, or indeed anything imaginable."

11. For example, the high Christology of Hebrews 1:1-14 serves to support the author's unfolding argument for resisting the temptation to renege one's faith in Christ for the security and peace of the former Jewish community and tradition (compare Heb. 10:32-39). This application points to the theological understanding of the superiority of God's new covenant relationship with His people in order that one might be encouraged to endure in faith. In 1 Peter 1:10-12, the relationship between the ministry of the prophets of the old covenant and the people of God of the new covenant is designed to support the admonition to maintain one's confidence in the future in order to live lives of faith-produced obedience and joy in the present, even in the midst of adversity (compare 1 Pet. 1:3-9,13-21). This application undergirds the theology of hope outlined in 1 Peter 1:3-9, which in turn leads to the praising of God's glory (compare 1:3,7). The creedal affirmation in 1 Corinthians 8:6 serves to support Paul's argument concerning meat offered to idols. In doing so it gives the explicit theological basis for the conviction of the "strong," who "know" enough to be able to eat it. It also provides the basis for the admonition to them to be "loving" enough to forego doing so for the sake of those "weaker" in the faith, since giving up their rights for others is an expression of dependence upon the one, true God. Similarly, the apparent maxim-like statement in 2 Corinthians 3:6, "the letter kills, but the Spirit makes alive," actually functions to support Paul's legitimacy as an apostle (2 Cor. 2:16-3:5) in the face of the accusations against him made by the so-called "super apostles" in Corinth (compare 2 Cor. 11:5,12-15). As such it provides the foundation for Paul's arguments concerning the genuine work of the Spirit in transforming God's people into the image of God in Christ (compare 3:18-4:6), which in turn leads him to call to repentance those who substitute the miraculous for sanctification as the ultimate sign of the genuine work of God (compare 2 Cor. 13:1-10). And Paul's general declaration in Romans 1:16 that he is "not ashamed of the Gospel, because it is the power of God," finds its context in Paul's desire to win support from the Romans for his message and upcoming mission to the West in view of the controversy surrounding Paul's ministry among the churches (compare Rom. 1:10-15; 15:20-24, 28f.). Paul's confidence in the face of this controversy highlights the truth of his conviction concerning the way in which the righteousness of God is now being revealed in the world through the Gospel, so that one can and must trust in it to avoid God's wrath (compare Rom. 1:17f; 3:21-26; 15:14-19). Finally, even the gnomic-like statement, "God is love," in 1 John 4:16 is an integral part of

John's larger argument for the distinguishing marks of true believers. His purpose is to make it clear to his readers that those who have left the church and its way of life, based on her confession of the manifestation of the love of God in the incarnation of God's Son, Jesus Christ, have indeed left the one true people of God (compare 1 John 2:18-29; 4:1-12). The direct theological statement concerning God in 1 John 4:16 thus calls attention to the way in which the love of God is manifested in one's life in 1 John 2:15-17, with its implied call to forsake the way of sin, as well as the implicit promise that God's love frees one from such a love of the world and its sinful consequences (compare 1 John 3:1-24).

12. Hence, for example, a sermon on Romans 1:16ff. ought not to degenerate into a history lesson on Paul's missionary journeys in order to support missions and call for personal evangelism, just as a series of sermons on Hebrews 1 should not become a tour through the angeology of post-biblical Judaism and the continuing societal, political, and theological appeal of Judaism for recent Jewish Christian converts in order to criticize modern Judaism. A sermon on 1 Peter 1:3-9 ought not to focus on the reality and kinds of persecutions faced by Christians then and now. Sermons on 1 Corinthians 8 should not become a lesson on idol worship and idol meat in ancient Corinth in order to solve directly a current church dispute. Second Corinthians 3:6 should not be an opportunity to delineate one's most recent theory on the pseudo-charismatic theology of Paul's opponents (and the church down the street), while 1 John 4 should not be used primarily to outline the illegitimate religious frauds of John's day, or one's own.

13. Greidanus, *The Modern Preacher and the Ancient Text,* 103. Compare his helpful discussion of preaching the intention of the human and divine authors of Scripture and the theocentric nature and purpose of Scripture on pp. 106-121.

14. Compare the theological responses to a historical problem (for example, the delay of the return of Christ in 2 Pet. 3), a social custom (for example, hair length and veils in 1 Cor. 11:2-16), a controversy (for example, the demand for Gentiles to "live like a Jew" as encompassed by circumcision, ritual purity laws, and food regulations in Gal. 2:11-21; 5:2-12), a relational problem (for example, the strife between Euodia and Syntyche in Phil. 4:2-3), an ecclesiological concern (for example, the role of women and the function and qualifications of elders and deacons in 1 Tim. 2:8-3:13), a societal issue (for example, the relationships within the household in Eph. 5:21-33; Col. 3:18—4:1), and a personal circumstance (for example, the change in Paul's travel plans in 2 Cor. 1:15-2:13).

15. *Hermeneutics,* unpublished syllabus, 1969, IV-2. This invaluable practical handbook on how to ascertain the flow of an author's argument has not been published, but is available through Fuller Theological Seminary's book store. Recently, its basic approach has been adapted and supplemented by the other important aspects of interpretation in Schreiner's *Interpreting the Pauline Epistles.* See also Peter Cotterell and Max Turner, *Linguistics and Biblical Interpretation* (Downers Grove: InterVarsity Press, 1989) 188-229, for a more philosophical, as well as practical, treatment of analyzing the relationship between clauses in discursive literature.

16. For a helpful discussion of the "root fallacy," as well as the many other grammatical, logical, and historical fallacies that often plague modern interpreters, see D. A. Carson, *Exegetical Fallacies* (Grand Rapids: Baker Book House, 1984).

17. See Fee and Stuart, *How to Read the Bible,* 51: "We simply cannot stress enough the importance of your learning to THINK PARAGRAPHS, and not just as natural units of thought, but as the absolutely necessary key to understanding the argument in the various Epistles" (emphasis theirs). For the relationship of this insight to preaching, see Haddon W. Robinson, *Biblical Preaching: The Development and Delivery of Expository Messages* (Grand Rapids: Baker Book House, 1980), 54, who bases his method of preaching in the Epistles on the fact that "In the New Testament letters . . . texts will usually be selected by paragraph divisions, since paragraphs delineate the building blocks of thought."

18. As Aune points out in *The New Testament in Its Literary Environment,* 160, after the first century B.C. ancient letters "functioned not only as means of communication but also as sophisticate instruments of persuasion and media for displaying literary skill."

19. Hence, for example, in Romans 5:1 the prepositional phrase "through our Lord Jesus Christ" indicates the manner or instrument by which the peace we have with God is brought about. In view of Paul's earlier argument in Romans 3:21-26, this is an important summary statement and deserves to be given its own propositional status, with its own subject and verb. In interpreting and preaching this verse, therefore, one ought to view

this phrase as a separate assertion and translate the sense of it as, "The way in which we have this hope is through our Lord Jesus Christ." This is confirmed by the fact that the very next clause in Romans 5:2 is based upon this prepositional phrase as the argument continues. In the same way, in Romans 8:3 the accusative absolute clause, "the incapability of the Law," functions as the crucial ground clause for the fact that God condemned sin in the flesh through the cross of Christ, and ought to be rendered, "because the Law was incapable . . . therefore God."

20. For example, series, progression, alternative, manner or instrument, comparison, negative-positive, general-specific, fact-interpretation, inference, ground, result, conditional, purpose, temporal, locative, adversative, question-answer, and situation-response. For these relationships and the ways in which one relates them together in order to follow the flow of an author's argument, see the works of Fuller, Schreiner, and Cotterell and Turner in note 15.

21. For example, in verses 3a and 3b (that is, on God's call and how it brings about a life lived by the power of God, that we might become sharers in the divine nature); 4a (that is, on God's call and how it brings about a life lived by the promises of God, that we might become sharers in the divine nature), and 4b-4c (that is, on how the power and promises of God enable one to escape the corruption in the world caused by passion, that we might become sharers in the divine nature).

22. This failure to distinguish clearly between the theme of the text and its main point is the prevailing weakness of most books and articles on preaching in the Epistles, or any other genre for that matter.

23. Compare Haddon W. Robinson, *Biblical Preaching*, 33, who argues that "sermons seldom fail because they have too many ideas; more often they fail because they deal with unrelated ideas. . . . Ideally each sermon is the explanation, interpretation, or application of a single dominant idea supported by other ideas, all drawn from one passage or several passages of Scripture." Robinson thus follows those who argue that the sermon should be based upon and revolve around the development of one specific thought and that this thought should be taken from the central idea or main thought of the text (compare 33-37). My point is that this central idea or main thought ought to correspond directly with the main point of the passage, rather than being the preachers own "distillation of life that abstracts out of the particulars of experience what they have in common and relates them to each other" as expressed in the text (p. 45). Robinson himself, however, rightly goes on to argue that in order to determine the subject and complement that combine to make up the main point of the sermon one "must become aware of the structure of the passage and distinguish between its major and supporting assertions" (p. 68).

24. Using the word of Greidanus, *The Modern Preacher,* 324. But I would state the case much stronger than he does when he writes: "Whenever feasible the preaching-text should also include the textual substantiation of a particular claim or demand" (p. 324). In my view, it should always do so! For Greidanus himself rightly emphasizes that "in the Epistles the imperatives never function without the indicative. . . . After a detailed study, Herman Ridderbos concludes that 'the imperative is grounded on the reality that has been given with the indicative, appeals to it, and is intended to bring it to full development' " (p. 326, quoting Ridderbos, *Paul,* pp. 254 ff.). Moreover, Greidanus follows Allen Verhey in stressing the "intimate connection" between the imperative and the preceding indicative, so that "this connection is more than the one flowing from the other" (p. 326). Rather, as Verhey has rightly pointed out: " 'the imperative is by no means merely an addendum to the indicative or even exactly an inference drawn from the indicative. Participation in Christ's cross and resurrection (the important priority of the indicative) and anticipation of the new age of God's unchallenged sovereignty (the important finality of the indicative) are constituted here and now by obedience to God's will (the imperative)" (p. 326, quoting Verhey, *Great Reversal,* 104 ff.).

25. See Herman Ridderbos, *Paul: An Outline of His Theology* (Grand Rapids: Eerdmans Publishing Co., 1975), 254-256: "it is immediately clear that the imperative rests on the indicative and that this order is not reversible. . . . Indicative and imperative thus do not represent a certain division of property in the sense that the indicative denotes the divine and the imperative the human share in the new life, or that the imperative arouses the believer to what God has done for him so that from his side, too, he not fail to give an answer. All this would set next to each other those elements in the gospel and in reality

which lie in each other, and would thus lead to a new legalism. The imperative is grounded on the reality that has been given with the indicative, appeals to it, and is intended to bring it to full development . . . the imperative not only has the function of bringing the new life denoted by the indicative to manifestation, but is also a constant touchstone for the latter . . . it repeatedly places the new life itself under the condition of the manifestation of life demanded by the imperative. . . . This making of the indicative conditional on the execution of the imperative (compare Gal. 6:7ff.) does not reverse the order and is likewise not intended only to unmask hypocrites . . . In the new obedience the new life must become evident, and without the former the latter cannot exist. The explanation of this relationship lies in the fact that the reality described by the indicative, however much to be appreciated as the gift of God and the new creation, yet exists in the way of faith . . . while, conversely, the execution of the imperative is not in the power of man himself, but is no less a matter of faith. . . . For this reason the connection between the two is so close and indissoluble. They represent two 'sides' of the same matter, which cannot exist separated from each other."

26. Compare Robinson, *Biblical Preaching,* 108: "But pity the man who fails to understand that his sermon should change lives in some specific way."

31

Richard Melick, President
Criswell College
Dallas, Texas

Preaching and Apocalyptic Literature

Preachers either love apocalyptic literature in the Bible or stay away from it. Perhaps this is normal. The language poses difficulties; the medium has no exact counterpart in modern life; and the symbolism seems to have little referent. Because of these difficulties, preachers often either shy away from apocalyptic because they do not understand it, or despair because the subjective element in interpretation arises so easily. Too often, personal attitudes and ideas are substituted for clear exposition.

Some preachers love apocalyptic texts. The literary form opens the door to speculations, and many see little need to do serious exegetical study. The themes of apocalyptic bring obvious joy to the hearts of the oppressed, but they may be preached with the triumphalism of one who possesses what everyone wants and only he has. Sometimes preachers even preach the apocalyptic texts as an ultimate vindication against their personal enemies—those who oppose the work of God.

Nevertheless, apocalyptic passages need proclamation. First, the Bible contains many apocalyptic passages. The whole counsel of God, therefore, includes them. Second, they graphically encapsulated Christianity. The genre captures the spirit of the Judeo-Christian heritage and ethos as well as any form of writing. Third, people need the message. The message of apocalyptic brings hope as it calls us to consider realities that people overlook because of the blinding effects of modern life. People need hope. They need to see a reality beyond their own sphere of understanding. Spirits are lifted in realizing that good will defeat evil, that God will triumph over Satan, and that someday the world will see the reign of the Lord of hosts.

In actuality, few apocalyptic texts occur in Scripture. The various suggested texts may differ according to one's definition of apocalyptic. Assuming, however, that a high degree of symbolism is a necessary ingredient to apocalyptic, the genre occurs in both the Old and New Testament. Old Testament texts include Daniel 2,7,8; Ezekiel 37:1-14; and Zechariah 1—6.[1] Some would add Isaiah 24—27, 56—66, and Joel 2. New Testament passages include Revelation 4—22, Matthew 24—25, Mark 13, Luke 21, 1 Thessalonians 4:13—5:11, and 2 Thessalonians 2.[2]

The biblical preacher cannot avoid preaching apocalyptic. How do we preach it? What do we say about it? How do we communicate its message? What relevance does it have for contemporary persons? These and many other questions demand serious reflection.

Preliminary Considerations

Since there are many approaches to the subject, some orientation is necessary. Conclusions in the following areas directly affect the preaching of apocalyptic.

The Definition of Apocalyptic

Scholars continue to debate the nature of apocalyptic. Apocalyptic literature first appeared in about the fifth century B.C. and continued until about the second century A.D. As a basically Jewish phenomenon, it found its way into Jewish Christian writings as a helpful tool to express Christian hope.

Two helpful avenues of approach define apocalyptic. Using the first approach, many define it by its literary form and characteristics. First, it is cosmic. It has characters and a plot that include both the supernatural and natural. In apocalyptic, the drama moves easily between these two realms. Second, it is dualistic. The drama pits evil against good, and God against Satan. Third, the message is normally eschatological. It points toward the ultimate triumph of God at the end of time. It assumes that in the present turmoil hope arises from realizing what lies in the future.

Fourth, it is delivered in a vision or dream. The form of revelation emphasizes the divine origin of the message. Fifth, apocalyptic is symbolic. Perhaps its most well-known characteristic, this one receives the most popular emphasis. The symbols demand interpretation, since they are usually bizarre, otherworldly creatures or mutated creatures of earth. Sixth, the plot is carefully stylized so that the reader immediately identifies with someone in the drama, and a carefully constructed movement carries them to a victorious end.[3]

Using the second approach, others define apocalyptic by its content. Naturally, there is no apocalyptic without apocalyptic forms, but beyond that, the messages of apocalyptic writings bear a striking similarity. They include a universal battle with intensifying warfare so that even cosmic forces participate in the drama. Apocalyptic culminates in the decisive triumph of God which leaves evil punished and good vindicated. The focus of apocalyptic is the sovereign God who in time comes to the aid of His people, delivering them from a repressive oppression.[4]

Further, the focus of apocalyptic needs clarification. Scholars debate whether the genre emphasizes eschatology (the end), or the heavenly mysteries which God chooses to disclose to people on earth (the present). This means that apocalyptic may take a future perspective (what will be), or it may take a present perspective (what is now). In actuality, both elements appear, and both contain implications for the modern preacher. God will triumph in history someday, but His people also need to see that He rules this present life from His heaven.[5]

Prophecy or Apocalyptic

How does prophecy relate to apocalyptic? Although the two are different, many preachers do not understand their differences. One of two mistakes often occurs. First, some treat apocalyptic like prophecy. They attempt to interpret it as though it predicts the future with the same degree of accuracy and detail that prophecy does. The symbols and bizarre creatures are treated as real, and the interpreters seek to find parallels in contemporary events. The eagerness with which those who approach apocalyptic in this fashion describe and proclaim the parts sometimes causes them to miss the whole picture.

Second, some distinguish too sharply between apocalyptic and prophecy, assuming that apocalyptic has no prophetic overtones. For them, apocalyptic imparts only a present hope in the most general terms. They see few glimpses of future realities. The preacher must avoid both of these extremes. Apocalyptic forms communicate through their own genre, but they speak consistently of ultimate victory.

Vision or Literary Form

A third factor in interpreting apocalyptic is whether or not it is a real vision. Any cursory reading of the material reveals that the spokesperson claimed to receive a vision, which was communicated exactly as it was received. Non-canonical written apocalyptic is normally either anonymous or pseudonymous, so the reader has to judge the integrity of the claim on its own merits.

Others stress the literary genre to such an extent that they invalidate the author's testimony. They argue that the speakers/writers carefully constructed apocalyptic visions, and that what they claim as visions cannot be spontaneous like real visions are. They assume that statements such as "I was caught up in the Spirit" cannot be taken at face value.

This introduces a major tension. Are the authors correct in their statements that their visions came from God through the Spirit, or did the visions really spring from the speaker's own mind? Is the claim to have a vision analogous to the modern speaker saying, "Once upon a time"? In other words, was this an accepted way of introducing what everyone knew was like a fairy tale?

Several factors suggest taking the words at face value. First, one should consider the origins of these literary introductions. Why would a claim to be a vision ever be associated with an apocalyptic vision? The obvious answer is that they came from an original speaker who had a real vision.

Second, the canonical apocalyptic literature identifies the writer/speaker. In most non-canonical apocalyptic writings, the writer was anonymous or used a pseudonym to substantiate the message. Biblical apocalyptic has authority because the readers knew the writer/speaker, and that writer/speaker commanded respect. Daniel, Ezekiel, Joel, and other Old Testament prophets enjoyed such honor. In the New Testament the apocalyptic elements came from Jesus (Gospels), Paul (Thessalonians), and John (Revelation).

Third, the patterns of including the apocalyptic texts suggest that authentic visions occurred. In each of the canonical writings, the apocalyptic sections occur imbedded *within the text*. Many of the non-canonical apocalypses *are the text*. The fact that the biblical apocalypses occur as pieces of the text, and not the entire text, suggests that the material is in some sense illustrative. Apocalyptic sections may constitute the primary message of a text, but they gain their authority from the text as a whole.

Fourth, why did the writers select the symbols they did? The various apocalyptic symbols have a striking similarity in the various writings. Often nations occur as beasts and supernatural beings occur as cosmic figures. The sources of these symbols must be considered.

Futurist or Preterist

Another consideration about apocalyptic is the primary application of the message. Many assume it has a future orientation. For them, the message presents the ultimate triumph of God at the end of time. Some extend this futuristic orientation to the specifics of the text. For them, the text predicts detailed events foreseen by the prophet. The futuristic interpretation describes the culmination of world history and the expectation that right will triumph over wrong. The text describes a time when God's people will reign victorious.

Others conclude that apocalyptic takes a contemporary glance at historical events occurring at the time of writing. They point out that the symbols refer to ancient persons and events. Rather than describing the future, apocalyptic, for them, simply brings hope to the audience of the speaker/writer. The message has relevance to all readers as they extend that message by applying it through first-century symbols to more modern applications. By application, any oppressed people may take heart as they read about the triumph of God over His enemies and theirs.

Preaching Apocalyptic

With these preliminary concerns in mind, some basic suggestions regarding preaching apocalyptic arise.

Enter the World of Apocalyptic

The most important aspect of preaching is to enter the world it describes. Interpreters will find this difficult for several reasons. First, we have no exact parallel to apocalyptic in our world. The medium lasted a brief period of time, about 500 years. Since we do not naturally understand the forms, we may make mistakes interpreting them. Second, the perspectives of our contemporary world draw us away from appreciating apocalyptic. Our world appreciates technology and scientific mediums. On the surface, we have little tolerance for such bizarre, imaginative descriptions. Third, today many trust in economic answers to life rather than spiritual answers. Historically, the oppressed have longed for spiritual satisfaction, but that has changed in the 20th century. Now many people aspire to material blessings, and nations engage in economic as well as military warfare.

More than ever, we need to be called to a more comprehensive outlook. Preachers must enter into a world view different from their natural perspective. This means that something must guide them. The modern world must see that there are spiritual realities which demand consideration. In actuality, they are the ultimate concerns, and civilization will crumble without them.

Apocalyptic calls us to spiritual concerns. The apocalyptic medium establishes its own world. The reader is lifted beyond the routine of everyday existence and is taken to a world revealing God's perspective. Even secular literature takes people to another world in this sense. People often retreat into a world of literature, the arts, and nature. In so doing, they find solace by dreaming of "another time and another place." Many escape the boredom of existence by immersing themselves in science fiction. For example, *Star Wars* devotees often see the themes of life in bigger-than-life scenarios. By immersing themselves in such art forms, people often expand their understanding and sometimes sharpen their commitments to good against evil. From that perspective, they may apply their insights to everyday life.

In the harsh existence of first century oppression, people needed to see a higher reality. As they heard the apocalyptic message, they were able to enter a reality beyond what they saw around them. They could identify with the timeless truth that God will defeat all His (and their) enemies.

The first task for preachers, therefore, is to understand the apocalyptic outlook. Since we do not naturally understand apocalyptic pictures—largely because of the symbolic forms—we must do what we can to enter that world. The following suggestions may help. First, read the apocalyptic section repeatedly at one sitting. The end will help illuminate the beginning. The mature state of the characters helps one understand the development process of these same characters and themes. While immersing oneself in the text, the imagination begins to move toward what is described. The movements and characters take on a visionary reality, and their actions flow naturally from the literary development. In essence, what is described becomes an alternate statement of reality for the reader.

Second, outline the plot. From the beginning, trace the movements so that the pieces blend together into a whole. Outlining the plot after repeated reading enables one to see how the individual movements fit naturally into the whole.

Third, imagine what it would be like to live as one or more of the characters. What are their tensions, their ambitions, their frustrations, and their triumphs? Like an actor reading a script, imagine how the drama could be worked out on a stage.

Two principles emerge here. First, preachers must know what they are communicating. To do so, it will be helpful if they can feel like the characters of the text must have felt. Second, they must find some way to communicate that reality to contemporary persons.

Consider the Impact of the Whole

Having entered into the world of apocalyptic, preachers need to consider the impact of the whole of the drama expressed. Here the "exegetical circle" emerges. In doing an exegesis, the specific texts build an understanding of the whole. The whole in turn illuminates the parts. This may be visualized as an upward and downward flow. From the particulars (the specific texts), the understanding flows upward to build a concept of the whole. From the whole (the entire text), the understanding flows back to put the particulars in perspective. This will keep one from excessive isolationist interpretations which have no connection to the drama. It also enables the specific texts to come alive with meaning.

Remember the Illustrative Value of Apocalyptic

Biblical apocalyptic lies embedded within other biblical texts. For example, in Daniel the apocalyptic sections occur embedded in a narrative text. The apocalyptic dreams support the writer's historical and biographical interests. The story of the Jewish heroes revealed the fact that God had not forgotten His people. If these men could triumph individually over pagan rulers, surely God could cause the people to triumph corporately over oppressive nations.

In Daniel, the Jewish heroes embody the message the book teaches. Similarly, the apocalyptic visions project the symbolism to more universal themes. In this, two complementary patterns emerge. First, God gave the visions to great men who proved their faith in their stand before pagan rulers. The readers accepted the visions because of the authority of the spokesperson through whom they came. Second, the visions coordinated with the book's obvious biographical interests by enlarging the impact of these men. Their lives affirmed God's truth. Similarly, the visions they received demonstrated that God sovereignly controlled the affairs of this world. God's triumph in the lives of these men symbolized His triumph in the world at large.

In the New Testament the primary apocalyptic materials occur in a similar setting. The Book of Revelation has two decidedly different sections. The first four chapters fit a typical epistolary style. Seven letters addressed to seven churches, similar to the Pauline letters and churches. Then, in a striking change of style, John presented his message in apocalyptic terms. The vision enhanced his letters, and at the same time it extended the message to universal audiences. The same Lord who spoke through John in didactic epistolary terms (1—3) spoke through a vision to confirm His message (4—21). Through the apocalyptic message, the churches were motivated to a more sober understanding of their situations. In the midst of difficult circumstances, apocalyptic called them to bear witness. In so doing, they would be faithful to the universal task of the people of God. Thus, apocalyptic materials confirm the message of the other literary forms used with them (biographical/historical and epistolary), and they extend the message to other contexts.

Approach Apocalyptic Like Parable

Hermeneutically, apocalyptic resembles parable.[6] Parables have a twofold function. They illustrate the truth, and they extend the knowledge of the truth by making it understandable to a broader audience.

Apocalyptic resembles parable in at least the following ways. First, parable and apocalyptic illustrate and extend the truth. Second, parables and apocalyptic both contain elements that do not demand interpretation. In the parables, main themes and characters are clear, but secondary elements are not always so clear. Some details simply carry the story. Third, both communicate a main point. Most scholars look for the one main point of parables, and they develop that point. Apocalyptic is similar—no one needs to relate the "shapes of the beasts," for example, to history. On the other hand, the "ten toes" of Daniel are quite significant. The text treats them as such. Fourth, apocalyptic and parable contain many minor points as well. Most parables contain several points the author intended to make.[7] Similarly, in apocalyptic materials, many supporting points correspond to reality. They should be interpreted for what they are: supporting points. Fifth, parables and apocalyptic create a world of their own. The story form of parables draws the readers into the world of the parable. The interpreter must appreciate the details of the historical/social setting in which parables occur. Apocalyptic should be approached by the interpreter in the same manner.

One more parallel must be made. In addition to parable, the closest genre to apocalyptic is prophecy. Prophecy, in looking beyond the present situation, predicts the future, is concerned with eschatology, and has relevance to the present by reminding the hearers of their destiny. This means that one would expect the events of apocalyptic to correspond to the overview of prophetic passages.

Interpret Biblically

Although many examples of apocalyptic occur in non-canonical literature, the primary source for interpreting canonical apocalyptic is the Bible. Two reasons suggest this. First, the Bible contains ample apocalyptic material to provide a biblically based context. God in His providence preserved the apocalyptic materials we have because they uniquely communicate His message. The church recognized that and included these books, and not others, in their canons. Second, the writers of Scripture gave themselves to the study of the Bible, and the various portions of Scripture saturated their thoughts.

For example, the Book of Revelation is filled with Old Testament imagery.[8] This principle means that the interpreter must consider the Bible as the primary resource for understanding, rather than historical events. Many interpreters look to a correlation between historical events and specific biblical interpretations to substantiate the meaning. Many have been overly specific in identifying persons and movements behind the symbols of apocalyptic. They quickly identify contemporary events as specific predicted fulfillments. However, it is only in retrospect that the interpreter sees such clear correlations. For example Daniel's vision of the four kingdoms refers to world kingdoms, but the specific identification of these kingdoms was not revealed until after their fulfillment. The interpreter, therefore, must be careful not to draw parallels to historical events too quickly.

This means that the clear biblical texts will illuminate what is illustrative. Correctly, therefore, preachers should construct a scheme of history from other biblical texts. Further, they should expect that the illustrative passages, such as apocalyptic, would present these same truths in alternative literary forms. Following this principle, an interpreter should affirm the major portions of apocalyptic which correspond to other didactic passages. Their interpretation seems evident. On the other hand, they should avoid specific interpretations of what is unique to apocalyptic, since, like parables, they are open to subjectivity or ego-expressive interpretations.

For example, the Bible clearly teaches a basic structure of human history. Among other texts, Daniel, Matthew, and 2 Thessalonians speak to this concern. They reveal a coming deterioration of morality, an increase in irreligious conduct, and an ecological devastation. Further, they describe the end of history as a climactic tension between Christ and the Antichrist. From texts other than apocalyptic texts, therefore, interpreters may construct a basic understanding of the course of events. The apocalyptic texts also present this historical scheme; however, they do not demand precise interpretations of details which support these movements. Preachers should preach their understanding in proportion to the full development of the themes in the whole of Scripture.

Be Doxological

Apocalyptic is doxological. The foundation and goal of all of the imagery and movements is the glory of God. In apocalyptic visions, God controls. Although Satan and his envoys exercise intermediate control, even their actions result ultimately in God's glory. God overrules them. The apocalyptic windows into heavenly scenes reinforce this perspective. Heaven is the place of God's throne, and there He alone is worshiped.

Surely a major point of preaching apocalyptic is the worship of Christ. He is to be worshiped on earth as He is in heaven. He orchestrates all events and persons so that in the end they all recognize His majesty. No message on apocalyptic is complete without that perspective.

The doxological perspective has several implications for preachers. First, God is the center of the drama. Every message must be related to divine activity in the world. Second, preachers cannot preach apocalyptic with a defeatist attitude. The people of God will triumph, and that message must be communicated. Third, preachers cannot preach apocalyptic with a sense of triumphalism. Unbelievers will be punished and all who oppose God with receive their just rewards. Nevertheless, servants of God cannot rejoice in the destruction of their friends and countrymen. Their punishment is the necessary outcome of the triumph of God's justice. As always, preachers should preach these themes with compassion and heartfelt concern for those who reject God.

Be Christological

Canonical apocalyptic focuses the vision on Jesus Christ. In this, all apocalyptic has a theocentric focus. The vision revolves around God's reign. In biblical apocalyptic, however, God's work occurs in and through Jesus Christ. Consistent with the Epistles, Christ governs and administers the concerns of the Godhead. The doxological element of biblical apocalyptic, therefore, is really Christological. Everything focuses on Jesus. In the Book of Revelation, the climax is the Second Coming of Christ. Anticipating that, every portion of the book provides glimpses of the glory of Jesus and the honor due Him.

This means that preachers must preach Christ. Each message must be Christological or it does not conform to the message of the Book. In sum, if apocalyptic does not produce a great appreciation and worship of Jesus Christ, preachers have not understood it correctly and do not proclaim it biblically. The Christian hope is more focused than the general truth that right triumphs over wrong, or that God triumphs over Satan. The Christian hope is the reign of Jesus Christ which brings the kingdom of God.

Proclaim the Text

Preaching is proclamation. The preacher must guard against assuming that the explanation of the text or even a correlation of the texts with history is proclamation. Explanation forms the foundation for the message. It is the heart of the sermon, and without it the message suffers from pure emotionalism. Further, preachers must attempt to correlate the text with contemporary life. Without that, Scripture has no relevance. However, correlation is not the primary task of preaching. Preachers must proclaim the message so graphically described by apocalyptic. All good preaching calls the hearers to submit to God's Word. Further, it compels hearers to get personally involved in the world view of apocalyptic. Each person responds by playing a role in the drama of history, thereby participating in the ultimate triumph of God. If preachers cannot proclaim the text relevantly, they fail in their calling.

Affirm the Theology

Apocalyptic graphically presents theology. Preachers must affirm that theology. Their minds must be submissive to both its message and the way the text presents it. Authentic preaching begins in the hearts and attitudes of preachers. They must live the message in their daily lives. They must preach with the kind of integrity that focuses the message, the preacher's life, and the activities of the congregation.

Interpret the Symbolism

Apocalyptic symbols are particularly difficult to interpret. Many want to see them literally, while others see no reference to reality. The crucial question is: What did the author intend?

Interpreters should isolate the symbols that have a significant place in the portion of the vision they are studying. They must know which symbols are the significant ones.

Gordon Fee recommends the following steps in interpreting symbols. First, one must be sensitive to the rich background of apocalyptic ideas. Second, note the different kinds of symbols. Some are permanent; some change. Some are specific; some are general. Third, when the writer interprets the symbols, his interpretation becomes the normative starting point for interpretation. Fourth, the vision as a whole must be the guide, not the specifics.[9]

The symbols remain a constant problem to the interpreters, yet the message is carried largely by the symbols. As a byproduct of immersing oneself in the drama of the whole, a sense of the nature of symbols will emerge. With some reading in good, exegetical commentaries, interpreters may gain a knowledge of the likely historical reference points of the symbols. However, the deeper meaning must be ascertained from a personal study.[10]

Conclusion

Some years ago a group of theology students were playing basketball in a high school gymnasium. They played beyond the normal hours the janitor worked, but he waited patiently for them to finish. Being a devout Christian, he quietly read the Bible. When they finished and came to thank him for his patience, they noticed he was reading the Book of Revelation. One asked jeeringly, "Do you understand what you're reading?" They knew the complexities of the book, and he shocked them with his answer. "Yes, it's clear. Jesus is going to win!"

Apocalyptic must be preached. It is a part of Scripture, graphically presenting the message of the Bible. While excesses must be avoided, the parallels of the text with clear Scriptures reveal that apocalyptic has much to say to any age. It calls us to consider a world other than, yet simultaneous, with ours. It is the real world. It is the world of our destiny. Apocalyptic reminds us that no matter what happens in time, some day Jesus is going to win. People of every age need to hear that word.

Notes

1. Ezekiel 40—48 seems apocalyptic, but (1) there is no symbolism, and (2) there are numerous allusions to literal phenomena in Israel.

2. Noncanonical apocalyptic includes Egyptian, Akkadian, Greek, Latin, and extrabiblical Jewish apocrypha and pseudepigrapha.

3. Most definitions are based on the form. For a good survey of definitions, see Robert M. Kuykendall, "The Literary Genre of the Book of Revelation: A Study of the History of Apocalyptic Research and Its Relationship to John's Apocalypse" (Ph.D. dissertation, Southwestern Baptist Theological Seminary, 1986). See also John J. Collins, *The Apocalyptic Imagination: An Introduction to the Jewish Matrix of Christianity* (New York: The Crossroad Publishing Co., 1984).

4. Many add this dimension to the definition. See, for example, Philip Vielhauer, "Apocalypses and Related Subjects: Introduction," vol. 2 in *New Testament Apocrypha*, eds., Edgar Hennecke and Wilhelm Schneimelcher (Philadelphia: Westminster Press, 1965). Also, George E. Ladd, "Apocalyptic Writings," *The International Standard Bible Encyclopedia* (Grand Rapids: Wm. B. Eerdmans, 1977).

5. These issues are discussed thoroughly in the 1979 edition of *Semeia*, "Apocalypse: The Morphology of a Genre," ed. John J. Collins. Also, The International Colloquium of Apocalypticism in Uppsala, Sweden, in 1979, published by David Hellholm, ed. *Apocalypticism in the Mediterranean World and the Near East* (Tubingen: J. C. B. Mohr, 1983).

6. This very helpful suggestion was made by Dr. William Larkin of Columbia Theological Seminary in Columbia, South Carolina. I have had many fruitful hours developing his suggestion.

7. For a good recent discussion of multiple point parables, see Craig Blomberg, *Interpreting the Parables* (Downers Grove: InterVarsity Press, 1990).

8. Most scholars conclude this, even though it is recognized that no specific Old Testament passage is quoted.

9. Gordon D. Fee and Douglas Stuart, *How to Read the Bible For All Its Worth: A Guide to Understanding the Bible* (Grand Rapids: Academie Books, 1982).

10. Some helpful material on symbolism includes: Adela Yarbo Collins, "Read the Book of Revelation in the Twentieth Century," *Interpretation* (July, 1986); The entire volume is very helpful. W. Randolph Tate, *Biblical Interpretation: An Integrated Approach*, 139, presents a simple chart of some of the possible Old Testament sources; See also Michael Lee Ruffin, "Symbolism in Zechariah: A Study in Functional Unity" (Ph.D. dissertation, The Southern Baptist Theological Seminary, 1986); Paul Porter, *Metaphors and Monsters: A Literary-Critical Study of Daniel 7—8* (Lund, Sweden: C. W. K. Gleerup, 1983); G. B. Caird, *The Language and Imagery of the Bible* (Philadelphia: Westminster Press, 1980); and Austin Farrer, *A Rebirth of Images: The Meaning of St. John's Apocalypse* (Glasgow: University Press of Glasgow, 1949).

Part V
Presenting the Sermon

Henry Ward Beecher (1813-1887)
"America's National Chaplain"

Phillips Brooks, himself considered one of the premier preachers in the history of the church, once described Henry Ward Beecher as "the greatest preacher of America and of our century" and later as "the greatest preacher Protestantism has ever produced."

Born into the remarkable family of revivalist Lyman Beecher, Henry grew up in an atmosphere dominated by ecclesiastical and theological controversy. In his own ministry, Beecher would reject his father's Calvinism, substituting a faith that stressed the love of God and preaching sermons that appealed to the emotions of his listeners.

In 1847 he accepted a call to the newly–founded Plymouth Church in Brooklyn, a growing suburb of New York City. Within a decade, the church had grown to more than 1,500 members, making it the largest in the city (and for a time, the nation's largest church). So many visitors sought to attend services that Beecher encouraged members not to return Sunday evening to leave room for others. His preaching was clear, heavily illustrated, and spontaneous; transcriptions of his sermons often bore little relation to the notes he carried into the pulpit!

His sermons reflected much of the romantic spirit of the Victorian era. Beecher became best known for taking on the social issues of his day in his sermons—from slavery to women's suffrage. He was known nationally for his eloquent opposition to slavery. His sermons were widely reproduced and distributed throughout the nation making Beecher something of a "national chaplain" in the mid-19th century.

Henry Ward Beecher came to see ethics, not theology, as the heart of Christianity, and he used the pulpit as a tool to change lives.

32

Joel Gregory, Pastor
First Baptist Church
Dallas, Texas

The Voice in Preaching

A sermon is not a sermon until it is a delivered or preached sermon. Sermons are not intended to be compositions for reading; rather, they are declarations in which the communicator, the thing being communicated, and the recipients of the communication are involved in an unusual triadic relationship.

Preaching is a word event. The language of preaching ought to be different from other kinds of language. It is not merely a cognitive, cerebral, informing task; it creates a speech event. After that speech event, those hearing pulpit discourse ought not to be the same. When one stands at the altar and speaks the vows, "I take you to be my wedded wife," that is effective language. When those words are spoken, it affects the human situation forever thereafter. When you stand in a courtroom with hand upraised to say that you are about to tell the truth, those words are charged with life and death, guilt and innocence. Pulpit speech partakes of that. It is effective language—language like that of a marriage service, like an oath in a court of law. Those words cause something to happen. On paper a sermon is a creation; on Sunday morning it ought to be a resurrection.

Delivery does matter. We turn our attention here to the verbal aspect of preaching.

Verbal Delivery

Cultivation of the speaking voice for the minister is well addressed in Al Fasol's little handbook, *A Guide to Self Improvement in Sermon Delivery.*[1] He discusses exercises for diaphragmatic breathing—the kind of deep breathing that enables you to originate speech not with a raspy, thorasic-type of quality but the kind of breathing that enables you to maintain the projection (or the throwing forward) of pulpit speech in the place where you are preaching.

Even with modern sound reinforcement, using lavalier microphones or pulpit microphones, you still need to master projection, or throwing forward the voice as you speak. What are some factors in oral delivery in the pulpit to which we must attend?

Variety of Pace and Pitch

One element is using variety in pace and variety in pitch. Have you counted the words per minute in your sermon in sections? The normal rate for preaching discourse is 125-190 words per minute. Theoreticians say that at 200 words per minute—into the rate of an auctioneer—individuals lose comprehension; that is they can no longer follow the significance of delivered speech. So the normal range ought to be 125-195 words per minutes. George W. Truett, late pastor of the First Baptist Church in Dallas from 1898 until 1944, was considered to be one of the masters of pulpit speech and delivery. At Southwestern Seminary, graduate students analyzed some of his sermons in terms of the variation of rate in the sermons. They found that at the beginning of his sermons he used an extremely slow rate of about 80 words per minute—a very deliberate, paced, commanding delivery. As he moved into the heart of the message, he was usually 140-180 words per minute, but they counted sections of his sermons where he was speaking in passages of oratory at 240 words per minute—actually surpassing comprehension, sweeping over people with emotion, and passion. All of that in the same message. Not only baseball pitchers but preachers as well need deliberate changes in pace. There are some obvious places where that needs to happen.

The exposition of the Word of God—that is, the cognitive explanation of the text—deserves a slower pace. Through the illustrative story and the narrative anecdote there is a natural quickening of pace. It is my opinion that when you come to the application function of preaching—when you are making an assault on the will of people to change the parliament of their personality—that needs to be the fastest pace. It is as if you are firing shots, trying to lay siege to their will—explaining at a slow rate, illustrating at a mid rate, seeking to change behavior at a fast rate.

The deadliest combination of pulpit speech is no variation in rate of delivery and no variation in pitch—up or down—reaching the higher ranges and the lower ranges of your pitch.

First, you will need to find your normal pitch for sermon delivery. Go to a piano (according to Dr. Fasol) and find the lowest comfortable voice in which you can speak; then, match that pitch to a key on the piano. For you who are tone deaf, get a musician to help you. Those who study such things as pitch and inflection say one-third of an octave above that identified note ought to be the normal pitch for sermon delivery. Working down and working up, one-third of an octave above the lowest comfortable speech, without straining the vocal apparatus is the vocal range where pitch is most comfortable for both preacher and congregation. If you have not found that range, you might check it and compare it against your normal pitch of delivery.

In listening to delivered sermons in seminary preaching labs, I found that in nervousness and agitation pitch rides up as the sermon continues. By the end of the sermon, rather than having a controlled, circumflexed kind of speech pattern that is appealing and filled with pathos, many preachers are at the highest part of their vocal register and are raspy, hoarse, and breathless at the very time when the message ought to be under control and calling decision and verdict from the congregation.

Patterns of Ministerial Speech

I want to address for a moment patterns of ministerial speech. Whether we like it or not we are in a cybernetically competitive environment. We who are preaching are not only being compared with the likes of Lloyd Ogilvie and Chuck Swindoll ubiquitously present on radio, but also with network news commentators, Tom Brokaw and others, who have established the kind of consensus of American public conversational speech. Because of that, our speech patters are under the evaluation of congregations as never before.

I come from a part of the country where there was an established kind of holy twang; that is, the unction of God was on a message because of a very specific kind of speech pattern. Preachers were not preaching with anointing unction, or even real biblical authority, unless that speech pattern was implied. That approach to the use of the voice is lethal to preaching. For example, there is the Beethoven's Fifth Symphony kind of approach. "Dearly beloved we have gathered *here,* to open the word of *God*"—at the end of every sentence there is dropping off of pitch and a slowing of pace. If you want to know how that affects people in contemporary communication you might want to run an experiment that I ran one time. I drove up to a McDonald's to those speaker phones where you order hamburgers remotely, and I employed that kind of stylized pulpit pattern. "I would like a Big *Mac* and an order of *fries.*" The girl there opened the window and looked around. I was closely examined when I came up to the pay window. (Avoid a preacher's tone, a ministerial melody that raises inflections or lowers them at the end of sentences.) No one communicates that way in the real world.

C. H. Spurgeon's sermons to us today read as if they were victorian compositions, but in reality Spurgeon spoke the common language of his day. He spoke the popular language of the southern section of London. People crowded in to hear him, not because he sounded different from street language but because he sounded unlike any other preacher in London. There were other pulpits full of purple passages of rhetoric. Henry Perry Lidden preached himself hoarse in St. Paul's Cathedral trying to project his voice and literally fainting back out of the pulpit with the task. However, Spurgeon spoke the *koine* of the day and avoided unusual patterns of pulpit speech.

Expressiveness in Delivery

Added to that is the matter of expressiveness. People should sense that the gospel matters to us as we preach, and I do not mean the assumed expressiveness of a preacher who has had one drama course too many. I mean the expressiveness that comes from a genuine engagement with the text until you stand and say the sermon with more pathos than that with which you would read a telephone book or the stock quotations. People sense that the subject matters to you. Remember the famous quote that Benjamin Franklin, the sometimes deist, made concerning the preaching of Whitefield. He said he went to hear him, not because he believed what Whitefield preached; but, when he heard Whitefield, he sensed that Whitefield believed it. When people come to hear us preach, raw pagans or secularists, they may not believe what we say but they ought to leave with the sense that the person in the pulpit believes the message being preached.

This expressiveness means there should be no lifeless or lackluster sermons. There is something questionable about a minister who is excited about sports but not excited about the gospel. Whose fault is it if there is no pathos at all in our preaching? It is not the fault of the gospel. The gospel is an exciting presentation of good news. It is not the fault of the congregation—they like some excitement at church! If there is any blame for our preaching lacking excitement, it rests within us. It may be because we are too self-conscious, not wanting to be vulnerable in the pulpit, standing there as the pillar and the ground of truth, objectified so that there is not much difference between us and one of those columns. We are there as the objective embodiment of truth, or, worse still, we ourselves have not been transformed by the very message that we proclaim. The gospel is an exciting word and by the pace, the pitch, and the projection of our delivery we should communicate that kind of excitement.

Diction in Delivery

One other minor matter that I will touch on—because I've heard it so often evaluating preaching in seminary laboratories—has to do with diction. Careful attention should be paid to the articulation of words. The omission of syllables or letters—saying "preachin'" instead of "preaching"—or the substitution of vowels should be avoided. I had been preaching in the South Pacific and I was speaking of the necessity of sending missionaries to the "Euthanasia." They heard me saying one thing when I was saying quite another thing about taking the gospel to "Youth in Asia." Good delivery does matter. It matters non-verbally and it matters verbally.

Preaching involves logos, ethos, pathos, the Word, the context, the passion. We need to understand that there is nothing artificial or contrived in any of those that guarantees power in preaching. There is no system of outlining, no method of structuring sermons that has implicit in it the guarantee that there will be power in the moment of preaching. Such power, in my observation, comes when the world of the then and the world of the now come together in the pulpit. The biblical revelation and the contemporary culture are brought together, and like negative and positive charges they create lightning. When those two come together, preaching happens.

Note

1. Al Fasol, *A Guide to Self-Improvement in Sermon Delivery* (Grand Rapids: Baker, 1983).

33

Roy DeBrand
Professor of Preaching
Southeastern Baptist Theological Seminary
Wake Forest, North Carolina

The Visual in Preaching

"I see what you're saying," is a common expression. People really do not "see" what we are saying, do they? They "hear" what we are saying. Or do they? "See" in this sense means to understand, to comprehend intellectually, to communicate. We preachers surely want that. There is more to effective communication than just hearing; people "seeing" what we say—the visual in preaching—is vitally important to communication.

Along with the spiritual, oral, emotional, and rhetorical elements in sermon delivery, visual factors play a major role in how well we communicate God's Word to our hearers. Whether we are seasoned veterans of pulpit prowess or raw recruits to this awesome task, there are certain visual aspects of preaching we would all do well to bear in mind. How do we enable our listeners to "see" what we say?

Initial Impression

The first visual impression preachers make on a congregation is general appearance, including how we dress, the way we sit, how we stand when it is time to preach, walking to the pulpit, and our posture in the pulpit. Believe it or not, people notice how we do all these things (especially pulpit committees, who notice everything).

Clothing/General Appearance

Congregations notice how preachers dress. While clothing is more a factor in some congregations than others, people do notice it, so we should pay careful attention to it, too. Clothing should be neat, clean, well-fitting, coordinated, and appropriate to the audience and occasion. This means we would not wear an expensive suit, silk tie, and alligator shoes in a church where everybody else is dressed in work clothes, nor would we show up in blue jeans at an upscale, affluent church.

In an important article entitled "How to Dress for the Pulpit," Bill Bruster points out that clothing has been important through the ages, and fashion consciousness is heightened in our generation. He cautions against wearing clothing that calls attention to itself. Advising that our manner of dress can enhance our role in the pulpit, Bruster explains that darker colors project authority while lighter colors exude warmth, intimacy, and personableness—a more supportive image. He also advises on how clothing can in some instances enhance certain physical characteristics while covering others, how to accessorize for variety and appeal, and he even deals with healthy diet and hair/beard care. The article concludes with this true story.

> A few years ago a great church in a capital city invited a man to preach "in view of a call." He preached a trial sermon in a white coat, black slacks, and white shoes. The church did not call him as pastor. One long-time member told me, "No one said anything about his sermon. They couldn't hear it for looking at him. People voted against his appearance." Like it or not—many vote on our appearance every week.[1]

It may not always be fair, but it is true: people notice how we dress, so how we dress is important. We do not want to do anything to hinder the gospel.

Sitting/Standing

Folks also notice how we sit and stand before we ever approach the pulpit. Most traditional pulpit furniture is extremely uncomfortable. Nevertheless, we should sit up straight in it, never slouching or fidgeting around. If we cross our legs, which in my opinion should be done sparingly, it might be better to cross them in X fashion rather than in figure-four fashion.[2] If not robed, men need to keep their socks pulled up and women need to keep dresses down over their knees. When we stand for prayers or to sing, stand up straight, neither stiffly nor slouchingly, but naturally and comfortably. We are being watched. Modesty and decorum must be kept in mind at all times.

Walking/Posture

People also observe the pace at which we walk, the posture by which we carry ourselves, even the heaviness or lightness of our step. These factors all communicate with those who "see" what we say. Walking too fast may belie either a lack of self-confidence, or over-confidence. On the other hand, dragging oneself to the pulpit may indicate unpreparedness, nervousness, or illness on our part. Generally speaking, it is best to stand up straight, walk at a comfortable, normal pace, and stand naturally and comfortably behind the pulpit.

At this point you might be asking yourself: "How can I sit, walk, and stand naturally when I am so nervous?" Well, sometimes you can't. You will be nervous and show it. At other times, even when the old nerves jingle you all the way down to your toes, you can look calm on the outside by the way you think about yourself and your message. If you have prepared well—the best you could with the time you had—if you are confident your message came from God, and if you are comfortable with the biblical relatedness between your text and sermon, then you will have a better chance at looking cool, calm, and collected than if any of these aspects are weak or missing. So think to yourself: "Yes, I am scared. But I am also prepared. These folks need to hear this sermon. I am going to do the best I can to deliver it. God will help me. I know it is a biblically-based message. It is God's word to them today. I can and must do this." With this assuring attitude, you can then think about the message from God and not about what you are going to say, how you will say it, how you look, or what they will think or say about it when you are through.

Take one or two deep breaths just before you get up to preach. Be sure to take just one or two, no more, and make sure they are deep, not shallow, so you will not hyperventilate. Then relax your entire body for an instant, like a baseball player might do just before stepping into the batter's box. Then walk confidently (not cockily) to the pulpit, stand erect with shoulders, arms, and legs in comfortable positions, and speak naturally.

There will undoubtedly be times in certain sermons when, for particular reasons, we might not want to do the obvious, "normal" thing. I remember seeing Carlyle Marney preach one time. He strode confidently to the pulpit, but instead of standing up straight, he leaned over on one elbow and began slowly, with a low voice, looking intimately at the audience: "Hark, hark, the dogs do bark, the beggars are coming to town, some in rags and some in tags, and some in velvet gowns."[3] He had us! We were captivated by his relaxed posture, as much as by the tenor of his sonorous voice, as much as by the words he spoke. It was quite a visual/verbal feast. That is good preaching! When we have good reasons to, we might slouch on an elbow, lean in close to the microphone, or do whatever we need to do to accomplish our goal. Be advised that these times are the exceptions, and unless we have good reason not to, we need to stand up and speak naturally and comfortably.

How We Look While Preaching

The most important visual aspect of preaching is how we look when we are engaged in the actual event of delivering a sermon. People relate to the way we look and move when we preach, so how we look and move are important. We give visual signals anytime, anywhere we preach. Preaching is at one and the same time an art and a craft, a devotion and a discipline, an exercise in spirituality and scholarship, an exciting and exhausting task. Creative visual movement in the pulpit greatly enhances communication, or it detracts from communication. The difference is how we move when we preach. Let us consider how we use our hands, our face, and our eyes when we preach.

Gesturing

A gesture is any movement of the head, body, or limbs to emphasize something we are saying.[4] Some gestures are natural and spontaneous, while others are planned. Even planned gestures should be so natural and fitting to what we are saying that they appear to be unplanned. When we gesture effectively, communication is greatly benefitted.

Gesturing means using our hands effectively. This is hard to do. Some preachers wave their hands without purpose, or move one hand or both in some habitual way, like a hacking or chopping motion. This is called "restless gesturing" and it can detract from, rather than ennoble, communication. Others hang onto the pulpit until their knuckles turn white, or hold onto their Bible while preaching, or put their hands into their pockets. This effectively robs those who do so of the possibility of using their hands for creative gesturing. I would advise against doing these things. Rather, we should seek creative uses for our hands, gestures that will add visual meaning to the words we speak.

Areas for Gestures

Gestures can indicate people, places, things, or ideas. If we think of them in spacial terms we might better be able to visualize which gestures might enliven which concepts as we communicate. Look with me at two horizontal planes for gesturing, then at three vertical planes we might use.

Horizontal Planes—Think of two horizontal areas for gesturing—center horizontal, and off to either side.

First, if we are making appeals, emphasizing or applying some truth directly to our congregation, or challenging people directly, then we will want to gesture in the area immediately in front of us, the center horizontal area. When we use our hands right out in front of us, then we are indicating people and ideas directly.

If we want to indicate people and ideas indirectly, then we will want to make our gestures off to the left or right side on a horizontal plane, rather than right in front of us. If we are preaching about dividing sheep from goats then we probably do not want to move our hands toward the congregation, but off to one side or another. The same would be true about gesturing anything negative or condemnatory, or even things off at a distance like scenery. Anytime we want to indicate indirectness, it is best to use the side horizontal planes.

Vertical Planes—Consider three vertical planes for gesturing. First, from the shoulders upward, the upper vertical area, might denote lofty ideas, people, places, and things. Use this upper area to communicate about God, heaven, prayer, goodness, the Christian life, and high ideals/morality. Next, the middle area, from the shoulders to the hips, could be used to indicate people, especially children. We could also think of this space as the plane in which to make direct appeals and applications to the congregation. Third, we may use the lower vertical region, from the hips down, to gesture about baser ideas—sin, Satan, evil, lower standards of living, and low morality.

Types of Gestures

When we are preparing our sermons for delivery we need to bear in mind not only areas for gesturing but three general types of gestures we might employ to help people picture what we are saying.

Partial/Descriptive Gestures—First, there is the partial or descriptive gesture, which gives a hint of the idea with which we are dealing. H. C. Brown described one effective sermon in which he saw this done.

> I saw a speaker on one occasion describe in imaginative terms how Adam hid from God in the Garden. Speaking for God, the speaker said, "Perhaps Adam is behind that bush!" and then used his hand as if to push the bush back. Next he said, "Perhaps Adam is up this tree!" and then used both hands as if to part the branches of the tree up over the head. It was a dramatic use of the partial gesture.[5]

How well I remember my first sermon preached before Dr. Brown, my beloved professor, in seminary. I preached about Eutychus, the young man who fell out of a lofted window while Paul preached long into the night (Acts 20). As I said, "Eutychus fell from the third story to the ground," I waved my hands one over the other in the manner of a "safe" signal by a baseball umpire. Later, during the critique, Dr. Brown asked me why I did not raise one hand above my head slightly when talking about the third story, then lower it suddenly to show Eutychus falling while I was telling about the fall. My only answer was that I had not thought about it. He advised me to think about it next time. Dr. Brown was right. Thinking about it makes all the difference. We need to think about how to gesture in ways and areas that picture what we are saying. Partial gestures effectively describe falling, rising, speed, and a multitude of ideas with the flick of a hand or nod of the head.

Descriptive Gestures—Descriptive gestures show shape or size. Billy Graham uses this one when speaking of the cross of Christ while stretching out his arms as if on a cross. We may talk about catching a nice-sized bass and people will not know what size we actually mean, or we may hold our hands 12-15 inches apart and then they will know. Descriptive gestures help people see what we are saying.

Emphatic Gestures—The third type of gesture is the emphatic and may take one of several forms. Pointing with our index finger will show specificity, exactly who, what, or where. A closed fist illustrates anger, power, or strength. When we gesture with our palms down we indicate rejection or negativity. Palms up accentuates the positive—acceptance, appeal, invitation, affirmation, and similar qualities. Parallel palms with either one or both hands demonstrates cutting something off, the end; it is called the "wood-chopping" gesture. Putting our hands flat toward the audience symbolizes holding them off at a distance, rejection, while open arms indicates the exact opposite. There are many varied and creative ways to use emphatic gestures, as well as partial and descriptive ones. These are intended to be suggestive, not exhaustive.

Ideally, the way we move and use our hands while preaching should be both planned and spontaneous. We need to visualize our sermon contents in terms of gestures, both in areas and types. Avoid being mechanical when gesturing. Mental planning is the key to effectiveness. Practice gestures as the sermon is rehearsed orally. Decide the best place in the sermon for certain gestures, the best way to do them, and the best time for them. Keep restless movement to a minimum. Communication can be greatly affected by the way we use our hands, head, and body while preaching. Make meaningful, creative, communication-enhancing movement in the pulpit.

Facial Expressions

A few months after I had assumed the pastorate of one of the churches I served, a church member who had become a friend asked me if she could tell me something that had been bothering her. I assured her she could. She told me that she did not vote for me to become the pastor of that church when I preached in view of a call. Then she told me why. She said: "You scared me to death when you preached. You looked so stern and angry, and I didn't want such a person as my pastor. But, after you were called and got here and I got to know you, I realized I was mistaken about you. You aren't like you seemed to be the first time you preached here."

In trying to analyze what gave this sister the impression I was stern and angry, when I was not and am not, I figured out it was my facial expression caused by my extreme nervousness in that service. Preaching in view of a call is a terrible experience through which to put preachers. So much rides on the results of one sermon that it is an extremely nerve-racking experience. My fright exhibited itself through my face. I looked angry.

We must learn to let our facial expressions mirror our words. We generally want to have a pleasant expression on our face when we are in front of people; not silly or inane, just pleasant. Then, as we speak, we need to reflect what we are saying by our facial expressions. We will avoid looking stern and angry unless we are. When addressing happy subjects we should inform our face about it and look happy. On the other hand, we do not want to be smiling when addressing sad or serious subjects. Avoid at all costs the "frozen face," or wooden expression. Saying, "I'm so happy in Jesus," while displaying a dead-pan facial expression does not lend itself to effective communication.

Our faces are great tools for communicating. We should think about how our faces look as we prepare and deliver our sermons. The keys to effective facial expression are naturalness and variety. We need to get into the habit of letting our faces reflect our words in all conversations. We develop this habit by being conscious of the need for it, then doing it consciously. Thinking about it is the way to improve. Practice also helps.

Eye Contact

Where do you look when you preach? Directly at your listeners? Just above their heads? Just below their shoulders? At a fixed point in the back or along the sides of the room? Some preachers look anywhere except directly at the people to whom they preach. My personal feeling about this is it robs preachers of one of their most natural and important visual tools—eye contact. To look people directly in the eye when we preach is to say: "I care about you."

Moreover, we need to look at people in all parts of the room in which we are speaking. This shows interest, concern, and individualized attention. Sometimes I will be aware of someone in the congregation who is particularly "tuned in" to what I am saying. Direct eye contact with this listener, and with similar listeners around the sanctuary, will boost the confidence of the one speaking, and people immediately around the "key listener" will think we are looking at them also. If we use this method, however, we should not focus on anyone until that person begins to get uncomfortable. Keep the eyes moving.

To have good eye contact we need to be relatively free from our notes. It is okay to preach with notes, manuscript, sermon brief, or whatever written form feels comfortable to us individually. Yet we must bear in mind that people do not want to be read a sermon; they want to be spoken to through a sermon.

One good way modern technology enables us to do some self-evaluation in the area of gestures, facial expressions, and eye contact is by a videotape review. Periodically have someone videotape you preaching. As you look at the tape, note your movement in each area discussed. Then rewind the tape and look at it again, this time on "fast forward." This really shows us how we move while preaching, especially if we have some habitual gesture or movement, such as flailing the air or rocking from side to side. It also shows us how we look when we preach (facial expression), where we look, and how much we look away from notes (eye contact). It is a helpful exercise that can assist us in improving our visual impact in preaching.

Other Visual Factors

While it is important to review the traditional aspects of the visual element of preaching, it is equally important to think about some new aspects of visual impact, such as multimedia enhancement of sermons, using objects as reinforcement, and pulpit design.

Multimedia Enhancement

Several popular preachers today use overhead projectors while preaching, with great effect. On them they will write key words to be explained, definitions of those words, key ideas or subjects in the sermon, major points they want to communicate, or the entire outline of the message. Often they will use prepared cels with Scripture texts, illustrations depicting what they are trying to get across, or words to hymns or poetry. Other preachers use slides, projected as they speak, depicting the subject they are addressing or art related to it. In a few of our larger churches an image of the pulpit area is projected onto screens conveniently located around the sanctuary, or in other rooms where overflow crowds can be accommodated. This can be done easily and fairly inexpensively by way of closed-circuit television. Why not try using contemporary technology to advance the age-old gospel message? Such visual assistance could be very effective when well done.[6]

Using Objects

Often we explain, illustrate, or apply truth in a sermon by talking about some object, any object which can be used to get the point across. Instead of merely talking about it, why not actually take the object with you and show it while referring to it? Some do this regularly in children's sermons. It need not be limited to children's sermons, however. Objects can be a strong reinforcement to truth in any sermon. They are powerful visual aids for preaching.[7]

Pulpit Design

One final aspect of the visual in preaching I would like to mention is pulpit design. Many of our traditional pulpits hide the preachers behind them, thus hampering communication as much as helping it. Perhaps the time has come for some communication-enhancing innovation in pulpit design. I notice that some of the preachers on TV use clear lucite-type pulpits, so audiences can see the preacher—feet, legs, and all. While these may not be in keeping with the decor in many of our sanctuaries, perhaps we could come up with designs to fit our particular decor that would accomplish the same purpose. A pulpit which does not hide the preacher behind it would be desirable. A semi-circle note-rest type, of sufficient width to hold a Bible and sermon notes, but on thin posts without bulky furniture below would work well.

We also need to get the microphones out of our faces. There are new types which do not have to be right up in our faces—and do not cast shadows over our notes—which may be worth checking into. Finally, we must be sure to have proper lighting on the pulpit so we can be seen. A sermon is no good if it is not heard, but it is even better when it is both seen and heard!

Conclusion

The next time we preach, and every time we preach, people should be able to say, "I see what you are saying." We must do everything within our power to assure that they do. This includes being aware that people watch everything we do when we preach, from the moment we enter until the moment we leave, including how we dress, sit, stand, and even walk.

As we preach, we must plan and execute movements that will pepper our sermons with meaning. We must be open to new ideas, new ways, better means to get the message of Jesus Christ across to people. This is our sacred calling and task. May our hearers be able to respond, "Yes, I see what you are saying!"

Notes

1. Bill Bruster, "How to Dress for the Pulpit," *Church Administration* 26:7 (April 1984): 29-30.
2. By X fashion I mean crossing legs with the back of one knee immediately over the other knee. By figure four I mean the side leg adjacent the shin of one leg resting on the knee of the other.
3. Carlyle Marney, *Beggars in Velvet* (New York: Abingdon Press, 1960), 47-50.
4. H. C. Brown, Jr., *A Christian's Layman's Guide to Public Speaking* (Nashville: Broadman Press, 1966), 65. Much of what I know about preaching in general and the visual in preaching in particular I owe to Dr. Brown, my major professor and dear friend, through his classroom notes, critiques, conversations, and writings. His influence is heavy here, as in all my homiletics. I sincerely hope this honors his memory.
5. Ibid.
6. See Harold Freeman, *Variety in Biblical Preaching* (Waco: Word Books, 1987), 161-171, for further suggestions on media-augmentation.

7. For more on the use of objects to explain, illustrate, or apply sermonic truth, see Roy E. De Brand, *Children's Sermons for Special Occasions* (Nashville: Broadman Press, 1983); and De Brand *Children's Sermons for Church Celebrations* (Nashville: Broadman Press, 1991); see also De Brand and C. W. Bess, *Bible-Centered Object Sermons for Children* (Grand Rapids: Baker Book House, 1985).

John A. Broadus (1827-1895)

"Professor and Preacher"

John A. Broadus has influenced the preaching of thousands of ministers through his textbook, On the Preparation and Delivery of Sermons. *First published in 1870, the book became the standard American homiletics text for several generations of seminarians, and continues (in revised editions) to be read and appreciated today.*

A Virginia native, the gifted young preacher was one of the original faculty of The Southern Baptist Theological Seminary when it was founded in 1859. During the Civil War, he preached often to Confederate troops; then, he rejoined his colleagues after the war to attempt to reestablish the fledgling seminary with few students and virtually no resources.

In one of his first preaching classes in those difficult years, only one student enrolled—a young blind man—but Broadus carefully prepared his lectures as if they would be delivered to a class of hundreds. It was those same lectures which became the basis for his famous textbook.

Although prominent pulpits and presidencies were offered to him, Broadus was committed to the young Baptist seminary where he taught and would later serve as president. In 1889, he was invited to present the Lyman Beecher Lectures on Preaching—one of only two Southern Baptists ever invited to participate in the famous Yale lectures.

A brilliant scholar and careful biblical expositor, Broadus was nevertheless best known for the remarkable compassion and tenderness reflected in his preaching. Whether as a professor or preacher, he was used by God to touch hearts and change lives.

34

Ralph Lewis
Professor of Preaching, Emeritus
Asbury Theological Seminary
Wilmore, Kentucky

Preaching With and Without Notes

Which is better—preaching with or without notes?

While this question might prompt an interesting theoretical discussion in seminary preaching classes, I recall a vivid experience of my own which forced me to face this question on a very concrete and practical level.

I had been invited to preach at a community-wide worship service in a Michigan resort town. About 600 people gathered in front of the town's bandshell in a beautiful outdoor setting. I had hardly begun to preach when a gusting lake breeze from behind me snatched up my note cards and scattered them into the crowd.

As I scurried, red-faced, to retrieve my sermon crutches, the host pastor good-naturedly called after me: "That's okay. The cows won't eat 'em!"

Which is better—preaching with or without notes?

At that moment I might have said: "The answer, my friend, is blowin' in the wind." The question is one every preacher needs to consider seriously. Neither fresh breezes nor old habits should be the primary determinant of our answer.

Why is this an important question for preachers today? Because our answer has broad implications for our delivery, and the importance of delivery can hardly be overemphasized. Demosthenes, the Sophists, the Elocutionists of the last century, as well as famous preachers throughout the ages illustrate the point. No speaker is very effective without good delivery. Your twenty minutes of delivery can instantly negate your twenty hours of sermon preparation. So anything that can help (or hurt) your delivery needs to be considered carefully.

What makes for a better, more effective delivery—preaching with or without notes? Let us see if a little historical perspective will shed some light on this question.

The reading of speeches was rare among the Greeks and Romans. While we regard Paul's epistles as written sermons for the early church intended to be read by whatever congregation he was addressing, there is no indication Paul ever read a sermon to any of his congregations.

It is difficult, if not impossible to picture Jesus reading the Sermon on the Mount, or His parables of the good Samaritan, the lost coin, the lost sheep, or the prodigal son, just as it is hard to imagine Paul reading his sermon to the philosophers on Mars Hill, or Peter unrolling a scroll on the day of Pentecost to read the divine summons to repent and believe.

The preaching patterns of Jesus and other early Christian preachers were very inductive—drawing on shared, everyday experiences, homilies, simple stories, parables, and concrete examples from Scripture, history, and life. In such inductive presentations, examples lead, questions overarch the evidence, and the accumulative process guides both the preacher and his listeners to the convincing conclusion. The commonsense flow of inductive structure with its accumulative evidence mounting toward a conclusion didn't require manuscripts or extensive notes to guide early Christian preachers.

A shift took place before the end of the fourth century. By A.D. 400 most Christian preaching had absorbed the principles of Greek rhetoric. In the centuries since, most preachers trained in rhetorical studies have abandoned the simple structure popular in the New Testament church for the more formal structure of the learned Greek model. The logical intricacy and the rhetorical structures of these deductive arguments are not as easy to remember without the prompting of written notes.

The use of complete manuscripts was not introduced into the pulpit until the 16th or 17th century. Manuscripts were popularized in the English establishment as a backlash against the Independents and the Puritans, whose impassioned preaching scandalized and scared royalty and clergy alike. Anything approaching extemporaneous preaching met with such official disfavor that one cleric was driven from his London pulpit because he lifted his eyes from his manuscript and looked at his congregation like the Dissenters did when they preached.

Scripted sermons maintained their popularity with preachers through all the centuries since. Of course there have been some notable exceptions—many of the great orators of the late 19th and early 20th centuries memorized their sermons, and others prepared merely the framework from which they soared to heights of seemingly spontaneous eloquence. The technological development of radio and television has prompted an even greater reliance on manuscripts because precise timing is paramount in broadcasting and a manuscript allows for the necessary control.

As we look back through the history of preaching to decide which would help us be better preachers—notes or no notes—we find great and effective preachers who have used every method of delivery.

Jonathan Edwards began by reading his sermons early in his ministry. He delivered his famous sermon, "Sinners in the Hands of an Angry God," from a minuscule manuscript. A young man held a lantern at his shoulder while his near-sighted eyes tried to decipher the writing. People clung to trees and posts to keep from falling into the yawning chasms of perdition. Later in life, Edwards advocated memorized or extemporaneous sermons.

Thomas Chalmers, the popular Scottish preacher, seemed equally at home with contrasting styles. For some time he felt he was unable to extemporize and always used a manuscript in his churches. He found it impossible, however, to use a manuscript when he addressed crowds of poor people on the outskirts of Glasgow. Contemporary observers testified that Chalmers' sermons to the plain folk seemed more effective and even more eloquent than those he delivered to so much acclaim in the pulpit of his own church. Perhaps he adapted to both styles because he wrote his sermons as if he were speaking them, at least in feeling, if not in actual sounds. He claimed to write everything "with an audience glaring in his face."

G. Campbell Morgan and Alexander Maclaren, like so many able expositors, felt notes or manuscript would interfere with needed eye contact. F. W. Robertson took a few notes into the pulpit, but almost never glanced at them. I have known some very effective preachers who would not think of standing in the pulpit without a complete manuscript and others who never glance at a note. Which would be the best course for you?

Actually John A. Broadus, whose book, *The Preparation and Delivery of Sermons*, was the most widely used homiletics book in American seminaries for a hundred years, speaks of three methods of delivery: reading, reciting, and extemporaneous speaking. Broadus acknowledges recitation is the least popular method. I find myself agreeing with Phillips Brooks who speaks of reciting sermons as "a method some men practice, but I hope nobody commends."

So in our discussion we are going to focus on the other two methods—manuscript and extemporaneous. Realize: (1) there are variations on these methods; (2) they both can be effective; and (3) your effectiveness may depend as much on how you execute your preference as which technique you use. Let us take a closer look as we consider some of the strengths and weaknesses, the advantages and disadvantages of the methods themselves.

Manuscript

The danger of a manuscript sermon is that it is more often read than preached. For any preacher who *can* read a sermon well, there are thousands who *think* they can. For too many ministers, a written and complete copy of their sermon resting on the pulpit in front of them acts as a very effective non-conductive material between them and their congregation. Often, even the power of God's Word and the life-changing force of His Spirit fail to burn through those pages of insulation.

Yet there is some important advice for those hoping to make the most of a manuscript. Keep your eyes on your hearers. Attention is largely kept through the eyes. "Look on us!" Peter and John said to the man begging at the Beautiful Gate of the temple (Acts 3:4). When Jesus gave His sermon in Nazareth, "the eyes of all were fastened upon Him" (Luke 4:20).

One of the most ridiculous sights in 30 years of teaching preachers was the student bending over his manuscript while he was gesturing behind his head. The kindest word to describe the scene would be "awkward"! Some thought it was hilarious—despite his earnest words.

If you preach from a manuscript, forget yourself. Lose sight of everything but your message and your hearers. Your chief task is to deliver the message to the waiting people. Church people today are sick and tired of being read to; like Dennis the Menace, they "want you to talk the book to me!"

How do you get and keep listeners involved? You can use directness, human interest, and your best oral style. That differs from the writing style you had recommended to you in your English composition classes. Oral style can be incorporated into the writing of a sermon. We need to include elements of oral style in every paragraph.

Practice until you can maintain direct eye contact with your hearers at least 90 percent of the time. Rehearse until you can enlarge the visual span of each glance. Slide the sheet down and inch or so as you near the end of the page. In this way you can escape any awkward transition when you go from one page to the next.

Some even recommend writing on only the top half of the pages. You may find it helpful to mark your script to indicate emphasis, pauses, and vocal phrases. Try to rethink and recreate the sermon at the time of presentation. Be conscious of rate, people, and your message. Focus on meaning, rather than words.

If you use a manuscript, do not apologize for it. Many of the most distinguished and successful preachers have read their sermons. Gregory, Augustine, Chrysostom, Baxter, Payson, and Jonathan

Edwards read manuscript sermons. Were they great because of their manuscript or in spite of it?

Try to be free. Work at it. Write for the ear, not for your own eye. Can you imagine a lawyer pleading his case by reading off a page of print? No, he must communicate with the jury eye to eye. He must face the people with warm earnestness. The eye on the written page surely is not as effective as the eye fixed on a human face.

Monotony is one of the most serious dangers of reading a sermon. Often, the only difference between a manuscript sermon and a memorized message is that one is read from a piece of paper and the other from the back of your mind. Engage your listeners. Establish personal contact. The voice is rarely monotonous in conversation. If the preacher feels what is being said, then monotones are far less likely. Charles G. Finney warned: "Any monotonous sound, great or small, if continued, disposes people to sleep."

Manuscript preaching imposes more limitations on our flexibility. Adjustment in word choice, phrasing, or content, or a shifted emphasis to meet an unexpected or different audience response tends to be limited. Ineffective oral and physical delivery of manuscript sermons are so common as to prompt a broad negative response. Why do so few ever seem to master the method?

Circumstances may warrant or even urge us to speak from a manuscript. What are the advantages of a written sermon? Precise statement, higher literary tone, accurate timing, and reduced emotional strain.

If you must have a manuscript, use your best active voice instead of passive voice. Use personal pronouns just as you would if you were speaking extemporaneously. Use colloquial words and short sentences. Remember, you are depending on material and style to hold attention.

Using a Manuscript

Advantages	*Disadvantages*
• Closure, confidence	• Often too much reading
• Finished form and style	• Does not seem natural, easy
• Timing is easier	• Emotional distance
• Accuracy is assured	• Easy to sound stilted
• Less emotional strain	• Less emotional involvement
• Fail-safe material	• Cannot insert inspiration
• Preacher at ease earlier	• Instant revision impossible
• Can be more literary	• Less personal, more distant
• More polished vocabulary	• Impossible to adjust, adapt
• Printed copy available	• Cannot change to fit hearers
• Easy to check structure	• Less eye contact
• Easy to rehearse	• Tends to monotone
• Can rely on manuscript	• Can be too cognitive

Make it easy to listen to. Keep the sermon alive and fresh by returning often to it after it is written. Study the manuscript at spaced intervals. Check for personal elements and human appeal. Make sure the light is favorable for reading.

Choose clear, objective, vivid, and impressive words. Avoid long complicated sentences. Exercise economy of words. Do not write an essay. Keep your outline constantly before you. A complete, well-developed outline will make your preparation simpler.

Read it aloud. How does it sound? Check for oral style. Revise so it sounds right. Does it move? Flow? Strive for short paragraphs? Write only on one side of your paper or you invite disaster. Number your pages to avoid confusion and embarrassment when you deliver it.

Extemporaneous Preaching

Some preaching professors advise: "Write out your sermons for the first few years, then you can extemporize." I disagree. What is apt to happen is that our manuscripted ways will soon be set in concrete and we will never bring ourselves to follow the advice of Broadus, who said of extemporaneous preaching: "Plunge in trembling knees and all." Good things can happen when we do.

Clarence Macartney, that great Presbyterian preacher, tells of his experience in a remote Canadian province a thousand miles from home. When he arrived at his destination he discovered an empty file folder where he was sure his manuscript had been. After his initial shock he decided to take a leap of faith and preach without any notes. After all, he was a long way from home. His triumphal experience made him resolve never to preach from a manuscript again. So he wrote his book *Preaching Without Notes*.

The forgotten manuscript at first seemed a calamity, but preaching without notes proved to be a great success. He said the human contact was so improved he could scarcely believe it. The purpose of preaching was gloriously fulfilled in a new and profound freedom, in a new and powerful contact with the people.

After nearly 25 years of teaching preaching courses in seminary, I introduced a drastic change. I decided to repeal the traditional demand for full manuscripts and it resulted immediately in better sermons. Suddenly trial sermons were less of a trial. They produced better relations with hearers, better emotional responses, better contact. The freedom of seminary students was spectacular. The content improved, too.

Perhaps one reason more people do not take the risk of preaching without notes is a critical disregard for the concept of extemporaneous preaching. Many people tend to misunderstand extemporaneous speaking. To them it means *impromptu*. Actually, a drastic difference distinguishes the *extemporaneous* sermon from an off-the-cuff *impromptu* sermon. The extemporaneous sermon is well prepared. It is prepared one big step beyond the manuscript—beyond mere writing out, and very much beyond spur-of-the-moment impromptu attempts.

In actuality it does not mean less preparation, but requires an extra step beyond manuscript preparation—becoming familiar enough with the material to convey it without reading. Time saved in not writing out exact words may be simply traded for extra time spent becoming familiar with the basic sermon ideas so we can convey them without merely reading them.

An obvious danger is we can get sloppy or lazy in preparation. Some running commentaries on Sunday morning are almost impromptu Bible reading. They may show directness, informality, flexibility, personal appeal, and even persuasiveness. Yet they show little respect for God or our listeners.

Edgar DeWitt Jones, in his book, *The Royalty of the Pulpit,* tells of an instance where the poorly prepared preacher took twenty minutes to ad lib his comments about the morning Scripture reading. This most promising graduate from seminary fizzled into oblivion because he had a gift of gab but failed to work at his potential.

If we are careful not to succumb to those temptations there are many benefits to be found: more interest, more friendliness, more agreement, more appreciation. Along with the temptation to prepare less comes the tendency not to think through, not give care or full attention to detail. Also, the temptation for some is to be content with mediocrity, with less care given to the examples, to style, and to conclusions in the moment of delivery.

More casual delivery may reduce esteem, respect, and even the reception of the preacher. Some persons may attach the importance of the message to a formal manuscript. A casual or more informal message may seem less important to hearers. More directness, eye contact, and intensity can balance this out.

Extemporaneous preaching can utilize extensive notes or none at all. As a rule, the fewer we need, the more we benefit from the advantages this method offers. No one demands a solo flight with no notes. Judiciously used, notes can serve as reminders to guide the preacher to a proper conclusion by noon. Many noted preachers through the ages used the extemporaneous method. For example, Whitefield was called a reciting preacher by some. In later life he seldom wrote any of his sermons. He insisted no preacher had preached his best until he had preached a sermon 42 times. As a traveling evangelist he had the opportunity to practice what he preached.

Henry Ward Beecher was an extemporaneous preacher who did not sacrifice preparation. Someone asked him how long it took him to prepare one of his sermons. "I've been working on that sermon for forty years," he said. Then he went out to remove last Sunday's "Standing Room Only" sign from the front of his church. For forty years they had pleaded with people *not* to come back Sunday night in order that those who were turned away from the morning service might be able to get in for the evening service.

John Calvin's hearers were more interested in his sermons than they were in his formal theological writing. As influential as his *Institutes* may have been over the ensuing centuries, his sermons found a more popular response with laity in Geneva. Calvin preached daily from the overflow of his study and writing. He questioned whether the Holy Spirit could redeem or even use a manuscript sermon. Some have criticized his lack of precise structure, his informal, colloquial style, his lack of strict logical reasoning in his extemporaneous sermons. Yet his extemporaneous endeavors brought out the Swiss people daily to hear him.

Preaching Extemporaneous Sermons

Advantages	*Disadvantages*
• Encourages rapid thinking	• Can educate away from people
• Saves time for other work	• Tends to neglect preparation
• Allows immediate response	• Hinders the habit of writing
• Transforms and warms material	• Demands renewed preparation
• Allows for altered responses	• Cannot quote so extensively
• Enables your best delivery	• Style may be less finished
• Definitely the popular preference	• Structure may seem loose
• Gains instant popular sympathy	• May reduce sermon scope, depth
• Rise to your highest potential	• May seem to be off-the-cuff
• Rise to best delivery possible	• May be too stressful for some
• Responds to inspiration of moment	• May seem too casual for some
• Quotes only vital material	• May lack exactness, specificity
• Facilitates easier speaking	• Neglects writing which promotes accuracy
• Saves time for difficult parts exactness	• Neglects writing which promotes exactness

So should you be preaching with or without notes, using a manuscript or extemporaneously? A couple of additional considerations might help you decide.

The Attention Factor

A young preacher complained to Spurgeon about one of the deacons in the front pew who would stop his ears with his fingers and lower his head when the pastor began to preach. It so upset him he did not know what to do. Spurgeon said: "I'd ask the Lord to send a fly to light on his nose."

Short of asking God to send a fleet of flies to rouse your drowsy congregations, what can you do to get your listeners' attention and involvement while you preach? Could the notes/no-notes delivery discussion apply here? How can the preacher capture the attention and sustain the interest of hearers? If you do not have attention, you do not have much hope as a speaker. H. A. Overstreet says: "The person who can capture and hold attention is the person who can effectively influence human behavior."

The duration of human attention varies from 3 to 24 seconds, according to tests. Most listeners may try to focus on the sermon; but unless the preacher helps, the cause is lost. The center of clear vision normally shifts at a rate of at least 100 times each minute. The rate is much greater if one reads or drives a car. Auditory attention also shifts. So every sermon must battle for human interest.

Attention must be captured, held, and recaptured many times during a sermon. Perhaps we need to take a lesson from the cinema. Most movies aim for an emotional climax at least every five minutes or they lose audience attention and quickly fade at the box office.

Eye contact and facial expression contribute to or detract from our hearers' attention. The American average of watching TV 50 hours a week prepares our people for direct engagement when they come to church. Whether the pastor reads the Bible or preaches the message of the week, listeners have come to expect a personal encounter in church services.

Indeed, the left-brain focus of the marketplace today cries for the renewal of warm human relationships when people come to church. The need for happy human memories, satisfying human contact, feelings of worth and worship mark most listeners in our day. The Bible is more than cognitive stuff. The effective sermon is more than reading the Bible and sharing our cognition.

Roger W. Sperry, Nobel prize winner in 1981 for his brain research, says one thing we know for sure: Americans neglect the right-brain in their formal education. "Readin,' 'ritin,' and 'rithmetic" all major on left-brain activity. Left-brain does the chores as the "day brain." It analyzes, catalogs, creates rules, and orders the minutia. It defines, divides, abstracts, reasons, and commandeers words as it speaks.

Our right-brain relates, remembers, responds emotionally, feels, and sees the pattern of the whole. It sings, dramatizes, makes metaphors and denotes similarities, comparisons, designs, and constructs. It synthesizes, creates visual imagery, discovers, explores, knows by experience, and dreams.

Obviously our people bring both halves of the brain to church. Some

70 percent of them prefer to learn from concrete experiences. Only 30 percent prefer to learn by abstracting, conceptualizing.

Sharing concrete experiences is far more interesting for most of us than merely abstracting sermons in theological terms. Jesus is a good example of this accent on shared experience from daily life. "Without a story He wouldn't preach, and the common people heard Him gladly" (see Mark 4:33-34).

The personal, practical, emotional, and right-brain aspects of the sermon have a harder time shining through a manuscript. Extemporaneous sermons make it easier to include the right-brain emotional images and feelings so necessary today. As a general rule, the fewer the notes the easier to achieve involvement by the people; that makes preaching a shared endeavor and not just a canned presentation by the preacher.

The Earnestness Factor

An urgency has marked all the great preachers. Some called it "unction." "I can't rightly tell you what it is, but I can tell you when it ain't." It grew out of their devotion, dedication, and prayer.

It is the quality John Wesley ascribed to his personal life-changing enlightenment at Aldersgate when his heart was "strangely warmed." It was nothing he induced or manipulated. He believed it was heaven-sent. The experience transformed the Oxford don's life; his sermons then began to electrify his growing outdoor congregations. Whitefield, the youngest Episcopal preacher in all England, preached to miners early in the morning when his sermons washed rivulets of tears down their sooty faces.

Yet their individual personalities were drastically different. Wesley was a polished, stainless steel tube; Whitefield was a spring thunder storm when he preached. He fell in a puffing heap with peroxisms, threatening a heart attack as he finished.

In the Lyman Beecher Lectures on Preaching at Yale, speakers repeatedly refer to a certain transcendent quality of the best preaching. This heightened feeling is so difficult to find in the responses given to most manuscripted sermons. Henry Ward Beecher, giving the first lectures, spoke of *enthusiasm*. Other lecturers through the years spoke of "earnestness," "conviction," "a soul aflame," "vigor," and "virility."

Brooks could not give "it" a name, but as an Episcopalian, he spoke of "enthusiasm," "eloquence," "magnetism," and "the gift of preaching." John Watson spoke of "intensity" and "spiritual passion." Broadus, in his textbook on preaching, spoke of "energy," "force, " "passion," and "animation." Others trace back to St. Augustine's "fervor."

This urgency was not always the most popular of attributes. Halford

E. Luccock said the highest tribute of the 18th century was to speak of the preacher as being "pious without enthusiasm." Then quickly he added if preaching stood in apostolic succession it must show "two of the basic laws of propaganda—first, reiteration . . . and second, *passionate affirmation.*"

Some discuss "*authentic* passion" arising from the process of discovery. Others warn against a specious, false, worked-up emotion. John M. Stapleton discusses the metaphor *turn-on* as it relates to electronic media. He talks of highly motivated and interested preachers who produce turned-on congregations by their inspired and inspiring sermons.

Traditional propositional form or points of our sermons may generate little emotion or passion either in the preacher or congregation. Our electronic "galaxy" today demands more involvement, more participation and more real excitement from its turned-on preachers.

Why add to the communication problems of the day by trying to filter our sermons through the pages of a manuscripted sermon? With the trained and skillful communicators on our satellite dishes, why do we think a pastor can survive if the warmth, earnestness, and personal impact are hindered by insulated paper sermons?

The less insulation between preacher and people, the clearer the earnestness comes through, and the greater opportunity for God to speak through the integrity and passion of His spokesperson.

Part VI Preaching and the Ministry

Charles Haddon Spurgeon (1834-1892)

"Proclaiming the Cross"

Asked once to describe his preaching method, Charles H. Spurgeon said, "I take my text and make a bee-line to the cross."

Few if any preachers in the history of the church have proclaimed the cross with such power and effectiveness as Spurgeon, the great British Baptist preacher of the nineteenth century. Even a century after his death, his sermons and other writings are still widely read and quoted.

Growing up in the home of his grandfather, a Congregational minister who had an extensive library, Spurgeon spent many hours reading classic Puritan writers. Those materials shaped the theological direction of Spurgeon whose preaching demonstrated careful theological thought along with clear presentation and illustrations drawn from everyday life.

Spurgeon's natural pulpit gifts were recognized early. Before age 20, he was called as pastor of the historic New Park Street Baptist Church in London. The congregation had declined to about 100 before his arrival; soon, Spurgeon's preaching had filled the 1200–seat sanctuary. Within eighteen months the church was forced to move to accommodate thousands who came to hear the cross proclaimed. In 1861, the congregation shifted to the new Metropolitan Tabernacle where the congregation numbered more than 6,000 per week for the next thirty years.

His magnificent voice and popular preaching style attracted Londoners across class and economic lines. As Helmut Thielicke would later relate, "He worked only through the power of the Word which created its own hearers and changed souls."

35

John A. Huffman, Jr., Pastor
St. Andrews Presbyterian Church
Newport Beach, California

The Role of Preaching in Ministry

Preaching is front and center for those of us called into the pastorate who have as part of our position descriptions the regular teaching and preaching of the Word of God. There are those who would depreciate the role of preaching, arguing for their own particular area of expertise under the headings to follow in this section: Worship; Pastoral Care; Administration; Education; Missions; and Church Growth. All of these areas are of vital importance in the life of a church. There is a place for persons who devote their whole professional lives to the study and practice of each of these. Not every ordained minister is called to have preaching as his or her foremost specialty.

However, I would encourage us to never minimize the importance of preaching and our role as preachers in our total ministry as leaders in Christ's church. During the past thirty years I have been approached by numerous pastoral nominating committees asking my guidance toward potential candidates. My first question is: "What are you looking for as the number one qualification in a prospective pastor?" In every case they have listed preaching as the highest priority. They are quick to qualify this statement, noting that these other areas are important. The strong presupposition which comes across is that churches are intent on calling pastors who they perceive as concentrating on preaching. This central focus of preaching in ministry does not minimize and can actually enhance the way in which they are carried out.

For example, preaching is not the same as individual, indepth psychotherapy. However, healthy preaching provides a superb environment for pastoral care. The best preachers will realize that significant pastoral care is carried out through sensitive, honest, vulnerable, self-disclosing preaching. Harry Emerson Fosdick was one of the first to articulate that pastoral counseling was one of his objectives in the pulpit.

Healthy preaching is an encourager of worship, pastoral care, administration, education, music, missions, and church growth. It provides an environment in the life of a faith community where all of these important ministries happen. Preachers are called to proclaim a holistic gospel which incorporates each of these areas. The degree to which they do this will substantially influence the extent to which the people of God will be able to grow towards wholeness in each of these areas, both within the specific context of worship and in the environments of these specialized ministries.

It appears to me that the major issue is encapsuled in the word *congruence*. It is in the proclamation of the preached word that biblical themes derive a contemporary authenticity. Week in and week out, faithful preaching—as nowhere else—brings together all of these other dimensions in a way that builds up both individual believers and strengthens the corporate community of faith. Faithful, biblical preaching, sooner or later, addresses all of these topics and many more. How they will fit together in the church will be greatly determined by how they have been handled in the preaching moment.

Church history reveals an ongoing dialogue of human personas with the Word of God as revealed in the Bible. This is a continuous struggle to define biblical authority and to establish ground rules for the meaningful communication of that truth. Central to this struggle is the interplay of pastoral authority and the authority of the Bible. The preached word blends through a hermeneutical process the objective, written Word with all of the intellectual, spiritual, social, physical, and psychological resources the preacher's selfhood brings to that process.

One who takes seriously the role of preaching in ministry is constantly asking himself or herself: "Just what is that blend for me and how am I doing in bringing about this interaction of biblical revelation with my personhood in a way that God's eternal Word is declared in helpful ways to all of life?"

I observe some preachers who refuse to let dogma reign over personalistic values. I observe others who see it necessary to define faith in terms of creedal fidelity. One stresses human-centeredness while the other stresses God-centeredness. One stresses natural revelation while the other stresses special revelation. One stresses a social gospel while the other stresses spiritual concerns. This has recently developed into a more-subtle tension between those who are doing relational theology and those who stress cognitive theology. These themes and variations on these themes are evident in contemporary preaching.

The issue is more complicated than it first appears. Neither of these traditions is completely consistent. There is a personalistic objectivism and a cognitive subjectivism reflected in the life-styles, communication methods, and biblical hermeneutics of both. Nonetheless, the tension continues. The issue at its core is that theological content has been and will continue to be the result of an ongoing dialogue of human persons with the biblical Word, which dialogue ultimately produces preaching.

I see human personality as relativistic, elastic, dynamic, and subject to constant change. On the other hand, I see biblical truth as having to some extent a propositional, final, "once-delivered-to-the-saints" quality.

During the entire course of my ordained ministry I have struggled with what place my preaching should take within the context of the rest of my ministry. I am convinced that preaching is central and highly determinative of what else happens within my ministry. This leads me then to a continuing struggle with what place my selfhood should take in the practice of ministry, especially in preaching. I view the Bible as "the only infallible rule of faith and practice." Propositional truth is important to me, as it has been to the Church throughout its entire history. I believe that there is much which God has chosen to reveal about Himself in the Bible which can, to some extent, be captured in propositional statement.

Yet I am convinced that the cognitive restatement of those propositions, while necessary, is never exhaustive. There is mystery. There is that special personhood of God and humans which refuses to be reduced to cognitive statements. Truth, to be communicated, needs to be filtered through divine and human personality. This has produced an internal creative tension which puts me through the range of feelings from exhilaration to anxiety. A major feature of my preaching as well as pastoral style has been a self-revelatory expression, both in terms of identification with others and personal illustrations of the truth I am endeavoring to share.

Approximately two decades into my ordained ministry I took a study leave and worked through some of the Yale/Lyman Beecher Lectures on Preaching, looking for insights which would authenticate or repudiate what had evolved as my own understanding of the role of preaching and the preacher in ministry, specifically as it related to my basic personal/professional self-expression. Phillips Brooks' emphasis on preaching as "communication of truth by man to men," having the two essential elements of truth and personality has fascinated me. I sense my need to come to a better awareness of what it means to have the truth "come really through the person, not merely over his lips, not merely into his understanding and out through his pen. It must come through his character, his affections, his whole intellectual and moral being. It must come genuinely through him."[1]

What does this really mean? How is it fleshed out in our preaching? To what extent does our use of personal experience as content and illustration in preaching enhance or detract from the communication of biblical truth? I am convinced of the truth conveyed in Brooks' concept. God has chosen to use the very person of those of us who communicate His truth to be an integral part of that truth. Who we are and how we live cannot help but detract from or enhance our preaching, which in turn impacts every other area of our ministry. However, I believe that there is also a separateness of the Word from our personhood. We dare not identify truth so closely with our own selfhood that we relativize it in our preaching to the point that the Word of God preached is a human word cut free from the written Word. We must be careful to examine the complexities of this matter, especially in the light of the narcissistic tendencies of our present culture's glorification of celebrity and our own vulnerability to this. We need to assess the extent and appropriateness of our homiletical endeavor to communicate truth by self to the self of others.

Not only is this a struggle for the preacher. Every person hearing the preached Word should be involved in this same struggle to find a creative intersection of biblical truth with one's own personhood. The preacher's task is to convey, with the help of the Holy Spirit, a dynamic blend of his or her person and biblical truth in a way that will facilitate a similar dialogue and ultimate intersection of the two within the hearer of the Word.

As men and women called to professional ministry, we need to be constantly measuring our effectiveness in bringing about this intersection by comparing our own evaluative reflections of what we are trying to do with some kind of reality testing as to how effective we are in doing it. As a pastor installed with responsibilities for a local congregation, I am called to serve persons who themselves are significant participants in this divine human interaction called preaching. It is appropriate that I listen to them, not only to judge my own effectiveness, but also to take seriously what they, in their priesthood as fellow believers, have to teach me. I have to constantly be asking myself how effective a job am I doing at designing, delivering, and evaluating preaching which intends to bring about an intersection between the persons of both the preacher and hearer with biblical truth. I try to constantly keep my ear to the ground so as to hear honest feedback as to how effective a job I am doing. On one occasion, I formalized this feedback enterprise in a five-stage process over a five-week period.

Stage one was the preparation of five sermons in which I entered into an active dialogue with myself; in them I dealt with the biblical text in a hermeneutical and homiletical way which proposed to mediate biblical truth through personal experience. I kept a journal describing the various ways which I, through each sermon, endeavored to help the person in the pew wage this same struggle to blend biblical truth with personal experience.

Stage two was the preaching of the sermon as best I could. Each sermon was audiotaped and also produced in written form.

Stage three was my evaluation. I reflected critically in a journal on how successful I was in accomplishing my ultimate intentions as journaled in stage one. This involved a specific statement of what I perceived to be my strengths and weaknesses in bringing about the desired intersection of biblical truth and person in this particular preaching act of ministry.

Stage four was small group sharing. A carefully chosen group of twelve lay persons from my church shared the ways in which they as hearers experienced the sermon. This group represented a variety of ages, theologies, genders, and intimacy with me. They were bound together by one common trait, their past record of willingness to speak up in honest communication. They committed themselves to meet for five, two-hour sessions in the afternoon of the Sunday in which each sermon was preached. The discussion was moderated by a lay person, without me present. I did not ask this group to evaluate the sermon in any way except to critically share their experience of how the sermon, in its content and delivery, enhanced or detracted from this desired intersection of biblical truth and their human persons. It was made clear that they were not primarily evaluating me or my sermon but what transpired or did not transpire in this act of preaching to bring about this desired intersection. I listened to the cassette recordings of their discussions in an evaluation procedure, comparing what they said with my own journal entries in stage one and stage three. I dealt only with the matter of the intersection of biblical truth through and to human persons and the congruence or lack of congruence of the intention with my personal evaluations and the group evaluations.

Stage five was to conclude how effective a job I had done in designing, delivering, and evaluating preaching which intended to bring about an intersection between both the person of the preacher and the hearer with biblical truth in a way that would enhance worship, pastoral care, administration, education, music, missions, and church growth.

Let me share with you the results of this ongoing process of reality testing in a way that you might find helpful for yourself. I will try to express it in terms of three specific areas.

First, I am learning that my use of personal experience, illustration, and selfhood as a person in preaching does considerably enhance my communication of biblical truth. However, in certain situations, it does detract. Therefore, I must develop a continuing, positive use of my person within restraints cautioned by lay observations and my reading and research. This lesson speaks to the issue of pastoral authority.

When Phillips Brooks articulated his concept that real preaching is truth through human personality, he emphasized his conviction that truth must come through the very character affections, the whole intellectual and moral being of the preacher. This conveyance of truth through personality is not a mechanical function. He distinguished between two kinds of preachers.

> I think that, granting equal intelligence and study, there is the great difference which we feel between two preachers of the Word. The Gospel has come *over* one of them and reaches us tinged and flavored with his superficial characteristics, belittled with his littleness. The Gospel has come *through* the other, and we receive it impressed and winged with all the earnestness and strength there is in him. In the first case man has been but a printing machine or a trumpet. In the other case he has been a true man and real messenger of God.[2]

I discovered that people sense our desperate desire to apply the biblical message to ourselves and our problems prior to sharing that word with them. This builds a personal identification factor. They want to identify the preacher who is a real person dealing with the real world in his or her own life. The hearers of the Word want to sense "believability," "credibility," and "integrity" in their preacher. Nonverbal gestures, physical bearing, eye contact, vocal variety, and the use of comic relief, all within one's normal communication style, are important to the hearer. I discovered that books of sermon illustrations are not very helpful.

Some listeners are turned off by anything that smacks of self-aggrandizing. Humility provides the counterbalance to the narcissistic tendencies of our times. Christopher Lasch puts his finger on this problem as he notes the emotional shallowness, the fear of intimacy, the false self-insight, the distorted sexuality, the dread of old age and death, which give evidence of the narcissism of many in our culture.[3] True humility demands that we preachers see ourselves as we are—sinners saved by God's grace, called to renounce our era's temptation toward self-absorption, replacing it with a genuine concern for others. The preacher who is untouched by a genuine humility is extremely vulnerable to a self-delusionary narcissism.

The preacher is always incomplete. The apostle Paul talked about "knowing in part" in a way that frees us not to worry about the fact that we do not have the complete knowledge of an erudite theological professor. Humility helps us realize that our preaching is partial, our best efforts at producing the definitive sermon on a particular topic fall short. Charles Bartow emphasizes the point that a particular sermon is:

> A product of our biography, as much as it is a product of our critical theological and biblical reflection upon issues and conditions of human life. Consequently, it is a partial but not a comprehensive statement of the gospel.[4]

Humility increases our capacities to laugh at ourselves as we more clearly see our own weaknesses. We are not to be the heroes. William Willimon writes:

> The goal of sharing personal feelings, experiences, stories and anecdotes is to link people with one another, and with the text—not to link them to the preacher. It is good to ask, "Who is the hero of this story?" If the hero is the preacher, something is wrong. The hero of most biblical texts is *God*, not us. The heroes of the church are not the clergy.[5]

We have the need for integrity. Although all of us may stumble into a kind of self-deception, our urgent quest must be for integrity. I have discovered that I must be who I am. I can be no one else. I must face up to my strengths and my weaknesses. How liberating this is. This integrity conveys itself to our people, most particularly through our preaching. Then it spills over into all these other areas of our ministry. We must distinguish between the form and the message. There is a substance to be communicated which the form must not block. The stress on "total image" can develop a person who is strong on form but weak on content. We may gesture rightly, express ourselves well, have the right opinions, and appear to be consummately successful while having only memorized what looks good, not what really *is* good.

Humility and integrity are crucial safeguards to help ensure the proper use of experience, illustration, and selfhood in preaching.

Second, let me share what I am learning about biblical authority as it relates to preaching.

Although I am firmly committed to a view of biblical authority which comes under the general label "the plenary view" (a very high view of Scripture), I am discovering that I need to more carefully refine the implications of that for my preaching. I need to be increasingly aware of where my congregation is in its acceptance of biblical authority. I need to distinguish for myself between my view of Scripture as authoritative, and my use of Scripture, hermeneutically and homiletically, realizing that my preaching can be increasingly instructed by theological conclusions drawn by persons whose presuppositions and methodologies relating to biblical authority differ from mine.

I am discovering that people are hungry to hear what the Bible has to say as it relates to where they live today. There is great variety on any given Sunday morning in a congregation as to various views of biblical authority. The pluralism of our society has impacted the makeup of the average congregation. David H. C. Read has emphasized that there are three component parts to preaching. The first is the proclamation of the gospel. The second is the teaching of what the believer needs to know of what God has revealed. The third is ethics which tell us how to live in relationship with others. He urged that we see each sermon we preach as having all three of these elements, although the main thrust will fall into one of these three categories.

I have discovered that when I have done my exegetical research, have exposed myself to non-traditional ways of looking at the text, and have made my evaluation as to their appropriateness, I must trust the Holy Spirit to help me focus in on the key message God is trying to communicate to me and through me from that text and build the preached word around that truth, ascertaining what is the most creative, helpful, and homiletical expression of that truth. I would agree with Phillips Brooks who wrote: "Definers and defenders of the faith are always needed, but it is bad for a church, when its ministers count it their true work to define and defend the faith rather than to preach the Gospel."[6]

Our highest calling is not that of defending the truth but proclaiming it in a proactive way with the help of the Holy Spirit, commending that eternal truth to life where it is lived today.

Third, let me share what I am learning about the Holy Spirit's capacity to use my strengths and weaknesses as a person *in process*, preaching to persons in process who are also speaking to me.

I am learning I need to trust more in the Holy Spirit's capacity to use my honest efforts and be more secure in my strengths and less afraid of my weaknesses. To state this in a slightly different way, you and I are privileged to recognize the process of sanctification in which the Holy Spirit takes our pastoral authority and when placed in tension with the authority of the written Word, produces a dynamic, developmental process in and through both as they intersect with the needs of a congregation.

There is a lot you and I need to know and can learn from our congregations about issues affecting preaching which we might never think to raise unless we dedicate ourselves to hearing their concerns. I am discovering I have run a little bit too scared throughout my entire ordained ministry. I am discovering that the Holy Spirit has the capacity to use my honest efforts in a way that uses my strengths and my weaknesses to positive ends. I need to listen to my critics but not let them get me down. I must reflect on my own struggle with pride and discouragement. I have a tendency to take full blame for that part of my ministry which is not well received and at the same time want to take the full credit for my accomplishments. Although you and I must be willing to learn from criticism, we need to manage our tendency to allow other persons to project their pathologies onto us. Most preachers have a need to please and, in the process, can be orchestrated in ways that minimize our effectiveness in ministry.

Our honest acknowledgement of our own human failures and our desire to uphold Jesus Christ and the Scriptures, while relating both to human need, is a tremendous safety factor. We are privileged to trust more fully the Holy Spirit to get His message across as we exegete the text to the best of our ability and integrate that with the existential circumstances to which we are preaching. I was caught short by J. Randal Nichols' suggestion that some minsters are over and underprepared. This, on occasion, has been my experience. I have wanted so much to do a great job of preaching that I have over-researched the commentaries, tried to pack too much into an individual sermon, and missed some of the spontaneity and delightful freshness which comes from less formal study and more musing integration of the biblical message into my own experience and the experience of my congregation. To put this in Nichols' words:

> In a word, preachers have a tendency to depend too obsessively and too long on commentaries and secondary materials and to brood and imagine too fearful and too little about what way a text or subject is trying to have with them. So you get the paradoxical and embarrassing situation of a sermon you just know had twenty hours behind it landing dead as a doornail as any kind of invitation to the Bible's world of transcendent presence, while the half-finished product of someone's insight while strap-hanging between subway stops soars like an eagle with its hearers close behind.[7]

In conclusion, the preacher and congregation must see themselves as persons whose humanness and Christian experience is lived out in community. Hell is alienation, isolation from God and each other in both this world and the next. The preacher's task is to place himself or herself and the hearers in the context of the immediate community and in the context of the broader church universal—past, present, and future. *My* message cannot be separated from *our* message, *my* story from *our* story. Both my story and our story are continually challenged, corrected, and transformed by *God's* story of how He works in, with, and through us. He is the God who created community—and the preacher speaks from, with, for, and to that community—as a person through whom God speaks from, with, for, and to persons. In these ways, our preaching and our roles as preachers impact every area of ministry.

Notes

1. Phillips Brooks, *Lectures on Preaching,* The Yale Lectures on Preaching, 1877 (Grand Rapids: Baker Book House, 1969), 8.
2. Ibid.
3. See Christopher Lasch, *The Culture of Narcissism* (New York: W. W. Norton & Company, 1978).
4. Charles L. Bartow, *The Preaching Moment* (Nashville: Abingdon, 1980), 62.
5. William H. Willimon, "A Funny Thing Happened to Me on the Way to the Pulpit," *The Christian Ministry* (January, 1982): 7.
6. Brooks, *Lectures on Preaching, 21.*
7. J. Randall Nichols, *Building the Word* (San Francisco: Harper & Row, Publishers, 1980), 31.

36

John Killinger
Distinguished Professor of Theology and Culture
Samford University
Birmingham, Alabama

Preaching and Worship

Church members in the Protestant traditions have often used the phrase "going to preaching" as if it were synonymous with "going to worship." This is because of the inordinate weight given in their churches to the theology of conversion and the concomitant importance of preaching, which often consumes as much of the liturgical agenda as all the other elements of worship combined. In Puritan New England, for example, sermons which extended to "twenty-fifthly" and "twenty-sixthly" usually ran to one-and-three-quarters to two hours in length, while the psalm singing and praying that formed a prelude to it took only an hour or an hour and a half. In many non-Catholic churches today, especially among blacks and Pentecostals, the sermon still exceeds the length of all other liturgical items by a noticeable margin.

Are the members of these churches less worshipful than members of churches which devote more time to such formal liturgical matters as Introits, Litanies, Prayers of Confession, Lectionary Readings, and the observance of the Lord's Table? Not necessarily. They may be mightily given to prayer and communion with God throughout the service and leave with a sense of having been cleansed and renewed for holy living. It is just that their vision of worship is different from that of persons who prefer a more sacramental order in which the preacher is less visible and dominant.

To distinguish between the two types of vision, it is necessary to remember the origins of Christian worship and the various uses of preaching among the first followers of Christ.

The Beginnings of Christian Worship

Inasmuch as the first Christians were Jews accustomed to regular attendance at synagogue, and who actually continued throughout their lifetimes to worship in synagogues wherever they went, it was natural that their experience of Christian worship should become modeled on the way they worshiped as Jews. Synagogue worship consisted of psalms, prayers, readings from the Torah and the Prophets, and interpretations of what was read. When Jesus attended the synagogue at Nazareth (Luke 4:16-30), He read from the scroll of Isaiah and, according to the custom, proceeded to give an interpretation of what He had read.

It is clear from the earliest references among Christian writings that those who worshiped as Christians merely adapted these general practices for their own services. They expanded them to include the invention of new hymns (scholars have shown that the New Testament is filled with snatches of these), the increased use of the prophetic books *plus* readings from the apostolic letters and the Gospels as these became available. Also, from the very beginning, the observance of the Lord's Supper remained a remembrance and reconstitution of Christ in their midst.

The Earliest Christian Preaching

Christian interpretation or preaching had from the beginning one primary aim, and that was to substantiate the claim that Jesus was indeed the Messiah, or Christ, predicted by the prophets of old. C. H. Dodd's now classic book *The Apostolic Preaching* establishes the seldom-varying theme and subthemes of this preaching. The unvarying *kerygma*, says Dodd, consisted of the following assertions:

> The prophecies are fulfilled, and the new Age is inaugurated by the coming of Christ.
> He was born of the seed of David.
> He died according to the Scriptures, to deliver us out of the present evil age.
> He was buried.
> He rose on the third day according to the Scriptures.
> He is exalted at the right hand of God, as Son of God and Lord of the quick and dead.
> He will come again as Judge and Saviour of men.[1]

How all of this was orchestrated and amplified surely depended to some extent on the context in which the preaching occurred. We can imagine that it differed in tone and argument when an apostle was proclaiming the faith in a heathen setting, as Paul did at Mars Hill in Athens (Acts 17:22-31), and when the gospel was being rehearsed in a setting of Christian worship, where virtually all of those present were already convinced of the Lordship of Christ. It is easy enough to conclude that interpretations in the Christian community began to be less repetitive and to expand from apologetics into the realm of the faith's implications for Christian behavior in both interpersonal and public realms.

Preaching and Worship in the Middle Ages

After Emperor Constantine legalized Christianity and made it the official religion of the empire early in the 4th century, the character of Christianity changed dramatically. There was a flurry of church building throughout the empire, and liturgies began to be adapted to more public display than had been necessary in smaller, more intimate settings. I use the plural form, "liturgies," because liturgical usages differed widely according to locale and tradition.

As the centuries passed, however, the numerous usages became consolidated into only a few, with the rite according to the church at Rome predominating in the West. Then, when the Roman Empire was finally demolished by "barbarian" armies in the fifth century, Latin ceased to be the common tongue of the lands that had once constituted the Empire. The church's worship in every rural and city church in the West continued to be conducted in Latin, and the sermon to be preached in Latin, but only the clerics (and not all of them!) understood the language being used. Thus developed an unprecedented cleavage between ritual and intelligibility, with the result that the Reformers of the 16th century would accuse the Roman Catholic liturgy of "superstition" and "magicalism."

The sermon, under such conditions, naturally became relatively unimportant. If it could not be understood by the people who worshiped because it was in a foreign tongue, it could hardly be called "interpretation" of the Scriptures or Word of God. In fact, the very Scriptures themselves were for centuries unintelligible to the common people because they could not understand the language in which they heard them read. The mere ritual itself became the essence of worship, and the sheer *number* of masses said or attended became more important than what they contained.

Alongside this emasculation of meaningful or understandable worship there very naturally arose traditions of vernacular preaching *outside* the churches, as from time to time great popular preachers made their way through the countrysides, drawing enormous crowds and electrifying the people by talking about faith, piety, and morality in language they could understand. Peter the Hermit, who was at least partially responsible for engendering enthusiasm for the First Crusade, and

Bernard of Clairvaux, who presided over the rise of the Cistercian monasteries, were two such celebrated figures, as were a number of the Dominican and Franciscan friars, members of preaching orders that spread throughout Europe to promote the faith through simple exposition in the languages of the people.

Yet little of this popular preaching, any more than the obscure homilies in liturgical setting, compared in its contents with the preaching of the early church. It lacked the theological focus of the early church on the saving work of Christ and tended to center instead on saints' legends, many of which were extremely farfetched and ridiculous, and pieties derived more from local custom than from biblical understanding. It remained for the Reformation to restore preachers' thinking to the biblical understanding of redemption and the declaration of the gospel as it had been proclaimed by the first Christians.

In the *German Mass* devised by Martin Luther and presented in 1526, the extreme ritual of the Roman mass was greatly simplified, the vernacular language was restored, modern hymns were introduced, a Christ-centered sermon was preached, and the magical character of the Lord's Supper was eliminated, with an insistence on the faith of the partaker. Preaching played a far more important role than it had enjoyed in the Middle Ages, but it was still viewed as subordinate to the liturgy as a whole and as providing a necessary introduction to the liturgy of the Upper Room.

Now even the Roman Catholic preaching tradition takes seriously the work of the Reformers and their attempts to correct both the excesses of late medieval worship and the errors and misapplications of what then passed for preaching.

The Effect of the Left-Wing Reformation and the American Frontier

Among the followers of Huldrich Zwingli, his enemies the Anabaptists, and other so-called "left-wing" or "radical" reformationists, whose emphasis was increasingly on the role of human intelligence and the work of the Holy Spirit in worship, the *form* of worship became less and less important. If the Lord's Supper, which had been the focus of Catholic worship and was still the primary concern of Lutheran liturgy, was merely symbolic, reminding us of the Lord's death, then the actual shape of ritual was of far less consequence than what was understood by it. These groups therefore tended to emphasize preaching and interpretation, often to the neglect of other liturgical usages.

A similar effect occurred on the American frontier, where, due to the ecumenical nature of frontier existence and the simplification of liturgical usages encouraged, if not dictated, by the facts of frontier living, the proclamation of the Word easily took precedence over complicated, historical rituals. The famous Cane Ridge camp meetings, as well as subsequent revival gatherings, featured the singing of popular hymns (of the sort written a few years earlier by Charles Wesley) and fervent evangelistic preaching centering on the redemptive work of Christ. Following the meetings, churches of various denominations would gather the "saved" into their own groups and observe baptism and the Lord's Supper in their own manners. The stamp of the general meeting, with its twin emphases on loud music and strong preaching, was set upon mainstream American worship for years to come, and the "Great Preacher" syndrome has tended to dominate North American religion ever since.

Recovering Worship

Since the middle of the present century, when liturgical studies in seminaries and universities began to produce more objective reflections on the nature and meaning of Christian worship and worship committees began to be formed and to become active in several major denominations, producing position papers, study books, and new hymnals and aids to worship, there has been an attempt in many church quarters to restore preaching to a more subordinate role and recapture a sense of *transcendence* in the liturgy. This effort reflects the fact that we no longer live in a frontier situation where life was elemental and simple and where a visiting preacher was more learned, authoritative, and spiritually aware than the local congregation and therefore to be heard with great reverence.

What worshipers in many communions want now is not only evangelistic preaching in the old sense, by which they are brought under conviction and led to Christ, but also evangelistic preaching that sensitively explores the ways in which God's work in Christ affects our self-understanding, our interpersonal relationships, our theology of the world, and our attitudes toward life, work, and others.

Accordingly, there is among several denominations a new emphasis on corporate worship as what we offer to God in response to the knowledge that God was in Christ effecting our salvation and that God's Spirit is still at work in our midst directing us in paths of holy and meaningful living. Proportionately more of the average worship hour is given to prayers and responses in which worshipers acknowledge the worth and majesty of God and offer themselves to God as grateful servants. There is widespread use of jointly planned lectionaries, whereby the churches of several denominations read each week the same passages of Scripture. This magnifies their sense of unity in God's Spirit and their desire to respond to the *whole* Word of God and not merely to favorite passages of their individual ministers or other congregational leaders. Ministers are encouraged to preach sermons based on the lectionary readings, using effective homiletical aids prepared by interdenominational resource teams, instead of merely relying on their own intuitions, training, and inclinations.

In many churches, the old 30- or 45-minute sermon of 50 years ago has given way to a 15- or 20-minute sermon today, and this in itself has altered the character of the presentation. There is no longer time for the elaborate development of complex sermon themes or the narration of several stories in the course of the sermon. Now the sermon must be sharply defined from the outset; the preacher must introduce it succinctly and effectively; and the development must be quick, clear, and to the point. Illustrations must be relatively short and the conclusion or call to commitment must be swift and efficient, without the emotionalism and lingering appeal of the old evangelistic style. The overall effect, when compared with the former way of preaching, is subdued and lends itself well to the more vertical spirit of general worship.

The Contributions of Worship to Preaching

Christian preaching, I have said, is historically of two kinds: preaching done in the context of worship and preaching done in other, usually secular, contexts. When we consider preaching done in the context of worship, we may well ask what effects the context has upon the sermon and, reciprocally, what effects the sermon has on worship.

Worship, it seems to me, should contribute to the effectiveness of the sermon in three specific ways:

A Spirit of Receptivity

The entire liturgical act should prepare a spirit of receptivity in the worshipers, so that the preacher does not have to struggle to make emotional contact with them. Any speaker knows how valuable this service is. It is much easier to cut to the heart of one's intentions in a speech or sermon if the groundwork has already been laid in the audience's "listenability." Even well known comedians and country music stars wait to come on to the stage until lesser known personalities have "warmed up" the crowd. Stump speakers and itinerant evangelists used to begin their presentations with several minutes' worth of jokes, pleasantries, and compliments to their hosts, because they knew that their audiences had to be wooed and won before they could get down to serious business. However, the minister who stands to speak in the midst of a liturgical situation where people's minds and hearts have already been focused on God by the hymns and prayers is able to move quickly and easily to the center of their attention.

A Specific Theme

More particularly, a well-planned worship service not only directs people's minds and hearts to God but can also, if the minister and other service planners wish, direct them toward a specific theme or area of concern, making it even easier for the minister to speak to the congregation's hearing. Howard Stevenson, Minister of Music at First Evangelical Free Church in Fullerton, California, where Chuck Swindoll is the Senior Minister, says in the book, *Mastering Worship* that he consults regularly with Rev. Swindoll about the themes or purposes of Rev. Swindoll's upcoming sermons, so that he can organize the music, readings, and transitional materials of the service to form as perfect a setting as possible for each sermon. Even ministers who do not choose to orchestrate their entire services around sermon topics usually select the hymns that precede or follow their sermons, and announce their topics to the ministers of music in order that the anthems for the service may be coordinated with them. This recognizes the importance of the sermon as the personalized word people will hear in the midst of the liturgy and tilts other variables in the service toward its success.

Aids to Devotion and Commitment

A good worship service surrounds the sermon with other aids to devotion and commitment that "make" the service. If the sermon was not captivating in a frontier worship service, people went away feeling disappointed and unhappy. Not so with a service in which people sing thoughtful and meaningful praises to God, wait before God in silence and prayer, participate in well-chosen litanies or readings, make their offerings of self and substance, receive the bread and cup of Christ's communion, and generally experience the presence of the Holy through the resourceful coordination of liturgical elements. Such a service, gracefully conducted, can well allay the need for a dynamic sermon. Many worshipers through the centuries have contentedly made their way to and from divine services in their local churches while knowing full well that their ministers were not stunning or even very capable preachers; given orderly and well-conceived liturgies, they did not require the inspiration of a great speaker to satisfy their spiritual needs. Realizing this, preachers in such happy situations are freed from anxiety, permitting the Holy Spirit to order their thoughts and command their language for the most fortuitous response to the gospel and the dawning reign of God.

The Contributions of Preaching to Worship

The worship service is clearly helpful to preachers as they interpret the Scriptures and speak to the needs of the congregation. On the flip side of that, what exactly should the sermon contribute to the liturgy?

The sermon, above all other aspects of worship, can be expected to interpret and amplify the Scriptures, which are our primary guide to doctrine and understanding in the faith. Typically, worship services are filled with Scripture references—hymns and anthems fashioned from psalms and other bits of Scripture, allusions in litanies and prayers, the words of institution at the time of the Lord's Supper, the reading of the lections. However, it is in the sermon that a particular portion or portions of Scripture are broken apart like a loaf of bread and fed to the congregation in bite-sized, digestible pieces. Worshipers are often struck by isolated words, phrases, or ideas from Scripture in other parts of the liturgical service. This is part of the serendipity of worship, and the Holy Spirit surely plays a part in achieving it. In the sermon, lingering attention can be focused on a pericope, so that it is interpreted, contemporized, and illustrated for the worshipers, thus "speaking" to them as a living, continuing Word.

The sermon is the minister's opportunity to inject into an otherwise more general and ecumenical service an element of personal communication that is only for the worshipers themselves. When it is time for the sermon, it is as if ministers turn from facing the altar, where their concentration had thus far been on God, and say in confidential tones to each person present: "Now, this is for *you*. I want *you* to hear this. I am going to interpret the Scriptures to *you* and talk to *you* about *your* life, *your* problems, *your* aspirations, and *your* possibilities. God has done something for *you*, and *you* are now going to learn what it is and how it is worked out at this time in *your* existence." The sermon is where ministers point a finger at each worshiper and say, like Nathan of old: "Thou art the man" or "Thou art the woman."

It is the preaching of the gospel that reminds us, in many subtle ways, that the Spirit of God is still operative in our time, laying demands on our lives and even calling some of our number to special training and service. The preacher is a vital symbol of this, called and set aside for the proclamation of the gospel and the care of the church. By merely standing in the midst of God's people as those who have dedicated their lives to the ministry, and who have spent the past week visiting the sick, counseling the confused, praying and studying and preparing a sermon, preachers reassure worshipers that God is active in the world, claiming minds and hearts, rearranging life-plans, and ushering in the divine rule. When the sermon itself is particularly successful, conjuring up collective memories of the faith and reestablishing hope for the future, the worshipers are even more assured. Then they are induced to confront their own situations and to ask if they are living as God wants them to live, and, if they are not, to resubmit themselves to the Spirit's counsel about what they should do.

What the Preacher Can Do

Given the important relationship between preaching and worship, what can you do as an individual preacher to enhance it and promote a stronger sense of spiritual reality in worship? Here are some suggestions:

1. Prepare every sermon you preach in a spirit of prayer and worship. This way you can be certain that the tone or style of the sermon will not negate or vitiate the sense of worship experienced by the congregation. I once heard Elam Davies, who was for many years pastor of the Fourth Presbyterian Church in Chicago, say that he always spread out the pages of his sermon manuscript on a table or sofa when he had completed work on them and prayed: "Here, Lord, this is the best that I could do this week." In this manner, he said, he always felt that his sermon was an offering he made to God. When he went into worship, he did not go empty-handed. Personally, I have found it helpful to ask as I begin the preparation of a sermon: "God, what do you want me to say in this sermon? Guide my mind and heart that I may say what You wish and not what I would say." To the extent that God is indeed in the sermons we preach, they will support and not destroy the spirit of worship in the service.

2. Ask of the sermon when you have completed it: "Could I preach this as an introduction to the Lord's Supper?" If you could—if the substance and tone of the sermon are fitting to be used at the table where we remember our Lord's death—then the sermon is probably suitable for preaching in the service of worship. If the sermon seems unsuited for such a purpose, then you might do well to reexamine it and consider whether you ought not to lay it aside and construct another. The Lord's Supper was from the earliest times a central feature of Christian worship; it is still a plumbline for testing the authenticity of what we do in our services.

3. Remember that the worshipers are waiting in the presence of God for a revelation that will change their lives and inspire them to take a higher road than the one they are on. Except in rare and justifiable instances, preach inspirationally and encouragingly to them, not harshly and judgmentally. There are rare times of exception, when congregations need to hear the prophetic word of condemnation for broken promises, false desires, and cheap commitments; and when these times come and are dealt with faithfully, they do not interrupt the sense of true worship. Generally speaking it is easier to draw flies with honey than it is to drive them with a swatter, and we shall help the average worshiper far more by showing him or her the advantages of moving toward God than by warning of God's wrath or displeasure.

One woman said of her pastor: "He paints such wonderful pictures of what God wants me to be that I always go off singing, confident that that's what I can become." A man said: "I always feel better when I go to worship, like I finally got a base hit and have made it to second, and then our minister gets up and hits a home run and we come in to score together!"

4. Keep the sermon relatively brief and to the point, so that it does not distract from the rest of the liturgy or overstay its welcome with the worshipers. Robert Browne, in *Be Brief About It*, says that people who watch 20 to 30 hours of television a week have learned to glean a lot from a 15-second commercial. They do not need half an hour of sales pitch to get the gist of a product's appeal. By the same token, says Browne, they do not need a 30-minute sermon to convince them of eternal truth. He believes that an eight- or ten-minute homily, if well planned and effectively preached, is just as effective as a much longer sermon in terms of what people retain and how it affects their lives. "Well planned and effectively preached" are perhaps the key words. A well planned sermon will take advantage of everything that happens during the worship service, building on the hymns and prayers to lead people to an encounter with God and a sense of commitment that will change their lives. An effectively preached sermon is one that people hear and remember, even if it is very short.

5. Preach a majority of your sermons from lectionary texts, choosing either the Old Testament, Epistle, or Gospel text designated for each particular Sunday. This will keep you at least partially mindful of preparing a sermon around thoughts that will be basic to the sermons of thousands of other clergy on a given day, and thus enhance your sense of being part of the Church Universal and of participating in the worship paid to God by millions of people. Ministers who make a practice of lectionary preaching attest that they feel an unusual sense of invisible support as they prepare and then deliver their sermons, as if they are joining a great band of spirits all moving in the same direction.

I remember the experience I had on one of the occasions when I went to preach in the Duke University Chapel and was asked if I would please observe the lectionary readings. I was rather busy at the time and considered preaching a favorite sermon that was not based on one of the lectionary texts, but finally decided to submit to the request and write a new sermon. As I did so, I had the feeling that I was being carried along in my thoughts and words by a great indefineable current, and that all I needed to do was to say a prayer and ride that current to the completion of the sermon. It was a good feeling, and I recommend the practice.

6. If the sermon customarily follows the offering and a hymn or anthem, as it does in so many American churches, consider reordering the liturgy to place the reading of the Word and the preaching of the

sermon earlier in the service. This allows the offering and general prayers to follow the sermon instead of preceding it, so that they may be viewed as responses to the proclamation and interpretation of God's movement toward us. This may seem to be a very simple matter with almost no weight at all, but you will be surprised at how it begins subtly to affect the way you regard the sermon as an integral part of worship and not as the climax of the service. It allows the motion of what is done in worship to follow its natural rhythm, which is for us to act upon the knowledge of God's gracious intervention in the human situation, instead of the other way around.

7. Having prepared the sermon in a spirit of prayer and humility, approach the actual preaching of it in the attitude of a servant-leader, not as a know-it-all who has come to talk about his or her own life or to speak authoritatively about an intellectual matter. Martin Luther recalled the way Johann Staupitz, his old teacher, always doffed his hat on entering the classroom because, he said, he never knew what great men of the future sat before him. We are in the limelight when we step into the pulpit, it is true; but we are not there as the smartest or best-informed or even the holiest persons in the congregation. We are there as those called to share Christ's presence with others, many of whom may be far worthier than we are. We may even have the privilege of addressing some little child who will one day rock the world with her writings or discoveries.

There are two lines that intersect in our beings when we stand to preach. One line is historical and vertical, running back to Brooks and Wesley and Zwingli and Francis and Chrysostom and Paul and Peter. The other is contemporary and horizontal, stretching out to all of those present in the congregation with us, and to all our brothers and sisters around the world who can also bear witness to the saving grace of God. The two lines form a cross, and we are on that cross when we preach. As ministers of the gospel, we forget this only at our peril. What did Paul say to his sophisticated friends at Corinth?

> I did not come proclaiming to you the testimony of God in lofty words or wisdom. For I decided to know nothing among you except Jesus Christ and him crucified. And I was with you in weakness and in much fear and trembling; and my speech and my message were not in plausible words of wisdom, but in demonstration of the Spirit and of power, that your faith might not rest in the wisdom of men but in the power of God (1 Cor. 2:1b-5, RSV).

This is why it is a good test for the sermon to ask if it could be preached as an introduction to the service of Communion. Our faith is about what God has done for us in Christ Jesus, and that is exactly what the Communion depicts. If the sermon is suitable as a preparation for our approaching the Lord's Table, then it is a proper response to God's activity in Christ and an integral part of true Christian worship.

Note

1. C. H. Dodd, *The Apostolic Preaching and Its Developments* (New York: Harper and Brothers, n.d.), 17.

Phillips Brooks (1835-1893)
"Truth Through Personality"

He had few of the traditional characteristics expected of great preaching: his delivery was clumsy, rushed, and he stared at the ceiling as he preached. Yet Phillips Brooks was considered one of the finest preachers of his age, attracting large crowds.

What Brooks lacked in traditional eloquence and polish, he made up for in boldness and substance of thought. His preaching helped listeners understand and apply God's Word in their own lives.

A native of Boston and a graduate of Harvard University, Brooks entered the ministry only after initially failing as a school teacher. Though his life–long shyness and insecurity brought similar failure to his initial preaching attempts, he persevered as a preacher because of the encouragement of teachers and fellow seminarians.

After serving two small Episcopal parishes in Philadelphia, in 1861 he became rector of Holy Trinity Church in Boston, and quickly became the city's best–known preacher. Through his preaching and other speaking, particularly against slavery, he became known as a prophetic voice in the pulpit.

His 1877 presentation of the Yale lectures on preaching is still considered one of the finest ever in that prestigious series; it was in those lectures that Brooks provided his now-famous definition of preaching as "truth through personality." Two years before his untimely death at age 57, Brooks became the Episcopal bishop for Massachusetts.

The ministry of Phillips Brooks offers ample evidence that power in preaching is less a matter of eloquence than of courageous proclamation and a pastor's love.

37
Wayne E. Oates
Professor of Psychiatry and Behavioral Sciences
University of Louisville School of Medicine
Louisville, Kentucky

Preaching and Pastoral Care

Both the practice of preaching and that of pastoral care are inseparable functions of the Christian pastor. Even in large, multi-staff churches where there are associate pastors of pastoral care, the preaching pastor will have pastoral care to do that cannot be delegated and the associate pastor needs periodic preaching opportunities. Preaching and pastoral care are woven together as one spiritual tapestry. Therefore any discussion of preaching and pastoral care must be from a synoptic angle of vision.

Preaching and Pastoral Care as Relational Events

Both preaching and pastoral care are *relational* events. They are face-to-face relationships between the pastor and the congregation, family, small group, or individual. In both preaching and pastoral care this can be easily forgotten or ignored by the pastor. The kind and quality of relationship is the medium through which the wisdom and care of the pastor reaches or does not reach other people.

Sermon preparation is a sweaty task when rightly done. The preacher may be so concentrated on the sermon itself that the audience is neglected in the effort to present a meticulously prepared sermon. This is *sermon*-centered preaching. The audience-centered sermon, on the other hand, focuses on the people themselves. Even a so-called "life-situation" sermon can be the exposition of a "problem" of people in general to the neglect of the personal kind and quality of relationship between the preacher and the congregation. Is the relationship warm and empathetic or is it detached and distant? Is the relationship one of trust and respect or of suspicion and distrust? Is the tone of the preacher's voice a carping, complaining tone or is it one of simple honesty, humor free of hostility, and filled with compassion for human frailty? Is the relationship one in which the preacher "lords it over the flock" or is it one in which he or she is an example to the flock, as 1 Peter 5:2 puts it? The letters of Paul are replete with his attention to his relationship to the audience to whom he is speaking. Philippians 1:1-11 is an excellent example of Paul's clarification of his relationship to the Philippians before he said anything else to them.

Even in sermons in which some very painful ethical confrontation may be necessary, it is wise, as Paul said, to restore the congregation in a spirit of gentleness looking to oneself, lest we also be tempted (Gal. 6:1). If the finger is pointed at others, call attention to the three other fingers pointing back at oneself. A very wise physician told a group of us once: "When you confront someone you should do so the way a surgeon operates on a patient's hand. He or she always upholds the hand with one hand while cutting with the other!" Confrontation is usually thought of as a hostile relationship. The most effective confrontation is speaking the truth in love (Eph. 4:15) as we grow together into Christ. Our relationship is an edifying or building up of each other, not tearing down each other.

Pastoral Care as a Source of Homiletical Inspiration

The personal and private pastoral care of individuals and families involves their life stories. These stories are the stuff of which life is made. Caring ministers often receive as much or more than they give in pastoral care of persons. These life stories are often dramatized vividly in metaphors that people use. These stories and metaphors are often—but not always—of such a nature that they can, *with the permission of their authors,* become the stuff of which sermons are made. For example, I was the pastor of a rural church in the tobacco farming area of Kentucky. I heard that the fourteen-year-old son of one of our church members had run away from home. I went to see the father—a father of thirteen other children! I sought to comfort him in this crisis. He thanked me for my visit and said: "I have checked carefully on his whereabouts. He is on the other side of the county, living and working with a good family that we know. He is safe and out of harm's way."

Then he said, as if to change the subject: "You see, Brother Oates, you can't raise a crop of tobacco in the plant bed. Plants have to be pulled up and planted in the field or they will cease to grow." He was giving me a metaphor of how the plant bed is sterilized with fire, cultivated carefully, and planted with seeds. When they become tender shoots, a canvas is spread over them lest the sun be too hot for them. When they can stand the sun, the canvas is removed. They grow to a height that they can be uprooted and planted in the wide open field, each plant standing on its own.

The plant bed was a metaphor for his home. He had the wisdom of years to be patient with his own and to look upon his son's "leaving home" as a step in his growth. After all, it was Jesus who said that in responding to His call to discipleship a person leaves father and mother (Matt. 19:29). In marriage, a person leaves father and mother and cleaves to his or her spouse (Matt. 19:5-6).

The metaphor my church member used is an earthly illustration of the texts to which I have just referred. It calls attention to the order of creation in which spiritual growth calls for children growing up and learning to be independent of parents. It also notes the way in which neighborhoods, church fellowships, and other adult mentors can participate in this process for each other.

Of course, the use of such a metaphor must be done with the parishioner's full consent, foreknowledge, and in such a way that the young son is not embarrassed. With care, good taste, and empathy this inspired bit of wisdom can edify the whole congregation. My basic point in this illustration is that pastoral care with individuals, families, and small groups can provide inspiration and wisdom for the preaching task.

Pastoral care through a sermon is different from the pastoral care of an individual. In the latter case, a pastor is searching with the individual counselee for the *uniqueness* of his or her plight. In pastoral care through a sermon, the pastor is searching with the congregation for the testings and temptations which are *common* to all of the congregation (see 1 Cor. 10:13). He or she is seeking those great universal concerns. For example a sermon could be entitled "Living Under Threat." Paul Tillich's three great threats common to all of us could be an outline:

1. The Threat of Fate and Death
2. The Threat of Emptiness and Meaninglessness
3. The Threat of Guilt and Condemnation.[1]

Preaching As a Form of Pastoral Care

Many pastoral care needs of a congregation can be met through the preaching event itself. Congregations go through severe crises as a whole community of faith. For example, more and more congregations as a whole are facing the crisis of having members afflicted with human immune virus, commonly known as AIDS. Pastors are called upon to sort through and work through the ambiguous ethical issues and provide compassionate ministry to the AIDS member and his or her family. The congregation responds as a whole. William Amos has written a documentary which includes his work as a preacher in the face of such a crisis in his book, *When AIDS Comes to Church.*[2]

I recall also how the church building where the congregation of which my wife and I are members burned early one bitterly cold Sunday morning. We gathered for the regular 11 o'clock service in the unheated Southern Baptist Seminary chapel. It was 10 below 0 degrees outside. All of us huddled together in our top coats. Our pastor asked me to lead the pastoral prayer. These are the words given to me to say:

> O God our help in ages past, Our hope for years to come, Be thou our shelter from the stormy blast and our eternal home. We give Thee our thanks, our Heavenly Father, for the gift of fire to keep us warm, even as the warmth radiates up from the floor of this building to keep us warm. We thank Thee for the gift of fire that helps us prepare our foods so that they will be warm and edible and nourishing. We thank Thee for fire which is a symbol, a picture, of the Power of Thy Holy Spirit descending upon us in a Pentecostal way separating itself to the foreheads of each of us. In fire Thou hast endowed us with the gift of understanding. Through the power of Thy Spirit Thou dost create on earth, in spite of sin, in spite of man's inhumanity to man. We humbly believe we are the body of Christ, the church against whom the gates of Hell shall not prevail. Yet we thank Thee our Father for the fear that fire strikes into our hearts when it is out of control. We give Thee our thanks that bodily all of us are here, and no one has been sent to a burn unit. We thank Thee for the firemen who risked their lives, who withstood more cold and exposure than any of us may ever do. We thank Thee for their families who share them with us. May we never take the work of firemen, of policemen, of doctors and nurses, and hospitals for granted.
>
> We thank Thee our Father that we are gathered together in this holy place. Our church is not a building. We the people of God where we come together *are* the church. As we come here because fire, out of control, has been meant to us for evil, Thy Spirit and Thy Power to guide us in such a fellowship wilt fulfill Thy intention that this tragic happening shall be unto us for good. May it cleanse our motives and sharpen the direction of our ministry. May it empower us to reach out to those people in this community who never have enough heat, who never have enough food, who never have enough medicine, who never have enough care. Make us instruments of that kind of caring, through Jesus Christ whose we are, whom we serve, and whom we adore. Amen.

The pastor then had the task of preaching in such a way as to stabilize the shocked congregation and to undergird them for the sufferings ahead of us. He started the sermon with an affirmation, "St. Matthews Baptist Church is alive and well! Thank God!" He drew us together in a common resolve to be the church at work in ministering to others and each other as we rebuilt the buildings.

Congregations go through corporate grieving, as was the case of a church in Pennsylvania where twenty-eight members of a quartermaster reserve unit were killed by a scud missile attack that destroyed their barracks during the Gulf War.

Another example is the church from which a bus load of teen-agers was killed in a fiery crash when a drunken driver was driving at a high speed going the wrong direction on a freeway. A whole church and town were thrown into acute grief that deepened into chronic grief over a two-year period because of the trial and conviction of the man who, in a drunken state, caused the wreck.

In stress research we have a concept called *endemic* stress. This is the stress of an unremitting nature that affects whole populations of people. The stress of the ordinary people of Iraq is an example. The threat of death on crowded city streets in this country is an endemic stress. The sermon that addresses these stresses is a form of pastoral care from the pulpit. A careful expository sermon on Romans 5:1-5 would provide the framework for such a sermon.

The Sermon as a Stimulus for Seeking Counseling

It is said that Jonathan Edwards' powerful sermons stimulated people to seek his spiritual guidance in his study during the week. Harry Emerson Fosdick measured the effectiveness of his preaching by the number of people it prompted to seek his counsel on a personal basis. The nineteenth-century evangelists used the "enquiry room" for people to present personal concerns after the service was over. These are examples of the integral relationship between preaching and pastoral care. The invitation has become a threadbare ritual and could be rewoven by pastors who are committed to meeting people at the depths of their need.

For example, a pastor could extend an invitation to the congregation for as many as felt led to do so to meet him or her at a stated time to discuss issues that the sermon raised in their minds. Also, a periodic encouragement of the congregation to seek their pastor's spiritual encouragement would be an enrichment of the invitation. The invitation should be an instrument of pastoral care and not just a ritual for recruitment of new members.

Conversely, the ritual of the invitation as a time when people join the church can be the culmination of a series of pastoral conversations with the person, the end result of pastoral care rather than the stimulus of pastoral care situations. The invitation in many churches needs enrichment. It seems to me that to relate the invitation to the pastoral care needs of the people is an effective way to enrich it. One thing that militates against this and other means of pastoral care is the aura of "busyness" that surrounds many pastors. Such initiatives as I have just mentioned have a way of saying to the congregation that the pastor has time for them. The sermon and the invitation can be a means of grace whereby pastor and people can connect at the point of their deepest needs for pastoral care.

Life Situation Preaching

As early as the middle forties and fifties, a particular kind of sermon was crafted. Charles Kemp, a pastor and pioneer in pastoral care and counseling, gathered together a collection of sermons by homiletical greats of many decades: Horace Bushnell, "Dissolving Doubts"; Phillips Brooks, "The Purpose and Use of Comfort"; Charles Jefferson, "Shadows"; Harry Emerson Fosdick, "Handicapped Lives"; Walter Russell Berne, "Greatness Under Difficulty," and many others. He outlined the criteria for life-situation preaching: "Is the problem 'common to all people'? Does it deal with a true life situation? Does the sermon grow out of human experience? . . . Would it lead people to go to the one who preached the sermon for personal guidance and help?"[3] The entry of the psychological influence upon preaching took the form of this kind of preaching.

We can accurately say that the modern pastoral care movement had its beginnings in the pulpits of this country before it took root in hospital visitation of the sick. The preaching of Horace Bushnell, Washington Gladden, Harry Emerson Fosdick, Leslie Weatherhead, and Theodore Adams heralded a conscious effort of these persons to extend pastoral care to their congregations from the pulpit. The present practice of pastoral care in hospitals and in pastoral counseling centers could be enriched greatly by the historical examination of these homiletical origins. The work, for example, of Fosdick and Weatherhead, encompasses the years of World War II and all the endemic stress of those years.

One raises the question, however, as to the basic doctrinal substance of such preaching. Does it so concentrate on the plight of humankind that the divine-human encounter in Jesus Christ is ignored or made incidental? Is the heart of the gospel made incidental to the problems of people? Are these sermons purely psychological exercises?

The answers to these questions are clear. Such sermons can indeed be exhortations of self-help. However, they need not be so. The life situation sermon has a serious doctrinal approach; however, it is a different kind of approach to doctrine. As Gaines Glenn Atkins says of Horace Bushnell: "The age he inherited approached life through doctrine. He approached doctrine through life."[4] The presence of the Lord Jesus Christ in crucial human situations is at work revealing the nature of God and the mission of human beings to the pastor who has eyes to see and ears to hear. After a heavy day of care of people in dire circumstances, preachers can bathe their minds in the pure, refreshing words of the

Bible. The distilled essence of the Christian faith will be more concrete and clearer as they do so.

Preaching and Pastoral Care as Consciousness Raising

A powerful dynamic of the unified task of pastoral care and preaching is the way it can raise the consciousness of a congregation to encompass the dispossessed, disfranchised, and outcasts of our world.

Divorce

Churches are reaching out in great numbers to divorced persons in and out of the church. This past Sunday I heard a superb sermon by our pastor, William Tuck, on the biblical teachings about divorce. He described the "difficult teaching of Jesus" as setting forth the ideal of Christian marriage and the compassion of Jesus in including the Woman at the Well in His spiritual redemption.

The Mentally Ill

Another group of the dispossessed is the mentally ill. Early in this century, Anton Boisen, a recovered mentally ill person himself, established a chaplaincy in a mental hospital. He had regular worship services for these patients. He even composed a hymn book for these services called, *Hymns of Hope.*[5]

Likewise, the problems of the mentally ill such as depression, suspicion, suicidal impulses, and personality disorders are becoming topics for series of sermons. For example, William Turner, pastor of South Main Baptist Church in Houston, Texas, recently preached a series of sermons on the personality disorders described in the *Diagnostic and Statistical Manual of Mental Disorders.* He probed deeply the biblical significance of these self-defeating ways of life. He brought the "character disorders" or patterns of living under the light of the good news of God in Jesus Christ. The subjects of his sermons and their texts are as follows:

> Getting Free from Dependency: "I Want to Stand on My Own" —Galatians 4:1-20
>
> Getting Free from Pretense: "I'm Bored and Restless and Fed Up with Faking It"—Mark 10:17-22
>
> Getting Free from Pride: "It's Tough Being Master of the Universe" —Luke 18:9-14.
>
> Getting Free from Angry Aggression: "I'm Tired of Getting Mad and Getting Even"—Luke 9:51-56
>
> Getting Free from Aimlessness: "To Be or Not To Be—I'm Sick of the Question"—Genesis 3:1-13

Getting Free from Perfectionism: "Help! My Conscience is Overheated!"—Matthew 23:23-24

Getting Free from Shame and Emptiness: "Must I Always Be a Loser?"—Luke 18:9-14

Getting Free from Suspiciousness: "I Wish There Was Somebody I Could Trust"—John 13:21-30

Turner brought the issues of mental illness and health out of the domain of psychiatric hospitals and into the everyday experience of the average church-going person. He did so without putting people down but by edifying them in the more personal meaning and claims of the gospel.

Moral Confusion about Sexuality

The consciousness of congregations is being raised from within and without about the massive amounts of moral confusion about sexuality. Whereas the Bible is forthright and outspoken about these issues, the preaching of today tends to look this way and that for severe criticism if he or she should or should not approach such issues as promiscuity or "recreational" sex, the "living together" phenomenon, homosexuality, and sexual abuse of children and women. Yet, all the while the pastor is conferring in personal counseling with people who are caught in the confusion these behaviors create.

The emergence of the AIDS epidemic has brought many of these problems—though not all of them—to the consciousness of people in and out of the church. Some pastors have presented sermons on AIDS and raised their congregations' awareness that this can happen to almost anyone who is not educated to prevent it.

However, two basic issues in human sexuality pervade all the problems that have been mentioned: *commitment* and *fidelity.* The opposite of these is promiscuousness and infidelity, deception and betrayal. Whatever form sexuality takes, these issues lie at the heart of the relationship. A cardinal principle of the mature, responsible personality is the capacity to form and maintain lifelong relationships. Sermons on this subject will go to the heart of the matter and apply to all forms of sexual covenants between people. The febrile threat of abandonment pervades shallow sexual liaison. The threats of unwanted children and the contracting of deadly diseases still hover over irresponsible sex.

Another basic issue pervades all forms of sexuality: responsibility. The right of all children being born into the world is to be wanted and to have their mother *and* father be responsible for them who teach them to be responsible for themselves in adulthood. A report released in June, 1991, by a 34-member bipartisan panel chaired by Senator John D. Rockefeller, says this concerning children in poverty (one in five American children): "Children do best when they have personal involvement . . . of a father and a mother, and when both parents fulfill their responsibility to be loving providers."

Homiletical approaches to human sexual behavior in terms of commitment, fidelity, and responsibility cut through the biases and prejudices of people and get to the heart of what it means to be sexual. Excellent background reading for preaching on these subjects can be found in C. Lloyd Rediger's, *Ministry and Sexuality: Cases, Counseling, and Care.* [6]

Preaching on topics about which a congregation does not think much and about which they speak only in private (if at all) can provoke questions and uneasy feelings. The pastor who preaches on these subjects is well-advised to organize teaching and discussion groups in which feedback can be expressed. Otherwise, the feedback may never reach the pastor or, if it does, it comes in a second, third, or fourth-hand way, getting distorted as it is retold again and again.

The common fulcrum used by pastoral care and preaching is the teaching and learning group. This feedback has a free and circular flow. Distortions are clarified. Wisdom and understanding have a chance to prevail.

Exegetical Preaching and Pastoral Care

We often assume that the relationship between preaching and pastoral care must be a preaching that draws its inspiration and subject matter from life situations, psychological issues, and/or self-help books. Far from it! A direct search of the Scripture provides biblical materials hurting to be preached that are distinctly related to contemporary pastoral care. Look then at a few examples.

One major issue in church conflict situations is that church people do not talk directly to the person with whom they have an ax to grind. If you take Matthew 18:15-20, you find Jesus teaching that a person should (1) go privately, one-on-one, face-to-face to a person who has sinned against them. (2) The objective is to get them to listen. (3) If this fails, then a person is instructed to take a third person with him or her. Again, the objective is to get them *to listen.* (4) If this fails, then one can bring the matter to the attention of the church. The objective is still to get them to listen.

This is not to be done in a punitive way. The apostle Paul suggested further in Galatians 6:1: "If a man is overtaken in any trespass, you who are spiritual restore that person in a spirit of gentleness. Look to yourself, lest you too be tempted" (RSV). These passages deal with a pastoral care issue that persistently presents itself to a pastor. A sermon entitled, "Face-to-Face Living," or "Listening: The Healing of Conflict," or "Restoration Through Gentleness and Self-Examination" would be in order.

Another pastoral care concern in every church is the ministry to and the ministry of widows. This concern appeared early in the post-Resurrection community of faith. In Acts 6:1-6 murmurings of the Hellenists against the Hebrews arose because their widows were being neglected. In response new leaders were chosen to minister to the economic situation of Greek widows. Furthermore, in 1 Timothy 5:3-16, explicit instructions are given to us concerning the pastoral care of widows of different types and stations in life. Yet this ministry is full of temptations to exploit widows and their children. Hence, James 1:27 says: "Religion that is pure and undefiled before God is this: to visit the widows and orphans in their affliction, and to keep oneself unspotted from the world" (RSV). These are just two of the numerous examples of texts that good exegesis will provide clear guidance and pastoral care for a congregation, families, and individuals. We as pastors are called upon to, as 1 Peter 5:2-4 says:

> Tend the flock of God that is in your charge, not by constraint, but willingly, not for shameful gain but eagerly, not as domineering over those in your charge, but being examples to the flock. And when the chief Shepherd is manifested you will obtain the unfading crown of glory (RSV).

Even this passage can be the basis of a sermon interpreting your relationship to your people as their undershepherd of Jesus Christ.

Conclusion

We have discussed preaching and pastoral care as relational events, pastoral care as a source of homiletical inspiration, preaching as a form of pastoral care, the sermon as a stimulus for seeking counseling, life situation preaching, preaching as a consciousness raising event, and exegetical preaching as pastoral care. Other dimensions of preaching and pastoral care could be discussed, but the initial assumption of the unity of preaching and pastoral care is the theme that binds all of these together into a coherent and compassionate ministry.

Notes

1. Paul Tillich, *The Courage to Be* (New Haven: Yale University Press, 1952), 40-51.
2. See William Amos, *When AIDS Comes to Church* (Louisville: Westminister/John Knox Press, 1988).
3. Charles Kemp, *Life-Situation Preaching* (St. Louis: Bethany Press, 1956), 28-29.
4. Quoted in Kemp, *Life-Situation Preaching*, 219.
5. See Anton Boisen, *Hymns of Hope*, rev. ed. (Elgin, Ill.: Brethren Publishing House, 1950).
6. See C. Lloyd Rediger, *Ministry and Sexuality: Cases, Counseling, and Care* (Minneapolis: Fortress Press, 1990).

38

James Emory White, Pastor
Mecklenburg Community Church
Charlotte, North Carolina

Preaching and Administration

A recent survey of "Fortune 500" top executives revealed that the quality considered most important for leadership was communication skill.[1] James C. Humes writes that the difference between mere management and leadership is "communication. And that art of communication is the language of leadership."[2] The language of leadership is one of the greatest needs in contemporary preaching and is the essence of the relationship between preaching and administration in the life of the church.[3] In order to move beyond mere efficiency to a ministry of effectiveness, the preaching task must include the ability to communicate the church's mission, goals, and programs with clarity and impact.

Learning the Language of Leadership

There are six major components to the relationship between preaching and administration: mission, vision, values, strategy, goals, and programs. Each must be addressed and communicated in such a way that those listening both understand and are motivated toward action and support.

Mission

The foundational communication is that of mission—the church's reason for existence. Proclaiming "why we exist" is the foundational platform for any church's administration. Understanding the purpose of the church is not something that should be taken for granted, but should be continually communicated as a regular staple of the preaching regimen. Many pastors meet this need through an annual sermon or sermon series on the mission of the church.

For most churches, the mission of the church is understood to involve four primary activities: worship, ministry, evangelism, and discipleship. Regardless of a church's understanding of its purpose, that purpose needs to be proclaimed from a biblical base if it is to be perceived as authentic. During my years as a pastor, I scheduled an annual sermon series on the purpose of the church, using such summary passages on the early church as Acts 2:42-47.

Many churches have developed this to the point of a "Mission Statement" that succinctly captures the purpose of the church. To be effective as a common understanding of the church's mission or purpose, such statements must be communicated on a regular basis.[4]

Vision

The business world has long understood the importance of vision, for if administration is the management or governing of institutional affairs, a guiding vision must be in place to serve as the molding force of the organization's activities. George Barna has defined vision for ministry as a "clear mental image of a preferable future, imparted by God to His chosen servants, based upon an accurate understanding of God, self, and circumstances."[5] Vision is distinct from mission, Barna adds, as vision is more strategic in nature. Mission states the broad purposes for which the ministry exists; vision details the particular strategy and unique nature of that mission as it manifests itself in a particular context.[6]

Guy Kawasaki has given a unique perspective to the communication of vision, calling it "selling the dream." He observes that selling a dream means "transforming a vision . . . into a cause and getting people to share that cause."[7] It is doubtful that there could ever be a better description of the relationship between preaching and administration.

A church's vision, therefore, involves how that church will uniquely fulfill its mission. Who will the church reach? How will this church be distinct from other churches? Where is our mission taking us? What are we trying to develop into as an organization and as a community of faith? Communicating a vision that speaks to these concerns is indispensable in terms of preaching's relationship to administration.

Values

Values are important to preach in terms of church leadership. Describing values answers three questions: What is considered important to a community of faith? Where do those values come from? Why are those values held by the church? Sometimes called "value amplification," what is at hand is the "process of elevating certain values as basic to the overall mission."[8] For example, if the mission of the church includes the evangelistic task, and the vision incorporates innovative strategies to reach out to the non-believer, then the preaching task must undergird the administrative efforts to structure for the fulfillment of that mission and vision by proclaiming the foundational value that lost people matter to God.

Strategy

A decisive component to the relationship between preaching and administration is the strategy of the church. In essence, the preacher's task involves sharing the following: *why* we do *what* we do the *way* we do it. The communication of methodological philosophy is decisive because few churches have their methodology divorced from their mission, vision, and values.

At this point it is important to discuss how preaching supports the administrative dynamics of change, for it is over methodology that resistance to change is most often manifest. The reason why change is often resisted is simply a lack of communication. As John Maxwell rightly notes, people change when they learn enough that they either *want* to change or understand and accept the *need* to change.[9] If the mission is clearly communicated, supported by the clear articulation of the church's vision and values, then methodological innovation that is clearly formulated in light of the church's mission, vision, and values will seldom be resisted.[10]

Goals

Effective leadership and administration inevitably involve setting goals and then striving for their attainment. Preaching is indispensable to these tasks, for if a goal is to be achieved, it must be clearly communicated and understood. Goals are distinct from both mission and vision, though mission and vision can be put forth as qualitative goals. Goals are usually specific, quantitative targets set for the church and its members in light of the church's mission, vision, values, and strategy.

Perhaps the most typical annual goal for most churches is the budget. Attendance figures are another common goal in many churches. The preaching task makes these goals known to the church, sets them in the context of the church's purpose and vision, and then issues the challenge and gives the motivation necessary for their actualization.

To effectively support such goals, the language of leadership must be sensitive to why people support causes, which usually involves the following: to do the right thing, to feel good about something, to contribute to society, to prove themselves, to join a social group, and to enrich their lives.[11] As James M. Kouzes and Barry Z. Posner note, "what is rewarding gets done."[12]

Programs

The average church calendar is filled with a wide variety of events that would benefit greatly from direct pulpit support and often receive such support. Most programs are brought into the life of the church to directly support the church's mission, vision, values, strategy, and goals. This relationship should be clearly articulated.

The key factors preaching offers to programs are validation and motivation. The program must be biblically validated in light of the church's mission, and then individuals must be motivated toward a level of involvement and support.

Perhaps the most common type of program that receives sermonic encouragement is that connected with stewardship. Many stewardship programs in the life of the church depend on effective pulpit support, such as the popular "Prove the Tithe" day held annually in many churches. For such a program to be effective, the biblical basis of the tithe and God's promises connected with giving must be clearly communicated and timed to coincide with the invitation to participate in the blessings God has promised to those who live in financial obedience to His word.

It is important to note that the six components mentioned above should be seen as somewhat sequential in terms of their implementation. It is a clearly articulated understanding of the church's mission that sets the church's administrative agenda. Most of the conflict in churches today can be traced to disagreement over the purpose of the church, not disagreement over the theology of the church.[13] The church's vision determines the direction the church takes in regard to its mission. The values and strategies of the organization offer further definition to the administrative activities of the community of faith. The church's goals and programs are then seen as the logical and accepted manifestation of what has already been made clear in light of the church's orientation. At every step the preaching task offers the indispensable language of leadership to ensure the effectiveness of the church's activities.

Communicating the Language of Leadership

Nine general categories mark the actual communication of the language of leadership. Each is an important vehicle for effectively using the preaching task to complement the administrative task.

Stories

Perhaps the most powerful tool for communicating the language of leadership within the preaching event is the use of stories that capture the essence of the vision, methodology, goal, or program that is being promoted. Stories engage our mind and spirit and are much more effective at conveying vision and goals than didactive material. Illustrations, as Reg Grant and John Reed note, have a way of "sneaking past the defenses of the heart."[14] They add that a "good story doesn't permit casual observation."[15] As a result, stories are extremely powerful communication tools for the preacher to use in support of the administrative task.

Conviction

The appearance of conviction and passion is indispensable in any preaching which has motivation as its goal. Simply put, if you do not *seem* to care, they will not *bother* to care. Enthusiasm is as infectious as negativism. Convictional preachers convey their message with emo tional force. In terms of traditional Greek rhetoric, an individual's pathos is the gateway to their ethos and logos.[16]

Positive Attitude

A positive, optimistic attitude breeds enthusiasm, which is desperately needed in the life of most churches. A positive spirit as conveyed through the preaching task is also extremely important to effective church administration. Studies of baby boomers have revealed that they simply are not motivated by guilt. In other words, negative preaching is ineffective for the support of the administration. I am not sure of its source, but a friend once shared with me the following truism: "A pat on the back, though only a few vertebrae removed from a kick in the pants, is miles ahead in results."

An interesting study was carried out by Flavil Yeakley for a dissertation research project at the University of Illinois at Urbana-Champaign. Yeakley studied over 1,000 churches in order to determine the dynamics of persuasion in religious conversion. His research revealed that there was a decided difference in effect between "negative" and "positive" styles of preaching in terms of church growth:

Effect of Preaching Style on Church Growth[17]

Low Growth Churches:
75% Negative
Medium Growth Churches:
81% Negative
High Growth Churches:
97% Positive

From an extremely pragmatic perspective, if the preaching style is decidedly negative, then the church is being trained to be negative. In this kind of environment members become more comfortable and familiar with knowing what they are "against" than what they are "for."

From an administrative perspective, the "negative" preacher should not be surprised when business meetings are less than supportive of new ideas or innovation.

Corporate Terminology

One of the most important shifts in terminology that can take place in terms of the relationship between administration and preaching is from the use of "I" to the use of "we." E. M. Kelly observes the following difference between a boss and a leader: "a boss says, 'Go!'—a leader says 'Let's go!' "[18]

Repetition

One of the most important methodological understandings in regard to implementing the language of leadership is repetition. Assuming that the church's mission is well understood can lead to a rude awakening for the church leader who discovers that not only is it not understood, but the understanding that *is* in place is far from the one desired.[19]

Simplicity

It is a mistake to assume that profundity is tied to complexity. Brevity marks effective communication. The Declaration of Independence is no more than 1,322 words; Lincoln's Gettysburg Address has 268 words; the Lord's Prayer contains only 56 words. These communicated messages which impacted the world beyond description, but did not need length to do so. The world of sales has an acronym that many preachers could stand to learn: KISS—"Keep It Short and Sweet" (or, less flatteringly, "Keep It Simple, Stupid").[20]

Many individuals strive for simplicity through the use of slogans. There can be little doubt that slogans have been incredibly successful in communicating vision throughout history. One has only to think of Patrick Henry's "Give me liberty or give me death," Martin Luther King's "I have a dream," or John F. Kennedy's "Ask not what your country can do for you; ask what you can do for your country." As a communication tool to support administrative goals and programs, slogans can be extremely effective. They should never be used, however, without more substantive sermonic support.

Appeal to Mission

An important habit is to tie goals and programs to the wider mission of the church. The mission of the church should serve as the justification for the activity at hand. The sheer number of programs can breed inattention. A clear relationship between the specific program and the wider mission of the church is instrumental for effective motivation.

Appeal to Action

If preaching is to support the administration and embody the language of leadership, it must be specific in its appeal to action. Four important components constitute the essence of any sermon that wishes to be practical in its application: 1) aim for a specific action; 2) be sure to tell your listeners why they should take this specific action; 3) most importantly, show them how; and 4) strongly consider making your application points your sermon points.

Target Your Audience

The background of your congregation should form *how* you communicate *what* you communicate. Speakers who target their audience are seeking answers to important questions: Who are these people? Where are they from? What are they thinking? How are they feeling? What are their needs? What are their hurts? What are their interests? What presuppositions do they carry about the church and its ministry? Even the most basic demographic data, such as the average level of education, can prove helpful in formulating a message for greatest impact.

Implementing the Language of Leadership

The final task for preaching and administration is to implement the language of leadership into your preaching calendar. Three suggestions include an annual "State of the Church" sermon, an annual series on the mission of the church, and the coordination of at least one major program with a sermon or sermon series.

"State of the Church" Sermon

Many pastors include a "State of the Church" sermon in their annual preaching calendar. This sermon usually involves the following dynamics: 1) explanation of the mission of the church; 2) description of the vision of the church; 3) analysis of how the church is doing in light of the mission and vision of the church; and 4) a challenge to renew corporate commitment to the mission and vision of the church for the coming year.

Annual Series on the Mission of the Church

The purpose of the church is such an important item to keep before the church that many preachers include an annual series on the mission of the church in their sermon planning. Whether its form takes shape as four sermons on the four tasks of the church (worship, ministry, evangelism, and discipleship) or as an exposition of the book of Acts in light of the mission of the early church, such a series serves as an annual reminder that everything the church engages itself in relates to the mission of the church.

Coordination of Preaching and Program

Many programs depend heavily on pulpit support. Examples include, but are far from limited to, the following: sermon series on stewardship to coincide with budget promotion; sermon on the importance of social action to support the beginning of a food pantry; sermon series on the importance of world missions prior to a missions offering drive; and a sermon on the importance of evangelism in light of a city-wide series of evangelistic meetings. The goal is to reflect on the calendar of the church and coordinate the preaching calendar with major administrative events that would benefit from direct pulpit support in the form of a sermon or sermon series. Themes that are highly relevant to administration should be espoused regularly, whether in direct connection with a particular program or not, such as stewardship and servanthood.

An example from my own pastoral background was "Reaching Your Potential," a sermon series which focused on the importance of discovering, developing, and then deploying your spiritual gift(s) for ministry in the life of the church. This series intentionally served as an introduction to a planned administrative shift toward the use of spiritual giftedness for the staffing of church leadership positions. The administrative program was designed to enroll individuals into a spiritual gifts awareness class, then train individuals according to their spiritual gift. The final step was to build the ministry and leadership of the church according to the spiritual gifts of our members. The preaching task was to introduce the biblical basis of spiritual gifts, highlight their importance in the life of the believer and in the life of the church, and lay the foundation for the administrative program to be effectively implemented and accepted into our community of faith.

In conclusion, the relationship between preaching and administration is what is known as the "language of leadership." When preaching supports church administration, the ministry of the church flows more smoothly and more effectively.

Notes

1. Cited by Marlene Caroselli, *The Language of Leadership* (Amherst, Massachusetts: Human Resource Development Press, Inc, 1990), 39.

2. James C. Humes, *The Sir Winston Method: The Five Secrets of Speaking the Language of Leadership* (New York: William Morrow and Company, 1991), 14.

3. Books on church administration are abundant, including, but not limited to, the following: Kennon L. Callahan, *Effective Church Leadership* (San Francisco: Harper and Row Publishers, 1990); Edward R. Dayton and Ted W. Engstrom, *Strategy for Leadership: Planning, Activating, Motivating, Elevating* (Old Tappan: Fleming H. Revell Company, 1979); Peter F. Drucker, *Managing the Nonprofit Organization: Principles and Practices* (New York: HarperCollins Publishers, 1990); Kenneth O. Gangel, *Feeding and Leading: A Practical Handbook on Administration in Churches and Christian Organizations* (Wheaton: Victor, 1989); Bruce P. Powers, ed., *Church Administration Handbook: Resources for Church Leaders*

(Nashville: Broadman Press, 1985); Lawrence O. Richards and Clyde Hoeldtke, *Church Leadership* (Grand Rapids: Zondervan, 1980); and Charles A. Tidwell, *Church Administration: Effective Leadership for Ministry* (Nashville: Broadman Press, 1985).

4. See the excellent discussion of a church's mission statement by John Yarbrough in *Visionary Leadership for Church Growth,* J. Truman Brown, Jr., comp. (Nashville: Convention Press, 1991), 69-85.

5. George Barna, *Without a Vision, the People Perish* (Glendale, CA: Barna Research Group, 1991), 28.

6. Ibid., 145.

7. Guy Kawasaki, *Selling the Dream: How to Promote Your Product, Company, or Ideas - and Make a Difference - Using Everday Evangelism* (New York: HarperCollins Publishers, 1991), 4.

8. Jay A. Conger, *The Charismatic Leader* (San Francisco: Jossey-Bass, 1991), 87.

9. Quoted in Elmer Towns, *Ten of Today's Most Innovative Churches* (Ventura: Regal, 1990), chapter 1.

10. The classic text on communicating and implementing change in the life of the church remains Lyle E. Schaller, *The Change Agent: The Strategy of Innovative Leadership* (Nashville: Abingdon, 1972). See also Leith Anderson's *Dying for Change* (Minneapolis: Bethany House Publishers, 1990).

11. Kawasaki, *Selling the Dream,* 53-54.

12. James M. Kouzes and Barry Z. Posner, *The Leadership Challenge: How to Get Extraordinary Things Done in Organizations* (San Francisco: Jossey-Bass Publishers, 1991), 44.

13. Such a statement, however true, should not be construed as discounting the importance of theology for the life of the church.

14. Reg Grant and John Reed, *Telling Stories to Touch the Heart: How to Use Stories to Communicate God's Truth* (Wheaton: Victor Press, 1990), 7.

15. Ibid., 9.

16. An excellent discussion of this dynamic, as espoused in classical Greek rhetoric, can be found in Mortimer Adler's *How to Speak, How to Listen* (New York: Collier, 1983).

17. Flavil Ray Yeakley, Jr., "Persuasion in Religious Conversion" (Ph.D. dissertation, University of Illinois at Urbana-Champaign, 1975).

18. Quoted in Kawasaki, *Selling the Dream,* 27.

19. See Benjamin B. Tregoe, John W. Zimmerman, Ronald A. Smith, and Peter M. Tobia, *Vision in Action: How to Integrate Your Company's Strategic Goals into Day-to-Day Management Decisions* (New York: Simon and Schuster, 1990), 158-159.

20. Sheila Murray Bethel, *Making a Difference: 12 Qualities That Make You A Leader* (New York: Berkley, 1990), 195.

39

Charles Fuller, Pastor
First Baptist Church
Roanoke, Virginia

Preaching and Education

Most who preach remember the occasion of their ordination to the Gospel Ministry. Whatever else may have been included in that service of recognition, these words of Scripture were most likely read: "In the presence of God and of Christ Jesus, who will judge the living and the dead, and in view of his appearing and his kingdom, I give you this charge:

> Preach the Word; be prepared in season and out of season; correct, rebuke and encourage—with great patience and careful instruction. For the time will come when men will not put up with sound doctrine. Instead, to suit their own desires, they will gather around them a great number of teachers to say what their itching ears want to hear. They will turn their ears away from the truth and turn aside to myths. But you, keep your head in all situations, endure hardship, do the work of an evangelist, discharge all the duties of your ministry" (2 Tim. 4:1-5, NIV).

Inherent in the call to preach is the assignment to correct, rebuke, and encourage, and to do it with great patience and careful instruction. Certainly we can presume that there is at least a partial definition of preaching entwined with Paul's charge to preach. Hence, we conclude preaching is to be consistent, unapologetic, uplifting, and patient, and to have a teacher's touch.

In our attempts to make distinctions in preaching styles, we sometimes refer to didactic or instructional preaching. In light of Paul's classic charge to Timothy, a reference to didactic preaching is a virtual repetition in terms. To instruct or to educate was woven into the very fabric of preaching to Paul. In fact, he underscored the inseparability of a pastor's role as preacher and educator when he described the assignments and gifts given to those who are to serve the church: "It was he who gave some to be apostles, some to be prophets, some to be evangelists, and some to be pastors and teachers" (Eph. 4:11, NIV).

Most commentators agree that the roles of pastor and teacher, by grammatical construction in this passage, refer to one person. Indeed, the pastor is to be an educator, not in the formal and professional sense in which we use the term today but in the biblical sense of one called "to prepare God's people for works of service, so that the body of Christ may be built up until we all reach unity in the faith and in the knowledge of the Son of God and become mature, attaining to the whole measure of the fullness of Christ" (Eph. 4:12-13, NIV).

Certainly there is no suggestion here that pastoral preaching is to be neglectful of evangelistic and prophetic content and character. To the contrary, Paul admonished Timothy and all preachers to do the work of an "evangelist" and to discharge "all" the duties of our ministry.

Paul modeled his own admonition about consistent preaching, evangelizing, and teaching, when he reminded the Ephesian church leaders about his previous ministry in their midst:

> "When they arrived, he said to them: 'You know how I lived the whole time I was with you, from the first day I came into the province of Asia. I served the Lord with great humility and with tears, although I was severely tested by the plots of the Jews. You know that I have not hesitated to preach anything that would be helpful to you but have taught you publicly and from house to house. I have declared to both Jews and Greeks that they must turn to God in repentance and have faith in our Lord Jesus' (Acts 20:18-21, NIV).

However, our Lord provides the unsurpassed model for preaching. In a day of many rabbis, He was one who astonished people with the authenticity and authority of His "doctrine." He was known to His own as Master. Today we call Him the Master Teacher. Interestingly enough, His last command upon leaving this earth was this: "*Teaching* them to observe all things whatsoever I have commanded you: and, lo, I am with you always even unto the end of the world" (Matt. 28:20, author's emphasis).

So we have our marching orders. We are to evangelize a world, and we are to instruct the redeemed. What, then, are some essentials which bind preaching and education?

A Timeless Textbook

We are to preach the Word. Let there be no question, the word we are to preach is the written Word, the Bible. Though it is not the burden of this chapter on preaching and education to deal with the nature and origin of the Bible, it must be said that how the Bible is viewed has everything to do with how it is preached and heard.

In his book, *A Minister's Obstacles,* Ralph Turnbull offered a commentary on the Bible's place among a preacher's resources:

> Here is a preacher's workshop where he sharpens and uses his tools. First of all, there is his use of and attitude toward the Bible. This is our textbook, above all others. It is not for us to spend hours with commentaries and a few minutes with a text. We should be men of our Book! Let the Word of God be central as the hub of the wheel, and then we shall place other works at the proper circumference in their true perspective.[1]

For this preacher, the Bible is not a text of theory or technicality; it is the collective, written revelation of Him who is Absolute Truth. Just as there would have been no visible revelation of God in Christ had God not conceived the incarnation, there would be no trustworthy scriptural revelation of Him without the initiative of divine inspiration. Though the personalities, experiences, and styles of those who penned the words of Scripture are respected and utilized, the content of the Bible is sacred text. Thus, the Word we preach is authentic, authoritative, infallible, and timeless. Presented as God's written voice, the Bible is not information to be considered and admired; it is Truth to be obeyed and applied.

If impressions are the better part of conclusions, the pulpit is responsible to impress its hearers with four vital conclusions about the Bible: it is believable; it is understandable; it is applicable; and it is inexhaustible.

The Bible needs no endorsement, but it will be more readily perceived as believable when preachers approach the Bible as their authority rather than themselves as an authority on the Bible.

When preaching communicates the Bible in the spirit and enthusiasm of its purpose—God *wanting* to make Himself known—it prompts its own hearing. It is when the Bible is handled as difficult material, fully known only to the spiritually elite, that it is deemed elusive to those for whom it is meant.

Separating biblical texts from the subjects being approached in preaching can create the impression of the Bible's impracticality. Not all matters addressed in preaching can be confined to Scriptural settings, but preachers should never short-sell the Bible's relevance to any human experience. It is for this reason that expository, exegetical, and textual preaching should be the mainstays of the pulpit.

It is the studious preacher—who enthusiastically shares the fresh discoveries of his own adventure in the Scriptures—who more readily convinces his hearers that the Bible is one of those books you simply cannot put down. One of the basic principles of teaching is that you cannot teach what you do not know. In no realm of learning is that principle more important than when it applies to one whose calling it is to "preach the unsearchable riches of Christ."

An Authentic Pulpit

Learning the gospel not only requires that those who preach it make it understandable and presentable, but also that they make it believable. Reginald E. O. White said it succinctly: "Only as we obey can we understand; only as we express the truth in Christlike living can we make it plain, especially to men puzzled by theoretic Christianity. Without the adornment of sound Christian character, fragrant, delightful, attractive and true, the doctrine is obscured, the truth is disfigured, and Christ is betrayed."[2]

When writing the church in Thessalonica, Paul reminded them that he had not only delivered the gospel to them verbally but that it was reinforced by the Spirit's power and by a behavior which authenticated his message: "For we know, brothers loved by God, that he has chosen you, because our gospel came to you not simply with words, but also with power, with the Holy Spirit and with deep conviction. You know how we lived among you for your sake" (1 Thess. 1:4-5, NIV).

Think of it! The gospel presents indisputable credentials in the influence of those whose behavior has been fashioned by the example of their preacher! That is, doubtless, what was on Paul's mind when he instructed Titus, the pastor in Crete: "But as for you, speak up for the right living that goes along with true Christianity" (Titus 2:1, TLB).

Authentic preachers are also teachable. They are subject to their own lessons. They handle the text as a student before attempting to handle it as a teacher. It is possible to exhaustively examine a Bible passage, while never allowing it to apply to the pulpit, only to the pew. The preacher should know his text—even become saturated with it—yet it is seldom emphasized that, while coming to know the text, the preacher also needs to find himself *in* that text. Though it may seem a small thing, a preacher can enhance a teachable mentality by simply using pronouns like "we" and "us," rather than "you" and "them," when making applications of biblical truth.

Where to draw lines of limitation is always debatable with respect to confessional preaching. Some confessions should be made only unto the Lord, and to put them on public display can so sensationalize them, they become distractions. To parade admissions of failure, or to exaggerate them for effect, can feature weakness and indulgence rather than repentance and grace. There is, however, a need for vulnerability to be found in the spirit of the preacher. It encourages those who seek to learn the gospel to have teachers who not only understand the gospel, but also understand people. To know the preacher has hurts makes his lessons on comfort authentic. To know the preacher has failed makes his messages on restoration far more assuring. To sense the preacher has had to learn some of the hard lessons makes others want to know what he knows.

The Mystery of Comprehension

For all our study, pulpit prowess, and example setting, we must remember we cannot teach what cannot be learned. In communicating God's truth, certain elements must be in place. In other realms of knowledge learning can come by exposure, experiment, explanation, exchange, and examination, but an in-depth education of God's people is accomplished through an indwelling potential:

> However, as it is written: "No eye has seen/no ear has heard/no mind has conceived/what God has prepared for those who love him"/but God has revealed it to us by his Spirit. The Spirit searches all things, even the deep things of God. For who among men knows the thoughts of a man except the man's spirit within him? In the same way no one knows the thoughts of God except the Spirit of God. We have not received the spirit of the world but the Spirit who is from God, that we may understand what God has freely given us. This is what we speak, not in words taught us by human wisdom but in words taught by the Spirit, expressing spiritual truths in spiritual words. The man without the Spirit does not accept the things that come from the Spirit of God, for they are foolishness to him, and he cannot understand them, because they are spiritually discerned. (1 Cor. 2:9-14, NIV).

Just as the convicting presence of the Holy Spirit is necessary for the prompting of belief unto salvation, the indwelling presence of the Spirit is essential to the comprehension of truths which lie beyond the conversion experience. Regardless of how bright the audience or how excellent the sermon, God's deeper truths are perceived as the Spirit empowers the speaker and illumines the hearer. Preaching plans, sermon content, and expectations of outcome should be approached with the "mystery of comprehension" in mind. Church programs of Bible study and discipleship training should reflect an awareness of this truth.

Sunday Schools in most churches are not designed to be in-depth discipleship seminars. They are outreach and fellowship oriented, using Bible study as the centerpost of activity. Though professing Christians dominate such settings, there may be non-Christians present, as they should be. There needs to be sensitivity, then, about presenting lessons in applied Christianity so that they do not bypass the necessity of personal conversion. By the same token, whether in a Sunday School setting, worship experience, or seminar atmosphere, Christians should be constantly challenged to grow in grace and in the knowledge of our Lord because they have the capacity and command to do so, enlightened by the indwelling Spirit.

A Few Tools of Learning

Understanding that the content of preaching must be founded in God's revelation, and that the comprehension of His truth is dependent upon the Spirit's illumination, there are tools the preacher can use to enhance learning in the house of God.

Illustrations

Those who heard Him said Jesus spoke as one who had His own authority. Indeed He did, for the truth He spoke was original and ultimate truth. He spoke divine truth in language which could be understood by human ears. He was the master story teller, using parables to clarify His lessons and to underscore His points. No less useful to us as preachers are well-chosen and well-timed illustrations.

Though some preachers are effective in the use of illustrations drawn from history, the arts, and literature, I am drawn to observations of human behavior and current events. In my view, the more people can identify with the illustration used, the more readily they can apply its point.

Notepages

It is not uncommon to see Sunday church bulletins with a page provided for notes to be taken on the sermon. More often than not, the notepage is blank, simply providing space for as much (or as little) as the note-taker wishes to write. The practice of providing a brief outline of the sermon on the notepage is an even more helpful tool. Providing a sermon outline for the Sunday bulletin early enough to get it into print may require more thorough preparation on the part of the preacher. That, however, may be a discipline which benefits the pulpit as well as the pew. There may be limited complaints that note-taking in worship services turns sanctuaries into classrooms, but the argument is weak.

Bibles

A biblical preacher has the responsibility of firmly binding what he says to what the Bible says, and to do so in a way his hearers can retain it. Without doubt, the most simple and effective way to accomplish that goal is for a Bible to be in the hands of both preacher and hearers. When the Bible is little used in the course of a sermon, there is little reason for Bibles to be brought by members of a congregation. To the extent the Bible is utilized in preaching, it becomes needful to those who follow the sermon. Preachers should be careful and thoughtful to identify passages to which they refer and take time, in the interest of those who need to learn, for those passages to be found. In the process of using the Bible a simple but important education process of Bible learning is enhanced.

Sermon Series

Though sermons preached in series are not readily thought of as *tools* to assist in learning, they can serve that purpose. A series of sermons on a book of the Bible, or charting the Bible through a sequence of subjects, can help systematize and crystalize the process of knowing the Word of God. Long, exhaustive sermon series can become laborious, overlapping, and repetitious, but the sequential approach to preaching can be effectively used to "equip the saints."

Visuals and Object Lessons

Working on the principle that we remember more of what we see than what we hear, there are numerous other tools of learning which preachers can employ. There are visuals and object lessons which can be effective. Some preachers are effective in the use of dramatic monologue. Whatever the tool used in communicating the gospel, however, it should never be so prominent it fails to convey the message of Him whom we preach.

Lessons in Language

Having served one church for over thirty years, I have discovered some of the "upsides" of longevity. Needless to say, there are obvious downsides to a lengthy pastorate. From the standpoint of preaching, longevity can breed and feed the temptation to coast. It has been my practice throughout my ministry to begin weekly sermon preparation with a blank sheet of paper. For me, such a practice is healthy discipline, an investment in the attempt to avoid repetition and staleness. On the other hand, an extended pastorate allows time for the development of such things as a pulpit vocabulary as familiar to the congregation as to the preacher. Certain words and phrases have been so often explained and employed that to use them is to communicate whole ideas and bodies of thought.

Commonplace to my preaching is a reference to the Bible as "God's Written Voice," or "God's Voice put to print." In the reference there is the essence of the meaning of divine inspiration. The term "twice-born" is like a thumbnail explanation of salvation's nature. Another phrase which captures the meaning of salvation is the description of Christians as "walking residences of the Holy Spirit." Other terms in this glossary, which are condensations of accumulated teaching, include "the table of forgiveness" and "the memorial meal" (the Lord's Supper), "the church family" (an intentional replacement for references to the congregation), and "the *Lord's* tithe and *our* offerings."

It is significant to reinforce the teaching of God's omnipresence by expressing thanks for His presence when leading a congregation in prayer. A careful use of words, which capsulate and harmonize with what is preached, contribute to the process of a congregation's doctrinal education. When those words become familiar by repetition, they help to fortify understanding.

Pulpit Affirmations

The pulpit has both an opportunity and a responsibility to strengthen the programs of Christian education in the church. A pastor should not only be familiar with those programs, he should be able to endorse and commend them. Sermons which touch on subjects or passages being dealt with in Sunday School classes or discipleship groups help to reinforce what others are doing to teach and train in the life of the church, resulting in a sense of unity. When focusing on Christian growth or calling for commitments to discipleship, it would be helpful for the preacher to commend specific programs and ministries in the church designed to facilitate the very challenges he has given.

Pulpit affirmations of staff members and those who work in the educational ministries of a church are not only endorsements of them, they help to encourage others to involve themselves in those programs and to push out the borders of their own Christian growth. As small an item as it may seem, it is important for the preacher to be accurate in references to educational events and structure and to evidence enthusiasm for that which he commends. Simply stated, there needs to be a healthy relationship between what is said in the pulpit to cultivate a hunger for spiritual growth and what is done in the church's program-life to implement that growth.

Opportunities Not to be Forfeited

Preaching opportunities are not just confined to the usual settings of Sunday worship, revivals, and conference programs. Actually, some of the best chances to communicate lessons of faith are occasions when preaching is not the cause of the gathering. Wedding and funeral services are just such occasions. Obviously, the style and approach of preaching is different, but it is no less preaching.

If ever there are attentive and pliable minds on the subjects of eternity, salvation, and assurance, it is in the midst of bereavement. Understandably, those who grieve most are helped most by truths of comfort. Those who are a step removed from the heaviest grief may well be ready to learn what they have not previously sought to hear. A funeral, then, allows the preacher to be a gracious instructor, comforting, evangelizing, and even correcting mistaken ideas.

To stand at a wedding altar and not seize the opportunity to at least briefly apply the instructions of Scripture to the occasion is a real forfeiture. Not only are there the obvious biblical references to home and family to be mentioned, there is the parallel of Christ as the spiritual bridegroom and Christians as the bride of Christ. A wedding is replete with opportunities for the preacher to entwine a ceremony for two with lessons for all present.

Always a Verdict

Ultimately, wherever it takes place, preaching is done to obtain a verdict. The gospel by its very nature demands more than interest; it calls for obedience. However else preaching and the church's education mission may be linked, their mutual goal is to draw all who hear to an obedient commitment to Jesus Christ, who is, Himself, The Gospel. "And I will give you pastors according to mine heart, which shall feed you with knowledge and understanding." (Jer. 3:15, KJV).

Note

1. Ralph G. Turnbull, *A Minister's Obstacles* (Old Tappan, NJ: Fleming H. Revell Co., 1959), 23-24.
2. Reginald E. O. White, *The Upward Calling* (Grand Rapids: Wm. B. Eerdmans Publishing Co., 1961), 18.

Dwight L. Moody (1837-1899)

"Preaching God's Love"

Among the great preachers of the Christian church, few would be considered less well prepared than Dwight L. Moody. Raised in poverty with little formal education, he moved to Boston as a teenager and became a sales clerk in a shoe shop. It was in that shop, however, that a faithful Sunday School teacher led young Moody to faith in Christ and helped launch the remarkable ministry that would touch thousands of lives on two continents.

Following his conversion, Moody moved to Chicago and his sales career blossomed. Determined to share his faith, he organized a Sunday School which grew rapidly. Moving into Christian service full–time, he devoted himself to the YMCA movement and eventually became its president. His growing demand as a speaker precipitated his transition into a revival preacher.

Joined by musician Ira Sankey, Moody's revivals had a profound effect on major cities in the U.S. and England. His quiet and simple presentation of the Gospel, combined with Sankey's music, drew great crowds. Moody's preaching was characterized by an emphasis on the greatness of God's love. As an evangelist, his preaching called on men and women to acknowledge and accept that love through faith in Jesus Christ.

Moody's sermons are far from being polished homiletical gems. Rather, they tend to be essentially collections of stories gathered about a central biblical theme (though without much biblical exposition). Whatever they lacked in polish, they clearly had in impact on the crowds of working people who came to hear him and who responded to God's love as a result of his powerful testimony of faith.

40

Charles Bugg
Carl E. Bates Professor of Christian Preaching
The Southern Baptist Theological Seminary
Louisville, Kentucky

Preaching and Missions

At the risk of some oversimplification, we may say Christian preaching has two fundamental tasks. The first is to proclaim what God revealed in Jesus Christ wants to do *in* us and *for* us. This is a vital aspect of proclamation. After all, we do preach the Christ who said: "I have come that they may have life, and have it to the full" (John 10:10b, NIV).

People today are searching for peace, purpose, and power in life. The shelves of secular bookstores are filled with promises of happiness, health, and heaven on earth. The preacher who does not listen to this longing in the lives of people will preach sermons that seem to have no relevance. While our answers as Christian ministers, hopefully, will be different from some of the "fluff" that is being offered these days, we still need to pay attention to these hungers of the human spirit. This is a vital part of proclamation. We must preach a Christ who wants to do something *in* us and *for* us.

Yet, this is only a part of our preaching. This same God in Christ also has called us to do something *with* Him and *through* Him in this world which He loves so deeply. The words of the Great Commission forcefully bring this truth home. "Therefore," the Risen Christ said to His disciples, "go and make disciples of all nations, baptizing them in the name of the Father and of the Son and of the Holy Spirit, and teaching them to obey everything I have commanded you" (Matt. 28:19-20a, NIV).

The command is clear. Jesus gives His disciples power, but it is an enabling power. It is not a power simply to be enjoyed by its recipients. It is not just something that Jesus does *in* and *for* His disciples. Rather, it is a power that moves the followers of Christ into the world to reach and to teach, to baptize and to nurture.

When this happens—when the power of Christ moves the church into the world with the good news of God's love in Jesus Christ—we call this missions. This is the picture of the church at its best—receiving the grace of God and then being gracious in sharing that message with others.

Those of us who preach, therefore, have as a part of our task to call the "called" out of themselves and into the lives of others. How do we do that? How do we call people to a vision of this world which God loved and for which Jesus died? I want to look at the subject of preaching and missions through the lens of several questions. Hopefully, we will all see again this God who wants to do something *in* and *for* us as well as *with* us and *through* us.

The Why of Our Preaching

Why preach missions? This is a question of motivation. Why even bother to try to call the church out to be the "church to the world?"

The most fundamental answer to this is that the nature of the God who formed and fashioned a people is to involve and invest Himself in creation. In 1979 *Time* Magazine selected what it considered to be the seven best preachers in America. Gardner C. Taylor, then pastor of the Concord Baptist Church in Brooklyn, New York, was one of those chosen. When asked to summarize the message of the Bible, Taylor said: "It is the story of a God who is out to get back what belongs to Him."

Could a better summary of the Bible be given? God creates. Humankind sins. God seeks to recreate. The seeking climaxes in the coming of Jesus to the world; and for Christians, the gospel is captured in those unforgettable words: "For God so loved the world, that He gave His only begotten Son, that whosoever believeth in Him should not perish, but have everlasting life" (John 3:16).

Preaching begins with the minister's concept of God. If God is small, our message is small. People hunger for size, but the God we often preach is too small for the tough issues of life. Sometimes we preach a God who loves only our kind. This was the sin of Jonah. He had no trouble believing that God could love Israel. But the Assyrians? That was out of the question. The pouting prophet never did understand the inclusive love of his God.

As a preacher I have to keep in mind that the God whom I preach is not a God fashioned in my image. The God of the Bible explodes my limited ideas of love and calls me to look at the world through new eyes. This is revolutionary. God refuses to be domesticated or limited to those whom we like or who live on our street or have the same color skin or the same ideas that we have.

What about a series of sermons on the God of the Bible? Why not let our churches hear again about this God of initiative who is constantly moving toward the world with reconciling love? Start with the doctrine of creation. God created us for relationship with Him, and the Bible is the story of how God seeks to bind up what humankind has broken in sin.

Preach the narrative of God's call to Abraham. "I will make you into a great nation," God said to the stunned patriarch, "and I will bless you;/I will make your name great,/and you will be a blessing" (Gen. 12:2, NIV). Here is God calling a people to Himself. "I will bless you," God said, and from that point on, the lives of Abraham and his descendants are forever changed. This is a God of size and strength, a God where "blessing" will no longer allow us to live life as usual.

The blessing has a requirement along with it. Something is done *in* and *for* Abraham, but now he is called to do something *with* and *through* God. "And you will be a blessing," God said. Do our churches understand this? The people of God are a people on mission. God does not give Abraham a choice. Do you want to receive a blessing or be a blessing? This is not either/or. It is both/and.

What about the Psalms? "The earth is the Lord's, and everything in it,/the world, and all who live in it," declares Psalm 24:1 (NIV). Think about that for a minute. Everybody, everything, the whole world belongs to God, and God is trying to get everyone to acknowledge that He is Lord. The mission is ours. *With* God and *through* God's power and provision, we move out into the world to let all people know that God is the sovereign Lord of all creation.

Consider the size of the God whom we preach. God has the whole world on His heart, and we are called to have the same heart for the world. God does not look out at the world and see Americans, Russians, Iranians, and Israelites. God sees people. God does not see brown skin, black skin, yellow skin, and white skin. God sees people. God does not see the ins and the outs, the haves and the have nots. God sees all people as needing the same thing—a relationship to Himself as known through Jesus Christ.

We also need to let people know that God's own heart is broken by the rejection of His love. To talk about the size and strength of God is not to make people think that God is impervious to the pain and problems of life. The decision of God to involve and invest Himself in life means that God opens Himself to our rejection. When a hand of love is extended, people may respond with a "yes" or a "no." They may take our hand in theirs or they may turn their backs on our expression of care.

The Old Testament book of Hosea is a powerful portrait of a God who loves us in a risky way. Hosea is called to marry Gomer, a prostitute. Gomer is unfaithful to Hosea, but he continues to pursue her with his love. Suddenly we see that this is more than just the story of a husband and wife. It is a penetrating picture of God's love for an unfaithful people. As Hosea expressed it: "The Lord said to me, 'Go, show your love to your wife again, though she is loved by another and is an adulteress. Love her as the Lord loves the Israelites, though they turn to other gods and love the sacred raisin cakes' " (Hos. 3:1, NIV).

While the book of Hosea presents a beautiful picture of the compassion of God, nowhere is this divine love seen more clearly than in the cross of Christ. For a time God attempted to communicate His heart through words. Through the patriarchs, through the psalmist, through the prophets—the message was that God was out to get back what belonged to Him. Yet, the words seemed to fall on deaf ears. They were eloquent, moving, tender words, but something was missing. What had happened to the vision of God who wanted to do something *in* us and *for* us, and then *through* us and *with* us? Where were the people who heard both sides of the call—to receive a blessing and to be a blessing?

It was time for *the Word* from God. To obscure parents in an obscure place, Jesus came. His childhood seems to have been relatively uneventful. At the age of twelve, Jesus did amaze the teachers at the Temple at Jerusalem; then He disappeared from public view.

When Jesus was about thirty, he emerged from obscurity; for the next three years He gave a new shape to history. Even His adversaries admired the way Jesus taught. They were ready to address Him as Rabbi although He had no formal training. Jesus was not content to be known only as "Teacher." He was the fullness of God, Son of Man and Son of God. Jesus had a mission—to the Jews and Gentiles, men and women, Greeks, Samaritans, lepers—and all of the barriers which separated people came tumbling down as Jesus proclaimed the boundless love of God. However, the young Nazarene made enemies. To some His words were blasphemy and to others He sounded like a political revolutionary. So Jesus' enemies sought to silence Him on the cross.

For a time these adversaries were successful. Jesus was dead, and so were the dreams of His followers to make a difference in the world. The disciples retreated to the darkness of the upper room or went back to fishing to try to forget that dark day when their hope died as Jesus died. It was all over. The Galilean was gone, and His words had stopped. The followers of Christ were left with silence, and their motivation for mission was gone.

Yet as Christians we know the rest of the story. Early on Sunday morning, some disciples of Jesus make their way to the borrowed tomb to try to find His body, but Jesus could not be found.His body was gone. He was a missing person. His followers could not find Jesus, but He found them. Suddenly the realization dawns. This is no mere man, no mere miracle worker or just an outstanding teacher. This is the resurrected Christ. Jesus is the living Lord, and the cross, which symbolized defeat, now represents the victory of God's love.

No wonder Paul wrote to the Corinthians that the pivot of his preaching was the cross. "We preach Christ crucified," Paul declared, "a stumbling block to Jews, and foolishness to Gentiles, but to those whom God has called, both Jews and Greeks, Christ the power of God and the wisdom of God" (1 Cor. 1:23-23, NIV).

Paul, the apostle to the Gentiles and the one in the early church most responsible for the message of God's inclusive love, found the focus of his faith in the cross. Why was Paul concerned to preach the good news to everybody? What motivated him to go from place to place to proclaim God's reconciling love to all persons? Where did the great apostle find the strength to endure persecution and prison so that he could tell people that God had come fully in Jesus?

Paul said the heart of his preaching was the cross, because it is in that event that the love of God for all people is most clearly seen. Why preach missions? Paul would answer that we preach because we understand at the cross God plays no favorites; that more than anything else, this God wants to favor us with His love in Jesus Christ.

The What of Our Preaching

What do we preach about missions? By this, I mean what kind of vision do we give our hearers of the world? What do we call the church to see as the object of its love? What constitutes missions?

The Book of Acts provides a clear answer to the question. Before His ascension Jesus instructed His disciples: "You will receive power when the Holy Spirit comes on you; and you will be my witnesses in Jerusalem, and in all Judea and Samaria, and to the ends of the earth" (Acts 1:8, NIV). In effect, these words of Jesus became a table of contents for the whole book of Acts. It is the story of the church's moving out from being perceived as another Jewish sect to embracing all of the world with the love of God. Persecution from the outside and strong disagreements on the inside—the church moves on and out "to the ends of the earth."

This is our vision of missions. It is both near and far, close and distant, the person next door and the person on the other side of the world. The challenge of the preacher is to call believers to this vision of missions.

Some of us are "farsighted" when it comes to the mission of the church. Missions seems more important the more distant it is from us. We love to give money to missionaries who serve in primitive places. We are stirred by accounts of what God is doing in some distant place.

A Christian is a citizen of the world in the sense that all people are created in the image of God and are loved by the same God who has loved us. We need to preach that. As ministers we need to help people distinguish between the actions of governments and the needs of their citizens. I may strongly disagree with the actions of leaders in places like

Libya, Iraq, or Iran, but the people are still those whom God loves and for whom Christ died.

Preach the Book of Acts as the gospel is extended, and as the good news encounters the lives of those who had been excluded or marginalized. Samaritans, a eunuch, women, Gentiles—some were hated and some distrusted by the religious establishment of the first century, but all were included as the objects of God's deepest affections. The gospel is for all people. Nobody is a second-class citizen in the kingdom. Christ comes to all, and all may come to Christ.

Jonah is also an excellent book to preach when we want to emphasize the inclusive love of God. The prophet hated Nineveh, and he had good reason. Nineveh was the capital of Assyria, and they had devastated the land of Israel and killed many of the people of God. As far as Jonah was concerned, the issue was revenge, not reconciliation. He decried the positive response of the Ninevites to his preaching because this meant that God would probably forgive them. Most of us ministers would feature it on our resumes if we ever had a response like Jonah's. Remember, the whole city repented. Yet Jonah became angry with God because Jonah wanted retribution, not redemption.

Part of the task of preaching in missions is to to overcome the "Jonah complex" among people. Preaching is the call to see the world through God's eyes and not through our own eyes. Because all persons are precious in God's sight, they become precious in our sight. Paul expressed it so powerfully in his second letter to the Corinthians:

> Therefore, if anyone is in Christ, he is a new creation; the old has gone, the new has come! All this is from God, who reconciled us to himself through Christ and gave us the ministry of reconciliation: that God was reconciling the world to himself in Christ, not counting men's sins against them. And he has committed to us the message of reconciliation. We are therefore Christ's ambassadors, as though God were making His appeal through us. We implore you on Christ's behalf: Be reconciled to God (2 Cor. 5:17-20, NIV).

The distinguishing characteristic of the life of the person reconciled to God through Christ is a life committed to the ministry of reconciliation. No option seems to be given to the Christian. "We are . . . ambassadors," Paul clearly wrote, as if there is no choice. According to Paul, to be reconciled is to become a reconciler. We are given the gift of grace; we are called to give that gift to others.

What about the ministry of reconciliation to those who live close to us? The risen Christ's words to His disciples were to be witnesses "in Jerusalem, and in all Judea and Samaria, and to the ends of the earth." Some people become far more excited about the ends of the earth than they do the "end" of their neighborhood or city.

Some of us remember the difficult days when many churches experienced great problems in the integration of their congregations. Several congregations which were near university campuses experienced a particular dilemma. African students, who had been converted through the efforts of missionaries, came to the United States. When they attempted to join a church, some were denied because their skin was a different color.

The irony is that many of those people who blocked the entrances to their churches were the ones who gave generously to the work of foreign missions. Prejudice causes us to make strange judgements. As long as folks were on the other "end" of the earth, they were the object of grace and giving. Next door and up close, however, these same people were forbidden to be a part of Christ's church.

Fortunately, this sad segment of the church's story seems to be ending. More and more churches are recognizing the inclusive nature of the church. Yet the issue still remains—what about missions to those who are closest to us?

For those of us who preach, this challenge demands specificity. Generalized preaching against hunger, injustice, bias, and other evils usually will receive a nod of affirmation from the congregation. It costs nothing to nod. It allows me to identify with God's side but not make any investment of my life. I can vote against sin without really taking up the cross.

When a preacher moves to the specifics and calls people to action, then that minister becomes prophetic in the best sense of that word. For example, I want the church where I am minister to see *all* of the people who are without Christ who live within the circle of the members' lives. What do I do? Pound the pulpit, plead the case, shout and scream about how we ought, must, and should be concerned? Or do I preach that concern and then share some specific strategies about how we can reach those closest to us? This is a prime example of how preaching and teaching can be interwoven. I may want to employ the pulpit to call the congregation to a new vision, but I also want to make certain that there are training opportunities to equip the members.

The same is true of other issues—poverty, hunger, oppression—it costs the preacher nothing to be against these things in general. When that same minister calls people to specific involvement, it becomes riskier but it certainly becomes more Christian. The hardest place for some of us to be concerned about missions is not in "Judea and Samaria, and to the ends of the earth." Rather, the most difficult challenge is to be concerned in the backyard of our own "Jerusalem."

The Who of Our Preaching

The question that many ministers ask is: "What shall I preach?" *What* in preaching is important. People are hungry for some substance in the sermons. They want to be fed. Few people are content with a steady diet of cotton candy. They want some calories in the sermons that they hear. Living life demands a lot of energy. We need something to sustain and to strengthen us on the journey. So the *what* of the sermon is an important concern.

I want to consider the "who" of the sermon in relationship to mission. Fundamentally, preaching is relational. The preacher is calling people to a new relationship to Jesus Christ. Doctrine is important, but it is not doctrine that saves us. The call of the New Testament is a call to "follow," and that word points to the relationship that the disciple has to his or her Master. We grow in our understanding of Jesus, but that understanding is built on the commitment of a personal relationship to Him.

When we look at the "who" of our preaching, we need to ask: "What was the center of Jesus' ministry?" If I am going to follow Him, I need to know where Jesus went and where I need to go. According to Luke's Gospel, Jesus shared the roadmap of His life early in His ministry. The setting was the synagogue in Nazareth. It was the Sabbath. Jesus was asked to read from the scroll of Isaiah, and this is the passage that He selected:

> The Spirit of the Lord is on me,
> because he has anointed me
> to preach good news to the poor.
> He has sent me to proclaim freedom
> for the prisoners and recovery of
> sight for the blind,
> to release the oppressed,
> to proclaim the year of the Lord's favor
> (Luke 4:18-19, NIV).

This is a powerful statement of mission, and several things need to be emphasized. First, Jesus pointed out: "The Spirit of the Lord is on me." Jesus said that He had been "anointed" to do the work of ministry, which is a way of saying that He was not functioning out of His own impulses or initiative. The Spirit had moved upon Him and was moving with Him to do the work.

Trying to meet human needs can be overwhelming. The stories are legion of people who set out to make a difference in the world and whose spirits were broken by the sheer size of the problems which they faced. Good intentions are not sufficient motivation for missions. Jesus did not just begin with what He had been called to do; He began with the divine resources that He had been given to do the work.

What a word for those of us who preach! Often, we major on the work that needs to be done, and preaching becomes nothing but exhortation. Like cheerleaders at a football game, ministers jump up and down and yell at the team to work harder, play better, and look like you are enjoying it whether you are or not. The problem is that some people on the field have lost their heart for the game and are simply going through the motions. We ministers plead for more perspiration from the team. What the team needs, however, is more inspiration.

"The Spirit of the Lord is upon me," Jesus said, "because he has anointed me," and then our Lord spelled out His mission. And what a mission it was! Who was it that received His ministry? The poor, the prisoners, the blind, and the oppressed.

Another part of the "who" of our mission is those to whom we minister. Missions is relational. It is born and nurtured out of relationship to Christ, and it finds an expression in the lives of those whom God loves. In a sense, Jesus is calling us to a new vision of people. Those who are often overlooked; those who sometimes are pushed to the perimeter of society; those who are frequently blamed for creating their own troubles—these are the ones that Jesus said were the particular focus of His ministry.

Yet all of us can be included in the poor, the prisoners, the blind, and the oppressed. Poverty of spirit exists in the big house in the best neighborhood. Some of us are imprisoned by habits, addictions, shame, fears, or a thousand other things that become the bars through which we peer wishing for the more abundant life. Blindness is rampant in our day. We become blind to the things that truly matter, blind to the needs of our families, blind to the things that make a life as we pour ourselves into making a living. Many of us are among the oppressed. We may be seen as having power, but we feel powerless to change even some things about ourselves. The rapid growth of substance abuse in our society is testimony to the fact that instead of dealing with the sources of our pain, we often seek to deaden our nerve endings.

All of this is to say that missions involves people: people who come from all walks of society but have the common need of finding full life in Jesus Christ. Some of these people live in distant places. Some have no houses and little food. Many are oppressed by structures that give them no power and no voice. Some of these people live in the inner cities sleeping in cardboard boxes, cold, dirty, smelling of clothes that are seldom changed.

Other people live in affluent suburbs. They seem to have it all. Nice houses, nice cars, designer clothes; scratch the surface of many of these folks, and you will discover a longing to know a life that is really worth living.

When we talk about missions, we are talking about bringing all of these people into a vital, personal relationship with Jesus Christ. We are talking about churches that care about all of the needs of people, and these churches care because they represent the Christ who weeps at the needs of His children.

Tragically, many people think of missions simply in terms of boards, structures, or organizations. Of course, we need institutional forms to facilitate our ministry, but these institutions must be the means to the end of serving Christ by serving the needs of people.

The challenge for the preacher in approaching missions is to remember the personal dimension of it. Jesus Christ gives us strength. Our Lord gives us direction. Then go out to those for whom He so deeply cares.

What a great calling we have as ministers. To stand to proclaim this One who wants to do something *in* us and *for* us, and then to preach that He has called us to do something *with* Him and *through* Him. That is truly a calling worthy of giving our very best.

Leslie Newbigin, for many years a missionary in India and a Bishop of the Church of South India, closed his book, *Mission in Christ's Way,* with these striking words:

> It is the Holy Spirit who is the primary missionary; our role is secondary. Mission is not a burden laid upon the church; it a gift and a promise to the church that is faithful. The command arises from the gift. Jesus reigns and all authority has been given to him in earth and heaven. When we understand that, we shall not need to be told to let it be known. Rather, we shall not be able to keep quiet. [1]

Note

1. Leslie Newbigin, *Mission in Christ's Way: A Gift, A Command, an Assurance* (New York: Friendship Press, 1987), 40.

41 *Nelson Price, Pastor*
Roswell Street Baptist Church
Marietta, Georgia

Preaching and Church Growth

As a lovely flower grows into full bloom, it matures in form and essence. It releases its fragrance as its beauty is beheld. Likewise, a church grows in its form by numerical increase and in its essence by evidencing spiritual attributes—the fruit of the Spirit.

Good preaching is essential to both aspects of church growth. There can be good preaching without growth but there cannot be growth without good preaching. It is conceivable that there could be numerical growth without good preaching but spiritual growth without good preaching cannot be envisioned. With preaching the church rises or falls, because it is the proclamation of the good news. When it is presented as good news it attracts and growth is spontaneous.

The early church had great preaching as its sanctified midwife. The Book of Acts, which chronicles the emergence and growth of the young church, focused on Peter's preaching on the occasion of Pentecost as the time of the first quantum leap in growth by the church. In passing the baton from the first generation of believers to the second, Paul exhorted Timothy: "Preach the word; be instant in season, out of season; reprove, rebuke, exhort with all longsuffering and doctrine" (2 Tim. 4:2).

Apostolic preaching was centered around the person and work of Christ. It was the focal point around which the emerging church rallied. In that era they had no glitzy advertising campaigns, no clever promotions, no dog and pony shows, and no goldfish to give away in order to grow. It was their message or nothing. It worked.

There would have been no Reformation or great spiritual awakenings without great preaching, and there has never been church growth without it. Every great awakening and every period of reformation has not only been given birth by great preaching but has spawned great preaching. The significance of great preaching is well established. Preaching needs to be given primary attention.

Conversely, it should be noted that every period of decadence within the church has been at a time when the primacy of preaching was neglected by the church. Often, attention swings to some other admirable aspect of church life before the holy craft of preaching degenerated as a result of the divergence. The decline of positive work in the pulpit means failure to apply God's Word to the world situation. As a result, the church develops a secular world view and not a scriptural world view. When this happens church growth stops, as surely as vegetation stops growing when water is withheld.

The statistics are amazing. One group of statisticians asserts that each Sunday about 720,000,000 supposedly inspirational words are issued from 237,000 pulpits and fall on the ears of some 45,000,000 worshipers. That means the pulpits of America can still be the greatest influence in our society for moral reform and spiritual change. If churches are to grow—and if America is to survive as a morally governed society—this opportunity must not be fumbled. If this sacred trust is allowed to fall into the hands of a dullard who is impassive or an intellect who is indifferent, there will be no church growth.

Personalization

The preacher must live with a John the Baptist complex: "He must increase, but I must decrease" (John 3:30). In every way, the preacher must do and be his best and then transfer all the praise, glory, and credit to the Lord. Paul, in returning from his first missionary journey, realized the Lord had given the grace, so he gave the Lord the glory (see Acts 14:27). Increasingly, the world is looking at preachers when they are out of the pulpit to know what they mean when they are in it. The preacher must live so as to assure his congregation of his unblemished morality and personal piety.

Ralph Waldo Emerson said: "Tell me what a person believes and I'll tell you what he'll do." Indiscrete or immoral ethical practices that betray professed sound theology discredit what is preached. As Satan's decoys, such inconsistency impedes church growth, often leading to regression.

No membership will long follow a preacher who does not evidence to them that he lives for a single purpose—to bring honor and glory to God through whatever service is rendered and in all that is preached. Single-minded devotion must be indisputable.

God has not chosen to build a great church without calling upon a preacher to plant his life in it for a prolonged time as a means of doing it. Longevity, not a common virtue, is an element in growth.

Preparation

For a preacher to remain productive for a protracted period, he must grow personally. This requires disciplined devotion. There is no way to remain fresh in the same pulpit without personal, spiritual, and intellectual growth by the preacher. Two basic essentials aid this growth.

One is a regimen of time alone with the Lord. Years ago while working in Brazil with a saintly missionary, Rosalee Mills Appelby, she gave me a book in which she had written this inscription: "One can't expect to amount for much for the Lord who isn't long alone with Him." Time alone with the Lord is a price to be paid for spiritual freshness. W. H. Griffith Thomas said: "We do not get close enough to men because we do not get near enough to God."

A minister should inform the congregation of his desire to serve them. He should then explain this cannot be done without time alone with the Lord in His Word. It is expedient to define this time for the congregation. Most congregations admire a minister who exercises self-discipline in his personal spiritual life. They need to be led to understand that he is working at these times, doing some of his most constructive work. In order to be at his best when available to them, he must at time be unavailable to them. Even our Lord in His human form knew He could not minister from a bleached-out spirit. He retreated when a group of people were ready to make Him their King by force (John 6:15).

J. H. Jowett quoted a noted English jurist as saying that "cases are won in chambers;" that is, "So far as the barrister is concerned, his critical arena is not the public court, but his own private room." In his study—on occasion on his knees and at times pouring over the Word of God—the preacher prepares "his case." It there becomes "bone of his bone"; while it is in the pulpit, it becomes "flesh of his flesh."

A second essential for personal pulpit growth is a growing library. James Stewart urged his students to spend their money on books, not clothes. He concluded people would see the need of clothing and provide it. They would realize the need for books but not know how to provide it.

Motivational speaker Charlie "Tremendous" Jones contends: "You are the same today as you'll be in five years except for two things, the people you meet and the books you read." A minister cannot remain static personally and be fresh in the pulpit. Growth through study is elemental. Through study a mind is amalgamated with all the great authors read. Thus, one's field of knowledge is multiplied by the number of sources utilized.

Bible study is a must for preachers. P. T. Forsyth observed: "The Bible is the supreme preacher to the preacher." As the student of the Word studies it, the Holy Spirit simultaneously searches the student's heart. Hence, as the preacher prepares the sermon, the sermon prepares him.

Church growth must be biblically based or it has no lasting foundation. In major cities across America, there are large, former church facilities where church gatherings emerged overnight and once evidenced great energy. They were built around a personality, on emotion, or media-based sensations. Unfortunately, without spiritual maturity resulting from biblical preaching, they have become as dust.

The advantage in study is not just to learn the thoughts of others but to stimulate yourself to think. Christopher Morley astutely noted: "The real purpose of books is to trap the mind into doing its own thinking."

The minister should not wait until he gets to the study to study. Every moment from the cradle to the pulpit is preparation time. There should be no "off" switch on a minister's homiletical mindset. It is necessary to view all of life from the vantage point: "How can this preach?" Allow everything—from the fall of an empire, as indicated by a fallen wall, to an infant's laughter—to be a catalyst for preaching. Record these thoughts. Don't let the anemia of "I'll never forget this gem" sap you of some of your most creative thought.

Members of our society will not follow a person spiritually they cannot respect intellectually. Conversely, they will not follow a person they cannot understand. For this reason, the Word must be palatably prepared and attractively presented. Charles Spurgeon sounded this word of warning: "Habitually coming into the pulpit unprepared is unpardonable presumption." A congregation will forgive its pastor of almost anything other than being unprepared to be his best every time he comes into the pulpit. Staying up all night with a family might impress that one family, but if it robs the pastor of preparation time the rest of the congregation will not be forgiving.

The preacher should approach the pulpit with the mindset of Paul who wrote: "I ... came not with excellency of speech or of wisdom, declaring unto you the testimony of God. For I determined not to know any thing among you, save Jesus Christ, and Him crucified" (1 Cor. 2:1-2).

Presentation

Style is "in" for this generation of church-goers. They seek it in clothing, cars, and life-style. Therefore, the style of preaching is decisive. Style refers to the manner of delivery, not the matter delivered.

"Give me the right word and the right accent and I will move the world," said Joseph Conrad.

This does not suggest compromising on Bible content. Styles change but the message does not. For example, there was a day when oratory was a popular pulpit style. Today's audience has little appetite for oratory unless it is of the highest quality. Any style will appeal if of high enough quality. However, since today's listener is rarely exposed to some styles like oratory, it is less likely to be accepted by most.

Some pulpits are veering away from messages with heavy Bible content. This is a critical error, for unless the Bible is preached to this generation, the next will suffer from spiritual amnesia. The Bible, even in-depth doctrine, can be stylistically presented. Without it, even the present generation of church-goers will be Bible illiterates.

Pulpit artistry minus the Bible might be delivered by such a charismatic speaker that numerical church growth will occur. Personal magnetism might draw a crowd. However, unless they are tutored in the timeless truths made applicable to today, the pastor will soon be facing a congregation that knows no Scripture. Since theology and ethics go together, the moral temperament of such church-goers will evidence no spiritual growth.

A style that blends emotionalism with pragmatism attracts. The mention of emotionalism causes some arched eyebrows. It need not for emotion simply refers to feeling. A previous generation played on emotions and gave the word a bad name among viewers of the church scene. Some of the most savory "fruit of the Spirit" noted in Galatians 5:22-23 involve emotions such as love, joy, peace, and kindness. Other emotions such as laughter, glee, happiness, elation, and a sense of thanksgiving are admirable also. Conversely, the pulpit can work to convert negative emotions, such as dejection, depression, despair, and despondency. A commendable word craftsman in the pulpit can apply God's Word in a manner so as to convert negative emotions. This is emotionalism at its best.

While extreme emotional exploitation should be avoided, the principle of emotional involvement must not be neglected. Ours is a sensate society. We are dramatically influenced by our emotions in every area of our lives. The pulpit must not overlook this. It is expedient in sermon preparation not only to seek a well-outlined message with pungent points, but to review it prior to delivery for emotional flow. This flow should be associated with the listening habits of people. More mature listeners have an attention span of approximately seven minutes. After this time, attention begins to stray. With this in mind, there needs to be an attention-grabbing thought and emotional change at five-to seven-minute intervals or the listener is lost.

Passion in the pulpit leads to persuasion in the pew. Dismiss the traditional image evoked by the word *passion*. It is not being used here for the prototypical fire-breathing, emotion-stripping, heart-rending, high-strung preacher who victimizes his hearers. *Passion* is used here to mean that a person should not preach as though there is nothing at stake. Proper passion projects a sense of importance and urgency about what is being shared. It conveys a sense of feeling about what is being said and for the people to whom it is said.

Pragmatism focuses on realism and stirs the intellect. By blending emotionalism and pragmatism, two facets that impact the will are combined for optimum effect. It is at the point of the will that growth occurs. First, personal growth in the essence of the faith transpires. Second, this moves persons to resolutely act, and that results in numerical growth. Of necessity, the preacher must put his whole mind into his preparation, his whole life into his illustration, and his whole soul into his presentation. Thus, a congregation is stirred to action.

People are looking for the practical that is born out of realism. Canned illustrations can be used only sparingly to be effective. Excessive use betrays the user as not being involved enough personally in contemporary life to draw applicable truths from the listener's world. A mild blend of historical events and facts with present happenings in a relevant manner is palatable. Biblical illustrations are a superior to most and tend to stir the listener's overall interest in Scripture. People tend to resent use of unrealistic illustrations being used to portray reality. They also detract from the supernatural that itself is hard for the secular mind to absorb. Nothing should detract from the divine.

Proclamation

For a church to grow, the proclamation of the "word of His grace" must be clear, contemporary, and compelling. It must speak to needs and offer relevant solutions that are understandable. It must be encouched in the language of the people and not the "language of Zion."

The message must be the "gospel once delivered" but delivered so "gospel" is understood to mean "good news." For the message to be vogue, it does not have to be vague. It must be attractive to attract. This does not hint of doctrinal compromise. It shouts of the necessity of applying the word so it can be comprehended and practiced.

As a child, one of my chores on our farm was feeding the chickens. They loved crushed corn. I soon learned I could use the corn to scare them away by throwing it at them. I also observed they would come running and gather around my feet if I simply scattered it so as to attract them. Many pulpits frighten people away with the same message that attracts others. The difference is in how it is presented.

With warmth and love, Charles Kingsley used to lean over his pulpit and say to his people: "Here we are again to talk about what is really going on in your soul and mine." That is the type of preaching that results in church growth. Church growth is not aided by the type of preaching described by one observer of preachers: "He's supernaturally dull. No one could be that dull without divine aid!"

A church service should be a gathering of the people around a minister of the Word in order to have an encounter with the living Word. Anything less than that is not preaching and will not grow a church. The pulpit must deal with basics. The world marveled over the success of the sophisticated weapons of America during the Persian Gulf War. Smart bombs and guided missiles amazed imaginative people. Many of them were made by Raytheon Corporation whose slogan is: "Excellence begins with Fundamentals."

There are foundational fundamentals that must be preached in an understandable way, such as:

- The veracity of God's Word
- The virgin birth of Jesus Christ
- The virtuous life of our Lord
- The vicarious death of Christ on the cross
- The victorious resurrection of the triumphant Christ
- The valedictory ascension
- The vindicating return of our Savior

These themes need to be interwoven with contemporary fundamentals found in the marketplace and school corridors, such as, but not exclusively:

- The sanctity of life
- The imperative of integrity
- Money management
- A biblical understanding of self-worth
- Sexual morality
- Interpersonal relations
- Ideals of family life
- Concepts of contentment
- How to deal with inordinate emotions
- Principles of peace of mind

People will respond to *candid* preaching who are repelled by *candied* preaching. People do not seek sugar-coated compliments, but the salt that will preserve them in a corrupt culture. They search for a voice as definitive as that of Isaiah who said: "This is the way, walk in it" (Isa.

30:21, NIV). That voice must ring with realism and reverberate with relevancy.

A preacher must know his "market." It is needful to know who will be present. It would not be prudent to preach a didactic message to a congregation consisting primarily of unchurched persons. Likewise, it is not discerning to preach an evangelistic message to a congregation of mature church members. For this reason, a study of the audience is as important as the study of the Word. This avoids trying to sell aluminum siding to people who live in glass houses.

A timeless poll taken by George Gallup in the early 90s identifies meritorious targets.[1] The broad-based survey dealt with the needs of the average American outside the church. Those polled revealed seven needs:

- The need for shelter and food.
- The need to be led to believe life is meaningful and has purpose. Seventy percent noted this need. Two-thirds said the church is not meeting this need.
- The need for help in establishing a sense of community and relationships. One-third say they have been lonely for a long time.
- The need to be appreciated and respected. Gallup concluded that the closer people feel to God, the better they feel about themselves.
- The need to be listened to and heard.
- The need for a growing faith.
- The need for practical help in developing a more mature faith.

Every minister should place his pulpit in the midst of these needs and pitch his mental tent over them. By addressing them, needs will be met. Happily, people return where they are fed.

Congregants should feel the message is not being delivered to "occupant," but has a personal address on it. One new convert said to her pastor: "The first several times I came to this church I felt you had either tapped my phone or had been reading my mail. You were inside my head!" That is the route to the heart.

As it is obligatory to change message subjects, so it is imperative to change types of sermons. Applied exposition should wisely form the core type of message in order to feed the people. Inductive sermons, a narrative format, topical, typological, and biographical forms are among styles to be used for variety in approach.

Even the type of delivery can change as circumstances and conditions dictate. The Lord did both "roar in Zion" (Amos 1:2) and "gather the lambs in His arms" (Isa. 40:11). Jesus preached repentance in light of approaching judgment (Mark 1:14-15), and was tactful not to break a bruised reed (Matt. 12:17-21).

For there to be church growth resulting from preaching, there must frequently be an evangelistic flavor. For there to be growth, preaching must be solicitous of response. It must be designed to get expressive reaction.

The proclamation of God's Word must include pressing for a verdict by the listener. The Methodist *Discipline* (1784) posed the following question and answer: "What is the best general method of preaching?" Answer: "(1) To invite. (2) To convince. (3) To offer Christ. (4) To build up, and to do this in some measure in every sermon."

Those four facts should flash on the marquee of the minister's mind in the study and in the pulpit. They are still foundational to church growth. Sermons should be baptized in them. To ensure growth, each message should be reviewed in the preparation stage to assure all four factors are included.

The pulpit that addresses the needs noted by Gallup, in the manner suggested by the "Discipline," will stand within the walls of a growing church consisting of spiritually growing members.

Notes

1. George Gallup, *National and International Religion Report*, Edward E. Plowman, ed. (Roanoke, Virginia: Stephen M. Wiko, Publisher, May 20, 1991), 1.

Part VII Preaching to the Needs of People

G. Campbell Morgan (1863-1945)
"Prince of Expositors"

G. Campbell Morgan once wrote that preaching is the "supreme work of the Christian ministry." His own ministry was devoted to faithfully teaching the Word of God in the pulpit.

As a young man, Morgan sought ordination in the Methodist church, but was rejected because he seemed to show little potential as a preacher! He instead became pastor of a series of Congregational churches, culminating in the pastorate of Westminster Chapel in London. Under his leadership and preaching, the congregation experienced new life and growth.

After a period of itinerant preaching and teaching in England and the United States, Morgan assumed the pastorate of Tabernacle Presbyterian Church in Philadelphia. At age 72, Westminster Chapel invited him to return as pastor; he returned to serve the London congregation for the final eight years of his ministry.

Wherever he preached, crowds came to hear Morgan's exposition of Scripture. His sermons often lasted an hour and displayed a carefully crafted development of his chosen text. His sermons reflected diligent study, but he preached from notes rather than a manuscript to allow freedom of delivery. As he preached, he became absorbed in the text and the sermon took on a remarkable power.

Morgan's sermons and other writings continue to provide ample resources for the contemporary preacher who seeks to communicate the truths of God's Word.

42

Michael Duduit, Editor
Preaching *Magazine and*
Director of Development and Church Relations
Samford University Birmingham, Alabama

Preaching and the Family

As you step into the pulpit, look out on the congregation filled with families—some of them traditional families, with two spouses and children, some couples, some single-member households, but all are families nonetheless.

Over on the left sit the Pattersons, who recently moved into your community. As he adjusts to his job transfer, she is growing more frustrated in her job search, and that creates added pressures. With two teenagers getting used to a new school and trying to make new friends, the last thing they need is more pressure at home.

Look to the other side of the sanctuary and notice Bob and Cheryl, who are planning to get married in a few weeks. You've begun counseling them in anticipation of their marriage, and it's clear they have some issues through which to work. He wants four or five kids, while she's not convinced she wants any—at least not for a long time. Bob is big on wifely submission, though Cheryl thinks it's something he'll get over soon. For now, all differences are ignored in the warm glow of romance.

Looking around, you notice that Mary Alice didn't make it to church this Sunday. She grew up in the church and used to be so involved, but since her divorce she's become fairly erratic in her attendance. She'll show up at singles events on Friday or Saturday night, but her Sunday morning appearances are growing farther apart.

As you stand in the pulpit week after week, what do you have to say to the tremendous needs of families—all kinds of families—that come on Sunday seeking a word from the Lord?

Stay Rooted in the Word

When preaching to family needs, one of the greatest temptations is the desire to become a psychologist. While the insights of Christian counselors and psychologists may be of great help to persons in our congregations, we are not called to dispense pop psychology (or any other kind) from the pulpit; we are called to proclaim God's Word so that the Holy Spirit can apply it to the hearts of people. That does not mean we do not learn from the insights of others, and it does not mean we may not use comments or ideas from such books as contemporary illustrations of the biblical message. Yet the message we preach must be rooted in Scripture; the sermon is not a place for group therapy.

By faithfully proclaiming God's Word on a systematic basis, we will regularly deal with critical issues affecting families in our congregations. Adam and Eve help us understand the foundations of the marriage relationship. Jacob's life is certainly illustrative of the potential for deceit and manipulation in families. David helps us understand the dangers of adultery and the pain that can be caused by broken parent-child relationships. The examples could go on.

In addition to using a systematic textual approach to preaching on families, it is also possible to be more topical, either through a series on the family or through individual, targeted sermons on specific marriage and family issues. Frank Harrington, pastor of Atlanta's Peachtree Presbyterian Church, preaches an annual sermon series on relationships; such a series would provide a pastor an excellent opportunity to address family concerns from a biblical foundation.

Face Contemporary Realities

The preacher who always refers to families in the context of a mother, father, and 2.5 children all living happily under the same roof is ignoring the situation of a majority of American families in the 1990s. Even within the church, the traditional nuclear family (much less the extended family, involving grandparents and other relatives) is becoming more and more something found in scrapbooks rather than daily experience.

The "traditional" family—where the husband is the breadwinner, the wife is a homemaker, and two or more children play happily ever after—represents only about 7 percent of American households. In the other 93 percent of American families, there may be a single parent in the home (usually the mother), or both husband and wife work at jobs outside the home.[1] The increasing prevalence of both divorce and out-of-wedlock births means that when we use only images of the "traditional" family in our sermonic language (such as in illustrations), we are ignoring substantial numbers of persons in our congregations who need to sense they are loved and wanted in the family of faith.

Likewise, if our only illustrations containing women involve the kitchen or childcare, we overlook the growing number of women (probably a majority in most congregations) who also hold jobs outside the home. We are well advised to "mix it up" in our language, so that sometimes the "banker" or "doctor" in our illustration is a "she" rather than always being a "he."

While we are facing realities in our own preaching, it is important to help families face the realities of marriage and family life as well. Too many persons enter marriage with a distorted perspective based on overdoses of television and movies. Preaching is one of several tools through which we can help families understand that they are not alone in their feelings of frustration and anxiety—that real families do not always look and act like many TV shows cast them. Using biblical as well as contemporary models, we can help people learn that marriage and family life is hard work, that it requires patience and understanding, and that we will often make mistakes in our relationships. Nevertheless, with God's strength and direction, Christian homes can be wonderful, nurturing places of acceptance and love.

One of the real challenges that faces the contemporary preacher is overcoming the cultural accretions that surround that word *love*. With the misuse and abuse of *love* that takes place throughout the media—from popular music to novels to movies—those who enter our congregations on Sunday need to relearn the meaning and significance of divine love and how that shapes loving relationships within families. Where, other than the church, will people learn that love has responsibilities as well as rewards? Preaching may be the only place many Christians will learn that real love is far more than the shabby substitute they have seen displayed so often in the popular media.

Another contemporary reality we face is the increasing devaluation of children in our society. In a nation where more than 1.5 million abortions take place every year, where millions of children live below the poverty level, and where even offspring of affluent families often become "latchkey children" because parents are too busy with their own careers and interests—preaching must boldly proclaim the value and significance of children as gifts of God deserving of our time and investment. What better way than to preach those texts in which Jesus drew the children to Himself and cautioned against harming the little ones? Those texts have profound implications for parental responsibility in our day and should be stated clearly and decisively from the pulpit.

Shifting attitudes about personal morality also deserve attention in our preaching. Bombarded as we are by messages of moral relativism throughout the culture—messages that sanction pre-marital sex and even adultery as normal and acceptable conduct—the pulpit must work to counteract that through preaching that demonstrates the implications of Christ's Lordship in our lives.

As we face the contemporary realities of attitudes and behavior relating to marriage and families, our preaching can point to a greater and higher reality that challenges us to seek Christ and His righteousness. In that seeking we will find a deeper and richer satisfaction than anything we might find elsewhere.

Note

1. Wayne E. Oates, "Preaching to Marriage and Family Needs," *Preaching*, Vol. I, no. 4 (January-February 1986), p 13.

43

William Hinson, Pastor
First United Methodist Church
Houston, Texas

Preaching and the World of Work

From the Sanctuary to the Salt Mine

The *Los Angeles Times* (July 26, 1991) carried an article with a banner headline declaring, "When God Goes to Work." The first sentence in the article read: "When God shows up at work, there often is hell to pay." The paragraphs that followed contained recitations of well-meaning persons from computer programmers to professional ball players who experienced problems in the work place because they are Christian.

Must people in the pews compartmentalize their faith—have a Sunday faith that leaves the larger portion of their lives untouched? Can preaching save our people from such schizophrenia? Have preachers, by emphasizing a dualistic view of the world, inadvertently contributed to the gap between the sanctuary and the "salt-mine"?

Lay people and clergy alike need to know that their work is vested with deep significance. When I began collecting materials in preparation for writing this chapter, I learned from my son-in-law about a book called, *Your Work Matters to God*.[1] I checked with personnel at the leading bookstores in the city of Houston where I live, and discovered all of them knew the book but had no copies available. I finally was able to secure a copy of the helpful volume from the publishers. I learned during my research that there is a real scarcity of materials relating to faith in the market place.

Our working people, in almost quiet desperation, are searching for divine significance in their work. Their search is complicated by a lack of materials and the silence of the press and the pulpit on this vital issue. They need the unique help that can be afforded by the pulpit to guide them in their search and to help them avoid the faulty views of work that drive them more deeply into despair.

If work is to be rescued from the present state of misunderstanding—if, as Halford Luccock suggests, we must relate a vertical gospel to a horizontal world in order for Christianity to flourish—the persons occupying our pulpits must point the way.

What are God's intentions for us in the working world? The first verse in the Bible tells us that God is a worker. "In the beginning God created the heaven and the earth" (Gen. 1:1). Passages like Psalm 104 outline in vivid detail the ongoing work of God. God is consistently portrayed in the Scriptures as a mighty worker. Job declares that rich and poor alike "all are the work of his hands" (34:19).

Very early in Genesis, we learn that "the Lord God took the man, and put him into the garden of Eden to dress it and to keep it" (Gen. 2:15). This divine assignment to "dress and keep" the creation as God's ruling representatives, as God's co-laborers, is beautifully clarified in the eighth Psalm. Speaking of man as having been made only "a little lower than the angels" (v. 5), the psalmist elaborated, saying: "Thou madest him to have dominion over the works of thy hands; thou hast put all things under his feet. All sheep and oxen, yea, and the beasts of the field; The fowl of the air, and the fish of the sea, and whatsoever passeth through the paths of the seas" (Ps. 8:6-8).

The Bible says we are workers for and with God from the beginning. The concept of work as a "curse" (see Gen. 3:17-19) must be interpreted as the direct result of sin—the disobedience of Adam and Eve in the garden. Interpreting one's labor as a "curse" from God is to overlook the initial command to "tend" and "keep," which was the principle directive God gave to Adam and Eve following their creation.

The meaning of God's initial directive to Adam is instructive for the preacher. Yahweh's command to "tend" indicates our responsibility to "conserve." The second instruction, to "till," directs Adam to "create." Interestingly, the two components of worship are tradition and innovation. Was Adam's gardening "work" or "worship"? How could two terms, used so closely in the beginning, become so divergent in our time as to indicate "sanctuary" and "salt-mine"?

Work and worship were obviously meant to be integrated by our Creator. Helping today's people find a new approach to work that integrates it into worship is badly needed. This is an especially pressing need as the shape of work is changing. Some 5.5 million persons are getting into a new form of "homework" where one's home and office (*hoffices*) are the same.

Jesus reinforced the concept of our being co-laborers with God when He declared: "My Father has been working until now, and I have been working" (John 5:17). One of His final declarations was: "I have glorified You on the earth. I have finished the work which You have given me to do" (John 17:4).

The apostle Paul, like Jesus, drew strength and inspiration from the conviction that he was a co-laborer with God. He cupped his hands and shouted to the Mediterranean world that he was a co-laborer with God (see 1 Cor. 3:9). Yet, is what Jesus and Paul did to be described as "work" in the traditional sense in which that word is used today?

In Benedicta Ward's translation of *The Sayings of the Desert Fathers (Apophthegmata Patrum),* she notes that the term "work" is used in two ways—it may mean manual labor or spiritual exertion. Jesus did not "work" during His itinerate ministry but was cared for by some wealthy women (Luke 8:1-3). He labored strenuously, however, in completing our redemption. Our task, as preachers, is to help our people understand the closeness, even the oneness, of manual labor and spiritual exertion.

Another biblical insight concerning work is the understanding of our labor as a limited gift. As Elton Trueblood has stated: "The chief glory of work lies in the fact that it is really the only thing we can give that is our *own.* We do not produce our talents as the natural resources with which we work, but we do produce our *toil* . . . . We may be stewards of our talents, but we are donors of our labor."[2]

Trueblood's statement is certainly in keeping with the parable of the talents (Matt. 25:14-30). We *receive* our talents but we *give* our labor. Our work, therefore, has a precious quality about it. As Jesus reflected on His own toil, He exclaimed: "I must work the works of Him who sent me while it is day; the night is coming when no one can work" (John 9:4, AT).

Our reward for faithful service during our daylight hours is more service to render in the next life (Matt. 25:20-23). Obviously our Lord had a high, holy understanding of labor. His understanding was lodged in the belief that God has a purpose for every person's life. Unfortunately, however, such a lofty understanding of daily toil has not permeated the living of many in our society. Some of our own people are struggling with faulty views of work.

The Christian Work Ethic

Atlantic Monthly carried a front-page story entitled "The Invention of the Weekend." The article accurately described the views of those who find their weekly labor boring and lacking in any significance. Their weekly cry is: "Thank God it's Friday" (TGIF). They work all week just to earn a paycheck and make it to the weekend. Real life is celebrated on the weekends. "Work which has no other incentive than the paycheck is," as Trueblood observes, "closer to slavery than it is to freedom."[3]

Here in Texas we have recently fought and lost the battle against legalized gambling. Voters had earlier approved betting at horse and dog races; now we have approved a state lottery. Many believe that boredom in the work place is one of the driving forces behind the pernicious evil of gambling. Those who spend sixty percent of their lives performing a task that is empty of meaning and fulfillment are desperate to add the element of excitement that risk-taking provides.

Victor Frankl, a prominent psychiatrist, has written that in any city Sunday is the saddest day of the week. On Sunday the tempo of the working week is suspended and the poverty of meaning and the emptiness of their existence rises up before urban dwellers once more.

The "working to live" view of work is what J. A. Walter has called the "instrumental work ethic." Those who express this understanding "see the purpose of work to be the earning of a wage or salary, and [it] is by far the most widespread view of work in contemporary society."[4]

Our post-Christian culture assumes that the chief reason people work is to make money. We talk about a job "not being worth it" because most of the extra revenue is heavily taxed. Or, on the other end of the economic scale, another says, "Why should I take a job? I can draw just as much in unemployment or through welfare." Our understanding of "vocation" as a holy calling or summons from God has been surrendered to a wholly secular understanding that defines our work as an occupation, just a job.

Jesus pitied those persons who worked only for pay. In Jesus' parable of the laborers in the vineyard, a part of the pain the owner of the vineyard must have felt related to what the long-term laborers had missed. They had worked from sun to sun, all day long, bearing the burden of the day and the scorching heat for a denarius, the agreed upon wage. When the workers came to the vineyard later, some much later, the long-term workers grumbled because all received the same pay. Not only did they resent the owner's generosity, and his right to do what he chose with what was his, but they missed altogether the privilege of working in the vineyard all day long. They had been spared the grief of those who grieve that they so late did come. The words of the householder, the owner, are devastating when he says to those who worked only for pay: "Take that thine is, and go thy way" (Matt. 20:14).

Preaching has, in some unfortunate incidents, contributed to the compartmentalization of work and "real living." In our eagerness to save our people from secularism and worldly values, we have sometimes adopted an enclave mentality and made God's creation, the world, a bad place. Instead of presenting the world as the arena in which Christ is served and in which faith is to be lived out, some preaching has made the world the enemy from which we take our living during the week and then hurry to the church on Sunday—the only place where true religious work is done.

Robert Calhoun, a professor at Yale, has pointed to the significance of ordinary work and the fallacy of the position described above when he said that devoted work is the very flesh and bone of living religion, without which worship cannot live and grow. Such an understanding of work closes the gap between worship and work, thereby increasing the possibility of Christianity being carried into the marketplace. Unless that happens there is little hope for our cause in our post-Christian Western culture.

A second faulty view of work includes those persons who "live to work." While their number is not as large as those who "work to live," every pastor is nonetheless acquainted with "workaholics."

Workaholics thrive on the strokes from work and the sense of control. As bosses, and workaholics are usually eventually bosses, they can speak and people will jump. At home, and in a marriage, one has to consider the other's well-being, which can be terribly inconvenient.

Complete preoccupation and absorption with work can be a way of shutting out reflection that might remind one of troubling considerations like one's place in the universe and the final end of life. God, after all, makes demands on all of us which, apart from grace, are impossibly uncomfortable. It is much easier, for some, to go on playing the American game whose rules, according to the bumper sticker, are: "He who dies with the most toys wins."

Materialism reduces work to a means to an end, and robs it of the lofty conviction that workers are sharing with a working Creator in the shaping of our world. Anyone who is acquainted with the Christian understanding of vocation as a holy calling cannot be deeply satisfied with the sole incentive of making money or accumulating toys.

A balanced life requires fruitful labor and fruitful rest. We must, in our feverish society, reintroduce the concept of the Sabbath as a basic part of the created order. "We cannot recover the true glory of work," says Trueblood, "unless we likewise recover the glory of rest."[5]

After thirty years of ministry, I can understand more clearly the importance of what Howard Thurman taught us at Boston University. Dr. Thurman insisted that the first five minutes of every class be spent in total silence. At the end of what seemed like an eternity to those of us who had been running in all directions, he would softly say: "Now young gentlemen (there were no women), if you are looking at the world through quiet eyes we will proceed."

The preacher must teach today's feverish, fragmented people to see their world through quiet eyes. They must be taught the benefits of being meaningfully disengaged. Jesus provides the paradigm in His ability, even when there were bodies waiting to be blessed, to go aside and "rest a while" (Mark 6:31).

Making The Gospel Relevant

How does the preacher make the gospel relevant to the world of work and rescue his or her people from faulty understandings of work? We must begin by learning about the work environment of our people.

How many times have you ever been in a "white room" where computer technicians live? How can a preacher preach to laity without any idea or sense of where they spend the greater portion of their lives? I have, for example, an entirely different understanding of one man who, all day long, simply monitors a small screen with numbers on it. Only rarely does he move, let alone punch a button.

I consider it a blessing to have worked at an assortment of jobs in my early years, ranging from coaching and teaching to cutting pulpwood and working on a telephone line crew. There is great value in having supported oneself while working on a commission. Many in our congregations base their economic survival on the ability to make the next big sale. We cannot address the spiritual needs of such people until we familiarize ourselves with the pressures that surround them.

Preachers must demonstrate authenticity in their sermons. The ministry is not exempt from stress; indeed, an official at the Menninger Foundation has recently stated that there is no vocation more susceptible to stress than the ministry. When we candidly share our own struggle in the gray areas, our people are especially attentive. We must remember that in the final analysis our people learn more from our struggles than from some of our affirmations.

We must demonstrate a feel for what it is all about in the economic world, a knowledge of what our people are up against in that world. This knowledge must include the moral struggles involved.

Each Thursday morning I have breakfast and prayer with about a dozen of my leading business men. One of their most emphasized requests of me is that I include in my preaching a restatement of Christian morality. There has never been a time when a Christian leader could assume that everyone knows it is wrong to lie or steal. To assume even a rudimentary knowledge of Christian values in our culture is to trust that we have not yet exhausted the moral capital of a previous generation. Rampant relativism, not only in society but also in the church, makes it essential for every conscientious preacher/teacher to teach the essentials of our faith.

A new Christian shared with me that he had, along with several other contractors, been involved in some bid rigging involving lucrative contracts. "The problem now," he said, "is that as a Christian I can no longer do anything that is dishonest." After much conversation and prayer, he told me that he was breaking off his illegal activities with the other contractor. To do so would, however, jeopardize his own company because they would undercut his bids and, because of his previous involvement, he could not turn to the legal authorities for help.

My parishioner, the new Christian, did the Christian thing and ultimately went bankrupt when he lost the ability to garner large contracts. His experience reminded me that the gospel makes a huge difference in the marketplace. People become willing to face boldly and with courage the consequences of a position that is taken on the authority of Scripture.

We must be bold enough to help those who work at jobs with evil consequences or in positions that do not in any way contribute to the well-being of another, to find the courage to change their job or get out of it. God does not want any of us to go to our graves feeling that our lives have been fruitless.

The Saint Sargius Church in Cairo, Egypt, has a number of impressive columns inside the nave. There is a column for each of the twelve disciples of Jesus. On the face of each column, there is a painted scene from the life and work of that particular disciple. On the column dedicated to Judas, however, there is absolutely nothing. It bears mute testimony to the tragedy of a poorly lived life that gathers no fruit. All persons need to believe that what they do is significant in the sight of God. If *their work* has no value in God's sight, *they* have no value.

We must help our people recover the glory in their jobs. I have been struck by the meaning of the phrase *Opus Dei* or "work of God." What makes something a work of God? Something is a work of God not because God does it. In the terminology of Benedict, for example, the work of God is not a work done *by* God but a work done *for* God. This means that absolutely nothing is more an *Opus Dei* than another if it is done for the glory of God—whether washing wounds or washing windows.

If this is God's world, any honorable work that contributes to the quality of life is a sacred task and should be undertaken with this aspect in mind. The really crucial decision for all of us comes, not when we decide what we will "be," whether a preacher or a plowman, but when we decide whether or not we will live our whole lives in what the late Thomas Kelly called "holy obedience."

According to an often-told story, Henry III, king of Bavaria in the eleventh century, grew tired of his heavy responsibility. One day he traveled to a local monastery, presented himself to the prior, and announced that he wanted to live the rest of his life in the monastery as a contemplative. The prior asked, "Your majesty, do you understand that this is about obedience? Whatever I tell you under authority you must do." King Henry replied, "Yes, father, I understand." "Then, your majesty," said the prior, "in obedience to me go back to your throne and serve in the place God has put you." King Henry, according to the story, went back to the throne and served the rest of his reign in a magnificent way.

Aquila and Priscilla, well-known companions of the apostle Paul, made tents for a living (Acts 18:1-3). Their evangelistic zeal was so great, however, that they are mentioned in three books of the New Testament. Surely they were listening when Paul told the Corinthians: "Whether therefore ye eat, or drink, or whatsoever ye do, do all to the glory of God" (1 Cor. 10:31).

When our people are persuaded that they are servants of God regardless of their work, the working world and our churches will be transformed.

Bach, the great composer, signed all of his compositions a.m.d.g., for *ad maiorem dei gloria*, "for the greater glory of God." Our task as preachers is to persuade our people, and ourselves, to "do all to the glory of God."

Notes

1. See Doug Sherman and William Hendricks, *Your Work Matters to God* (Colorado Springs: Navpress, 1987).
2. Elton Trueblood, *Your Other Vocation* (New York: Harper & Row, 1952), 62.
3. Ibid., 62.
4. J. A. Walter, *Sacred Cows* (Grand Rapids: Zondervan, 1979), 30.
5. Trueblood, *Your Other Vocation*, 75.

Harry Emerson Fosdick (1878-1969)

"Life–Situation Preaching"

Harry Emerson Fosdick's life spanned from the "pulpit princes" of the nineteenth century to the shaping of the modern scientific era. His preaching reflected the efforts of mainline Protestantism to preach the faith of the former in a language acceptable to the latter.

As a young man, Fosdick adopted liberal theology as a way to relate his Christian faith to the truths of modern science. After serving as pastor of a Baptist church, he returned to New York City to become professor of homiletics at Union Theological Seminary, his alma mater. For several years he also preached at the city's First Presbyterian Church, but left that post in the face of attacks on his liberal theology by conservative Presbyterian leaders. For years, Fosdick would engage in a rhetorical war with those in the conservative and fundamentalist camps.

While continuing his teaching role at Union, in 1926 he added the pastorate of Park Avenue Baptist Church, which moved and was renamed Riverside Church. Under his leadership, Riverside became the preeminent pulpit of mainline Protestantism in this century. Even those who disagreed with his theology recognized in him a preacher of remarkable gifts.

Fosdick taught and practiced what he called "life–situation preaching," examining life issues in light of the life and teaching of Jesus. He believed the purpose of preaching was to produce a positive change in the lives of listeners. Though he made extensive use of the Bible in his sermons, he discounted the value of traditional expository preaching.

Fosdick used many models in his own ministry, and his sermons provide unique and worthy models of study in our own day.

J. Alfred Smith, Pastor
Allen Temple Baptist Church
Oakland, California

44 Preaching and Social Concerns

Preaching on social issues is taboo among many popular preachers. They recoil from addressing social issues with the skill of persons fleeing from dangerous serpents. Alvin C. Porteous talks about a popular preaching which talks incessantly in "perpetual Sunday twaddle" in a multitude of words which have little of the bite of reality about them because they correspond to nothing in the real world in which we put our lives. Porteous says that this kind of preaching is the essence of profanity in that it takes the Lord's name in vain. It is a sort of vacuous verbalization about God.[1]

Pious profanity in preaching avoids social issues. This kind of a moral preaching can be escapism, entertainment, or egocentrism, or it can be the immoral preaching of sectarianism, biblicism, or authoritarianism. Such preaching can be a cowardly act or the reflection of ignorance about the great issues which affect the lives of those who sit in the pews.

Some of the characteristics of this bland preaching to homogeneous audiences of status quo conformity are as follows:

- preaching peace of mind
- preaching a prosperity gospel
- preaching the psychology of self-esteem
- preaching Jesus as the supplier of every need without explaining how Jesus supplies human needs
- preaching a gospel of cheap grace

- preaching a legalistic gospel of duty
- preaching a gospel of dogma unrelated to life
- preaching a gospel which proof texts the biases of the preacher
- preaching a gospel of personal piety that excludes social responsibility
- preaching from a limited number of themes and texts in the New Testament, and preaching almost exclusively from the Old Testament the perspectives of prophecy, typology, and dispensationalism.

Perhaps these preachers are better than those angry fire and brimstone preachers who are against the world and whose sermons on social issues are characterized by "negative bashing." Ill-prepared persons preaching about the gospel and social issues can be more deadly and destructive than those timid souls who strive to explain biblical texts without offering any social application.

Special preparation is necessary in order to preach on social issues. Responsible preachers must practice continuing education. These preachers must study correct biblical interpretation, theology, sociology, and church history. They must seek an understanding of both sides of issues like AIDS, abortion, human sexuality, euthanasia, bio-ethics, economics, nuclear waste, ecology, affirmative action, race and racism, science and scientism, third world and minority group concerns, apartheid, divestments of church bodies in financial institutions for religious/social/political reasons, the failure of the criminal justice system, non-violence, war, and the religious baptizing of partisan politics.

Most preachers took no more than one seminary course in Christian ethics. Very well written texts, journals, and magazines are available in the area of Christian ethics. While it is not possible to read all of the material in the field of Christian ethics, responsible preachers will read consistently and critically the literature in an attitude of prayerful objectivity.

In visiting preachers, I cannot help but notice how narrow is the selection of books which adorn the shelves of their libraries. Few magazines, periodicals, journals, and books address the socio-economic or political issues which erode compassion and concern. There is a need to read widely and to open minds and hearts to publishers and authors of other disciplines, traditions, and ethnic groups. Read works written by disciplined scholars who are women and who represent African-American, Asian-American, and Hispanic viewpoints. Be aware of viewpoints of integrity that are different from the controlling and dominant philosophers and theologies of those who hold the power and have held the control of conceptual thinking in the schools, universities, and seminaries of America. With the rapid increase of minority groups and the diminution of the population of Anglo Americans, if for no other reason than that of reconciliation in the human community, gospel preachers of redemption should expose their minds to the best thinking of "Samaritan" scholars in the household of faith.

Read the prayerful reflections of ethnic minority Christian thinkers who have perspectives on ethical issues such as affirmative action, social justice, the changing role of women, the middle class tax revolt, attacks on housing to achieve integration, domestic efforts to improve the lot of the deprived and disadvantaged, funding of public education, the inadequacy of health care, and the plight of seniors. Help your people to hear the cries of those in your urban Macedonia who are homeless, hungry, and helpless. Any gospel that neglects these concerns is guilty of neglecting the sinful now and now for the abstract, sweet by and by of a utopian New Jerusalem.

Eternal life in the Koine Greek is concerned about the quality of life in the now as well as in the hereafter. Such questions were not ignored by eighth-century preachers like Amos, Hosea, and Micah. Surely these prophets are a part of the preaching canon of modern day preachers. A gospel of love and justice, a gospel of grace and righteousness must address the indifference and antipathy to the plight of blacks and other oppressed groups. Preachers of good news cannot preach love without being concerned about the embracing of consumerism, preoccupation with self, or cultural narcissism. Preachers of good news must address the meanness mania, neo-racism, and ethnocentrism that have gained acceptability and conformity among too many church people.

Gerald R. Gill challenges preachers of good news:

> While meanness is a strong categorization, it is an apt one to explain the current mood among much of the American populace. For meanness denotes selfishness, stinginess, and malice.... These denotations—selfishness, stinginess, and malice—are expressions of an increasing unwillingness and hostility upon the part of many citizens to share more equally the benefits of American society. [2]

How does 1 Corinthians 13, Luke 4:14-20, and Luke 10:25-37 address the meanness mania?

While attending a seminar for senior pastors of very large churches, I was painfully surprised that the nationally recognized authorities on church growth who lectured us on making our large congregations larger ignored the ministry of our churches to our members as it relates to applying the principles of Christian social ethics to the world beyond the large church campuses. The goal of the classes was to master sociological principles of homogeneous church growth. No Zaccheus-type conversions of repentance and restitution as it relates to economic justice were mentioned. The thesis was to grow into "Super Churches" by ignoring preaching on social issues. The cultural captivity of preaching to cultural captives had a greater priority than preaching the Christ of the four Gospels. In vain, I listened to hear about the Christ who became flesh and pitched a tent among us.

Karen Lebacqz, professor of Christian ethics at the Pacific School of Religion, has written a book to help preachers escape the trap of cultural captivity which presents Jesus Christ as an intellectual abstraction or a cold dispenser of propositional doctrines. Her book is *Justice in an Unjust World*.

This work gives a broad, biblically rooted presentation of the justice of God and God's call for us to heed the cry for justice in the churches and communities where we preach and serve. Dr. Lebacqz also parallels the biblical content with the narratives of persons who have been and who are victimized by injustice. No attempt is made to intensify feelings of guilt. Every chapter provides a framework for enabling and empowering Christians to work in the spirit of Jesus Christ in changing injustice into justice. Dr. Lebacqz's sober and logical Christian realism offers no utopian illusions. She writes:

> Justice in an unjust world may be characterized as a renovation incorporating radical openness to new structures and possibilities. But it is never perfect justice. It is incomplete and fragile. Sometimes it will fail. It will yield new injustices that require resistance and redress. Justice is therefore never a total accomplishment but always a process and a vision.[3]

This awareness of human imperfection in the quest for justice does not in any way excuse preachers from preaching about living and working for righteousness and justice until the kingdom of God comes in its fullness. This fact should also motivate preachers to speak in humility and love on social issues. Preachers do not have the ultimate word.

Understanding is always partial. First Corinthians 13:9 reminds us: "For we know in part and we prophesy in part" (NRSV). As long as our hearers know that we preach in humility and sincerity, we can be forgiven by them when we fail to untie the "Gordian Knot of truth" in our exegesis, interpretation, and application of Scripture to the complexities of burning social issues. Henlee H. Barnette, Professor Emeritus of Christian ethics at The Southern Baptist Theological Seminary, shares an ancient Hebrew prayer to help preachers who preach on social issues:

> From the cowardice that shrinks from new truths, from the laziness that is content with half truths, and from the arrogance that thinks it knows all truth, O God of Truth deliver us. [4]

Preaching on social issues call for humility and an understanding that those who preach do not have the penultimate word. "Prudence is necessary since intelligent, planned action is called for, and common sense is essential if the battle is not to be lost for the wrong reasons. Many a good idea has been defeated because the strategies were faulty."[5] Paul Simmons, professor of Christian ethics at The Southern Baptist Theological Seminary, suggests that preachers should be wise as serpents and harmless as doves and should strive to persuade hearers rather than offend persons as they preach on social issues.

In preaching, God speaks, people hear, and are moved to act in a new way. Preaching on social issues should help persons see reality in a new light and the event of preaching should lead to personal transformation. The personality of those who preach must be loving and winning, especially if preachers are to address social issues. In Denver, Colorado, in January of 1981, at a meeting of the Association for Theological Field Educators, I shared this story in my address:

> A particular church in a hierarchical denomination had become well known as a graveyard for ministers. The internal conflicts of the church usually resulted in requests to transfer the pastors after a brief residence. A new bishop arrived on the scene and immediately sent to this church one of the brightest and apparently most capable ministers in the district. True to form, within a year the chairperson of the personnel committee called the bishop and informed him that the church wanted the minister moved on to another setting.
>
> "What's the problem?" asked the bishop. "Well," came the reply, "all he does is get up every Sunday and tell us that we are going to hell." Reluctantly, the bishop arranged for the transfer of the minister to another church. This time he sent a much older person to be the minister of the church and settled back in partial contentment that he had eliminated one of his problems in his headache churches. But alas, within six months, the chairperson of the personnel committee was back on the phone to the bishop.
>
> "This preacher's no better than the rest of them. All he does is get up every Sunday and tell us all that we are going to hell." Totally exasperated, the bishop decided to fight fire with fire. He sent to the church an aggressive, young, recent seminary graduate who had been known for championing every cause from abortion to draft evasion. The bishop grimly dug in his heels and waited for the thunder and lightning to strike. But three-and-a-half years passed and he never heard a word. The annual reports indicated that the congregation had grown substantially in attendance and budget and had embarked on a few social programs. The bishop's curiosity peaked and he called the chairperson of the church's personnel committee.
>
> "How do you like your minister?" he asked. "He's wonderful," came the reply. "I don't get it," said the bishop. "I thought that certainly this minister would prophetically tell you that you're going to hell if you don't change your warp." "Oh," said the lay person, "hardly a Sunday passes that our minister doesn't tell us that we're going to hell, but he cries about it. The others were glad about it." [6]

In telling this story to theological educators of the Association of Theological Schools, I was stressing that those who teach seminarians to preach on social issues should help students to preach with anguish rather than anger. People accept challenge and criticism if they are spoken to in humility and love, and with a broken and burdened heart. Such a spirit may help to build relationships with persons in the congregation. When relationships are intact, it is easier to preach about social issues or matters that are controversial. Some preachers make the mistake of preaching confrontationally or on ethical issues without prophetic anguish and before they have had ample time to build relationships of trust with the congregation.

Not all sermons should be prophetic. Some sermons should heal the broken hearted, nurture disciples, or call persons into an acceptance of the Lordship of Jesus Christ. Warren H. Stewart, Sr., in *Interpreting God's Word in Black Preaching,* says that from Professor James Sanders he learned to adopt two basic hermeneutical modes that Sanders called the "constitutive" and the "prophetic." Whereas the prophetic challenges, the constitutive supports, gives identity, and purpose. In order to balance the constitutive and the prophetic, some pastors use the lectionary. However, Dr. Stewart points out the uniqueness in African-American preaching is that these preachers have not preached the constitutive one Sunday and the prophetic the following Sunday. Stewart says that these classic preachers have a dual usage of the constitutive and the prophetic in the same sermon. [7]

The use of hermeneutical methodology in preaching on social issues is the ethical responsibility of preachers who inspire the confidence and trust of people who come Sunday after Sunday to hear what God has to say on the issues which make their lives complex. They come not so much to hear preachers whose feet are made of clay, but to hear persons whom they trust to allow God to speak through them. Responsible preachers listen in to the message as they give it, for they, too, need the voice of God to challenge them to *be* good news and to *do* good news in order to have integrity in *proclaiming* good news.

Ethical preachers are good news persons who do good work in preparing themselves to preach on social issues. They study the issues carefully. They study the needs of their preaching audience. They prepare both head and heart to preach with humility and love. They prepare their text with exegetical expertise and hermeneutical excellence. Perhaps the best coaching plan that I have seen for preaching responsibly on social issues comes from Raymond Bailey. He encourages preachers to avoid:

- Poor preparation and faulty exegesis
- Glittering generalities
- Loaded language and name calling
- Emotional manipulation
- Misrepresentation and partial truth. [8]

In *Preaching As a Social Act,* Arthur Van Seters challenges preachers to expand beyond the five fallacies Bailey cites. Seters would not deny Bailey's suggestions; he simply points out the need for preachers to look at the wider context of preaching. Preachers should ask the following questions:

- What is happening in the world as this sermon is being prepared?
- What news report are we talking about most?
- What issues or events are we avoiding?
- How do we as a congregation/parish view the world, and what are our attitudes toward change?
- On which views of what is going on around us do we find a consensus and which are controversial?
- What is the general mood of life in our community as this sermon is preached?
- What forces of evil in the world do we specifically identify as needing to be addressed by preaching?[9]

In preaching to persons who may resist attitudinal change, preachers need to find images and metaphors that will draw persons into engaging the text so that they will create a new openness to persons and to the power of the Holy Spirit who alone brings about human transformation. Preachers may want to lead their hearers into thinking about specific ways they can concretely respond to the call and claims of God that emanate from the text. There is the need to make abstract ideas come to life with pulsating images and then to make sure that pulsating images are filled with content and substance.

Preachers may master communication theory and understand the technique of the delivery of sermons. They may sharpen homiletical skills and hermeneutical processes. They may update themselves on the theories of Christian ethics and learn the sociology and traditions of the texts selected for sermonic development. Yet preaching must come from hearts touched with both the burdens of the hearers and the urgency to speak as God's messengers. With the combination of burden and urgency, preachers can face the challenge of preaching on social concerns.

The San Francisco Chronicle (August 26, 1991) gave an inspiring example of preaching on social concerns by John Allin, the pastor of President George Bush. The sermon was preached on August 25, 1991, at St. Ann's Episcopal Church in Kennebunkport, Maine. It was preached in a positive spirit in the presence of President Bush. The preacher said: "While we have been preoccupied with the evils of communism, we have failed to examine the problems of our own system. What would it be like if we bent our total efforts to feed and to heal as we have bent our total efforts to defend against a perceived Soviet military threat? The United States complained about Japanese barriers to U.S. rice imports, but ignored the fact that its own sugar subsidies hurt poor Central American countries." Pastor Allin called for reforms of the U.S. prison system, which he said is growing more rapidly than new schools. Urging that inmates be taught to read and work before they are released, he said: "Turn those prisons into schools, places of industry." This sermon was delivered with some humor and with constructive suggestions as well as an analysis of the problems which need correcting. This is an example of preaching on social issues at its best. Students should study this skillful art of preaching which majors on reconciliation and not alienation.

In his last major public appearance, while he was terminally ill, the pathos, ethos, and logos of Orlando Costas, Dean of Andover Newton Theological School sent home the transforming power of God's message as he prayed with social sensitivity and personal piety a prayer from the peasants of Central America:

> Sent by the Lord am I, my hands are ready now to help construct a just and peaceful loving world. Angels cannot change a world of hurt and pain into a world of love, of justice and peace. This task is mine to do. Make it reality. Oh, help me God obey, help me to do your will. [10]

Preachers like the late Orlando Costas have reminded us that there need be no taboo on preaching on social issues. Jesus in Luke 4:14-21 inaugurated His ministry by preaching on social concerns.

The African-American pulpit, which shaped and nurtured my religious formation, adopted Jesus Christ as the model for preaching on social issues. This legacy never had the option of deciding whether or not to preach on social issues. Without preaching bitterness or hostility, without being self-righteous or judgmental, early African-American preachers declared that the battle against slavery was not between the slave and the master, but between the system of oppression and the system of liberation. Therefore, their sermons presented, as David Shannon states, "the basic biblical theme of divine presence in the midst of oppression and suffering as a basis for hope." [11] This was the foundation upon which persons like Martin Luther King, Jr. could preach a gospel of reconciliation which appealed to both whites and blacks during the era of legalized segregation. The social issues of today are legion but preachers can preach about them with the mind and spirit of Jesus Christ. The task is ours to do. May God help us make it reality.

Resources for preaching on social concerns:

Armstrong, James. *Telling Truth: The Foolishness of Preaching in a Real World*. Waco: Word Books, 1977.

Aycock, Don M, ed. *Heralds to a New Age*. Elgin, IL: Brethren Press, 1985.

Bailey, Raymond. "Ethics in Preaching." *Review and Expositor.* 1989.

Barnette, Henlee H. "The Minister as a Role Model." *Review and Expositor.* 1989.

Barry, James C., ed. *Preach The Word in Love and Power.* Nashville: Convention Press, 1986.

Brown, Robert McAfee. *Spirituality and Liberation: Overcoming the Great Fallacy.* Philadelphia: Westminster Press, 1988.

Brown, Robert McAfee. *Saying Yes and No, On Rendering to God and Caesar.* Philadelphia: Westminster Press, 1986.

Brown, Robert McAfee. *Unexpected News: Reading the Bible with Third World Eyes.* Philadelphia: Westiminster Press, 1984.

Felder, Cain Hope, ed. *Stony the Road We Trod: African American Biblical Interpretation.* Minneapolis: Fortress Press, 1991.

Gill, Gerald R. *Meanness Mania, The Changed Mood.* Washington, D.C.: Howard University Press, 1980.

Lebacqz, Karen. *Justice in an Unjust World.* Minneapolis: Augsburg Publishing House, 1987.

Porteous, Alvin C. *The Search for Christian Credibility.* Nashville: Abingdon Press, 1971.

Proctor, Samuel D. *Preaching About Crises in the Community.* Philadelphia: Westminister Press, 1988.

Schaull, Richard. *Naming the Idols, Biblical Alternatives for U.S. Foreign Policy.* Oak Park, IL: Meyer-Stone Books, 1988.

Schulz, William F., ed. *Transforming Words.* Boston: Skinner House, 1984.

Simmons, Paul. "The Pastor as Prophet, How Naked the Public Square," *Review and Expositor,* 1989.

Smith, Kelly Miller. *Social Crisis Preaching.* Macon, GA: Mercer University Press, 1984.

Seters, Arthur Van, ed. *Preaching as a Social Act: Theology and Practice,* Nashville: Abingdon Press, 1988.

Warlick, Harold C. *How To Be a Minister and a Human Being.* Valley Forge, PA: Judson Press, 1982.

Wiesel, Elie. *Messengers of God: Biblical Portraits and Legends.* New York: Summit Books, 1976.

Notes

1. Alvin C. Porteous, *The Search for Christian Credibility* (Nashville: Abingdon Press, 1971), 28.
2. Gerald R. Gill, *Meanness Mania: The Changed Mood* (Washington, D.C.: Howard University Press, 1980), 1.
3. Karen Lebacqz, *Justice in an Unjust World* (Minneapolis: Augsburg Publishing House, 1987), 147.
4. Henlee H. Barnette, "The Minister as a Role Model," *Review and Expositor,* Vol. 86, no. 4 (1989): 509-510.
5. Paul Simmons, "The Pastor as Prophet: How Naked the Public Square," *Review and Expositor,* vol. 86, no. 4, (Louisville: The Southern Baptist Theological Seminary, 1989), 519.
6. J. Alfred Smith, quoted by Harold C. Warlick, Jr., *How to Be a Minister and a Human Being* (Valley Forge, PA: Judson Press, 1982), 71-72.
7. Warren Stewart, *Interpreting God's Word in Black Preaching* (Valley Forge, PA: Judson Press, 1984), 33.

8. Raymond Bailey, "Ethics in Preaching," *Review and Expositor,* Vol. 86, no. 4 (1989): 536.
9. Arthur Van Seters, ed., *Preaching as a Social Act: Theology and Practice* (Nashville: Abingdon Press, 1988), 264.
10. Prayed at the biennial of the American Baptist Churches, U.S.A., June 18, 1987, at the convention center in Pittsburgh, Pennsylvania, by Orlando Costas.
11. David T. Shannon, "An Ante-bellum Sermon: A Resource for an African American Hermeneutic," *Stony the Road We Trod,* Cain Hope Felder, ed. (Minneapolis: Fortress Press, 1991), 122.

45

Ken Hemphill
Church Growth Consultant, Home Mission Board of the Southern Baptist Convention
Atlanta, Georgia

Preaching and Evangelism

"Preacher, we hired you to do that!" A sobering and unexpected response to a young preacher who thought he knew how to make his church hum.

I had just accepted the call to be the pastor of my first church. I was full of zeal and short on knowledge or experience. During my college years at Wake Forest I had worked on the staff of Calvary Baptist Church as youth pastor. Pastor Mark Corts had led me through a program of evangelism training much like Continuous Witness Training. I had seen what this training had done to equip laymen to share their faith. I had witnessed the exciting growth of that church.

Now that I had a church of my own, I was sure that it was just what was needed to turn things around. Without any warning, I announced to the church my intention to teach this class on personal evangelism during the Church Training hour. Everyone nodded approvingly since at that time we had no Church Training. Attendance was good on the first evening of class, with about 18 adults attending. On the second week attendance began a steady decline and by the fourth week only a few hearty souls remained.

Right in the middle of my lecture a deacon interrupted me in the most unceremonious way. "Preacher, why are you telling us about witnessing?" I was dumbfounded. Surely my interrogator was kidding. Confused and obviously rattled, I managed to mumble something about witnessing being every Christian's job. It was at that precise moment that he informed me: "Preacher, we hired you to do that!"

First, it was unsettling to think that in their mind I was just a hired hand. Beyond that I could not believe the preacher was viewed as a professional evangelist, a hired gun.

I had just returned from graduate work in Cambridge and was the pastor of the First Baptist Church in Galax, Virginia. The church was growing and everything was going smoothly. The church had welcomed me with open arms and had been most complimentary about my ministry. I suppose that is why an off-handed remark by one of my deacons hit me like a stun gun.

"Pastor, you just don't preach enough about hell!"

At first I was rattled by the comment. I could not understand why this very supportive deacon wanted me to preach on hell with greater frequency. When I questioned him about his remark, he explained that he had been saved when an evangelist had given a graphic portrayal of hell. He was confident that the lack of baptisms in the church during recent years was the lack of enough hang-'em-over-hell messages. For this deacon, the pastor could fulfill his work as evangelist by preaching on hell.

These two events may help us to focus on the questions that this chapter title raises. What is the relationship between preaching and evangelism in the local church? Does the preaching of evangelistic sermons enable the pastor to satisfy Paul's injunction to young Timothy to fulfill his ministry by doing the work of an evangelist? After all, the immediate context in 2 Timothy 4:2-5 is about preaching the Word. How many of our laypeople think that the heart of the church's evangelistic ministry is fulfilled by a few evangelistic messages? For that matter, what percentage of our laity views evangelism as a task confined to professionals? What is the role of pastors in evangelism? How do they communicate this to the church at large?

Defining Evangelism

Before addressing preaching and evangelism, we need to define evangelism. Sometimes the term *evangelism* is used loosely to describe virtually any church or pastoral activity. Those who use the term in this way define evangelism as *presence evangelism*. Persons who accept such a definition reason that social action should be called evangelism regardless of whether it is accompanied by a verbal witness about Christ. Christian presence and social involvement are critical, but devoid of verbal witness they are insufficient.

Others hold to a *proclamation* view of evangelism. They insist that a verbalization of the gospel must accompany good works. Once the proclamation has been heard and understood, the evangelist has fulfilled his or her duty. A frequent motto of those who hold such a definition is "share Christ and leave the results to God." This concept of evangelism is an improvement over presence evangelism because it includes the spoken *evangel*. It also rightly acknowledges that the results of evangelistic activity are the sovereign work of the Holy Spirit. Yet we must ask whether the proclamation definition gives sufficient consideration to the Lord's command: "Go out into the highways and along the hedges, and compel them to come in, that my house may be filled" (Luke 14:23, NASB). Or consider the passion of the apostle Paul: "We beg you on behalf of Christ, be reconciled to God" (2 Cor. 5:20, NASB).

Persuasion evangelism goes a step beyond proclamation evangelism. Persuasion evangelism does not consider a person to be evangelized until he or she responds to the good news of the gospel, becomes a disciple of Christ, and a responsible member of a local church. The persuasion definition best fulfills the great commission: "Go therefore and make disciples of all nations, baptizing them in the name of the Father and the Son and the Holy Spirit, teaching them to observe all that I commanded you" (Matt. 28:19-20, NASB).[1] It has the advantage of pulling together that which has traditionally been called evangelism and discipleship. When personal evangelism is understood and embraced, balanced church growth occurs.

How then does your preaching impact the evangelistic activity of the church?

Preaching to Create a Climate for Evangelism

How would you describe an evangelistic church? Is it a church that has a good outreach program, or one that has a tradition of great revivals, or perhaps one with a pastor who preaches great evangelistic sermons? Any and all of these elements may be present in an evangelistic church, but evangelism is more of an environmental issue than it is a programmatic one. An evangelistic church, above all else, has a climate that enhances both personal and corporate soul-winning. Seven elements that must be present to create a healthy climate for evangelism are:

1. A Warm Evangelistic Atmosphere

The staff, the leaders of the church, and the members must believe in the priority of evangelism. It must be a natural part of church planning and conversation.

2. A Pervasive Spirit of Love

The members of the church must love one another and actively love the lost. When lost persons visit the church they must feel embraced as a person and not as a prospect.

3. A Spirit of Excitement and Expectancy

When Christians are genuinely excited about what God is doing in their lives, they will naturally communicate this to their unsaved friends. This excitement about the things of the Spirit leads to expectancy. The people come praying for and expecting evangelistic fruit.

4. A Sense of Urgency

When one fully understands the awful fate of lost persons and their own responsibility for sharing the good news, it will create a sense of urgency.

5. An Awareness of the Supernatural at Work

One of the great side benefits of seeing evangelistic results in the local church is a first-hand encounter with the supernatural work of the Holy Spirit. People today hunger to see the hand of God in their own lives and churches.

6. A Team Spirit

For the body to function properly in evangelism, members must serve according to their spiritual gifts. All members must be led to accept responsibility for the Great Commission, and all must be led to share in the joy of the harvested fruit.

7. A Shared Vision

Without a vision, the people perish. It may not be physically possible for my church to reach every person in our area, but I hope no one tells my people. Our vision is to permeate our community with the gospel so that none shall be lost.

The Pastor Sets the Pace

Here is the first place that our preaching and the church's evangelistic health are interrelated. The pastor sets the pace for the evangelistic spirit of his church. In my own ministry I can track the months where my zeal for reaching the lost has been shoved onto a back burner because of heavy schedule demands. The impact on our church's effectiveness is immediate. The people seem to sense that the pastor's priorities have changed. Pastors have the greatest responsibility and opportunity to create and maintain an evangelistic climate in the church through their preaching.

The evangelistic climate can be greatly influenced through the weekly preaching ministry. For example, take each element in the list above and construct a series of messages designed to challenge the church body to allow the Spirit to transform their thinking and behavior in a particular area.

Deal with what it means for the members of the body to love one another. This series of messages should be biblically based and practical. Consider passages such as 1 John 3, Romans 12:9-21, Romans 15:1-7,

Galatians 6:1-11, and John 13:5-17. If, through preaching, the church family is moved toward a more loving spirit, the evangelistic climate of the church will be impacted.

Further, preach about the team spirit necessary for balanced church growth and effective evangelism. Spend several weeks in 1 Corinthians 12 alone. The pastor should share his heart and vision on these practical issues related to evangelism. People want to know where the pastor believes God is leading the church, and they will respond to God's Word when it is expounded with integrity. For the church to have a shared vision for fulfilling the Great Commission, the pastor must communicate that vision from the pulpit.

Preaching to Call Others to Witness

The most effective pattern for total church evangelism is still one-to-one, person-to-person sharing of the gospel. This approach enables all the members of the church to be salt and light in the marketplace. It allows the church to penetrate the community and reach those who would never come to the church to hear the good news. Many of the popular concepts of evangelism in our day are built on the proposition of getting the unsaved to our buildings and functions so that they may hear the good news. Experience reveals that some will attend, but both Scripture and practical knowledge reveal that we must "go" if we are to fulfill the Great Commission. The church will not experience long-term evangelistic success unless it motivates and equips the laity to share their faith in Christ outside the church building.

First, pastors cannot preach effectively and convincingly about evangelism if they are not personally doing evangelism. There is a hollow ring to the sermon on personal soul-winning when there is no evidence that the pastor himself is a soul winner. I am personally involved in our weekly outreach program and in training others to witness. I enjoy sharing with our church family about the opportunities that God gives me to witness. I join them in praying about lost friends and family members. Because my church family knows that I am personally committed to sharing my faith on a regular basis, I can with integrity call them to involvement.

How then do pastors preach in such a way that they can encourage others to witness? Pastors will not get lasting results by haranguing and harassing or by heaping loads of guilt on those who are not presently involved. Pastors must patiently and positively allow God's Word to transform hearts and minds concerning the need to witness.

When preparing to preach on witnessing, pastors first might ask: Why do the great majority of Christians not witness? Most of the reasons or excuses given can be summarized in three categories: lack of understanding, fear, and personal life-style.

1. Lack of Understanding

Many Christians are like the deacon who thinks the pastor is a hired professional for evangelism. Although it is true that some individuals have a gift for evangelism, it is equally true that all believers are called to be witnesses. Through their preaching ministry, pastors can lovingly and biblically help remove the confusion that keeps many laity from witnessing.

Another issue of understanding that must be dealt with effectively from the pulpit is the condition of human sin, one's plight without God, and God's singular answer for the sin problem. I am continually amazed at how many people in our churches are "hopeful" universalists. They hope that their husband or neighbor, who is a good person, will get to heaven. This lack of understanding will be resolved only by good doctrinal preaching.

Some believe that doctrine must be watered down if the church is to grow. This view is both untrue and unbiblical. The early church experienced healthy growth and, according to Acts 2:42, continually devoted themselves to the apostles' teaching. Healthy, long-term church growth and evangelism will be enhanced by doctrinal preaching.

Consider doing a series of messages on the important doctrines of the faith. Deal with issues such as God, Christ, the Holy Spirit, the fallen nature of humankind, heaven and hell, and God's plan of salvation. Develop healthy believers. Dispel the ignorance that keeps many church members from sharing their faith. Look at Paul's personal testimony in 2 Corinthians 5:14-21. Note that his conviction about man's condition and God's solution moved him to beg people to be reconciled to God. It takes both a personal encounter with God and a clear understanding of God's plan to provide lasting motivation for witnessing.

2. The Fear Factor

Many Christians confess that they are afraid to share their faith. They fear personal rejection. As a pastor, be honest about your own fears and those of the early disciples. Fear is overcome by perfect love. Such love originates in the Holy Spirit being poured out in one's heart. Many Christians are ignorant of the ministry of the Holy Spirit who gives boldness in witnessing for Christ. Consider a series of messages on the ministry of the Holy Spirit.

3. The Life-style of the Christian

Thomas G. Long argues that many people have spiritual laryngitis because they are not walking the walk and, therefore, are unwilling to talk the talk of the Christian life. Thus he concludes: "Preachers who do not address ethical concerns forfeit their ability to address evangelistic concerns."[2] Preaching for evangelism requires that we deal honestly and openly about issues of personal holiness and the Christian life-style.

Biblical Exposition for Evangelism

Thus far we have dealt with "Preaching and Evangelism" without yet addressing preaching evangelistically. This study would not be complete without considering this important issue. Think about the evangelistic impact in weekly preaching as well as special evangelistic messages.

Weekly Evangelistic Emphases

Most preachers in evangelical traditions have felt a responsibility to make a weekly evangelistic emphasis. Usually this is accomplished by making an appeal at the end of the message. This method is done ritualistically even in small churches where the pastor may know the personal testimony of every person present. Genuine concern for the lost is laudable, but such vain repetition may, in fact, dull the sensitivity of the congregation to the call for decision.

A more extreme version of the weekly evangelistic appeal is found in the pastor who feels led to preach an evangelistic message weekly. I once knew a young person who was regular in attendance at a Friday night youth Bible study, but who rarely attended church on Sunday morning. When I asked her about this seeming contradiction in her commitment, she told me she had accepted Christ under the preaching of her pastor when she was just nine. "I love my pastor, but I have heard the same message for seven years now." I began to listen more attentively and discovered that she was correct. No matter what text was selected, the pastor usually preached a similar message detailing how to receive Christ. Not only was he not producing evangelistic results, he was impoverishing believers. Pastors need not preach an evangelistic message weekly to see regular evangelistic results.

When the climate for evangelism exists, Christians witness and bring unsaved persons to church, the Bible is preached, and results are seen regularly. John Bisagno makes this same observation: "Strange as it may seem, any preaching can be evangelistic if one creates a proper setting, finishes with an evangelistic appeal, and gives a good invitation. One of the surprising things I discovered upon entering the pastorate was the ease with which the Holy Spirit blessed any type of preaching with evangelistic results when things were right."[3]

Alan Walker, in his book *Evangelistic Preaching*, argues for "existential evangelism." By this he means that the pastor can give a call to commitment in many specific and concrete ways. He gives an example of how he gives such an invitation after preaching a message on marriage and purity. His evangelistic appeal came directly from the challenge to marital holiness.[4]

I have had numerous experiences where the Holy Spirit produced unexpected evangelistic results. One Sunday morning I preached a message on commitment to service. I extended the invitation and the first person down the aisle was my next door neighbor. His wife had been led to Christ some months earlier by one of our visitation teams. He had listened to the gospel that evening but did not respond. He did, however, begin attending church with his family. After he made his public commitment that day he remarked to me about why he came on that particular Sunday. He told me that he had heard the gospel on several occasions and knew how to be saved, but he had never seen the real point of salvation until I preached on total commitment.

Regular evangelistic results are possible without preaching weekly evangelistic messages. Create the environment, train the people, preach the Bible, and extend an invitation with confidence. Giving a special appeal to receive Christ may depend on the size of the church, the pastor's specific knowledge of a person's needs, and the prompting of the Holy Spirit in the worship service. When you give an evangelistic appeal, do not just tack it onto the sermon in a cold and ritualistic manner.

Preaching the Evangelistic Message

Every pastor should regularly preach messages which are clearly and identifiably evangelistic. According to V. L. Stanfield: "Evangelistic preaching is presenting 'Jesus Christ in the power of the Holy Spirit, that men may put their trust in God through Him, accept Him as their Savior, and serve Him as their King, in the fellowship of His church.' "[5] As James Clarke writes: "It is a mystery and privilege to have the opportunity to be a channel for the passage of life of God to man, to be the living contact point of the Holy Spirit, the human agents of divine power. The Spirit-filled preacher can touch the conscience, change the motives, and awaken the deep, dormant powers of the human heart as can no other man."[6]

Here are seven reasons for preaching evangelistic messages:

1. Preaching the gospel is God's chief instrument for saving people (Rom. 10:14; 1 Cor. 1:21-24). The evangelistic pulpit is complementary to the pastor's personal soul winning efforts (Acts 20:20).

2. It is an issue of obedience to Christ (Luke 24:47). We have the privilege to stand in God's stead and urge people to be reconciled to God (2 Cor. 5:18-20).

3. Lost persons are in critical and urgent danger.

4. Preaching produces the crisis that brings decisions. It provides the

atmosphere in which the Holy Spirit can produce the harvest from the seed sown in personal evangelism.

5. It enables people to see the supernatural work of the Holy Spirit through the preached word.

6. Evangelistic preaching energizes the church's soul-winning ministry. It becomes the rallying point for all other evangelistic activity.

7. It gives Christians a clearer view of the gospel, reviewing basic doctrines and granting assurance.[7]

Writers who have listed the characteristics of good evangelistic preaching generally fit them into two categories: theological and practical. Theologically, the evangelistic sermon should be thoroughly biblical in content, pressing the claims of the living God, exalting Christ, being dominated by the cross, magnifying grace, attacking the doctrine of salvation by works, and aiming at producing repentance. Practically, it should be positive, clear, brief, intellectually respectable, conforming to good ethics, appealing to the whole personality, amply illustrated, urgently declared in the power of the Holy Spirit, and climaxed with a public call to commitment.[8]

Best results will be obtained from the evangelistic message in the local church when the people have been trained to share their faith and to bring their unsaved friends with them to church. It makes little sense to preach a powerful evangelistic sermon without first preparing the church. Prayer meetings should be scheduled where the lost are prayed for by name. A specific date or series of dates should be given so that people could encourage unsaved friends to attend church with them for that particular service. Plans should be made to have sufficient altar counselors to deal with those responding to the invitation.

Offering the Evangelistic Invitation

The drawing of the net with a call to public commitment is certainly one of the central elements of evangelistic preaching. The invitation must provide closure to the message, apply the truth of the message to the listeners, and offer an urgent and immediate call for action and response. The preacher must make adequate preparation for the invitation if it is to be effective.

The first element of preparation is sowing the seed through personal witnessing and praying for the unsaved by name. Second, the preacher should work to ensure that the invitation is integral to the message itself. Often the invitation looks as if it is an afterthought to the message. Preachers are sometimes guilty of closing their Bible before actually extending the invitation, visually saying, "The message is over; now let me add the invitation." The conclusion, application, and invitation of the message should be prepared with diligence. Throughout much of my preaching ministry I have worked hard at the introduction and body of the sermon and have given little thought to the actual closure. In recent years I have worked to make the closure and invitation integral to the message itself. Work to make it flow naturally out of the body of the sermon so that you do not lose the congregation's attention before you bring closure.

As for the mechanics of a good invitation, be clear, brief but thorough, courteous, honest, confident, expectant, patient, authentic, and urgent. Haddon W. Robinson compares the giving of the invitation with the landing of an airplane. It requires thoughtful preparation because it calls for a verdict. Robinson gives several practical suggestions such as the use of a brief summary of the message, a clear illustration, a quotation that is short and to the point, a question, an honest prayer, and specific instructions concerning what one must do.[9]

All alike urge integrity in giving the evangelistic invitation. Never use a bait and switch technique where you ask the congregation to do one thing and use that response to lead to a different one. One evening I took a youth group to hear a well-known speaker. After the initial impact of the invitation, he asked everyone to bow their heads. He then requested that anyone unsure about their salvation raise their hand so that he could pray with them for their assurance. Having completed the prayer, he reminded the participants that God had seen their response and that if they had doubts about their salvation it was likely that they had not been saved. He then began the invitation again with a special focus on persons who had raised their hands. The evangelistic invitation is a divine moment where the Holy Spirit works through us to draw persons to Christ. Pastors must prepare well, but should not resort to trickery or replace the work of the Spirit with human technique.

Specific help with giving the invitation is found in Roy Fish's *Giving a Good Invitation* or *The Effective Invitation* by R. Alan Street.

Preaching and evangelism should be partners in the life of every pastor and every church. The pulpit provides the God-given opportunity to create a vision for evangelism, fan the flame of passion for soul-winning, and harvest the results of powerful preaching and personal witnessing. It is absolutely essential that the church know that the pastor's evangelistic life-style and preaching are in harmony. If the pastor does not do the work of an evangelist, he will not be effective in preaching evangelistically. "Be sober in all things, endure hardship, do the work of an evangelist, fulfill your ministry" (2 Tim. 4:5, NASB).

Notes

1. For a more complete discussion of the definition of evangelism, see Ken Hemphill and Wayne Jones, *Growing an Evangelistic Sunday School* (Nashville: Broadman Press, 1989), 26-29.
2. Thomas G. Long, "Preaching About Evangelism: Faith Finding Its Voice," *Preaching*

In and Out of Season, Thomas G. Long and Neely Dixon McCarter, eds. (Louisville: John Knox Press, 1990), 86.

3. John Bisagno, *The Power of Positive Evangelism* (Nashville: Broadman Press, 1968), 7.
4. Alan Walker, *Evangelistic Preaching* (Grand Rapids: Francis Asbury Press, 1983), 21.
5. V. L. Stanfield, *Effective Evangelistic Preaching* (Grand Rapids: Baker Book, 1965), 11.
6. James W. Clarke, *Dynamic Preaching* (New Jersey: Fleming H. Revell Company, 1960), 41-44.
7. For similar lists, see Stanfield, *Effective Evangelistic Preaching*, 12-16, and Faris Daniel Whitesell, *Evangelistic Preaching and the Old Testament* (Chicago: Moody Press, 1947), 22-28.
8. For a more extensive discussion of the evangelistic message, see Whitesell, *Evangelistic Preaching*, 29-41 and Stanfield, *Effective Evangelistic Preaching*, 20-22.
9. Haddon W. Robinson, *Biblical Preaching* (Grand Rapids: Baker Book House, 1980), 168-170.

Martyn Lloyd–Jones (1899-1981)
"Expositor of the Word"

Few churches have been as blessed as London's Westminster Chapel. It has enjoyed the ministry of not one but two of the finest preachers in the history of the Christian church.

Martyn Lloyd–Jones, a native of Wales, served as Associate Pastor during G. Campbell Morgan's second term as pastor of that historic London church. When Morgan retired in 1943 at age 80, Lloyd–Jones became the pastor and continued the remarkable tradition of expository preaching for which Westminster's pulpit is known. He assumed the pulpit when war–time London was still experiencing regular bombing; in a setting of fear and hostility, Lloyd–Jones attracted great crowds by faithfully proclaiming a "word from the Lord" to His people.

For Lloyd–Jones, expository preaching was not a dry, running commentary on a biblical passage. Though his sermons emerged out of the text and made clear the message of the chosen passage, he believed the preacher must give a distinctive homiletical form to his message to aid communication. Lloyd–Jones' sermons were well illustrated, using a variety of sources; as a former medical student, he was often able to share a fitting illustration from the world of medicine. He was always careful to provide a contemporary application of the biblical truths he preached.

Lloyd–Jones employed a commanding use of the English language. Yet his power in preaching grew out of something altogether greater: his listeners sensed they were in the presence of one empowered by the Holy Spirit.

B. Clayton Bell, Pastor
Highland Park Presbyterian Church
Dallas, Texas

46 Preaching and Conflict

The good news of Jesus Christ is based upon conflict—the conflict of God against Satan, good against evil, truth against falsehood, heaven against hell. Once a person has been chosen for the side of God, he or she is automatically opposed to the forces of the evil one. However, once a person has opted for God it does not eradicate the old nature that is inclined away from God. Latent vestiges of the "old Adam" linger on to raise an ugly head in the fellowship of believers.

To further complicate matters, in a society where church membership is still relatively popular and widely acceptable, people who are unregenerate will become members of a church for the wrong reasons. So in addition to the not-yet-mature children of faith, there is the mix of not-yet-children of faith. It makes for a built-in potential for conflict.

Conflict in the church should come as no surprise. Human nature is fallen, and people have latent hostilities just waiting to break out. Human beings are finite in understanding and judgment; therefore they will differ in opinion on what is negotiable and not negotiable. More basic to conflict is the assertion by James who asks: "What causes fights and quarrels among you? Don't they come from your desires that battle within you" (4:1, NIV)?

When conflict looms, it is important to start by identifying the cause of conflict. There are five that immediately come to mind: theological, ethical, personality, aesthetic, and leadership.

The Causes of Conflict

Theological Cause

Theological conflicts may be conflicts over doctrine. If so, is the doctrine central or peripheral to the faith? Whether Jesus is coming again before, during, or after the great tribulation is not as important as whether Jesus is truly God. Preaching in this kind of conflict should put issues in biblical and eternal perspective.

Ethical Cause

Conflicts over ethical and moral issues should be simple to resolve. Yet witness the struggle over abortion and homosexuality, and we find severe conflict. Never mind that some Christians reject the full authority of the Scripture and come to differing opinions about this. There are Christians who are fully agreed on the inspiration and authority of the Bible who do not agree on certain facets of the debate on abortion, or how to deal with gay persons in the church.

Personality Cause

Personality conflicts are probably the most difficult with which to deal. Egos in tension, power struggles between certain individuals or families, or between the preacher's ego and the egos of other persons are often subtle and hard to identify. For the minister whose own ego is not involved in the struggle, preaching must be accompanied with much prayer that the Holy Spirit will bring conviction and determination to live and work in mutual love, respect, and esteem.

Aesthetic Cause

A fourth area of conflict is in the area of aesthetics—conflicts over taste, (i.e. color of choir robes), volume of organ, decor of parlor, style of worship, choice of hymns for worship, and other such things. The resolution of these differences is usually worked out through patience and compromise.

Leadership Cause

The final area of conflict that comes to mind is in the area of leadership, goal setting, and the direction of a church's program and mission.

Preaching in the Face of Conflict

Start with Personal Self-Examination

The preacher should willingly ask: Am I the cause of the conflict? Am I espousing a viewpoint, a strategy, a cause, or an objective that is personal rather than mandated by God?

Be Focused on the Will of God, Not Personal Desires

To focus on the will of God in conflict means focusing on the objective(s) God has in mind. It also means focusing on the way in which God wants us to achieve His objective(s).

What are some things that are clearly God's will?

• God is "not wanting anyone to perish, but everyone to come to repentance" (2 Pet. 3:9, NIV);

• "It is God's will that you should be sanctified: that you should avoid sexual immorality; that each of you should learn to control his own body in a way that is holy and honorable, not in passionate lust like the heathen, who do not know God" (1 Thess. 4:3-5, NIV);

• God clearly wants the body of Christ united, not divided!

"How good and pleasant it is when brothers live together in unity!" (Ps. 133:1, NIV).

"So in Christ we who are many form one body, and each member belongs to all the others" (Rom. 12:5, NIV).

"You are all sons of God through faith in Christ Jesus, for all of you who were baptized into Christ have clothed yourselves with Christ. There is neither Jew nor Greek, slave nor free, male nor female, for you are all one in Christ Jesus" (Gal. 3:26-28, NIV).

"Make every effort to keep the unity of the Spirit through the bond of peace" (Eph. 4:3, NIV).

God does not use the devil's methods to achieve His ends, though He may overrule bad methods for His own glory. God does not use fear and lies to accomplish His ends:

> There are six things the LORD hates, seven that are detestable to him: haughty eyes [pride], a lying tongue [disregard for truth], hands that shed innocent blood [disregard for life], a heart that devises wicked schemes [commitment to planning evil], feet that are quick to rush into evil [rash participation in evil], a false witness who pours out lies [subversion of justice] and a man who stirs up dissension among brothers [disregard for unity in the community, or the communion of saints] (Prov. 6:16-19, NIV; explanatory notes in brackets are the author's).

Preaching to a church in conflict must aim at and emphasize the importance of maintaining the unity of the body of Christ.

Put Issues in Eternal Perspective

I was told that James Reston, the syndicated columnist, said to his minister: "I come to church to get life put in perspective." In light of a person's eternal destiny, what is really important? What is peripheral? In light of the clear mandates of God in Scripture, what are the things upon which we should concentrate? What can take second place? In light of our Lord's prayer for His church (John 17), what are the issues He deemed most important for His disciples?

Over the 34 years I have been in the ministry, there are three major arenas of conflict in which I have had to preach. Let me share briefly what I learned.

The *first* arena of conflict was in Alabama from 1958-1968. Race relations in society and in the church was the major issue. How does one preach on such an emotional issue with any effectiveness? Some preachers I knew were so outspoken they lost their pulpits. They became vocational martyrs. They were replaced by preachers who supported the status quo. God only knows what impact for change the martyrs had, but they certainly lost any chance they had for continuing influence with their congregations.

In 1961 I attended a biracial meeting in Birmingham to talk about race relations. An older black man took his seat beside me, and during the afternoon he made a comment I have never forgotten. Placing his hand upon my knee he said: "*There is no law in the land that can make this brother want me to sit next to him.*" The man was Martin Luther King, Sr., and he was right. Laws must be just, but laws cannot control the attitudes of the heart. I chose to preach the gospel of God's love and grace that can soften hard hearts, warm cold ones, and convert perverse ones. He did, but not overnight. The preachers of the Word must never lose confidence in the power of the Holy Spirit to change hearts.

In teaching and in preaching, I stressed the biblical doctrine of sin and grace and forgiveness; and then stressed the doctrine of the church as the body of Christ made up of redeemed sinners. One summer, vacationing in the mountains of North Carolina, I had the privilege of visiting with a former seminary professor. He was aware of the racial tensions in Alabama, so he asked me: "Clayton, how are things going with you?" I shared with him my frustration over the fact that I was the first preacher in the history of that church who had said that the church belonged to Jesus Christ and anyone who wanted to worship and follow Him should be included in any local church. "In fact," I said, "I don't think there will be much change until some of the older generation pass on." He was thoughtful for a moment, and then replied with a memorable line: "Yes, where there's death, there's hope!"

The *second* arena of conflict is the ongoing tension of ministering in a pluralistic denomination that often gets bad press because of actions or statements by a very few high-profile people. The "conflict" comes when a local congregation reacts to the perceived position or statement with which they disagree. The role I have sought to play in such conflict has been two-fold.

First, the minister must be on the side of truth. What is true? What is rumor? What is exaggerated? It is terribly important to ferret out the facts and not act in fear or on hearsay. Helping people understand the uniqueness of our form of church government and the high degree of freedom and autonomy allowed a local church sometimes assuages unnecessary anxiety about the powers of those with whom one may disagree.

Second, I emphasize the importance of being a witness for what one believes is true in a denomination where there is diversity of viewpoints. The New Testament clearly states that all Christians have a responsibility for one another. We are to exhort one another, admonish one another, love one another, forgive one another, correct one another, and provoke one another to good works. When we find things going on in the church with which we disagree, does that give us the right to separate ourselves from it? Or do we have the obligation to exhort (and be open to exhortation), to admonish (and be open to admonishment), to love (and be open to be loved), to forgive (and be open to being forgiven), to correct (and be open to correction), and to provoke (and be open to being provoked) to good works! One of the sins of the American mind is to split when we disagree. The mind of Christ is to love and sacrifice for those with whom He had the greatest disagreement, namely us sinners.

The *third* arena of disagreement has been the recent conflict and division in Highland Park Presbyterian Church. This arose, to a large degree, because of the very conservative nature of this congregation and its differences with some of the positions expressed by leaders of the denomination. Some of the people sought to take the church out of the denomination. After much prayer and soul searching, I became convinced that the place for Highland Park Presbyterian Church was to stay in the heritage where God had placed it. My preaching emphasized: (a) the importance of being faithful where we had been placed; (b) not giving in to fear of denominational coercion, but to act in faith; (c) accepting in love the role of responsibility for one another; and (d) preserving the unity of the body of Christ. I also urged people to differentiate between the perceived errors of some Presbyterian people and the soundness of a system of theology and government under which we operate.

Yet there was a more subtle spiritual issue in the struggle. Many of the leaders in the secessionist movement were independent-minded entrepreneurs who could not live under the perceived threat of having anyone—namely the Presbyterian hierarchy—telling them what to do. This was accompanied by an almost arrogant pride that we have all the truth we need and will not listen to anyone outside of our own enclave.

An interesting issue arose out of the debate, and that was the role of the pastor in the life of the church. Is he or she the paid servant of the congregation? Or is the pastor the called leader of the congregation? It very quickly became obvious that those who wished to secede from the denomination thought the staff were the paid servants of the congregation and should not be involved in the decision. I was repeatedly reminded of the warning of Paul to Timothy: "For the time will come when men will not put up with sound doctrine. Instead, to suit their own desires, they will gather around them a great number of teachers to say what their itching ears want to hear" (2 Tim. 4:3, NIV).

A noted preacher went to his new parish in New York City and on the first Sunday introduced himself to the congregation by saying: "I want you to know that I am here as a servant to all of you—but none of you is my master." That expresses the balance a minister must have in any church, whether it is in conflict or not: a servant to all, but obedient to only one Master, Jesus Christ.

47

Kenneth L. Chafin
Pastor Emeritus
Walnut Street Baptist Church
Louisville, Kentucky

Preaching and Human Crises

All who preach are dealing with people in crisis whether they are aware of it or not. This is true irrespective of the size, age, location, or makeup of the congregation. Any time people gather for worship, some of them will be dealing with a life crisis which they have brought to church with them. It may be a woman who is waiting for a report from a laboratory on tissue taken from a tumor, a couple who just discovered that their son is taking drugs, a man who must make a decision this week on what to do with his mother who has Alzheimer's disease, a young couple whose marriage is in trouble, a fifty-eight year old man who is being forced to take early retirement, a fifteen-year-old daughter of a church leader who learned the day before that she is pregnant, or a single parent who has lost her job.

Often there is no way the preacher could be aware of the special burdens which individuals bring with them. More often there is an awareness of needs but no clear idea what role the pulpit ought to take in dealing with those crises. Some ministers feel that these are matters for counselors and try to refer them to trained professionals. Others count on the ministries which grow out of the fellowship of a loving congregation to be the encouragement and support to those going through difficult times. While the insights of counseling and the support of the community of faith are important, they do not eliminate the need for the pulpit to be a source of help to people in times of crisis in their lives.

Address People's Needs

Authentic biblical preaching should address the needs of the people. There is no conflict between the idea that the sermon should be rooted in an accurate understanding of the Scriptures and that it should seek to meet the needs of those who hear it. The idea that one must choose between preaching the Bible or being helpful sets up a false dichotomy and lays the foundation for irrelevant preaching. Our best definition of preaching should take the eternal Word of God and relate it to the real needs of people in the context of worship. This means that the faithful preacher can never ignore those in the congregation who are in crisis in their lives.

When I was a young professor I was invited to do a series of daytime Bible studies with a group of older adults in a church which also had an elementary school for kindergarten through fifth grade. The adults were all mature Christians and had requested that I teach John's First Epistle. All went well until Thursday morning when the pastor informed me that they were going to bring the children from the school in to be a part of the Bible study—more than a hundred boys and girls between five and eleven years of age. When I suggested to the pastor as diplomatically as I could that I doubted if these children would get much out of a study of 1 John, he suggested in all seriousness: "Just pretend they aren't there." Preachers who really care cannot be insensitive either to levels of understanding or to crises which are a part of the lives of those who listen.

This is not a suggestion that the preacher must "make the gospel relevant," because there is an eternal relevance to what God has done in Jesus Christ to save us. The word of the gospel is the only word we have which speaks to the deepest and most profound need of all people—the need for love, acceptance, forgiveness, meaning, and hope. Nor does it ignore the role of the Holy Spirit in applying truth to needs of which the preacher may not have been aware. It is an affirmation that the more the preacher understands the human lot in general—and the circumstances of those in the congregation in particular—the easier it will be to help them through their crises from the pulpit. This places a burden upon the preacher to know what is happening in the lives of the people; that effort will be amply repaid by the response of those who will be helped.

Be Aware of Personal Crises

To be effective in preaching to those in crisis, the minister needs to be alert to the pressures life brings to them, and to the crises which are created. These crises are as varied as life. Pastors preach to people who face critical health problems which call for extensive tests, hospitalizations or home confinements, chemotherapy or radiation, physical or occupational therapy, counseling, special diets, expensive medication, and radical surgeries. Any one of these can create financial stress, emotional overload, and a spiritual crisis for the individual or for the family. A lingering health problem can undermine one's self confidence, strain relationships, and cause a person to doubt God.

Be Aware of Death in Many Forms

Pastors also preach each week to people who are dealing with death in one form or another. While people grow up accepting the certainty of death eventually for all people, when it touches their lives and their families it creates a crisis. Even when a parent who dies has lived a long and fruitful life and their death comes as a relief to suffering, it still creates a sense of loneliness and a renewed sense of mortality. When a spouse dies, a part of the one who is left is torn away, creating great pain, loss, and loneliness. When the death is of a child or a teenager, in addition to the normal sense of loss, there is the added feeling that things are out of order. Parents are not supposed to bury their children, and it seems so unfair that those who have lived such a short time should die. When the death comes suddenly and without warning, the stress is greater. When the death is self-inflicted, it creates a sense of guilt for all who were close to the person. The only thing more traumatic than dealing with the death of a loved one is contemplating one's own death.

Pastors also preach each week to persons who are dealing with many forms of death other than physical. The death of a relationship can create crisis. A person going through a divorce will experience all the symptoms of a person whose spouse has died—without much of the support system which is available to a widow or widower. People who retire often face a real crisis because so much identity is attached to what people do; when they are no longer doing it, they do not know who they are. The loss of independence for an older adult, whether it involves moving out of one's home or having to quit driving, is for most people a very traumatic experience. Not being able to function on their own, having to move in with children or move into a nursing home, creates a major crisis for most people. These are but a few of the many things which can bring an awareness of death into the lives of the people to whom ministers preach.

Deal with "Why" Questions

Before pastors can help people find resources for dealing with the crises in their lives, they often have to help them deal with the question of why. It is second nature for people to wonder why things happen to them. Ever since the days of Job people have had friends who have given them bad answers to that question—the most prominent one being that bad things happen as punishment for sins. Even the apostles assumed that a man's blindness was a result of someone's sin (see John 9). It is not uncommon to hear someone discussing something terrible which happened and then say: "I'm sure God had a reason for this happening."

One of the most helpful things a preacher can do is to help people get rid of the idea that all that happens to them is punishment for something they have done, or that everything which happens to them is what God purposes for their lives. Both of these popular assumptions are false, and left unchallenged they create a sense of guilt which only adds to the problems people already have. People often quote Romans 8:28 to suggest that everything which happens to us is a part of a divine plan and that to question anything shows a lack of faith. A better interpretation of the verse is to affirm that not everything which happens to us is good or of God, but that if we turn to God with what has happened He will work with us to bring good out of it.

This is the redemptive principle which permeates the Bible—the idea that God salvages good for our lives from that which is evil. This was Joseph's interpretation of his brother's actions against him. This is what turns an instrument of death like the cross into a symbol of life and hope. Preachers do not know why people suffer, but they can help them know what to do with their pain and where to turn with the crises of their lives.

The preacher does not have to neglect the whole congregation in order to minister to those in crisis from the pulpit. While there are very few times when everyone will be dealing with the same crisis, what one person experiences will ultimately be experienced by most people. This means that the faithful pastor who deals over a long period of time with the crisis issues of life will be helping some people process what has happened to them in the past, encouraging others about what they are going through at the time, while preparing some for what may lie in the future for them.

The preacher does not need to give the pulpit over to preaching solely on crises. It would be a mistake for each week's sermon to deal with the previous week's crisis in the life of the church or one of its members. This would not give time for reflection and would create a kind of "hand-to-mouth" diet of sermons which would lack both balance and depth. The preacher begins by taking an awareness of the things which are happening to the people as he or she plans for the year's preaching. This will make it possible to bring the insight of the Scripture to bear on those inevitable experiences and events which create crises for people.

A good system would be to take pencil and paper in hand and make an inventory of the crises which the people in the congregation had to deal with during the past year. It will be safe to assume that some of these same experiences will be repeated in the lives of others. This awareness can be taken to the study week by week as sermons are prepared. It will serve to remind the preacher of what is happening in the lives of those who will be listening. It may affect how a point is stated, how a story is told, the different areas of application, even how the sermon is delivered. Dealing with the crises in people's lives from the pulpit is as much an attitude or a style of relating to people as it is the preparation of individual sermons.

Deal with Crises in Context

The pulpit does not have to bear the whole load, but it must deal with the crises in the lives of people in the context of all the personal and corporate ministries which take place. The message at a funeral will be heard against the backdrop of visits to the hospital, cards written from prayer meeting, food brought by the Sunday School class, phone calls full of concern, and many other loving contacts. The sermon which affirms that the failure of a marriage is not an unforgivable sin must be reinforced by the teaching in the Sunday School class and by the attitude of the church members. The pulpit's reassurance that God will not abandon His children in the times of their trouble needs to be fleshed out in the church's love and prayers.

The pulpit is not the only part of the hour of worship which can address people in crisis. There are times when the choice of the Scripture reading speaks in a personal and powerful way to an individual who carries a heavy load. Some of the greatest comfort and wisest counsel is often found in the lyrics of the hymns which are sung as a part of worship. The pastoral prayer offers a context for bringing the special needs of the people to God in the context of worship.

It is the pulpit which must create the atmosphere in which people are able to deal in the context of their faith with that whole range of emotions which are created by the crises in their lives. They need to be made free to engage in denial, to vent anger, to ask questions for which there are no good answers, to hurt, and even to doubt. The notion that good Christians do not hurt or get discouraged is unhealthy and untrue and can be very destructive. The idea is so persistent that the pulpit needs to constantly contradict it.

Model Openness and Honesty

One of the best ways to make people comfortable dealing honestly with what is going on in their lives is for preachers to model an openness and honesty about their own feelings. One of the strengths of a confessional approach to preaching is that it presents the preacher as a human being who lives in the same world as the parishioners and must cope with the same problems. The preacher who feels the need to play God and tries to have simple answers to all of life's problems will create a false sense of security for many people. It will not speak to the needs of those in crisis and it will send a clear message to them that their feelings have no place at church.

I remember the response of a dying friend to the oversimplified answers to life's ultimate question. Each day she was in the hospital I dropped by with flowers from my garden and sometimes a snack from my kitchen. We talked of life—the things going on in the world, items from today's paper, people we both knew. She knew she was dying but worked hard at living each day to its fullest, and she transformed her bed of pain into a place of authentic witness by her spirit. One day as I was leaving she thanked me for coming and said: "There are two kinds of people who visit me who make me want to throw up—those who just sit and stare at me and those who cover me up with pious platitudes."

Within a person's relationship with God and in the fellowship of the church there are vast resources for helping people deal with life's ups and downs, and the preacher needs to lead the way in reminding people of this fact. One way a preacher fulfills God's command to comfort His people is by creating an open, honest, caring atmosphere in which people may surface—without fear—all the things which threaten them.

Suggestions for Dealing with Death

The ultimate crisis which the pulpit must deal with is death. Since the Garden of Eden people have been dealing with this reminder that we are creatures and not the Creator. Since to forget that fact is still a temptation, the pulpit must continue to deal with death in all its forms. Death raises questions about life and after life. Death disrupts relations and leaves unfinished business. Death creates great pain and a sense of loss. It reminds us of our own mortality. It surfaces feelings and fears which are difficult to control.

While the funeral message is the most pointed way in which the preacher deals with death, its effectiveness is tied with how death has been dealt with in the regular flow of the year's preaching. The things which people have heard from the pulpit on Sundays will create the backdrop from which they will hear what is said at a funeral. This should not be difficult since the Bible is filled with material on the theme.

The Old Testament narratives are full of accounts which make strong texts as we deal with issues related to death. I once had a stronger-than-usual response to a series of sermons from 1 and 2 Samuel based on the life of King David. In trying to deal with the feelings which the series evoked, I discovered that three of the twelve sermons dealt with some emotion relating to death.

A sermon dealing with the death of David and Bathsheba's first son (2 Sam. 12:15-23) was entitled *Learning to Turn Loose*. It developed the theme of learning to turn loose of those things which we cannot change and go on with our lives. David's actions in the story speak to the feelings of all those people who are clinging to what is dead and who need to let go and move on.

A sermon entitled *Grief That Immobilizes* was based on David's response to Absalom's death (2 Sam. 18:31—19:8). This message developed the nature of grief but also used David's experience to show what happens to honest grief when it is mixed with guilt. It spoke to those people who were not able to get over things that had happened to them. It helped some to see that they had short-circuited the grief process by mixing in other feelings.

A third sermon in the series dealt with David's learning that God was not going to allow him to fulfill his life's ambition of building the temple (2 Sam. 7:1-14). It was entitled *Living With a Dream Postponed* and developed the question of what a person should do when he or she realizes that they will not accomplish in life what they had hoped to do. The strong response to this particular sermon suggested that there are more people who are grieving the death of a dream than one would imagine.

One of the great narratives in the New Testament which is built around a death can be preached during Holy Week, as we consider the death of Christ. It is the story of the death of Christ's friend Lazarus and the impact which his death had on everyone (John 11:33-37). I prepared a sermon on this text as a part of a series on the family and entitled it *When Death Touches the Family*. The fact that it was removed from the immediate context of a particular death seemed to make it possible for people to hear it.

The writings of the apostle Paul are filled with texts which relate the hope people have in Christ to the experience of death. There are few passages which are more powerful than when he discussed the possibility of his own death in Philippians (Phil. 1:19-26). While preaching a series of sermons based upon Philippians, I used this text to deal with death under the title of *Life Which Transcends Death*. A sermon on facing one's own death in the context of finding joy in all of life puts death in a more wholesome perspective for the Christian.

The funeral message is but a part of the ministry to a family at the time of a death, but it is an important part. It should attempt to accomplish at least three things. First, it should free those who are present to remember the one who has died. If a person is made to be accountable to God, is the object of God's eternal love, and is capable of fellowship with God, then it honors God and the departed for those who have gathered to spend some time thinking about that person as he or she really was. The preacher who knows the person well can draw out of personal observations and experiences to model for the group the kind of honest remembering which needs to be done. If the pastor does not really know the person, it might be wise to interview several people who knew the deceased well. Then the preacher might say: "As you know I was not well acquainted with the deceased, but I talked to some who knew him well and want to share with you some of their memories."

The funeral message also needs to help those who are there to set their grief in a context that will free them to go on living. This part of the message needs to deal head on with the nature of grief, elements which contribute to our sense of loss, how individualized grief is in its expression, and how God uses the process to deal with our losses and to prepare us to go on with life's responsibilities. If the death was of a young person, the result of a suicide, or some other catastrophic event, these add to the complexity of the grief; that fact ought to be surfaced so that people will feel free to think and talk about it.

More than anything else, the funeral message needs to put the remembering and grieving against the backdrop of the Christian's hope in Jesus Christ. This is not the time to be clever or subtle but to articulate in plain language what the Bible affirms. Death shakes people to the core of their being, and on the day they bury someone they love they need to be reminded of the words of Jesus: "I am the resurrection, and the life: he that believeth in me, though he were dead, yet shall he live" (John 11:25). The only hope anyone has for life which transcends the grave is based on God's power and love, so that at a funeral everyone's hope needs to be focused on that day when death shall be no more and all tears are wiped away (Rev. 21:4).

While the ultimate question which the pulpit deals with is death, there are many forms of death and the pulpit needs to discover creative and redemptive ways of dealing with them. Once the preacher begins to be more aware of these many deaths, the easier it will be to help from the pulpit. For instance, to a young person, a senior adult selling her home and moving to live with a daughter and her family may not seem like much. To the senior adult it is the death of independence and the beginning of the reversal of roles between parent and child. It has all the trappings of a death, and it should be treated seriously.

The eighty-three-year-old man who had to give up his car and driver's license lost much more than transportation. He needs help with his very real grief. One of the great fears of older adults relates to the quality of life. I was surprised at the response I got when I preached a sermon on *Staying Alive Your Whole Life* from Deuteronomy 34:7—"Moses was an hundred and twenty years old when he died: his eye was not dim, nor his natural force abated." There are many deaths which are tied to the aging process, and the sensitive minister will use the pulpit as a source of insight, encouragement, and comfort for the older adults.

While the church holds forth the biblical ideals for marriage it also becomes a source of comfort for those who have been wounded by the failure of a marriage. Parts of the church have always been nervous about ministering to the formerly married for fear that it sent a mixed signal about God's ideal for marriage. Those people fail to understand the very nature of the church's calling—to both lift up God's ideals for our lives and to preach God's grace to all who fall short. This is what made it possible for Christ to set impossibly high standards for marriage (Matt. 19:1-9) and also reach out in love to a woman who had been married five times and at the time of her conversation had a live-in boyfriend (John 4:1-26).

For years I did a series of sermons on the family that began on Mother's Day. In looking back over several of the series, it dawned upon me that I had never preached on divorce in one of the series even though it played an increasingly significant part in the state of the family today. The following year one of the sermons in the family series developed the theme *Is There Life After Divorce?* It began by pointing out that next to one's own physical death, nothing has more potential for undermining a person's sense of self worth and raising questions about their relationship with God than the failure of a marriage. There were more requests for tapes of that sermon than any others in the series—suggesting that it was an issue which needed to be preached.

Be a Comforter

The task of being a preacher is a wonderful and awesome responsibility. Nowhere is the vastness of the task clearer than in the angel's instruction to the apostles after they had opened the doors of the prison where they were incarcerated—"Go, stand and speak in the temple to the people all the words of this life" (Acts 5:20). There are many words about the Christian life which the faithful preacher must speak. Among those many themes there must be words of encouragement about God's love and concern for those in crisis.

When I began to preach in the rural community where I was reared my only models were "fire and brimstone" preachers. The preaching was long on judgment and the people did not feel as if they had been to church if they had not been made to feel guilty. My first preaching copied their model, which led my Aunt Lillian to reply when asked what my preaching was like: "Kenneth rips our hides and pours salt in the wounds." At the time I thought she was bragging on me. Across four decades of living and sharing the burdens of God's people I have found a better model.

I have heard God's Word to His prophet: "Comfort ye, comfort ye my people, saith your God" (Isa. 40:1). I have found God's comfort in Jesus' invitation: "Come unto me, all ye that labour and are heavy laden, and I will give you rest" (Matt. 11:28). Consequently, when I go to the pulpit with healing words for those in crisis I know that on that day I am doing the work of my God.

Part VIII
Special Concerns in Contemporary Preaching

Helmut Thielicke (1908-1985)

"Preaching in the Face of Evil"

It would be hard to imagine a more difficult time and place to become a pastor than 1941 in Nazi Germany. Yet Helmut Thielicke used his pulpit to oppose the evil of his age and to offer hope to a war–torn people.

Thielicke's intended career was teaching theology; this he did at the University of Heidelberg until 1940 when the Nazi leadership forced him out for his criticism of their regime. He was forbidden to publish and his travel was restricted, so he became a pastor. Rather than a punishment, however, those years of pastoral service became an important ministry and a profound influence on his future theological development.

Much like Martyn Lloyd–Jones in London, Thielicke preached to people facing the burden and pain of war—bombings, death of loved ones, and the hardships of daily life. Unlike his Welsh counterpart, however, Thielicke preached to a people whose nation was defeated and occupied. Amidst devastation and opposition, he faithfully proclaimed the hope available through Christian faith.

There is a remarkable eloquence to Thielicke's preaching that is as moving in our own day as in his. Though his preaching style was not expository in form, he effectively related biblical principles and themes to the everyday concerns of his listeners. Thielicke used illustrations masterfully; often an illustration introduced his sermons.

In an age when many preachers are called to stand in forceful opposition to both personal and social evil, Helmut Thielicke is a worthy model of courageous preaching.

48

Raymond Bailey
Professor of Preaching
The Southern Baptist Theological Seminary
Louisville, Kentucky

Ethics in Preaching

The disillusionments suffered by the public during the eighties may make the nineties the decade for the rediscovery of public ethics. The S&L scandals, insider trading, exposure and censure of breaches of public trust by congressional leaders, and a presidential candidate forced out of the campaign for plagiarism all combine to make the American people suspicious of all public figures. Surveys by the Gallup organization indicated that the electorate was concerned about honesty in government and business. Elected officials and sales persons ranked at the bottom of confidence polls. Major universities expanded curricula to include ethics courses in nearly every field. Lost trust is not easily restored.

The clergy did not escape public scrutiny. Modern mass media has made it possible for contemporary preachers to reach audiences in the millions. The TV evangelists have become celebrities contending with the liabilities of public attention and sometime adoration as well as the benefits. Moral lapses by "stars" cannot be easily hidden or quickly forgiven or forgotten. The failure of one congressman can result in ridicule of the whole body, and a *60 Minutes* expose of a television evangelist can have a negative impact on established religious institutions and on the local pastor. In all fairness it should be noted that mainline churches and local priests and pastors have not avoided the investigative reporters and litigation in the courts for sexual and financial misconduct. Many laity have been outraged to discover clerical misconduct overlooked and covered up by ecclesiastical bodies. Trust is no longer (if it ever was) automatic for the local parish minister. It is not unreasonable to expect the minister to earn the trust of those she or he would lead and then to treat that trust as sacred. While religious interest and devotion remains high, organized religion has a credibility problem.

The problems of immorality and dishonesty are not new in this age. The Old Testament is replete with warnings about false prophets. The twenty-third chapter of Jeremiah provides one example of rebuke of religious leadership. "'Woe to the shepherds who destroy and scatter the sheep of my pasture!' says the Lord" (v. 1, NRSV). Prophets were indicted for indulging in the corruptions prevalent in the society at large. Popular preachers were chided for endorsing dangerous lifestyles and creating false hopes. Their weakness was traced to the lack of personal spirituality. Jeremiah specifically attacked those "who steal my words from one another" (23:30, NRSV). The sins of personal infidelity to the way of God and plagiarism were not invented in the twentieth century.

American history and literature have kept the human frailty of clergy before the public. From Hawthorne's *The Scarlet Letter* and Sinclair Lewis' *Elmer Gantry* to Arthur Miller's *The Crucible*, clergy have suffered from the dramatic portrayal of their failure to live up to the ideals they espoused. Long before television, the names of leading American preachers such as Beecher and Sunday were linked to accusations of sexual and financial scandal. The most widespread and dangerous ethical shortcomings of the clergy, however, may be those of the subtle variety. This is particularly true of the preaching function of ministry. A rash of recent books address clergy morality and issues of interpersonal relationships, but few lines are given to integrity in the pulpit.

Preaching cannot be separated from the personal and professional life of the preacher. Emerson observed long ago: "What you are stands over you the while, and thunders so that I cannot hear what you say to the contrary."[1] If the life of the minister is known to the audience, the credibility of his or her words will depend on whether or not the preacher practices what is proclaimed. Authentic living makes for authentic preaching. A congregation has a right to expect the preacher to live by the standards explicit and implicit in the message proclaimed. A preacher who declares "thus says the Lord" is rightfully expected to have a relationship with the Lord. The preacher should be not only a moral person and a good human being, but also a spiritual person. "Although the ministry is a profession, the special standing of the minister has more to do with personal qualities than with professional role."[2] The minister is presumed to live by the transcendent ethic implicit in the gospel. The preacher should be a person of prayer whose words are backed up by his or her life. The minister differs from other professionals in that life and work are inextricably intertwined.[3]

This is not to say, however, that ministry is not a profession that should adhere to the characteristics of a profession including extensive training, a body of specialized knowledge, services that benefit society, and placing the interest of the constituency above personal interest.[4] A sense of vocation does not exclude a professional attitude with appropriate standards commonly accepted by the community.

With this in mind we turn to the practice of the art of preaching and what appears to me to be obvious and reasonable ethical standards broadly accepted by those involved in public communication and persuasion and intensified by the high purpose of preaching and the special character of the content.

Homiletics books allot little space to the ethics of sermon preparation and presentation. Perhaps this is because they assume that the common standards of propriety for academics, politics, business, and literature with regard to respect for the audience, the work of others, and the truth will prevail. Surely the minimum standards of honesty for high school and college students writing term papers would be honored by women and men committed to ultimate truth. The standards for ministers of the gospel should meet and exceed those applied to the lawyer and legislator. Unfortunately, some ministers appear to believe that their noble purpose sets them above the rules that apply to others. We do well to remember that we are accountable to the Source of all truth.

The ethical issue most discussed with regard to sermons is that of plagiarism. Positions vary widely. Augustine proposed that those better at delivering sermons than composing them should preach the wisdom of others but added that such should be done "without deception."[5] If one chooses to read someone else's sermon, that should be acknowledged to the congregation. Not many congregations are willing to pay for such preaching. John Broadus wrote of the "shameless stealing" of the work of others by those unwilling to apply themselves to the difficult labors of careful preparation and thought. His conclusion to the matter was that "it is a good rule never to make use of another's contribution in a way that would be embarrassing to confess in public if the author were present."[6] The problem is not a new one. Surely all ministers would agree that to steal the words of others without crediting the source is unethical. Likewise, to take the creative idea or special insight of another without citing the source is unacceptable. Jamie Buckingham has shared an experience that illustrates the potential for embarrassment when one "borrows" from others:

> I remember when Charles Allen came to preach in the little South Carolina town where I was pastor of the Baptist church. I had read all Allen's books of sermons—and preached most of them. Some of our folks went down to Main Street Methodist to hear Dr. Allen. One of them came back and told me, "You'll never believe it, but that lanky old Methodist is preaching your sermons." The substance only is borrowed. From flagrant exhibition of stealing both thought and language, plagiarism shades off into less serious things such as unconscious borrowing, borrowing of minor elements, and mere imitation."[7]

A form of plagiarism commonly practiced by preachers is the appropriation of someone else's experience as their own. When a congregation hears a variety of "prophets of God" describe verbatim the same experience as a personal one, should they not be expected to be skeptical of everything that preacher says? John Killinger advises that "it takes nothing from the sermon to preface an illustration, 'someone has said,' or 'a colleague has told this story.'"[8] Credibility requires appropriate acknowledgement of borrowed material. This certainly does not deny the existence of commonplace topics and illustrations freely exchanged and used. The problem occurs when originality is claimed or when one presents the experience of another as one's own.

Most writers on the subject of preaching who address the subject at all limit their discussion to the issue of plagiarism, the most obvious and common but neither the only form of intellectual dishonesty nor the most dangerous. For in-depth treatment of unethical practices of ignorance and intent we must turn to the field of public address. I have elsewhere sought to advance the idea that preaching is a branch or form of rhetoric.[9] Ethics has been an important topic in classical and modern rhetorical works. Plato contended that truth must be the primary concern of the public speaker. Contemporary rhetorical critics have observed that "the cultivation of a sense of responsibility for the uttered statement is a crying imperative for speakers today."[10] Does not every congregation have the right to expect of any preacher "intelligence, character, and good will," the reasonable expectations Aristotle assigned to any audience that a speaker seeks to influence? His list of causes for the loss of credibility sounds like a review of the work of some televangelists.

> Speakers are untrustworthy in what they say or advise from one or more of the following causes. Either through want of intelligence they form wrong opinions; or, while they form correct opinions, their rascality leads them to say what they do not think; or, while intelligent and honest enough, they are not well-disposed [to the hearer, audience], and so perchance will fail to advise the best course, though they see it. . . . It necessarily follows that the speaker who is thought to have all these qualities [intelligence, character, and goodwill] has the confidence of his hearers.[11]

Ignorance, particularly when it is the result of laziness, is no excuse for misrepresentation, misleading, or half-truths. Just as a parent should not punish in anger or for revenge, the preacher should not seek in any way to harm a congregation through poor advice or deception. The sins of speakers have changed little over the centuries. Audiences are still misled by ignorance and connivance.

Years of reading and listening to sermons from ministerial students as well as sermon collections, conferences, and church services have led me to identify recurring specious sermonic fallacies and persuasive devices. Five of the most common weaknesses are:

- poor preparation and faulty exegesis
- glittering generalities
- loaded language and name calling
- emotional manipulation
- misrepresentation and partial truth

Poor Preaching and Faulty Exegesis

The first failure of preaching integrity may be the source of all the others. Inadequate preparation may indicate willful ignorance, a lack of respect for the message, a lack of respect for the audience, or mere laziness.

James T. Cleland identified four homiletical sins of preachers.[12] First is ignorance or rejection of biblical criticism, higher or lower. Any serious student of the Bible can make use of multiple modern translations, commentaries, biblical encyclopedias, and the like. A minister has the responsibility of keeping up in the disciplines related to his or her work. As a good doctor is expected to keep abreast of the latest medical discoveries, a good preacher will be aware of the latest developments in biblical studies and theology. Continuing education is required of any "professional." Many choose to trust intuition rather than the demanding task of investigation. Research requires sufficient time and effort. The preacher owes it to the congregation to find time to prepare. The preacher who waits until the end of the week to prepare for Sunday demonstrates a disrespect for preaching and for those who must suffer ill-prepared sermons.

Inspiration should be supported by investigation. A passionate search for truth should motivate the pastoral theologian, the truth that *lies in* the text as opposed to a "truth" *brought to* the text. A congregation is entitled to a preacher who is as well informed and as skilled in theology as a surgeon is in medicine. The preacher should do all in his or her power to understand the Bible, the environment in which it was produced, and the culture to which it is proclaimed. The preacher is a theologian who should use every tool available, including those of archaeology, hermeneutics, exegesis, and communication.

Cleland's second homiletic sin is "slovenliness," the careless or utilitarian handling of Scripture. Those who are fearful of critical tools and would censure those who do use them are often careless in their use of Scripture. They use the Scripture to serve their purpose without regard for biblical or theological context. A preacher, known for his literal approach to Scripture, speaking at a national conference, quoted Genesis 2:25 as a call for complete honesty between husband and wife. Couples, he said, were to be transparent to one another and tell everything about their relationship with one another. Such an interpretation strains the text unreasonably. When questioned about his interpretation, the minister laughingly responded that he had only "spiritualized" the passage. The person who reveres the Scriptures will not "use" them. Is it not disgraceful that "ministerially speaking" is a phrase synonymous with gross exaggeration?

A third homiletical transgression is the outright lie. Such drastic distortion is sometimes practiced in the name of preserving a denominational doctrine or avoiding an unpleasant or unpopular Scripture. A preacher may deny the clear sense of the text because that meaning is at odds with a revered doctrine. It is an easy way to avoid the thorny theological issues raised by discrepancies in Scripture. More often the lie is at the expense of a human target. There is more than one way to lie in a sermon. A certain seminary professor was publicly attacked on the basis of points of views of others summarized in a book he wrote. The ideas of others were taken out of context and attributed to him.

Another example of poor exegesis is the instance of a well-known pastor speaking before a national gathering of thousands who took Leviticus 2:11-13, a passage dealing with leaven in the meal offering, and used it as a typology for Christian proclamation in the modern world. Such a use strains even the most liberal understanding of typology. With only one exception leaven is treated as negative throughout the Scriptures. In this passage it has nothing to do with human qualities or practices. The preacher used the text as an excuse for elaborating his own standards of purity and orthodoxy.

The Sadducees were portrayed in the same sermon as the liberals of their day and used as an analogue for contemporary theological progressives. The Pharisees were identified with the modern literal interpreters of Scripture. In truth, the Sadducees were the literalists of Jesus' day, denying such doctrines as the resurrection because they could not be found in the Torah. The Sadducees were unwilling to accept any doctrine that could not be defended by their canon. In both instances a faulty methodology misled the audience.

An early sermon that I preached was supposed to be on the text Luke 2:41-52. A dear friend and loving pastor helped me exegete the Scripture. We ended up with a three point sermon: (1) They lost Jesus in the Temple (church). (2) They did not know they had lost Him until it got dark (crisis). (3) They found Him right where they left Him. It was an outline that would "preach." The only problem was that the sermon had nothing to do with the text.

The fourth category of homiletical sin cited by Cleland is allegorical interpretation of Scripture. Allegory was for a long time officially disdained as a method of biblical interpretation. The current emphasis on literary criticism and narrative preaching encourages examination of texts for cues that would suggest appropriate allegorical interpretation.

There is, however, a difference in interpretation and flights of fantasy imposed on a text.

A recent issue of a widely distributed religious periodical provides an example of such fantasy at work. The text under consideration was Acts 7:41-43. The writer identifies preachers with "full treasuries" as modern "golden calves." The reference to the worship of "the host of heaven" (7:42) and "the star of the god Rephan" (7:43) is applied to modern astrology and the idolization of contemporary celebrities.

Some literalists employ bizarre allegory in identifying figures and symbols in apocalyptic literature like Ezekiel and Revelation. In the early days of Social Security, some preachers identified Social Security numbers with the mark of the beast (Rev. 13:17; 14:9). Babylon in Revelation has at various times been applied to Jerusalem, Rome, Moscow, and other cities in different periods. It follows that the beast (Rev. 13:11-18) has been "exposed" to be medieval popes, Napoleon, Hitler, Stalin, and even some presidents of the United States. One's interpretation should be carefully examined when it conveniently contributes to the condemnation of a person or people politically or ethnically different from the interpreter.

Glittering Generalities

The most common weakness I see and hear in sermons is that of glittering generalities or gross generalizations. Undocumented assertions and unfocused problem-solution sermons abound. The following two generalities appeared in the same sermon: "America is dying! Why? . . . The one major problem . . . concerns 'easy-believism Christianity.' . . . Christianity is giving her balloons and bribes. The people of America are lost and dying and bound for hell." Only a few lines later the writer asserts that "through all the fun and games, shallow 'decisions' are being made, instead of heart-felt changes." How are such conclusions fairly drawn? Where are the standards written down?

Preachers who promise prosperity to all tithers and easy solutions to all human problems to those who "trust Jesus" are out of touch with reality and Scripture. Few pastors would deny that there are Christians who suffer from hunger and sickness. Progressive preachers who characterize all fundamentalists as uncaring and insensitive are no more ethical than right wingers who characterize liberals as immoral or nonevangelistic. Generalizations fail listeners in one of two ways. There is the broad statement that makes undocumented accusations and sweeping promises that go beyond the Scriptures. An example of an unfounded generalization is the preacher's assertion that "down through the years, the one device most used by Satan to destroy God's work has been a gathering together of all churches into one big one." The clear implication is that those who reach out across denominational lines are doing the devil's work. Such suggestions appeal to the fears people have of those who are different from them. Ecumenism ranks alongside secular humanism as a favorite standard target for certain preachers.

The second failure is the failure to offer specific application to contemporary life. Week after week some ministers proclaim empty theological propositions that sound religious but offer little challenge or help to listeners. Preachers owe something to people they expect to come and listen to them once or several times a week. Integrity requires diligent examination of theological assertions in the light of the problems of particular audiences. Incarnational preaching should be marked by the scandal of particularity: A particular truth for a particular audience at a particular moment in time.

A campus preaching competition asked entrants to identify the audience for their sermon in order to evaluate how they spoke to particular audiences. One entry included a note that assured the committee that this sermon was for anyone, anywhere, anytime. Can you imagine a doctor suggesting that one pill would fix everyone's illness? Jesus and Paul set a good example for the modern preacher by speaking to specific needs of individuals and groups. There are preachers who seem to have only one message which they repeat week after week in meaningless generalities.

Loaded Language and Name Calling

Loaded language and name calling have become a fine art in American religious rhetoric where they should have no place at all. "Redneck," "fundamentalist," "secular humanist," and "liberal" are almost as common as favorite biblical terms. Religious periodicals advertise conferences on "real" evangelism and for "real" women, implying of course that some are unreal. Name calling is intensified when a strong contrast is made. An example of such contrast occurred in the context of a debate within a Southern Baptist association meeting. Referring to the preceding speaker, a pastor declared that he was not surprised at the speaker's position because the speaker was "a neo-orthodox Barthian but I am an evangelical Christian." Of course few people in the assembly knew what neo-orthodoxy or Barthism were but all knew what "an evangelical Christian" was.

> "Name calling" is a device to make us form a judgment without examining the evidence on which it should be based. Here the propagandist appeals to our hate and fear. He does this by giving "bad names" to those individuals, groups, nations, races, policies, practices, beliefs, and ideals which he would have us condemn and reject.[13]

Name calling shifts the focus away from critical analysis of issues to emotional prejudices and is usually a form of emotional manipulation.

Philosopher and rhetorician Kenneth Burke has discussed this issue in depth and addresses the bifurcation of language into "God-terms" and "devil terms." Craig Loscalzo explains Burke's terminology:

> God-terms are generalized terms that summarize positive . . . terms. . . . God-terms . . . stand at the top of a hierarchy of terms. . . . The devil function of a term can be seen by finding a term that causes divisions within a social order designating what is known as a common enemy.[14]

A "sermon" delivered by the Black Muslim leader Malcolm X provides some excellent examples of this technique. The speech was delivered before an overwhelmingly white audience. Freedom was assumed to be the ultimate virtuous state. He proceeded to set up conflict between slave-victims (his race) and master exploiters (the audience). Such a simplistic dichotomy between good guys and bad guys is a common device for Christian preachers. Wrong identification is another way proclamation is compromised—we lead the audience to identify with the wrong group in Scripture and thus miss the message. For example, middle-class Americans often identify with the Hebrews in bondage when their status and life-style places them squarely in the camp of the Egyptians.

More recently in a widely distributed periodical, a preacher wrote about "a Bible-believing preacher" and "Bible-believing Christianity" with the clear implication that some preachers and Christians are not Bible believers. "Bible-believing" is an obvious ultimate phrase in certain ecclesiastical circles. In the same sermon the writer associates "super churches" with "anti-Bible," "humanism" and "easy-believism." The pressure for numerical growth is said to drive "hundreds of godly pastors" from the ministry. Do we identify "godly" and "ungodly" pastors by the size of their congregations?

Emotional Manipulation

The zeal of evangelists to convert the lost often leads to unethical emotional manipulation. The line between rational persuasion, genuine religious emotional appeal, and manipulation is sometimes a fine one. Clyde Fant offers a helpful distinction:

> Manipulation . . . may be defined as persuasion that is deliberately not in the best interest of the individual involved but is deceptively intended for the advantage of the persuader; or that attempts to get people to do something they would not do if they had the facts.[15]

Of course an eager evangelist might argue that getting a person down the aisle to make a public profession is always in the "best interest" of the professing person, but the millions of inactive religious converts suggest that some of those lured down the aisle hated themselves and the evangelists the next morning. Seduction was the way of the serpent, not the way of Christ. The use of conversion statistics for personal promotion implies a scalp-gathering mentality that is for the advantage of the persuader. In a sermon contrasting the orthodox and liberals, the preacher climaxed his harangue with the emotionally charged story of a family trapped in a burning car and a bystander who let the family die rather than become involved. Theological differences were portrayed as absolutes with life and death meaning. The story was not germane to the subject and apparently included only for sentimental appeal. Another popular pulpit orator reported the scene of a hotel tragedy where "a man leaped out the window. . . . Women took babies to the windows and dropped them to certain deaths below. . . . Grown, intelligent people leaped to their deaths from those windows." The scene is then used as an analogy for the experience of hell.

Manipulation has been developed into a fine art in the twentieth century. Research into psychology and human behavior has produced techniques for conditioning human beings to do just about anything. Duane Litfin's article that appeared some years ago in *Christianity Today* reported an experiment at a large eastern university that demonstrated that after three sessions using hypnotic suggestion a persons' religious attitudes could be completely changed. Ethical questions prompted the investigators to discontinue their research.[16] One wonders if this means of conversion would not be acceptable to some soul hunters. Litfin cited some familiar techniques of holy motivators:

1. Slick and flashy evangelism centered around a flamboyant, pseudo-celebrity type of evangelist.
2. The familiar machine-gun, pulpit-pounding style . . . that tends to rev up the emotions but bypass the rational faculties.
3. Sad-story laden messages lacking any real biblical substance.
4. Interminable invitations designed to wear down resistance until someone, *anyone* responds.
5. Such widespread techniques as asking people to raise their hands to be prayed for and then asking all who raised their hands to come forward (. . . having publicly admitted his need by raising his hand, the person is placed under tremendous social and psychological pressure to comply when the second invitation is given).[17]

Surely our task is to present the gospel in the clearest terms in order to allow the listeners to make a free and intelligent choice. The truth of God should not require subterfuge. I cannot think of a single biblical narrative that records God's entrapment of a convert. Deceit is not a divine technique.

Misrepresentation and Partial Truth

Misrepresentation and partial disclosure are the final forms of questionable preaching practices to be considered here. Misrepresentation may involve taking a statement out of context and distorting the intention of the author or it may simply distort a statement or position of someone else in order to further the cause of the speaker. Partial disclosure is presenting only the part of the truth that favors the preacher's position.

A prominent Baptist pastor quoted Reinhold Niebuhr to support his argument that "some Baptists believe that in recent years the state has moved away from being neutral about religion and has become increasingly hostile to religion and in its place has endorsed another religion—secularism." The source is an excellent one, but the implication was that Niebuhr was a Baptist, which he was not. The overall sermon was an excellent one, and it might be argued that such matters are insignificant, but I would contend that the nature of preaching requires the greatest fidelity to correctness. Next time it might matter.

Great care should be exercised in attributing motives to those with whom one disagrees. A thinly disguised attack on Catholicism appeared in this form: "There is a heretical religion that has created a diabolical, mind-terrorizing doctrine of purgatory as a scheme to raise money and manipulate the minds of men. . . . It is a diabolical scheme to raise money and to control the minds of men." Note the use of charged language, "heretical, mind-terrorizing, diabolical" which intensifies the charge that the doctrine is only a money-making "scheme."

David Buttrick has wisely observed that "all preachers serve Christ in brokenness, trusting in grace alone."[18] All of us have erred at one time or another in the use of sources or in reasoning. This fact does not, however, excuse us from observing the highest standards for truth and fairness. We must earn the right to be heard, and this means absolute credibility.

Kenneth E. Andersen, in his Presidential Address before the Speech Communication Association of America in 1983, presented six principles as an ethical code for speakers.[19] This code provides a minimum standard for preachers who claim to communicate the most important message for the welfare of humanity.

1. *Accept proper burden for the communication activity.*

The preacher seeks a hearing. The nature of our calling is such that we should do all in our power to ensure quality content and performance. The preacher is accountable to his or her audience and to God. Preaching is an awesome responsibility which should not be taken lightly.

2. *Act so that the potential effectiveness of all future communication is enhanced.*

The preacher wants to continue to be an influence on those who hear her or him. A high level of trust is necessary for a healthy pastor-parishioner relationship. If an ongoing dialogue is not possible the speaker will want to act in such a way that those who come later will find receptive hearers. Once a preacher has abused the office the re-establishment of trust is extremely difficult. The television evangelists have created great material for stand-up comics, but all proclaimers suffer from the fall-out. Once a congregation has been hurt by an immoral or dishonest preacher they tend to filter the message of all preachers through that experience.

3. *Act to maximize individual freedom of choice and responsibility.*

People cannot be tricked into the kingdom of heaven. The effects of manipulation are usually short-term. God created us as responsible persons. The dignity of divine creation requires respect for the individual's responsibility to make a free, informed decision. Preachers of every age should follow the apostle's example and renounce "disgraceful, underhanded ways . . . refuse to practice cunning or to tamper with God's word, but by open statement of the truth we would commend ourselves to every man's conscience in the sight of God" (2 Cor. 4:2, RSV). Jesus showed respect for His hearers and gave them the right of decision. He did not hesitate to make clear the consequences of choosing to follow Him. The gospel of Jesus was never deceptive or candy-coated.

4. *Act so that the respect of each participant for self and others is maximized.*

The nature of the gospel requires worthy means to achieve its goals. Paul warned that we should not be "peddlers of God's word; but as men of sincerity" (2 Cor. 2:17, RSV). The preacher should honor all persons as those created in the image of God.

5. *Act so as to improve yours and others' communication ability and understanding.*

Communication is a process which should be respected. Errors in ethical judgment often result from impatience. The preacher should strive to equip the listener with keys to discernment that will respect intellect, feeling, and will.

6. *Enforce this code upon self and all others.*

The nature of preaching should require a strict code of ethics with regard to handling the revelation that is entrusted to the preacher. The Bible is replete with examples of false and misguided prophets. Every effort should be made for individuals and the community of proclaimers to adhere to the highest standards of research, fairness, and persuasive integrity that demonstrates a respect of the image of God in all those who listen.

Let each person who would bear the awesome responsibility of speaking for God join with Paul in a bold declaration: "We have renounced disgraceful, underhanded ways; we refuse to practice cunning or to tamper with God's word, but by the open statement of the truth we would commend ourselves to every man's [person's] conscience in the sight of God" (2 Cor. 4:2, RSV).

Such a pledge and practice among the society of proclaimers would do much to restore credibility in our message among those who need its truth.

Notes

1. Ralph Waldo Emerson, *A Field of Diamonds*, ed. Joseph S. Johnson (Nashville: Broadman Press, 1974), 32.

2. Owen Brandon, quoted in Karen Lebacqz, *Professional Ethics: Power and Paradox* (Nashville: Abingdon Press, 1985), 64-65.

3. Ibid., 145.

4. Michael D. Bayless, *Professional Ethics* (Belmont, California: Wadsworth, 1981), 4-9.

5. Augustine, *On Christian Doctrine*, trans. J. F. Shaw, *Great Books of the Western World*, Vol. 18 (Chicago: William Benton, 1952), 62.

6. John Broadus, *On the Preparation and Delivery of Sermons*, 3rd ed. (New York: Harper and Row, 1944), 87.

7. Jamie Buckingham, "Pulpit Plagiarism," *Leadership* (Summer, 1983): 62-63.

8. John Killenger, *Fundamentals of Preaching* (Philadelphia: Fortress, 1985), 130.

9. Raymond Bailey, "Proclamation as a Rhetorical Art," *Review and Expositor*, Vol. LXXXIV, no. 1 (Winter, 1987): 7-21.

10. Lester Thonssen, A. Craig Baird, and Weldo Braden, *Speech Criticism* (Malabar, Florida: Robert Krieger Co., 1981), 558.

11. Aristotle, *The Rhetoric*, trans. Lane Cooper (Englewood Cliffs, New Jersey: Prentice-Hall, 1932), 92.

12. James T. Cleland, *Preaching to Be Understood* (Nashville: Abingdon Press, 1965), 64-70.

13. *Propaganda Analysis*, Vols. 1, 2, published by Institute for Propaganda Analysis (November, 1937), 1.

14. Craig Loscalzo, "The Rhetoric of Kenneth Burke as a Methodology for Preaching," (Ph.D. dissertation, The Southern Baptist Theological Seminary, 1988), 147-148.

15. Clyde Fant, *Preaching for Today*, 2nd ed. (San Francisco: Harper & Row, 1987), 117-118.

16. A. Duane Litfin, "The Perils of Persuasive Preaching," *Christianity Today* (Feb. 4, 1977): 15.

17. Ibid., 17.

18. David Buttrick, *Homilectics: Moves and Structures* (Philadelphia: Fortress, 1987), 459.

19. Kenneth E. Andersen, audiotape of SCA 1983, General Session: "A Code of Ethics for Speech Communication." The tape is available from Speech Communication Association of America, 5108 Backlick Road, Annandale, VA 22003.

49

Craig Skinner
Professor of Preaching
Golden Gate Baptist Theological Seminary
Mill Valley, California

Creativity in Preaching

"A sermon grows as an apple grows, and what it needs is sun and time. You may pick it green if you are in a hurry, and if you do it will set your people's teeth on edge. You may pick it half ripe and lose something of the flavor, or you may wait until it becomes mellow, rich, and juicy, and then the saints are glad."[1]

Sermon Preparation

Maturing the Crop

Truly ripe thoughts add fresh dimensions of reality to any pulpit. A calm confidence and a deep joy inhabit our sermons as we share genuine harvests of thought instead of immature ideas. Pulpiteers of previous generations called this desirable ethos "preaching out of the overflow." Such a phrase pictures a quality of spiritual unction, an evident power of proclamation, and an impactive sense of composure, all arising because the strength of the reservoir behind our streams of thought add new energy to their flow.

So while sermons need not be scintillating to be attractive, they must be mature. If ripeness nourishes reality in sermons, then superficial thoughts and shallow ideas destroy it. Yet Saturday nights find too many pastors so paralyzed by the proximity of their pulpit demands that they content themselves with the repackaging of borrowed thoughts, and so become echoes instead of authentic voices of God.

Getting the Harvest to Market

The farmer who hopes to deliver a fresh crop to market each week must plan for sequential harvesting. This, in turn, depends upon an extended program of plowing, planting, and cultivation which schedules consecutive stages of development over an extended period of time suitable to his production goals. Yet we too often expect to plant ideas every Monday (or later), and then reap a full harvest from them every Friday (or earlier). We ought to plant fertile sermon seeds, but we must also be ready to tend them over a timely period designed to cultivate their responsible growth.

The growth of an authentic pulpit reality loses its mystery when we consider the role of the subconscious human self in the association of ideas, and remember how many of life's other creative discoveries arise quite naturally.

Creativity in Preparation

It may seem strange to some that the passive subconscious self can be a supporting resource for the conscious self. Psalm 39 appears to reflect just such a process. The early verses talk of guarding speech in the presence of the wicked from whom logical judgment demands only vengeance. Under such discipline distress grows worse, and the psalmist's heart became "hot" within him. In verse 3 he confessed: "While I was musing the fire burned; then I spoke with my tongue (NASB).

He sat in quietness after a period of struggle with the facts as he initially saw them. During that quiet time of withdrawal, an inner light broke across his experience so that his final words were *not* those of vengeance. He allowed all the realities to incubate while he withdrew from conscious reasoning about the situation and, as a result, an inner discernment arose which cooled his inflamed spirit and allowed him (in the remainder of the psalm) to be content with expressing his trust in God's sovereignty and grace. Thus the creative capacity of his inner spirit, led by God's Spirit, enabled him to replace the hot and angry passion of his initial reasoning about the wicked with a more positive response of faith and hope.

Automatic Preparation

Mark 4:26-29 presents Jesus' picture of kingdom growth as akin to a farmer who carefully plants his seed in prepared soil, and then leaves it entirely alone as he goes about other ordinary duties. Anxiety will not hasten the harvest so the farmer waits patiently for the seed's natural growth through successive stages until it finally becomes ripe for harvest.

Jesus asserted that, while sowing and harvesting belong to us, all that lies between belongs to God. The seed produces its crop "by itself" (the Greek is *automatē*—automatically).[2] This spontaneity of growth remains a mystery for the farmer. Development occurs, but just how "he himself does not know" (v. 27, NASB). What he does know is how to cooperate with God's principles of natural growth to secure a good harvest.

If Jesus asserted that the maturation of God's kingdom parallels His design for growth in the natural world, we may also consider such a model as a paradigm for the spiritual cultivation of our messages about kingdom truth. The parable spotlights several significant principles: (1) growth arises from the creative nature of the seed itself; (2) enduring patience within an unhurried time frame is needed, along with an absolute faith in the self-generating capacity of the seed to develop; (3) although growth may be slow, the harvest is sure; and (4) our part in the task is to plant the seed well, and then to reap the harvest with courage as it ripens.

Every farmer plants seeds knowing they will multiply many times over by harvest time. As in nature, so also in the intellect, *we always reap more than we sow* after we plant a fertile idea. Growth develops as we fulfill our assigned tasks, and then leave the Lord to undertake those for which He assumes responsibility. Made in the image of a Creator-God, humankind alone among all His creatures possesses the capacity to think, to plan, and to communicate—all functions of creativity. Ideas sent down to the subconscious can sprout, develop, and evolve to fruition *automatically*, establishing themselves creatively in fresh and original dimensions if we are willing to plant them in faith.

Logic and Perception

Recent research convinces many scientists that the human brain operates simultaneously on two major levels. Obviously all men and women possess a capacity to memorize and to reason. We also appear to possess a second facility which processes and synthesizes the data we receive and precipitates perceptions from that data. We are able to sense realities intuitively which are beyond those which we must reason out to purely logical conclusions. Some research suggests that our rational awareness centers in the left hemisphere of the brain, and that our intuitive awareness centers in the right.

Left Brain and Right Brain

The left brain appears to gather and logically analyze facts and other raw data. Mathematical abilities appear to locate here, and this is the agency for the communication of our ideas. Information is processed sequentially, and then stored in connective banks which enable it to be recognized and recalled. Left brain functions seem strongest among scientists, and within similar rationally oriented minds.

Creative ideas appear to synthesize in the right brain. From a variety of inputs we determine the significance of the data gathered by the left brain as we consider it all holistically, and then distill the implications and inferences of all of which we have become aware. We make connections that extend the left brain's factual information into areas of fresh relevance. This intuitive sensing leads to new perceptions and fresh insights. The right brain represents the emotional and imaginative you which feels, designs, and creates. Right brain strengths appear at highest levels among writers, artists, poets, musicians, and other very creative persons.

In order to function in the fullness of our humanity we must use the cognitive, rational functions of the left brain. Yet we equally need the intuitive and creative connections of synthesized insight which flow from the right.

The Creative Cycle

Psychologists use many different terms to portray the production of a creative idea within the human mind. A general agreement exists that imaginative development involves a sequential advance of thought through a group of definable processes which cover its conception, gestation, and birth. These may be described as deliberately chosen intellectual behaviors. They can be defined as the five purposeful mental activities of the mind we know as informing, exploring, withdrawing, discovering, and verifying.

1. Informing

This is the mind's initial locating function concerning the topic or problem upon which the mental reflection is being undertaken. The basic essentials of its nature are thoroughly investigated, and the main areas of thought and directions of consideration are ascertained. During this process of collation every fact or idea considered is to be accepted without any judgment as to its relevance.

2. Exploring

A discernable second phase in creative thought is that of a penetrative investigation of all the latent associations available between the facts and materials gathered under stage 1. An incredible variety of such potential relationships between the materials previously collated can develop here if the human mind's creative capacity is totally freed to imagine possible combinations and invent fresh connections. Through such a process we consider the concern in view from every potential perspective and think through all the possible ways in which it may be linked to other facts and ideas, expanded, developed, or applied.

In order to implement such a "brainstorming" function of exploration, the primary essential is a disciplined commitment to a nonjudgmental response to the suggestions thus generated. Unless such a discipline is rigorously applied, the ongoing process of imaginative creativity will certainly be truncated, and possibly entirely destroyed. Logical thought must be suspended in favor of the free association of ideas.

Creative invention is an extension of other ideas. As a wide variety of differing facts and concepts come into fresh associations with each other they create new offspring. These couplings breed original ideas which grow out of the fresh connections between the old ones. All the pieces of information gathered must be thrown against each other, and cast into as various a number of connections as is possible. We note what breeds from their cohabitation, remaining open to accept any suggestion, recording everything, and deliberately refusing to reject anything no matter what its character may be.

This exploration function must continue until all constructive thought finally grinds to a frustrating halt, often producing feelings of anxiety, disappointment, and even fatigue, over the lack of final conclusions. Only when the frustration level of our exploring becomes almost unbearable should we move on to subsequent stages of the process. The heights of ecstasy experienced when the creative insights finally arrive bear a direct relation to the depths of agony experienced to this point.

3. Withdrawing

The third step in the creative process appears to many to be both the strangest and the most difficult. This demands a complete (although temporary) abandonment of the task and a total surrender of it to the inner creative self. Everything which has passed through our minds in stages 1 and 2 is deliberately sent underground and left there to lie alone. You must renounce it completely, and act for a period as if the entire concern simply did not exist. A minimum of three to seven days (including relaxed evenings of sleep)—more if possible—should intervene before you reconsider the matter. Unless a green shoot sprouts unexpectedly during this period, forcing you to jot it down, you should be content generally to turn to other tasks and leave what you have sown quite alone, allowing ample time for it to germinate, just as the farmer has buried his seed and turned his attention entirely to other pursuits. The intention of this phase is to put the matter entirely out of the conscious mind and, through such chosen forgetfulness, to plant it firmly in the subconscious where our natural (but hidden) creative capacities may function unhindered.

While attention focuses on other tasks—as you sleep, read, travel, fellowship, or talk—powers lodged in an inner basement of the mind labor on secretly. Now and then that subconscious self may reach up to grab your attention as it suddenly links a present experience with some past reality you have planted by faith. A green blade may sprout into view as you read a newspaper, watch TV, or notice something fresh in a situation you have not before perceived. Other surprising growth can appear spontaneously while your mind is working in a completely different area of theology, or biblical study, or history. The stage of withdrawal acts as an incubator nourishing the creative life within, and it leads naturally (and, *given enough time*, almost automatically) into the next phase where insights tumble in.

4. Discovering

Here spontaneous intuitive discernments commonly arrive as ecstatic "aha" experiences. They must be written down immediately—however wrong, irrelevant, or even "off-the-wall" they may appear. Again we temporarily suspend all critical judgment in favor of recording those creative thoughts, to be evaluated later. The longer you work with such processes the more adept you will become at locking down such connections quickly.

A new insight may often leap into conscious awareness through a seemingly accidental coincidence, such as when Isaac Newton watched an apple fall, or Galileo grasped the law of the pendulum as he viewed swinging lamps in the Pisa Cathedral. Whenever this happens, however, it is initiated by the subconscious whose inner forces of creative production have been patiently working with seeds previously planted in our minds and memories and left there to germinate and grow. The "coincidental" occasion then becomes a fresh dynamic, spotlighting our inside thinking which is thereby seen to show signs of an exciting coming harvest.

Each of these illuminating shafts of light, however unusual they may first appear, contain some truth which we may not immediately "see" logically, as they reflect our intuitive capacity to perceive before we reason. As they first arrive in unfinished or unacceptable forms, the ideas thus discovered may still require hard labor to bring them into a finality of form acceptable to the reasoning mind, and suitable for use in a sermon. A final phase then allows us to confirm which of the discoveries we have made we may finally accept, as we judge them in the light of their logical maturity.

5. Verifying

In this last phase we "try on" each of the ideas we have generated by working them through to a full development and application. Such details validate and refine them, and the truth of each idea is either confirmed or denied. In the previous phase a lightning flash illuminated a pathway before us for just a few brief seconds. Now we must move inch by inch over the freshly focused terrain, examining it all minutely to see if it is possible for us to journey across it with safety. We select and exclude materials. We check and verify facts. We focus the whole matter out of its initial fuzziness into an ordered structure and craft a precision of expression which best communicates our ideas.

Implementing the Plan

Long Range Design

One of the best ways to initiate a continuity of cycled creativity is to find a mountain cabin or some other place by yourself—away from the office telephone and all other persons—for four days or more during one of the last weeks of every summer. Many rich resources exist for the planning of sermon series, special days, and other self-chosen themes.[3] Take some good ones with you. Spend this time preplanning all your services for the year ahead.

You can simply collate ideas, one to a page in a small loose-leaf notebook, filing them as "hot for early use," or otherwise. Many find it useful actually to rough out a full schedule of topics and approaches for the year ahead, Sunday by Sunday, using the Christian Year, and including local church needs. Planning sermon subjects, topics, and biblical portions for future preaching helps you plant the ideas which will then have time to grow.[4]

Once your sermon garden is readied, and the seeds are sown, you need no longer face a weekly crossroads without directional signs. Instead you begin each sermon preparation time with the conviction that *the actual decision to preach on that matter is already taken*. The question, "Upon what shall I preach?" now resolves itself into a much simpler one: "Of all the matters about which I have already decided to preach, which one is suitable to schedule next, and how close to harvest has it grown?"

A lectionary may suggest helpful preaching themes, but only as these are reviewed, listed, and scheduled well beforehand will you actually plant them, and therefore be able to nourish their growth to a ripe maturity. Also, while most lectionaries do cover main biblical contents over a three-year cycle, their help with the specific needs of your local congregation may be quite minimal.

Daily Schedule

In their zeal to be family oriented, too many pastors forget that some of the best times to give themselves to spouses and/or children lie in the late hours of the afternoon. For most families adequate mornings simply require a quick breakfast, then all members have to "get up and go" for their appropriate tasks of the day. So a well-disciplined pastor can claim the most productive period of each day (the early morning hours) to schedule concentrated work in the sermon garden. By so doing you may facilitate a life of great freedom from other competing and distracting responsibilities.

If most employees in your congregation, along with their children, start for work or school around 7:15 a.m., why not you? Begin then in your study (at the church and away from home distractions[5]) around 7:30 a.m. Train your office secretary to respond to all inquiries (except emergencies) with the information that you are engaged, but also to promise that you will return phone calls promptly at 10:30 a.m. (That's when you will break for coffee, although callers need not know this!) You will then enjoy three clear hours each morning stacked only with opportunities for plowing, fertilizing, watering, planting, weeding, nourishing, and harvesting a great diversity of crops. In those early hours you can complete four times the work in half the time you would take if you attempted it during the lazy hours of the afternoon.

From 10:30 a.m. to noon you may deal with correspondence, administrative matters, and even a counseling appointment if desired. After you break for lunch, and make a few hospital or other calls as needed, you can then go home from 3 p.m., and spend two or three of the late afternoon hours relaxing with the family, going to the store, or whatever. This is all well justified if you began your day at 7:30 a.m. It also gives time to rest and change before any evening responsibilities.

Each day in the week (or portions of each of the study periods) can be scheduled for reflection upon a variety of ideas, and if one appears closer to harvest than another this can be moved up to be delivered earlier than originally planned if desired.

The "verification" phase of any preparation should be scheduled for the week *prior* to the one which ends with the Sunday of delivery. This leaves the last week before delivery for the finalization of the actual sermon manuscript or notes. Each preacher needs to determine a creative schedule which fits best with his or her personal program. I find that an allowance of one week for each of the five creative stages works well. I must therefore have completed my "information" phase by at least one clear month prior to delivery. Currently published examples of creative results arising from such a staged process are readily available.[6]

In its essence, then, creativity is simply a matter of faith. In its operation it requires time and patience. Poor sermons are such because they lack the richness that only unhurried growth can impart. The universal testimony of those who trust the Holy Spirit's guidance by sensitizing themselves to the creative powers of their own human spirits is that they find a mind-exploding relevance in what is prepared at long range, where before they assumed that this could not be. Sermons planned at long range fit smoothly into contemporary contexts when the week prior to their delivery is left for the final harvesting and presentation of the fruit.

God *does* work with us on Saturday nights, but we do better if He is helping us polish the apples then rather than seeking to plant and harvest them all at one sitting.

Notes

1. Charles Edward Jefferson, *The Minister as Prophet* (New York: Crowell and Co, 1905), 76.

2. A term used only once elsewhere in the Scriptures, in Acts 12:10 where the city gate opened to Peter of "its own accord."

3. Annual *Minister's Manual* volumes are available each year from Zondervan, Abingdon, and Harper, which provide hundreds of sermon seeds, lists of potential pulpit emphases and a multitude of other resources. I find Harper to be the most useful (see note #6, below). Every theological library usually has an abundance of these. Also see Lloyd M. Perry, *A Manual for Biblical Preaching* (Grand Rapids: Baker, 1991). This is another old classic, whose homiletic theories may be outdated, but a resource still incredibly rich in analyses of biblical materials, suggestions for special days, and abundant sermon series ideas. I consider it to be an indispensable "idea book" for the beginning biblical preacher, and a valuable tool for the seasoned one. A more recent volume which presents content ideas for preaching from biblical books, and faces critical questions associated with them, is James W. Cox, ed., *Biblical Preaching* (Philadelphia: Westminster, 1983). Major preaching help for balanced and responsible interpretation in the difficult area of biblical prophecy can be found in an insightful new volume by Walter C. Kaiser, Jr., *Back Toward the Future* (Grand Rapids: Baker, 1989).

4. See J. Winston Pearce, *Planning Your Preaching* (Nashville: Broadman Press, 1967). This material has remained in print, and in demand, for 25 years.

5. You will also need a small "study corner" at home with a reference volume or two, where you can put some finishing touches to a roughed out sermon if needed. Normally, when home you should *be* at home, and not at work!

6. Brainstorming the parable of Luke 15:11-32 suggested that it could be the story of *two* prodigal sons. Because only one brother left home and travelled to the far country, the idea first appeared to be strange, but (as the process requires) this logical judgment was rejected in favor of open acceptance of anything the imagination suggested. Further detailed reflection on the biblical materials revealed that the elder brother's pride and envy drove him away from *faith* in his father, and that his selfishness and neglect drove him away from *fellowship* with his father. [The completed creative sermon on Luke 15 may be viewed in James W. Cox, ed., *The Ministers Manual* (New York: Harper, 1992), 262-264. Likewise a consideration of the narrative of Micah found in Judges 17 and 18 yielded a fresh understanding of his private religion as typical of those we all create—*superficial, self-righteous, unstable, and unnecessary*. The full sermon is in James W. Cox, ed., *Best Sermons No. 5* (New York: Harper, 1992) where it appears as one of the assigned models, and is titled "Back Yard Religion."]

50

William E. Hull, Provost
Samford University
Birmingham, Alabama

The Contemporary World and the Preaching Task

We begin with an awkward question: Why is "great preaching" so often dull? In 1971, Clyde E. Fant, Jr. and William E. Pinson, Jr., published a thirteen volume anthology, *20 Centuries of Great Preaching,* which included sermons from more than ninety pulpit masters of the ages.[1] For the last two decades I have consulted this encyclopedic resource but seldom found material which I thought would be interesting and powerful if used today. This limitation is obviously not due to any lack of ability or spiritual depth on the part of the authors, for every sermon is a carefully selected masterpiece. Nor is it due to the absence of the preacher's personality, for sermons can be gripping even in written form. My conclusion is that the sermons lack sparkle and punch today precisely because they were written for another generation.

Fant and Pinson begin their vast enterprise with these words: "Great preaching is relevant preaching"[2]—and I could not agree more! Yet in making their sermons relevant to an earlier age, these giants utilized a different rhetorical style. Their words carried nuances and suggested allusions which set off associations unfamiliar to us today. Most importantly, they addressed different urgencies; they aimed at different targets; they grappled with problems defined by different contexts. In order to be relevant, their message had to be, not timeless, but timely! In some cases the very language which they used required translation, for instance from Greek or Latin or German into English, but it was not possible to translate the living situation into which their proclamation was flung. Rather than being viewed as a criticism, it is a compliment that these sermons were so carefully crafted for their own time that they no longer resonate with the temper of our time. If the greatest preaching in Christian history is dated to its own day, should that not be true of our sermons as well?

Even though the attribute of timeliness is characteristic of all great preaching, many pulpiteers today openly resist the challenge of being relevant to the world in which they live. Immediately the reply comes that to be "relevant" is to risk accommodating or even compromising the gospel to contemporary thought. In the name of integrity, they refuse to tamper with the traditional language of the pulpit, choosing rather to glory in the *irrelevance* of their message. Yet, to their chagrin, the forceful idiom of one generation becomes the tired cliché of the next. Static formulations become increasingly impotent as the times are inexorably transformed. Finally they find themselves speaking in a language that is no longer fresh about concerns that no longer matter to a generation that no longer exists!

The risk of restating the gospel is neatly summarized in a somewhat sardonic comment of Dean Inge: "If you marry the Spirit of your own generation you will be a widow in the next."[3] Two clarifications are in order. First, our homiletical task is not to embrace the modern mood but to contend with it on behalf of the claims of Christ. The urgent issue is not whether the church capitulates to contemporary culture but whether it confronts that culture with a proclamation which makes unmistakably clear the radical demands of the gospel upon the totality of concrete human existence as it is lived today. Second, Inge appears to have overlooked the fact that we are not eligible even for widowhood in the next generation. He is correct that the spirit of our age will die, but he forgets that we will die with it. Mercifully, we are not required to anticipate what may meet the needs of tomorrow, since only God knows what that day may bring (Matt. 6:34). Rather, we are to take up the task that never changes, that of fashioning our finest understanding of the biblical message for the one generation we are given to serve.[4]

Taking the Contemporary World Seriously

Those preachers who like to ignore the contemporary world often do so in the name of fidelity to the Bible. However, when we go in search of the meaning of the Bible, we are helped immeasurably by an understanding of its own world. Most breakthroughs in biblical interpretation have come as the result of a better grasp of the actual situation with which the various writers of Scripture were originally dealing. Think, for example, of the flood of light thrown on the New Testament from our study of apocalyptic Judaism in the pseudepigraphical literature, or of sectarian Judaism in the Dead Sea Scrolls from Qumran, or of rabbinic Judaism in Mishnah and Talmud, or of esoteric Judaism and Hellenism in the early Gnostic writings discovered at Nag Hammadi. These and other contributors to biblical "backgrounds" do not provide the *content* of our message but they do provide the *context* within which we may clarify both its distinctiveness and its strategy.

The theological reason why this is true is because divine revelation was not disclosed in some transcendent moment as a disembodied truth from "beyond" history. Such Gnostic notions were steadfastly repudiated by the conviction that "the Word became *flesh*" (John 1:14); that is, God's disclosure became an integral part of first-century Palestinian history, participating fully in the scandal of temporal and spatial particularity. Far from ignoring the specific human situation, the Word was addressed directly to it. The particular character of the world into which the Word was thrust determined the shape it assumed and the way it was understood.

For example, when the story of Jesus took root in various Christian centers, it was transmuted into at least four distinctly different Gospels, each an attempt to make the message relevant in the milieu where it was planted. Although there was only one "gospel" (*euaggelion*) from God, it was always taken "down" (*kata*) according to various interpreters who drew out its significance for the readers they addressed. Again, Paul was determined to preach the only true gospel (Gal. 1:6-9), yet his formulation of the faith in Galatians and Romans differed markedly from that in Colossians and Ephesians. The explanation lies not in some evolutionary hypothesis which posits a developmental principle in Pauline thought, but rather in the creative interpenetration of his *kerygma* with strikingly different historical situations.

This means that preaching is fashioned in a dialogical relationship between the divine Word and the human world which it addresses. The biblical message is inescapably bound to its own situation in the unity of proclamation and response. The same should be true of our preaching today as it seeks to confront the twentieth century with the claims of Christ. The form of our message cannot be the same as that of the biblical message because our modern world is scarcely identical to the first century world. We do not demonstrate our fidelity to Scripture by preaching today the same thing that the Bible did about circumcision (Gal. 5:2-12), veiling women (1 Cor. 11:2-16), and meat offered to idols (1 Cor. 8:1-13), not because these sections of the Bible are untrue, but because these practices have a quite different meaning in modern America. Neither are we to ignore these passages as outdated, for they contain the very heart of the gospel. Rather, the enduring authority of the whole Bible requires that we learn to preach on these topics in such a way that our message will impinge upon our day with exactly the same intentions that the biblical message impinged upon its day: declaring the same purpose, demanding the same verdict, delivering the same impact.

The inseparable connection between the message and its matrix means that we may not limit the definition of our task simply to that of discovering the content of the ancient faith and then attempting to state it in contemporary fashion. Rather, since the biblical revelation cannot be stated adequately at all apart from *its* unique historical setting, we must instead seek to make that message relevant for *our* unique historical setting. In other words, there are four factors involved in the act of proclamation, not two. These may be expressed schematically in a homiletical formula which describes preaching thus.[5]

$$\frac{\text{Biblical Message}}{\text{Biblical World}} = \frac{\text{Our Message}}{\text{Our World}}$$

On the upper side of the formula, the Christian message in any age is seen, not as a set of self-contained timeless propositions, but as the address of God set over against the world in dialogue, a confrontation in which truth is disclosed in encounter. On the underside, the particular character of the temporal situation into which the Word is thrust determines the way in which the revelation is understood and the form it assumes. Relevance is to be found in the juxtaposition between the Word and its world. Each element taken separately is inescapably time-bound. The enduring factor is the significance of the relationship between the two parts. A message shaped to address one specific situation may not be relevant in a different situation unless it is reshaped. Relevance is disclosed by the way in which the message engages its own world and seeks to transform the situation which it presents.

Dietrich Bonhoeffer has well summarized our attempt to provide a biblical and theological justification for the preacher taking seriously the contemporary world. Said he:

> A word can only be authoritatively and convincingly spoken to me when it springs from the deepest knowledge of my humanity and strikes me here and now in the total reality of my human existence. Any other kind of word is powerless. Hence the Church's message to the world, if it is to be authoritative and convincing, must be declared with the deepest knowledge of the world's life and must concern the world in the full scope of its present reality.[6]

Understanding the Contemporary World

If we are required by the nature of the biblical message as an address to its own world to become witnesses of that same truth to our quite different world, how may we better understand the life situation in which we minister? A major problem arises from the neglect of this agenda in the training of preachers. Most seminaries offer no in-depth study of contemporary life anywhere in the theological curriculum.[7] Standard textbooks on homiletics are largely silent on strategy questions of how to engage the modern mind with the gospel.[8] The wider literature on preaching in books and journals may contain a few scattered references of an inspirational or hortatory nature but very little solid analysis of the current *Zeitgeist*.[9] Nor do continuing education workshops on preaching devote any significant attention to this issue. In my judgment, the single weakest link in present efforts to equip ministers to preach is the almost complete lack of resources to help them understand the world to which they will witness.[10]

Both the magnitude and the irony of the problem may be glimpsed by comparing the training which ministers receive to study the ancient biblical message with the training which they receive to prepare their own contemporary message. Before trying to interpret the New Testament gospel, students are given a rather comprehensive introduction to the historical dynamics of the first-century world including the impact of exile and resettlement, conquests of Alexander and subsequent rule by his Ptolemaic and Seleucid successors, rise of the Maccabean revolutionaries and the Hasmonean dynasty, and the intervention of Rome and Herodian rule. They will know clearly such religious movements as Pharisees, Sadducees, Zealots, and Essenes; institutions such as temple, synagogue, and Sanhedrin; cultural trends such as Hellenization; philosophical trends such as Stoicism; and political trends such as emperor worship. They can distinguish apocalypticists from Gnostics and talk intelligently about the significance of the fall of the Jerusalem Temple in A.D. 70. More crucially, they can relate all of these developments to the ways in which the New Testament message was formulated and proclaimed in such a world.

Yet when they cross over twenty centuries and begin to hammer out a message for today, they are left to understand their own world presumably by intuition or osmosis. Nor does it help much to watch television and read the daily paper plus a weekly news magazine. Most seminary-trained preachers do not understand the impact of the Vietnam war on the American mind as well as they do the corruption and collapse of the Hasmonean dynasty on the Jewish mind. They do not know the religious assumptions of the modern New Age movement as well as they do those of the ancient Gnostic movement. They cannot explain the social causes which gave rise to early twentieth-century American dispensationalism as well as they can explain the rise of intertestamental Jewish apocalypticism. They have not analyzed the shifting patterns of church-state relations since the emergence of New Right religion in the 1970s as carefully as they have traced tensions between the Tobiads and the Oniads in the Jerusalem high priesthood. I hope the point is clear: students of preaching need as much training in the twentieth-century world as students of New Testament need in the first-century world, but that training has not been provided.

So what is the preacher to do? First, realizing the deficiency, set priorities on your time in order to give balanced attention to a study of modern life. A good rule of thumb might be to divide your study time equally between the biblical message and your modern message, in each of these two areas devoting about half as much time to a study of the world as you do to a study of the Word. Resolve to work on the gaps in your training until you honestly feel that you understand the contemporary world *at least as well* as you understand the biblical world. With this commitment firmly in place, set up a systematic program to study the world you are trying to change. You can probably get some help by talking over your plans with a good journalist, especially an editorial page writer at a major newspaper; with a good reference librarian specializing in American studies; and with professors whose disciplines or personal interests are focused on current events. Once you gain an overview of your task, begin reading the books, journals, and newsletters that will fill in the missing pieces.

Unfortunately, there is not space here to outline the field or to identify a basic bibliography, but let me suggest a few leads that may prove promising. Pollsters such as Gallup, Roper, and Yankelovich issue trend reports which usefully sample public opinion but are often expensive. Many newsletters take the contemporary pulse; one of the more insightful from a Christian perspective is *Context*, a somewhat miscellaneous "commentary on the interaction of religion and culture" written by Martin E. Marty. Periodicals that may be counted on to have something of worth in most issues include *The Atlantic Monthly, Harpers*, and *The New Republic*. Faith traditions inform cultural critique from a Protestant perspective in *Christianity and Crisis*, from a Catholic perspective in *America*, from a Jewish perspective in *Commentary*, and from an interfaith perspective in *First Things*. Analysis in greater depth and more sophistication is found in journals such as *The American Scholar, Daedalus*, and *The Wilson Quarterly*. Most of the better books on contemporary life intended for the general reader rather than the specialist are reviewed, advertised, or mentioned in these serials as well as in the *New York Times Book Review*, the *New York Review of Books*, and the *Times Literary Supplement*.

Admittedly the field of study is enormous and I have barely hinted at the resources available. For example, the standard bibliography limited to books written on American studies in this century through 1983 has 12,044 entries covering Anthropology, Art and Architecture, Autobiographies and Memoirs, Folklore and Folklife, History, Literature, Music, Political Science, Popular Culture, Psychology, Religion, Science/Technology/Medicine, and Sociology.[11] Doubtless many preachers are daunted at the prospect of self-study in so vast an arena—it seems almost like teaching oneself to swim in the middle of the ocean! Yet do we neglect the New Testament world simply because thousands of books have been written on first-century Judaism and Hellenism? Surely the better course is to be highly selective in studying works on both worlds which provide a broad overview and which integrate insights from many disciplines.

Shaping Relevant Sermons

To assist you in following a productive path of study, I want now to offer seven practical suggestions designed to help preachers understand their world in ways that will shape relevant sermons.

1. *Set the contemporary era in a spacious context of past and future.* We usually define the "present" in terms of a generation involving thirty or forty years, but it is unwise to wear blinders that restrict your purview to that time frame. Understanding our nation today is still profoundly influenced by insights from Alexis de Tocqueville's *Democracy in America,* published 1835-40.[12] The Civil War (1861-65) and the two World Wars (1914-18, 1941-45) unleashed forces that are still working beneath the surface of public life.[13] Likewise, we are already being influenced by developments which will not come to fruition for several years into the future, such as microtechnology, robotics, space travel, genetic engineering, and globalization.[14] In this slippery field, the preacher will do well to rely on the more sober studies of The World Future Society[15] than on the over-simplified sensationalism of popularizers such as John Naisbitt and Alvin Toffler.[16]

2. *Within the present generation, look for studies that probe the underlying meaning of social change rather than merely chronicle the most prominent current events.*[17] For example, no Southern preacher can escape the influence of the civil rights struggle on this era, a story well told by Taylor Branch in his two-volume study of *America in the King Years.*[18] Massive dislocations in the public psyche require close attention to those tumultuous years between the assassination of John F. Kennedy and the abdication of Richard M. Nixon (1963-1974).[19] Equally important is the rise of the New Right in the late seventies and its triumph in the so-called Reagan Revolution of the eighties.[20] While it is premature to take the pulse of its uneasy aftermath in the nineties, a number of essays are beginning to diagnose the pervasive malaise which Jimmy Carter tried unsuccessfully to get the nation to face a dozen years earlier.[21]

3. *In addition to tracking the time-line of the present era, give equal attention to the meaning of place.* Begin at home by learning what resources the public library has on the history and demographics of your city, county, and state. While census reports and metropolitan planning studies are important, move beyond such statistical analyses to learn the lore of your community as reflected in the work of local poets, novelists, and

artists. Dare not neglect wider regional studies, especially if you live and work in Dixie![22]

4. *In approaching the culture of a particular time and place, be sure to look for the level where most of the people live to whom you are preaching.* Some academics seem to operate on the principle of "the higher the culture the better" and so they write at length about a rarefied intellectual climate which may be found in pockets of New York, London, and Paris, plus a few large universities, but scarcely anywhere else. Such writers may refer condescendingly, if not contemptuously, to "mass culture" or "pop culture," but this is a perfectly legitimate and relevant area of study, especially for those working at the grass roots level where local congregations flourish.[23] For example, over the past generation Vance Packard has often been accused of writing "pop sociology" with journalistic over-simplification, yet he has been able, not only to popularize, but also to influence the perception of significant trends such as motivational research, upward mobility, conspicuous consumption, invasion of privacy, nomadic anonymity, and biogenetic manipulation.[24]

5. *Balance your study of contemporary culture, not only between "high" and "low," but also between public and private.* Clearly the preacher needs to struggle with that elusive reality called the American character.[25] Some of the most helpful analysis now appearing is by Robert Bellah and his students, especially on civil religion and on individualism/communitarianism in America.[26] The preacher will want to trace the latter trend by comparing *The Organization Man* to its sequel, *The New Individualists*.[27] The profoundly personal nature of religion also demands a special focus on the understanding of individual selfhood which comes from studying private life in its historical, psychological, sociological, and cultural aspects.[28] A helpful typology for categorizing the values inherent in various American life-styles has been provided by the VALS (Values and Lifestyles) study of SRI International.[29]

6. *Since there are so many complex dimensions to contemporary culture, look for integrative studies that approach significant change from a synoptic viewpoint.* For example, every preacher will need to understand the rise of American Fundamentalism in the late nineteenth and early twentieth centuries. Rather than viewing this movement as an isolated religious development, let Martin Marty tell the story against a broad historical backdrop which relates Fundamentalism to the new America of immigration, industrialization, and urbanization.[30] Even better, let Jackson Lears set it in the cultural context of an antimodernism that expressed itself in politics, psychology, the arts, business, family life, and gender roles.[31] Only in this way will Fundamentalism be perceived as a corporate life-style and not just a belief system. One of the best ways to draw all of the relevant strands together is through the continuous study of biography since, finally, the whole spectrum

of cultural dynamics are assimilated and acted upon one life at a time.[32]

7. *Finally, once you have gained a unified understanding of American culture from top-to-bottom and inside-out, look for recurring patterns by which the present is illuminated by historical parallels.* History does not repeat itself, but there are fairly predictable cycles by which the pendulum of change swings in corrective fashion. Arthur Schlesinger, Jr., for example, has argued for an alternation between public purpose and private interest at generational intervals[33] which helps us to explain the rise and fall of altruism in counterpoint with materialism[34]—an undulation of crucial importance to any preacher with stewardship responsibilities for raising the church budget! One parallel which I have found particularly instructive is that between the 1920s and the 1980s in Southern white Protestantism, especially in controversies that wracked the Southern Baptist Convention during both decades.[35] Only time will tell whether the troubled 1990s will reproduce some of the religious characteristics of the depressed 1930s,[36] but at least we know where to look—without forcing the evidence to fit any preconceived theory.

Preaching With New Understanding

The preacher does not become intimately familiar with the contemporary world in order to deliver learned discourses on American culture any more than the New Testament exegete studies the first-century world in order to become an expert on ancient history. In both cases, this knowledge is used to determine how the gospel message was originally proclaimed, and how it can be proclaimed today so as to accomplish its unchanging intentions. The ideal is for the preacher to keep one foot in the biblical world and the other in our own world so that the message to those two worlds is united in everything proclaimed. Some have described this bi-polar approach to preaching as working with a Bible in one hand and today's newspaper in the other, fostering a never-ending dialogue between the two. While the task is more complicated than that, the preacher must ever labor to translate what the gospel *meant* in its own world into what it must *mean* in our world if it is to accomplish the same divine purposes.[37]

An entire book could and should be written on how to use an understanding of the modern world to address its deepest needs with the gospel. Here there is space only to be suggestive. I begin by urging that your scriptural study for preaching be based on commentaries and related resources that emphasize the historical context of each passage. Actually this is a rather recent development—and therefore a primary reason why older commentaries are of limited usefulness—coming as a result of the development of form criticism between the two world wars.

Originally, form criticism was a technical discipline devoted to identifying and classifying each unit (*pericope*) of Scripture in its earliest oral form. With this methodology came an emphasis on the life setting (*Sitz-im-leben*) of the passage and thereby an analysis of how the passage functioned in that context. The preacher would do well to build a working library around commentaries that analyze the *intentionality* of each passage and not just the meaning of any obscure terms and grammatical constructions in the text.[38]

Armed with a life-centered understanding of Scripture, the preacher should then ponder contemporary pulpit strategies and how they may best be assisted by the structure of the sermon. Here let me caution against two common approaches which are almost always weak. One is to introduce the sermon with some current issue or event that will arrest the hearer's attention, then devote the body of message to a biblical homily that never really addresses this modern agenda. Do not "use" the modern world merely for illustrative purposes, as if you are borrowing from it but not really talking to it in responsible fashion.

The other dubious approach is to reverse the procedure and begin with a biblical theme, devoting the body of the sermon to its textual or topical treatment, then using the conclusion to "apply" your findings to modern life. The problem here is that such a move comes too late in the sermon for the hearers to work out the proper relationship between the several biblical truths which they have just heard and the many complex worlds in which they daily live.

If it does not take the contemporary challenge seriously enough merely to tack it on to the beginning or the ending of a sermon, how may the preacher construct a more authentically dialogical encounter? Go back to the homiletical formula analyzed above and consider its four parts both in their vertical and their horizontal relationships. This will suggest several ways to put structure in the service of strategy.

Putting Structure in the Service of Strategy

1. When the key need is to clarify some strange biblical teaching that could easily be misunderstood, you may wish to begin with the biblical problem, then show how it made sense in its own world. Then move to our world to find meaningful parallels, concluding with the kind of contemporary response that preserves the original biblical intention. For example, you could show how Paul passionately opposed circumcision in Galatians 5, then explain how this practice had come to function as the badge of Jewish nationalism in the years leading up to the war with Rome. After clarifying Paul's intention to free his worldwide mission from political partisanship that would exclude Gentiles, you could then search for the types of nationalism/nativism/tribalism that restrict mis-

sion outreach today, ending with suggestions as to how the church may offer a salvation purged of any cultural prerequisites. The structure of such a sermon would look like this:

I. The Crisis of Circumcision in the Early Church
   1. Paul's attack on circumcision in Galatians 5
   2. The role of circumcision in Jewish exclusiveness
II. Hindrances to a Universal Gospel Today
   1. Cultural barriers in WASP-Christianity
   2. Proclaiming salvation for all in Christ alone

2. In the previous example, we started with the biblical situation because circumcision is not an issue in American Christianity. There are times, however, when we may need to begin in the past precisely because some present issue is too controversial to be faced directly. I well remember when many Deep South congregations in the 1950s and 1960s could not confront the evils of racial segregation realistically because they felt that their whole way of life was being threatened. This became a good time to talk about the ancient Samaritans, contrasting the revolutionary attitude of Jesus (John 4:1-42) with the prevailing Jewish prejudices of that day. Only then was it time to talk about contemporary Christian attitudes toward despised minorities in the ghettos of America. The structure here inverts the sequence in each section as compared with the previous example:

I. The Early Christian Breakthrough in Samaria (Acts 1:8)
   1. The bitter history of Jewish-Samaritan hostilities
   2. The transformation wrought by Jesus (compare Luke 9:51-56 and Acts 8:14-17)
II. The Gospel of Modern "Samaritans" in Our Midst
   1. Patterns of ancient prejudice in the church today
   2. Learning to discover the "Samaritans" in our community

3. Not only may we reverse the order in which we treat the homiletical formula viewed vertically, we may do the same horizontally by treating the modern scene first and then the biblical scene. In this age of media saturation, some events so dominate the news that they are on everyone's mind. It would have been almost unthinkable to go to church on the Sunday after John F. Kennedy's assassination, or after Neil Armstrong landed on the moon, or after a nuclear reactor exploded at Chernobyl and not hear a sermon that spoke directly to such momentous developments. For example, when the Berlin Wall fell in November, 1989, I preached a sermon that first traced the ugly history of that barrier from its erection in 1961, then described the irresistible yearning for freedom that finally breached its defenses without a shot being fired. After asking the congregation to live behind the Iron Curtain for half the sermon, we then turned to repressive structures in the first century (for instance, male/female, slave/free, clergy/laity) and ended by showing

how Jesus achieved "break-throughs" by His ministry of "peace" (Eph. 2:14). Note how this structure rearranges the formula:

I. The Wall Came Tumbling Down
   1. The Berlin Wall: an epitaph (1961-1989)
   2. The triumph of freedom over bondage
II. The New Joshua as Wall-Breaker
   1. The wall-weary world of ancient Palestine
   2. Jesus as the reconciler of enemies then and now

4. The first three examples are not meant to imply that every sermon which takes modern life seriously must have two parts, then/now or now/then, with the relation of Word and world variously arranged under each part. When preaching to a congregation already deeply interested in the Bible, it is possible to devote the entire sermon to the teachings of Scripture and yet show how important it is to adapt religion to the needs of the day. This approach is especially helpful in presenting the New Testament as the fulfillment of the Old Testament. For example, we all know that temple, priesthood, and sacrifice played a dominant role in Old Testament religion, yet disappeared almost immediately in New Testament religion. The same kind of transformation reshaped important concepts, for example, Old Covenant/New Covenant, Old Israel/New Israel, Jerusalem below/Jerusalem above. A generic outline designed to show that God's truth does not stand still any more than time stands still—even in the Bible—might look like this:

I. Biblical Truth for an Old Age
   1. The original form of the teaching
   2. The value of this teaching for its day
II. Biblical Truth for a New Age
   1. The limitations of an old teaching to meet the needs of a new day
   2. The new form of the teaching as a fulfillment of the old (compare Matt. 5:17-48)

5. Many preachers prefer to prepare textual or expository sermons with three or more parts corresponding to the main points in the scriptural passage, feeling that this approach anchors their message very directly in the Bible. While this popular method allows the scriptural content to determine the structure of the sermon, such an approach need not ignore the contemporary world.

For example, suppose that I am preaching on how to conquer tragedy by closely following the text in John 9:1-4. The first part might talk about the human approach to tragedy as reflected in the response of the disciples to the man born blind (vv. 1-2), but their debate over "who sinned" could be related to the very same arguments today between conservatives and liberals over individual responsibility versus collective guilt. The second part would contrast the response of Jesus in treating the blind man, not as a problem to be explained by assessing blame, but as a life to be changed for the glory of God (v. 3). That approach can be seen at work in our world today by those willing to light a candle rather than curse the darkness (Abraham Lincoln, Albert Schweitzer, Mother Teresa). Finally, the imperative to work while the opportunity exists (v. 4) could be emphasized by showing how apathy and delay on the part of well-meaning religionists have plunged our inner cities into darkness. In this structure, the biblical point is first discovered from the text but then its contemporary relevance is clearly defined before moving on to the next point.

6. Another popular structure is the topical sermon which treats some theme in light of its constituent parts or by some principle of logical analysis. Here it is not as important to "make room" for the modern world within the structure of the sermon because the topic itself is usually of contemporary interest. For example, this might be a sermon on how to overcome the stress or loneliness or anxiety of modern life by drawing on a number of scripture passages for guidance. The strength of such a message will depend, not only on the forcefulness with which the Christian answer is given but on the clarity and depth with which the human problem is understood. Such insight does not have to be segregated in a separate section of the sermon in order to be effective. Often the shape of the problem is best inferred by indirection, reading between the lines," or hearing as an "overtone" to what is said. George Buttrick, for example, was a master of the quip, the aside, the terse retort which would forcibly remind his hearers that he knew exactly what the world was doing to them even though it was his main business to declare what the gospel could do for them.

What I have been trying to say both here and throughout this chapter is that people come to respect preaching which shows that the preacher does know where they really live—that the preacher is deeply involved in that world himself and not confined to some protective clergy bubble! People want solid answers, but they also want to know that the minister has wrestled with solid questions. In one sense, gaining a profound knowledge of the world in which we work entitles us to proclaim the Word through Whom that world was made, the Word Who gives that world its life and light (John 1:3-4).

Notes

1. Clyde E. Fant, Jr. and William M. Pinson, Jr., *20 Centuries of Great Preaching*, 13 vols. (Waco: Word Books, 1971).
2. Ibid., vol. 1, v.
3. W. R. Inge, *Diary of a Dean* (New York: Macmillan, 1950), 12.
4. Comments on relevance in this section and in the one to follow are drawn from two longer studies by the author: William E. Hull, "The Relevance of the New Testament," *Review and Expositor*, vol. 62, no. 2 (Spring, 1965): 189-200; and "The Theological Task of

Baptists Today," *The Truth that Makes Men Free*, ed. Josef Nordenhaug (Nashville: Broadman Press, 1966), 445-452.

5. This formula, in slightly different form, was suggested by Robert M. Grant, "Commentaries," *Interpretation*, 2:460, 1948, reprinted in Balmer H. Keller and Donald G. Miller, eds., *Tools for Bible Study* (Richmond: John Knox Press, 1956), 105. Grant attributes the formula without documentation, to his teacher, Henry J. Cadbury.

6. Quoted by Heinrich Ott, *Theology and Preaching* (Philadelphia: Westminster, 1965), 12.

7. The problem is accentuated by the large number of free-standing seminaries where neither faculty nor students have any intimate daily contact with those working in other disciplines, such as modern history, psychology, or sociology, whose job it is to study trends in contemporary life. Sad to say, even some divinity schools related to comprehensive universities neglect the opportunity to engage their faculty and students in the full range of intellectual concerns represented across the campus.

8. Notice the indifference to the modern world in the most widely used homiletics textbooks of this generation: David Buttrick, *Homiletic* (Philadelphia: Fortress, 1987); Fred B. Craddock, *Preaching* (Nashville: Abingdon, 1985); H. Grady Davis, *Design for Preaching* (Philadelphia: Fortress, 1958). These manuals almost give the impression that preaching is a self-contained event conceived in the mind of the preacher and completed upon delivery to a congregation as if "the world out there" scarcely exists!

9. For a typical example see James S. Stewart, "The Preacher's World," *Heralds of God* (New York: Charles Scribner's Sons, 1946), 9-57. Most such treatments look at contemporary life through homiletical lenses, searching only for those features of the modern world that obviously merit a sermon (for instance, doubt, despair, loneliness, corruption). Approached in this fashion, the resulting portrait is almost always incomplete, distorted, and pessimistic. Methodologically, it is better to begin with the modern world as it understands its own reality before highlighting those features that seem to deserve a pulpit response.

10. The semi-annual review journal *Homiletic*, which has been available since 1976, contains a brief section in most issues called "Human Sciences and Culture" which provides three or four entries on modern life of interest to scholars in the Academy of Homiletics. However, almost none of the works cited are written to help preachers or to relate preaching to the contemporary world. The two standard bibliographies on homiletics each contain two sections on "The Setting of the Sermon," one "Liturgical" and the other "Special Occasions," but both consider only the type of worship service in which preaching takes place. Out of 4,035 listings, there is virtually nothing that relates preaching to the modern condition! See William Toohey and William D. Thompson, eds., *Recent Homiletical Thought: A Bibliography, 1935-1965* (Nashville: Abingdon, 1967); and A. Duane Litfin and Haddon W. Robinson, eds., *Recent Homiletical Thought: An Annotated Bibliography, 1966-1979* (Grand Rapids: Baker, 1983). Not surprisingly, this chapter was not a part of this book as originally projected but was added as a result of my pleadings by an editor willing to risk a topic almost never treated anywhere in the literature on preaching.

11. Jack Salzman, ed., *American Studies: An Annotated Bibliography*, 4 vols. (New York: Cambridge University Press, 1986, 1990).

12. Alexis de Tocqueville, *Democracy in America*, 2 vols. (New York: Alfred A. Knopf, 1945). For the background of this landmark study, see James J. Schleifer, *The Making of Tocqueville's Democracy in America* (Chapel Hill: University of North Carolina Press, 1980); and Richard Reeves, *American Journey: Traveling with Tocqueville in Search of Democracy in America* (New York: Simon and Schuster, 1982). On the life of the author, see André Jardin, *Tocqueville: A Biography* (New York: Farrar, Strauss, and Giroux, 1988).

13. On the impact of the Civil War on American life, see James M. McPherson, *Battle Cry of Freedom: The Civil War Era* (New York: Oxford University Press, 1988); and *Abraham Lincoln and the Second American Revolution* (New York: Oxford University Press, 1990). On the impact of the two world wars on global history, see Paul Johnson, *Modern Times: The World from the Twenties to the Eighties* (New York: Harper & Row, 1983).

14. For a Christian critique of such trends, built on his earlier *The Mustard Seed Conspiracy* (1981), see Tom Sire, *Wild Hope* (Dallas: Word, 1991).

15. The most valuable publication of the World Future Society is a compact bibliograph-

ical review, *Future Survey*. It also publishes a scholarly journal, *Futures Research Quarterly*, and a popular periodical, *The Futurist*. Also helpful and dependable are the more business-oriented projections of Peter Drucker in such works as *The New Realities* (New York: Harper & Row, 1989).

16. John Naisbitt, *Megatrends: Ten New Directions Transforming Our Lives* (New York: Warner, 1982); and with Patricia Aburdene, *Megatrends 2000: Ten New Directions for the 1990s* (New York: William Morrow, 1990). Alvin Toffler, *Future Shock* (New York: Random House, 1970); *The Third Wave* (New York: William Morrow, 1980); *PowerShift* (New York: Bantam, 1990).

17. Examples abound, but I select Robert Nisbet, *The Present Age: Progress and Anarchy in Modern America* (New York: Harper & Row, 1988) because of its breadth of synthesis in a few pages and the substance it gives to themes often treated superficially by social conservatives.

18. The first volume has been published as *Parting the Waters: America in the King Years, 1954-1963* (New York: Simon and Schuster, 1988). The second volume, to be titled *Pillar of Fire*, will span "the LBJ years, the agony of Vietnam, and the eclipse of American liberalism" (publisher's announcement).

19. This pivotal period has been the object of intense analysis. See Tom Shachtman, *Decade of Shocks: Dallas to Watergate, 1963-1974* (New York: Poseidon, 1983); and Charles R. Morris, *A Time of Passion: America 1960-1980* (New York: Harper & Row, 1984). More mature assessments of Vietnam are just beginning to appear. See Loren Baritz, *Backfire: A History of How American Culture Led Us into Vietnam and Made Us Fight the Way We Did* (New York: William Morrow, 1985).

20. The literature on the New Right is already enormous. For a sampling, see Sidney Blumenthal, *The Rise of the Counter-Establishment: From Conservative Ideology to Political Power* (New York: Times Books, 1986); and Jerome L. Himmelstein, *To the Right: The Transformation of American Conservatism* (Berkeley: University of California Press, 1990). For an analysis of the resulting ideological polarization, see James Davison Hunter, *Culture Wars: The Struggle to Define America* (New York: Basic Books, 1991). An audit of the Reagan years is just beginning. See Haynes Johnson, *Sleepwalking through History: America in the Reagan Years* (New York: W. W. Norton, 1991); and Lou Cannon, *President Reagan: The Role of a Lifetime* (New York: Simon and Schuster, 1991).

21. On Sunday evening July 15, 1979, following a ten-day "domestic summit" at Camp David, President Jimmy Carter addressed the citizenry on a "crisis of confidence" which he attributed to a "national malaise." Not many of his hearers were prepared to accept charges of worshipping "self-indulgence and consumption" and the speech was vigorously rejected, especially by presidential aspirants and media pundits. It is interesting that this is exactly the diagnosis that dominates interpretations of the early nineties (for instance, *Future Survey*, vol. 14, no. 1 (January, 1992.):1). Compare John Taylor, "Nervous About the Nineties: The New Angst," *New York*, June 20, 1988, 28-35; Molly ONeill, "Words to Survive Life With: None of This, None of That," *New York Times*, May 27, 1990, 1-Y, 14-Y; David R. Gergen, "An Age of Indifference," *U.S. News & World Report*, June 25, 1990, 68.

22. For a recent overview of regional distinctives, see Joel Garreau, *The Nine Nations of North America* (Boston: Houghton Mifflin, 1981), which is regrettably weak on Dixie (128-166). Literature on the South is enormous but perhaps more evocative than on any other region. Just as American studies begin with de Tocqueville, modern Southern studies begin with W. J. Cash, *The Mind of the South* (New York: Alfred A. Knopf, 1941). On the regional self-consciousness of the South, see Carl N. Degler, *Place Over Time: The Continuity of Southern Distinctiveness* (Baton Rouge: Louisiana State University Press, 1977). A convenient guide to the riches of Southern studies is provided by three one-volume encyclopedias: David C. Roller and Robert W. Twyman, eds., *The Encyclopedia of Southern History* (Baton Rouge: Louisiana State University Press, 1979); Charles Reagan Wilson and William Ferris, eds., *Encyclopedia of Southern Culture* (Chapel Hill: University of North Carolina Press, 1989); Samuel S. Hill, ed., *Encyclopedia of Religion in the South* (Macon: Mercer University Press, 1984).

23. For an introduction to the debate over the morality of mass culture, see Patrick Brantlinger, *Bread & Circuses: Theories of Mass Culture as Social Decay* (Ithaca: Cornell Univer-

sity Press, 1983). For an example of insightful analysis in this area, see Marshall W. Fishwick, *Seven Pillars of Poplar Culture* (Westport, Conn: Greenwood Press, 1985).

24. Vance Packard, *The Hidden Persuaders* (New York: David McKay, 1957); *The Status Seekers* (New York: David McKay, 1959); *The Waste Makers* (New York: David McKay, 1960); *The Pyramid Climbers* (New York: McGraw-Hill, 1962); *The Naked Society* (New York: David McKay, 1964); *The Sexual Wilderness* (New York: David McKay, 1968); *A Nation of Strangers* (New York: David McKay, 1972); *The People Shapers* (Boston: Little, Brown, 1977); *Our Endangered Children* (Boston: Little, Brown, 1983); and *The Ultra Rich* (Boston: Little, Brown, 1989).

25. Popular surveys in the generation just ending include Henry Steele Commager, *The American Mind: An Interpretation of American Thought and Character Since the 1880's* (New Haven: Yale University Press, 1950); and Max Lerner, *America as a Civilization* (New York: Simon and Schuster, 1957). More recent probes are more pessimistic. See Marvin Harris, *America Now: The Anthropology of a Changing Culture* (New York: Simon and Schuster, 1982); and Michael Crozier, *The Trouble with America* (Berkeley: University of California Press, 1984).

26. On civil religion, see Robert N. Bellah, *Beyond Belief* (New York: Harper & Row, 1970); and *The Broken Covenant* (New York: Seabury, 1975). On individualism and communitarianism see Robert N. Bellah and others, *Habits of the Heart* (Berkeley: University of California Press, 1985); and *The Good Society* (New York: Alfred A. Knopf, 1991).

27. William H. Whyte, Jr., *The Organization Man* (New York: Simon and Schuster, 1956); Paul Leinberger and Bruce Tucker, *The New Individualists: The Generation After The Organization Man* (New York: HarperCollins, 1991).

28. Under the general editorship of Philippe Ariès and George Duby, *A History of Private Life*, 5 vols., covers the twenty centuries from Pagan Rome to the present (Cambridge: Belknap Press, 1987-1991). For an historical/psychological interpretation, see Christopher Lasch, *The Culture of Narcissism: American Life in an Age of Diminishing Expectations* (New York: W. W. Norton, 1978); and *The Minimal Self: Psychic Survival in Troubled Times* (New York: W. W. Norton, 1984). For a more sociological approach, see Daniel Yankelovich, *New Rules: Searching for Self-Fulfillment in a World Turned Upside Down* (New York: Random House, 1981); and Joseph Veroff, Elizabeth Douvan, and Richard A. Kulka, *The Inner American: A Self-Portrait from 1957 to 1976* (New York: Basic Books, 1981). For a cultural analysis, see Philip Slater, *The Pursuit of Loneliness*, 3d ed. (Boston: Beacon Press, 1990); and Peter Clecak, *America's Quest for the Ideal Self: Dissent and Fulfillment in the 60s and 70s* (New York: Oxford University Press, 1983).

29. Arnold Mitchell, *The Nine American Lifestyles: Who We Are and Where We're Going* (New York: Macmillan, 1983).

30. Martin E. Marty, *The Irony of It All, 1893-1919*, vol. 1 in *Modern American Religion* (Chicago: University of Chicago Press, 1986).

31. T. J. Jackson Lears, *No Place of Grace: Antimodernism and the Transformation of American Culture, 1880-1920* (New York: Pantheon Books, 1981).

32. To cite but two ministerial examples in a vast field: Robert Moats Miller, in *Harry Emerson Fosdick: Preacher, Pastor, Prophet* (New York: Oxford University Press, 1985), shows how his subject's life was a prism refracting every hue of American culture from late Victorianism (which Fosdick never fully abandoned) to post-World War II reconstructionism. Marshall Frady and William Martin have told the story of Billy Graham in such a way that it illumines the interaction of neo-evangelicalism and American culture from mid-century to the present. See Marshall Frady, *Billy Graham: A Parable of American Righteousness* (Boston: Little, Brown, 1979); and William Martin, *A Prophet with Honor: The Billy Graham Story* (New York: William Morrow, 1991).

33. Arthur M. Schlesinger, Jr., *The Cycles of American History* (Boston: Houghton Mifflin, 1986), 23-48.

34. See David E. Shi, *The Simple Life: Plain Living and High Thinking in Americana Culture* (New York: Oxford University Press, 1985); Lewis H. Lapham, *Money and Class in America* (New York: Weidenfeld & Nicolson, 1988); James Lincoln Collier, *The Rise of Selfishness in America* (New York: Oxford University Press, 1991); and Warren Johnson, *The Future Is Not What It Used to Be: Returning to Traditional Values in an Age of Scarcity* (New York: Dodd, Mead, 1985).

35. General parallels between the 1920s and the 1980s are obvious in Kenneth K. Bailey, *Southern White Protestantism in the Twentieth Century* (New York: Harper & Row, 1964), even though the book was written years before the eighties! Striking similarities between the 1920s and the 1980s in the SBC are anticipated by James J. Thompson, *Tried as by Fire: Southern Baptists and the Religious Controversies of the 1920s* (Macon: Mercer University Press, 1982).

36. Robert T. Handy, "The American Religious Depression, 1925-1935," *Church History*, vol. 29, no. 1 (1960): 3-16.

37. On the distinction between what the Bible *meant* and what it *means*, the preacher should ponder deeply the famous article by Krister Stendahl, "Biblical Theology, Contemporary," *The Interpreter's Dictionary of the Bible*, vol. 1. (Nashville: Abingdon Press, 1962) 418-432.

38. Let me illustrate using the Gospel of Mark. At the beginning of this century, the standard commentary of Henry Barclay Swete (1898) was a treasure-trove of close linguistic analysis, patristic parallels, and astute exegetical insights, but the reader learns almost nothing about the kerygmatic character of the text, about how Mark was being "preached" and what issues were being addressed. The impact of form criticism can begin to be seen in Rawlinson (1925) and Branscomb (1937), becoming an explicit methodology in the encyclopedic commentary of Vincent Taylor (1952) but still not being utilized to bring out the full kerygmatic implications of the text. Only in more recent treatments by Schweizer (1970), Lane (1974), Anderson (1976), and Guelich (1989) has form criticism, supplemented by redaction criticism, enabled the exposition to become truly life-centered. With the innovative work of Ched Myers, *Binding the Strong Man: A Political Reading of Mark's Story of Jesus* (Maryknoll, NY: Orbis, 1988) we come full circle and intentionality threatens to overwhelm exegesis.

Part IX Resources for Preaching

Billy Graham (1918–)
"Preacher to the World"

William Franklin (Billy) Graham has preached to more persons than any Christian preacher in history, both in the United States and around the globe.

Born in North Carolina, young Graham made a commitment to Christ in a tent revival. While a student at a Florida Bible college, he felt God's call to preach and began to practice alone in the woods near campus. After further education at Wheaton College, he became a pastor and became involved in a radio program which spread his popularity. Invited to become an evangelist with Youth for Christ, Graham began preaching to increasingly larger crowds.

Graham's 1949 Los Angeles crusade propelled him to national attention, and major crusades followed in the largest cities throughout the United States and around the world—a ministry of mass evangelism that has continued for more than four decades. Such is Graham's reputation and recognition around the globe that when formerly Communist nations were again opened to the Gospel in the late 1980s and early 1990s, Graham was normally the first invited to preach.

While his sermons are not noted for eloquence in the sense of many other great preachers, they are marked by a forceful and direct proclamation of the Gospel. His sermons are simple, clear, and well illustrated, often with items drawn directly from the day's newspaper headlines. In recent years, Graham has also more readily discussed the implications of Christian faith on various social issues of the day.

Through his crusades, television, radio and other media, Billy Graham has been an effective and faithful spokesman for Christ to the entire world.

51

Richard Allen Bodey
Professor of Practical Theology
Trinity Evangelical Divinity School
Deerfield, Illinois

Bibliography

I. THE PREACHER

Adams, Jay E. *Shepherding God's Flock: A Preacher's Handbook on Pastoral Ministry*. (3 vols. in 1). Grand Rapids: Baker, 1979.

Garvie, Alfred E. *The Christian Preacher*. New York: Scribner, 1928.

Geest, Hans van der. *Presence in the Pulpit: The Impact of Personality in Preaching*. Translated by Douglas W. Stott. Atlanta: John Knox, 1982.

Humbert of Romans. *Treatise on Preaching*. Edited by Walter M. Conlon. Westminster, MD: Newman, 1951.

Jabusch, Willard Francis. *The Person in the Pulpit: Preaching as Caring*. Nashville: Abingdon, 1980.

Jenkins, Daniel T. *The Gift of Ministry*. London: Faber & Faber, 1947.

John Chrysostom, St. *On the Priesthood*. New York: Macmillan, 1955.

Morgan, G. Campbell. *The Ministry of the Word*. 1919. Reprint. Grand Rapids: Baker, 1970.

Stott, John R. W. *The Preacher's Portrait*. Grand Rapids: Eerdmans, 1961.

Switzer, David K. *Pastor, Preacher, Person: Developing a Pastoral Ministry in Depth*. Nashville: Abingdon, 1979.

Turnbull, Ralph G. *A Minister's Obstacles*. Rev. ed. Grand Rapids: Baker, 1972.

II. BIBLICAL AND THEOLOGICAL FOUNDATIONS FOR PREACHING

Allen, Ronald J. *Contemporary Biblical Interpretation For Preaching*. Valley Forge: Judson, 1984.

Beaudeau, John William, Jr. *Paul's Theology of Preaching*. Macon: Mercer University Press, 1988.

Best, Ernest. *From Text to Sermon: Responsible Use of the New Testament in Preaching*. Atlanta: John Knox, 1978.

Clowney, Edmund P. *Preaching and Biblical Theology*. Grand Rapids: Eerdmans, 1961.

Dodd, C. H. *The Apostolic Preaching and Its Developments*. 1936. Reprint. Grand Rapids: Baker, 1980.
Fisher, Wallace E. *Who Dares to Preach: The Challenge of Biblical Preaching*. Minneapolis: Augsburg, 1979.
Fuller, Reginald H. *The Use of the Bible in Preaching*. Philadelphia: Fortress, 1981.
Grasso, Domenico. *Proclaiming God's Message: A Study in the Theology of Preaching*. Notre Dame: University of Notre Dame Press, 1965.
Greidanus, Sidney. *The Modern Preacher and the Ancient Text: Interpreting and Preaching Biblical Literature*. Grand Rapids: Eerdmans, 1988.
———. *Sola Scriptura: Problems and Principles in Preaching Historical Texts*. Toronto: Wedge, 1970.
Hayes, John H., series ed. *Knox Preaching Guides* (on individual biblical books). Atlanta: John Knox; Louisville: John Knox/Westminster, 1981-.
Jungmann, Josef A. *The Good News, Yesterday and Today*. New York: Sadlier, 1962. Adapted translation of *Die Frobotschaft*, 1936.
Kaiser, Walter C., Jr. *The Old Testament in Contemporary Preaching*. Grand Rapids: Baker, 1973.
———. *Toward an Exegetical Theology: Biblical Exegesis for Preaching and Teaching*. Grand Rapids: Baker, 1981.
Keck, Leander E. *The Bible in the Pulpit: The Renewal of Biblical Preaching*. Nashville: Abingdon, 1978.
Knox, John. *The Integrity of Preaching*. Nashville: Abingdon, 1957.
Lischer, Richard. *A Theology of Preaching: The Dynamics of Preaching*. Nashville, Abingdon, 1981.
Marcel, Pierre Charles. *The Relevance of Preaching*. Translated by Rob Roy McGregor. 1963. Reprint. Grand Rapids: Baker, 1975.
Mays, James Luther, series ed. *Interpretation: A Bible Commentary for Teaching and Preaching*. Atlanta: John Knox; Louisville: John Knox/Westminster, 1982-.
Mounce, Robert H. *The Essential Nature of New Testament Preaching*. Grand Rapids: Eerdmans, 1960.
Ott, Heinrich. *Theology and Preaching*. Translated by Harold Knight. Philadelphia: Westminster, 1965.
Patte, Daniel. *Preaching Paul*. Philadelphia: Fortress, 1984.
Philibert, Michael. *Christ's Preaching and Ours*. London: Edinburgh House, 1963.
Rust, Eric Charles. *The Word and Words: Towards a Theology of Preaching*. Macon: Mercer University Press, 1982.
Scherer, Paul. *The Word God Sent*. 1965. Reprint. Grand Rapids: Baker, 1977.
Smith, Dwight Moody. *Interpreting the Gospels for Preaching*. Philadelphia: Fortress, 1980.
Thompson, Claude H. *Theology of the Kerygma: A Study in Primitive Preaching*. Englewood Cliffs, NJ: Prentice-Hall, 1962.
Thompson, William D. *Preaching Biblically: Exegesis and Interpretation*. Nashville: Abingdon, 1981.
Von Rad, Gerhard. *Biblical Interpretation in Preaching*. Translated by John E. Steely. Nashville: Abingdon, 1977.
White, Richard C. *Biblical Preaching: How to Find and Remove the Barriers*. St. Louis: Christian Board of Publishing, 1988.
Wilder, Amos N. *Early Christian Rhetoric: The Language of the Gospel*. Cambridge, MA: Harvard University Press, 1971.
Wolf, Hans Walter. *Old Testament and Christian Preaching*. Philadelphia: Fortress, 1986.

Worley, Robert C. *Preaching and Teaching in the Earliest Church*. Philadelphia: Westminster, 1967.

III. THE ART OF PREACHING

Adams, Jay E. *Preaching with Purpose: A Comprehensive Textbook on Biblical Preaching*. Phillipsburg, NJ: Presbyterian and Reformed, 1982.
———. *Sermon Analysis: A Preacher's Personal Improvement Textbook and Workbook*. Denver: Accent, 1986.
Barry, James C., comp. *Preaching in Today's World*. Nashville: Broadman, 1984.
Barth, Karl. *Homiletics*. Translated by Geoffrey W. Bromiley and Donald E. Daniels. Louisville: Westminster/John Knox, 1991.
Baumann, J. Daniel. *An Introduction to Contemporary Preaching*. Rev. ed. Grand Rapids: Baker, 1979.
Beale, Lawrence L. *Toward a Black Homiletic*. New York: Vantage, 1978.
Blackwood, Andrew W. *Preaching from the Bible*. 1941. Reprint. Grand Rapids: Baker, 1974.
———. *The Preparation of Sermons*. 1948. Reprint. Grand Rapids: Baker, 1980.
Bodey, Richard Allen, ed. *Inside the Sermon: Thirteen Preachers Discuss Their Methods of Preparing Messages*. Grand Rapids: Baker, 1990.
Bonhoeffer, Dietrich. *Worldly Preaching: Lectures on Homiletics*. Edited and translated, with critical commentary, by Clyde E. Fant. New York: Crossroad, 1991.
Braga, James. *How to Prepare Bible Messages: A Manual on Homiletics for Bible Students*. Portland: Multnomah, 1971.
Broadus, John A. *On the Preparation and Delivery of Sermons*. New York: Armstrong, 1870.
———. 2nd ed. Revised and edited by Edwin C. Dargan. New York: Armstrong, 1901.
———. 3rd ed. Revised and edited by Jesse Barton Weatherspoon. New York: Harper, 1944.
———. 4th ed. Revised and edited by Vernon L. Stanfield. New York: Harper & Row, 1979.
Brown, H. C., Jr., H. Gordon Clinard, and Jesse Northcutt. *Steps to the Sermon*. Nashville: Broadman, 1963.
Buttrick, David. *Homiletics: Moves and Structures*. Philadelphia: Fortress, 1987.
Caemmerer, Richard R. *Preaching for the Church*. St. Louis: Concordia, 1959.
Caldwell, Frank H. *Preaching Angles*. Nashville: Abingdon, 1954.
Chappell, Clovis G. *Anointed to Preach*. Nashville: Abingdon, 1951.
Claude, Jean. *An Essay on the Composition of a Sermon*. 1779. Reprinted in Charles Simeon, *Expository Outlines on the Whole Bible*. Vol. 21. Grand Rapids: Zondervan, 1956.
Cox, James William. *Preaching*. San Francisco: Harper & Row, 1985.
Craddock, Fred B. *As One Without Authority: Essays on Inductive Preaching*. 1971. Reprint. Nashville: Abingdon, 1979.
———. *Preaching*. Nashville: Abingdon, 1985.
Crum, Milton, Jr. *Manual on Preaching: A New Process Of Sermon Development*. Valley Forge: Judson, 1977.
Dargan, E. C. *The Art of Preaching in the Light of Its History*. New York: Doran, 1922.
Davis, H. Grady. *Design for Preaching*. Philadelphia: Fortress, 1958.
Delnay, Robert G. *Fire in Your Pulpit*. Schaumburg, IL: Regular Baptist Press, 1990.

Drakeford, John W. *Humor in Preaching*. Grand Rapids: Zondervan, 1986.
Edwards, Otis Carl, Jr. *Elements of Homiletic: A Method for Preparing to Preach*. New York: Pueblo, 1982.
Eslinger, Richard L. *A New History: Living Options in Homiletic Method*. Nashville: Abingdon, 1987.
Fant, Clyde E. *Preaching for Today*. Rev. ed. New York: Harper & Row, 1987.
Farra, Harry. *The Sermon Doctor: Prescriptions for Successful Preaching*. Grand Rapids: Baker, 1989.
Francis de Sales, St. *On the Preacher and Preaching*. Translated with introduction and notes by John K. Ryan. New York: Regnery, 1964.
Freeman, Harold. *Variety in Biblical Preaching: Innovative Techniques and Fresh Forms*. Waco: Word, 1987.
Hall, E. Eugene, and James L. Heflin. *Proclaim the Word: The Bases of Preaching*. Nashville: Broadman, 1985.
Hoefler, Richard Carl. *Creative Preaching and Oral Writing*. Lima, OH: C.S.S., 1978.
Hostetler, Michael J. *Introducing the Sermon: The Art of Compelling Beginnings*. Grand Rapids: Zondervan, 1986.
Howard, J. Grant. *Creativity in Preaching*. Grand Rapids: Zondervan, 1987.
Hunt, Ernest Edward. *Sermon Struggles: Four Methods of Sermon Preparation*. New York: Seabury, 1982.
John Wesley on Pulpit Oratory. Revised and abridged by Ross E. Price. Kansas City, MO: Beacon Hill, 1955.
Jones, Ilion T. *Principles and Practice of Preaching*. 1956. Reprint. Nashville: Abingdon, 1974.
Killinger, John. *Fundamentals of Preaching*. Philadelphia: Fortress, 1985.
Knoche, H. Gerard. *The Creative Task: Writing the Sermon*. St. Louis: Concordia, 1977.
Kooienga, William H. *Elements of Style for Preaching*. Grand Rapids: Zondervan, 1989.
Larsen, David L. *The Anatomy of Preaching: Identifying the Issues in Preaching Today*. Grand Rapids: Baker, 1986.
Lenski, C. H. *The Sermon: Its Homiletical Construction*. 1927. Reprint. Grand Rapids: Baker, 1968.
Lewis, Ralph L., and Gregg Lewis. *Learning to Preach Like Jesus*. Westchester, IL: Crossway, 1989.
Lischer, Richard. *Theories of Preaching: Selected Readings in the Homiletical Tradition*. Durham: Labyrinth, 1987.
Lloyd-Jones, D. Martyn, *Preaching and Preachers*. Grand Rapids: Zondervan, 1971.
Logan, Samuel T., Jr., ed. *The Preacher and Preaching: Reviving the Art in the Twentieth Century*. Phillipsburg, NJ: Presbyterian & Reformed, 1986.
Luccock, Halford E. *In the Minister's Workshop*. 1944. Reprint. Grand Rapids: Baker, 1977.
Macartney, Clarence Edward. *Preaching Without Notes*. 1946. Reprint. Grand Rapids: Baker, 1976.
Martin, O. Dean. *Invite: Preaching for Response*. Nashville: Discipleship Resources, 1987.
Massey, James Earl. *Designing the Sermon: Order and Movement in Preaching*. Nashville: Abingdon, 1980.
Mawhinney, Bruce. *Preaching with Freshness*. Eugene, OR: Harvest House, 1991.
Miller, Calvin. *Spirit, Word, and Story: A Philosophy of Preaching*. Waco: Word, 1989.

Mitchell, Henry H. *Celebration and Experience in Preaching*. Nashville: Abingdon, 1990.
Perry, Lloyd M. *Biblical Preaching for Today's World*. Rev. ed. Chicago: Moody, 1990.
Piper, John. *The Supremacy of God in Preaching*. Grand Rapids: Baker, 1990.
Pitt-Watson, Ian. *A Primer for Preachers*. Grand Rapids: Baker, 1986.
Radecke, Mark William. *In Many and Various Ways: Explorations in Sermonic Form*. Lima, OH: C.S.S., 1985.
Reierson, Gary B. *The Art in Preaching: The Intersection of Theology, Worship, and Preaching with the Arts*. Lanham, MD: University Press of America, 1988.
Reu, Johann Michael. *Homiletics: A Manual of the Theory and Practice of Preaching*. Translated by Albert Steinhaeuser. 1922. Reprint. Grand Rapids: Baker, 1967.
Roen, William H. *The Inward Ear: A Sermon Evaluation Method for Preachers and Hearers of the Word*. Washington, DC: Alban Institute, 1989.
Rossow, Francis C. *Preaching the Creative Gospel Creatively*. St. Louis: Concordia, 1983.
Sangster, William Edwin. *The Approach to Preaching*. 1952. Reprint. Grand Rapids: Baker, 1974.
———. *Power in Preaching*. 1958. Reprint. Grand Rapids: Baker, 1976.
Sittler, Joseph. *The Anguish of Preaching*. Philadelphia: Fortress, 1966.
Skinner, Craig. *The Teaching Ministry of the Pulpit: Its History, Theology, Psychology, and Practice for Today*. Grand Rapids: Baker, 1973.
Sleeth, Ronald E. *God's Word and Our Words: Basic Homiletics*. Atlanta: John Knox, 1986.
Spring, Gardiner. *The Power of the Pulpit*. 1866. Reprint. Edinburgh: Banner of Truth, 1986.
Spurgeon, C. H. *Lectures to My Students*. Series 1-3. 1894. Reprint. Grand Rapids: Zondervan, 1955.
Stevenson, Dwight E. *In the Biblical Preacher's Workshop*. Nashville: Abingdon, 1967.
Stott, John R. W. *Between Two Worlds: The Art of Preaching in the Twentieth Century*. Grand Rapids: Eerdmans, 1982.
Taylor, Gardner, C. *How Shall They Preach?* Elgin: Progressive Baptist Publishing House, 1977.
Turnbull, Ralph G., ed. *Baker's Dictionary of Practical Theology*. Grand Rapids: Baker, 1967.
———. *The Preacher's Heritage, Task, and Resources*. Grand Rapids: Baker, 1968.
Ward, Ronald A. *Royal Sacrament: The Preacher and His Message*. London: Marshall, Morgan & Scott, 1958.
Wardlaw, Don M., ed. *Preaching Biblically: Creating Sermons in the Shape of Scripture*. Philadelphia: Westminster, 1983.
Whitesell, Faris D., and Lloyd M. Perry. *Variety in Your Preaching*. Westwood, NJ: Revell, 1954.
Wilson, Paul Scott. *Imagination of the Heart: New Understanding in Preaching*. Nashville: Abingdon, 1989.
Young, Robert D. *Be Brief About It: Clues to Effective Preaching*. Philadelphia: Westminster, 1981.

IV. TYPES OF SERMONS

Abbey, Merrill R. *Living Doctrine in a Vital Pulpit*. Nashville; Abingdon, 1965.
Baab, Otto J. *Prophetic Preaching: A New Approach*. Nashville, Abingdon, 1958.

Bennett, Bill. *Thirty Minutes to Raise the Dead: How You Can Preach Your Best Sermon Yet - This Sunday* (expository preaching). Nashville: Nelson, 1991.
Blackwood, Andrew W. *Biographical Preaching for Today*. Nashville: Abingdon, 1954.
———. *Doctrinal Preaching for Today*. Nashville: Abingdon, 1946.
———. *Expository Preaching for Today*. Nashville: Abingdon, 1953.
Brown, David Mark. *Dramatic Narrative in Preaching*. Valley Forge: Judson, 1981.
Carl, William J. *Preaching Christian Doctrine*. Philadelphia: Fortress, 1984.
Coleman, Richard J. *Gospel-Telling: The Art and Theology of Children's Sermons*. Grand Rapids: Eerdmans, 1982.
Cox, James W., ed. *Biblical Preaching: An Expositor's Treasury*. Philadelphia: Westminster, 1983.
DeBrand, Roy. *Guide to Biographical Preaching*. Nashville: Broadman, 1988.
Ellingsen, Mark. *Doctrine and Word: Theology in the Pulpit*. Atlanta: John Knox, 1983.
———. *The Integrity of Biblical Narrative: Story in Theology and Proclamation*. Minneapolis: Augsburg Fortress, 1990.
Holbert, John C. *Preaching Old Testament: Proclamation and Narrative in the Hebrew Bible*. Nashville: Abingdon, 1991.
Horne, Chevis, T. *Preaching the Great Themes of the Bible: Stimulating Resources for Doctrinal Preaching*. Nashville: Broadman, 1986.
Howe, Reuel L. *The Miracle of Dialogue*. New York: Seabury, 1963.
———. *Partners in Preaching: Clergy and Laity in Dialogue*. New York: Seabury, 1967.
Koller, Charles W. *Expository Preaching Without Notes*. Grand Rapids: Baker, 1962.
Larsen, David L. *The Joyful Sound: Evangelistic Preaching Today*. Westchester, IL: Crossway, 1992.
Leavell, Roland Q. *Prophetic Preaching Then and Now*. Grand Rapids: Baker, 1963.
Liefeld, Walter L. *New Testament Exposition: From Text to Sermon*. Grand Rapids: Zondervan, 1984.
Lowry, Eugene L. *Doing Time in the Pulpit: The Relationship Between Narrative and Preaching*. Nashville: Abingdon, 1985.
———. *The Homiletical Plot: The Sermon as Narrative Art Form*. Atlanta: John Knox, 1980.
———. *How to Preach a Parable: Designs for Narrative Sermons*. Nashville: Abingdon, 1989.
MacLennan, David A. *Pastoral Preaching*. Philadelphia: Westminster, 1955.
McEachern, Alton H. *Dramatic Monologue Preaching* (with model sermons). Nashville: Broadman, 1984.
Meyer, F. B. *Expository Preaching: Plans and Methods*. 1912. Reprint. Grand Rapids: Baker, 1974.
Perry, Lloyd Merle, and John R. Strubhar. *Evangelistic Preaching*. Chicago: Moody, 1979.
Perry, Lloyd M., and Charles M. Sell. *Speaking to Life's Problems: A Sourcebook for Preaching and Teaching*. Chicago: Moody, 1983.
Robinson, Haddon W. *Biblical Preaching: The Development and Delivery of Expository Messages*. Grand Rapids: Baker, 1980.
Salmon, Bruce C. *Storytelling in Preaching: A Guide to the Theory and Practice*. Nashville: Broadman, 1988.
Shoemaker, H. Stephen. *Retelling the Biblical Story: The Theology and Practice of Narrative Preaching*. Nashville: Broadman, 1988.

Smith, W. Alan. *Children Belong in Worship: A Guide to the Children's Sermon*. St. Louis: Christian Board of Publishing, 1984.
Stanfield, V. L. *Effective Evangelistic Preaching*. Grand Rapids: Baker, 1965.
Steimle, Edmund A., Morris J. Niedenthal, and Charles L. Rice. *Preaching the Story*. Philadelphia: Fortress, 1980.
Stibbs, Alan M. *Expounding God's Word*. London: InterVarsity, 1960.
Stratman, Gary D. *Pastoral Preaching: Timeless Truth for Changing Needs*. Nashville: Abingdon, 1983.
Thompson, William D., and Gordon C. Bennett. *Dialogue Preaching: The Shared Sermon*. Valley Forge: Judson, 1969.
Thulin, Richard L. *The "I" of the Sermon*. Philadelphia: Fortress, 1989.
Walker, Alan. *Standing up to Preach: The Art of Evangelical Preaching*. 1983. Reprinted as *Evangelistic Preaching*. Grand Rapids, Zondervan, 1988.
Whitesell, Faris D. *Evangelistic Preaching and the Old Testament*. Chicago: Moody, 1947.
————. *Power in Expository Preaching*. Westwood, NJ: Revell, 1963.
————. *Preaching on Bible Characters*. Grand Rapids: Baker, 1955.

V. ILLUSTRATION AND APPLICATION

Adams, Jay E. *Truth Applied: Application in Preaching*. Grand Rapids: Zondervan, 1990.
Deffner, Don. *The Real Word for the Real World: Applying the Word to the Needs of People*. St. Louis: Concordia, 1977.
Flynn, Leslie B. *Come Alive with Illustrations: How to Find, Use and File Good Stories for Sermons and Speeches*. Grand Rapids: Baker, 1987.
Hostetler, Michael J. *Illustrating the Sermon*. Grand Rapids: Zondervan, 1989.
Kuhatschek, Jack. *Taking the Guesswork out of Applying the Bible*. Downers Grove: InterVarsity, 1990.
Lehman, Louis Paul. *Put a Door on It! The "How" and "Why" of Sermon Illustrations*. 1975. Reprinted as *How to Find and Develop Effective Illustrations*. Grand Rapids: Kregel, 1985.
Macpherson, Ian. *The Art of Illustrating Sermons*. 1966. Reprint. Grand Rapids: Baker, 1976.
McQuilkin, J. Robertson. *Understanding and Applying the Bible*. Rev. ed. Chicago: Moody, 1992.
Robertson, J. D. *Handbook of Preaching Resources from English Literature*. New York: Macmillan, 1962.
Sangster, William E. *The Craft of Sermon Illustration*. Philadelphia: Westminster, 1950.
Tan, Paul Lee. *Encyclopedia of 7700 Illustrations—Signs of the Times*. Garland, TX: Bible Communications, 1979.

VI. PERSUASION

Bernard, Edmund I. *The Appeal to the Emotions in Preaching*. Westminster, MD: Newman, 1944.
Berkley, James D., ed. *Preaching to Convince*. Waco: Word, 1986.
Ford, Leighton. *The Christian Persuader*. Minneapolis: World Wide Publishers, 1988.
Griffin, Em. *The Mind Changers: The Art of Christian Persuasion*. Wheaton: Tyndale, 1979.
Hendricks, Howard G. *Teaching to Change Lives*. Portland, OR: Multnomah, 1987.

Jackson, Edgar N. *A Psychology for Preaching*. 1961. Reprint. New York: Hawthorn, 1974.
Lewis, Ralph L. *Persuasive Preaching Today*. Wilmore, KY: Ashbury Theological Seminary, 1982.
McLaughlin, Raymond M. *The Ethics of Persuasive Preaching*. Grand Rapids: Baker, 1979.
Sleeth, Ronald E. *Persuasive Preaching*. 1956. Reprint. Berrien Springs, MI: Andrews University Press, 1981.
Walter, Otis M. *Speaking to Inform and Persuade*. 2nd ed. New York: MacMillan, 1982.

VII. COMMUNICATION, RHETORIC, AND DELIVERY

Abbey, Merrill R. *Communication in Pulpit and Parish*. Philadelphia: Westminster, 1980.
Achtemeier, Elizabeth R. *Creative Preaching: Finding the Right Words*. Nashville: Abingdon, 1980.
Adams, Jay E. *Communicating with Twentieth-Century Man*. Phillipsburg, NJ: Presbyterian & Reformed, 1979.
Aristotle. *Rhetoric*. Translated by W. Rhys Roberts. New York: Modern Library, 1954.
———. *Poetics*. Translated by Ingram Bywater. New York: Modern Library, 1954.
Bartow, Charles L. *The Preaching Moment: A Guide to Sermon Delivery*. Nashville: Abingdon, 1980.
Burke, Kenneth. *The Rhetoric of Religion: Studies in Logology*. 1961. Reprint. Berkeley: University of California Press, 1970.
Chartier, Myron R. *Preaching as Communication: An Interpersonal Perspective*. Nashville: Abingdon, 1981.
Cicero on Oratory and Orators. Edited by J. S. Watson. Carbondale: Southern Illinois University Press, 1986.
Davis, Ken. *Secrets of Dynamic Communication: Preparing and Delivering Powerful Speeches*. Grand Rapids: Zondervan, 1991.
Fasol, Al. *Guide to Self-Improvement in Sermon Delivery*. Grand Rapids: Baker, 1983.
Fenelon's Dialogues on Eloquence. Translated by Wilbur Samuel Howell. Princeton: Princeton University Press, 1951.
Flesch, Rudolf. *The Art of Clear Thinking*. 1951. Reprint. Harper Collins, 1973.
Flesch, Rudolf. *The Art of Readable Writing*. Rev. ed. New York: Macmillan, 1986.
———. *How to Write, Speak and Think More Effectively*. New York: NAL-Dutton, 1963.
Garrison, Webb B. *The Preacher and His Audience*. Westwood, NJ: Revell, 1954.
Kennedy, George A. *Classical Rhetoric and Its Christian and Secular Tradition from Ancient to Modern Times*. Chapel Hill: University of North Carolina Press, 1980.
Kraft, Charles H. *Communication Theory for Christian Witness*. Nashville: Abingdon, 1983.
Litfin, Duane. *Public Speaking*. Grand Rapids: Baker, 1981.
Massey, James Earl. *The Sermon in Perspective: Communication and Charisma*. Grand Rapids: Baker, 1976.
Murphy, James J., ed. *A Synoptic History of Classical Rhetoric*. Davis, CA: Hermagoras, 1983.

Nichols, J. Randall. *Building the Word: The Dynamics of Communication and Preaching*. San Francisco: Harper & Row, 1980.
Nichols, Sue. *Words on Target: For Better Christian Communication*. Louisville: Westminster/John Knox, 1963.
Ong, Walter J. *Orality and Literacy: The Technologizing of the Word*. New York: Methuen, 1982.
Perelman, Chaim. *The Realm of Rhetoric*. Notre Dame: University of Notre Dame Press, 1982.
Quintilian. *On the Teaching of Speaking and Writing*. Edited by James J. Murphy. Carbondale: Southern Illinois University Press, 1970.
Reid, Clyde H. *The Empty Pulpit: A Study in Preaching as Communication*. New York: Harper & Row, 1967.
Stevenson, Dwight E., and Charles F. Diehl. *Reaching People from the Pulpit: A Guide to Effective Sermon Delivery*. 1958. Reprint. Grand Rapids: Baker, 1978.
Strunk, William, Jr., and E. B. White. *The Elements of Style*. 3rd ed. New York: Macmillan, 1979.
Vines, Jerry. *A Guide to Effective Sermon Delivery*. Chicago: Moody, 1986.
Weaver, Richard M. *The Ethics of Rhetoric*. Davis, CA: Hermagoras, 1985.
———. *Language Is Sermonic: Richard M. Weaver on the Nature of Rhetoric*. Edited by Richard L. Johannsen, Rennard Strickland, and Ralph T. Eubanks. Baton Rouge: Louisiana State University Press, 1970.
Welsh, Clement. *Preaching in a New Key: Studies in the Psychology of Thinking and Listening*. Philadelphia: United Church Press, 1974.
Whately, Richard. *Elements of Rhetoric*. Edited by Douglas Ehniger. Carbondale: Southern Illinois University Press, 1963.

VIII. PREACHING IN WORSHIP

Babin, David E. *Week in Week out: A New Look at Liturgical Preaching*. New York: Seabury, 1976.
Bass, George M. *The Renewal of Liturgical Preaching*. Minneapolis: Augsburg, 1967.
Bosch, Paul. *The Sermon as Part of the Liturgy*. St. Louis: Concordia, 1977.
Burke, John, ed. *The Sunday Homily: Scriptural and Liturgial Renewal*. Washington, DC: Thomist, 1966.
Coffin, Henry Sloane. *Communion Through Preaching*. New York: Scribner, 1952.
Doyle, Stephen C. *The Gospel in Word and Power: The Biblical Liturgical Homily*. Wilmington: Glazier, 1982.
Fuller, Reginald H. *What Is Liturgical Preaching?* London: SCM, 1957.
Macleod, Donald. *Word and Sacrament: A Preface to Preaching and Worship*. Englewood Cliffs, NJ: Prentice-Hall, 1960.
Rice, Charles L. *The Embodied Word: Preaching as Art and Liturgy*. Minneapolis: Augsburg Fortress, 1991.
Skundlarek, William. *The Word in Worship: Preaching in a Liturgical Context*. Nashville: Abingdon, 1981.
Sloyan, Gerard Stephen. *Worshipful Preaching*. Philadelphia: Fortress, 1984.
Stewart, James S. *Exposition and Encounter: Preaching in the Context of Worship*. Birmingham, England: Berean, 1957.

IX. PLANNED PREACHING, THE CHURCH YEAR, AND OTHER SPECIAL OCCASIONS

Abbey, Merrill R. *The Shape of the Gospel: The Bible Through the Christian Year*. Nashville: Abingdon, 1970.

Asquith, Glenn H. *Preaching According to Plan*. Valley Forge, PA: Judson, 1968.
Blackwood, Andrew W. *Planning a Year's Pulpit Work*. 1952. Reprint. Grand Rapids: Baker, 1975.
Gibson, George M. *Planned Preaching*. Philadelphia: Westminister, 1954.
Johnson, Howard A., ed. *Preaching the Christian Year*. New York: Scribner, 1957.
Long, Thomas G., and Neely Dixon McCarter. *Preaching in and out of Season*. Louisville: Westminster/John Knox, 1990.
Pearce, J. Winston. *Planning Your Preaching*. Nashville: Broadman, 1967.
Steel, David. *Preaching through the Year*. Atlanta: John Knox, 1980.

X. TOPICS OF PREACHING

Achtemeier, Elizabeth. *Preaching About Family Relationship*. Philadelphia: Westminster, 1987.
———. *Preaching from the Old Testament*. Louisville: Westminster/John Knox, 1989.
Adams, Jay E. *Audience Adaptations in the Sermons and Speeches of Paul*. Phillipsburg, NJ: Presbyterian & Reformed, 1976.
Bailey, Raymond. *Jesus the Preacher*. Nashville: Broadman, 1990.
———. *Paul the Preacher*. Nashville: Broadman, 1991.
Blackwood, Andrew W. *Preaching from Prophetic Books*. Nashville: Abingdon, 1951.
———. *Preaching from Samuel*. 1946. Reprint. Grand Rapids: Baker, 1975.
Bond, A. R., *The Master Preacher: A Study of the Homiletics of Jesus*. New York: American Tract Society, 1910.
Capps, Donald. *Pastoral Counseling and Preaching: A Quest for an Integrated Ministry*. Philadelphia: Westminster, 1980.
Colquhoun, Frank. *Preaching on Favourite Hymns*. London: Mowbray, 1986.
Fisher, Wallace E. *Preaching and Parish Renewal*. Nashville: Abingdon, 1966.
Foster, John. *The Preacher's Use of Church History*. Birmingham, England: Berean, 1958.
Handy, Francis J. *Jesus the Preacher*. Nashville: Abingdon, 1949.
Hayden, Eric W. *Preaching Through the Bible* (sermons on each biblical book as a whole). Grand Rapids: Zondervan, 1964.
Hessel, Dieter, ed. *For Creation's Sake: Preaching, Ecology, and Justice*. Philadelphia: Geneva, 1985.
Hughes, Robert. *A Trumpet in Darkness: Preaching to Mourners*. Philadelphia: Fortress, 1985.
Jones, Maurice. *St. Paul the Orator*. London: Hodder & Stoughton, 1910.
Kemmer, Dieter Werner. *Faith and Human Reason: A Study of Paul's Method of Preaching as Illustrated by 1-2 Thessalonians and Acts 17: 2-4*. Leiden, Holland: Brill, 1975.
Killinger, John. *The Centrality of Preaching in the Total Task of the Ministry*. Waco: Word, 1969.
Kinlaw, Dennis F. *Preaching in the Spirit*. Grand Rapids: Zondervan, 1985.
Leggett, Donald A. *Loving God and Disturbing Men: Preaching from the Prophets*. Grand Rapids: Baker, 1990.
Leonard, Bill J. *Word of God Across the Ages: Using Christian History in Preaching* (model sermons). Nashville: Broadman, 1981.
McCabe, Joseph E. *How to Find Time for Better Preaching and Better Pastoring*. Philadelphia: Westminster, 1973.

Mummaw, John R. *Preach the Word: Expository Preaching from the Book of Ephesians.* Scottdale, PA: Herald, 1987.
Murphy-O'Connor, Jerome. *Paul on Preaching.* New York: Sheed & Ward, 1963.
Nichols, J. Randall. *The Restoring Word: Preaching as Pastoral Communication.* San Francisco: Harper & Row, 1987.
Proctor, Samuel D. *Preaching About Crises in the Community.* Philadelphia: Westminster, 1988.
Robertson, A. T. *The Glory of the Ministry: Paul's Exulatation in Preaching.* New York: Revell, 1911.
Sider, Ronald J., and Darrel J. Brubaker, eds. *Preaching on Peace.* Philadelphia: Fortress, 1982.
Sider, Ronald J., and Michael A. King. *Preaching About Life in a Threatening World.* Philadelphia: Westminster, 1987.
Sollitt, Kenneth W. *Preaching from Pictures.* Boston: Wilde, 1938.
Stapleton, John Mason. *Preaching in Demonstration of the Spirit and Power.* Philadelphia: Fortress, 1988.
Stevenson, Dwight E. *Preaching on the Books of the New Testament.* New York: Harper, 1956.
———. *Preaching on the Books of the Old Testament.* New York: Harper, 1961.
Willimon, William H. *Preaching About Conflict in the Local Church.* Philadelphia: Westminster, 1987.
Wagley, Laurence A. *Preaching with the Small Congregation.* Nashville: Abingdon, 1989.
Willimon, William H., and Robert L. Wilson. *Preaching and Worship in the Small Church.* Nashville: Abingdon, 1980.
Young, Robert D. *Religious Imagination: God's Gift to Prophets and Preachers.* Philadelphia: Westminster, 1979.

XI. HISTORY AND SOCIOLOGY OF PREACHING: GROUPS AND PERIODS

Bayley, Peter. *French Pulpit Oratory, 1598-1650: A Study in Themes and Styles, with a Descriptive Catalogue of Printed Texts.* New York: Cambridge University Press, 1980.
Blaikie, W. G. *The Preachers of Scotland from the 6th to the 19th Century.* Edinburgh: T. & T. Clark, 1888.
Blench, J. W. *Preaching in England in the Late Fifteenth and Sixteenth Centuries.* New York: Barnes & Noble, 1964.
Brastow, Lewis O. *Representative Modern Preachers.* 1904. Reprint. Freyport, NY: Books for Libraries, 1968.
Brilioth, Yngve T. *A Brief History of Preaching.* Philadelphia: Fortress, 1965.
———. *Landmarks in the History of Preaching.* London: Society for the Propagation of Christian Knowledge, 1950.
Broadus, John A. *Lectures on the History of Preaching.* New York: Armstrong, 1907.
Dargan, Edwin C. *A History of Preaching.* 2 vols. 1904. Reprint. 2 vols. in 1, Grand Rapids: Baker, 1959.
Davies, Horton. *Varieties of English Preaching, 1900-1960.* Englewood Cliffs, NJ: Prentice-Hall, 1963.
Downey, James. *The Eighteenth Century Pulpit.* Oxford: Clarendon, 1969.
Elliott, Emory. *Power and the Pulpit in Puritan New England.* Princeton: Princeton University Press, 1975.
Friedenberg, Robert V. *"Hear O Israel:" The History of American Jewish Preaching, 1654-1970.* Tuscaloosa: University of Alabama Press, 1989.

Gammie, Alexander. *Preachers I Have Heard*. Glasgow: Pickering & Inglis, 1945.
Hicks, H. Beecher, Jr. *Images of the Black Preacher: The Man Nobody Knows*. Valley Forge: Judson, 1977.
Holland, DeWitte T., ed. *Preaching in American History: Selected Issues in the American Pulpit, 1630-1967*. Nashville: Abingdon, 1969.
———. *The Preaching Tradition: A Brief History*. Nashville: Abingdon, 1980.
———. *Sermons in American History: Selected Issues in the American Pulpit*. Nashville: Abingdon, 1971.
Hood, Edwin Paxton. *The Throne of Eloquence: Great Preachers, Ancient and Modern*. London: Hodder & Stoughton, 1885.
Hoyt, A. S. *The Pulpit and American Life*. New York: Macmillan, 1921.
Hunter, David G., ed. *Preaching in the Patristic Age*. Mahweh, NJ: Paulist, 1989.
Jeffs, Ernest H. *Princes of the Modern Pulpit in England*. Nashville: Cokesbury, n.d.
Jones, Edgar DeWitt. *American Preachers of Today: Intimate Appraisals of Thirty-two Leaders*. 1933. Reprint. Freeport, NY: Books for Libraries, 1971.
———. *Lincoln and the Preachers: How Lincoln Influenced the Preachers and How the Preachers Influenced Lincoln*. New York: Harper, 1948.
Ker, John. *Lectures on the History of Preaching*. Edited by A. R. Macewan. London: Hodder & Stoughton, c. 1890.
Kerr, Hugh T. *Preaching in the Early Church*. New York: Revell, 1942.
Laymon, Charles M. *They Dared to Speak for God: Great Preachers in the Bible*. Nashville: Abingdon, 1974.
Lessenich, Rolf P. *Elements of Pulpit Oratory in Eighteenth-Century England (1600-1800)*. Köln, Germany: Böhlau, 1972.
Marchant, Sir James. *British Preachers*. New York: Putnam, 1928.
Mitchell, Henry H. *Black Preaching*. Philadelphia: Lippincott, 1970.
Mitchell, W. Fraser. *English Pulpit Oratory from Andrewes to Tillotson: A Study of Its Literary Aspects*. London: Society for the Propagation of Christian Knowledge, 1932.
Neale, J. M. *Medieval Preachers and Medieval Preaching*. London: Mozley, 1856.
Newton, Joseph Fort. *Some Living Masters of the Pulpit*. New York: Doran, 1923.
Nicoll, W. Robertson. *Princes of the Church*. London: Hodder & Stoughton, 1921.
Owst, G. R. *Preaching in Medieval England, 1350-1450*. Cambridge: University of Cambridge Press, 1926.
Pattison, T. Harwood. *The History of Christian Preaching*. Philadelphia: American Baptist Publishing Society, 1903.
Petry, Ray C. *Preaching in the Great Tradition: Neglected Chapters in the History of Preaching*. Philadelphia: Westminster, 1950.
Rosenberg, Bruce A. *The Art of the American Folk Preacher*. New York: Oxford University Press, 1970.
Sinclair, Hugh. *Voices of Today: Studies of Representative Modern Preachers*. London: James Clarke, 1912.
Smith, Hilary Dansey. *Preaching in the Spanish Golden Age: A Study of Some Preachers of the Reign of Philip III*. New York: Oxford University Press, 1978.
Smyth, Charles. *The Art of Preaching: A Practical Survey of Preaching in the Church of England, 747-1939*. London: Society for the Propagation of Christian Knowledge, 1953.
Stout, Harry S. *The New England Soul: Preaching and Religious Culture in Colonial New England*. New York: Oxford University Press, 1986.
Szarmach, Paul E., and Bernard F. Huppe, eds. *The Old English Homily and Its Backgrounds*. Albany: State University of NY Press, 1978.

Thompson, Ernest Trice. *Changing Emphases in American Preaching*. Philadelphia: Westminster, 1943.
Turnbull, Ralph G. *A History of Preaching*. Vol. 3, continuing the work of Edwin C. Dargan, vols. 1 and 2. Grand Rapids: Baker, 1974.
Webber, F. R. *A History of Preaching in Britain and America*. 3 vols. Milwaukee: Northwestern, 1952-1957.
Weidman, Judith L. *Women Ministers*. San Francisco: Harper & Row, 1985.
Wiersbe, Warren W. *Listening to the Giants*. Grand Rapids: Baker, 1980.
————. *Walking with the Giants: A Minister's Guide to Good Reading and Great Preaching*. Grand Rapids: Baker, 1976.
Wiersbe, Warren W., and Lloyd M. Perry. *The Wycliffe Handbook of Preaching and Preachers*. Chicago: Moody, 1984.
Wilkinson, William Cleaver. *Modern Masters of Pulpit Discourse*. New York: Funk & Wagnalls, 1905.
Worley, Robert C. *Preaching and Teaching in the Earliest Church*. Philadelphia: Westminster, 1967.

XII. HISTORY OF PREACHING: INDIVIDUAL PREACHERS

Adams, Jay E. *Sense Appeal in the Sermons of Charles Haddon Spurgeon*. Nutley, NJ: Presbyterian & Reformed, 1975.
Attwater, Donald. *St. John Chrysostom: Pastor and Preacher*. London: Harvill, 1959.
Blackwood, James R. *The Soul of Frederick W. Robertson, the Brighton Preacher*. New York: Harper, 1947.
Chamberlin, John S. *Increase and Multiply: Arts-of-Discourse Procedure in the Preaching of Donne*. Chapel Hill: University of North Carolina Press, 1976.
Crocker, Lionel, ed. *Harry Emerson Fosdick's Art of Preaching: An Anthology* (and analyses). Springfield: Thomas, 1971.
————. *Henry Ward Beecher's Speaking Art*. Westwood: Revell, 1937.
Doughty, William. *John Wesley, Preacher*. London: Epworth, 1955.
Gundry, Stanley N. *Love Them In: The Proclamation Theology of D. L. Moody*. Chicago: Moody, 1976.
Hoogstra, Jacob T., ed. *John Calvin, Contemporary Prophet*. Grand Rapids: Baker, 1959.
Jenkins, R. B. *Henry Smith: England's Silver-Tongued Preacher*. Macon, GA: Mercer University Press, 1983.
Kiessling, Elmer C. *The Early Sermons of Luther and Their Relation to the Pre-Reformation Sermons*. 1935. Reprint. New York: AMS, 1971.
Linn, Edmund Holt. *Preaching as Counseling: The Unique Method of Harry Emerson Fosdick*. Valley Forge: Judson, 1966.
Lossky, Nicholas. *Lancelot Andrewes The Preacher, 1555-1626: The Origins of the Mystical Theology of the Church of England*. Translated by Andrew Louth. Oxford: Clarendon, 1991.
McLean, Alexander. *Campbell as a Preacher*. 1908. Reprint. Grand Rapids: Baker, 1955.
Meuser, Fred W. *Luther the Preacher*. Minneapolis: Augsburg, 1983.
Mueller, William R. *John Donne: Preacher*. Princeton: Princeton University Press, 1962.
Nixon, Leroy. *John Calvin: Expository Preacher*. Grand Rapids: Eerdmans, 1950.
Parker, Thomas L. C. *The Oracles of God* (John Calvin's theory of preaching). London: Lutterworth, 1947.
Ray, Charles. *A Marvelous Ministry: The Story of C. H. Spurgeon's Sermons, 1855 to 1905*. Pasadena, TX: Pilgrim, 1985.

Ross, Bob L., comp. *An Introduction to the Life and Ministry of Charles Hadden Spurgeon (1834-1892) and a Catalog of His Sermons and Books*. Pasadena, TX: Pilgrim, 1985.

Ryan, Halford R. *Harry Emerson Fosdick: Persuasive Preacher*. Westport, CT: Greenwood, 1989.

———. *Henry Ward Beecher: Peripatetic Preacher*. Westport, CT: Greenwood, 1990.

Simpson, W. J. Sparrow. *St. Augustine the Preacher*. London: Society for the Propagation of Christian Knowledge, 1912.

Turnbull, Ralph G. *Jonathan Edwards, the Preacher*. Grand Rapids: Baker, 1958.

Wagner, Don M. *The Expository Method of G. Campbell Morgan*. Westwood, NJ: Revell, 1957.

Westra, Helen. *The Minister's Task and Calling in the Sermons of Jonathan Edwards*. Lewiston, NY: Mellen, 1986.

White, W. D. *The Preaching of John Henry Newman*. Philadelphia: Fortress, 1969.

XIII. HISTORY OF PREACHING: HOMILETICAL THEORY

Alan of Lille. *The Art of Preaching*. Translated by Gillian R. Evans. Kalamazoo: Cistercian Publications, 1981.

Augustine, T. *On Christian Doctrine*. Book 4. Translated by D. W. Robertson, Jr. Indianapolis: Bobbs-Merrill, 1958.

Humbert of Romans. *Treatise on Preaching*. Edited by Walter M. Conlon. Westminster, MD: Newman, 1957.

Perkins, William. *The Art of Prophecying*. London: Kyngston, 1607; available on microfilm, Ann Arbor, MI: University Microfilms International.

XIV. SERMON ANTHOLOGIES

Allen, R. Earl, and Joel Gregory, comps. *Southern Baptist Preaching Today*. Nashville: Broadman, 1987.

———. *Southern Baptist Preaching Yesterday*. Nashville: Broadman, 1991.

Atkins, Glenn, ed. *Master Sermons of 19th Century*. Chicago: Willett, Clark, 1940.

Bayley, Peter, ed. *Selected Sermons of the French Baroque, 1600-1650*. New York: Garland, 1982.

Benn, J. Solomon, comp. *Preaching in Ebony*. Grand Rapids: Baker, 1981.

Blackwood, Andrew W., ed. *The Protestant Pulpit: An Anthology of Master Sermons from the Reformation to Our Own Day*. Nashville: Abingdon-Cokesbury, 1947.

Chandos, John, ed. *In God's Name: Examples of Preaching in England, 1534-1662*. Indianapolis: Bobbs-Merrill, 1971.

Cox, James W., ed. *Best Sermons*. Vol. 1. San Francisco: Harper, 1988 (published annually).

———. *The Twentieth Century Pulpit*. 2 vols. Nashville: Abingdon, 1978, 1981.

Crotwell, Helen Gray, ed. *Women and the Word: Sermons*. Philadelphia: Fortress, 1978.

Fant, Clyde E., Jr., and William M. Pinson, Jr. *Twenty Centuries of Great Preaching*, 13 vols. Waco: Word, 1971.

Farmer, David Albert, and Edwina Hunter, eds. *And Blessed Is She: Sermons by Women*. San Francisco: Harper, 1990.

Fish, Henry C., ed. *Pulpit Eloquence of the Nineteenth Century*. New York: Dodd & Meade, 1872.

The Foreign Protestant Pulpit: Sermons by Eminent Preachers of France, Germany, Holland, and Switzerland. 1st series. London: Dickinson, 1869.
Gifford, Frank D., ed. *The Anglican Pulpit Today: Representative Sermons by Leading Preachers of the Anglican Communion*. New York: Morehouse-Gorham, 1953.
Mead, Frank S. *The Pulpit in the South*. New York: Revell, 1950.
Morrison, Charles Clayton, ed. *The American Pulpit: A Volume of Sermons by Twenty-five of the Foremost Living American Preachers*. New York: Macmillan, 1926.
Motter, Alton, M., ed. *Sunday Evening Sermons*. Preached before the Chicago Sunday Evening Club. New York: Harper, 1950.
Petry, Ray C. *No Uncertain Sound: Sermons That Shaped the Pulpit Tradition*. Philadelphia: Westminster, 1948.
Sadler, William Alan, Jr., ed. *Master Sermons through the Ages*. New York: Harper, 1963.
Sampson, Ashley, ed. *Famous English Sermons*. London: Nelson, 1940.
Wiersbe, Warren W., comp. *Treasury of the World's Great Sermons*. Grand Rapids: Kregel, 1977.

XV. LYMAN BEECHER LECTURES ON PREACHING AT YALE UNIVERSITY
(Representative Selections)

Baxter, Batsell Barrett. *The Heart of the Yale Lectures*. New York: Macmillan, 1947.
Jones, Edgar DeWitt. *The Royalty of the Pulpit: A Survey and Appreciation of the Lyman Beecher Lectures on Preaching Founded at Yale Divinity School 1871*. New York: Harper, 1951.
1871-72 Beecher, Henry Ward. *Yale Lectures on Preaching*. First series. *Personal Elements in Preaching*. New York: J. B. Ford, 1872.
1872-73 Beecher, Henry Ward. *Yale Lectures on Preaching*. Second series. *Social and Religious Machinery of the Church*. New York: J. B. Ford, 1873.
1873-74 Beecher, Henry Ward. *Yale Lectures on Preaching*. Third series. *Methods of Using Christian Doctrines in Preaching*. New York: J. B. Ford, 1874.
1874-75 Hall, John. *God's Word Through Preaching*. New York: Dodd & Meade, 1875.
1876-77 Brooks, Phillips. *Lectures on Preaching*. New York: Dutton, 1877.
1877-78 Dale, R. W. *Nine Lectures on Preaching*. New York: Anson D. F. Randolph, 1878.
1878-79 Simpson, Matthew. Lectures on Preaching. New York: Anson D. F. Randolph, 1879.
1879-80 Crosby, Howard. *The Christian Preacher*. New York: Nelson & Phillips, 1880.
1885-86 Taylor, William M. *The Scottish Pulpit: From the Reformation to the Present Day*. New York: Harper, 1887.
1890-91 Stalker, James. *The Preacher and His Models*. New York: Armstrong, 1891.
1895-96 Van Dyke, Henry. *The Gospel for an Age of Doubt*. New York: Macmillan, 1896.
1899-00 Brown, John. *Puritan Preaching in England*. New York: Scribners, 1900.
1906-07 Forsyth, P. T. *Positive Preaching and the Modern Mind*. New York: Hodder & Stoughton, 1907.
1911-12 Jowett, J. H. *The Preacher: His Life and Work*. New York: Doran, 1912.
1913-14 Horne, Charles Sylvester. *The Romance of Preaching*. New York: Revell, 1914.

1914-15 Pepper, George Wharton. *A Voice from the Crowd*. New Haven: Yale University Press, 1915.
1922-23 Brown, C. R. *The Art of Preaching*. New York: Macmillan, 1922.
1929-30 McConnell, Francis John. *The Prophetic Ministry*. New York: Abingdon, 1930.
1930-31 Buttrick, George A. *Jesus Came Preaching*. New York: Scribner, 1931.
1935-36 Park, John Edgar. *The Miracle of Preaching*. New York: Macmillan, 1936.
1937-38 Sperry, Willard Learoyd. *We Prophesy in Part*. New York: Harper, 1938.
1940-41 Sockman, Ralph Washington. *The Highway of God*. New York: Macmillan, 1942.
1942-43 Scherer, Paul. *For We Have This Treasure*. New York: Harper, 1944.
1943-44 Oxnam, Garfield Bromley. *Preaching in A Revolutionary Age*. New York: Abingdon-Cokesbury, 1944.
1946-47 Phillips, Harold Cooke. *Bearing Witness to the Truth*. Nashville: Abingdon-Cokesbury, 1949.
1951-52 Stewart, James. *A Faith to Proclaim*. New York: Scribner, 1953.
1952-53 Luccock, Halford E. *Communicating the Gospel*. New York: Harper, 1954.
1953-54 Kennedy, Gerald. *God's Good News*. New York: Harper, 1955.
1958-59 Sittler, Joseph. *The Ecology of Faith*. Philadelphia: Muhlenberg, 1961.
1960-61 Bartlett, Gene E. *The Audacity of Preaching*. New York: Harper, 1962.
1962-63 Barr, Browne. *Parish Back Talk*. Nashville: Abingdon, 1964.
1972-73 Read, David H. C. *Sent From God: The Enduring Mystery of Preaching*. Nashville: Abingdon, 1974.
1973-74 Mitchell, Henry H. *The Recovery of Preaching*. New York: Harper, 1977.
1975-76 Taylor, Gardner C. *How Shall They Preach?* Elgin, IL: Progressive Baptist Publishing House, 1977.
1976-77 Buechner, Carl Frederic. *Telling the Truth: The Gospel as Tragedy, Comedy and Fairy Tale*. San Francisco: Harper, 1977.
1977-78 Craddock, Fred B. *Overhearing the Gospel*. Nashville: Abingdon, 1978.
1978-79 Claypool, John R. *The Preaching Event*. Waco: Word, 1980.
1982-83 Smith, Kelly Miller. *Social Crisis Preaching*. Macon, GA: Mercer University Press, 1984.
1984-85 Muehl, William. *Why Preach? Why Listen?* Philadelphia: Fortress, 1986.
1985-86 Forbes, James. *The Holy Spirit and Preaching*. Nashville: Abingdon, 1989.
1988-89 Breuggemann, Walter. *Finally Comes the Poet: Daring Speech for Proclamation*. Minneapolis: Fortress, 1989.

XVI. THE WARRACK LECTURES

Established 1920
Delivered at the Theological Colleges
of the Church of Scotland
(Representative Selections)

Berry, Sidney M. *Vital Preaching*. London: Independent, 1936.
Black, James. *The Mystery of Preaching*. 1924. Reprint. Grand Rapids: Zondervan, 1978.
Burnet, Adam. *Pleading with Men*. Westwood, NJ: Revell, 1935.
Cairns, Frank. *Prophet of the Heart*. New York: Harper, 1935.
Cleland, James T. *Preaching to Be Understood*. Nashville: Abingdon, 1965.
Coffin, Henry Sloane. *What to Preach*. New York: Doran, 1926.
Cowan, A. *The Primacy of Preaching Today*. New York: Scribner, 1955.
Craig, A. C. *Preaching in a Scientific Age*. New York: Scribner, 1954.

Farmer, Herbert H. *The Servant of the Word*. 1941. Reprint. Philadelphia: Fortress, 1964.
Gossip, Arthur John. *In Christ's Stead*. London: Hodder & Stoughton, 1925.
Hutton, John. *That the Ministry Be Not Blamed*. London: Hodder & Stoughton, 1921.
Jarvis, E. D. *If Any Man Minister*. London: Hodder & Stoughton, 1950.
Jeffrey, George J. *This Grace Wherein We Stand*. London: Hodder & Stoughton, 1949.
Keir, Thomas H. *The Word in Worship*. Oxford: Oxford University Press, 1962.
Macgregor, H. C. *The Making of a Preacher*. Philadelphia: Westminster, 1946.
Mackenzie, Hamish C. *Preaching the Eternities*. Edinburgh: St. Andrew, 1963.
MacLennan, David A. *Entrusted with the Gospel*. Philadelphia: Westminster, 1956.
Macleod, George. *Speaking the Truth - in Love*. London: SCM, 1936.
McIntyre, R. E. *The Ministry of the Word*. London: Nelson, 1950.
McWilliam, Stuart W. *Called to Preach*. Edinburgh: St. Andrew, 1969.
Menzies, Robert. *Preaching and Pastoral Evangelism*. Edinburgh: St. Andrew, 1962.
Niles, Daniel T. *The Preacher's Calling to Be Servant*. London: Lutterworth, 1959.
Pitt-Watson, Ian. *Preaching: A Kind of Folly*. Philadelphia: Westminster, 1978.
Read, David H. C. *The Communication of the Gospel*. London: SCM, 1952.
Reid, James. *In Quest of Reality*. London: Hodder & Stoughton, 1924.
Scott, W. Boyd. *Preaching Week by Week*. New York: Richard R. Smith, 1928.
Small, R. Leonard. *With Ardour and Accuracy*. Edinburgh: St. Andrew, 1960.
Stewart, James S. *Heralds of God*. 1946. Reprint. Grand Rapids: Baker, 1972.
Watt, Lauchlan Maclean. *The Preacher's Life and Work*. London: Allenson, c.1931.
Wright, James. *A Preacher's Questionnaire*. Edinburgh: St. Andrew, 1958.

XVII. BIBLIOGRAPHY

Litfin, A. Duane, and Haddon W. Robinson, eds. *Recent Homiletical Thought: An Annotated Bibliography. Vol. 2, 1966-1979*. Grand Rapids: Baker, 1983.
Toohey, William, and William D. Thompson, eds. *Recent Homiletical Thought: A Bibliography, 1935-1965*. Nashville, Abingdon, 1967.